Boston MBTA
Oak Grove
Malden
Wellington
Sullivan Square
Community College
Wonderland
Revere Beach
Beachmont
Suffolk Downs
Orient Heights
Wood Island
Airport
Maverick
Logan International Airport
Alewife
Davis
Porter
Harvard
Central
Kendall/MIT
Charles/MGH
Lechmere
Science Park
North Station
Haymarket
Bowdoin
Gov't Center
Park St
State*
Aquarium
Downtown Crossing
Chinatown
South Station
NE Medical Center
Boylston
Arlington
Copley
Hynes/ICA
Kenmore
Fenway
Boston College
Cleveland Circle
Riverside
Woodland
Waban
Eliot
Newton Highlands
Newton Centre
Chestnut Hill
Reservoir
Beaconsfield
Brookline Hills
Brookline Village
Longwood
Prudential
Symphony
Back Bay
Mass Ave
Ruggles
Roxbury Crossing
Jackson Sq
Stony Brook
Green St
Forest Hills
Heath
Dudley Sq
Broadway
Andrew
JFK/UMass
Savin Hill
Fields Corner
Shawmut
Ashmont
Cedar Grove
Butler
Milton
Central Ave
Valley Rd
Capen St
Mattapan
North Quincy
Wollaston
Quincy Center
Quincy Adams
Braintree
To Quincy & Hull
To Hingham
LEGEND
Transit lines & stop
Commuter rail & station
Terminal station
Free interchange with other lines
Accessible Station
Parking
*Chinatown: Accessible July 2002
*State: Not accessible for Blue line inbound.
Boston Harbor Ferry Services
1 Lovejoy Wharf to Charlestown Navy Yard
2 Lovejoy Wharf to U.S. Courthouse to World Trade Center
3 Long Wharf to Charlestown Navy Yard
4 Hingham Ship Yard to Rowes Wharf, Boston
5 Quincy Shipyard and Pemberton Point, Hull to Long Wharf, Boston
For schedule & fare information, call (617) 222-3200 or visit our website at www.mbta.com
© MBTA 2002

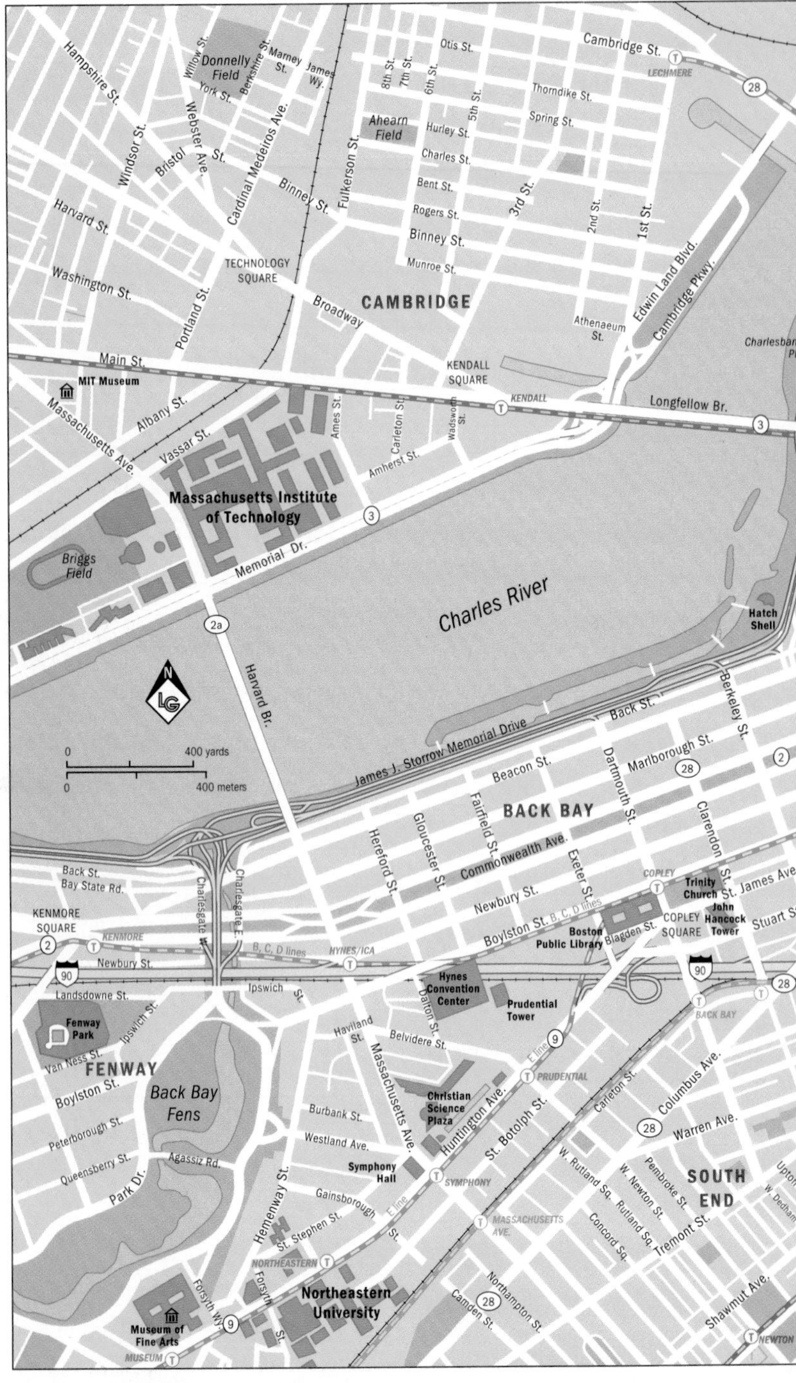

CAMBRIDGE
Cambridge St.
LECHMERE
Otis St.
Thorndike St.
Spring St.
Hurley St.
Charles St.
Bent St.
Rogers St.
Binney St.
Munroe St.
8th St.
7th St.
6th St.
5th St.
3rd St.
2nd St.
1st St.
Hampshire St.
Willow St.
Donnelly Field
Berkshire St.
Marney St.
James Wy.
York St.
Windsor St.
Bristol St.
Webster Ave.
Cardinal Medeiros Ave.
Ahearn Field
Fulkerson St.
Binney St.
Harvard St.
Washington St.
Portland St.
TECHNOLOGY SQUARE
Broadway
Athenaeum St.
Edwin Land Blvd.
Cambridge Pkwy.
Charlesbank Pk.
Main St.
MIT Museum
KENDALL SQUARE
KENDALL
Longfellow Br.
Massachusetts Ave.
Albany St.
Vassar St.
Ames St.
Carleton St.
Wadsworth St.
Amherst St.
Massachusetts Institute of Technology
Memorial Dr.
Briggs Field
Charles River
Hatch Shell
Harvard Br.
N
LG
0
400 yards
400 meters
James J. Storrow Memorial Drive
Back St.
Berkeley St.
Marlborough St.
Beacon St.
Dartmouth St.
Fairfield St.
Gloucester St.
Hereford St.
Clarendon St.
BACK BAY
Commonwealth Ave.
Exeter St.
Newbury St.
Boylston St.
B, C, D lines
COPLEY
Trinity Church
St. James Ave.
John Hancock Tower
Stuart St.
COPLEY SQUARE
Boston Public Library
Blagden St.
Back St.
Bay State Rd.
Charlesgate W.
Charlesgate E.
KENMORE SQUARE
KENMORE
HYNES/ICA
Newbury St.
Ipswich St.
Landsdowne St.
Hynes Convention Center
Dalton St.
Prudential Tower
BACK BAY
Fenway Park
Ipswich St.
Van Ness St.
FENWAY
Boylston St.
Back Bay Fens
Peterborough St.
Queensberry St.
Agassiz Rd.
Park Dr.
Haviland St.
Belvidere St.
Massachusetts Ave.
E line
PRUDENTIAL
Christian Science Plaza
Huntington Ave.
St. Botolph St.
Carleton St.
Columbus Ave.
Warren Ave.
Burbank St.
Westland Ave.
Symphony Hall
SYMPHONY
Gainsborough St.
Hemenway St.
St. Stephen St.
E line
W. Rutland Sq.
W. Newton St.
Pembroke St.
Rutland Sq.
Concord Sq.
Tremont St.
SOUTH END
Upton St.
W. Dedham St.
MASSACHUSETTS AVE.
NORTHEASTERN
Forsyth St.
Forsyth Wy.
Northeastern University
Northampton St.
Camden St.
Shawmut Ave.
NEWTON ST.
Museum of Fine Arts
MUSEUM

■ THE RESOURCE FOR THE INDEPENDENT TRAVELER

"The guides are aimed not only at young budget travelers but at the independent traveler; a sort of streetwise cookbook for traveling alone."

—The New York Times

"Unbeatable; good sight-seeing advice; up-to-date info on restaurants, hotels, and inns; a commitment to money-saving travel; and a wry style that brightens nearly every page."

—The Washington Post

"Lighthearted and sophisticated, informative and fun to read. [Let's Go] helps the novice traveler navigate like a knowledgeable old hand."

—Atlanta Journal-Constitution

"A world-wise traveling companion—always ready with friendly advice and helpful hints, all sprinkled with a bit of wit."

—The Philadelphia Inquirer

■ THE BEST TRAVEL BARGAINS IN YOUR PRICE RANGE

"All the dirt, dirt cheap."

—People

"Anything you need to know about budget traveling is detailed in this book."

—The Chicago Sun-Times

"Let's Go follows the creed that you don't have to toss your life's savings to the wind to travel—unless you want to."

—The Salt Lake Tribune

■ REAL ADVICE FOR REAL EXPERIENCES

"The writers seem to have experienced every rooster-packed bus and lunar-surfaced mattress about which they write."

—The New York Times

"A guide should tell you what to expect from a destination. Here Let's Go shines."

—The Chicago Tribune

"[Let's Go's] devoted updaters really walk the walk (and thumb the ride, and trek the trail). Learn how to fish, haggle, find work—anywhere."

—Food & Wine

LET'S GO PUBLICATIONS

TRAVEL GUIDES

Alaska 1st edition **NEW TITLE**
Australia 2004
Austria & Switzerland 2004
Brazil 1st edition **NEW TITLE**
Britain & Ireland 2004
California 2004
Central America 8th edition
Chile 1st edition
China 4th edition
Costa Rica 1st edition
Eastern Europe 2004
Egypt 2nd edition
Europe 2004
France 2004
Germany 2004
Greece 2004
Hawaii 2004
India & Nepal 8th edition
Ireland 2004
Israel 4th edition
Italy 2004
Japan 1st edition **NEW TITLE**
Mexico 20th edition
Middle East 4th edition
New Zealand 6th edition
Pacific Northwest 1st edition **NEW TITLE**
Peru, Ecuador & Bolivia 3rd edition
Puerto Rico 1st edition **NEW TITLE**
South Africa 5th edition
Southeast Asia 8th edition
Southwest USA 3rd edition
Spain & Portugal 2004
Thailand 1st edition
Turkey 5th edition
USA 2004
Western Europe 2004

CITY GUIDES

Amsterdam 3rd edition
Barcelona 3rd edition
Boston 4th edition
London 2004
New York City 2004
Paris 2004
Rome 12th edition
San Francisco 4th edition
Washington, D.C. 13th edition

MAP GUIDES

Amsterdam
Berlin
Boston
Chicago
Dublin
Florence
Hong Kong
London
Los Angeles
Madrid
New Orleans
New York City
Paris
Prague
Rome
San Francisco
Seattle
Sydney
Venice
Washington, D.C.

COMING SOON:

Road Trip USA

BOSTON

Megan R. Smith Editor
Stephen L. Mott Associate Editor

Christine C. Yokoyama Map Editor
Matthew K. Hudson Managing Editor

St. Martin's Press New York

HELPING LET'S GO If you want to share your discoveries, suggestions, or corrections, please drop us a line. We read every piece of correspondence, whether a postcard, a 10-page email, or a coconut. **Address mail to:**

Let's Go: Boston
67 Mount Auburn Street
Cambridge, MA 02138
USA

Visit Let's Go at **http://www.letsgo.com,** or send email to:

feedback@letsgo.com
Subject: "Let's Go: Boston"

In addition to the invaluable travel advice our readers share with us, many are kind enough to offer their services as researchers or editors. Unfortunately, our charter enables us to employ only currently enrolled Harvard students.

Distributed outside the USA and Canada by Macmillan.

ISBN: 0-312-31980-0

First edition
10 9 8 7 6 5 4 3 2 1

Let's Go: Boston is written by Let's Go Publications, 67 Mount Auburn Street, Cambridge, MA 02138, USA.

Contents

bold denotes a map

ABOUT LET'S GO

GUIDES FOR THE INDEPENDENT TRAVELER

Budget travel is more than a vacation. At *Let's Go*, we see every trip as the chance of a lifetime. If your dream is to grab a knapsack and a machete and forge through the jungles of Brazil, we can take you there. Or, if you'd rather enjoy the Riviera sun at a beachside cafe, we'll set you a table. If you know what you're doing, you can have any experience you want—whether it's camping among lions or sampling Tuscan desserts—without maxing out your credit card. We'll show you just how far your coins can go, and prove that the greatest limitation on your adventure is not your wallet, but your imagination. That said, we understand that you may want the occasional indulgence after a week of hostels and kebab stands, so we've added "Big Splurges" to let you know which establishments are worth those extra euros, as well as price ranges to help you quickly determine whether an accommodation or restaurant will break the bank. While we may have diversified, our emphasis will always be on finding the best values for your budget, giving you all the info you need to spend six days in London or six months in Tasmania.

BEYOND THE TOURIST EXPERIENCE

We write for travelers who know there's more to a vacation than riding double-deckers with tourists. Our researchers give you the heads-up on both world-renowned and lesser-known attractions, on the best local eats and the hottest nightclub beats. In our travels, we talk to everybody; we provide a snapshot of real life in the places you visit with our sidebars on topics like regional cuisine, local festivals, and hot political issues. We've opened our pages to respected writers and scholars to show you their take on a given destination, and turned to lifelong residents to learn the little things that make their city worth calling home. And we've even given you Alternatives to Tourism—ideas for how to give back to local communities through responsible travel and volunteering.

OVER FORTY YEARS OF WISDOM

When we started, way back in 1960, Let's Go consisted of a small group of well-traveled friends who compiled their budget travel tips into a 20-page packet for students on charter flights to Europe. Since then, we've expanded to suit all kinds of travelers, now publishing guides to six continents, including our newest guides: *Let's Go: Japan* and *Let's Go: Brazil.* Our guides are still annually researched and written entirely by students on shoe-string budgets, adventurous travelers who know that train strikes, stolen luggage, food poisoning, and marriage proposals are all part of a day's work. Even as you read this, work on next year's editions is well underway. Whether you're reading one of our new titles, like *Let's Go: Puerto Rico* or *Let's Go Adventure Guide: Alaska*, or our original best-seller, *Let's Go: Europe*, you'll find the same spirit of adventure that has made *Let's Go* the guide of choice for travelers the world over since 1960.

GETTING IN TOUCH

The best discoveries are often those you make yourself; on the road, when you find something worth sharing, please drop us a line. We're Let's Go Publications, 67 Mt. Auburn St., Cambridge, MA 02138, USA (feedback@letsgo.com).

For more info, visit our website: www.letsgo.com.

HOW TO USE THIS BOOK

PLANNING YOUR TRIP. *Let's Go Boston* has plenty of info and advice that will be useful even before you visit Boston, handily collected at the back of this guide. **Planning Your Trip** is chock full of practical info on passports, plane tickets, and more. Hostels and hotels in Boston fill up quickly, so reserve far in advance of your arrival. (Check **Accommodations** for lodgings in all price ranges.) For those interested in doing more than just seeing the sights, there's **Alternatives to Tourism,** which has info on studying, working, and/or volunteering in Boston.

You can strategize your sightseeing with **Discover Boston,** which has suggestions on things to see and do in the city, plus a detailed run-down of the can't-miss attractions in every neighborhood. Read up on Boston's history and culture in **Life & Times,** a thumbnail sketch of the city—both past and present.

ONCE IN BOSTON. Upon arrival, **Once in Boston** will be an invaluable resource, with info on everything from maneuvering the subway system (known as the "T") to withdrawing money from your bank account. You'll spend most of your time in Boston flipping through the chapters that follow Once in Boston: **Sights, Food & Drink, Nightlife, Shopping,** and **Sports & Entertainment.** Establishments in these chapters are usually grouped by neighborhood and plotted in the **Maps** section at the back of this guide, marked off with a black stripe down the side. Useful numbers and services are listed in the **Service Directory.**

FARTHER AFIELD. Boston is great, but what makes it really great is its proximity to soft beaches, great skiing, rigorous hiking, historic battlefields, and other diversions that make perfect day-long or weekend getaways from the city. Whether you want to scale New Hampshire's Mt. Washington or sun with celebrities on Martha's Vineyard, the **Daytrips from Boston** chapter has what you need.

THE INSIDE SCOOP. Black boxes scattered throughout this guide offer insider tips for making the most of your stay in Boston—everything from advice on where to go for a gourmet blowout to info on getting cheap tickets to a Red Sox game.

PRICE RANGES & RANKINGS. Within each neighborhood, *Let's Go Boston* ranks all establishments by value; the best places get a thumbs-up (☒). At the end of each food and accommodation listing in this guide, you'll find a marker indicating a price range, as follows:

	①	②	③	④	⑤
ACCOMMODATIONS based on average rate per person, per night, double occupancy	under $35	under $55	under $75	under $95	$100+
FOOD based on average price for an entree (main dish) at dinner	under $7	under $11	under $16	under $22	$23+

A NOTE TO OUR READERS The information for this book was gathered by *Let's Go* researchers from May through August of 2003. Each listing is based on one researcher's opinion, formed during his or her visit at a particular time. Those traveling at other times may have different experiences since prices, dates, hours, and conditions are always subject to change. You are urged to check the facts presented in this book beforehand to avoid inconvenience and surprises.

❶❷❸❹❺

PRICE RANGES >> BOSTON

Our researchers list establishments in order of value from best to worst; our favorites are denoted by the Let's Go thumbs-up (☒). Since the best value is not always the cheapest price, we have incorporated a system of price ranges for quick reference. Our price ranges are based on a rough expectation of what you will spend. For **accommodations,** we base our price range on the cheapest price for which a traveler can stay for one night, double occupancy. For **restaurants** and other dining establishments, we estimate the average amount that you will spend for an entree. The table below tells you what you will *typically* find in Boston at the corresponding price range; keep in mind that a particularly expensive ice cream stand may be marked a ❷, because the symbol is based on a normal entree price.

ACCOMMODATIONS	RANGE	WHAT YOU'RE *LIKELY* TO FIND
❶	under $35	Camping; most dorm rooms, such as HI or other hostels. Expect bunk beds and a communal bath; you may have to provide or rent towels and sheets.
❷	$35-50	Lower end B&Bs or guest houses. Expect a semi-private bathroom on the hall, or a small private bath.
❸	$50-70	Most B&Bs, and country inns. Private baths and uniquely decorated, spacious rooms. Should include breakfast.
❹	$70-90	Similar to 3, but may have more amenities, larger rooms or be in a more touristed area.
❺	above $90	Upscale B&Bs, expect perfect service, large rooms, private baths, wonderful included breakfasts and a convenient location.
FOOD	**RANGE**	**WHAT YOU'RE *LIKELY* TO FIND**
❶	under $7	Mostly cheap sandwiches or falafel from greasy diners and bakeries. Rarely ever a sit-down meal.
❷	$7-11	Vegitarian fare, good sandwiches or low-priced entrees. You may have the option of sitting down or taking out.
❸	$11-16	Mid-priced entrees, cooked to order. Tip will bump you up a couple dollars, since you'll probably have waitstaff.
❹	$16-22	A somewhat fancy restaurant, or sushi bar. Expect more than one fork. Few restaurants in this range have a dress code, but some may look down on t-shirt and jeans.
❺	above $22	Excellent food, a decent wine list, and and a famous chef. Dress nicely, and be ready to spend more than you ever imagined for ordinary things like water, bread and beer.

RESEARCHER-WRITERS

Stephen L. Mott III *Boston, Cape Cod, Nantucket, Pioneer Valley*

Steve came out of nowhere, a loose cannon with an unconventional style and a desire to shake things up. A plucky upstart, Steve brought a fresh vibe and outside-the-box type thinking to the book. He does things his way, take it or leave it. A native of the mean streets of Norwell, MA and hardened in the fires of the Harvard sociology department. Steve has learned that if you don't play by the rules, sometimes you have to make up your own. When he's not busy watching the Red Sox, he's gripping it and ripping it—in the surf, in the snow, or on the rugby pitch.

Megan Smith *Boston, Cape Cod, Martha's Vineyard*

Bursting onto the travel guide scene last year with her hugely successful debut: *Let's Go: USA 2003*, Megan began the *Boston* book under a lot of public pressure. Could she duplicate the subtle humor and deft writing style that were the trademarks of her last effort? The critics were confident, and *Let's Go* was banking on it. For her sophomore effort Megan chose a more introspective topic, hoping to experiment with a softer, more personal style in her writing. A senior member of the Radcliffe crew team, Megan used her first three years at Harvard and a championship crew season as fodder to produce an artful masterpiece that is destined to eclipse even the blockbuster that was her debut.

CONTRIBUTING WRITERS

Rohit Chopra is a senior government major, with an emphasis on city planning, at Harvard University, where he also serves as President of the Undergraduate Council and is an active member of Adams House.

Ankur Ghosh wrote and edited the previous edition of this guide and is the former capo (a.k.a. Editor-in-Chief) of the second best-known criminal organization in Boston, the Mount Auburn Gang (a.k.a. Let's Go Publications).

Derek Glanz is currently earning a Ph.D. in political science and is a freelance writer covering the St. Louis Cardinals.

RESEARCH CONSULTANTS

The Pascavage Family	*Falmouth & Woods Hole*
Will Riffelmacher	*Freedom Trail & Jamaica Plain*
The Schiller Family	*Martha's Vineyard*
Ella Steim	*Nantucket*
Arielle Jones	*Pioneer Valley*
Dustin Lewis	*Provincetown*

ACKNOWLEDGMENTS

Megan thanks: To Steve for putting up with the stress of the job and staying laid back to the end. To Matt for having the wisdom to let us buck the system every so often. To Christine for answering more questions than any human should have to. To prod for being rock stars. To the pod for the free miles and jolly ranchers as well as the unsolicited musical advice. To Radcliffe for starting the summer in style and keeping it rolling on and off the rooftops—watch that last step. To Will for the "misty June island," Bruce, and a vacation that was worth all the hours. To Ella, Cait, and Travis for making the most of the best summer apartment...ever. To the BGD for being so pomo. And finally, to my family, for being there at the end, the much clichéd light.

Steve thanks: I should begin by thanking the researchers, me and Megan, nice work: you guys were the soul of this book. Megan especially, thanks for the hard work, unwavering patience and hours spent formatting my copy. Sarah, Megan (the other one), Dave, Mike, Dunia, thanks for the distractions, the obscure/uber-cool music (Dave and Sarah) and the sandwich (Megan). Matt, thanks for leaving the cool stuff in the book, Christine thanks for being so cool. Arielle thanks for Nantucket, I couldn't have done it without you. Thanks roommates, Ron and Adam for being sweet dudes; Mom for the moral support; Dad for the best food in Boston; and Nick and Claire cause what the hell I had one more line. Oh, thanks to my dogs too, nice.

Christine thanks: Many thanks to Megan and Steve for being helpful and all-around awesome. Thanks also to Brian E. for the map proof and the daily serenade, to Brian F. for the housing, to my parents for making me go home sometimes, and of course, to my roommates for everything and then some.

INSIDE

Discover Boston

Boston is what I would like the whole United States to be.
—Charles Dickens

For a long time, Boston *was* the United States. In the 17th and 18th centuries—America's formative years—the city played a starring role in the country's fight for independence. In the 19th century, some of America's most influential doers and thinkers called Boston home, unabashedly dubbing it the "Hub of the Universe." In the 20th century, the Biggest Small Town in America experienced—writ large—the same growing pains sweeping the rest of the nation, including immigration booms, civil rights battles, and problems with urban expansion and renewal.

On this side of the millennium, Boston at times seems to trump up its illustrious past too aggressively. Indeed, many visitors think the city is little more than the Freedom Trail (p. 43), a walking tour through Boston's most important historical landmarks. But while the well-trampled Trail does revisit some exciting moments in US history, this most American of American cities didn't earn the title of "America's Walking City" for one measly 2½ mi. stroll. Boston is a restless stew of compact neighborhoods, dramatically distinct communities, winning cultural attractions, and acres of urban parks—all of which are best sampled on foot. While the Freedom Trail is a nice place to start, wandering around Boston's many different districts, its jumble of streets, and its (rarely square) squares will give you a glimpse of a still-evolving metropolis where tired history is less important (and less fascinating) than the lives of those who live in the city today.

A CITY OF NEIGHBORHOODS

THE LAY OF THE LAND

Boston is the capital of the state of Massachusetts and the largest city in New England. The city's easily navigated patchwork of neighborhoods is situated on a peninsula jutting into the Massachusetts Bay (bordered to the north and west by the **Charles River** and to the east by **Boston Harbor**). The city proper is centered on the grassy expanse of **Boston Common;** the popular **Freedom Trail** (p. 43) begins here and runs through what most package tourists consider "Boston." The Trail heads east of the Common through **Downtown** (still the same compact three square mi. settled in 1630), skirting the city's growing **Waterfront** district to the southeast. The Trail then veers north to the **North End,** Boston's Little Italy, and finally crosses the Charles River to the far-flung but historically significant neighborhood of **Charlestown.**

Boston Common is sandwiched between aristocratic **Beacon Hill** to the north and the nation's first **Chinatown** to the south. (Much of Chinatown overlaps with the tiny **Theatre District,** to the west.) The rest of the city spreads out westward from the Common, much of it ringed by a string of parks and green spaces known as the **Emerald Necklace** (p. 44). Just west of the Common are the grand boulevards and brownstones of the chic **Back Bay,** separated from the artsy and predominantly gay **South End** (to its south) by the Mass. Turnpike (I-90). West of the Back Bay are **Kenmore Sq. & Fenway,** home to baseball's Red Sox as well as the city's major museums. Just west of this area is student- and budget-friendly **Allston,** an oft-neglected pocket of the city popular with bar crawlers and clubbers.

South of the Fenway are Boston's largest and most green neighborhoods, which don't see many visitors. Heading west to east, these outlying regions are: vibrant, cheap, and queer-friendly **Jamaica Plain;** sprawling and often racially charged Roxbury and **Dorchester;** and predominantly Irish **South Boston** (a.k.a. "Southie"), unsurprisingly a pubber's paradise.

This guide includes all of Boston proper (as described above), plus select coverage of three nearby cities. The upscale (and largely Jewish) suburb of **Brookline** is just west of Jamaica Plain (and south of Allston). The area's most inventive food and most diverse nightlife are just across the Charles River in **Cambridge,** a Bohemian town that's home to brainy MIT and prestigious Harvard University. Just north of Cambridge is the working-class suburb of **Somerville,** centered on hip Davis Sq.

Within each chapter, neighborhoods and cities are listed alphabetically.

INNER NEIGHBORHOODS

BACK BAY

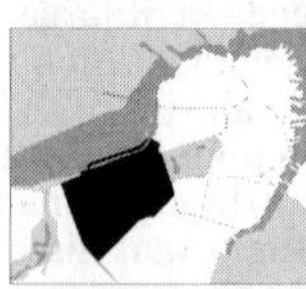
see map p. 314-315

T: *Hynes/ICA (Green-B,C,D) lets out onto Newbury St. at Massachusetts Ave. T: Copley (Green) serves Copley Sq., and T: Symphony (Green-E) serves the Christian Science Plaza.* ***Sights:*** *p. 57.* ***Food:*** *p. 105.* ***Nightlife:*** *p. 135.* ***Shopping:*** *p. 172.* ***Accommodations:*** *p. 184.*

Though it began as a stinky tidal flat, Back Bay has come a long way. Today, **Newbury St.** embodies everything yuppie about Boston—posh bars, expensive restaurants, and (of course) shopping like you've never seen before. Highlights include:

Sights: The beauty of the Boston Public Library (a museum disguised as a book repository) is matched only by the dramatic expanse of Christian Science Plaza, home to the unusual Mapparium and Mary Baker Eddy Library.

Food: Boston's best curries at Kashmir, wild Rock 'n' Roll Sushi at Gyuhama, and garlicky *tapas* in the cozy bar at Tapéo.

Nightlife: Rub elbows with Boylston St.'s endless parade of scenesters at dim Bukowski's, or toast them at celeb-endorsed Whiskey Park.

Shopping: Newbury St. is the closest Boston gets to Rodeo Dr. Choose from hand-me-down designer duds at Second Time Around, gourmet soaps at fresh, or museum-worthy goods (at museum-worthy prices) at Louis Boston.

Accommodations: With some of the best options in the city, the standout establishments are the Oasis and Newbury St. Guest Houses—both in the heart of the action.

BEACON HILL

see map p. 317

T: Charles/MGH (Red) lets out at the corner of Cambridge St. and Charles St. ***Freedom Trail Sights:*** *p. 44.* ***Other Sights:*** *p. 63.* ***Food:*** *p. 107.* ***Shopping:*** *p. 172.* ***Accommodations:*** *p. 186.*

Amid elm trees, gas lanterns, and winding cobblestone streets, the wealthiest families in Boston live in the cramped brick townhouses of Beacon Hill. Beacon Hill's quaint center is **Charles St.,** lined with antique shops and conservative clothiers. Highlights include:

Sights: The Shaw Memorial and State House face off at the foot of Beacon Hill, while the Nichols House—frozen in time at the turn of the century—crowns the hill's summit.

Food: Lavish Persian food in a romantic setting at Lala Rokh.

Shopping: Find all those "unexpected necessities" for your home—fake sushi, garlic-shaped salt shakers, personal chill-out bubbles—at Black Ink or Koo de Kir.

Holidays & Festivals: All eyes are on the Charles River Esplanade for the 4th of July, where a concert of patriotic tunes by the Boston Pops culminates in a dazzling display of fireworks and live cannon fire.

CHINATOWN

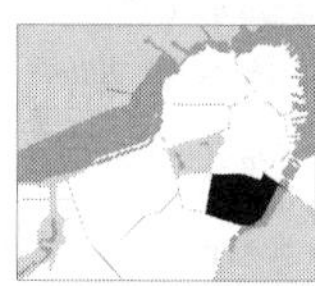

see map p. 322

T: Chinatown (Orange) lets out onto Essex St. at Washington St., 1 block north of Chinatown's main thoroughfare, Beach St. ***Sights:*** *p. 78.* ***Food:*** *p. 114.* ***Shopping:*** *p. 172.*

Overshadowed by Financial District skyscrapers is the nation's first Chinatown, where some of the cheapest and tastiest food in Boston can be found well into the wee hours of the night. Highlights include:

Food: A Nirvana for East Asian food lovers. Try the sleek cuisine at Shabu-Zen, some of the city's best sushi at Ginza, or fin-flapping fresh Chinese at Jumbo Seafood—just don't skip town without a tapioca ball drink from the Chinatown Eatery & Juice Bar.

Shopping: Chinatown's selection is as chaotic as its streets, with countless Asian grocers, bulk fabric stores, and gift and toy shops selling the wackiest imported trinkets.

DOWNTOWN

see map p. 324-325

T: Park St. (Green/Red), Downtown Crossing (Orange/Red), and Government Ctr. (Blue/Green) all serve Downtown. ***Freedom Trail Sights:*** *p. 46.* ***Other Sights:*** *p. 80.* ***Food:*** *p. 117.* ***Nightlife:*** *p. 141.* ***Shopping:*** *p. 172.* ***Accommodations:*** *p. 189.*

With the shopping hub of **Downtown Crossing** and the historic hub of the **Freedom Trail** (which starts here and runs through most of the neighborhood; see p. 43), Downtown is usually the first and often only place visitors to Boston get to see—which is a shame, because the shiny skyscrapers and countless shops peddling "ye olde" tourist dreck are not at all typical of this intimate city. Highlights include:

Sights: The informative Old State House (a museum chronicling Boston's history), the chaotic Haymarket (a multi-block farmers' market), and the haunting Holocaust Memorial are not to be missed.

Nightlife: The newly hip "Ladder District" is home to some of the most unusual nightlife spots in Boston, including the Bollywood-meets-Hollywood "hookah" den (which has unfortunately gone smoke-free with the rest of Boston) at Mantra.

Shopping: Downtown's major attraction. Faneuil Hall & Quincy Market (p. 50)—a giant chain mall and food court—vie for tourist dollars with Downtown Crossing, best known as the site of the legendary Filene's Basement (a cut-rate department store).

Holidays & Festivals: Government Ctr. hosts 2 popular all-you-can-eat summertime food-fests—the Scooper Bowl (ice cream) and the Chowderfest (take a wild guess).

KENMORE SQUARE & THE FENWAY

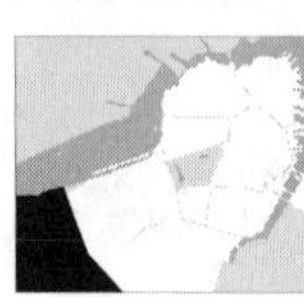
see map p. 330-331

T: Kenmore (Green-B,C,D). The Green-B and Green-E Lines run through the area. ***Sights:*** *p. 84.* ***Food:*** *p. 120.* ***Nightlife:*** *p. 145, p. 144.* ***Shopping:*** *p. 172.* ***Accommodations:*** *p. 190.*

The thrill of the pennant race and the glory of a 60 foot gasoline advertisement mean as much to Bostonians as the delicate sound of a world class orchestra and the world's largest Monet collection outside of France, and it can all be found here. Dominated to the north by the historic **Fenway Park,** to the south by the **Avenue of the Arts** and split in half by Olmstead's rolling park the Fens, Kenmore and the Fenway are remarkably peaceful neighbors. Highlights include:

Sights: Just around the corner from the epic Museum of Fine Arts is the delightful Isabella Stewart Gardner Museum.

Food: Not 1 but 2 outposts of the Brown Sugar Café, the city's best Thai restaurant.

Nightlife: Lansdowne St. is Boston's clubbing central—from flashy, trashy Avalon to super-sized game room-*cum*-disco Jillian's, plus the dueling karaoke pianos at Jake Ivory's.

Sports & Entertainment: You haven't really seen Boston until you've been to a baseball game at storied Fenway Park, where the best team in baseball plays every summer.

Accommodations: The HI-Boston Fenway is the city's best hostel, housed in a former hotel—too bad it's only open in summer.

NORTH END

see map p. 332

T: Haymarket (Green/Orange). Follow signs through the construction and across the Fitzgerald Expwy. (I-93). Turn right onto Cross St. (which runs parallel to the Expwy.), then left up Hanover St., the North End's main street. ***Freedom Trail Sights:*** *p. 52.* ***Food:*** *p. 121.* ***Shopping:*** *p. 172.*

As Boston's Italian-American enclave, a leisurely trip through the North End's winding, narrow streets (centered on **Hanover St.**)—lined with rustic *trattorie*, Old World bakeries, and cramped *salumerias* (corner grocers)—will make you forget the traffic snarls and tourist hordes of Downtown. With such famous residents as patriot leader Paul Revere, it is only appropriate that most North End sights are on the Freedom Trail. Highlights include:

Sights: The Freedom Trail runs through the entire neighborhood, passing by such highlights as peaceful North Sq. and the surreal reliquary in the gift shop of the Old North Church.

Food: The North End's red sauce-slinging spots differ little in quality and atmosphere, so it's best to let your wallet—not your nose—be your guide. Our favorites include the homestyle favorites at Trattoria Il Panino and the mouth-watering French/Italian delights at Sage.

Holidays & Festivals: In summer, the largely Catholic North End hosts many saints' feast days, marked by parades, dancing, and carnivals.

SOUTH END

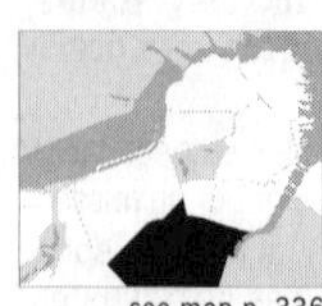
see map p. 336

Centered on parallel Tremont St. and Washington St. ***T:*** *Back Bay (Orange) is a few blocks from Tremont St., while the T's new Silver Line runs along Washington St.* ***Sights:*** *p. 92.* ***Food:*** *p. 125.* ***Nightlife:*** *p. 149.* ***Shopping:*** *p. 172.* ***Accommodations:*** *p. 191.*

Once a poor merchant suburb and a working class slum, the **South End** has since become an arts community, a yuppie hangout, and Boston's most gay-friendly all inclusive neighborhood. Home to the trendy boutiques and boisterous bars of **Tremont St.,** the ultra-experimental galleries below **Washington St.,** and hands-down the best restaurants within 300 mi., this is the place to shop, drink, eat and explore. Highlights include:

Sights: Hot contemporary art at the galleries in the SoWa Building.

Food: Given the amazing line-up of gourmet eateries here, it's hard to go wrong. Standouts include Addis Red Sea's affordable and unforgettable Ethiopian, Sister Sorel's full-blown gourmet at deflated prices, and Flour's otherworldly pastries.

Nightlife: The South End is where the boys (who love boys) are, though most bars feature a mixed crowd. Whether it's free live jazz at down-home Wally's, divey decor at the Delux, or sexy cocktails at Bomboa, you're guaranteed a good time.

Shopping: Tremont St. is lined with countless trendy clothiers and gift shops, but nobody beats Market for the widest selection of *prêt-à-partay* designer goods.

THEATRE DISTRICT

see map p. 322

T: Boylston (Green) lets out onto Tremont St. at Boylston St. All clubs and theaters are within 1-2 blocks. ***Nightlife:*** *p. 151. For nearby* ***Food*** *and* ***Shopping,*** *see* ***Chinatown*** *(p. 3).*

After the Puritans (who thought theater was sinful) faded from prominence in Boston, the city's miniscule (2-block) Theatre District grew into the preeminent pre-Broadway tryout spot. The Theatre District was once the site of over 30 theaters that saw countless major American premieres (including Tennessee Williams' *A Streetcar Named Desire* and Rogers & Hammerstein's *Oklahoma!*). Now only the most prestigious theaters remain, and most feature touring productions or small-scale premieres anyway. The neighborhood has also blossomed into an entertainment district of a whole other sort: it's now one of the most chic, sleek nightlife spots in the city, with crowds of well-dressed, well-funded international folk crowding its many upscale bars and dance clubs. Highlights include:

Nightlife: Conspicuous consumption abounds at Commie-chic Pravda 116, just steps from the thumping, gay-friendly beats of Europa/Buzz.

Sports & Entertainment: The giant Wang Ctr. (p. 163) hosts Broadway blockbusters year-round and the country's most-visited production of *The Nutcracker* in the winter, while the smaller Charles Playhouse (p. 162) is home to the fun-but-freaky Blue Man Group.

WATERFRONT

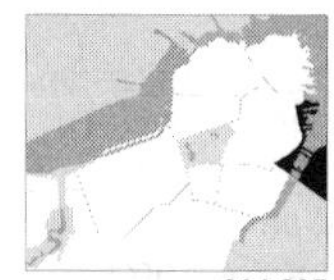
see map p. 324-325

T: South Station (Red). Follow traffic up Atlantic Ave., turn right onto the pedestrian-only Northern Ave. Bridge, and cross the Ft. Point Channel. Northern Ave. becomes Seaport Blvd. after crossing the Ft. Point Channel. Alternatively, take the free shuttle that runs along Seaport Blvd. from South Station to the World Trade Ctr., which is on one of the Waterfront piers (5-7min., M-F 6am-12:30am). ***Sights:*** *p. 93.* ***Food:*** *p. 128.*

Both visitors and Bostonians know the Waterfront is the best place to gorge on great seafood. Trolley tours and boat tours (see **Tours,** p. 97) depart from the heavily touristed **Long Wharf.** Highlights include:

Sights: The New England Aquarium delights visitors of all ages, while those of a more outdoor mind ferry from Long Wharf to the Harbor Islands.

Food: No surprises here—the Waterfront is the place for incredibly fresh (and incredibly expensive) seafood. The wallet-friendliest spots include No Name and Jimbo's Fish Shanty, while Legal Sea Foods ladles up the city's best chowder.

OUTER NEIGHBORHOODS

ALLSTON

see map p. 313

T: Harvard Ave. (Green-B; "Night Owl" Green Boston College) lets out at Commonwealth Ave. and Harvard Ave. Walk up Harvard Ave. (with McDonald's on your right) to get to the intersection with Brighton Ave., Allston's main drag. Bus #66 (p. 21; also a "Night Owl") from Harvard Sq. runs along Brighton Ave. to Harvard Ave. ***Food:*** *p. 103.* ***Nightlife:*** *p. 134.* ***Shopping:*** *p. 172.*

A great place to look for long-term accommodations (p. 191), Allston is a budget-friendly (though somewhat run-down) neighborhood filled with cheap ethnic eateries and hopping, bountiful nightlife. Populated by countless college students, tragic hipsters, and working-class families, Allston is the place for travelers in the know. Highlights include:

Food: An array of budget ethnic restaurants, from hearty Colombian mountain food at Camino Real to the city's cheapest Vietnamese at V. Majestic.

Nightlife: Popular (and populated) with college students, Allston is a barfly's dream, with cheap booze and wild young crowds most nights of the week.

BROOKLINE

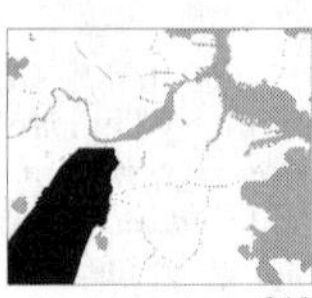
see map p. 318

T: Coolidge Corner (Green-C) lets out at Coolidge Corner, at the intersection of Harvard St. and Beacon St. #66 bus (p. 21) from Harvard Sq. runs along Harvard St. through Coolidge Corner. ***Food:*** *p. 108.* ***Shopping:*** *p. 172.* ***Accommodations:*** *p. 186.*

Generally known as an upscale "streetcar suburb" for wealthy Boston professionals, Brookline is not as monochromatic as you might imagine. A substantial Jewish population also calls Brookline home, as the numerous kosher delis, synagogues, and Judaica shops attest. Of most interest to travelers is bustling **Coolidge Corner** (at Harvard St. and Beacon St.), a popular dining and shopping destination presided over—like its funkier northern counterpart, Davis Sq. (p. 8)—by a revival cinema, the Coolidge Corner Moviehouse. Highlights include:

Food: It's no surprise that Brookline has great delis and Boston's best bagels (try Kupel's)...but how to explain it being home to some of the city's best sushi (at FuGaKyu)?

Shopping: Blink and you'll miss Grand Opening!, the Greater Boston area's most comfortable and earnest sex shop.

Entertainment: The eclectic lineup of films, events, amateur pornography, and author readings at the Coolidge Corner Moviehouse is hard to beat.

DORCHESTER

see map p. 334-335

All sights are on Columbia Point. ***T:*** *JFK/UMass (Red). From there, take free shuttle #2, marked "JFK Library" (daily every 20min. 8am-5:30pm).* ***Sights:*** *p. 97.*

Among the oldest and historically most troubled neighborhoods in Boston, Dorchester is now dominated by locals who live, work and go to school together in this economically and racially diverse setting. Though not geared towards or generally appropriate for tourists, Dorchester remains a vibrant, important part of Boston's landscape with a strong sense of community. Highlights include:

Sights: Experience the legacy of one of the nation's most beloved presidents and take a moment to enjoy the best view of Boston's unique skyline at the JFK Library and Museum.

JAMAICA PLAIN

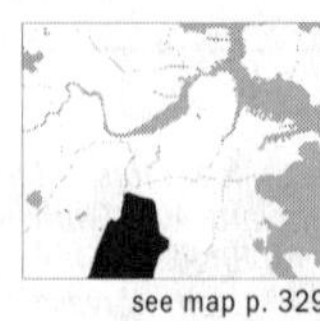
see map p. 329

T: The Orange Line runs through JP 5-6 blocks east of Centre St., the main thoroughfare. ***Sights:*** *p. 82.* ***Food:*** *p. 118.* ***Nightlife:*** *p. 144.* ***Shopping:*** *p. 172.*

Jamaica Plain's slew of vegetarian-friendly restaurants and expanses of green spaces are perhaps Boston's best kept secrets. Recently revitalized, JP is full of character with many area artists and a sizeable queer community lending itself to a liberal environment of come-as-you-are food and nightlife spots along busy **Centre St.** Highlights include:

Sights: Work up a sweat sailing on Jamaica Pond or running around the spacious Arnold Arboretum—then quench your thirst at the Sam Adams Brewery (free beer!).

Food: Cheap eats with a side of entertainment. Tacos El Charro stands out among the neighborhood's many authentic *taquerías* with its live mariachi music, while heavenly Bella Luna offers karaoke and bowling alongside their delicious gourmet pizzas.

Nightlife: As diverse and vibrant as JP's terrain—from the traditional (Brendan Behan's Pub) to the non-traditional (Dyke Night at the Midway Café).

Holidays & Festivals: Aromatic Lilac Sunday comes every May to the Arboretum.

SOUTH BOSTON

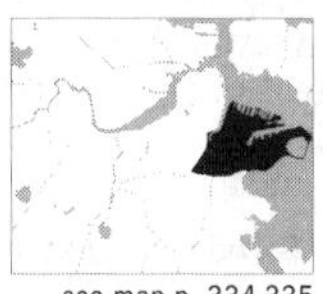

see map p. 334-335

T: Broadway (Red). Exit right onto W. Broadway, which becomes E. Broadway at Dorchester Ave. Alphabetical streets (from A to P St.) intersect Broadway. ***Sights:*** *p. 97.* ***Nightlife:*** *p. 148.*

Home to Boston's large, tightly-knit, working-class Irish community and subsequently some of the best Irish bars, filled with the best Irish people, "Southie" is a destination that is not to be missed in the pursuit of inebriation. Southie also houses enjoyable parks and historical monuments, oft overlooked by visitors and locals alike, and quite enjoyable in the daylight hours. Highlights include:

Sights: Castle Island (neither an island nor a castle) is the closest of the islands in the Harbor Islands National Park, a string of fantastic woodlands floating in Boston Harbor.

Nightlife: Forget the boisterous "pubs" around Faneuil Hall—the dark, gloomy, neighborhood joints lining Broadway are the real deal, and Lucky's on Congress St. is the best bar in town.

Holidays & Festivals: Southie's raucous and bawdy St. Patrick's Day (Mar. 17) is hardly holy, but worth a trip. For a dose of ancient Celtic culture, stop in at the summertime *ceili* on Castle Island, an afternoon of dancing, music, and Irish cuisine.

ACROSS THE RIVER

CAMBRIDGE

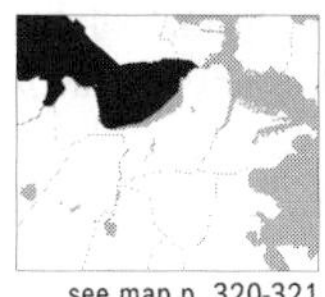

see map p. 320-321

T: Harvard (Red) lets out in Harvard Sq., at the chaotic intersection of Massachusetts Ave., Brattle St., JFK St., and Dunster St. The #69 bus (p. 21) runs from the T to Inman Sq. T: Central (Red) serves Central Sq. T: Kendall (Red) serves Kendall Sq. ***Sights:*** *p. 97.* ***Food:*** *p. 110.* ***Nightlife:*** *p. 137.* ***Shopping:*** *p. 172.* ***Accommodations:*** *p. 187.*

Like that guy next-door who feels comfortable mowing his lawn naked, and doesn't understand why you object, Cambridge is Boston's often clueless, always offbeat, liberal neighbor. Home to some of the most prestigious Universities in the country, **Harvard University** and **MIT,** Cambridge is generally populated by fun-loving nerds. Beyond the college scene, lie the other squares. Gritty **Central Sq.** is home to diverse ethnic restaurants—everything from Mexican to Tibetan—and Boston's most exciting nightlife. **East Cambridge**—centered on half-yuppie, half-hippie Inman Sq. and industrial gem Kendall Sq.—is an off-the-beaten-path hodge-podge of gourmet delights and laid-back nighttime diversions. Highlights include:

Sights: Harvard features the Carpenter Ctr. (a contemporary art mecca) and the Glass Flowers exhibit (delicate glass flower sculptures), among other delights. MIT counters with its unique campus and fascinating techno-museum.

Food: Where to begin? If the city's infinite Indian eateries and cozy cafés aren't your style, there's always hearty Tibetan at Rangzen, Boston's best falafel at Moody's, celebrity burgers at Bartley's, gourmet pizza at Emma's, spicy Afghani at the Helmand, and of course Oleana's otherworldly transcendence disguised as gourmet Mediterranean cuisine.

Nightlife: A night out in Central Sq. never disappoints, with everything from a Moroccan-themed chill lounge to a porn-filled gay dance club. Other great Cambridge watering holes include divey Charlie's Kitchen and the snazzy B-Side Lounge, a hidden neighborhood joint.

Shopping: Harvard Sq.—especially Harvard Book Store—is a book-lover's paradise. The jewel in Cambridge's multifaceted used clothing crown is the pink Garment District.

CHARLESTOWN

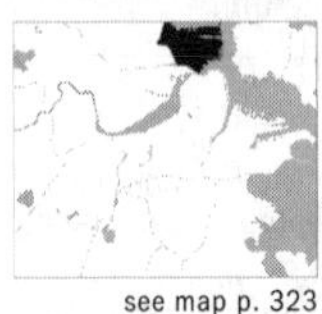

see map p. 323

T: Community College (Orange) is Charlestown's only T stop. It's easier to follow the Freedom Trail to Charlestown from T: Haymarket (Green/Orange). ***Freedom Trail Sights:*** *p. 55.*

Across the Charles River from Boston but incorporated into the city proper since 1873, Charlestown has long played an important part in the history of the Hub (and the rest of the United States) and is home to several historic sites, all of which are best visited on the **Freedom Trail** (p. 43). Highlights include:

Sights: It's a quick downhill trip from the rolling expanse of Bunker—wait, Breed's—Hill to the country's oldest watering hole, Warren Tavern.

Holidays & Festivals: Bunker Hill Day (June 17) brings parades, historic reenactments, and joyful partying in the streets.

SOMERVILLE

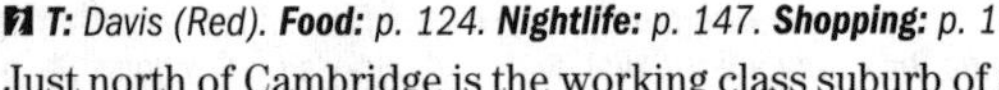

T: Davis (Red). ***Food:*** *p. 124.* ***Nightlife:*** *p. 147.* ***Shopping:*** *p. 172.*

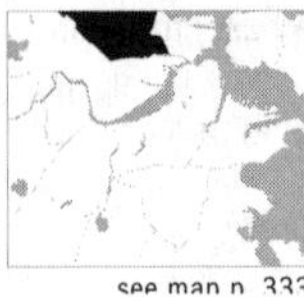

see map p. 333

Just north of Cambridge is the working class suburb of Somerville, made up of various distinctive town squares (Teele Sq., Ball Sq.) and centered on vibrant **Davis Square.** Recently voted one of the "15 hippest neighborhoods in North America," Davis is alive day and night: centered on the legendary Somerville Theatre (p. 166) and filled with plenty of superb and surreal public art and outdoor hangouts. It's a great place to spend an afternoon and evening just wandering around. In recent years, Davis has also become a mecca for queer females and their friends. Highlights include:

Food: The best branches of some of the city's best local chains—including savory Anna's Taqueria.

Nightlife: Irish eyes are smiling thanks to the divey Sligo Pub and the thick pints and traditional music at the Burren.

THINGS TO SEE & DO

Boston is so compact and walkable that you can see and do most everything you want on foot. To guide you in your travels, here's our list of can't-miss attractions:

20. New England Aquarium (p. 96). Children of all ages will delight in the Aquarium's array of Technicolor denizens of the deep, not to mention its lovable penguins and IMAX theater.

19. Boston Public Library (p. 61). A library disguised as a museum disguised as a park, the BPL (America's first lending library) draws bibliophiles, art snobs, and Internet addicts alike.

18. JFK Library (p. 79). This I.M. Pei-designed museum is both a well-appointed space and a moving reflection of one of America's most loved presidents.

17. Sam Adams Brewery (p. 83). All you ever wanted to know about beer and beer brewing, brought to you by America's winningest brew. Plus free beer! Oh, did we mention free beer?

16. MIT Museum (p. 78). A quirky, well-executed collection of robots, holograms, and other things that go <blip> in the night.

15. Haymarket (p. 81). The sheer chaos of Boston's multi-block farmers' market—right in the heart of Downtown—must be seen to be believed.

14. Faneuil Hall & Quincy Market (p. 50). The world's only shopping mall pretending to be a historical landmark, these twin colonial buildings are the most visited spots in the city.

13. Tremont St. (p. 125). It may not be as chic as Newbury St., but for gourmet food and fabulous shopping, the South End's main drag is nearly unbeatable.

12. Arnold Arboretum (p. 84). One of Boston's largest parks, the Arboretum's rolling expanses are the perfect escape from the cramped confines of the city.

11. Christian Science Plaza (p. 62). An epic expanse of grass and concrete, dominated by the ornate Mother Church, centered on a dramatic reflecting pool, and home to the fascinating Mary Baker Eddy Library.

10. Harvard Sq. Bookstores (p. 173). A must for readaholics, Harvard Sq. has some of the city's and the nation's best bookstores—from the Harvard Book Store to the creative Curious George Goes to Wordsworth.

9. Beacon Hill Brownstones. (p. 63). The city's oldest and snobbiest quarter is classic Boston, with winding cobblestone streets crammed full of gas lamps, private parks, and quaint brownstones with purple windows. See our walking tour of the neighborhood, p. 15.

8. Isabella Stewart Gardner Museum (p. 88). Well-maintained. Breathtaking. Extravagant....and that's just the atrium courtyard. Housed in a lavish turn-of-the-century mansion, the museum features the work of some of the past few centuries' most famous artists.

7. Museum of Fine Arts (p. 86). Impressive to the point of exhaustion, the globe-trotting MFA showcases every artistic and artisanal tradition known to mankind, including Japanese samurai armor, medieval musical instruments, and the largest Monet collection outside France.

6. Public Garden & Swan Boats (p. 46). A lush, beautifully manicured park smack dab in the middle of the city, the Public Garden offers year-round flowers, Boston's most beloved statue *(Make Way for Ducklings)*, and quiet sunset trips aboard the famed Swan Boats.

5. Newbury St. (p. 58). The exception to the Puritan rule, chic Newbury St. is an 8-block parade of high-priced attitude, diverse shops (from sleek luxury boutiques to musty used bookstores), and trendy outdoor cafés.

4. North End Trattories (p. 121). Charmingly Italian-American, eating in the North End is a must for visitors to Boston. Fill up on classic pasta and then grab a *cannoli* at one of the many pastry shops.

3. Harvard University (p. 71). Prestigious Harvard is the country's oldest and wealthiest university and has a historic campus and several world-class museums—showcasing the work of everyone from the Mayans to Mondrian.

2. Fenway Park (p. 85). Tourists may think Boston revolves around the Freedom Trail, but Bostonians know the city's heart lies just inside the gates of storied Fenway, America's oldest and smallest baseball park.

1. Freedom Trail (p. 43). 300 years in 2 mi.?! It's funny because it's true. Just follow the red brick road (and the camera-wielding tourist hordes) on this trip back in time to the country's exciting revolutionary beginnings.

SUGGESTED ITINERARIES

THREE DAYS

DAY 1: FREEDOM TRAIL. No trip to Boston is complete without a walk down the Freedom Trail (p. 43), which runs from the spacious **Boston Common** (p. 44) through busy **Downtown** (p. 46) and the charming **North End** (p. 52)—passing most of the city's major historical attractions en route. Boston's Italian-American quarter, the North End's twisted streets are perfect for nighttime promenading—before and after a hearty Italian meal at one of the neighborhood's *trattorie*. For a post-dinner stroll, consider aristocratic **Beacon Hill** (p. 14), an old-time neighborhood well-suited for walking after dark. Still rarin' to go after dinner? Downtown has plenty of nightlife options.

DAY 2: BACK BAY & ENVIRONS. Begin your trip through Boston's most elegant district at beautiful **Christian Science Plaza** (p. 62) and make your way northeast toward chic Newbury St. (p. 58), Boston's premier shopping destination. Pause to rest your feet (and your credit card) at breezy **Copley Sq.,** then coast into the evening

in one of the lush **Public Garden's** Swan Boats (p. 46). Though the Back Bay has its share of great restaurants, it's just a short walk (or subway ride) from here to the more affordable and phenomenal eats in **Chinatown** (p. 115)....Or maybe you'll want to hold off and return to Chinatown's late-night eateries after a night out on the Back Bay's hopping **Boylston St.** or the sexy **Theatre District** (p. 151).

DAY 3: CAMBRIDGE. Our **Walking Tour of Harvard Sq.** (p. 12) is a great way to spend a day in the heart of free-spirited Cambridge (p. 70). The tour begins with the sights and sounds of fun-filled **Harvard Sq.** and stately Harvard University, making its way east toward hip **Central Sq.,** a divey neighborhood with countless affordable ethnic eateries and Boston's most interesting nightlife. Serious foodies shouldn't even *think* of dining anywhere outside **East Cambridge,** a gourmet ghetto with countless award-winning restaurants.

FIVE DAYS

If three days just isn't enough, read on....

DAY 4: KENMORE SQ. & THE FENWAY. The Fenway is home to Boston's most cherished civic and cultural institutions—best sampled at the exquisite and intelligent **Gardner Museum** (p. 88) or through the exhausting collections of the **Museum of Fine Arts** (p. 86). Go from high-brow to low-brow in just a few blocks as you continue south along the Fenway to storied **Fenway Park** (p. 85), worth visiting on a tour even if you can't get tickets to a game. After dark, Kenmore Sq. and the Fenway play host to games of a different type: just follow the pretty young things flocking to the sweaty dance clubs along **Lansdowne St.** (p. 145).

DAY 5: SOUTH END & EMERALD NECKLACE. Ringed by a continuous string of parks known as the Emerald Necklace (p. 44), Boston is one of the greener urban spaces in the country. Consider spending the morning at one of the parks on or off the Necklace—like the Charles River Esplanade (p. 69) or Jamaica Plain's Arnold Arboretum (p. 84)—before making your way over to the trendy and gay-friendly **South End** (p. 4), a well-maintained neighborhood with some of the city's best art galleries, restaurants, and nightlife. While **Tremont St.** has long been the neighborhood's main thoroughfare, newly revived **Washington St.** is now one of the city's hottest destinations for food and fun after dark.

SEVEN DAYS

Still here? By now you're probably tired of the meager confines of the city, so it's time to branch out and leave Boston.

DAY 6: OUTER NEIGHBORHOODS. Though far from the city proper, **Dorchester's** Columbia Point (p. 79) sees many visitors thanks to the JFK Library—a thoughtful monument-*cum*-museum—and the engrossing Commonwealth Museum. Don't linger too long, though—the great outdoors await! Up the street from Columbia Point is South Boston's **Castle Island** (p. 90), a peninsula that was once part of the 30-odd wooded islands that make up the **Harbor Islands National Park** (p. 95)—a favorite destination of Boston-area outdoors enthusiasts. After a day out and about, retire to funky and gay-friendly **Jamaica Plain** (p. 6), fast becoming one of the city's most vibrant and diverse districts. With plenty of dining, shopping, and nightlife options hidden among its acres of parks and ponds, JP is a great place to finish out your trip to the Hub.

DAY 7: HISTORIC DAYTRIPS. The towns in the immediate vicinity of Boston offer a healthy dose of history and an enjoyable escape from Boston's cramped quarters. **Lexington and Concord** (p. 202) were major battlegrounds during the Revolutionary War and are not far from the natural beauty that inspired Thoreau at **Walden Pond.** For a different take on colonial America, head to witch-crazed **Salem** (p. 206).

SEASONAL HIGHLIGHTS

Boston has many different personalities, and the experience of visiting Boston varies depending on when you choose to come. While **summer** (late June-Aug.) is the busiest, **spring** (Apr.-early June) and **fall** (Sept.-early Nov.) are the most pleasant. **Winter** (late Nov.-Mar.) is to be avoided at all costs, as the cold in these northern reaches makes for a depressing landscape and even more depressed locals. For a list of official holidays and when they occur, see p. 38.

SPRING (APR.-EARLY JUNE)

There is a rumor that spring exists in Boston, but it passes by every year before anyone gets a chance to really enjoy it. However brief, the breezy, sunny pause between frigid winter and sweltering summer is one of the most exciting times to visit the city: aside from **Lilac Sunday** at the Arnold Arboretum (p. 84), there's the Red Sox opening their season at **Fenway Park** (p. 85) and the world's best runners enduring the **Boston Marathon** (p. 168). The Marathon is always run on **Patriot's Day,** which also brings reenactments of various colonial events and a traditional morning game at Fenway Park.

SUMMER (LATE JUNE-AUG.)

The scorching summer months are the most heavily touristed time of the year, as hordes of tourists spend their days walking the city's 300 years of history on the Freedom Trail (p. 43) and window-shopping along chic Newbury St. (p. 58). If you can brave the heat, don't miss the season's many **free concerts** and other outdoor events (including Government Center's **Scooper Bowl;** see p. 81), culminating in the spectacular music and fireworks of the annual **4th of July** festivities at the Hatch Shell (on the Esplanade; see p. 69). The days before and after the 4th are celebrated as **Harborfest,** when Boston hosts countless patriotic and maritime events, plus the annual chowder cook-off known as **Chowderfest.** Throughout the season, each neighborhood celebrates its heritage with music, food, and fun at various ethnic **festivals;** the most popular of these are undoubtedly the boisterous Catholic feast days in the North End (p. 121).

FALL (SEPT.-EARLY NOV.)

Fall begins with the attack of the minivans—when students flood the city and move in to dorms at Boston's numerous universities and colleges. The **Head of the Charles Regatta**—the world's largest boat race—brings preppies past and present to the shores of the Charles River for a weekend of fun in the sun. Autumn in New England is synonymous with **fall foliage,** when the trees turn stunning shades of red, orange, and brown. Though the truly amazing foliage is farther inland in western Massachusetts, Boston's many green spaces do put up a respectable show—remember that leaves change color in the city later than elsewhere.

WINTER (DEC.-MAR.)

The blustery, damp, and gray winter won't show you Boston (or Bostonians) at their best. There is a brief influx of travelers in late December, when crowds flock to the city to celebrate the nation's original **First Night,** an alcohol-free New Year's Eve celebration. Though the slopes and powder are nothing like the US Rockies or the Alps, New England's copious snowfall and craggy terrain make for some great **skiing** (for more info, see our **Skiing New England** chapter on p. 251). Many mark the end of winter and the start of spring on Mar. 17, better known as **St. Patrick's Day.** After a wild parade down Broadway in predominantly Irish Catholic Southie (South Boston; see p. 7), drunken revelers all over Boston dance in the streets and down pints in the city's many Irish (and faux-Irish) pubs; whatever you do, don't wear orange.

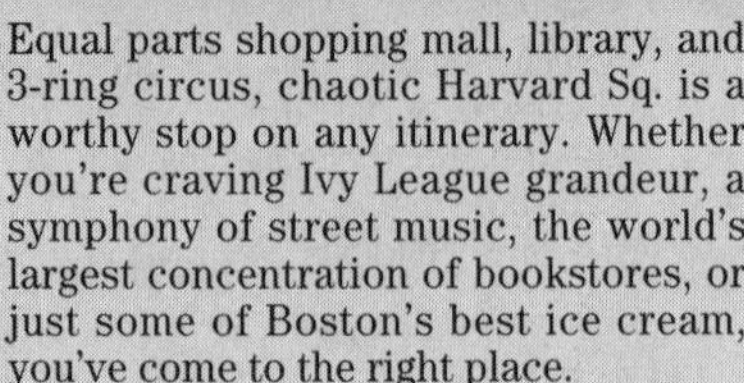

Equal parts shopping mall, library, and 3-ring circus, chaotic Harvard Sq. is a worthy stop on any itinerary. Whether you're craving Ivy League grandeur, a symphony of street music, the world's largest concentration of bookstores, or just some of Boston's best ice cream, you've come to the right place.

LENGTH: 0.6 mi. (1km)

DURATION: 3-4hr.

START: T: Harvard (Red)

FINISH: T: Harvard (Red)

1 THE PIT. You'll emerge from the Harvard T stop into what is affectionately referred to as "The Pit"—a stretch of brick that shows you Harvard Sq. at its funhouse best. Battle the hordes of tourists and gangs of pierced and disaffected youth for a prime viewing spot at one of the many impromptu street music performances—featuring everyone from Beatles impersonators and string quartets to guitar-strumming folkies. If you're a fan of bad puns or the radio show *Car Talk* (or both), look for the upper-floor offices of the fictitious law firm Dewey, Cheetham, & Howe (get it?); the silly auto advice show broadcasts from that building.

2 CAMBRIDGE COMMON. Walk north up Mass Ave to the large green park where history was made (a couple of times). Stop on the way to admire the statue of William Dawes, Paul Revere's midnight ride companion who rode through the park and was later shafted by Longfellow in his famous poem. Gaze across at the Washington Elm in the south corner, where Gen. Washington assumed control of the Revolutionary Army.

3 MEMORIAL HALL. As you walk across the street and towards the next stop, Harvard Law School lies to the left behind the giant marble Littauer Building, and Memorial Hall looms up ahead. Built in 1870 to commemorate those Harvard graduates who died fighting for the Union Army in the Civil War, Memorial Hall is now home Harvard's ridiculously epic freshman dining hall (closed to the public), and the gorgeous music and theater venue Sander's Theatre (p. 157).

4 JOHN HARVARD STATUE. Enter Harvard Yard and bear right; each building in this portion of the yard is a freshman dormitory. Presiding over it all is larger-than-life statue of Harvard's namesake John Harvard, known as the "Statue of the Three Lies" because (1) the statue was not modeled on John Harvard; (2) Harvard did not found the college, but only donated money to it; and (3) the college was founded in 1636, not 1638. Visitors often rub his well-shined shoe for good luck, but they'd think twice if they knew what Harvard tradition dictates every student do to him before graduation.

5 TERCENTENARY THEATRE. On the other side of the building behind John Harvard—University Hall, designed by Charles Bulfinch (p. 68)—lies the expanse of grass known as Tercentenary Theatre, site of Harvard's annual commencement ceremonies. To your left lies Memorial Church, built in 1932 to commemorate those who died in WWI and added to after each subsequent war. Opposite U-Hall is Sever Hall, a classroom building that's unremarkable save for its arched entranceway, where acoustics are such that a person whispering on one side can be heard perfectly on the other.

6 WIDENER LIBRARY. Looming ominously over Tercentenary Theatre is Harry Elkins Widener Memorial Library, named for a student who drowned on the Titanic and whose mother donated the money for the library on the condition that all matriculating Harvard students pass a swimming test (the rule has since been repealed). Home to 5.5 million volumes from Harvard's 13 million holdings (the world's largest university collection and the second largest total collection in the country), In winter, students sled down the snow-banked steps on cafeteria trays. The library is closed to the public for security reasons.

7 FOGG ART MUSUEM & CARPENTER CENTER. You're at Harvard—time for an education. From Widener, head left out the gates and across Quincy St. to the Fogg Museum (p. 74), which offers an excellent (if small) survey of the last few centuries in European and American fine art (all in a quiet, Venetian-inspired setting). Continue through the annals of art history at the Carpenter Ctr. (p. 96) next

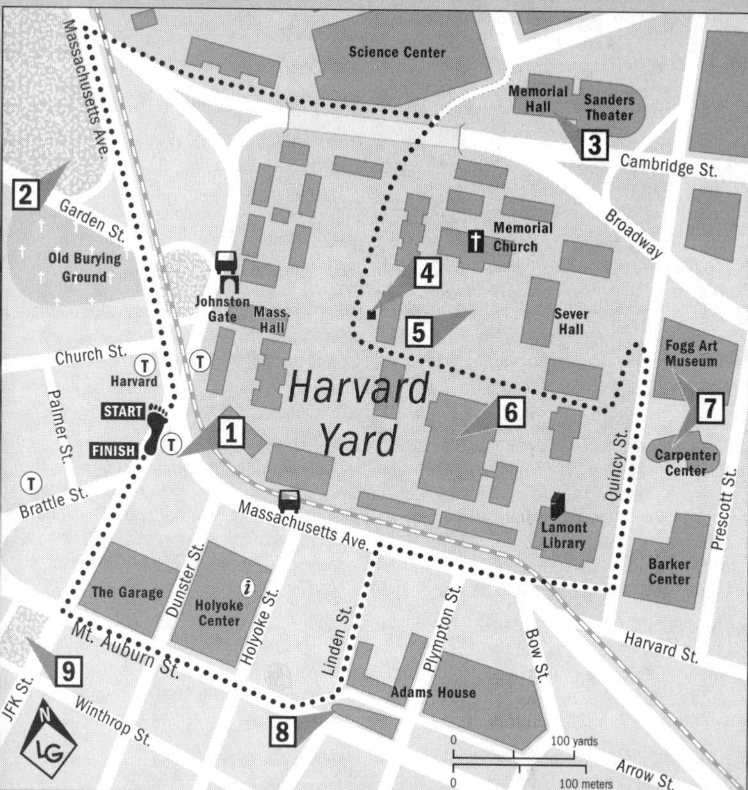

door. This unusual building—the only one in North America designed by Le Corbusier (and the only one to be described as "two pianos humping")—is home to 2 of the area's hottest contemporary art galleries, as well as the avant-garde Harvard Film Archive. Continue Down Quincy St. to Mass Ave., but before you get to far, grab an ice cream from Harvard's best scoopers, Toscanini's (p. 110). Continue down Linden St. to Mt. Auburn St.

8 LAMPOON CASTLE. No, you're not imagining things—the Lampoon Castle really *is* laughing at you. Although home to Harvard's humor magazine the *Lampoon*—which produced Conan O'Brien and spawned *Animal House*—the building's clownish façade (complete with beanie-shaped roof) may be the funniest thing about the place. The interior is only open to Lampoon members and their guests; if you really must see inside, backtrack to Schoenhof's and pick up a copy of *Babar Goes to America,* in which Babar tours the castle.

9 WINTHROP SQ. Head down Mt. Auburn St.—noting the *Let's Go* world headquarters at #67 on your right—to JFK St. There you'll find this small patch of grassy calm popular with resting bike messengers and lunching suits. Consider stopping in at Grendel's Den (p. 140)—on the edge of the square—to raise a pint to the separation of church and state: the dark underground bar/restaurant was the defendant in a 1982 US Supreme Court case that overturned a Massachusetts law, which had allowed churches to ban bars from selling alcohol. Now head up JFK St. (stopping when necessary to shop) and take the T back to the big city or to dinner in delectable Inman or Kendall Sq. (p. 113).

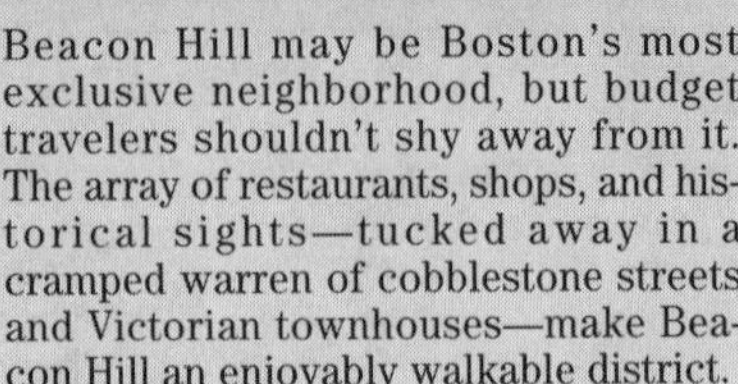

Beacon Hill may be Boston's most exclusive neighborhood, but budget travelers shouldn't shy away from it. The array of restaurants, shops, and historical sights—tucked away in a cramped warren of cobblestone streets and Victorian townhouses—make Beacon Hill an enjoyably walkable district.

LENGTH: 1 mi. (1.6km)

DURATION: ½ day

START: T: Park St. (Green)

FINISH: T: Charles/MGH (Red)

1 BOSTON COMMON & THE PUBLIC GARDEN. Exiting T: Park St., you'll find yourself in the heart of Boston, looking up at its skyscrapers through the green of Boston Common and the Public Garden (p. 46). Take your time meandering through the Common, while enjoying its quirky *Make Way for Ducklings* bronze sculpture and the kid-pleasing Frog Pond. The many benches are perhaps the best place in Boston to pause and absorb the feel of the city and its inhabitants. If you're feeling extra ambitious, stroll through the Common and into the Public Garden where you'll be greeted by Swan Pond and its famous boats. Both the Common and the Public Garden are classic settings for a picnic before you embark on the rest of your Beacon Hill explorations.

2 SHAW MEMORIAL. This larger-than-life bronze relief commemorates the 1863 death of Robert Gould Shaw and members of his 54th regiment, the first free black regiment recruited by the North during the American Civil War. Coming up the steps from Boston Common, your first sight of the memorial will be its backside, inscribed with a dedication by then-president of Harvard University, Charles Norton Eliot. Plaques in front of the memorial give details about the battle (at Ft. Sumter, South Carolina) where Shaw died, and offer historical information on the memorial's sculptor, Augustus St.-Gaudens. An alternate walking tour of Beacon Hill—the Black Heritage Trail (see p. 66)—departs from here as well. For more info on the memorial, see p. 46.

3 MASSACHUSETTS STATE HOUSE. The Shaw Memorial sits in the shadow of this gold-domed temple to democracy, just across the street. Even more striking than the stately exterior—modeled after Greek law courts (this is the Athens of America, after all)—is the lavishly decorated interior. Take a guided tour (every 40min.) of the inside or grab a self-guided tour pamphlet at the entrance. For more on the state house, see p. 67.

4 NICHOLS HOUSE. As you make your way up Beacon Hill away from the State House, you'll walk along countless streets lined with understated but ridiculously expensive townhouses (some are worth more than $5 million). These are once and forever the private homes of Boston's wealthy upper-crust, christened "Boston Brahmins" by one of their own, Oliver Wendell Holmes. The purple windows on some of the older houses are not an artistic statement, but an imperfection in the original 19th-century glass caused by exposure to sunlight. Charles Bulfinch (p. 68) is the man behind the townhouses' distinctive look. Unfortunately, Nichols House is the only Beacon Hill townhouse open to the public; its interior has been carefully restored and furnished with period artifacts, offering a glimpse into how the 19th-century elite once lived and a chance to become better acquainted with Bulfinch's style. For more on the Nichols House, see p. 67.

5 MT. VERNON STREET. This row of quiet townhouses—considered some of the most beautiful in all of Beacon Hill—oozes the 19th-century Victorian charm you came to the neighborhood to see. Why you may not be able to afford the cobblestone and red brick, antique lampposts and door knockers, miniature gardens, and (of course) purple windows, looking is always free.

6 LOUISBURG SQUARE. The supposed birthplace of door-to-door Christmas caroling is also one of the most elite and desirable addresses in the city. Boston Brahmins can't seem to agree on what part of Louisburg Sq. is the most valuable: Is it the elegant brownstones, the gated park in the middle (open only to Louisburg Sq. residents), or the guaranteed private parking in a city where even the mayor can't find a place to park? For more on Louisburg Sq., see p. 66.

7 CHARLES STREET. This busy street is the beating heart of Beacon Hill, and a great place to spend a sunny afternoon. (Note that this is mostly window-shopping territory—on Charles St., even the 7-11 is swank.) Having trouble picking from among the countless antique

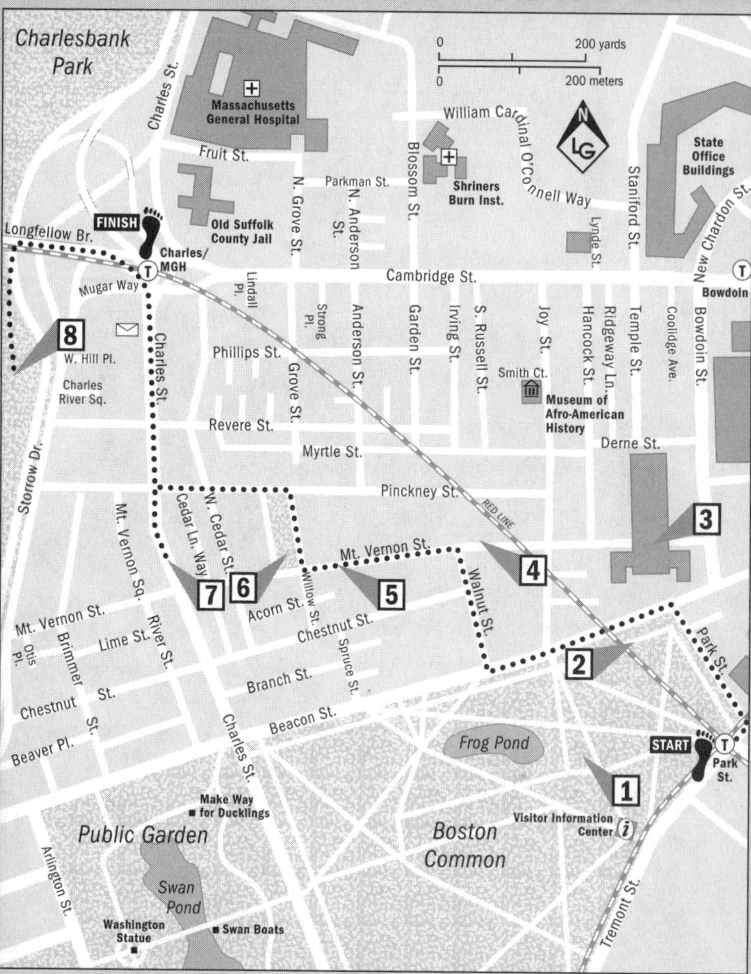

shops, restaurants for every budget, and numerous upscale boutiques with unbearably trendy names (good, wish, moxie, etc.)? Our vote is for the hip trinkets and "unexpected necessities" at **Black Ink** (p. 178), the eclectic furnishings (everything *including* the kitchen sink) at **Koo de Kir** (p. 179). For a pit stop, the cheap local diner the **Paramount** (p. 108), also infamous as one of the sites of a Boston Strangler murder has some greasy and filling breakfast options.

8 THE ESPLANADE. The best place to rest your feet after a day of climbing up and down Beacon Hill is the Charles River Esplanade, a lush stretch of park that runs along the Charles River (just beyond the Charles/MGH T stop, at the end of Charles St.). If you're still feeling active, join the masses of bikers, sunbathers, and dog owners as they tour the Charles River. Otherwise, plant yourself on the river bank and watch the sailing and rowing that enlivens the Charles River Basin. The Esplanade is also home to the Hatch Shell, a popular spot for free summertime concerts, including the Boston Pops' Fourth of July extravaganza. For more info, see p. 69.

E
HEATH STREET
HUNTINGTON AVE
3624

Once in Boston

ARRIVING & DEPARTING

LOGAN INTERNATIONAL AIRPORT

T: Airport (Blue). ***Contact:*** *☎800-235-6426 or 800-235-6486 US only; www.massport.com/logan.*

Every major national and international airline carrier serves Boston's only airport, Logan International (airport code BOS). For up-to-date weather, traffic, and flight delay info, call or check the website above.

GROUND TRANSPORT

Logan is a mere 5 mi. from downtown Boston. However, traffic and construction around the airport is so bad (thanks to the Big Dig; see p. 99) that it is often just as fast and much cheaper to travel by subway as it is to travel by taxi or private shuttle. Times and prices listed in parentheses below are for trips between the airport and downtown Boston.

BY T (30MIN.; $1). The subway (known as the T; p. 19) is by far the cheapest way to get to and from the airport, though maneuvering around if you have lots of luggage is difficult and may make a taxi or private shuttle worth the cost. The T closes at 1am (F-Sa 2:30am), so if your flight arrives or departs after 1am, you're stuck taking a taxi or shuttle.

To get to the airport from anywhere in Boston, take the T to **T: Airport (Blue),** about a 30min. ride from downtown. A free shuttle bus constantly makes the 10min. trip between the T station and the five **airport terminals,** lettered A-E. The board outside the T station lists which airlines fly out of which terminals. T fare is $1, regardless of distance, and trains run between downtown and T: Airport every 5-10min. To get from the airport to downtown Boston by T, follow the signs to ground transportation; the free shuttles back to T: Airport (Blue) leave from there.

If you're catching a late-night flight out of Boston and plan on using the T, your only option is the T's "Night Owl" service (which only runs F-Sa 12:30-2:30am; see p. 20 for more info). Take the poetic T: Wonderland (Blue), from T: Government Ctr. (Blue/Green), to T: Wood Island (Blue) where you can catch free shuttles for the five terminals.

BY TAXI (20-30MIN.; $15). Taxis are the most convenient and most expensive way of getting to and from the airport. Although taxis are usually also the fastest route to the airport, traffic and construction near Logan often means that a taxi ride can take longer than the T; expect up to 1hr. trips to and from downtown if you dare to brave Boston traffic during rush hour (M-F 6:30-9am and 4-6pm).

Taxis are available at Logan terminals daily 24hr. and provide service to all of New England. For those traveling to Logan, any taxi in the city will also be happy to take you to the airport. Trips between the airport and all parts of Boston, Brookline, Cambridge, and Somerville covered in this book (i.e. everywhere except places in the **Daytrips from Boston** chapter) are based on **metered rates,** a $1.50 airport fee, and all tolls (like the $3 Harbor Tunnel toll). Metered rates between Logan and popular destinations are approximately: Back Bay/Copley Sq., $16; Cambridge, $25-30; Downtown, $15; Kenmore Sq., $17. For more information on taxis, see p. 21. For a list of taxi companies, see the **Service Directory** p. 284.

BY SHUTTLE (20-30MIN.; $12). The popular **Back Bay Coach** (☎888-222-5229; www.backbay-coach.com) runs a door-to-door van service between Logan Airport and destinations in the Greater Boston area. They boast cheaper prices than taxis, but one must be willing to wait for a van to fill to reap the benefits. From the outer reaches of the city (Brookline, Cambridge, Jamaica Plain, Kenmore Sq. the Fenway, Somerville, etc.), their prices are 30-50% cheaper than taxis. It's best to reserve 24hr. in advance online or over the phone, but you can also call upon arrival for a shuttle if you're willing to wait a while. Rates are fixed by destination and payable using credit card or cash: to and from Downtown $9 each way; to and from Cambridge or Somerville $12-16.

SOUTH STATION (BUSES & TRAINS)

At Summer St. and Atlantic Ave. ***T:*** *South Station (Red).*

Most buses and trains traveling to and from Boston stop at South Station, just east of Chinatown and south of Downtown. The station has access to the T (Red Line), and there are city taxis waiting outside. At night, the area around the station is deserted and may be unsafe; all amenities (food, restrooms, gifts, even a bar) can be found inside the station.

The two other train stations in the city are: **North Station,** 135 Causeway St., T: North Station (Green/Orange), which serves some buses; and **Back Bay Station,** 145 Dartmouth St., T: Back Bay (Orange), which only serves Amtrak (see p. 264). Both stations are on subway lines, although neither is on a line with frequent trains or a central location. Your best bet if you're arriving by train or bus is to stay aboard until you reach South Station.

GETTING AROUND

ON FOOT

The best way to see Boston is on foot. From the Freedom Trail to Boston Common, the city is best understood by walking through the neighborhoods. Nicknamed "America's Walking City," Boston is small and centralized. The subway (T) goes everywhere, but its layout exaggerates the distances between destinations and taking it eliminates much of the "off-the-beaten trail" allure of walking. Boston drivers are among the most aggressive in the nation, but usually defer to pedestrians at crosswalks, who are even more aggressive, ignoring crosswalks altogether in favor of walking whenever and wherever they want.

BY PUBLIC TRANSPORTATION

***Massachusetts Bay Transportation Authority** (main switchboard ☎617-222-5000, routes and schedules ☎617-222-3200; www.mbta.com). Maps available at most T stops and on buses. The website has the most up-to-date schedules, maps, and fares.*

America's first public transportation system, the MBTA began in 1897 by ferrying a few thousand passengers from Park St. to Boylston St. along Boston Common (p. 44); today it moves 1.2 million passengers per day using subways (known as the "T"), buses, light rails, and ferries. Although at times it may feel as though the T still uses its original 19th-century tracks and cars, the entire system is relatively modern, clean, and very safe. It is by far the most inexpensive, convenient, and extensive means of travel within Boston and Cambridge.

The major drawback to public transport for travelers is that buses and trains only run 5am-12:30am. By 1am, all public transport shuts down, even though most nightlife establishments stay open until 2am. Most nights you'll be stuck taking a taxi (see p. 21); however, to accommodate late-night revelers on weekends, the T has instituted a "Night Owl" service that runs F-Sa until 2:30am (for more info, see p. 20).

BY SUBWAY (T)

The subway system is split into five colored lines—Red, Blue, Orange, Silver, and Green—that radiate out from downtown Boston (Park St. Station) in every direction. The Green line splits into four lettered lines, B-E. Trains run every 5-10min. on the Red and Green lines, and less frequently on Blue, Orange, and Silver lines. Stops on most lines are named intuitively (The Museum of Fine Arts is at T: Museum, Harvard University is at T: Harvard, etc.), so navigation is a breeze. This guide mentions the T stop and line closest to every establishment listed.

Trains on all lines travel in one of two directions toward either terminus of the line. Though the front of most trains lists the appropriate terminus, signs within the station only point to "inbound" and "outbound" trains. Check the color system map in the middle of this guide to determine which direction you want: **inbound** trains are headed in the direction of T: Park St. or T: Downtown Crossing, while **outbound** trains head away from those stops.

T FARE. A T ride costs $1 each way in most cases. (ages 5-11 40¢, seniors with a senior ID pass 20¢). Some outlying stations such as Braintree and Quincy Adams on (T:Red) cost $2 to travel inbound and require $1 to exit the station. Station attendants man token booths at underground stations; at above-ground stations, insert a token, coins, or a $1 bill into the machine at the front of the train. Contrary to posted signs, the machine takes bills, though drivers don't have change. At stations served by two or more lines, you can transfer freely between lines at no cost.

BY BUS

The MBTA also runs a fleet of buses along set routes throughout the city. Though not as reliable or safe as the T, buses are sometimes the most convenient option for getting around a certain neighborhood. **To get on a bus,** stand at a street-side bus stop, marked by a pole-mounted, T-emblazoned white sign with a list of the bus lines that pass by it; the bus should pull over. If a bus leaves from a T stop, it usually leaves from the street outside the entrance. **To get off a bus,** press the yellow tape by the windows. If you're unsure of where to get off, just ask the bus driver. T: Harvard (Red) and all the T stops downtown—Park St., Government Ctr., State, and Downtown Crossing—have schedules and maps. For a complete list of schedules and maps, check online www.mbta.com/traveling_t/schedules_buses. Here are the most useful bus routes and the major attractions and T stops they pass by:

Bus #1: Harvard Sq. - Dudley via Mass. Ave. Fastest route between Cambridge and the Back Bay/ Newbury St. Departs daily every 10min. 5am-1am from Harvard's Johnston Gate at T: Harvard (Red). **#1 Night Owl** (every 30min. F-Sa 1-2:30am) follows the same route. *T: Harvard (Red) - T: Central (Red) - MIT - Newbury St. - T: Symphony (Green) - Tremont St. (South End) - Dudley Station.*

Bus #66: Harvard Sq. - Dudley via Brookline. Fastest route between Cambridge, Allston, and Brookline. Departs daily every 10-15min. from Cambridge Common park (see p. 70) near T: Harvard (Red). **#66 Night Owl** (every 30min. F-Sa 1-2:30am) follows the same route. *T: Harvard (Red) - Brighton Ave. (Allston) - T: Coolidge Corner (Green-B) - Dudley Station.*

Bus #69: Harvard Sq. - Lechmere via Cambridge St. Runs to Cambridge's Inman Sq. (p. 7). Departs daily every 20-30min. 5:30am-12:30am from Harvard's Johnston Gate at T: Harvard (Red). *Harvard Sq. - Inman Sq. - Lechmere/CambridgeSide Galleria.*

BUS FARE. Most visitors will be able to get everywhere using the T, but buses may occasionally be useful. Bus fare is 75¢ (children and high school students 40¢, seniors with ID 15¢). The machine at the front of the bus takes both exact change and—despite the signs—$1 bills (just don't expect change back; slip your bill in the slot on the left side of the change machine). If you will be taking a different bus later in the day, ask the driver for a paper transfer. Unless you have a Visitor Pass or monthly combo pass (see below), you cannot transfer between a bus and the subway, or vice versa.

PASSES

If you're moving to Boston and live far from work and play, it's definitely worth investing in a **monthly pass** for unlimited travel each month on buses ($25), subways ($35), or both ($57 combo pass). Riding the T or a bus twice a day, a monthly pass pays for itself in just over two weeks.

For short-term visitors, the pass situation is different. The city is so small that you really can see and do most everything on foot. If you don't mind walking, you shouldn't need to ride the T more than 2-3 times per day, meaning you can probably do without the flashy unlimited-travel **Visitor Passes** (1-day $6, 3-day $11, 7-day $22). If you'll be in Boston for 5-7 days, the pass that will save you money is the **Weekly Combo Pass** ($12.50), good for unlimited bus and T travel for a week (always Su-Sa). These passes are only sold M-F and Su at the following T stations: Harvard (Red) and Park St. (Green/Red) 11am-7pm; Kenmore (Green-B,C,D) and Haymarket (Green) 6:30am-midnight; and Government Ctr. (Green) 4-7pm. All passes except the Weekly Combo Pass are available at stations, over the phone (☎877-939-0929 or ☎617-222-5218), or online (http://commerce.mbta.com).

BY "NIGHT OWL"

The "Night Owl" late-night transportation service starts when normal T service ends, running 1-2:30am on **Friday and Saturday nights,** technically Saturday and Sunday mornings. Specially marked above-ground buses ("rail buses") run to and from **Government Ctr.** (p. 81), following 10 routes almost identical to portions of the T's colored subway lines. The routes are named after their terminus and the color of their daytime line (i.e. "Red Alewife"). Stops are marked by white plaques on the side of the street, always featuring the "Night Owl" symbol of a bleary-eyed owl. Buses leave Government Ctr. headed for the 10 termini (as well as in the opposite direction) F-Sa every 30min. 1-2:30am.

NIGHT OWL FARE. Fare for a ride on the "Night Owl" is $1 and includes a free transfer at Government Ctr. to any of the other "Night Owl" lines. In the Nightlife chapter (p. 133), we list the "Night Owl" lines and stops that correspond to regular T stops.

OTHER TRANSPORT

BY TAXI

If you can't wait to hail a taxi on the street, see p. 284 for a list of local taxi companies; most bars also post local taxi companies' numbers.

Although they're not nearly as frequent or common as they are in other US cities, taxis can be hailed relatively easily on most streets in Boston, just raise your hand and wave one over. There are **taxi stands** near all major hotels, along Mass. Ave. in Harvard Sq., and outside train stations and all terminals of Logan Airport. Empty taxis are difficult to find after 1am (after 2:30am F-Sa), when public transportation shuts down and taxis are the only transport available. Arcane Puritan-era "blue laws" (see **Drugs & Alcohol,** p. 24) force liquor-selling establishments to close nightly at 2am, so if you want to flag down a taxi around that time, head to where they congregate, near Boston nightlife: Kenmore Sq., Harvard Sq. in Cambridge, Boylston St. in the Back Bay, and along Brighton and Commonwealth Ave. in Allston.

BY CAR

In an effort to keep tourists and other non-locals from driving in their town Bostonians have embarked upon an unmatched campaign of automotive terror. Through the cunning use of one-way streets, expensive parking that is always full, and confusing, badly maintained roads, Bostonians have made it almost impossible to drive in the city. Boston drivers, who smugly refer to themselves as "Massholes," are apt pugilists, with nothing but contempt for motorists with rental or out-of-state plates. They have a proudly cultivated reputation as the most careless and aggressive motorists in the nation. If you have a car, your safest (and in the long run, cheapest) bet is to pay for a spot in a parking garage and use your car sparingly.

To rent a car, you must be at least 21 years old (some places at least 25 years) and have a valid US or Canadian driver's license or an International Driving Permit (IDP; see p. 264). Insurance requirements in the US are complicated; ask your car rental agency. Prices and availability vary from day to day and agency to agency (check www.rentalcarguide.com/boston.htm to compare prices across companies). Popular agencies include the following; all are at Logan Airport (p. 17), unless another location is indicated.

Adventure Rent-a-Car, 139 Brighton Ave. (☎617-783-3825). **Allston.** T: Harvard Ave. (Green-B). From $34 per day (100 mi. included). Insurance $13. Must be 21+; $5 per day surcharge for under 25. Open M-Sa 8am-5:30pm.

Alamo (☎800-462-5266, in Boston ☎617-561-4100; www.alamo.com). Must be 21+; $25 per day surcharge for under 25. Open 24hr.

Avis (☎800-331-1212, in Boston ☎617-561-3500; www.avis.com). Locations throughout the city, including a 24hr. site at the airport. 25+ only.

Budget (☎800-527-0700; www.budget.com). Locations throughout the city. Must be 21+; $30 per day surcharge for under 25.

Dollar (☎800-800-3665, in Boston ☎617-634-0006; www.dollar.com). Locations throughout the city, including a 24hr. site at the airport. Must be 21+; $30 per day surcharge for under 25.

Enterprise (☎800-736-8222, in Boston ☎617-561-4488; www.enterprise.com). Locations throughout the city, including one at the airport (M-F 7am-10pm, Sa-Su 9am-10pm). Must be 21+; $25 per day surcharge for under 25.

Hertz (☎800-654-3131; www.hertz.com). Locations throughout the city. 25+ only.

National (☎800-227-7368; www.nationalcar.com). Two locations in the Boston area, one in Cambridge and another at the airport. Must be 21+; $30 per day surcharge for under 25.

Thrifty (☎800-847-4389, in Boston ☎877-283-0898; www.thrifty.com). Airport location. Must be 21+; $30 per day surcharge for under 25.

BY BICYCLE

MassBike (Massachusetts Biking Coalition) lists trails, shops, tips, and other bike-related info (like getting T passes for bikes) at www.massbike.org. ***Police:*** *stolen property ☎617-343-4240.*

Bikes are quite common and useful in Boston, which is so small that you can bike from one end of the city to the other in under an hour. Many nearby daytrips (p. 195)—such as popular Walden Pond—are also possible and rather enjoyable by bike. There are also many scenic bike trails in the Boston area, the most popular being the path along the Charles River.

The downside to the popularity of bikes is that they are also popular with thieves. Never leave your bike unlocked or unattended, as it will be stolen in a matter of minutes; buy a U-lock, and always remember to lock your front wheel as well as the bike frame.

Popular bike rental spots include:

Back Bay Bikes, 336 Newbury St. (☎617-247-2336; www.backbaybicycle.com). **Back Bay.** T: Hynes/ICA (Green-B,C,D). $20 per day. Open in summer M-F 10am-7pm, Sa 10am-6pm, Su noon-5pm; off-season M-Sa 10am-6pm, Su noon-5pm.

Bicycle Exchange, 2067 Massachusetts Ave. (☎617-864-1300). **Cambridge.** T: Porter (Red). $20 per day. Open Tu-Sa 9am-6pm, Su noon-5pm.

Cambridge Bicycle, 259 Massachusetts Ave. (☎617-876-6555). **Cambridge.** T: Central (Red). $25 per 24hr. Open M-Sa 10am-7pm, Su noon-6pm.

Community Bicycle, 496 Tremont St. (☎617-542-8623). **South End.** T: Back Bay (Orange) or T: E. Berkeley St. (Silver). $20 per 24hr. Open M-F 10am-7pm, Sa 10am-6pm, Su noon-5pm.

TOURIST OFFICES

The many tourist offices in the Boston area provide a logical starting point for anyone looking for more information on a particular part of the city.

Cambridge Office for Tourism (☎617-497-1630 or 617-441-2884; www.cambridge-usa.org) runs a Visitor Information Booth outside T: Harvard (Red). Open M-F 9am-5pm, Sa 10am-3pm, Su 1-5pm.

Greater Boston Convention & Visitors Bureau, 2 Copley Pl., #105 (☎617-536-4100; www.bostonusa.com). **Back Bay.** T: Copley (Green). Runs two info booths, one on Boston Common (p. 44) in **Beacon Hill,** just outside T: Park St. (Green/Red) and the other in the Prudential Center, T: Prudential (Green). Open M-F 8:30am-5pm.

National Historic Park Visitor Ctr., 15 State St. (☎617-242-5642; www.nps.gov/bost). **Downtown.** T: State (Blue/Orange). Freedom Trail info and tours. Open daily 9am-5pm. Another Visitor Ctr. in **Charlestown,** in the Charlestown Navy Yard. Open in summer 9am-6pm; off-season 9am-5pm.

HEALTH & SAFETY

MEDICAL CARE

Boston's many top-notch hospitals and medical facilities ensure that health services in the city are among the best in the country, if not the world; just make sure you have travel insurance (see p. 262). If someone is in a life-threatening situation, dial ☎**911** (toll-free) from any phone for police and/or ambulance services. For less acute situations, most Boston hospitals run 24hr. walk-in emergency rooms (ERs); see p. 283 of the **Service Directory** for the hospital nearest you.

For minor ailments (coughs, blisters, etc.), head to one of the many drugstores or pharmacies throughout the city (**CVS** and **Walgreens** are the biggest chains). Many convenience stores (7-11, Store24, City Convenience) also sell non-prescription drugs and remedies. If you're unsure of what you need, the trained pharmacist behind the prescription drugs counter can recommend medication. Unlike in other parts of the world, most drugstores and pharmacies in Boston are open late (until about 8-10pm) and on Sundays (until about 5-6pm). For Boston's 24hr. pharmacies, see p. 283:

PERSONAL SAFETY

Boston is as safe as any other large urban area in the United States. Theft is not that common, violence even less so. There is no sure-fire way to protect yourself from harm, but you should feel safe as long as you use common sense: travel in groups whenever possible; familiarize yourself with your surroundings before setting out; carry yourself with confidence; and duck into shops or inconspicuous places if you need to check a map or this guide.

PROTECTING YOURSELF

Boston and Cambridge are so small that you're never too far from safe neighborhoods and places where there are lots of people and activity. Nevertheless, use caution when in Dorchester, Roxbury, and the parts of the South End south of Washington St., and avoid walking in these neighborhoods at night. Most daytime outdoor gathering places—such as Downtown Crossing (p. 80), Boston Common (p. 44), and the paths along the Charles River—are deserted at night, and might be less safe for those traveling alone. The city's former red-light district (the "Combat Zone" between Chinatown and Downtown, near the Ladder District; see p. 141) has been recently cleaned up, but you should still be very cautious there at night.

MONEY & VALUABLES

Petty theft and pickpocketing on the T and in the streets is rare, but that doesn't mean you shouldn't be cautious. Don't keep all your valuables (money, passport, important documents) in one place: split your money and IDs and keep some locked up in a safe at your place of accommodation. If you have multiple ATM and credit cards, designate a certain credit card as your "emergency" card and don't carry it with you.

PUBLIC TRANSPORTATION

The T may not be spotless, but it is fairly safe, much safer than other US public transportation systems, such as the subways in Chicago or New York. Most lines and stations of the T are safe in the daytime, but at night, the Blue Line, Orange Line, and the southern stops on the Red Line are fairly deserted and may be less safe.

TERRORISM

In light of the September 11, 2001 attacks on New York City and Was[illegible], the national government has warned of an increased threa[illegible]rrorist activities in the United States. Terrorists often target la[illegible]ular with tourists (which explains the closing of the John Hanc[illegible]. 60); however, the threat of an attack is not specific enough to war[illegible]oiding certain places or modes of transportation. Stay aware of developme[illegible]s in the news and watch for alerts from law enforcement. Allow extra time for airport security procedures and do not pack sharp objects in your carry-on luggage, as these will be confiscated.

DRUGS & ALCOHOL

Boston can't shake the fact that it was built by Puritans: laws regarding the vices are strictly enforced, and penalties for breaking those laws are harsh.

The minimum **drinking age** in Boston and the rest of the US is 21, and that age limit is strictly enforced. Those used to the less vigilant carding in Europe and other parts of the US should consider themselves warned: unless you and everyone in your party looks over 35, you cannot purchase beer or hard liquor from a store or a bar until you show a photo ID that (1) says you are at least 21 and (2) is issued by a state, national, or international government. Holders of out-of-state driver's licenses or international IDs will most likely be asked for back-up ID (such as a student ID, ATM card, or credit card).

Massachusetts' **blue laws** have yet to be repealed, meaning that all liquor stores are closed Sundays and cannot sell liquor after 10:45pm the rest of the week (bars, pubs, and dance clubs are not affected by this). Equally old zoning laws dictate that some nightlife establishments serving liquor can only stay open until 1am (last call around 12:45am). Every place that sells liquor must shut down by 2am (last call 1:30-1:45am).

Drug possession of any sort is illegal, and penalties are severe (including fines and jail time), even in regards to drugs such as marijuana, which are less penalized or decriminalized in other countries. Tobacco products are not sold to anyone under 18, another strictly enforced law. This year legislation was also passed prohibiting smoking in all public buildings, restaurants, and bars. For more on the ban, see the In Recent News feature, p. 136.

EMBASSIES & CONSULATES

CONSULAR SERVICES IN BOSTON

All foreign embassies to the United States are in the nation's capital, Washington, D.C. Their contact numbers are listed below, but call or check www.embassyworld.org for hours. There are a few consulates in Boston, listed below. In an emergency, a consulate should be able to provide legal advice, notify family members of accidents, supply a list of local lawyers and doctors, and (in exceptional circumstances) may be able to provide citizens with cash advances.

Australia: Embassy in Washington, D.C. (☎202-797-3000).

Canada: 3 Copley Pl., #400 (☎617-262-3760). T: Copley (Green). Embassy in Washington, D.C. (☎202-682-1740).

Ireland: 535 Boylston St., 3rd fl. (☎617-267-9330), at Clarendon St. T: Copley (Green). Embassy in Washington, D.C. (☎202-462-3939).

New Zealand: Embassy in Washington, D.C. (☎202-328-4800).

South Africa: Embassy in Washington, D.C. (☎202-232-4400).

United Kingdom: 1 Memorial Dr. (☎617-245-4500). T: Kendall (Red). Embassy in Washington, D.C. (☎202-588-6500)

KEEPING IN TOUCH

BY MAIL

US Postal Service: *☎800-275-8777; www.usps.gov. Most branches open M-F 8am-5:30pm, Sa 8am-noon; all closed Su and state and national holidays (see p. 38 for a list of holidays). For a list of* ***post offices,*** *see p. 284.*

SENDING MAIL FROM BOSTON

The **postal rate** for letters under 1oz. headed anywhere in the **US** is 37¢; postcards and aerogrammes cost 23¢. Letters and aerogrammes to Canada cost 60¢, postcards 50¢. For Australia, Ireland, New Zealand, South Africa, and the UK, rates are 80¢ for letters and 70¢ for postcards or aerogrammes. All international mail should be marked "AIR MAIL" or "PAR AVION" on the front and will arrive by air at its destination in about 4-7 days. A post office clerk or the official online rate calculator at http://postcalc.usps.gov will give you rates on anything else.

Postage **stamps** for domestic and international letters and postcards can be purchased at all post offices as well as at most convenience stores, drugstores and pharmacies, and even at some ATMs.

All domestic and international mail that has proper postage and weighs under 15oz. can be dropped off in round-topped, dark blue mailboxes found on street corners. Postmen usually collect mail from these boxes M-Sa 5pm.

There are two **24hr. post offices** in Boston: one just behind South Station, T: South Station (Red), and the other at Logan Airport, T: Airport (Blue).

ESSENTIAL INFORMATION

PHONE FACTS

Emergency: ☎911 (toll-free).

Operator: ☎0 (toll-free).

Collect or Reverse-charge calls: ☎0 (toll-free).

Massachusetts-only Directory Assistance: ☎411 (toll-free).

National Directory Assistance: ☎1 + area code + 555-1212 (from a pay phone).

To call anywhere in the **US or Canada** from Boston, dial: ☎1 + area code + local number.

To call abroad from Boston, dial:

1. Int'l dialing prefix: **011**

2. Country code for the country you want to call: Australia 61; Ireland 353; New Zealand 64; South Africa 27; UK 44.

3. City/area code. If the first digit is a zero, omit it.

4. Local Number.

RECEIVING MAIL IN BOSTON

If you don't have a mailing address in Boston, you can still receive mail via **General Delivery,** known as *Poste Restante* in most other parts of the world. Mail addressed to you and sent to one of the following two addresses will be held for pick-up for up to 30 days. A photo ID is required for pick-up:

General Delivery
Fort Point Post Office
25 Dorchester Ave.
Boston, MA 02205

or

General Delivery
Cambridge Main Post Office
770 Massachusetts Ave.
Cambridge, MA 02139

The **American Express** travel offices in the Boston area also provide a free Client Letter Service. Though it's meant for cardholders or traveler's checks users, they will hold letters for any traveler as long as you contact them in advance. Mail should be addressed to "American Express," with your name on the second line and the office's address after that (for a list of AmEx offices, see p. 281). The letter should also have "CLIENT MAIL" written on it somewhere on the front.

BY PHONE

CALLING WITHIN BOSTON

The cheapest way to place a call to anywhere in the Greater Boston area is to use a coin-operated **pay phone,** commonly found on street corners. For calls to the Greater Boston area, most pay phones charge 35¢ for the first 3min. For long-distance calls, you can first dial the number and then wait to be told how much money to insert (pay phones only accept coins). It's cheaper, however, to call abroad from Boston using a prepaid phone card (see below).

All the neighborhoods and independent towns covered in the this book (excluding the **Daytrips from Boston** chapter) are in the 617 area code, which uses **10-digit dialing.** To place a local call within this area code, you must first dial the 617 area code as you would for a long-distance call, even though the call will be billed as a local call. To remind you of 10-digit dialing, all 617 numbers in this guide include the area code.

CALLING ABROAD FROM BOSTON

International calls are cheapest using **prepaid phone cards,** which are available at most convenience stores, drugstores, and pharmacies. *Let's Go* and ekit.com offer a calling card that provides a number of services, including email and voice messaging (visit www.letsgo.ekit.com for more info). These cards charge a certain per minute. list price (from about 12¢ and up) for a set amount of minutes; instructions on the card tell you how to place a call. Make sure any card you buy is issued by a reputable national phone service carrier, or phone service may be spotty. The street vendor-hawked prepaid cards with too-good-to-be-true rates usually are: many have unreliable service and may have hidden hardware and dial-up charges that make the prices no better than the more "reputable" cards sold at convenience stores and pharmacies.

No matter how you place a call, national and international phone rates tend to be highest in the morning, lower in the evening, and lowest on Sunday and at night.

BY EMAIL & INTERNET

Boston and Cambridge don't have many Internet cafes. Luckily, public libraries in Boston, Cambridge, and Somerville have terminals with **free Internet access.** Some travelers claim it is possible to use the computer terminals on the many college campuses around Boston, but campus terminals are technically restricted to the use of enrolled students. Below we list how and where to find Internet access in the area.

Adrenaline Zone, 40 Brattle St. (☎617-876-1314). **Cambridge.** Downstairs from the Algiers coffeehouse: exit T: Harvard (Red) onto Brattle St. and follow it as it veers right. Not exactly perfect for coffee and email, disaffected youth frequent this Internet cafe-*cum*-gaming room in droves. Internet access $5 per hr., $3 for 30min. Open daily 11am-11pm.

Boston Public Library, Copley Sq., 700 Boylston St. (☎617-536-5400; www.bpl.org). **Back Bay.** T: Copley (Green). Enter via Dartmouth St. Seven terminals of free 15min. Internet access. For more on the BPL, see p. 61.

Cambridge Public Library, 449 Broadway (☎617-349-4040; www.ci.cambridge.ma.us/~CPL). T: Harvard (Red). Walk against traffic up Massachusetts Ave., turn left onto Quincy St., then right onto Broadway. Free Internet access with sign-up for free library card. One first-come, first-served terminal with 15min. access. Reserve terminals with 1hr. Internet access by calling ☎617-349-4425. Open June-Aug. M-F 9am-9pm, Sa 9am-5pm; Sept.-May M-F 9am-9pm, Sa 9am-5pm, Su 1-5pm.

Somerville Public Library (West Branch), 40 College Ave. (☎617-623-5000). T: Davis (Red). Seven terminals with free 30min. Internet access. Limit 1hr. per day. Open M, W-Th 10am-9pm; Tu 10am-6pm; F 2-6pm.

THE MEDIA

LOCAL NEWSPAPERS

There was a time in Boston when newspaper reading was yet another front in the city's tense class war: whether you chose to read the more conservative, working class-favored **Boston Herald** or the cautiously liberal, snootier **Boston Globe** (each

50¢; both available at newsstands) said a lot. Those days are over though, and many young Bostonians now get their news from snappy free weekday commuter rag **Metro,** which claims to be able to be read cover to cover in 16.7min. and can be found at any T station or bus stop. Also popular in Boston is the *New York Times*, which is published by the *Boston Globe*'s parent company. If you're looking for the best nightlife and entertainment listings, we recommend:

Boston Phoenix (every Th; free from street-side boxes; www.bostonphoenix.com). Boston's alternative weekly paper, and indisputably the best resource for living cheaply but happily in Boston. Includes free movie passes, food and arts criticism, erotic personal ads, liberal news reporting, and the phenomenal *8 Days A Week*–Boston's most comprehensive and diverse nightlife and entertainment listings, with substantial queer info. Parent company publishes yuppie nightlife tab **Stuff@Night** (every other Tu; www.stuffatnight.com).

Improper Bostonian (every other W; free from street-side boxes; www.improper.com). This sassy Bible for the upwardly mobile, under-35 crowd has the most comprehensive rundown of gourmet food events and the best shopping coverage, from hot new shops to the latest trends. In addition, their nightlife listings include lots of gay and lesbian info, but are not as good as the Phoenix's (see above).

Boston Magazine (monthly; $3.95 from newsstands; www.bostonmagazine.com). Glossy lifestyle magazine only of interest to the budget traveler for its highly touted annual "Best of Boston" issue (published in Aug.; website has previous winners), which awards everything from the best cheap lunch to the best TV sportscaster.

***Boston Globe* Calendar** (every Th with *Boston Globe*; 50¢ from newsstands; www.boston.com/globe/calendar). The *Globe*'s exhaustive weekly listing of goings-on in the Greater Boston area, from ballet to baseball, plus articles on life in Boston and special features in summer on trips to the Cape, the Berkshires, and the beaches.

Life & Times

Most people come to Boston looking for tea and Paul Revere. Though both of these can be found in Boston, the city is not merely a piece of American history, as old and preserved as Pompeii. Contemporary Boston has an identity more complex than just history, a complexity reflected in its skyline, where the stone monuments and bell towers of the Freedom Trail shoulder their way through the thickening crowd of glass-faced skyscrapers. Boston is a study in contrasts, and it has been tension and contrast that has shaped the city since its inception.

The history of Boston is the story of how different communities united, fought, and eventually learned to live together; it is the story of progression and preservation. Each neighborhood has its own place in history---not just the history of colonial America, but the history of how a varied group of citizens have endeavored to inhabit the same small space. Understanding Boston's history is essential to a full appreciation of the city in the 21st century. Today Boston provides visitors and natives with far more than just a glimpse of the past, as its many neighborhoods provide a wide array of entertainment and nightlife options from a run along the Charles River to a drink in a Southie pub to an afternoon of shopping amid the upscale and worldly glitz of Newbury St.

HISTORY

Boston's story is the tale of a city cleverly expanding despite being constrained on three sides by water. Its five centuries in existence are paced by the continuous addition and renovation of outlying neighborhoods. Boston first began as a hilly outcropping and that land has literally been reshaped into the Boston that exists today. As Boston has expanded, a variety of neighborhoods, each with a unique identity, has emerged, making Boston a city with a layered history. The 17th and 18th centuries are the eras in history that most sights in Boston focus on—including the popular Freedom Trail (see p. 43), which runs through Downtown, the North End, and Charlestown, the oldest neighborhoods. However, Boston's more recent history is visible in the city as well with 19th century neighborhoods like Back Bay and modern construction projects like the Big Dig.

17TH CENTURY: COMING TO AMERICA

SETTLING DOWN

Native American tribes had already long populated New England's deep forests and rugged terrain when the first European settlers arrived. The 17th century brought a steady onslaught of white explorers to the New World, and when Britain's King James I chartered the **Plymouth Company,** a stable colony was founded. In September 1620, the **Pilgrims**—a group of rural separatists who wanted to worship away from the urbane Anglican Church—departed England under the auspices of the Plymouth Co., aboard the **Mayflower** (a recreation of the original boat now stands moored in Plymouth, MA, south of Boston; see p. 208). On Nov. 9, the Pilgrims landed near present-day Provincetown (p. 223), on Cape Cod, but soon headed inland to found a colony near what is today Plymouth, MA. Faced with the harsh New England winter, less than half the Europeans lasted until the spring. Those that survived did so largely because of the immense help and advice of the Indians.

With the aide of the native tribes, the colony eventually prospered. However, it would be several years before anyone headed north toward the three hills of the **Shawmut Peninsula**, which was attached to the mainland by a thin "neck" (later named **Dorchester Neck,** now part of South Boston). Perhaps realizing the strategic and economic importance of the peninsula, which was situated between a major river and the ocean, Rev. **William Blackstone** migrated there in 1624, building Boston's first house on the south slope of Beacon Hill (the only of the original three hills that remains today).

HOLIER THAN THOU

Continuing discontent with the domineering Anglican Church in England led to further settlement of the Boston area. This time it was the **Puritans**—a wealthy and well-educated group who wanted to either "purify" what they saw as a corrupt church or break from the church completely. In 1629, they used their wealth and clout to convince King Charles to charter the **Massachusetts Bay Colony,** which set sail from Southampton and settled on the Mishawum Peninsula, just north of the Shawmut Peninsula (what is now Charlestown). **John Winthrop** was chosen as the colony's leader and governed from the Great House in present-day City Sq. (see p. 57) until harsh conditions convinced the settlers to move across the river and join Rev. William Blackstone's growing group on Beacon Hill.

As the colony began to grow, the Puritans became the dominant force in 17th-century politics. A number of colonists, most notably **Roger Williams** and **Anne Hutchinson,** were kicked out of the Puritan colony because of their dissenting ideas. Both Williams and Hutchinson eventually made their way to the more liberal Rhode Island. **Mary Dyer** was not so fortunate—after being expelled from the colony because of her Quaker ideology, she returned to Boston and was executed in Boston Common.

Mary Dyer's execution was only the beginning in a dark trend of colony purification via persecution. The next victims of the Puritan watch were "witches." The Puritans, starting in 1655 with the hanging of Ann Hibbens, began executing the so-called witches. Accusations became common and mass hysteria ensued, culminating in the **Salem Witch Trials** (for more on Salem, see p. 206) in 1692. Over the course of the trials around 150 people were arrested and 19 hanged for being witches.

When they weren't executing heretics, the Puritans were busy setting up schools. As it was important to educate preachers in such a hyper-religious colony, the Puritans established their places of learning early on in Boston's history. The Public Latin School was founded in 1635 as a preparatory institution, and one year later Harvard College was founded. By the conclusion of the 17th century Boston was no longer a struggling colony, but a rapidly growing city in the New World. As the city of Boston and the rest of the American colonies become more independent, the distance between the American colonies would grow and conflict would ensue.

18TH CENTURY: THE AMERICAN REVOLUTION

REBELS WITH A CAUSE

Boston quickly rose to a place of prominence in the American colonies, due in large part to the peninsula's strategic position at the mouth of the Charles and the heart of the Massachusetts Bay. Fueled by economic successes in shipbuilding, fishing, and shipping, Boston came to dominate American colonial trade and was the fourth largest center of trade in all of the British Empire by the mid-1700s.

Looking to prosper from Boston's commerce, the British endeavored to enforce navigation laws and gain revenue from Boston trade. A series of taxation acts by the British government led to a string of protests from the increasingly angry citizens of Massachusetts Bay, who indulged in what they felt to be justified resistance against unlawful authority.

The **Stamp Act of 1765** was the Crown's first direct tax on the colonies and required mail, contracts, and newspapers to be stamped by the colonial governments before they could be purchased by the colonists. Unpopular for obvious economic reasons, this act was also intended to defray the cost of keeping British soldiers quartered in America—something else that didn't thrill Bostonians, whose flourishing city was filled with garrisons of British troops. Tensions between the quartered soldiers and colonists reached a head on March 5, 1770, when British Redcoats (the name given to the red-suited British soldiers) opened fire on several civilians near the site of the British colonial government (now the Old State House; p. 50). In a skirmish known as the **Boston Massacre,** the soldiers killed five civilians. Though most reports agree that the soldiers were egged on by hecklers, the Boston Massacre was seen by colonists as an unprovoked attack.

The fire of revolution lit by the Boston Massacre was further fanned by Britain's passage of the **Tea Act** of 1773, which placed heavy taxes on tea being shipped to New England. That year, after refusing to allow taxed tea to be unloaded from the ship *Dartmouth*, colonists disguised as Native Americans and armed with hatchets crept aboard the ship at night and dumped nearly 100 chests of tea into the harbor. This event—better known as the **Boston Tea Party**—was once recreated with a healthy dose of irony aboard the now closed Boston Tea Party Ship and Museum (see p. 94), moored on Boston's Waterfront.

The early half of the 1770s was marked by countless acts of rebellion by "Patriot" colonists, whose voice of protest grew louder under the strict rule of the British. Tensions rose as Britain punished Boston for their acts of rebellion by passing the **Coercive Acts.** Under the new act, military rule was set up to impose order on the city, and the port of Boston was closed. As colonial protests waxed stronger and the British acts harsher, America headed towards a revolution under the leadership of such Bostonians as: silversmith **Paul Revere;**

brewer **Samuel Adams;** and politico **John Hancock,** who is best known for signing the American Declaration of Independence with a dramatic, florid signature to show his devotion to the cause.

TALKIN' BOUT A REVOLUTION

The official start of what became known as the **Revolutionary War** came on April 19, 1775 during the **Battles of Lexington & Concord,** when British troops stationed at Embarkation Point planned to advance on a cache of artillery the Patriots had stored at Lexington, northwest of Boston. Paul Revere asked signal lanterns to be hung in the Old North Church (p. 53) as code for how the troops would be attacking ("one if by land, two if by sea"). When two lanterns were finally hung, he and fellow patriot William Dawes rode through the streets on horseback shouting the call to arms. Thanks to Revere and Dawes' work, Patriot troops were there to greet General Gage's British Redcoats on Lexington's Battle Green (p. 202). Though no one knows who fired that first volley, the "shot heard 'round the world" marked the start of several years of fighting.

The war raged across all 13 colonies, but as the official birthplace of the war, Boston remained at the heart of the Revolution. The first two years saw intense fighting in and around the city, including the famed **Battle of Bunker Hill,** actually fought on Charlestown's Breed Hill (p. 57). While the Patriots' governing body (the Continental Congress) met in Philadelphia, southwest of Boston, the Patriots' army—led by Virginia-born General George Washington—was headquartered mostly in Cambridge and even slept in Harvard University dorms (p. 71). The troops busied themselves keeping British General Gage at bay in Massachusetts until March 17, 1776 (now a city wide holiday known as "Evacuation Day"), when, repelled by Washington's artillery positioned on Dorchester Heights in present-day South Boston (p. 91), British troops withdrew from the city. On July 4th, the Patriots signed the "Declaration of Independence" from Britain. The colonies were finally free and independent states, facing the new challenge of governing themselves. A state constitution for Massachusetts was framed in 1780, and Hancock was elected the first governor of the Commonwealth of Massachusetts.

19TH CENTURY: BLUE-BLOODS & THE IRISH

OLD MONEY WHEN IT WAS NEW

Independence from Britain was hard-won, but life after the war was by no means easy. The British had left much of the city a shambles. As the city got back on its feet, Boston's merchant elite came to preside over Boston from their graceful brownstone homes high atop Beacon Hill, where Rev. Blackstone had first settled Boston just two centuries earlier. Dubbed the **Boston Brahmins** by writer Oliver Wendell Holmes, this upper upper-class, descended from the Puritans, was the dominant force shaping the city's political, intellectual, and social currents, as well as its architectural appearance. It was **Charles Bulfinch**—the architect of many of the aristocratic homes on Beacon Hill as well as the Massachusetts State House (p. 67)—who patented the simple red-brick "Federalist" style that has become one of the city's defining characteristics.

ABOLITION & THE CIVIL WAR

In the 19th century the issue of slavery would come to the forefront of American politics and eventually become a leading cause of the **American Civil War** (1861-1865). Despite the relatively conservative values espoused by Brahmins, Boston became a hotbed of anti-slavery agitation, regarded as an abolitionist stronghold by the rest of the country. Although cynics have alleged that Boston's interest in abolition was more economic than humanitarian, the city nonetheless boasts an extensive history of liberal, abolition-oriented thought.

Due to a clause in the state constitution that states, "All men are born free and equal," slavery was abolished in Massachusetts in 1783. By 1800, Boston had become home to the nation's largest free black community, and in 1809, the **African Meeting House** (now the Museum of Afro-American History; p. 65) became the nation's first church for black worshipers. By national law, blacks were not allowed to vote, but they did hold reasonably well paying jobs in Boston, living in communities in the old West End (now the northern slope of Beacon Hill, p. 64) and the North End, and eventually establishing a strong presence in Roxbury.

At the center of the abolitionist cause was **William Lloyd Garrison** and his magazine the *Liberator*, established in 1831 on the current site of Government Ctr. (p. 81). The *Liberator* was an influential anti-slavery journal, and Garrison was often persecuted for his liberal publication, including calls for its censorship from the governors of Virginia and Georgia. Even in the face of persecution, the abolitionist movement found a home in Boston, where, in addition to Garrison, outspoken leaders such as **Frederick Douglass** often came to promote the abolitionist agenda.

Despite its progressive abolitionist thinking, Boston had an infamously segregated school system. The city's struggle with segregation in schools began in 1849 when Benjamin F. Roberts brought a suit demanding public schooling for his black five-year-old daughter Sarah. Even with wealthy white lawyer and abolitionist Charles Sumner representing him, the Supreme Court ruled against Roberts and his daughter. Nearly 22 years later, the legislature would pass a law stating that no child be denied admission to a school on account of race or color, making Boston the first US city to pass such legislation. The law did not end Boston's segregation headaches, which would come to a climax in the 1960s with the forced busing crisis (see p. 36).

When the slavery debate finally exploded into the American Civil War, Boston again proved its commitment to the abolitionist cause. **Colonel Robert Gould Shaw** was asked to lead America's first black regiment. The all-black 54th regiment was organized on Beacon Hill and trained in Jamaica Plain. When Shaw was killed in battle near Charleston, South Carolina, Confederates buried him with his men in a mass grave. Though the Confederates intended the act as an insult, Shaw's family was honored by this burial and insisted that the Union not exhume his body. A memorial to Shaw and his regiment stands at the foot of Beacon Hill, just off Boston Common (see p. 46).

THE REDHEADS ARE COMING!

After the Civil War ended, immigrants—both African-Americans migrating north from the devastated southern states and Europeans crossing the Atlantic—flooded Boston. One of the largest groups was the Irish Catholics. Victims of British tyranny for hundreds of years and driven by starvation at the hands of the 1845 Irish potato famine, they came to Boston in large number. The influx was rapid, increasing from 3,900 in 1840 to more than 50,000 in 1855. Italians, German and Eastern European Jews, French Canadians, Poles, Lithuanians, Portuguese, and Chinese streamed into the metropolis as well. The immigration boom and Boston's concurrent annexation of the ethnically diverse neighborhoods of Roxbury, Dorchester, Charlestown, West Roxbury, and Brighton meant that by 1860 nearly 60% of the population of Boston had been born abroad.

Between 1800 and 1900, Boston transformed from a small, homogenous, English, Protestant seaport of 24,000 inhabitants to a polyglot city of more than 560,000 residents, almost half of whom were Irish. The Brahmins who once dominated the city were quickly becoming a minority; at the turn of the century, only 11% of Boston's residents had extensive family history in New England. The new Bostonians usually settled into tightly knit, ethnically segregated groups, staking out neighborhood demarcations that remain to this day.

BIRTH OF THE BACK BAY

Immigrant groups were greeted with a less than kindly reception from the Brahmins, who saw them as a threat to their Puritan hamlet on a hill. As the years wore on, the non-Brahmins, especially the Irish Catholics began to possess a significant portion of the city's social and political power. Sensing defeat when less-than-acceptable neighbors began creeping up onto Beacon Hill, some of the Brahmins evacuated and headed for new territory. They settled on the land that was being created by the filling in of Back Bay (for more on the filling of the Back Bay, see p. 57). Using earth from the other two of the Shawmut Peninsula's three hills, the efforts to fill wetlands and increase the habitable land in Boston had begun in the early 19th century. With the wave of immigrants, the project started in earnest in 1858, when hundreds of thousands of loads of gravel from Needham were transported to the city and dumped into the festering swamp west of Downtown Boston. Nearly four decades later, Boston had gained over 400 acres and the entirely new neighborhoods of the Back Bay and the South End. Moreover, the "First Families" gained a new place for their mansions, filling the Back Bay with luxurious palaces befitting their self-envisioned regal status.

ATHENS OF AMERICA

Despite their snobbery and eventual fall from prominence, the Brahmins left a significant legacy for the city of Boston and did much to improve the quality of intellectual life during their reign. The era of the Brahmins' rule was one of great cultural and artistic growth, centered mostly on the creation of important civic and cultural institutions in the long-neglected Fenway area. Private donations from deep blue-blood coffers provided most of the funding for the ventures. Between 1840 and 1880, the **Boston Public Library** (p. 61, which doubles as an art museum), the world-renowned **Museum of Fine Arts** (p. 86, eventually moved to the Fenway from its original Copley Sq. location), the **Boston Symphony Orchestra** (**BSO;** p. 156), and the now-defunct **Museum of Natural History** were all built. Also at this time, **Mary Baker Eddy** was building a following and starting the Christian Science Church of Christ, the only major religion founded by a woman. In 1892, she made Boston the world headquarters for the church, which it remains today, with the beautifully landscaped **Christian Science Plaza** (p. 62). This influx of high culture and the city's propensity for fostering high-minded thinking earned Boston the nickname "Athens of America." Indeed, around this time, Mark Twain noted: "In New York, they ask 'How much is he worth?' In Philadelphia, 'Who were his parents?' In Boston, they ask 'How much does he know?'"

LUCK O' THE IRISH

By the late 1800s, with the Brahmins fast fading from the limelight, the Irish population in Boston became the major political force in town. In 1885, **Hugh O'Brien** was elected the first Irish mayor of Boston. However, the state legislature made swift changes in city regulations to limit his, as well as overall Irish, power. A civil service law was passed to regulate the hiring and promotion of state and city employees, a move calculated to prevent O'Brien from handing out appointed positions to friends and relatives. The police department and liquor licensing were also taken out of the mayor's jurisdiction and placed under the control of a special commission appointed by the governor.

The failure of political Catholics (mostly Irish) and Protestants (mostly holdover Brahmins) to work together injured Boston's struggling economy and prevented the state and city governments from mobilizing against rising crime. The Irish had the numbers, the Brahmins had the money, and the two didn't see eye-to-eye on anything. Unofficial battle lines had been drawn between Protestants and Catholics, rich and poor, Boston "native" and immigrant, and the resulting political and social melee paralyzed Boston for decades. Moreover, the slick trickery and back-room dealing associated with O'Brien—as well as the maneuvering associated with the forces trying to keep him out of power—ushered in an era of nearly 50 years during which Boston politics would be synonymous with graft, corruption, and greed.

20TH CENTURY: FROM WICKED TO PISSAH

WHO'S THE BOSS?

After O'Brien, the next Irish mayor elected was **John "Honey Fitz" Fitzgerald** (who entered office in 1905). Largely unremarkable in his mayorship, his main claim to fame was is being an ancestor to John Fitzgerald Kennedy—Boston's favorite son and the 35th President of the United States, who was born 10 years later in nearby Brookline.

The most popular, influential, and controversial of the Irish Catholic politicians in Boston, **James Michael Curley** (otherwise known as "the Boss") led the Irish political machine through much of the 1920s, 30s, and 40s, serving as congressman, governor, and mayor. A law had been passed prohibiting consecutive terms as mayor, so Curley was re-elected four times, running and winning every other election starting in 1914. He was wildly popular, especially among the poor, on whose behalf he regularly pushed progressive social reforms. All of this success occurred despite—or perhaps because of—his status as the poster child for political corruption. He won his first bid for alderman in 1904 from prison, having been convicted for civil service exam fraud. This first brush with the law began a longstanding trend that continued through his final term as mayor (1945-1949) when he was charged with mail fraud. Throughout his political career, Curley was constantly plagued by new charges—some certainly trumped up by horrified Brahmins, but many supported by actual evidence. Curley's showmanship, appeals to ethnic pride, and promises of a more prosperous city captivated mainstream voters as easily as they enraged the old guard.

Quick to pick a fight with the rich—and even quicker to use their retaliation as a rallying point for his poorer constituents—Curley's most memorable stunt was his attempt in 1915 to sell the historic **Public Garden** (p. 46) for a paltry $10 million and use half of the proceeds to build smaller parks in poorer areas of the city. Of course, motives were rarely pure, as political capital was not the only capital Curley was earning in City Hall or on Beacon Hill. Some say there was never a contract that did not involve some kickback to "the Boss." Although he dramatically improved the conditions of the poor and took steps to beautify the city, taxes quintupled; all the while, Curley found the funds in his meager governmental salary to build a sprawling private mansion overlooking Jamaica Pond.

WARTIME WOES

With two World Wars and the Great Depression of the 1930s, the first half of the 20th century had not been very kind to much of the United States. During this time, Boston shouldered the added burden of trying to contend with severe Curley-era political corruption, a swiftly declining economic infrastructure, and a staggering increase in the crime rate. Economic problems were compounded by numerous strikes, the most violent of which occurred on September 9, 1919 when the Boston police went on strike. The strike left two boys dead in South Boston and another two people wounded in Scollay Sq.; both incidents were the result of a disproportionate National Guard response.

Further economic strife came from the city's loss of its superior port status to the expanding economies of San Francisco and Seattle on the west coast. Meanwhile, the manufacturing sector had migrated to the lower wages, better weather, and proximity to raw materials found in the American South. The city of Boston seemed to have hit rock bottom, and for the second half of the 20th century, Boston would expend most of its energy attempting to revamp the city.

UPLIFTING SHAPE AND SUPPORT

Boston's rebirth began in 1957 when the Massachusetts State Legislature and the Boston City Council established the **Boston Redevelopment Authority (BRA).** The BRA was responsible for urban renewal projects that would salvage Boston's image. They focused their efforts on three major areas: the West End, Scollay Sq., and the South End. Begun in 1958, the first project was a disastrous overhaul of the **West End,** wherein the entire neighborhood was demolished and whole communities displaced to make way for the Charles River Park Apartments. Developers were more attentive to the wishes of the community during their second project—the restoration of **Faneuil Hall & Quincy Market.** Perhaps the most successful plan was the BRA's third project—the demolition of **Scollay Sq.** and subsequent construction of **Government Ctr.** (p. 81). Completed in 1968, the sprawling plaza is a perfect example of the group's aim to bring innovative architecture and civic design to renewal projects. With the development of Government Ctr., the city was able to eliminate the red light district that had long inhabited Scollay Sq. Another city project of the 1950s was the **Central Artery Project.** Originally designed to provide a systematic highway system into and around Boston via two highways (the Central Artery and the Inner Belt), only half of the Central Artery could be completed before the project was halted because it was too disruptive, having displaced 20,000 people from their homes.

The city's image was further cleansed when nonpartisan, unassuming, and seemingly corruption-free, Mayor **John Hynes** was elected in 1967, effectively ending the political corruption that had been status quo in the earlier part of the 20th century. During his tenure as mayor, the city received billions in federal funds and began planning massive economic growth. Around this time, several prominent politicians and businessmen began meeting to discuss the future of the city in the basement of the Boston Safe Deposit & Trust Co. Known as **The Vault,** both for their meeting place and their deep pockets, this group did much to jump-start the construction and development that continues in earnest (often to the point of exasperation) today.

But all was not perfect in this time of rapid rebirth. Social problems and unrest caused by the displacement of large communities were aggravated by growing racial tensions and a new force of insensitive bureaucracy.

FORCED BUSING

As the middle classes slowly and steadily defected to the suburbs, Boston was left a rotting urban core populated only by the very rich and the very poor. The wealthy sent their children to private and parochial schools, and the city's once great public schools fell sadly into disrepair. Children were assigned to schools according to their neighborhood, and while public schools across the city suffered from insufficient funding, the schools in Roxbury and Dorchester where the population was predominantly black showed the worst signs of neglect.

By the mid-1960s, Boston found itself in the embarrassing position of having a school system overwrought with ***de facto* racial segregation,** in which black children seemed to end up at the worst schools in the city. Though the 1954 landmark Supreme Court case of *Brown v. the Board of Education* declared segregation in schools illegal, the neighborhood system preserved racial separation. Parents in minority-dominated school districts raised their voices in protest of this discrimination, and the NAACP—a national minority rights watchdog group—brought the Boston School Committee to court. After two years of deliberating, Judge W. Arthur Garrity, Jr. handed down a controversial decision: the School Committee would be required to set in place and enforce a system of court-ordered, cross-town busing that would assign students to schools on the basis of racial quotas.

When the school year began in 1974, over 15,000 African-American children were bused every day from neighborhoods like Roxbury and Dorchester to predominantly white schools in places like Charlestown and South Boston, where it was made clear that they were unwelcome. Violent protests erupted in the streets of neighborhoods across the city, and police were brought in time and again to monitor the constant near-riot conditions. The scars busing left on Boston's neighborhoods have taken decades to heal; in fact, it was not until 2000 that the city stopped assigning students to schools on the basis of race.

BOSTON TODAY: STILL BUILDING

Bostonians always seem to be building something, and the new millennium is no exception with several major projects kicking into high gear. Here's a rundown of the major facelifts-in-progress:

WATERFRONT DEVELOPMENT

As the final frontier for the city of Boston, the South Boston Waterfront is the latest target of the BRA. Under the Public Realm Plan, the **Fan Pier Project** seeks to transform 20 acres of a former industrial zone into a new city park area, appropriately dubbed the Fan Pier. The Boston City Council has also approved land for a new convention center and home for the **Institute of Contemporary Art** (**ICA;** p. 58). The new ICA should open in 2005 at Fan Pier and will feature an museum's exhibition space that is triple the current building's size.

In anticipation of the Waterfront development, Boston's all-pervasive subway system, known as the "T" (p. 19), opened a portion of its new **Silver Line** in late 2002. It's not a subway proper, but rather a network of high-speed, low-emission buses that run above ground as frequently as subway cars. The Silver Line connects the farther reaches of the South End, Roxbury, and Dorchester to Downtown, and there are plans to split the line so that it connects Downtown to South Station and the Waterfront.

THE BIG DIG

Although only one-fifth of the Greater Boston area's population lives within the city's incorporated boundaries, the city produces over half of the area's goods. Commuters from the suburbs hold a large number of jobs in Boston, and the city's population more than triples during the workday. Boston has attempted many means of moving commuters into and out of the city, but traffic in Boston never seems to get any better. In 1959, the city opened the Central Artery, an elevated thoroughfare that was supposed to be for local travel only. When objections to construction halted the project, the supposedly calm road became instead a major expressway (I-93), which now tears through Downtown, making the city less elegant and no more accessible. Over 30 years after its construction, the Central Artery carries a whopping 220,000 automobiles each day, almost triple the number it was designed for. It has an accident rate four times the national average for an urban interstate, and cars sit in bumper-to-bumper traffic jams for hours every day.

City officials, fearing that clogged arteries might stop the heartbeat of economic prosperity, decided there was only one place to go: underground. This resulted in what locals refer to as the "Big Dig," a construction project begun in 1991 that should be under way through at least 2004. Thus far, the Big Dig has cost the city $15 billion, making it, per mile, the most expensive project of its kind in the history of mankind. When finished, the Big Dig should make city driving more manageable as well as reconnect neighborhoods cut off from Boston proper by the Central Artery—namely the charming North End and fast-growing Waterfront—to the city again. For details on the project, see p. 99.

SPORTS & RECREATION

With four major professional teams, innumerable college teams, the Boston Marathon, and the Head of the Charles, Boston is a fanatical sports town.

BASEBALL & THE RED SOX. Playing ball in the American League of Major League Baseball (MLB) for over a century, the Red Sox and Fenway Park are as much a city landmark as Boston Common. In recent years, one of the most impassioned city debates was over the push to build a new ballpark. Fans rallied around the cry to "Save Fenway" and plans were made to restore the old park. For more on the Red Sox, see p. 166.

BASKETBALL & THE CELTICS. One of the original franchises in the National Basketball Association (NBA), the Celtics, led by Larry Bird, were a dynasty in the 80s, winning four national championships. Though they aren't quite the contenders they were then, the team still packs in the Fleet Ctr. For more on the Celtics, see p. 167.

BOSTON MARATHON. Taking over the city every April, the Boston Marathon is the world's oldest annual marathon. Every year thousands of runners, ranging from the world's best to daring locals, take on Heartbreak Hill in hopes of completing the 26 mi. road race. For more on the Marathon, see p. 168.

FOOTBALL & THE PATRIOTS. Technically, the Patriots are New England's team and play in Foxborough, MA, but Boston likes to think of the National Football League (NFL) team as their own, having cheered them on to a Super Bowl victory in 2002. For more on the Patriots, see p. 167.

HEAD OF THE CHARLES REGATTA. The world's largest two-day boat race, the Head of the Charles draws over 300,000 spectators to the banks of the Charles River. For more on the Head of the Charles, see p. 168.

HOCKEY & THE BRUINS. Hockey may be the national pastime of Canada, but the Bruins and their fans give their rivals to the north a competent, if unsuccessful, challenge every year. The Bruins compete against Canadians and Americans alike in the National Hockey League (NHL). For more on the Bruins, see p. 168.

BOSTON'S FESTIVALS

Boston may be a city with a conservative tradition stretching back to the Puritans, but modern Bostonians pride themselves on breaking out of this mold. Below are a list of the major holidays and festivals the city celebrates.

DATE	NAME & LOCATION	DESCRIPTION
January 1st	First Night	Boston rings in the New Year with performances at over 40 locations and a huge pyrotechnics display.
March 17th	St. Patrick's Day	With a large Irish population, South Boston celebrates St. Patrick's Day in a rowdy and drunken block party.
Third Monday in April	Patriot's Day & the Boston Marathon	Commemorating the beginning of the Revolutionary War, Boston remembers the war with not only reenactments but also a 26 mi. marathon.
Mid-June	Provincetown International Film Festival	Liberal Provincetown hosts a film festival that represents close to 20 countries and spans 5 days.
July 4th	Independence Day	In celebration of America's independence, the Boston Pops play at the Hatch Shell, while a crowd listens on the banks of the Charles and watches a massive fireworks display.
First week of July	Harborfest & Chowderfest	Daily events, everything from colonial reenactments to a clam chowder contest, celebrate Boston's heritage.
Mid-October	Head of the Charles Regatta	Though it's technically a sporting event, the crowds of people and vendors turn the banks of the Charles into a weekend festival amid the fall foliage.
Mid-October	Vegetarian Food Festival	Exhibits from grocers, demonstrations from chefs, and free sampling amount to a frenzy of herbivores flooding the city.

BOSTON IN PRINT

Boston has long held the written word in high regard—a tradition begun by the well-read Puritans and continued today in Boston's many colleges and universities. With a thriving literary community, the city remains a haven for contemporary writers. Familiarizing yourself with Boston's literary heritage is an excellent way to have Boston's past identities—from the Puritan age of Anne Bradstreet to the transcendental times of Thoreau—come alive.

HISTORICAL WRITERS

Many famous American authors called the Boston area home. In the mid-19th century, the heart of the Transcendental movement was in Concord (p. 204), and the most important American writers would gather at their publishers' home, now the Old Corner Bookstore (p. 49). Below is a list of important historical literary figures from the Boston area.

POETS

Anne Bradstreet (1612-1672). As a Puritan woman, she wrote poetry about the trials of faith in the New World. Her poetry both describes the beauty of the New England landscape as well as the tragedies, like the death of her children, that occurred in the young Puritan colony.

Phillis Wheatley (1753-84). A colonial-era slave who began writing at the age of 14 at the encouragement of her master, she is recognized as a major female poet in American letters, though few of her works survive.

Henry Wadsworth Longfellow (1807-82). A longtime Cantabrigian, he immortalized largely mythologized accounts of great American events in verse, including *Paul Revere's Ride.* To tour his Cambridge abode (a popular literary gathering place), see p. 76.

Robert Lowell (1917-77). Descended from pure Boston Brahmin stock, Lowell wrote countless poems about life in Boston, the most famous (and cryptic) of which is "For the Union Dead," a horrifying depiction of the city in winter, centered on the Shaw Memorial off Boston Common (p. 46). Lowell spent much of his life in and out of McLean Psychiatric Hospital (in Belmont, just east of Cambridge), which also hosted poetess Sylvia Plath and was the setting for the book (and film) *Girl, Interrupted.*

AUTHORS

Ralph Waldo Emerson (1803-1882). The father of transcendentalism, Emerson has impacted writers from the 19th century to the present. Most of his works are essays on the relationship between man and society and make excellent daytrip reading.

Nathaniel Hawthorne (1804-1864). Though best known for his Puritan-era novel *The Scarlet Letter,* Hawthorne also contributed a wealth of novels and innumerable short stories to the American literary vault. He wrote *The Scarlet Letter,* while living in the Old Manse (p. 205) in Concord.

Henry David Thoreau (1817-1862). Under the tutelage of Emerson, Thoreau attempted to escape the fetters of society, by living self-sufficiently on Walden Pond. During his transcendental experiment, he recorded his experience in *Walden*, one of the most important American works and the greatest achievement of the transcendentalists. Today, Walden Pond and Thoreau's living quarters remain a pristine environment for travelers with a desire to escape the city. For more on Walden Pond, see p. 205.

Louisa May Alcott (1832-1888). Her novel *Little Women* was based on her own experiences growing up with three sisters. Alcott wrote the famous sisterly epic from the Orchard House (p. 204) in Concord where she and her family lived.

BOOKS ABOUT BOSTON

Fortunately for travelers with a desire to read on the road, Boston's love affair with good literature—and literature's love affair with Boston—didn't end with Thoreau. For those looking to read while exploring, here are some of our favorite books about the city.

FICTION

There are many classic novels set in Boston, from Hawthorne's *The Scarlet Letter (1850)* to Margaret Atwood's 1985 novel *The Handmaid's Tale*, set in a Cambridge of the future. Some lesser-known favorites include:

The Bostonians (1886). Bostonian Henry James pits traditional Brahmin values against "radical" feminist suffrage in a detail-riddled period novel about a supposedly pseudo-lesbian love affair.

Make Way for Ducklings (1941). Robert McCloskey's children's classic follows Mr. and Mrs. Mallard as they lead their brood of ducklings past countless Boston landmarks en route to the Public Garden, where today statues commemorate their fictional visit (see p. 46).

Asa, As I Knew Him (1987). Cambridge author Susanna Kaysen's witty novel perfectly depicts the bookish climate of her town (complete with an intellectual love affair), then suddenly flashes back in time to examine the privileged life of those living on Cambridge's old Tory Row (p. 76). Kaysen based her better-known *Girl, Interrupted* on her time at the McLean Psychiatric Hospital in nearby Belmont, MA, where Robert Lowell and Sylvia Plath also did time.

Johnny Tremain (1987). Esther Forbes' Newbury Award winner about a young silversmith's apprentice suddenly thrown into the thick of the Revolution is an excellent introduction to the historical events that shaped both Boston and the birth of a nation.

A Drink Before the War (1994). The first of Dennis Lehane's "Kenzie and Gennaro" detective novels follows the two Dorchester-based sleuths as they attempt to uncover corruption and racism in Boston's government. From Beacon Hill to Savin Hill, this often gruesome, always hard-boiled thriller paints a horrifying portrait of racial, political, and socioeconomic tensions in and around Boston (even after the demise of Mayor Curley).

Central Square (1998). A fascinating, quick parable from George Packer about community, race, and gentrification told through several disconnected characters, whose lives intersect in the Cambridge neighborhood of the title.

Interpreter of Maladies (1999). Boston University-educated Jhumpa Lahiri won the Pulitzer Prize for this slim volume of beautiful short stories about first- and second-generation Indians living in Boston and Cambridge.

Adams Fall (2001). Since Henry Adams' late-19th century autobiography *The Education of Henry Adams*, insider novels about life at elite Harvard University (p. 71) have been popular. This pulpy Harvard horrorfest by newcomer Sean Desmondis is the first to deal with ghosts, drugs, and killer underground libraries.

NON-FICTION

Boston's jumbled history—from the Revolutionary War to Mayor Curley to the Big Dig—has been the topic of many works of historical and social commentary. Some of the most insightful include:

Common Ground (1986). The late historian J. Anthony Lukas won a Pulitzer for this intelligent, troubling chronicle of the racially polarizing forced busing crisis (see p. 36), recorded here through three different area families (2 white, 1 black) caught up in the crisis.

Red Sox Century (2000). By Glenn Stout and Richard A. Johnson, the newest of the many Sox histories is arguably the best with its new takes on old franchise legends.

The Big Dig: Reshaping an American City (2001). Peter Vanderwarker uses photographs, blueprints, interviews, and more to lead readers deftly through the past, present, and future of Boston's confounding Central Artery Project (p. 35).

Anthony Mitchell Sammarco is a local historian who has written over 30 "neighborhood biographies," each using vivid prose, period photos, and countless artifacts to trace the history of a different district in the Boston area. The most interesting titles include *The North End, The South End, Roxbury,* and *Jamaica Plain.*

BOSTON ON FILM

Most movies about Boston are shot outside the city. There are, however, a few films worth seeing that really capture the Greater Boston area. Here are three great flicks actually shot in Boston:

Love Story (1970). Harvard PhD candidate Erich Segal based this passionate, if slightly sappy, tale of doomed romance and class struggle on his late 60s stint as an RA in the Harvard dorm where actor Tommy Lee Jones and former US vice president Al Gore were roommates (they are both supposedly the inspiration for the jock-with-a-heart-of-gold lead of the film). The movie's bitter weather and tragic, volatile, only-in-the-Ivy-League romance are both achingly accurate–albeit excessively sappy–depictions of life in Boston and Cambridge.

Good Will Hunting (1997). Written by and starring Boston natives Ben Affleck and Matt Damon, this is the story of a brilliant MIT janitor who woos a comely Harvard student all over Boston while receiving counselling from Bunker Hill Community College professor Robin Williams. Filled with scenes at many area sights, you can still solve math problems on napkins in Harvard Square and brood lovelornly on the Red Line inbound to Charles/MGH, but the spot where Matt delivers that famous line about "dem apples" has long since been covered over by a yuppie bar (see p. 140).

Next Stop Wonderland (1998). Brad Anderson's first outing is a whimsical and quite touching proto-*Bridget Jones's Diary.* This pseudo-chick flick chronicles the dating travails and fateful pratfalls of a determined single woman (the underrated Hope Davis), all against the backdrop of sights found almost exclusively on the T's Blue Line (the titular "Wonderland" is the line's northern terminus). Watch for scenes in Eastie (East Boston, an old neighborhood near the airport), the Aquarium, the swank Copley Plaza Hotel, and Davis Sq.

BOSTON RADIO & TV

FM RADIO	STATION	FORMAT
88.9	WERS	Emerson College
90.9	WBUR	Natl. Public Radio (news)
92.9	WBOS	Rock
94.5	WJMN	Top-40 R&B and rap
95.3	WHRB	Harvard (jazz/classical)
96.9	WKLB	Country
98.5	WBMX	Soft Rock
100.7	WZLX	Classic Rock
101.7	WFNX	Alternative Rock
102.5	WCRB	Classical
103.3	WODS	Oldies
104.1	WBCN	Alt-rock and Hard Rock
107.3	WAAF	Hard Rock and Metal
107.9	WXKS	Top-40 Pop

AM RADIO	STATION	FORMAT
680	WRKO	Talk
740	WJIB	Instrumental pop
850	WEEI	Sports
1030	WBZN	Talk, News
1090	WILD	Rap, Hip-Hop

TV	STATION	AFFILIATE
2	WGBH	PBS
4	WBZ	CBS
5	WCVB	ABC
7	WHDH	NBC
25	WFXT	FOX
27	WUNI	Univisión
38	WSBK	UPN
56	WLVI	WB

INSIDE

Sights

FREEDOM TRAIL

Begins at the City of Boston's Visitor Info Ctr. in Boston Common, facing Tremont St. (at West St.). ***Contact:*** *National Park Service Visitors Ctr., 15 State St. (☎617-242-5642; www.thefreedomtrail.org or www.nps.gov/bost/freedom_trail.htm), opposite Old State House (p. 50). For a list of tourist offices and their hours, see p. 22.* ***Open:*** *24hr. for walking; hours of individual sights vary.* ***Admission:*** *Free; some sights charge separate fees. Freedom Trail ticket, covering Old South Meeting House, Old State House, and the Paul Revere House is available. Adults $9.50, children $3.* ***Tours:*** *Free 90min. guided tours (approx. 1¼ mi.) of a portion of the Trail (from Old South Meeting House to Old North Church) leave from the National Park Service's Visitors Ctr. mid-Apr. to mid-June M-F 2pm; mid-June to Aug. daily 10, 11am, 1, 2, 3pm. Arrive 30min. before tour start time to get a required ticket. Limit 30 people per tour.*

The heart of the only urban national park in the country, the Freedom Trail is a 2½ mi. self-guided walking tour through parts of Beacon Hill, Downtown, the North End, and Charlestown. It aims to bring the colonial heyday of the city to life, running past 16 official sights (numbered below) that were important to the history of Boston and in the United States' struggle for freedom from Britain. Many of these stops are just empty buildings or commemorative plaques, but the overall experience of walking through the city's past, while catching glimpses of its chaotic present and renewed future, is not to be missed. Moreover, some of Boston's more interesting or controversial sights have been built on or near the Freedom Trail and are marked here as "Nearby Sights"

A walk along the Trail without stopping takes a little over 1hr.; plan around 4hr. for visits inside buildings as well as local distractions along the way. The Trail is a red brick path in the sidewalk; brass medallions along the Trail indicate important

the EMERALD NECKLACE

Olmsted's Emerald Necklace

Known for his design of NYC's Central Park and San Francisco's Golden Gate Park, Frederick Law Olmsted (1822-1903) is acknowledged as the founder of American landscape architecture. In Boston, he is revered as the designer of the Emerald Necklace.

In 1850, when the idea of the Necklace was first conceived, Boston's only major green space was the Boston Common, established in 1634. Olmsted's imaginative concept was a continuous string of 9 parks ringing the city: originating at the Boston Common and Public Garden (p. 46); continuing through the Commonwealth Avenue Mall, the Back Bay Fens and Riverway, JP's Olmsted Park (p. 83), Jamaica Pond (p. 83), and Arnold Arboretum (p. 84); before ending at Franklin Park (p. 83).

The result? Unlike in other smog-choked, crowded cities, you can hardly turn a corner in Boston without stumbling across a quiet park or patch of grass. The **Emerald Necklace** boxes throughout this chapter point you to the various green spaces of the Emerald Necklace.

stops (these are numbered below). Directions below are for those who wish to visit the sights independently of the Freedom Trail.

Opposite the Old State House is a US National Park Visitor Ctr. with info on the Freedom Trail and other parts of Boston. Rangers from the Visitors Center lead tours of the middle portion of the Trail, which depart from the Old State House.

BEACON HILL

***Discover Beacon Hill:** p. 3. **Other Sights:** p. 63. **Food:** p. 107. **Shopping:** p. 172. **Accommodations:** p. 186.*

As the first place settled in Boston (by Rev. William Blackstone in 1624), it is only appropriate that the Freedom Trail begin on the northeast corner of Boston Common on Beacon Hill.

1. BOSTON COMMON

***T:** Park St. (Green/Red). **Open:** 24hr. The Common is deserted after dark, so exercise caution.*

Originally a lowly cow pasture sold by Rev. William Blackstone to the Puritans for about $45, Boston Common was America's first public park and remains the heart of the city, a truly common place where visitors and residents from all over the city gather together to sunbathe, picnic, rest their feet, and let their children run wild. In nice weather, there is no better or more popular place to be in Boston.

The Common earned a spot on the Freedom Trail as a site for colonial protests, hangings, and burials. A plaque hidden in the grass marks the spot of the storm-toppled Great Elm, used for public hangings until 1876. During the British rule of Boston, troops camped out and trained here. When the British sailed for nearby Lexington and Concord for the first official battle of the Revolutionary War (see p. 202; these were the troops Paul Revere warned of on his midnight ride), they sailed from Charles St. (at the foot of the Common), then a waterfront port known as Embarkation Point.

Aside from a slew of small historical monuments, the Common is home to the large **Frog Pond,** which—depending on the time of year—serves as a reflecting pool (Apr.-July), a children's wading pool (July-Sept.), and the city's premier ice-skating venue (approx. Nov.-Mar.; skates available for rental). Also popular are the free **Shakespeare on the Common** (☎617-747-4468; www.commonwealthshakespeare.org) performances given on midsummer nights from mid-July to mid-Aug. at the **Parkman Bandstand.** In addition to being the start-

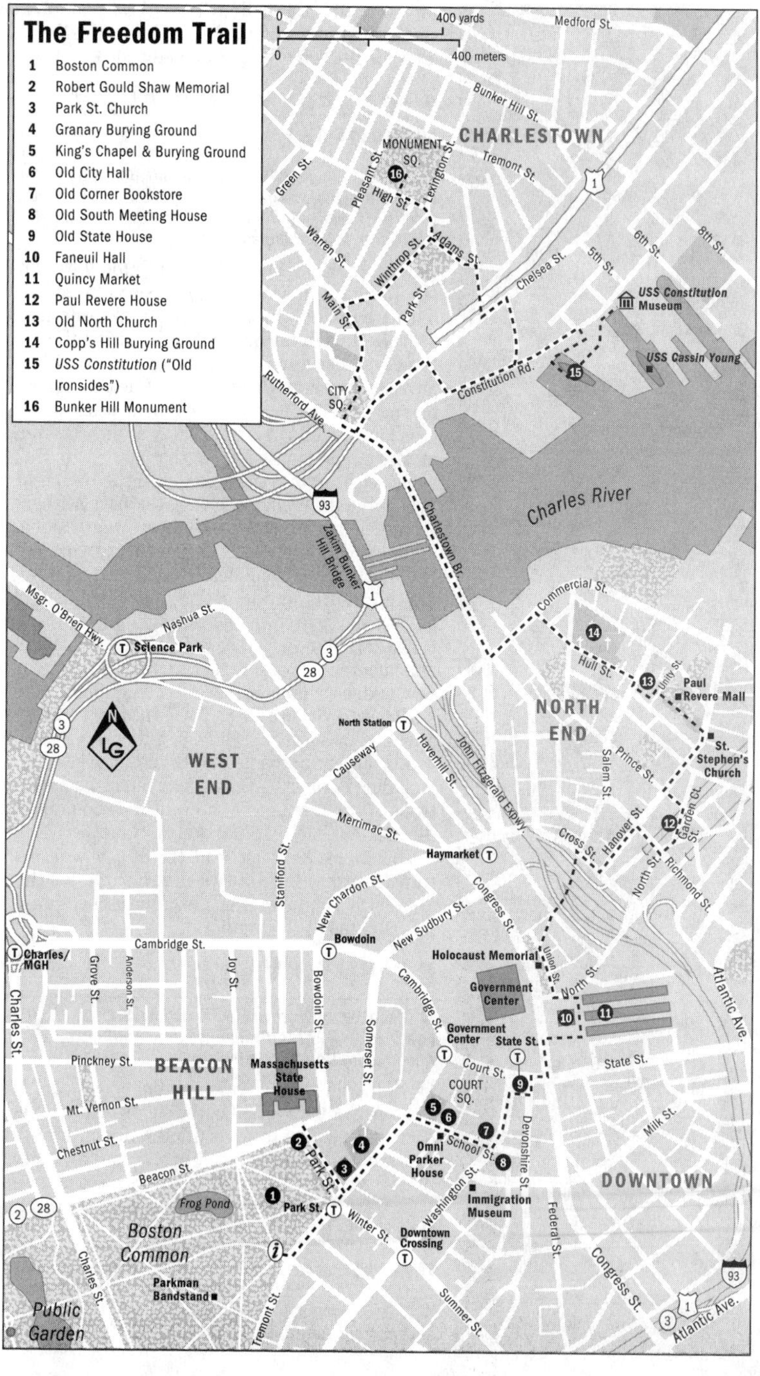
The Freedom Trail
1 Boston Common
2 Robert Gould Shaw Memorial
3 Park St. Church
4 Granary Burying Ground
5 King's Chapel & Burying Ground
6 Old City Hall
7 Old Corner Bookstore
8 Old South Meeting House
9 Old State House
10 Faneuil Hall
11 Quincy Market
12 Paul Revere House
13 Old North Church
14 Copp's Hill Burying Ground
15 USS Constitution ("Old Ironsides")
16 Bunker Hill Monument
0
400 yards
0
400 meters
Medford St.
Bunker Hill St.
CHARLESTOWN
MONUMENT SQ.
Tremont St.
Lexington St.
Pleasant St.
High St.
Green St.
Warren St.
Winthrop St.
Adams St.
Main St.
Park St.
Chelsea St.
5th St.
6th St.
8th St.
USS Constitution Museum
USS Cassin Young
Constitution Rd.
CITY SQ.
Rutherford Ave.
Charles River
Charlestown Br.
Zakim Bunker Hill Bridge
Msgr. O'Brien Hwy.
Nashua St.
Science Park
Commercial St.
Hull St.
Unity St.
Paul Revere Mall
NORTH END
St. Stephen's Church
North Station
Causeway
Haverhill St.
John Fitzgerald Expwy.
Salem St.
Prince St.
Garden Ct. St.
Hanover St.
Cross St.
North St.
Richmond St.
WEST END
Merrimac St.
Haymarket
Staniford St.
New Chardon St.
Congress St.
New Sudbury St.
Bowdoin
Cambridge St.
Charles/MGH
Holocaust Memorial
Union St.
Government Center
North St.
Atlantic Ave.
Grove St.
Anderson St.
Joy St.
Bowdoin St.
Somerset St.
Cambridge St.
Charles St.
Pinckney St.
BEACON HILL
Massachusetts State House
Government Center
State St.
Court St.
COURT SQ.
State St.
Mt. Vernon St.
Chestnut St.
Omni Parker House
School St.
Devonshire St.
Milk St.
Beacon St.
Park St.
Washington St.
Immigration Museum
DOWNTOWN
Frog Pond
Park St.
Winter St.
Boston Common
Downtown Crossing
Federal St.
Charles St.
Parkman Bandstand
Congress St.
Public Garden
Tremont St.
Summer St.
Atlantic Ave.

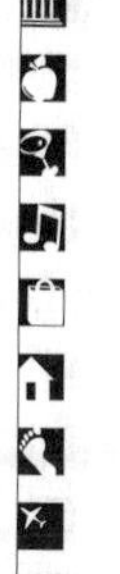

the EMERALD NECKLACE

Public Garden

Across Charles St. from the Common. ***T:*** *Park St. (Green/Red).*

As the first gem in Boston's Emerald Necklace, the exquisite 24-acre Public Garden is the nation's first botanical garden (opened in 1859) and one of the most pleasant green spaces in Boston, with elaborately manicured grounds and flowers blooming year-round. At its heart is the manmade Swan Pond, home to the famous **Swan Boats,** swan-fronted paddleboats that have ferried visitors around the pond since 1877. (☎617-522-1966. $2.50, ages 2-15 $1 for a 15min. ride. Open daily 10am-5pm, weather permitting.) Every spring, children flock here to see Romeo and Juliet—the live swans who inhabit the pond in warmer months—make their grand procession to the Garden from the nearby Ritz-Carlton.

The Public Garden's other famous avian attractions (equally beloved by children) are the bronze statues of **Mrs. Mallard & Her Ducklings,** who waddle around Boston looking for a home in Robert McCloskey's *Make Way for Ducklings* (see p. 40; they end up at the Public Garden). Little Jack was suddenly stolen in Nov. 1999, but was found 1 month later in a library at Boston University and returned to his proper home.

ing point of the Freedom Trail, the Common is the first jewel in Olmsted's "Emerald Necklace" of Boston-area parks (see p. 44).

2. ROBERT GOULD SHAW MEMORIAL

Beacon St., at Park St., opposite the Massachusetts State House (p. 67). ***T:*** *Park St. (Green/Red). From the T, walk up Park St. with the Common on your left.* ***Open:*** *24hr.* ***Admission:*** *Free.*

This memorial commemorates Colonel Robert Gould Shaw and the Massachusetts Infantry's 54th regiment, the first free black regiment recruited to fight for the North during the US Civil War. On July 19, 1863, Shaw led the 54th in an assault on Fort Wagner, South Carolina, where he and 62 members of his regiment were killed. (His battle uniform is on display at the Museum of Afro-American History, farther up Beacon Hill; see p. 65.) Among the soldiers in the regiment was Sergeant William Carney, the first African-American awarded the prestigious Congressional Medal of Honor for his bravery retrieving the Union flag from Confederate soldiers. (A photographic reproduction of the flag is on display across the street, in the Massachusetts State House's Hall of Flags; see p. 67.) The larger-than-life, high-relief bronze sculpture cast by Augustus St. Gaudens, a popular Boston-area sculptor, was dedicated on May 31, 1897 in a ceremony attended by surviving soldiers of the 54th as well as prominent activists and thinkers of the era, including Booker T. Washington. Small plaques in front of the monument offer information about the life and times of Shaw and St. Gaudens.

The **Black Heritage Trail** (p. 66), a walking tour through Beacon Hill that chronicles the area's 19th-century African-American community, begins at the memorial.

DOWNTOWN

Discover Downtown: *p. 3.* ***Other Sights:*** *p. 80.* ***Food:*** *p. 117.* ***Nightlife:*** *p. 141.* ***Shopping:*** *p. 172.* ***Accommodations:*** *p. 189.*

Downtown is the historic and financial heart of Boston. Containing half of the sights on the Freedom Trail, Downtown is filled daily with both tourists following the red brick road and city natives walking briskly to their offices.

3. PARK ST. CHURCH

1 Park St., at Tremont St. ***T:*** *Park St. (Green/Red).* ***Contact:*** *☎617-523-3383; www.parkstreet.org.* ***Open:*** *June-Aug. Tu-Sa 9am-3:30pm for tours, both self-guided and administered.* ***Admission:*** *Free.*

Built in 1809 on the site of the 18th-century town granary, the elegant Park St. Church (now a Congregational church) was once known as "Brimstone Corner" because gunpowder for the War of 1812 was stored here. Today, Boston's skyscrapers overshadow the church, but for many years the church was the first sight travelers saw when approaching Boston. Throughout the 19th century, the church was the site of some of the country's most impassioned anti-slavery speeches, including a famous 1829 speech delivered by prominent abolitionist William Lloyd Garrison.

4. GRANARY BURYING GROUND

Next to Park Street Church. ***T:*** *Park St. (Green/Red).* ***Open:*** *daily 9am-5pm.* ***Admission:*** *Free.*

Established in 1660, this cemetery takes its name from the grain warehouse that once occupied the site of the adjacent Park St. Church. It is the final resting place of the five victims of the Boston Massacre (which took place just outside the nearby Old State House; see p. 50), as well as such colonial notables as: Elizabeth "Mother" Goose (of nursery rhyme fame); Samuel Adams; florid "Declaration of Independence" signer John Hancock, whose suggestive tombstone is a favorite photo op; and silversmith-*cum*-midnight rider Paul Revere. (Revere's riding partner, William Dawes, lies down the street at King's Chapel; see below.)

5. KING'S CHAPEL & BURYING GROUND

58 Tremont St., at School St. ***T:*** *Park St. (Green/Red).* ***Contact:*** *☎617-227-2155.* ***Open:*** *Chapel open in summer daily 9am-4pm; in winter Sa 9am-4pm. Burying ground open daily in summer 9am-5pm; in winter 9am-3pm.* ***Admission:*** *Chapel donation $2. Burying ground free.*

Built in 1688 by order of King James II (hence the church's name), King's Chapel is the oldest Anglican parish in America. None of the Puritan colonists who lived in Boston at the time of its construction would sell the Royal Governor land to build a non-Puritan church—and especially not a church of the very denomination they had come to America to escape—so the chapel was built on a town burial yard. When the congregation of British soldiers who worshiped here became too large, America's first architect, Peter Harrison, was hired to design a grand new church. The result is the building you see today, considered the finest example of Georgian church architecture in North America. If the building seems to be lacking something, it's because it is. The governor ran out of money before construction was completed, so a spire was never added atop the bell tower, which houses the largest piece ever crafted by Paul Revere (who worked as a silversmith when not plotting revolution). In 1785, soon after the remodeling, King's Chapel became the first Unitarian Church in the Americas. Unitarian services are still held at the church today.

The small **burying ground** adjacent to the chapel was Boston's first. Fewer than 1% of bodies buried here are marked with headstones, and many graves are stacked four or more bodies deep. At the center of the plot is a cluster of graves including those of William Dawes, who rode with Paul Revere on his midnight ride (see p. 53), and Mary Chilton, the first Puritan to touch Plymouth Rock (in present-day Plymouth, MA; see p. 208).

6. OLD CITY HALL

45 School St. ***T:*** *Government Ctr. (Blue/Green).* ***Contact:*** *☎617-523-8678.* ***Open:*** *Courtyard open 24hr. Interior open M-F 9am-5pm.*

A smirking statue of Benjamin Franklin—the first portrait statue ever erected in the US—presides over the courtyard in front of the Old City Hall building. It was built on the former site of the **Boston Latin School,** which gives the street its name. A plaque in the ground commemorates the school, which is still in operation but has since relocated to the Fenway. Established in 1635, Boston Latin was the country's first public school and its first educational institution; famous alumni of the school include Benjamin Franklin, John Hancock, and

Granary Burial Ground

Old City Hall

Omni Parker House

Samuel Adams. (The latter two didn't venture far and are buried up the street at the Granary Burying Ground; see p. 47.) Brahmin-era architect Charles Bulfinch (see p. 68) built a county courthouse on the site in 1810, but the government outgrew the building by 1865, when it was demolished to make way for a new City Hall—the quite attractive French Second Empire building that stands today on Bulfinch's original foundation. The building served as Boston's City Hall until 1969, when the government moved to the breathtakingly bizarre inverted brick ziggurat in Government Ctr. (p. 81); the Freedom Trail passes by that City Hall between the Old State House (#9; p. 50) and Faneuil Hall (#10; p. 50).

Today, Old City Hall is filled with businesses, but even with all the businesses, it is worth walking through the building to see the architecture; pamphlets and guides are available on the ground level.

NEARBY SIGHT: OMNI PARKER HOUSE

60 School St., opposite Old City Hall. ***T:*** *Park St. (Green/Red).* ***Contact:*** *Restaurant ☎ 617-725-1600, hotel ☎ 617-227-8600; www.omnihotels.com.* ***Open:*** *Restaurant open Su 7am-noon, M-F 6:30am-2pm and 5:30-10pm, Sa 7am-noon and 5:30-10pm.* ***Admission:*** *Restaurant and gift shop are the only parts open to non-guests.*

If you're already sick of the Freedom Trail's yellowed colonial history, stop by the Omni Parker House, which is steeped in Boston's more recent—but no less revolutionary—history. One of the city's oldest hotels, the Parker House was the supposed birthplace of the Boston Creme Pie (today a slice is $5.75), which is not actually pie, but a custard-filled cake with chocolate icing. The dessert is prepared using the original recipe in the expensive Parkers Restaurant downstairs (entrees $20-28). The hotel also saw the creation of another Boston-born treat: it was from this hotel that John F. Kennedy announced his candidacy for US President.

The Parker House has also housed some of the past century's most influential characters (for good or bad): before Vietnamese revolutionary Ho Chi Minh's tenure as a busboy here and prior to civil rights leader Malcolm X's stint as a waiter, actor John Wilkes Booth spent a week here. He did so directly before traveling to Washington, D.C.'s Ford's Theatre to assassinate the 16th US President, Abraham Lincoln. Incidentally, Booth was in town to see his brother Edwin perform in a play.

7. OLD CORNER BOOKSTORE (BOSTON GLOBE STORE)

1 School St., at Washington St. ***T:*** *State (Blue/Orange).* ***Contact:*** *☎617-367-4000.* ***Open:*** *Su 11am-4pm, M-F 9am-5:30pm, Sa 9:30am-5pm.*

After Puritan religious agitator Anne Hutchinson's house on this site was destroyed by fire in 1711, Thomas Crease built the current red-brick building as a residence and apothecary (pharmacy). The building is referred to as a "bookstore" because, from 1845 to 1865, it was at the heart of Boston's once-thriving literary scene, when it housed the offices of the prestigious Ticknor and Fields publishing house. The house published such great American writers as Ralph Waldo Emerson, Nathaniel Hawthorne, Henry Wadsworth Longfellow, Harriet Beecher Stowe, and Henry David Thoreau. Today, it is home to the *Boston Globe* store and is filled floor to ceiling with Boston- and *Boston Globe*-themed tourist dreck.

ESSENTIAL INFORMATION

THAT'S THE TICKET

For those who really want to cover every inch of the Freedom Trail, the **Freedom Trail Ticket** will help save on admission to the mid-Freedom Trail stops. The ticket covers the Old South Meeting House (#8), Old State House (#9), and the Paul Revere House (#10).

The ticket is $9.50 for adults and $3 for children. Regular admission to these places totals $13 for adults, making the combo ticket a real bargain as well as a way to avoid the lines that invariably come with the Freedom Trail.

8. OLD SOUTH MEETING HOUSE

310 Washington St., at Milk St. ***T:*** *State (Blue/Orange).* ***Contact:*** *☎617-482-6439; www.oldsouthmeetinghouse.org.* ***Open:*** *daily Apr.-Oct. 9:30am-5pm; Nov.-Mar. 10am-4pm.* ***Admission:*** *Adult $5, students and seniors $4, ages 6-18 $1, under 6 free.*

Best known as a colonial meeting hall, the building has also served as a church, a British stable, a post office, and (currently) a museum of free speech. Early members of the church congregation included Samuel Adams, African-American poet Phillis Wheatley, and Benjamin Franklin (who was baptized here and went to school around the corner at the Boston Latin School). On the day after the Boston Massacre (which took place on March 5, 1770 outside the nearby Old State House; see p. 50), Faneuil Hall could not accommodate all the people who came to the town meeting to protest the event, so the crowd moved to Old South, which was the largest building in Boston at the time. There they drew up measures demanding the removal of British troops from the city, thus beginning the building's association with the public debate over various issues of religious, political, and social import. It was here that patriot rebels planned the Boston Tea Party. In 1876, the Old South Preservation Committee, which included *Little Women* author Louisa May Alcott and poet Ralph Waldo Emerson, was formed to preserve the building, then slated for demolition. Today, its spare church-like interior has been converted into a rather unimaginative museum, with exhibits about the various debates held here. It's not really worth the price of admission and pales in comparison to the Immigration Museum across the street.

Just up the street from the Old South Meeting House is Downtown Crossing. Boston's major outdoor discount shopping area (for more info, see p. 173), Downtown Crossing is a great spot to rest your feet, take a break from the Freedom Trail's musty history, and partake in another all-American activity—shopping.

NEARBY SIGHT: "DREAMS OF FREEDOM" IMMIGRATION MUSEUM

1 Milk St., at Washington St. ***T:*** *State (Blue/Orange).* ***Contact:*** *☎617-338-6022; www.dreamsoffreedom.org.* ***Open:*** *mid-Apr. to Dec. daily 10am-6pm; Jan. to mid-Apr. Tu-Su 10am-5pm.* ***Admission:*** *$7.50, students and seniors $6.50, ages 6-17 $3.50.*

Although most travelers know that New York City's Ellis Island is America's major immigration port (with half of all immigrants to the United States arriving there) few realize that Boston is the country's second most frequent point of arrival, with one in six immigrants having entered America through the city. To commemorate the struggles and triumphs of these immigrants, the interactive, kid-friendly Immigration Museum was built here, on the site of Benjamin Franklin's birth.

Subtitled "Dreams of Freedom," the museum is a flashy, 2 fl. multimedia extravaganza that uses chintzy special effects and interactive games—computerized quizzes, holograms, bright lights, and even an "immigration rap"—to chronicle the history of immigration in Boston and the role immigrants have played in the city. Visitors are issued a "passport" upon entrance, which is stamped by virtual "immigration officers" throughout the museum. The journey begins with an enjoyable 20min. interactive movie, narrated by an animatronic Franklin. The final portion of the museum, which includes the Bernard Chiu Gallery, a contemporary art space with rotating exhibits, encourages visitors to record their own immigrant stories.

9. OLD STATE HOUSE

206 Washington St., at State St. ***T:*** *State (Blue/Orange).* ***Contact:*** *☎617-720-1713; www.bostonhistory.org.* ***Open:*** *daily July-Aug. 9am-6pm; Sept.-June 9am-5pm.* ***Admission:*** *$5, students and seniors $4, ages 6-18 $1.*

Preserved and run by the Bostonian Society as a museum of the history of Boston, the Old State House is perhaps the most interesting and well-organized of the stops along the Freedom Trail. Built in 1713 as the headquarters of the British government, the building has—like the Old South Meeting House (p. 49) up the street—served many functions over the years, including a merchants' exchange, general meeting place, legislative building, and most famously, as the site of the Boston Massacre.

The museum's fascinating and unusually wide range of exhibits on colonial life include such diverse topics as colonial female diarists, British pirates, the changing architectural face of the city, and the 350-year history of firefighting in Boston and bring new life to the one-time headquarters of the colonial government (the building is the oldest existing courtroom in the Western Hemisphere). Every year on America's Independence Day (July 4), an actor in period clothing reads the "Declaration of Independence" from the balcony, where it was first read to Bostonians on July 18, 1776.

Stand under the Old State House balcony and look right for a ring of cobblestones in a traffic island; this marks the site of the **Boston Massacre,** an event that many claim sparked the American Revolution. On March 5, 1770, British redcoats and American patriots clashed in this small skirmish that left five civilians dead, including Crispus Attucks, the first black man to die in the Revolution. The night of the Boston Massacre is eerily recreated in a room inside the Old State House.

It's a bit of a walk from here to the next stop on the Trail, Faneuil Hall; the Trail passes by Boston's sleek Financial District en route, crossing behind Government Ctr. (p. 81), which is home to the current Boston City Hall.

10. FANEUIL HALL

15 State St., at Congress St. ***T:*** *Government Ctr. (Blue/Green).* ***Contact:*** *☎617-242-5675.* ***Open:*** *daily 9am-5pm (except when being used for public functions). US park rangers give talks about the history of the building and the city on the 2nd fl. every 30min. 9:30am-4:30pm.* ***Admission:*** *Free; enter through rear center doors, facing Quincy Market.*

Built in 1742 by merchant Peter Faneuil and given as a gift to the town, Faneuil Hall has served as a public meeting hall for over 250 years and was critical to sparking the Revolutionary War. It was here that angered patriots, known as **Sons of Liberty,** approved revolutionary measures, such as boycotts of English cloth and tea. The **Daughters of Liberty** helped enable these boycotts by weaving their own cloth and growing and brewing their own herbal teas. In the mid-19th century, Faneuil Hall was the chief rallying place of America's anti-slavery movement and played host to famous abolitionists like William Lloyd Garrison and Frederick Douglass, as well as slavery advocate and President of the Confederate side during the Civil War Jefferson Davis.

The only rallying cry heard in Faneuil Hall today is capitalism. Sure, you can take a peek inside the spacious restored meeting hall and adjacent exhibits on colonial history, but know that the real reason people come to this giant outdoor shopping plaza is to spend their money on the chain-mall goods and overpriced tourist crap for sale in the 1st fl. shops and in the stores of adjacent Quincy Market. The only place to escape the overly commercial ground floor is to head upstairs, where National Park Rangers give talks in a spacious meeting room, which has managed to retain the feel it must have had centuries ago when the nation's great orators spoke there.

11. QUINCY MARKET

Opposite Faneuil Hall. ***T:*** *Government Ctr. (Blue/Green).* ***Open:*** *Most retail stores open Su noon-6pm, M-Sa 10am-9pm. Restaurants and pubs usually open daily on Su-Th until midnight or 1am, F-Sa until 2am.*

Once Boston's major meat and fish market, Quincy Market (named for its commissioner, former Boston mayor and Harvard president Josiah Quincy) is now a giant three-building shopping mall and food court (meals $5-7) with such historically significant spots as the Gap and Victoria's Secret. Swarming with tourists and street performers throughout the year and almost unbearably packed in summer, it is perhaps the world's only shopping mall that also happens to be a National Park. Despite its chain-mall repulsiveness, this is the best place to grab an affordable lunch mid-Freedom Trail. Quincy Market is full of small scale versions of Boston's big name restaurants, like Legal Sea Foods. For what many claim as the best clam chowder in the city, stop by **Houston's.** Just be sure to leave Quincy Market quickly, before people mistake you for a tourist.

NEARBY SIGHT: HOLOCAUST MEMORIAL

Carmen Park, Congress St. ***T:*** *Government Ctr. (Blue/Green).* ***Open:*** *24hr.*

Completely out of place amidst the rowdy bars and tourist hordes of Faneuil Hall and Quincy Market, the sobering New England Holocaust Memorial was placed adjacent to the Freedom Trail to allow visitors to reflect on the meaning of freedom and oppression and to remember the freedoms many were forced to give up during the Holocaust *(Shoah)*. Said to represent everything from gas chamber smokestacks to candles in a menorah, each of the six luminous glass towers represents one of the six major Nazi concentration camps. Hauntingly lit at night, each tower is etched with

Faneuil Hall

Quincy Market

The North End Under Construction

quotations from Holocaust survivors and a pattern of 6 million numbers. The numbers are meant to recall the numerical tattoos given to concentration camp internees and to represent the estimated 6 million Jews who died in the camps.

NORTH END

T: Haymarket (Green/Orange) lets out just next to Big Dig construction on the Fitzgerald Expwy. (I-93), beyond which lies the North End. To get to Hanover St., the neighborhood's main artery, follow pedestrian signs through the construction work, turn right onto Cross St. (which runs parallel to the Expwy.), then left onto Hanover St. **Discover the North End:** p. 4. **Food:** p. 121. **Shopping:** p. 173.

Between Faneuil Hall/Quincy Market and the North End (site of the next stop on the Trail), the Freedom Trail runs over and around the chaos of the Big Dig, Boston's massive headache of a construction project (see p. 99). Although the journey is a bit of an unwanted adventure (thankfully, signs clearly mark the way), it does give you a taste of yet another epoch of change in the long history of Boston that the Freedom Trail examines and celebrates.

As another of Boston's old neighborhoods, it is only appropriate that the North End holds many of the Freedom Trail's sights. When the Puritans left their original settlement in Charlestown to settle on the Shawmut Peninsula, they ended up here, turning tangled cowpaths into streets (a confounding layout that remains to this day) and blanketing the area with wooden dwellings (like the **Paul Revere House**) and steepled churches (like the **Old North Church**). After the Revolution, Beacon Hill became the favored place to live, and various immigrant groups began flooding the North End; by 1910, the population was 90% Italian immigrants. Today, the neighborhood still feels "Italian," but high rents have driven many of the descendants of those original immigrants into the suburbs.

If you don't stop here for lunch while on the Freedom Trail, consider coming back at night for authentic, hearty Italian food followed by rich coffee (or *grappa*) and divine pastries.

12. PAUL REVERE HOUSE

19 North Sq. T: Haymarket (Green/Orange). Follow signs through the construction and across the Fitzgerald Expwy. (I-93), turn right onto Cross St. (which runs parallel to the Expwy.), then left up Hanover St., and right onto Richmond St., which dead-ends at North Sq. **Contact:** *Paul Revere House ☎617-523-2338, Pierce-Hichborn House ☎617-523-2338; www.paulreverehouse.org.* **Open:** *daily mid-Apr. to Oct. 9:30am-5:15pm; Nov. to mid-Apr. 9:30am-4:15pm; closed Jan.-Mar. M.* **Admission:** *$3, students and seniors $2.50, ages 5-17 $1.*

Built in the late 1600s, this modest building, just off quiet North Sq., is the oldest wooden house in Boston. On February 15, 1770, an unknown middle-class silversmith named Paul Revere acquired the then 90-year-old house. Five years later, it was from this house that Revere departed on his famous midnight ride to warn the colonists of the British attack on Lexington and Concord. This attack would mark the official start of the American Revolution. The building was slated for demolition in 1905, but Revere's great-grandson, John P. Reynolds, bought it and organized the Paul Revere Memorial Association to restore it. On April 18, 1908 (the 133rd anniversary of Revere's ride), the house opened its doors to visitors, fully restored and offering a glimpse of what everyday life was like in Revere's time.

Attached to the house (across a small courtyard) is the **Pierce-Hichborn House,** one of Boston's few remaining 18th-century brick buildings. It is only open by appointment and during limited tour times, making visiting difficult; you'll be just as well informed about 18th-century Bostonian life if you visit the more accommodating **Otis House** (see p. 64), in Beacon Hill.

NEARBY SIGHT: ST. STEPHEN'S CHURCH

401 Hanover St. T: Haymarket (Green/Orange). **Contact:** *☎617-523-1230.* **Open:** *M-Sa 8am-5pm; Su open for worship services only, 8:30 and 11am.* **Admission:** *Free.*

When the Freedom Trail reemerges onto Hanover St. from North Sq., it turns past St. Stephen's Church. Though not an official Freedom Trail site, St. Stephen's is both historically and architecturally significant. St. Stephen's is the only Boston church designed by **Charles Bulfinch** (p. 68) that remains standing. The first church on this site was built in 1714 and replaced in 1804 by a Bulfinch-designed building resembling the present structure. The church's bell was cast by silversmith and colonial rebel leader Paul Revere. It was christened St. Stephen's when it was sold to the Catholic Diocese in 1862. Almost 30 years later, it saw the baptism of Rose Fitzgerald Kennedy, mother of the first and only Catholic President of the United States, John F. Kennedy. Ravaged by fires in 1897 and 1929, St. Stephen's was finally restored to the original Bulfinch design in 1964. The exterior was inspired by Italian Renaissance churches, while the simple white interior shows Bulfinch's patented clean and austere "Federal" style (on display in full force in Beacon Hill).

Paul Revere Mall

NEARBY SIGHT: PAUL REVERE MALL

After traveling from North Sq. back on to Hanover St. (the North End's main thoroughfare), the Freedom Trail turns left toward the Old North Church, passing through a wide expanse of tree-shaded brick known as the Paul Revere Mall. At the mall's heart is an elegant bronze statue (designed in 1885, but not cast until 1940) of the North End native and rebel leader who lends his name to the mall. When it was laid out in 1933, this once green expanse was intended as a gathering place for North End residents seeking a wide-open respite from the cramped and dirty streets of their neighborhood. It remains important to the community, as plaques embedded in the brick walls honor North End men and women who contributed to Boston's rich history and culture.

On a sunny day, the shady mall is the most comfortable place in the North End to enjoy a must-have *cannoli* or other Italian sweet from one of the many bakeries or *caffés* on Hanover St. (for our picks, see p. 123).

Old North Church

13. OLD NORTH CHURCH

193 Salem St., at Hull St. ***T:*** *Haymarket (Green/Orange). Follow pedestrian signs through the construction on the Fitzgerald Expwy. (I-93), turn right onto Cross St. (which runs parallel to the Expwy.), then immediately left onto Salem St.; it's 8 short blocks up Salem St. on the right.* ***Contact:*** *☎ 617-523-6676;*

Copp Hill Burying Ground

Charles River Bridges

The dramatic Zakim Bridge (p. 55)—the world's widest suspension cable bridge and the first built asymmetrically—may be the most prominent bridge spanning the Charles, but it isn't the only unique one. Other bridges (heading east to west) include:

Longfellow Bridge: Connecting Cambridge's Kendall Sq. to Beacon Hill (the Red Line from T: Kendall/MIT to T: Charles/MGH passes over it), this bridge offers the best view of the Boston skyline from the Charles (it's most dramatic at sunset). Known as the "Salt & Pepper Bridge" for its shaker-shaped towers, the bridge was immortalized in the film *Good Will Hunting* (see p. 41).

Harvard Bridge: Despite its name, this bridge (which runs along Mass. Ave.) leads to MIT. Markers on the bridge note that it is 364.4 smoots long—after Oliver Smoot, a late-1950s MIT undergrad who was laid end over end across the bridge in a fraternity prank. The markings are repainted every few years.

Larz Anderson Bridge: Connecting Harvard's main campus with its business school (along Cambridge's JFK St.), this bridge offers the best vantage point during the Head of the Charles Regatta (p. 11), which starts at the BU Bridge to the east. The bridge was the site of Quentin Compson's fictitious suicide in Faulkner's novel *The Sound & the Fury;* a plaque commemorates this.

www.oldnorth.com. ***Open:*** *daily mid-June to Sept. 9am-6pm; Oct. to mid-June 9am-5pm.* ***Admission:*** *Suggested donation $3. Paul Revere Tonight performances $12, children $8.* ***Tours:*** *5-10min. talks when enough people gather; 40min. Behind the Scenes tours given by appointment or when there's enough interest.*

The Old North Church is the oldest church in Boston. Officially known as Christ Church Boston, it was built in 1723 in the style of British architect Sir Christopher Wren (most famous as the designer of London's St. Paul's Cathedral) and remains a functioning Episcopalian-affiliated place of worship. The church is on the Freedom Trail because of the important part it played in jump-starting the American Revolution. On the night of April 18, 1775, Paul Revere told the sexton of the Old North Church, Robert Newman, to hang lanterns in the church's belfry to signal to the colonials stationed across the river in Charlestown how the British troops would be advancing on a cache of military supplies the colonials were hoarding at Lexington (for more on Lexington, see p. 202). Newman was to hang "one if by land, two if by sea." When two lanterns were hung, Revere rode through the streets in a midnight dash immortalized in Longfellow's poem *Paul Revere's Ride.*

Since there are no historical exhibits in the small, sparsely decorated church, there's little to hold your interest in the church proper. For those with an overwhelming desire to see every inch of the church, the Behind the Scenes tour takes visitors into the crypts, steeple, and Clough House. Open to the public, the Clough House contains a bizarre **museum,** more accurately termed a Revolution-era reliquary. Aside from the various colonial ledgers and war artifacts on display, the jumble of objects under glass here include hair from George Washington's head and a bottle filled with tea from the original Boston Tea Party.

14. COPP'S HILL BURYING GROUND

Entrance on Hull St. ***T:*** *North Station (Green/Orange). With the river on your left, follow Causeway St. through the construction and under the Fitzgerald Expwy. (I-93); stay on the street as it heads past the Charlestown Bridge and becomes Commercial St. Turn right on Hull St.; the burying ground is just up the hill, past N. Hudson St.* ***Open:*** *daily dawn-dusk.* ***Admission:*** *Free.*

Just up Hull St. from the Old North Church, the 341-year-old Copp Hill Burying Ground is the 2nd-oldest cemetery in Boston (after the King's Chapel Burying Ground, farther back on the Freedom Trail; see p. 47). The hill is named for cobbler William Copp, who sold his land on the northernmost slope of the Shawmut Peninsula to the colonial government in 1659 (his children David and Thomas are buried here). The burying ground earned a spot on the Freedom Trail as the final resting place of more than 11,000 colonial Bostonians, among them 1000 free blacks, who settled at the bottom of Copp's Hill in a settlement known as New Guinea. Another notable grave is that of Robert Newman, who hung the signal lanterns in the Old North Church.

During the Battle of Bunker Hill (the site of which you'll be visiting soon on your Freedom Trail jaunt; see p. 57), a British battery fired on Charlestown from this vantage point. Today, the view of Charlestown is almost fully obscured, although you do get a glimpse of both the spires of the Zakim Bunker Hill Bridge (see below) and the pointy Bunker Hill Monument (p. 57) that inspired them.

NEARBY SIGHT: ZAKIM BUNKER HILL BRIDGE

From Copp's Hill Burying Ground, the Freedom Trail follows the Charlestown Bridge across the Charles River into Charlestown, running parallel to the cars-only Leonard Zakim Bunker Hill Bridge (on your left as you exit the North End). Opened in 2002, the bridge is one of the newest and most welcome additions to the Boston skyline. The elegant 10-lane bridge is the pride of the oft-maligned Big Dig (p. 99) and the world's widest suspension cable bridge. It is symbolically named for late Boston-area Jewish-rights activist Leonard P. Zakim, called "a master bridge builder and architect for justice and equality" by US Senator Ted Kennedy. The bridge is double-dubbed the Zakim Bunker Hill Bridge because the bridge's inverted Y-shaped towers are meant to resemble the Bunker Hill monument (p. 57), visible in the distance as you cross the bridge.

CHARLESTOWN

Discover Charlestown: *p. 8.*

After crossing the Charlestown Bridge into Charlestown and turning on to Constitution Rd., the Freedom Trail splits in two directions at the entrance gate to the Charlestown Navy Yard (it heads clockwise or counterclockwise on a circular loop). The right fork leads to the disappointing *USS Constitution* (#15; see below), while the left fork leads to picturesque Monument Sq. and the Bunker Hill Monument (#16; p. 57).

15. *USS CONSTITUTION* & MUSEUM

Charlestown Navy Yard. ***T:*** *Community College (Orange). Exit the T onto Austin St. and turn right onto Warren St. Follow Warren St. under the highway overpass and turn left onto Constitution Ave., which leads right up to the ship.*

USS CONSTITUTION ("OLD IRONSIDES")

Charlestown Navy Yard. ***Contact:*** *www.ussconstitution.navy.mil.* ***Open:*** *Tu-Su 10am-4pm.* ***Admission:*** *Free.* ***Tours:*** *Free 30min. tours every 30min. 10am-4pm; last tour 3:30pm.*

The *Constitution* was launched in 1797 from Boston and is now the world's oldest warship still in the water. The ship is now part of the US Naval Reserve. During the **War of 1812,** America's unofficial "second war for independence" from the British, cannonballs fired by Britain's HMS *Guerriere* supposedly bounced off the oak hull of the *Constitution*, earning it the nickname "Old Ironsides." After the War of 1812, the *Constitution* toured and fought all over the world, but was declared unseaworthy early in 1830. Later that year, Boston Brahmin intellectual Oliver Wendell Holmes composed an ode to the ship that raised a public outcry for its restoration and reinstatement as a symbol of national pride. Ironically, the ode praises the ship for being in ruins and wishes it well as it sinks heroically into the sea during battle.

U.S.S. Constitution

Bunker Hill Monument

View from the Anderson Bridge

Returned to Boston in 1970, the ship is now crawling with naval reservists who spend their days leading tours of the ship and busying themselves with the ship's upkeep. The ship is towed out to open water several times per year and rotated, to prevent it from weathering unevenly. The pomp and circumstance of these "Turnaround Cruises" (check website for dates) make them the best time to visit the ship.

Regardless of when you go, be ready for long, long lines, as the ship is popular with tour groups; recently increased security measures have also meant a bottleneck at the entrance (no metal objects are allowed on board). The self-guided tour is a disappointing 10min. walk around the small top deck, with reservists standing sternly in corners, eager for you to ask them questions. A free pamphlet on the ship offers some history, which is good because the ship's accompanying museum (see below) does little to clarify the *Constitution's* prominent place in American history.

USS CONSTITUTION MUSEUM

Charlestown Navy Yard, opposite the USS Constitution. ***Contact:*** *☎617-426-1812; www.ussconstitutionmuseum.org.* ***Open:*** *daily May-Oct. 9am-6pm; Nov.-Apr. 10am-5pm.* ***Admission:*** *Free.*

Not officially affiliated with either the US Naval Reserve or the *USS Constitution*, this museum's several disorganized rooms document the *Constitution*'s publicity tours, wartime campaigns, and restorations using historical information, period artifacts, a grade-B movie reenactment, and interactive exhibits. The bells and whistles (and cannon fire) of the exhibits will no doubt entertain young children, but those over the age of 12 will love the museum more for the comfort of its A/C.

USS CASSIN YOUNG

Moored behind the USS Constitution. ***Open:*** *daily in summer 10am-5pm; off-season 11am-3pm; hours can vary depending on availability of rangers.* ***Admission:*** *Free.* ***Tours:*** *Free 45min. guided tours daily; times vary depending on ranger availability, usually 10, 11am, 2, 3pm.*

Literally and figuratively overshadowed by "Old Ironsides," this *Fletcher*-class destroyer (commissioned in 1943) was *actually* ironsided, serving as the Navy's first line of defense in the US's World War II campaigns in the Pacific. Meant to stand in harm's way and protect the more fragile warships behind it, the *USS Cassin Young* was hit twice in 1945 by Japanese kamikaze pilots while patrolling the South Pacific. The ship is named after a captain who was awarded the Congressional Medal of Honor for bravery during the 1941 attacks on America's Pacific stronghold at Pearl Harbor, in Hawaii.

16. BUNKER HILL MONUMENT

Monument Sq. ***T:*** *Community College (Orange). Exit onto Austin St., turn right onto Warren St., and then left on to Monument Ave., which leads up to Monument Sq.* ***Open:*** *daily in summer 9am-6pm; off-season 9am-5pm.*

Crowned by the vaguely suggestive Bunker Hill Monument, the lush hilltop park Monument Sq. is a peaceful ending to the Freedom Trail's often arduous trek through the urban hubbub of Boston. Unfortunately, the park and monument are all a bit of a lie. As every Boston schoolchild knows, the famous Battle of Bunker Hill (June 17, 1775) that the site commemorates (where General Israel Putnam uttered the famous words "Don't fire until you see the whites of their eyes") was actually fought on nearby Breed's Hill. Although the British won the battle, their victory came at the high price of 1054 casualties, nearly half of those who fought. The skirmish was thus widely considered a moral victory for the rebels, and **Bunker Hill Day** is still celebrated each year (June 17) at the site. It's the culmination of a week-long celebration throughout Charlestown that features battle reenactments, street processions, and a doll carriage parade.

The 221 ft. granite obelisk of the Bunker Hill Monument is actually the second on the site. Visitors can climb the 294 steps to the top of the monument for a view of the Charlestown Harbor and Navy Yard (with the USS *Constitution* in profile), set against the tangle of the Big Dig (see p. 99). There is also a small but informative historical exhibit in the Visitors Ctr. (see p. 22) in the Charlestown Navy Yard.

From the Bunker Hill Monument, hungry history buffs can make their way down Pleasant St. to **Warren Tavern,** 2 Pleasant St. (☎617-241-8142). As the oldest existing bar in the US (est. 1780), the tavern has seen many historical events, including George Washington's funeral oration and the Mason meetings, where Paul Revere and other patriots first sowed the seeds of revolution.

NEARBY SIGHT: CITY SQUARE

Chelsea St. and Rutherford Ave. ***T:*** *North Station (Green/Orange). Exit the T onto Causeway St., walk a few blocks to the Charlestown Bridge, and turn left onto the bridge. The bridge lets out onto Rutherford Ave. on the Charlestown side of the river.* ***Open:*** *24hr.*

City Square is the unofficial last stop on the Freedom Trail. It occupies the same plot of land where, in 1629, the Massachusetts Bay Colony built its first public edifice—the "Great House," a private residence and place of governance for the colony's first governor, John Winthrop. The original foundation of this "Great House" is marked on the grass with large rocks. Charlestown sprung up around the Great House, and the area became so crowded that settlers moved across the river to the Shawmut Peninsula (present-day Boston). When the governor followed his constituents across the river, his house became the Three Cranes Tavern, now referenced in the crane-shaped weather vane atop the monument in the middle of the square.

OTHER SIGHTS

BACK BAY

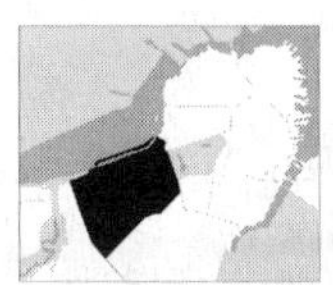

see map p. 314-315

Discover Back Bay: *p. 2.* ***Food:*** *p. 105.* ***Nightlife:*** *p. 135.* ***Shopping:*** *p. 171.* ***Accommodations:*** *p. 184.*

Now one of the most desirable and expensive neighborhoods in the city, the Back Bay was, until the late 19th century, an uninhabitable tidal flat tucked into the "back" corner of the bay surrounding the Shawmut Peninsula. A 37-year land reclamation project, begun in 1857, involved carting in dirt and sand from Beacon Hill and Greater Boston to fill in 400 acres of rancid-smelling marsh. Strict guidelines were set for both the street layout (based on the wide boulevards of Paris) and the architectural style of the buildings, which accounts for the neighborhood's uniformly picturesque look.

With stately brownstones and spacious, shady promenades laid out in an easily navigable grid, the elegant Back Bay is one of the city's most beautiful and eminently walkable districts. The heart of the Back Bay is **Newbury St.** (p. 58), lined with mid-range and upscale shops and restaurants as well as the city's most prominent art galleries. Cross-streets are conveniently labeled alphabetically, from Arlington to Hereford St. Another major point of interest, busy **Copley Sq.** is a popular resting spot smack dab in the middle of the city (p. 60). In Back Bay's southwest corner is the often overlooked, gorgeously designed **Christian Science Plaza** (p. 62).

NEWBURY ST.

T: ***T:*** *Hynes/ICA (Green-B,C,D) and the #1 bus from Harvard Sq. (p. 20) both let out onto the east end of Newbury St. at Massachusetts Ave. T: Arlington (Green) is a block south of the west end of Newbury St.* ***Contact:*** *www.newbury-st.com.*

Newbury St. is the ritziest promenade in Boston, a mile-long stretch of asphalt where tourists and locals alike go to see, be seen, and spend frivolously. In the eight blocks between Massachusetts Ave. and Arlington St., there are nearly 200 shops and art galleries, over 40 restaurants and outdoor cafés, roughly 100 salons, and countless well-groomed, mobile phone-toting trendsetters. There are few better places to spend a sunny afternoon, even though crowds often overflow the sidewalks.

A mix of sedately grand old architecture and flashy *nouveau riche* style, Newbury St. is laid out perfectly for an afternoon stroll. The T and bus let out at the east end of the street at Mass Ave.; as you walk west toward the Public Garden, stores and eateries get more and more upscale, ending with *très* chic Burberry and Hermès, just opposite the Four Seasons Hotel. Cafés and ice cream shops cluster halfway along the street for a mid-trip refueling, but polish off that coffee or cone before hitting the string of art galleries (p. 59) that line the latter half of the street.

INSTITUTE OF CONTEMPORARY ART (ICA)

955 Boylston St. ***T:*** *Hynes/ICA (Green-B,C,D). Exit left onto Massachusetts Ave., with the Virgin Megastore on your left, travel one block then turn left onto Boylston St.* ***Contact:*** *☎617-266-5152; www.icaboston.org.* ***Open:*** *W and F noon-5pm, Th noon-9pm, Sa-Su 11am-5pm. Closes unannounced for weeks at a time to install new exhibits; call ahead.* ***Admission:*** *$7, students and seniors (65+) $5. Free Th 5-9pm.* ***Special Events:*** *Lectures by artists on current exhibits 1st Th of every month 6:30pm (check website or call for specific dates); free with admission.*

Planning to move to a new building on Fan Pier in 2006, the ICA is currently found in an unassuming brick archway with three huge floors that can accommodate exhibits of any shape or size. The ICA is non-collecting, meaning all exhibits are temporary; there are typically 3-4 major shows per year (each running 3-4 months), featuring the work of both established artists like Cindy Sherman and Annie Leibovitz and lesser-known national and international artists. Bostonian tastes in art do not run to the avant garde, so the exhibits tend to be fairly traditional—thought-provoking, but hardly provocative. (Head to Cambridge's free Sert Gallery (p. 75) if you want to see cutting-edge work.) Giving the museum a technological edge is their multimedia approach to exhibits; each exhibit has an accompanying video projected on to the lower level wall and played on loop for institute-goers.

GALLERIES

All the following line Newbury St.; most galleries are on the west end of the street, between Exeter and Arlington St. ***T:*** *Arlington (Green-B,C,D), take Arlington St. one block north to Newbury.* ***Contact:*** *The invaluable* Boston/New England Gallery Guide *(www.galleryguideonline.com), available free at all galleries, has a map and description of most galleries in the Back Bay area as well as most of the region.*

The Back Bay has always been at the center of Boston's gallery scene—there are nearly 40 galleries on Newbury St. alone. However, most area galleries cater to more conservative tastes carrying work that is "easy on the eyes" and eminently traditional. The galleries below are the exceptions, specializing mostly in contemporary art or art that is non-traditional, regardless of period. Galleries are listed here from east to west, for easy navigation along Newbury St.

Barbara Krakow Gallery, 10 Newbury St., 5th fl. (☎617-262-4490; www.barbarakrakowgallery.com). The best and most well established gallery in Boston, the well-lit space draws the hottest work from New York City and focuses exclusively on contemporary conceptual art in all media. They cover everything from electronic painting to video sculpture, with an emphasis on printmaking. Open Tu-Sa 10am-5:30pm.

Howard Yezerski Gallery, 14 Newbury St., 3rd fl. (☎617-262-0550; www.howardyezerskigallery.com), only accessible by an elevator from the 2nd fl. One of the best regarded galleries in New England, their exhibits focus mostly on nearly impenetrable, though still interesting, abstract art drawn from all over the world and in various media. Open Tu-Sa 10am-5:30pm.

Chappell Gallery, 14 Newbury St., 2nd fl. (☎617-236-2255; www.chappellgallery.com). Watch where you step here–Chappell is the only local gallery devoted to glasswork, featuring delicate, unique works in a crowded space. Open Tu-Sa 11am-5:30pm. Also on the 2nd fl., **Alpha Gallery** (☎617-536-4465; www.alphagallery.com) has more standard works, mostly American prints and paintings, in a larger space. Open Tu-F 10am-5:30pm, Sa 11am-5:30pm.

Galerie d'Orsay, 33 Newbury St. (☎617-266-8001; www.galerie-dorsay.com). Invokes Paris's Musée d'Orsay in both name and holdings, with a phenomenal and diverse collection of small-scale masterworks (paintings, etchings, statuary, etc.) by big-name 15th-20th century artists–including Picasso, Matisse, Chagall, Rembrandt, and Miró. Their recent additions of sculpture and contemporary work are especially noteworthy. Open M-Sa 10am-6pm, Su noon-6pm.

Robert Klein Gallery, 38 Newbury St., 4th fl. (☎617-267-7997; www.robertkleingallery.com), across from the Pucker Gallery (see above). Though the staff may be the iciest on Newbury St., this gallery is the only spot in New England devoted exclusively to photography. They showcase over 3000 works by the greatest legends in the almost 180-year history of the medium–everyone from Ansel Adams to Zbigniew Zbajek. Open Tu-F 10am-5:30pm, Sa 11am-5pm.

Pepper Gallery, 38 Newbury St., 4th fl. (☎617-236-4497; www.peppergalleryboston.com), across from the Robert Klein Gallery. Pepper proves size doesn't matter: with just one exhibit every month or so, this tiny 1-room gallery spices up the small gallery space with an always thoughtful, always engaging, and often tongue-in-cheek mix of contemporary multimedia works by both established and emerging artists. Open Tu-F 10am-5:30pm, Sa 11am-5pm.

inside
SECRETS TO...

Galleries on Newbury St.

For most visitors, Newbury St. is merely a string of high-priced stores and even higher-priced bars and restaurants. However, the true beauty of Newbury St. is not the well-clad fashionistas sipping on martinis and eating on patios, it is the artwork in some of the city's most renowned art galleries.

Housed above and amidst the Newbury St. shopping scene, the art galleries provide a quiet respite from the designer brands and bags crowding the sidewalk. Many art galleries seem intimidating, with austere interiors, incomprehensible art, and stern-looking staff. But fear not: there's no dress code, and the usually friendly staff is perfectly happy for you to look around. The galleries are technically places of business trying to sell their artwork, but visitors are always welcome to stop in and browse, free of charge–making a gallery tour one of the cheapest and most enriching experience possible on Newbury St.

Our listings begin at the east end of Newbury St. (closest to the Public Garden).

Pucker Gallery, 171 Newbury St. (☎617-267-9473; www.puckergallery.com). This enormous collection includes work by recent European artists as well as arts and crafts from all over the globe, African masks to Japanese silkscreen prints. The entire collection is open (in addition to the temporary galleries on the ground floor): just tell the attendant what you want to see, and they'll lead you on an individual tour of those works. The work of Vienna-born Secessionist Friedensreich Hundertwasser is particularly interesting. Open Su 1-5pm, M-Sa 10am-5:30pm.

Nielsen Gallery, 179 Newbury St. (☎617-266-4835; www.nielsengallery.com). Taking up an entire converted townhouse, this is one of the Back Bay's largest galleries as well as the neighborhood's friendliest, least intimidating space. They specialize in contemporary painting, but it is arguably the space and not the art that is most impressive about the gallery. Open Tu-Sa 10am-5:30pm.

International Poster Gallery, 205 Newbury St. (☎617-375-0076; www.international-poster.com). Perhaps the leading poster gallery in the world, their vintage posters—mostly early 20th century Art Nouveau advertisements for everything from cars to chocolate—have long been popular with both serious and casual art collectors. This beautiful collection has over 10,000 posters, including the world's largest selection of vintage Italian works. Open M-Sa 10am-6pm, Su noon-6pm.

COPLEY SQ.

T: Copley (Green).

Named for painter John Singleton Copley, Copley Sq. is the lush stretch of grass between **Trinity Church** (p. 60) and the **Boston Public Library** (p. 61). Popular with both lunching businessmen and busy shoppers looking for a place to rest their feet (and their credit cards), Copley Sq. is surrounded by some of Boston's most beloved buildings.

MARATHON MONUMENTS

The legendary Boston Marathon (see p. 168)—the country's oldest and most respected foot race—ends in Copley Sq. every April, so it's only fitting that several works of art in the square commemorate the brutal 26.2 mi. run. A small monument embedded in Boylston St., near Dartmouth St., depicts a map of the marathon's course in granite, while the whimsical *Tortoise & Hare* (by Nancy Schön, who also created *Mrs. Mallard & Her Ducklings* in the Public Garden; see p. 46) race to the finish line in the middle of the pedestrian area in front of Trinity Church.

TRINITY CHURCH & HANCOCK TOWER

206 Clarendon St. Visitor entrance only through the church's bookshop; follow signs from the Clarendon St. side of the church. ***T:*** *Copley (Green).* ***Contact:*** *☎617-536-0944; www.trinitychurchboston.org.* ***Open:*** *daily 8am-6pm.* ***Admission:*** *$4, includes self-guided tour pamphlet.* ***Tours:*** *30-45min. guided tours $5, offered 2-3 times per day; check posted signs or call. Free tour offered after Su 11:15am religious service.*

Designed by noted architect Henry Hobson Richardson and erected between 1872 and 1877, the elegant Trinity Church, whose exterior is modeled on the French Romanesque style, remains the focal point of Copley Sq. Noted theologian and preacher Phillips Brooks—best known as the author of the Christmas carol "O Little Town of Bethlehem"—was rector here until 1891, and an oversized statue of him by Brahmin-era sculptor Augustus St. Gaudens (sculptor of the Shaw Memorial in Beacon Hill; see p. 46) stands out front. In comparison to the gorgeous sandstone and granite facade, the church's interior seems a bit mundane, but for the visitor seeking to indulge in the building's grand architecture without hearing the noise of Copley Sq., it is a worthwhile venture.

A popular photo op is the reflection of the church in the mirrored façade of the neighboring **John Hancock Tower.** Designed by noted architect I.M. Pei (who also designed the JFK Library (p. 79), the Christian Science Plaza (p. 62), and the pyramid in front of Paris's Louvre Museum) and incorporating almost 14 acres of glass, the 790 ft., 62-story Hancock Tower is the tallest building in New England. Once home to a public observation deck that offered the best views of the area (on clear days, you could see to New Hampshire), the building is now closed to the public, as a result of the events of September 11, 2001.

BOSTON PUBLIC LIBRARY

700 Boylston St. The artwork and courtyard are best accessed via the Dartmouth St. entrance, facing Copley Sq. ***T:*** *Copley (Green).* ***Contact:*** *☎617-536-5400; www.bpl.org.* ***Open:*** *M-Th 9am-9pm, F-Sa 9am-5pm; Oct.-May also Su 1-5pm.* ***Admission:*** *Free.* ***Tours:*** *Free guided "Art and Architecture Tours" M 2:30pm, Tu and Th 6pm, F-Sa 11am; Oct.-May also Su 2pm. Tours leave from the lobby of the Dartmouth St. entrance.*

Founded in 1848 by the Great and General Court of Massachusetts, the BPL was the first free public library in the United States and the first to allow patrons to borrow books. It now functions as both a lending library and a small but fascinating art museum. The entrance on Boylston St. (the Johnson Building) leads to the library half of the BPL, which has over 1 million books (128 of which are copies of *Make Way for Ducklings*), plus an additional 6 million non-circulating titles. In the catalog room at the rear of the 1st fl., there are 7 computer terminals, each with 15min. **free Internet access,** on the 2nd fl. there are 1hr. free Internet access terminals. There is also a reading room with hundreds of national and international newspapers available for free.

Flanked by statues representing Art and Science, the entrance on Dartmouth St. leads to the art holdings of the McKim building, named after architect Charles Follen McKim, who modeled this building on a Venetian *palazzo*—just like the Gardner Museum (p. 88) and Harvard's Fogg Art Museum (p. 74). The library is best known for the **Sargent Gallery** on the 3rd fl., home to 19th-century society portraitist John Singer Sargent's unfinished allegorical mural series, *Triumph of Religion (1890-1919)*. Pamphlets in the gallery explain the mural—which was criticized by some for its anti-Semitism—in detail. On the 2nd fl., the serene and slightly eerie **Abbey Room** is closed while undergoing construction. The Abbey Room renovations are the last stages of a renovation project that has been going on for over 10 years. The **Wiggin Gallery,** on the 3rd fl. in the Sargeant Gallery's south end, is a peaceful exhibition space with arched windows overlooking the courtyard.

The library tours end in the hidden, rarely visited interior **courtyard** (accessible via the Dartmouth St. entrance—just follow the hallway all the way around the corner): this sun-dappled, fountain-filled, colonnaded oasis of calm vies with the *palazzo* courtyard of the Gardner Museum for the title of most peaceful spot in Boston.

Newbury St.

Boston Public Library

Trinity Church & Hancock Tower

PRUDENTIAL CENTER TOWER & SKYWALK

800 Boylston St. ***T:*** *Prudential (Green-E) lets out into the lobby of the Prudential Ctr. To get to the Skywalk from there, go to the Prudential Tower section of the Prudential Ctr., which is in the middle of the mall, and check in with the lobby guard to take the elevator to the 50th fl.* ***Contact:*** *☎617-859-0648; www.prudentialcenter.com* ***Open:*** *Shops at Prudential Ctr. M-Sa 10am-8pm, Su 11am-6pm. Skywalk open daily 10am-10pm.* ***Admission:*** *Skywalk $7, seniors (62+) and ages 3-10 $4.*

Boston's small-scale answer to the Empire State Building is the Prudential Tower and its impressive **Skywalk,** a 50th fl. observation deck with a far-reaching 360° view of Boston and the surrounding area. Although Boston Harbor is partially obscured by the John Hancock Tower, the Skywalk nevertheless provides visitors to the city with the highest vantage point in Boston (at 700 ft. up) now that the Hancock Tower is closed. Placards beneath the windows point out popular Boston landmarks in the distance.

CHRISTIAN SCIENCE PLAZA

Bound by Massachusetts Ave., Huntington Ave., and Belvidere St. Enter on Mass. Ave. ***T:*** *Symphony (Green-E) lets out onto Mass. Ave.* ***Parking:*** *$5 with validation. Enter at the intersection of Mass. Ave. and Huntington Ave., next to the Horticultural Hall.*

The most well-designed and underappreciated public space in Boston, the 14-acre Christian Science Plaza is an epic stretch of grass and concrete dominated by the mammoth "Mother Church" and centered around a stunning reflecting pool. A renovation of the area that finished up in the fall of 2002 is the first step in a program to revitalize the area on and around Huntington Ave., now known as the Avenue of the Arts (for more info, see p. 85).

FIRST CHURCH OF CHRIST, SCIENTIST

T: *Symphony (Green-E) lets out onto Massachusetts Ave.; the church entrance faces Mass. Ave.* ***Contact:*** *☎617-450-3790; www.tfccs.com.* ***Open:*** *Sept. to mid-Apr. M-Sa 10am-4pm, Su 11:30am-4pm; mid-Apr. to Aug. M-Tu and Th-Sa 10am-5pm, Su 11:30am-4pm.* ***Admission:*** *Free.* ***Tours:*** *Free 30-45min. tours depart from the Portico on the hour M-F 10am-3:30pm, last tour departs 3:30pm); Su 11:30am; no tour W noon.*

Most of the buildings in Christian Science Plaza house the international headquarters of the First Church of Christ, Scientist, founded in 1879 by New Hampshire-born healer **Mary Baker Eddy** (1821-1910). Interested in medicine and health from an early age, Mrs. Eddy was healed of a serious injury as she read a Bible passage, leading her to discover a practice of prayer-based healing that she termed Christian Science. She wrote about her discovery in the landmark *Science and Health with Key to the Scriptures* (first published in 1875, but revised throughout her lifetime) and founded the Church of Christ, Scientist 4 years later.

In 1892, Mrs. Eddy oversaw the construction of a simple Romanesque **Mother Church** (designed by Franklin Welch), which stands in the middle of the Christian Science Plaza. This served as the headquarters of the rapidly expanding church until 1906, when the lavish, Byzantine- and Renaissance-influenced "extension" that presides over Christian Science Plaza was added on to the back end of the original. Noted architect I.M. Pei (who designed the JFK Library (p. 79), the Hancock Tower (p. 60), and the pyramid in front of Paris's Louvre Museum, among other edifices), created the Christian Science Plaza you see today. Pei's most dramatic contribution was the serene, perfectly smooth **reflecting pool and fountain,** which doubles and trebles the already repetitive architecture of the plaza in its waters. Running the length of the pool from the Mother Church to Belvidere St. is his **Colonnade Building,** which houses the offices of the many publications affiliated with the Church of Christ, Scientist, including the well-respected *Christian Science Monitor*—whose offices you can spy on at the Mary Baker Eddy Library (see below). The other side of the pool is not nearly as exciting, overlooked only by the rather drab **Administrative Tower** and the semicircular **Sunday School.**

MARY BAKER EDDY LIBRARY

*200 Massachusetts Ave., next to the Mother Church **T:** Symphony (Green-E) lets out onto Mass. Ave. **Contact:** ☎888-222-3711; www.marybakereddylibrary.org. **Open:** Tu-F 10am-9pm, Sa 10am-5pm, Su 11am-5pm. **Admission:** $5; students, seniors, and children $3.*

Opened in the fall of 2002 and intended to be both a museum and a research facility, this library entertains and informs with dazzling multimedia displays, including a trip through the freshly scrubbed Mapparium, one of the most beloved and often overlooked sights in Boston. The library's two lower floors of fascinating interactive exhibits explain why the complex is officially named the Mary Baker Eddy Library for the Betterment of Humanity. In addition to exhibits chronicling Mrs. Eddy's life and achievements, several galleries use cutting-edge technology to explore loftier topics—such as the contemporary search for life's meaning and the power of ideas to change the world—inspired by those very achievements.

On the 1st fl. in the imaginative **Hall of Ideas,** a heat-sensitive hologram fountain (built by MIT's Media Lab, who show off their other wares at the MIT Museum; see p. 78) pours forth a virtual "stream" of holographic words and letters that "splash" onto the floor and crawl around the room before resolving themselves on the walls into one of 800 quotes taken from thinkers throughout history. (The fountain was designed by Howard Ben-Tré, who also built the fountain at Downtown's Post Office Sq.; see p. 82.) Just off the Hall of Ideas is the enchanting **Mapparium,** a multistory stained-glass globe that depicts the world as it was in 1935. Though the recent renovation of the Mapparium has turned it into a cheesy light show celebrating global harmony, visitors still have the chance to walk through and enjoy its vibrant hues and crystal-clear, echoing acoustics, which allows someone standing in the center of the room to hear their own voice in perfect surround sound.

The highlight of the 2nd fl., the ***Christian Science Monitor* gallery** lets visitors see the working newsroom of the publication. The upper floors of the building (open only by appointment) house Mrs. Eddy's papers, which make up the country's largest collection of documents written by and belonging to a woman.

BEACON HILL

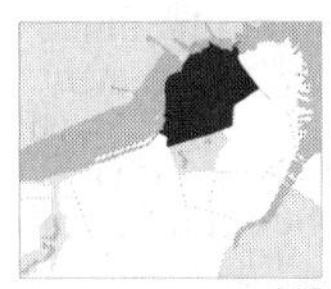

see map p. 317

***T:** Charles/MGH (Red) lets out at Cambridge St. and Charles St. **Discover Beacon Hill:** p. 3. **Freedom Trail Sights:** p. 44. **Food:** p. 107. **Shopping:** p. 172. **Accommodations:** p. 186.*

Upscale neighborhoods may spring up practically overnight in the rest of the US, but none of them will ever match the old-money allure of Beacon Hill. Amid elm trees, gas lanterns, and winding cobblestone streets, the wealthiest families in Boston (some of them descended from the founding "First Families of Boston") live in the cramped brick townhouses that have been in their families since their construction some 300 years ago. Shunning the gaudy mansions and fashionable lofts demanded by America's *nouveau riche,* these old school families live in a style reflecting their Puritan heritage: wealth is rarely flaunted, and austere values are still the norm.

Once a cow pasture, Beacon Hill was transformed when Charles Bulfinch built the Massachusetts State House on the hill's southern slope in 1797. The city's wealthy politicos flocked to the area to be close to work, and a real estate boom began, led by Bulfinch himself, who designed many of the area's brownstones and effectively patented the "Federalist" style of the neighborhood (for more on Bulfinch and the Federalist style, see p. 68). Before the rise of the hill, the 18th-century elite all lived in long-gone Bowdoin Sq. in homes close to and similar in style to the **Otis House** (p. 64). Beacon Hill is still the top choice for the well-to-do, and its central location remains key to its desirability. Situated south of Mass. General Hospital and Government Ctr., east of the Financial District, and north of the chic Back Bay, Beacon Hill boasts a population of 10,000, 70% of whom walk to work (although that may just be because parking on the hill is impossible).

GIVING BACK

Serving History

Kaitlyn Greenidge *is a National Park Service Ranger who leads tours of Boston's* ***Black Heritage Trail.*** *Below she discusses what she has learned during her time as a volunteer ranger. For more on volunteering, see* ***Alternatives to Tourism*** *(p. 269).*

LG: What do you do at the Museum of Afro-American History?

A: I work for the National Park Service. At our site we lead tours of the Black Heritage Trail and interpret the history of the Beacon Hill neighborhood and Boston's 19th century black community. Our primary focus is leading the tours, but we also do educational programs for teachers during the year and have smaller tours and a few events during the year to get people to come and explore our two main buildings–the Smith School and the museum.

LG: What role do you think the Black Heritage Trail plays in Boston's history?

A: It proves that Boston's history is varied, has a lot of layers, and involves a lot of people. Sometimes in history books it doesn't sound like there were the same complexities that we have today. Finding out that those complexities existed makes history more interesting.

The area has traditionally been divided into 3 districts: the **North Slope,** between Pinckney and Cambridge St., once socioeconomically divorced from Beacon Hill and called the West End; the **South Slope,** south of Pinckney St., abutting the Boston Common; and the **Flat of the Hill,** the area between Charles St. and the Charles River, once entirely underwater. The North and South Slopes are quaint but almost entirely residential, with a few historical points of interest scattered throughout. The Flat of the Hill, focused on Charles St., is home to antique shops, contemporary gift stores, boutiques, and restaurants of all price ranges—not to mention the Charles River Esplanade Park (p. 69)—making it a great place to spend an afternoon and/or a lot of money. Consider our **Walking Tour of Beacon Hill,** p. 15, if you're wondering how best to spend a day in the area.

NORTH SLOPE (OLD WEST END)

In the early 1900s, the North Slope of Beacon Hill (then known as the West End) was an interesting cultural stew created by the many Italian, Jewish, and Irish immigrants who settled in the area, already home to countless African-Americans. Although the North Slope was geographically quite close to the South Slope, socioeconomically it's dwellings were worlds away from those upper-crust Federalist-style homes. The area was poor and the buildings considered an eyesore by the city government. In the 1960s, the government decided it needed better infrastructure—hospitals, roadways, research centers, apartment buildings—and completely demolished the West End to accommodate new construction. In a matter of years, the entire community was displaced by belching bulldozers and backhoes.

The only original sight still intact is the first **Harrison Gray Otis House,** which was spared demolition when it was moved 42 ft. north to allow the city to widen the street in front of it. The self-guided **Black Heritage Trail** leads you through the history of the neighborhood's black community prior to their displacement from the hill.

HARRISON GRAY OTIS HOUSE

141 Cambridge St., at Lynde St. ***T:*** *Charles/MGH (Red). From the T, head away from the river down Cambridge St.* ***Contact:*** *☎617-227-3956.* ***Open:*** *W-Su 11am-4:30pm.* ***Admission:*** *$5. Admission by tour only.* ***Tours:*** *30min. tours on the hour and ½hr.*

This boxy Federalist-style house (built in 1796) was the first of three that Harrison Gray Otis commissioned his childhood friend Charles Bulfinch to design. Otis was a former Congressman and Boston mayor (1829-32) who encouraged the development of Beacon Hill's South Slope, including the construction of the Massachusetts State House (p. 67) also overseen by Bulfinch. When Otis moved elsewhere in the neighborhood, his home was carved up into a boarding house. The building has been completely restored—half as a Federalist mansion and half as a rooming house—and is now a museum describing how the Boston elite lived in the years just after the Revolutionary War. The tours of the house are excellent; there is seemingly nothing the volunteer tour guides don't know about Boston, then and now, and they lead you through all the various incarnations of the building, from mansion to run-down inn.

MUSEUM OF AFRO-AMERICAN HISTORY

46 Joy St. ***T:*** *Charles/MGH (Red). Head down Cambridge St. away from the Charles River, then turn right onto Joy St.; enter by turning right onto Smith Ct.* ***Contact:*** *☎617-720-2991; www.afroammuseum.org.* ***Open:*** *June-Aug. daily 10am-4pm; Sept.-May M-Sa 10am-4pm.* ***Admission:*** *Free.*

This tiny museum occupies the original site of the Abiel Smith School, an all-black school where, from 1839 to 1855, African-Americans started a movement to force the city to provide better education for black children. Protests here lit the fire of public debate over the segregation of Boston's public schools, a practice that officially ended in 1855 but a problem that has lingered in the city far into the 20th and 21st centuries. Indeed, segregation in schools reached its most fevered peak during the school busing crisis of the 1970s (see p. 36). The museum's emphasis is on historical efforts for equality through education, but it includes rotating exhibits on a wider variety of issues as well as period artifacts, like Robert Gould Shaw's uniform. It's best to start at the top floor—where an indispensable 17min. documentary traces the history of blacks and black protests for equality in the city—and work your way down through the other two floors of the museum.

The museum is on the Black Heritage Trail, a self-guided walking tour through sights on Beacon Hill significant to the city's 19th-century African-American community. However, although the museum is the *last* stop on the

(continued from p. 64)

LG: What would you say are the struggles in Boston today? What racial tensions still exist?

A: Boston's neighborhoods are still fairly segregated. In the last five years or so, I think it has come a long way, but it comes down to going the next step beyond legal desegregation and really integrating people's lives.

LG: How does the history of the Black Heritage Trail affect visitors today?

A: I think this [National Park] site is really unique because it's in a neighborhood in a city where people can come and really get a feel for a whole community and understand how a community can contribute to and really change history.

It's really a good way to understand and look at history—being in the place where it actually happened. I think a lot of times people forget that history takes place in a specific place and specific time. People think of history happening in this mythical land that you can't really get to, but when you walk around our site, you can actually see the houses and feel the streets and have the same feeling you might have had walking around then.

trail, it's possible to pick up a brochure and map of the trail at the museum and work your way backward on the trail to its starting point, the Robert Gould Shaw Memorial (part of the Freedom Trail; see p. 46).

Next door to the museum is the **African Meeting House,** the oldest black church in America and the original home to the school that moved into the Abiel Smith School house. The Meeting House is currently closed and will reopen in the summer of 2005.

BLACK HERITAGE TRAIL

Begins at the Robert Gould Shaw Memorial (p. 46), at Park and Beacon St. ***Contact:*** *☎617-742-5415.* ***Admission:*** *Free; self-guided tour maps available at the Museum of Afro-American History.* ***Tours:*** *Free 2hr., 1½ mi. tours led by US park rangers depart from the Shaw Memorial June-Aug. daily 10am, noon, 2pm; Sept.-May by appointment (call 24hr. in advance).*

As the first American city to abolish slavery (in 1783), Boston was a crucial stop on America's Underground Railroad, a network of households throughout the country that secretly helped blacks enslaved in the South escape to freedom in the North. Many free African-Americans moved to the city at the turn of the century, so that by as early as 1800, the 1100 African-Americans in the city made up one of the largest black communities in the country.

The Black Heritage Trail is a walking tour that explores the history of this 19th-century African-American community, passing by various buildings and locales important to the community's struggle for racial and social equality in Boston. All the sights on the trail except the last two, the African Meeting House and the Museum of African American History, are now private and not open to the public, so a self-guided trip along the trail is more of an architectural tour than a historically informative excursion. In the summer (June-Aug.), the National Park Service offers guided walking tours of the trail, with well-informed and witty park rangers who explain the history and significance of each stop along the way. One of the last stops, the **Holmes Alleyway** allows tour takers to walk the same path as fugitive slaves, who would run through the alleyway to escape slave catchers. At the end of the alleyway is the African Meeting House, where candles were always lit and beds always ready for the fleeing slaves.

SOUTH SLOPE

The southern slope of Beacon Hill, everything between Pinckney St. and Boston Common, is what most people think of when they think of the neighborhood: austere brownstones with purple windows and elm-shaded cobblestone streets just reeking of the old money that has lived on the South Slope since it was the only part of Beacon Hill that existed. (The remainder of the neighborhood was made by filling in tidal flats years later, as the city began to grow.)

Boston-born aristocrat and author Oliver Wendell Holmes first coined the term "Boston Brahmins" in reference to the elite class of 19th-century New England families who called Beacon Hill home. Many of the current brownstones are still occupied by descendants of those original Brahmin "First Families," but unfortunately, only the **Nichols House** (p. 67) is open to the public. Nevertheless, you can still get a feel for the neighborhood's charm by wandering around the area. You can try our **Walking Tour of Beacon Hill** (p. 15), or keep the following in mind: homes on Mt. Vernon St. and Chestnut St. are the most luxurious, though some on Beacon St. along Boston Common are valued at over $5 million because of their views of the Common. Small green placards indicate which homes housed famous folk.

LOUISBURG SQUARE

Between Mt. Vernon and Pinckney St. ***T:*** *Charles/MGH (Red). Follow traffic down Charles St. and turn left onto Mt. Vernon St.; it's 2 blocks uphill.* ***Open:*** *24hr.* ***Admission:*** *Free.*

This cobblestone-covered block is not only the supposed birthplace of door-to-door Christmas caroling, but also the most elite and prestigious address in the city. Previous residents have included the wealthy Vanderbilt family and *Little Women* author Louisa May Alcott; current "celebrities" who call Louisburg Sq. (pronounced Lewisberg) home include Massachusetts Senator John Kerry and his wife, ketchup heiress Teresa Heinz, who own a corner townhouse valued at a modest $2 million. Few can agree on what part of Louisburg Sq. is the most valuable: the elegant brownstones, the gated private park in the middle (only Louisburg Sq. residents get a key), or the guaranteed free private parking in a city where even the mayor can't find a spot for his car. Though the brownstones may be out of your price range, the square itself is a well-chosen diversion from the bustle of Charles St.

Beacon Hill

NICHOLS HOUSE

55 Mt. Vernon St. ***T:*** *Charles/MGH (Red). Follow traffic down Charles St. and turn left onto Mt. Vernon St.; it's several blocks up on the left.* ***Contact:*** *617-227-6993.* ***Open:*** *May-Oct. Tu-Sa noon-4:30pm; Nov.-Apr. Th-Sa noon-4:30pm.* ***Admission:*** *$5; by tour only.* ***Tours:*** *30min. tours every 30min.; last tour 4pm.*

The only Beacon Hill townhouse open to the public, Nichols House was given to the city of Boston in 1961 by the late Rose Standish Nichols, who lived in the house for most of her 88 years. She preserved much of the original late 19th-century decor to serve as a museum of turn-of-the-century Boston Brahmin life.

Several Brahmin-era artists have close ties to the house. The plot of land was originally owned by portraitist John Singleton Copley whose own portrait hangs in the house's parlor. Rose's uncle was noted sculptor Augustus St. Gaudens (of Shaw Memorial fame; p. 46), and his work is found throughout the house. Though not as well-known, Rose's own arts and crafts decorate the walls. Informative, docent-led tours of the charming, cramped quarters are the only way to see the house, and its artwork is definitely worth the admission price.

Boston Common

MASSACHUSETTS STATE HOUSE

Beacon St., at Park St. ***T:*** *Park St. (Green/Red). From the T, walk up Park St. with the Boston Common on your left.* ***Contact:*** *617-727-3676;*

The Mapparium

Charles Bulfinch

Best known as a designer of the US Capitol in Washington, D.C., Charles Bulfinch was also the most influential architect of 19th-century Boston—a time of great urban construction in the city.

After graduating from Harvard, Boston-born Bulfinch toured Europe before returning to his hometown, determined to bring European architecture to the states. However, the US had just gained freedom from Britain, and in designing buildings to house the newly independent government, city planners thought it more appropriate to break with past traditions and develop a new style that would reflect the new nation's confidence, distinct from the architecture of their ousted European oppressors.

Bulfinch designed the Massachusetts State House (see right) with this in mind, and soon his patented "Federal" style of architecture (reserved exteriors, massive size, plain lines, lots of brick and brown stone) began to be copied throughout Boston. He is responsible for Boston's very distinct, very staid architectural look, from the elegant brownstones of **Beacon Hill** (p. 63) to the stately grey stone of **University Hall** at Harvard (p. 72).

Other Bulfinch masterpieces include **Faneuil Hall** (p. 50), the **Harrison Gray Otis House** (p. 64), and **St. Stephen's Church** (p. 52).

www.state.ma.us/sec/trs (for tours only). ***Open:*** *M-F 10am-4pm; last tour 3:30pm.* ***Admission:*** *Free; self-guided tour pamphlet available at entrance.* ***Tours:*** *30-40min. guided tours available by appointment. They recommend calling at least 24hr. in advance.*

In the early days of the Massachusetts Bay Colony, the seat of government was the Old State House downtown (now a museum; see p. 50). After the colonists won independence from Britain in the American Revolution, area politicians wanted a new government building that would reflect the prosperity and prestige of their young democracy. They bought John Hancock's cow pasture on the south slope of Beacon Hill and hired a young selectman named **Charles Bulfinch** to design an appropriately impressive structure. Bulfinch went on to leave his spare, solid architectural mark on much of Boston, in a style known as the "Federalist" style, which looked distinct and confident, reflecting America's confident stance as a new nation.

Completed in 1797, the golden-domed state capitol covers 6¾ acres, or about two city blocks. Bulfinch's lavish topper supposedly inspired the tradition of putting a gold dome on every US state capitol building. The interior is just as splendid as the exterior, ornamented with stained glass and monumental statues. The guided tours aren't necessary, as the self-guided tour pamphlets available at the entrance more than adequately tell you about everything going on inside, including the famous "Sacred Cod."

Follow the senators to the **Capitol Coffeehouse,** 122 Bowdoin St. (facing the side of the State House) for a sandwich or sub ($3-5) to enjoy at nicely manicured **Ashburton Park,** behind the State House. The pillar in the middle of the park is a replica of the one that once sat at the top of the hill and served as a warning light to ships in the harbor (hence the name Beacon Hill). The original pillar fell when the land was leveled to build the State House.

BULL & FINCH PUB (*CHEERS* BAR)

84 Beacon St., at Brimmer St. in the basement of the Hampshire House, facing Boston Common. ***T:*** *Park St. (Green/Red) or T: Arlington (Green).* ***Contact:*** *☎617-227-9600; www.cheersboston.com.* ***Open:*** *Bar and downstairs gift shop open daily 11am-1 or 2am, depending on business. Upstairs gift shop open daily 10am-10pm.* ***Admission:*** *Free.*

Although it's billed as Boston's #1 tourist attraction, the Bull & Finch Pub is really the city's #1 tourist disappointment. Hollywood producers chose the Bull & Finch as the setting for the TV sitcom *Cheers*, which centered on the quirky characters at a neighborhood bar "where everybody knows your name." Despite its status as a popular local watering hole that had imported its furnishings from a British pub builder, the producers decided that the only thing about the Bull & Finch that said "neighborhood pub" was its exterior. A shot of the still-hanging "Cheers" sign opens every episode of the show and a replica of the cigar-store Indian statue from the show now stands inside the bar, but the interior where Sam and the gang swap jokes is a Hollywood soundstage (now home to *Cheers* spinoff *Frasier*) that doesn't remotely resemble the cramped and chintzy interior of this pub. The Bull & Finch recently opened up an equally cheesy Faneuil Hall branch (p. 50) that more closely resembles the show's interior. Tourists crowd into the bars at both locations for overpriced drinks and *Cheers*-themed bar food, like "E-Norm-ous Burgers" and "Diane's Desserts." Die-hard fanatics of the show can be found spending exorbitant amounts of money at one of the two gift shops (mug $8, $6 with purchase of a beer).

THE FLAT OF THE HILL

CHARLES RIVER ESPLANADE

Charles River. ***T:*** *Charles/MGH (Red) Cross the Footbridge and head towards the Charles River.* **Open:** *24hr.* **Admission:** *Free.*

The lush Esplanade—spread gracefully along the Charles— is popular with visitors and locals alike, and not only because it offers boat docks and running and biking paths. The Esplanade is home to the **Hatch Memorial Shell,** a free outdoor concert venue. Radio stations host free concerts here in summer, and every summer Friday brings "Free Friday Flicks," where family-friendly movies are screened at the Hatch Shell for free (beginning at sunset).

On the **4th of July,** the renowned Boston Pops (p. 156) give a free concert at the Hatch Shell, featuring patriotic music and Tschaikovsky's *1812 Overture* (with real cannon fire) and culminates in an extravagant multi-ton fireworks display (one of the country's best). Get to the Esplanade by 8am if you want a seat, or get a vantage point somewhere else (the fireworks are visible from anywhere in the city) and hear the concert broadcast live on WCRB 102.5 FM. The Pops also gives a free preview concert on July 3rd, but seating is limited, so get there early.

Louisburg Sq.

State House

Houses on Beacon Hill

Cheers

Joggers on the Esplanade

Cambridge

CAMBRIDGE

see map p. 320-321

T: Harvard (Red), T: Central (Red), and T: Kendall (Red) are close to all the major sights. ***Discover Cambridge:*** *p. 7.* ***Food:*** *p. 110.* ***Nightlife:*** *p. 137.* ***Shopping:*** *p. 172.* ***Accommodations:*** *p. 187.*

Although separated from Boston by only a small river, Cambridge (pop. 100,000)—often referred to as Boston's "Left Bank" for its liberal politics and Bohemian flair—has always been worlds away from the bigger city in history and temperament.

Cambridge was actually founded in 1630 by ultra-conservative Puritans and intended as a capital; when the capital was eventually built in Boston, the Cambridge settlement, then called Newtowne, separated from Boston and set out on its own. The city became home to the nation's first college in 1636, when Harvard University was established. Also home to the first independent printing press, Cambridge established itself early on as a place for innovation and education. During the Revolutionary War, Cambridge's **Tory Row** (present-day Brattle St.; p. 76) was home to many British sympathizers (referred to as Loyalists or Tories), who eventually fled to seek refuge from the Patriot rebels in Boston and Charlestown. By the 1960s, Cantabrigians had come a long way from the days of conservative Loyalists, becoming so radical that stodgy Bostonians disparagingly christened Cambridge the "Kremlin on the Charles."

Although its counter cultural vibe has died down since its first few centuries of anti-war sentiment, Cambridge is still a vibrant and exciting place to be, with dozens of bookstores and trendy shops, a large student population, and food and nightlife options on par with Boston. The city remains centered around **Harvard Sq.,** now a thrilling (but overdeveloped) gathering spot filled with awestruck tourists, angry local teenagers, over 300 street performers, and countless current and future (i.e. Harvard) yuppies living in the shadow of **Harvard University** (p. 71). Southeast of Harvard Sq., in Kendall Sq., is the equally prestigious institution of higher learning, the **Massachusetts Institute of Technology** (p. 77).

CAMBRIDGE COMMON

Between Massachusetts Ave. and Garden St. ***T:*** *Harvard (Red) lets out onto Mass. Ave.* ***Open:*** *dawn-dusk. Avoid walking alone here at night.*

From its humble origins as a cow pasture, the Cambridge Common has become a community gathering place with a certain historical prominence. The shifting boundaries of Cambridge itself have reduced the Common from its original 86 acres to a mere 16, but it is still large enough to accommodate soccer-playing Cantabrigians, baby carriages, and trekking tourists.

The main historical attractions are the towering monument to President Lincoln and the Civil War dead, the poignant memorial to the Irish Potato Famine (known as *An Gorta Mor—The Great Hunger*), and the large tree on the southern side of the park. Known as the Washington Elm, this is the spot where George Washington is supposed to have assumed command of the Revolutionary Army. On the sidewalk running along Mass Ave. are a set of hoofprints, marking the path William Dawes took on his midnight ride with Paul Revere.

Harvard Square Newsstand

MT. AUBURN CEMETERY

580 Mt. Auburn St., at Brattle St. ***T:*** *Harvard (Red). From inside the T, take bus #71 or #73 (10min., every 5-15min.) up Mt. Auburn St. to Brattle St. (ask for the cemetery stop). Alternatively, walk or drive 1.5 mi. up Brattle St. from the T, until it dead-ends (ahem) at Mt. Auburn St.* ***Contact:*** *☎617-547-7105.* ***Open:*** *Apr.-Oct. daily 8am-7pm, Nov.-Mar. daily 8am-5pm.* ***Admission:*** *Free.*

The Mt. Auburn Cemetery opened in 1831 as the country's 1st "rural cemetery," designed in the manicured style of late 18th-century English gardens. Some of Boston's most influential politicians, thinkers, and artists are interred here, including: Brahmin-era architect Charles Bulfinch (p. 68); founder of the Boston-based Church of Christ, Scientist Mary Baker Eddy, (p. 62); American painter Winslow Homer; abolitionist Charles Sumner; and American poet Henry Wadsworth Longfellow (who lived at nearby Longfellow House until his death; see p. 76). The highlight is the **Washington Tower** (in the cemetery's heart, on Mountain Ave.), which offers a breathtaking view of the Boston skyline.

An information booth immediately inside the Egyptian-revival gate (very similar to the Granary Burial Ground's gate; see p. 47) has a map of the plots.

Dunster House

HARVARD UNIVERSITY

T: *Harvard (Red) lets out at the intersection of Massachusetts Ave., Brattle St., JFK St., and Dunster St. Harvard Yard is across the street.* ***Contact:*** *Events &*

John Harvard Statue

Fogg Art Museum

Lampoon Castle

Mass. Hall

Information, Holyoke Ctr. (☎617-495-1573; www.harvard.edu). Enter next to Au Bon Pain, across Dunster St. from the T. ***Open:*** *M-Sa 9am-5pm.* ***Admission:*** *Free.* ***Tours:*** *Free student-led campus tours Sept.-May M-F 10am and 2pm, Sa 2pm; June-Aug. M-Sa 10, 11:15am, 2, 3:15pm.*

Established on October 28, 1636, Harvard is the oldest university in the US, and now one of the most prestigious institutions of higher learning in the country. The school is known the world over for its brilliant faculty, which has produced nearly 40 Nobel Laureates and includes such luminaries as biologist E.O. Wilson, economist John Kenneth Galbraith, and Pulitzer Prize-winning poetess Jorie Graham.

The college began as a meeting of a dozen men in a wooden house behind a cow pasture. They took the name Harvard in 1638 after Rev. John Harvard, a graduate of Britain's Cambridge University (from which the city of Cambridge took its name) who died in Charlestown and left his entire library and half of his estate to the college. (A statue of a man purported to be John Harvard now stands in the middle of Harvard Yard. Visitors often rub his shoe for good luck, but they'd think twice if they knew what unspeakable things Harvard pranksters over the years have done to the statue.) Today, the university has nearly 20,000 students, about 6600 of whom are undergraduates enrolled at Harvard College. The remaining students attend one of the university's many well-regarded graduate and professional schools.

In addition to famous graduates like philosopher and poet Henry David Thoreau, class of 1837, and former President John F. Kennedy '40, Harvard also boasts many famous almost graduates. These include Cambridge native and actor Matt Damon—who left his sophomore year to write the Oscar-winning screenplay for *Good Will Hunting*—and businessman Bill Gates, who also dropped out his sophomore year to start a little company named Microsoft.

HARVARD YARD

Harvard Yard is the heart of undergraduate life at Harvard, as well as the site of the university's annual commencement ceremonies. The Information Ctr.'s student-led tour is the best way to see the university's gorgeous red-brick campus and learn about its somewhat tumultuous history; they also have informational pamphlets ($1-3) for self-guided tours of the Yard, although the highlights are noted below and in our **Walking Tour of Harvard Sq.** (p. 12).

The college's oldest standing building (built in 1720) is **Massachusetts Hall;** once used for housing Revolutionary-era troops and now home to the President's offices, the building was occupied in 2001 for three weeks by student protesters. The east side of Mass. Hall faces the Charles Bulfinch-designed **University Hall,** also the site of a student occupation (in 1969) and fronted by the famous **John Harvard statue.** This is also known as "The Statue of the Three Lies" because: (1) the statue was not modeled on John Harvard; (2) Harvard did not found the college as the statue indicates, but only donated money to it; and (3) the college was not founded in 1638 as the statue indicates, but in 1636.

Graduation festivities take place in the vast green expanse behind University Hall, known as Tercentenary Theater. Across Tercentenary Theater from U-Hall is Sever Hall, a classroom building whose entrance arch is designed so that a person whispering on one side can be heard on the other side. Presiding over the area is massive Widener Library, which houses nearly 5 million volumes from Harvard's 13.3 million book collection and makes Harvard's the world's largest university library collection. None of the buildings described above are open to the public.

LAMPOON CASTLE

44 Bow St., at Mt. Auburn St. ***T:*** *Harvard (Red). Exit the T onto JFK St., walk 1 block, and turn left onto Mt. Auburn St.; you can't miss it up ahead.* ***Contact:*** *☎617-495-7801; www.harvardlampoon.com.* ***Open:*** *only to members of the Lampoon and their guests.*

One of the most distinctive buildings in Cambridge, the Lampoon Castle (hardly the size or stature of a true castle) is home to the offices and playrooms of one of Harvard University's humor magazines, the *Harvard Lampoon* (established in 1876). Though it has now lost much of its edge and even more (read: all) of its sense of humor, the *Lampoon* has over the years been the training ground of such rapier wits as George Santayana, John Updike, George Plimpton, and late-night TV host Conan O'Brien. In 1969, several alumni of the magazine founded *National Lampoon*—a national version of the college rag, and also the group behind such comedic film classics as *Animal House* and Chevy Chase's *Vacation* series.

The building itself was deliberately designed by *Lampoon* co-founder Edmund Wheelwright to resemble a laughing head, complete with a beanie cap roof, windows for eyes, a vibrantly colored door for a mouth, and heating vents for ears. The building looks cartoonishly "mad" in winter, when steam comes out of its "ears." Constructed in 1909 with monies donated by Isabella Stewart Gardner (see p. 88) and *Lampoon* alumnus-*cum*-newspaper millionaire William Randolph Hearst, the castle is only open to *Lampoon* members and their guests; the closest most tourists can get to the interior is the drawing and description offered by cartoon elephant Babar, who somehow manages to tour the castle in his *Babar Goes to America.*

HARVARD UNIVERSITY ART MUSEUMS (HUAM)

All 3 museums are on or around Quincy St. ***T:*** *Harvard (Red). From the T, walk against traffic up Massachusetts Ave. and turn left (at the Inn at Harvard) onto Quincy St.* ***Contact:*** *☎617-495-9400; www.artmuseums.harvard.edu.* ***Open:*** *All 3 museums open M-Sa 10am-5pm, Su 1-5pm.* ***Admission:*** *$6.50, seniors and students $5, under 18 free (includes all 3 museums). Free Sa 10am-noon.* ***Tours:*** *Free and vary by museum (see below).*

The Harvard University Art Museums (HUAM) feature an impressive collection of artwork of all styles and genres, ranging from ancient Near Eastern sculpture to contemporary works on video and film. Though each museum has a different focus, the three museums—the Sackler, the Fogg, and the Busch-Reisinger—share the same hours and admission fee. All are easily explored in an afternoon thanks to their small size and proximity to each other. Visiting the museums in the order listed below gives you a chronological survey of the collection—a chronology that can be continued at the nearby Carpenter Ctr. for the Visual Arts, which features the most contemporary work.

Harvard Street Performers

The Garage Mall

Church St. Cemetery

ARTHUR M. SACKLER MUSEUM

485 Broadway, at Quincy St. ***Tours:*** *M-F 2pm.*

The four floors of the Sackler are the least engaging and most disorganized of the Harvard art museums. The collection focuses almost exclusively on **non-Western art** (both ancient and contemporary), including pre-Columbian, Islamic, and Indian treasures and one of the country's leading collections of East Asian art. The artifacts on the 2nd fl. are superb (curators often juxtapose rotating contemporary Asian works with the ancient works on display), but the haphazard 4th fl. looks like a half-completed statuary excavation gone wrong. The ground floor features rotating shows by contemporary artists, often curated by Harvard doctoral candidates.

FOGG ART MUSEUM

32 Quincy St., at Broadway. ***Tours:*** *M-F 11am.*

Covering two floors of a building designed in the style of a Venetian *palazzo* (just like Boston's Isabella Stewart Gardner Museum; see p. 88), the Fogg is the oldest and most popular of the HUAM museums. It offers an excellent (if small) survey of all the major trends and styles in Western art, specializing in the work of artists from **Europe and North America** from the Middle Ages to the early part of the 20th century. The highlights of the Fogg collection include its preeminent selection of Impressionist works (everyone from Monet to Renoir) and its fantastic van Gogh self-portraits. On the 2nd fl., at the entrance to the Busch-Reisinger Museum (see below), are studies for John Singer Sargent's *El Jaleo*, which now hangs in its completed form in the Isabella Stewart Gardner Museum.

BUSCH-REISINGER MUSEUM

Entrance in the far right corner of the 2nd fl. of the Fogg. ***Tours:*** *M-F 1pm. Moholy-Nagy's sculpture* Light-Space Modulator *is demonstrated W 1:45pm.*

The best of the HUAM museums, the Busch-Reisinger is actually located inside the Fogg and picks up where the Fogg leaves off chronologically. The tiny museum is devoted to the art of the German-speaking countries of Central and Northern Europe and specializes in German Expressionism and Abstraction. Its six small galleries move chronologically from the turn of the last century to the recent past and follow the rise and subsequent repression of the avant garde movement Recently, the museum acquired several works by abstract artist Piet Mondrian. To the right of the entrance, a special exhibitions gallery showcases rotating exhibitions of 20th-century artists' work.

CARPENTER CENTER

24 Quincy St., next door to the Fogg. ***T:*** *Harvard (Red). From the T, walk against traffic up Massachusetts Ave. and turn left onto Quincy St.* ***Contact:*** *☎617-495-3251.* ***Open:*** *M-Sa 9am-11pm, Su noon-11pm. Sert Gallery open M-Sa 10am-5pm, Su 1-5pm.* ***Admission:*** *Free.*

The Carpenter Ctr. is the only building in North America designed by famous Swiss-born architect Le Corbusier and was hailed upon its unveiling in 1963 as both an architectural masterpiece and a poured-concrete vision of "two pianos humping." Most of the Carpenter Ctr. is occupied by the classrooms, offices, and studios of Harvard's Visual and Environmental Studies (a.k.a. art) department, but the building does house two of the best contemporary art galleries in New England. A visit to these galleries is the perfect continuation of the chronological survey begun in a tour of the three Harvard art museums. The **main gallery,** in the lobby, has constantly rotating exhibits by visiting faculty, who are some of the visual art world's hottest acts. The outside ramp (parallel to Quincy St.) leads up to the phenomenal **Sert Gallery** on the 3rd fl., a dark industrial space that hosts conceptual art exhibits and expositions of work by the biggest names in contemporary photography, video, and film. The basement of the Carpenter Ctr. is home to the diverse Harvard Film Archive (p. 165).

HARVARD MUSEUM OF NATURAL HISTORY & PEABODY MUSEUM

Both museums accessible from 26 Oxford St. ***T:*** *Harvard (Red). Walk north through Harvard Yard; pass between the Harvard Science Center (on the left) and Sanders Theatre (on the right). This puts you at the intersection of Oxford and Kirkland St.; turn left onto Oxford St.* ***Contact:*** *HMNH: ☎617-495-3045; www.hmnh.harvard.edu. Peabody Museum: ☎617-496-1027; www.peabody.harvard.edu.* ***Open:*** *Both open daily 9am-5pm.* ***Admission:*** *$7.50, students and seniors $6, children 3-18 $5 (includes both museums). Free year-round Su 9am-noon and Sept.-May W 3-5pm.*

Carrying on in the grand tradition of such European science museums as Vienna's Naturhistorisches Museum, the Harvard Museum of Natural History and the attached Peabody Museum contain far more information than any one could process in one visit. The dark and labyrinthine HMNH has three main galleries—one each on botany, comparative zoology, and geology (each confusingly labeled as a separate "museum"). The zoology and geology sections have the typical array of fossils and rocks, including the only assembled skeleton of *Kronosaurus queenslandicus*, a 42 ft. prehistoric, flesh-eating marine reptile. The undisputed main attraction of the museum is in the botany section, which is home to the internationally renowned **Glass Flowers,** officially known as the Ware Collection of Blaschka Glass Models of Plants. The exhibit contains over 3000 incredibly life-like and life-sized models of various plants and flowers made of colored or painted glass. The entire exhibit was renovated recently, making it much easier to walk through and examine the flowers up close.

Founded in 1866 by George Peabody, the **Peabody Museum of Archaeology and Ethnology** (accessible via the HMNH) also has three main galleries and a special exhibit hall, all dedicated to the study of indigenous peoples across the globe. Harvard's anthropology department is home to some of the world's leading experts on Mesoamerica (the ancient peoples who lived in modern-day Central America), so it comes as no surprise that the highlight of the museum is "Encounters with the Americas," which explores the native cultures of Mesoamerica (such as the Mayas, Incas, and Aztecs) before and after Spanish contact. Most striking among the myriad artifacts is the mammoth cast of a Mayan temple stairwell (found by Harvard archaeologists in Copán, Honduras), considered the longest hieroglyphic text in the world.

SEMITIC MUSEUM

6 Divinity Ave. ***T:*** *Harvard (Red). Walk through Harvard Yard towards the north; pass between the Harvard Science Center (on the left) and Sanders Theatre (on the right), take a right on Kirkland St. Follow Kirkland for 1 block and turn left onto Divinity Ave.; it's on the right.* ***Contact:*** *☎617-495-4631; www.fas.harvard.edu/~semitic.* ***Open:*** *M-F 10am-4pm, Su 1-4pm.* ***Admission:*** *Free.*

Pitser Great Dome

Memorial Dr.

MIT

Currently home to over 40,000 artifacts collected on expeditions to the Semitic language-speaking countries of Egypt, Jordan, Cyprus, Iraq, and Tunisia, the small Semitic Museum was founded in 1889 to house Harvard's ancient Near Eastern archaeological collections and the university's Department of Near Eastern Languages and Civilizations. As a result, exhibits focus on both the artifacts themselves and on the process of locating, excavating, preserving, and restoring them. The highlight of the three floor museum is the 1st fl., where visitors can follow the construction, destruction, and restoration of Egypt's Sphinx over hundreds of years.

TORY ROW (BRATTLE ST.)

T: Harvard (Red). Exit the T onto Brattle St. and follow it as it veers right. The truly lavish mansions begin after you pass the Loeb Drama Center (p. 161) and continue until Brattle St. dead-ends at Mt. Auburn St., at the Mt. Auburn Cemetery (p. 71). **Contact:** *Cambridge Historical Society ☎617-547-4252; www.cambridgehistory.com.* **Admission:** *All houses save the 2 listed below are private residences and are not open to the public.* **Tours:** *through the Cambridge Historical Society May-Oct. Sa 10am-noon. Reservations required. $10.*

Until the Revolutionary War began, tree-lined Brattle St. was referred to as "Tory Row" because the stately mansions along the street were home to British sympathizers, known as Loyalists or Tories. Nearly 300 years later, the homes still house Cambridge's most affluent, blue-blooded families, some descended from those original Tories. The architectural styles of the houses are very diverse, and a trip down Tory Row (en route to the Mt. Auburn Cemetery; see p. 71) is a pleasant way to spend an afternoon. To both see the houses and understand the area's historical context, take the walking tour "Tory Row: Brattle Street in the 18th Century."

LONGFELLOW HOUSE

105 Brattle St. **T:** *Harvard (Red). Exit onto Brattle St. and follow it for about ½ mi.* **Contact:** *☎617-876-4491.* **Open:** *June-Oct. W-Su 10am-4:30pm.* **Admission:** *$3, under 16 free. Admission by guided tour only.* **Tours:** *45min. tours 10:30, 11:30am, 1, 2, 3, 4pm.*

This elegant lemon-yellow Georgian mansion was the home of famous 19th-century American poet **Henry Wadsworth Longfellow,** who lived here for over 40 years, until his death in 1882. It is preserved exactly as it was when Longfellow lived here and the original furnishings help distinguish this site above those that merely use period antiques to replicate what life may have been like.

Offered a teaching fellowship at Harvard University in 1834, Longfellow began his time in the house as a boarder. When Longfellow married Fanny Appleton in 1841, her father purchased the house and gave it to the newlyweds as a wedding present.

Longfellow is considered by many to be one of the first truly "American" authors, as his epic-length poems draw on American themes and often commemorate important American historical events. His most popular works include *The Song of Hiawatha* (1885) and *Paul Revere's Ride* (1861), about his midnight dash through Boston (p. 53). This house was (unsurprisingly) a gathering place for prominent 19th-century American writers and artists.

Before Longfellow's time, during the Revolutionary War, the house served as the headquarters of the Continental Army (from July 1775 to April 1776); it was from this house that Gen. George Washington planned the siege on Boston.

HOOPER-LEE-NICHOLS HOUSE

159 Brattle St. ***T:*** *Harvard (Red). Exit the T onto Brattle St. and follow it for about ½ mi.* ***Contact:*** *☎617-547-4252; www.cambridgehistory.org.* ***Open:*** *Tu and Th 2-5pm.* ***Admission:*** *$5; students, seniors, and children $3. Admission by guided tour only.* ***Tours:*** *hourly Tu and Th 2-5pm.*

This house, which has undergone several architectural transformations in its 310-year history, supposedly incorporates portions of the oldest house in Cambridge (built in 1685). Named for the three families that have lived in the house since it was first built (physician Richard Hooper was the original owner), the house has been the headquarters of the Cambridge Historical Society since 1957.

MASS. INSTITUTE OF TECHNOLOGY (MIT)

T: *Kendall/MIT (Red). From the T, walk up Main St., turn left onto Vassar St., and left again onto Mass. Ave.; the Small Dome will be on your left. #1 bus from Harvard Sq. (p. 19) lets off in front of the Small Dome.* ***Contact:*** *MIT Info Ctr., Lobby 7 (Small Dome), 77 Massachusetts Ave. (☎617-253-1000; www.mit.edu).* ***Tours:*** *Free campus tours (includes a talk by the MIT admissions office) M-F 10am and 2pm; begin across the street from Lobby 7 (Small Dome).*

MIT is the world's leading institution dedicated to the study of science and technology, attracting brilliant minds and billions of private and government dollars. The 10,000 enrolled students are as well-known for their intellectual prowess as they are for their frequent campus pranks, known around school as "hacks." Famous hacks have included everything from reassembling a police car (complete with doughnut-chomping policeman) on top of a building to turning the campus' central Great Dome into R2D2 from *Star Wars*. One of the school's museums usually has a gallery of the most memorable hacks throughout history.

The campus is centered around the Great Dome-topped **Infinite Corridor,** a building accessible from Mass. Ave. via **Lobby 7** (home to the Info Ctr., campus maps, and info on the university). Lobby 7 is also known as the Small Dome to distinguish its smaller domed roof from the Infinite Corridor's Great Dome, a striking Neoclassical roof visible from Memorial Dr. and Boston.

As you walk around, you'll notice that everything at MIT—from the buildings to the majors—is given a number, so the entire campus seems like a giant math equation. In fact, several buildings at MIT have unique mathematical properties: the #66 building on Ames St. is a perfect 30-60-90° triangle, and the **Kresge Auditorium** (across from Lobby 7/Small Dome) touches the ground in only three places (it's an eighth of a sphere). In terms of sheer inventiveness do not miss the bizarre, Frank Gehry-designed **Stata Center;** facing inwards toward campus from Vassar St., the building can only be described as Dr. Seussian in its dimensions and design.

LIST VISUAL ARTS CENTER

20 Ames St. ***T:*** *Kendall/MIT (Red). From the T, walk up Main St. (with the Marriot on your right) and turn left onto Ames St. #1 bus from Harvard Sq. (p. 19) lets off in front of Lobby 7/Small Dome, where the Info Ctr. will direct you to the LVAC.* ***Contact:*** *☎617-253-4680; web.mit.edu/lvac.* ***Open:*** *Sept.-June Tu-Th and Sa-Su noon-6pm, F noon-8pm.* ***Admission:*** *Free.*

The MIT-affiliated List Visual Arts Ctr. features changing exhibits of national and international experimental works in all media and genres. Exhibits range from sculpture and performance art to photography and enigmatic explorations of the Internet, but always utilize cutting edge aesthetics and multimedia displays. The LVAC is housed in the striking I.M. Pei-designed Weisner Building (#E15), also home to the secretive MIT Media Lab, which built (among other things) the Mary Baker Eddy Library's hologram fountain (p. 63).

MIT MUSEUM

265 Massachusetts Ave., at Lansdowne St. ***T:*** *Central (Red). Walk 5min. down Mass. Ave. (with Starbucks on your left). From T: Kendall (Red), walk up Main St., turn left onto Vassar St., then right onto Mass. Ave. #1 bus from Harvard Sq. (p. 19) lets out in front of the museum.* ***Contact:*** *☎617-253-4444; web.mit.edu/museum.* ***Open:*** *Tu-F 10am-5pm, Sa-Su noon-5pm.* ***Admission:*** *$5; students, seniors, and ages 5-18 $2.*

If you can only go to one science-themed museum in Boston, skip the obvious choice and head to MIT. This little-known interactive museum showcases the most cutting edge technological innovations coming out of MIT and other research centers around the globe, all presented in dazzling interactive, multimedia exhibitions. In addition to the constantly changing lineup of temporary exhibits on science, technology, and visual media (advertised inventively in the windows looking out on Mass. Ave.), the museum has several permanent galleries, including an interactive history of MIT, a collection of robots and other artificially intelligent beings, and the **world's largest collection of holograms.**

The pinnacle of the museum is the ongoing exhibit highlighting the work of genius sculptor and engineer Arthur Ganson, whose ironic work in the medium of machines is most reminiscent of a cheeky Rube Goldberg.

MUSEUM OF SCIENCE

Science Park. ***T:*** *Science Park (Green).* ***Contact:*** *☎617-723-2500; www.mos.org.* ***Open:*** *Sept.-June Sa-Th 9am-5pm, F 9am-9pm; July-Aug. Sa-Th 9am-7pm, F 9am-9pm.* ***Admission:*** *Museum $13, seniors $11, ages 3-11 $10. Omni Theater, Planetarium, or Laser Show ticket $8.50, seniors $7.50, ages 3-11 $6.50; $3.50 discount on all shows after 6pm.*

The Museum of Science seeks to educate and entertain children of all ages with countless permanent and rotating interactive exhibits, divided up among three color-coded wings. Highlights of the permanent exhibits include: the giant *Tyrannosaurus rex* (Blue Wing, Lower Level); the wacky Theater of Electricity (Blue Wing, Level 1); the Soundstair, stairs that sing when you step on them (Red Wing, Level 1); and the Big Dig exhibit (Blue Wing, Lower Level). Attached to the museum is the **Mugar Omni Theater,** which shows various nature- and history-themed IMAX films on a five-story wraparound screen (check tickets.mos.org for hours and films). The **Hayden Planetarium** next door hosts trippy laser shows with music by everyone from Led Zeppelin to Britney Spears.

CHINATOWN

T: *Chinatown (Orange).* ***Discover Chinatown:*** *p. 3.* ***Food:*** *p. 115.* ***Shopping:*** *p. 173*

see map p. 322

Tucked away behind Financial District skyscrapers and amid Big Dig chaos is the nation's first Chinatown. Originally a garment and leather district, the neighborhood took on its ethnic character when the first waves of Chinese immigrants began arriving on the east coast of the US in the late 19th century in search of work. Seen as something of an urban eyesore throughout the 19th and early 20th centuries, Chinatown's reputation was further smudged when the long established red-light district at Scollay Sq. was relocated to its western border to make way for the new city hall (Government Ctr., see p. 81) A few sex shops whose leases have yet to run out remain in Chinatown, but this area once known as the "Combat Zone" is now almost entirely safe.

City planners left Chinatown untouched and against the odds the diverse Asian community (now encompassing ethnic Chinese, Japanese, Korean, Vietnamese, Filipino, and more) has survived and flourished. Spotless Japanese cars speed through graffiti covered streets, "Oriental" pagodas perch atop phone booths, and Chinese characters mark every business—even McDonald's.

CHINATOWN GATE

Beach St., at Hudson St. ***T:*** *Chinatown (Orange). Walk against traffic down Washington St. and turn left at the parking lot onto Beach St.; it's 3-4 blocks up.*

The elaborate pagoda gate, on the eastern end of Beach St., is the classic symbol found in Chinatowns throughout the US. Given by the Taiwanese government to the city in 1982 and guarded by Chinese lions, the side of the gate facing Harrison Ave. (visible as you walk from the T) is inscribed with the phrase *tian xia wei gong*, a saying often attributed to Sun Yat-sen that translates roughly to "everything under the sky is for the people." The opposite side of the gate (facing South Station) reads *li yi lian chi*, an ancient Chinese proverb with no direct translation that concerns being a good person in both familial and public spheres. Next to the gate is a small park dedicated to those who died in the 1989 massacre in Beijing's Tiananmen Sq.

DORCHESTER

see map p. 334-335

Settled in 1630, Dorchester is as old as Beacon Hill and the North End. Although it is now Boston's largest neighborhood, early Puritans settled only on tiny **Columbia Point;** that area is still home to the only sights of interest to the traveler—namely the **JFK Library** (p. 79) and the lesser-known **Commonwealth Museum** (p. 80), both near the campus of UMass-Boston. The most racially and economically diverse of Boston's neighborhoods—often the sight of the city's most racially and economically charged violence—Dorchester has long attracted large numbers of immigrants (most recently those of Jamaican, Vietnamese, and Haitian descent). Despite the economic decline of some Dorchester neighborhoods and the resulting troubles with school and street violence (such as the 1970s forced busing crisis; see p. 36), Dorchester residents strive to maintain their strong sense of community. Nevertheless, *Let's Go* suggests you avoid wandering around Dorchester unknowingly, especially at night.

JOHN F. KENNEDY LIBRARY & MUSEUM

Columbia Point. ***T:*** *JFK/UMass (Red). From there, take free shuttle #2, marked "JFK Library" (daily every 20min. 8am-5:30pm). By car, take Exit 15 (Morrissey Blvd./JFK Library) from Rte. 3/I-93S.* ***Contact:*** *☎617-929-4500 or 877-616-4599; www.jfklibrary.org.* ***Open:*** *daily 9am-5pm; film every 20min. until 3:30pm.* ***Admission:*** *$8, students and seniors $6, ages 13-17 $4, under 12 free.*

Commonly referred to as the JFK Library, this combo museum and research facility was dedicated in 1979 as one of only 10 Presidential Libraries in the US. Housed since 1993 in a stunning stone-and-glass tower designed by noted architect I.M. Pei—who also designed the Hancock Tower (p. 60) and Christian Science Plaza (p. 62)—the museum's main purpose is to pay tribute to the life and legacy of Brookline-born and Boston-educated former US president John Francis Fitzgerald Kennedy. Although he held the nation's highest office for less than a full term, his myriad accomplishments as the 35th President of the United States (1961-63) and tragic death have made him one of the most beloved men in American history. He and his fashion plate wife Jackie were the closest American politics came to royalty, and indeed, his time as president is often referred to as "Camelot," in reference to the mythical golden age of European rule.

A visit to this monument/museum begins with a 17min. film on Kennedy's youth and early political aspirations. From here, the museum proceeds chronologically through a series of rooms that both recreate important moments in Kennedy's life and trace the important issues of his presidency. Exhibits move from Kennedy's time in the US Navy to his extensive work with civil rights, his creation of the US Peace Corps (a program in which American youth apply to work in developing countries), and his involvement in the Cold War and the space race.

The highlight of each exhibit is the original documentation on display. The stunning Cuban Missile Crisis exhibit includes the spy photographs that began the crisis, the original drafts and notes of Kennedy himself, and the letter from Russia ending the standoff; all are declassified originals. Other historical gems include the painstaking recreation of the White House, especially the Oval Office (the president's office in Washington, D.C.), and the rotating special exhibits on Jackie Kennedy, whose consummate style and Oleg Cassini-tailored tastes defined an entire generation and continue to influence American culture and ideas of womanhood.

Touring the museum one can not help feeling a sense of impending doom, and in the penultimate room, that feeling is validated. Pitch-black, the room contains only TV screens. These constantly loop news reels telling of JFK's unexplained assassination in Dallas, Texas on Nov. 22, 1963 and footage of the subsequent funeral. Beyond this room and the following "Legacy Exhibit" is the Pavilion, a 115 ft. all-glass atrium with some of the most awe-inspiring views of the Boston skyline.

COMMONWEALTH MUSEUM

220 Morrissey Blvd., Columbia Point, opposite the JFK Library. ***T:*** *JFK/UMass (Red). From there, take free shuttle #2, marked "JFK Library" (daily every 20min. 8am-5:30pm). By car, take Exit 15 (Morrissey Blvd./JFK Library) from Rte. 3/I-93S.* ***Contact:*** *☎617-727-9268.* ***Open:*** *M-F 9am-5pm, Sa 9am-3pm.* ***Admission:*** *Free.*

Although the JFK Library across the parking lot attracts the lion's share of visitors, the Commonwealth Museum (housed in the State Archives Building) is worth a visit. For those whose appetite for American and Bostonian history was not sated by the Freedom Trail (p. 43), the tiny museum is run by the Massachusetts Historical Commission and maintains a series of rotating exhibits that illuminate and contextualize such musty but amazing archival materials as King Charles I's 1629 charter for the Massachusetts Bay Colony, the original Paul Revere engraving of the Boston Massacre (which took place outside the Old State House; see p. 50), and potsherds and quirky ancient artifacts, including America's oldest bowling ball, unearthed by the construction crews of the Big Dig (p. 99).

DOWNTOWN

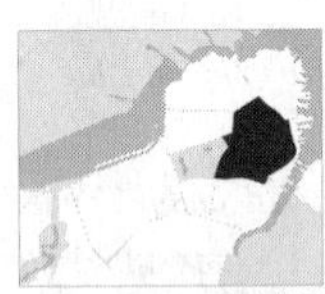
see map p. 324-325

T: *Park St. (Red/Green), Government Ctr. (Blue/Green), State (Blue/Orange), and Downtown Crossing (Red/Orange) are all within a few blocks of each other in the heart of Downtown.* ***Discover Downtown:*** *p. 3.* ***Freedom Trail Sights:*** *p. 46.* ***Food:*** *p. 117.* ***Nightlife:*** *p. 141.* ***Shopping:*** *p. 173.* ***Accommodations:*** *p. 189.*

At first glimpse, it seems like the downtown of any other city, with tall office buildings reflecting blue sky, cars jockeying with buses in the streets, and hordes of businessmen crowding into cafés during the lunch-hour rush. In reality, Downtown is a hodgepodge of very unusual districts. The area is home to many of Boston's major sights, most of which line the historic **Freedom Trail** (p. 43) that runs through **Downtown Crossing,** a major outdoor shopping area that overlaps with the glitzy nightlife district the elite have dubbed the **Ladder District** (p. 141). Eastward lie the Art Deco skyscrapers and faceless office buildings of the tangled Financial District, centered on the **Custom House Tower** (p. 82). North of Downtown Crossing, the municipal buildings of bleak **Government Ctr.** (p. 81) were built over the city's former red-light district (known as Scollay Sq.). Farther northeast is the Fleet Ctr., a giant sports and entertainment venue with its own **Sports Museum** (see p. 81) that's slowly being converted into a pubbers' paradise. Just east of this is tourist central—the outdoor shopping plaza at **Faneuil Hall & Quincy Market** (p. 50).

GOVERNMENT CENTER

T: Government Ctr. (Blue/Green). ***Open:*** *24hr., although it's fairly deserted at night.*

The sprawling brick expanse of Government Ctr. is home to the nondescript **JFK Building** and surreal **City Hall.** The upside-down ziggurat design of City Hall was intended to symbolically express the structure of government: the floors lowest to the ground house government offices used by the "common" public; the middle levels are home to the mayor's office and city council chambers (those who act as "middlemen" between the people and the government); and the far reaches of the upper floors hold the bureaucratic agencies with little or no direct contact with the public.

Hidden in the left corner of the plaza (in front of the JFK building) is a plaque and granite plinth marking the **birthplace of the telephone.** It is from a building on this spot that, on June 2, 1875, Alexander Graham Bell placed the first phone call to his assistant Thomas A. Watson. Thomas Edison invented the stock ticker in the same building. On the other side of Government Ctr., atop the Starbucks coffeeshop, is a giant (over 227 gallons) functional **tea kettle,** built in 1873.

In summer, usually in mid-June, Government Ctr. hosts the three-day ice cream-lovers' paradise known as the **Jimmy Fund Scooper Bowl** (☎800-525-4669; www.jimmyfund.org), where a $7 ticket gets you all the ice cream you can eat, provided by all the major New England ice cream distributors (from Ben & Jerry's to Brigham's; for a list of ice cream places, see p. 102). Several weeks later, the same spot is home to Harborfest's popular annual chowder cook-off known as **Chowderfest** (July 5, 2004; 11am-6pm).

SPORTS MUSEUM OF NEW ENGLAND

Fleet Ctr. Buy tickets at the Fleet Ctr. box office and enter through the Premium Club's private entrance nearby. ***T:*** *North Station (Green/Orange).* ***Contact:*** *for museum and exhibit info ☎617-624-1235, for hours ☎617-624-1234; www.sportsmuseum.org.* ***Open:*** *by tour only; hours vary drastically. Tours are usually M-Th every hr. on the hr. 11am-3pm.* ***Admission:*** *$6, seniors (60+) and ages 6-17 $4, under 6 free.*

Located on the 5th and 6th fl. of the flashy Fleet Ctr. (a gigantic performance venue also used for hockey and basketball games), this enjoyable museum is a must for all who understand or want to understand Boston's fanatical obsession with professional sports. The Fleet Ctr. itself was built on the site of the legendary Boston Garden, the original home of the Boston Bruins as well as the Boston Celtics (back in their glory days). In homage to the old Garden, the museum recreates a penalty box. Each of the interactive exhibits in the museum is dedicated to a different Boston sports franchise—basketball's Celtics, hockey's Bruins, American football's New England Patriots, and baseball's legendary Red Sox. Beyond Boston's big four, there are exhibits on figure skating, boxing, and even some college sports teams. In addition to displaying archival footage and authentic gear, awards, and other artifacts, the museum features life-size cut-outs accompanying reconstructions of lockers that belonged to Boston's sports legends, past and present—from the Celtic's Larry Bird to the Sox's Nomar Garciaparra.

HAYMARKET

On Hanover St. between Government Ctr. and the North End. ***T:*** *Haymarket (Green/Orange).* ***Open:*** *year-round F-Sa 7am-7pm, usually closes earlier Sa.*

An outdoor produce market has been held in the vicinity of the present-day Haymarket since the early 1700s (it's been along Blackstone St. since 1839). Known as one of Boston's best places to buy high-quality fruits and vegetables at low prices, the Haymarket has also inexplicably become one of Boston's major tourist attractions, as many as

100,000 people visit each weekend. A trip to this chaotic market of over 200 licensed vendors (it makes even the Big Dig look tame) is definitely a unique way to spend a weekend morning or to take a break from the Freedom Trail, which skirts the Haymarket en route to the North End (p. 52).

Some tips on navigating the market: in summer, mornings are most crowded, while winter crowds flock to the Haymarket in the afternoon. Produce is most consistently fresh early on Friday, while prices plummet and quality/freshness gets much spottier as Saturday progresses. Regardless of when you visit, don't touch the goods on display; tell the vendor how much or many you want and they'll pick it out. Don't worry: they'll replace anything you don't find up to par.

CUSTOM HOUSE TOWER

3 McKinley Sq., on State St. ***Contact:*** *☎617-310-6300.* ***T:*** *State (Blue/Orange). Walk against traffic down State St. to India St.* ***Admission:*** *$1 donation (given to charity) for entrance to observation balcony.* ***Open:*** *Entrance to balcony Su-F 10am and 4pm, Sa 4pm; always open for guests.*

Built in 1847, the 495 ft., 26-story Custom House was Boston's first skyscraper. Although it's now dwarfed by its sleek modern neighbors, the Custom House's Greek Revival tower, with its distinctive clock, is still one of the most unique buildings in Boston's skyline. Originally built to collect customs revenue, it was recently converted into a hotel by Marriott, who went to painstaking lengths to preserve the original architecture and interior design—including the restoration of the top-floor observation balcony, which offers views of the Boston Harbor.

Perhaps the most famous residents of the Custom House Tower are the pair of **Peregrine Falcons** who make their nest in the hidden upper reaches of the clock tower. Once prominent in the New England area, the Peregrine Falcon (one of the fastest birds on earth) faced extinction in the 1950s because of the pesticide DDT. To save the birds, state and federal wildlife agencies began setting up breeding pairs in select locations (the nest in the Custom House Tower was made in 1987). The Custom House falcons are one of the most productive nesting pairs in New England, having laid 64 eggs and raised 36 chicks. There most recent success was in spring of 2003, when the tower was actually closed to ensure a healthy nest. Thanks in part to the Custom House's efforts, the Peregrine Falcon was removed from the federal endangered species list in 1999.

PARK AT POST OFFICE SQ.

Along Congress St., between Milk and Franklin St. ***T:*** *State (Blue/Orange) or Government Ctr. (Blue/Green). Exit the T onto State St. and turn right onto Congress St.* ***Open:*** *24hr.* ***Admission:*** *Free.*

Laid out in 1992 by the City of Boston, the Park at Post Office Sq. (presided over by an elaborate Art Deco post office building) is an unexpected natural paradise hidden among the Financial District's skyscrapers. A favorite lunchtime picnic spot for local suits, the park is filled with the sound of birds chirping and trees rustling, making it easy to forget that you're in the heart of urban Boston. The park is dedicated to the humane treatment of animals, and one end is dominated by a circular fountain in which (presumably unharmed) bronze animals splash busily. The fountain was designed by Howard Ben-Tré, who is also responsible for the Eddy Library's virtual fountain (p. 63.) The other end of the park is home to the glass-walled, copper-domed **Milk St. Café** (sandwiches and wraps $6-7).

JAMAICA PLAIN

see map p. 329

T: *The Orange Line runs through JP about 5-6 blocks east of Centre St. (use the Jackson Sq., Stony Brook, Green St., or Forest Hills stops).* ***Discover Jamaica Plain:*** *p. 6.* ***Food:*** *p. 118.* ***Nightlife:*** *p. 144.* ***Shopping:*** *p. 172.*

Although incorporated into the City of Boston, Jamaica Plain offers everything quintessentially un-Bostonian—ample parking, good Mexican food, and acres of forests and outdoors opportunities. Although it fell into disrepair in the last century (when it was known as an immigrant ghetto with a rampant drug trade), JP has recently experienced a full-on revival and is now one of Boston's brightest and most diverse neighborhoods, with one of the area's more sizeable queer communities. With a vibrant arts scene, affordable housing, and seemingly unending woodlands just steps away, Jamaica Plain is becoming an ideal place to live. The creeping gentrification that usually accompanies such urban renewals—taking the form of rising prices, homogenized crowds, and multiplying Starbucks coffeeshops (*q.v.* the South End)—has been largely absent from JP.

Work up an appetite at the **Arnold Arboretum** (p. 84) or **Olmsted Park** and **Jamaica Pond** (see right), then sate your hunger at one of the many affordable and delicious restaurants lining Centre St. Wash it all down with a stop at the nearby **Sam Adams Brewery** (p. 83), where the free beer-making tour concludes with a taste test of the highly regarded brewery's latest concoctions.

FRANKLIN PARK & ZOO

1 Franklin Park Rd. ***T:*** *Forest Hills (Orange) or Andrew (Red), then take bus #16 to the Zoo's Zebra Entrance. By car, take Exit 15 from I-93.* ***Contact:*** *☎617-541-5466; www.zoonewengland.com.* ***Open:*** *Apr.-Sept. M-F 10am-5pm, Sa-Su 10am-6pm; Oct.-Mar. daily 10am-4pm.* ***Admission:*** *Park free. Zoo $9.50, seniors $8, ages 2-15 $5, under 2 free; Butterfly Landing $1 extra.*

This huge park (520 acres, the Emerald Necklace's largest) encompasses the Forest Hills Cemetery and the Franklin Park Zoo among its wide open green space. Aside from being the final resting place of such literary figures as e.e. cummings, Eugene O'Neill, and Anne Sexton, the **Forest Hills Cemetery** doubles as a creepy Victorian sculpture park. The livelier **Franklin Zoo** is a favorite of young visitors to Boston. In addition to exhibits like the beautiful Butterfly Landing (where more than 1000 butterflies flutter freely), the zoo's five main habitats let you walk through different regions of the world in miniature—from a kangaroo-filled Australian desert to a wildebeest-trampled sub-Saharan veldt. There's also a petting zoo and all those beasties kids love, like anacondas and bathing hippos.

SAM ADAMS BREWERY

30 Germania St. ***T:*** *Stony Brook (Orange). Turn left onto Boylston St.; after 2 blocks go right on Bismark St. at the Sam Adams sign. Call or check the website for driving directions.* ***Contact:*** *☎617-522-9080; www.samadams.com/beer/tour.html.* ***Admission:*** *Suggested donation $2.* ***Tours:*** *Th 2pm; F 2 and 5:30pm; Sa noon, 1, 2pm. Additional tour May-Aug. W 2pm.*

the EMERALD NECKLACE

Olmsted Park & Jamaica Pond Park

Both parks line the Jamaicaway, which runs parallel to Centre St. Olmsted Park runs from Rte. 9 to Perkins St.; Jamaica Pond Park runs from Perkins St. to Prince St. The Arborway runs from the edge of Jamaica Pond Park to the Arnold Arboretum. ***T:*** *Green St. (Orange). Turn left out of the T onto Green St., then right onto Centre St., and left onto Pond St., which runs into the Jamaicaway at Jamaica Pond.* ***Contact:*** *Ranger Station ☎617-635-7383, boathouse ☎617-522-6258.*

Named for Frederick Law Olmsted (p. 44), Olmsted Park connects Brookline to Boston and was designed with pathways and planting patterns that would highlight the dramatic land forms of the area. Adjacent to Olmsted Park, the 120 acre **Jamaica Pond Park** is home to beloved Jamaica Pond, Boston's largest natural body of water. The pond is a popular fishing spot and boating destination (the boathouse rents sailboats and rowboats, $10-15 per hr.). Although signs forbid swimming, illicit midnight skinny-dipping is a favorite sport among local students. August's **Jamaica Pond Concert Series** brings classical music to the pond.

the EMERALD NECKLACE

Arnold Arboretum

125 Arborway, Jamaica Plain. ***T:*** *Forest Hills (Orange). Entrance 1 block northwest of the T, along the Arborway. Also accessible from JP's Olmsted Park and Jamaica Pond.* ***Open:*** *daily dawn-dusk.* ***Contact:*** *☎617-524-1718; www.arboretum.harvard.edu.*

Run by Harvard University, the Arboretum's over 265 acres function as a living botany museum that is home to one of the largest selections of flora and fauna in the world. Unfortunately, few people ever take the time to venture out to JP, and as a result the Arboretum is perhaps the most underappreciated space in the city.

One of the most popular events at the Arboretum is **Lilac Sunday** (the 2nd or 3rd Sunday in May), when the 400 lilac plants burst into full bloom. The event officially began in spring of 1925 and has grown larger with the passing years, so that now English folk dancing, picnics, and tours enhance the seasonal spectacle and celebrate the arrival of the long-awaited lilacs.

The Arboretum also prides itself on the Larz Anderson Bonsai Collection, named after an early 20th century ambassador to Japan who donated his collection of miniature *bonsai* trees to the Arboretum in 1937.

Sam Adams' Harvard-educated CEO and founder Jim Koch used his great-great-grandfather's 150 year-old German recipe to brew a beer he named after Revolutionary War hero (and colonial brewmaster) Sam Adams, in hopes of starting a "revolution" that would free beer-swilling Americans from the harsh tyranny of imported beers. Sam Adams is now the most award-winning beer in the country (it is the only American brand to pass stringent European brewing competition regulations) and is a great source of pride for the city.

The brewery's free 40min. tour leads you through the original Sam Adams Brewery, now just a research and development office (the beer is brewed at various industrial plants all over the country). At the end of the tour, those who are 21+ and possess ID are escorted to a special brewery bar, where they receive a commemorative plastic pint glass, learn how to "taste" beer, and then try out their newly honed tasting skills on a few pints of beers currently being tested by the company.

KENMORE SQ. & THE FENWAY

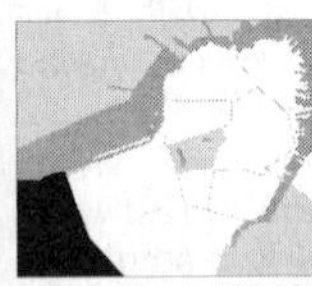

see map p. 330-331

T: *Kenmore (Green-B,C,D) serves Kenmore Sq. and Fenway Park, while the Avenue of the Arts (Huntington Ave.) runs between T: Symphony and T: Museum (Green-E); all are also "Night Owl" Green Line stops.* ***Discover Kenmore Sq. & the Fenway:*** *p. 4.* ***Food:*** *p. 120.* ***Nightlife:*** *p. 145.* ***Shopping:*** *p. 172.* ***Accommodations:*** *p. 190.*

It's a bit tricky to get around this area on the T, but if you're looking for the city's best art, finest music, and favorite pastime, look no further than Kenmore Sq. and the Fenway. The area is home to Boston's most cherished civic and cultural institutions, from museums and a world-class symphony to the beleaguered but much loved Red Sox.

The name Fenway comes from the marshy **Fens** (part of Frederick Law Olmsted's Emerald Necklace; see p. 44), a curving green space that splits the neighborhood in two. North of the Fens, **Kenmore Sq.** (dominated by the 60 ft. Citgo sign) is home to the dorms and classrooms of Boston University as well as the cherished baseball diamond **Fenway Park** (p. 85). South of the Fens, the **Fenway** neighborhood contains Northeastern University as well as Boston's major cultural spots, which line Huntington Ave., unofficially termed the **Avenue of the Arts** in 1998.

Here you'll find venerated Symphony Hall (p. 86), lavish Jordan Hall (p. 157), the exquisite Isabella Stewart Gardner Museum (p. 88), and the overwhelming Museum of Fine Arts (p. 86).

FENWAY PARK

Ticket office, 4 Yawkey Way. ***T:*** *Kenmore (Green-B,C,D). Walk down Brookline Ave. (with the Hotel Buckminster on your right) and turn left onto Yawkey Way.* ***Contact:*** *tickets ☎617-482-4769 or 617-267-1700, tours ☎617-236-6666; www.redsox.com.* ***Games:*** *Apr.-Oct. M-F 7:05pm, Sa-Su 1:05pm. Gates open 1½hr. before game time.* ***Admission:*** *If you're just touring the park, entrance is by guided tour only: $9, seniors $8, under 14 $7. Tickets can be purchased online or at the Ticket Office; for tips on getting cheap tickets, see p. 167.* ***Tours:*** *1hr. guided tours late May-Aug. every hr., 9am-4pm or until 3hr. before game time.*

Being the oldest and smallest park in Major League Baseball gives storied Fenway Park, built for the 1912 season and rebuilt in 1934, a tangible claim to fame. Despite the modernization of the ballpark (three new seating areas were added in 2003) and the very modern ticket prices (baseball's most expensive), a visit to Fenway is a time warp back to a long-gone era. With real grass, unique dimensions, and the most dedicated fans in the history of sports, being at Fenway feels a lot like stepping back to 1918 (the last time the Sox won the World Series). Unlike some newer parks, Fenway is full of history—from the red seat in the bleachers to the right field foul pole, every part of the park has a story. The best way to hear those stories is to take a tour. Tours are pricey, but worth it for the countless tales of Red Sox and Fenway lore recounted by the zealous guides. Fenway legends include the "Green Monster" (the in-play left-field wall), the quirky scoreboard (one of only two manual boards left), and the wretched Curse of the Bambino.

AVENUE OF THE ARTS

Huntington Ave. becomes "Avenue of the Arts" from T: Symphony to T: Museum (Green-E).

In 1998, Malcolm Rogers, the controversial current director of the Museum of Fine Arts (MFA), had the idea of renaming the stretch of Huntington Ave. between **Symphony Hall** (p. 86) and the **MFA** (p. 86) the "Avenue of the Arts" in hopes of jumpstarting a cultural revival of the area. The MFA committed to a multimillion dollar expansion and improvement of both its building and the streets and grounds around its stretch of the

in recent news

The New York Times Saves Fenway

Dwarfed by the soulless concrete monstrosity that is Yankee Stadium, Fenway Park, the smallest and oldest ballpark in the Majors, has always had trouble generating the type of revenue necessary to buy a world championship and overcome a curse. The math is simple, if Boston sells-out its 34,000 seats, they still stand to make less than the Yanks can make selling just ¾ of their 57,000.

This simple fact has placed storied Fenway at risk of demolition for the last 10 years. Hope, however, springs eternal, and now from the most surprising of places. In 2002 an ownership group dominated by The New York Times Co. purchased the team. With New Yorkers as the new owners, many thought the end was near for Fenway, but instead of a demolition crew a construction crew materialized and began the slow revamping of Fenway. Though ownership was quick to note that improvements do not necessarily mean Fenway will remain the home of the Sox, it is reassuring nonetheless to see new structures emerge from the old park. New features include: $200 a seat first row boxes with waitstaff, 2 cheap-seat roof boxes, $50 barstools atop the Green Monster, 2 open air concourses, and a much needed new coat of paint.

Symphony Hall

Museum of Fine Arts

Inside Symphony Hall

Avenue of the Arts. Nearby institutions, such as the unique **Isabella Stewart Gardner Museum** (p. 88), have yet to commit to improvements, but many are taking note.

SYMPHONY HALL

301 Massachusetts Ave., at Huntington Ave. ***T:*** *Symphony (Green-E).* ***Contact:*** *☎617-266-1492; www.bso.org.* ***Admission:*** *Free. Aside from concerts, entrance is by tour only.* ***Tours:*** *Free 1hr. tour Oct.-May W 4:30pm and 1st Sa of every month 1:30pm. Tour times change occasionally; call first and confirm.*

Home to both the world-renowned **Boston Symphony Orchestra** (p. 156) and its more casual companion the **Boston Pops** (p. 156), august Symphony Hall is a treasured Boston landmark. Built in 1900, this U-shaped hall is modeled on the most acoustically perfect hall in the world—the Gewandhaus in Leipzig, Germany. It features shallow balconies to prevent aurally "dead" spots, wood flooring to reflect sound, and an acoustically exact, but comfort-challenging five inches between rows of seats. The tours are great for classical music aficionados, as the guide spends as much time on the building as he does on the colorful history of the illustrious BSO. For information on getting tickets to a BSO or Pops concert, see p. 155.

Across Huntington Ave., **Jordan Hall** (p. 157) is the performance space of the prestigious New England Conservatory. It may host musicians who are not as famous as those who play at Symphony Hall (or those who aren't *yet* that famous), but its over-the-top gilded interior—viewable only during one of NEC's frequent free concerts—far outshines the Symphony's subdued balconies.

MUSEUM OF FINE ARTS (MFA)

465 Huntington Ave. ***T:*** *Museum (Green-E).* ***Contact:*** *☎617-267-9300; www.mfa.org.* ***Open:*** *M-Tu and Sa-Su 10am-4:45pm, W-F 10am-9:45pm; Th-F only West Wing open after 5pm. As a result of construction related to the museum's expansion and facelift (which broke ground in 2003 and will continue for nearly a decade), a number of galleries in the East Wing will be closed or relocated; check floor plan maps for the latest updates.* ***Admission:*** *M-F until 3pm $15, students (18+) and seniors (65+) $13, ages 7-17 $6.50. M-F after 3pm and all-day Su free. Suggested donation only W after 4pm; $2 off Th-F after 5pm. Ticket includes 1 additional admission within 30 days.* ***Tours:*** *Free 1hr. guided tours M-F 10:30 and 11:30am, 12:30, 1, 2, 3pm; W 6:15pm; Sa 10:30am and 1pm; Su 1:30pm.*

Boston's massive Museum of Fine Arts showcases artwork from all over the world and all throughout history, taking an encyclopedic and ethnographic approach to art and art history. Second in the US only to NYC's Metropolitan Museum of Art in quality and quantity of holdings, the MFA features nearly every artistic and artisanal tradition known to mankind, including Japanese samurai armor, contemporary American art, medieval musical instruments, Impressionist still-lifes, and even a selection of yellowed Mughal-era sheet music.

Bewilderment is not uncommon at the MFA: the museum's exhibits are well-explained and intelligently curated, but not laid out in any intuitive order (i.e. by style, period, etc.). Thankfully, both floors are designed similarly, with foreign art and artifacts in the southern half and American and European art to the north. The best way to tackle the museum is to enter through the southern Ionic temple entrance on Huntington Ave. (guarded by Cyrus Dallin's equestrian statue *Appeal to the Great Spirit*) and proceed counterclockwise around both floors. Descriptions below move counterclockwise.

FIRST FLOOR

The dramatic Huntington Ave. entrance is the original entrance to the museum. Just to the right of the grand staircase is the world's largest collection of **Nubian art and artifacts.** The Nubians lived in Sudan during the time of the ancient Egyptians, as a stroll through their familiar-looking pyramids and mummies makes evident. Nearby, the MFA's millennia-spanning collection of Egyptian artifacts was unearthed during a 1905 expedition to the Nile River Delta and the pyramids at Giza. The highlight is the eerie **Egyptian Funerary Arts** gallery, just beyond the Nubian art, a crypt-like room filled with actual mummies, burial coffins, and funerary statuary. Hidden around the corner, the **American Silver** collection lets you see what busy silversmith Paul Revere was up to when he wasn't planning a revolution, and the musical instrument room reveals what busy inventor Ben Franklin was up to when we wasn't flying his kite.

Double back through the rotunda and hang a right into the **Lane Gallery's** phenomenal contemporary art collection, with abstract works by Georgia O'Keefe and Arthur Dove, a demure drip painting by Jackson Pollock, and many other masterpieces. If you are having trouble grasping the meaning behind this particular brand of art, have a seat, (most of the benches in the museum are designed by famous artists like Wendell Castle) and read one of the books provided for novices. Once you feel rested and enlightened, move north to the **Evans Wing.**

ESSENTIAL INFORMATION

MUSEUMS

If you're planning a museum binge, consider a **CityPass,** which covers admission to (and lets you skip lines at) the Aquarium (p. 96), JFK Library, MFA, Harvard's Museum of Natural History, Museum of Science, and the Prudential Ctr. Skywalk (p. 62). Passes, available at the museums or www.citypass.com, are valid for 9 days after 1st use and cost $34 (ages 3-17 $19.50), which works out to a 50-55% discount.

To help with your museum blitz, here's a list of Boston's major museums by type:

ART MUSEUMS

Boston Public Library (61)
Carpenter Center (75)
Galleries–Back Bay (59)
Galleries–South End (92)
Gardner Museum (88)
Harvard U. Art Museums (73)
Inst. of Contemporary Art (58)
Museum of Fine Arts (86)

HISTORICAL MUSEUMS

Boston Tea Party Ship (94)
Commonwealth Museum (80)
HMNH & Peabody Museum (75)
Harvard Semitic Museum (75)
Immigration Museum (49)
JFK Library (79)
Mary Baker Eddy Library (63)
Museum of Afro-Am. History (65)
Old State House (50)
USS *Constitution* Museum (56)

OTHER MUSEUMS

Children's Museum Boston (94)
MIT Museum (78)
Museum of Science (78)
Sports Museum (81)

In the Evans Wing, you'll find one of the world's most impressive collections of American art, ranging from colonial times to the present and including all media, from textiles to photographs. The collection is arranged chronologically from east to west, and the best gallery is the room housing the **colonial portraits** at the easternmost end. The gallery is dominated by the work of Copley Sq. namesake John Singleton Copley. Don't miss Copley's *Watson and the Shark* or Gilbert Stuart's small unfinished portrait of George Washington, both in this room. If you do miss the latter, don't worry—it's also on the $1 bill.

Jog back through the Lane Gallery, pass through the rotunda, and turn right into the popular **Asian art** galleries, where you will find elaborate works in all media from China, the Indian subcontinent, Japan, Korea, and the Middle East; the fierce samurai warrior regalia in the Japanese galleries is especially notable.

SECOND FLOOR

The Asian art gallery continues on the 2nd fl.; follow the stairs within the gallery. The highlight of this floor (if not the entire museum) is the soothing **Temple Room,** a dimly lit, quiet gallery built to look like a Buddhist temple and presided over by ornate buddhas and other deities.

Make like Marco Polo and navigate your way out of the Asian art (a difficult task) to the 2nd fl. **Egyptian** galleries. (You'll pass through a rotunda decked out in murals by John Singer Sargent, which are nice, but pale in comparison to Sargent's allegorical mural *Triumph of Religion,* on display at the Boston Public Library; see p. 61.) The main Egyptian gallery has multi-story pillars, plinths, and statuary taken from temples and mausoleums throughout the Nile River Delta, while small side galleries lead to recreations of ancient Egyptian chapels.

Head back to the rotunda and pass through the **Koch Gallery** (a room piled high with forgettable European art that often hosts unforgettable free world music concerts) to the 2nd fl. of the **Evans Wing.** This dizzying array of 17th- to 20th-century European art is again organized chronologically from east to west. The delightful but tiny **Spanish Chapel,** a rough recreation of a frescoed Byzantine church from Catalunya, is a visitor favorite, but it's nothing compared to the **Impressionism** gallery, which ends your MFA visit with a bang. The room houses the MFA's 36-work Monet collection (the largest collection outside France), including the stunning studies of the *Rouen Cathedral.* There are also works by other great Impressionist and post-Impressionist masters, including Cézanne, Degas (you're greeted by his bronze *Ballerina*), Renoir, van Gogh, and Picasso; among these, the most intriguing is Picasso's dark, fragmented *Portrait of a Woman.* The gallery leads directly into the museum shop, which empties into the über-modern Cohen gallery. Here you will find *The Letting Go*, a freaky, vibrating installation constructed by young artist Sarah Sze. Stairs beneath this lead to the temporary exhibits and the I.M. Pei-designed West Wing exit.

ISABELLA STEWART GARDNER MUSEUM

*280 Fenway. **T:** Museum (Green-E). Walk down Huntington Ave. (with the MFA on your right) and turn right onto Louis Prang St., which becomes The Fenway 2 blocks down. **Contact:** ☎617-566-1401; www.gardnermuseum.org. **Open:** Tu-Su 11am-5pm. **Admission:** M-F $10, Sa-Su $11; students $5; under 18 and individuals named "Isabella" free. **Tours:** free guided tours F 2:30pm (limited to 20 people; reserve in advance); audio tours $4.*

The Gardner Museum is like nothing you've seen before. This striking Venetian *palazzo*-style mansion was built at the turn of the century by eccentric and outspoken socialite Isabella Stewart Gardner, who intended the building to serve both as her home and as a museum for her astounding personal collection of fine art and furnishings. The mansion now stands as a monument to her extravagant tastes: every room in the four-story mansion has been decorated and arranged by Ms. Gardner to perfectly complement the art on display in the room (e.g. delicate silk wallpaper for fragile watercolors, imported Spanish tiles for the Spanish-themed *El Jaleo*, etc.). Her will also stipulated that no major changes could ever be made to the museum, so the entire mansion remains exactly as Ms. Gardner left it. On St. Patrick's Day, 1990, paintings worth over $200 million (including one of only 32 Vermeers left in the world) were stolen—the largest unsolved art theft in US history—and their empty frames still hang on the walls. Many of the works were deliberately left unlabeled (thankfully, the guards know *everything* about the paintings and the mansion), so much of the pleasure of the place is in wandering from room to room and responding to works and settings on your own. The following are the must-see rooms:

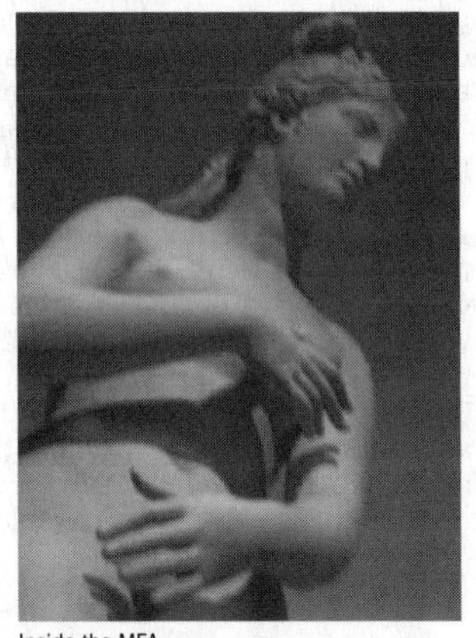
Inside the MFA

FIRST FLOOR

Opposite the ticket counter, the **Yellow Room** is filled with autographs, photographs, and manuscripts by and from musician acquaintances of Ms. Gardner's, including Brahms, Beethoven, Strauss, and Mendelssohn. The main entrance leads to the **Spanish Cloister,** one of the museum's most attractive rooms. Centered on John Singer Sargent's passionate, flamenco-themed painting *El Jaleo* (sketches for which hang in Harvard's Fogg Museum; p. 74), the room is lined with Spanish tiles from a 17th-century Mexican church.

Hidden near the coat check, the best room on the floor is the **Blue Room,** holding unsigned watercolors by John Singer Sargent. The true highlight of the museum is also on this floor, though not on the walls. Vying with the Public Library's *palazzo* courtyard (p. 61) for most soothing spot in Boston, the Gardner Museum's *palazzo* courtyard is a lush, flower-filled, impeccably manicured oasis where time seems to slip away. Visit after sundown to catch the courtyard's eerie candlelight.

Corridor in the MFA

SECOND FLOOR

Much of this floor is taken up by the dark and uninspiring Tapestry Room, which doubles as a concert hall. The north corner's lavish **Early Italian Room** and **Raphael Room** contain celebrated Italian Renaissance works. The undisputed champion of this floor is Rembrandt's self portrait, hanging in the **Dutch Room.** It was the first painting Gardner acquired and is considered by many to be the cornerstone of her collection.

THIRD FLOOR

The most impressive rooms are on the 3rd fl. First up is the **Veronese Room,** covered by an ornate gilded ceiling. Next comes the **Titian Room,**

Appeal to the Great White Spirit

a tribute to Ms. Gardner's favorite painting, Titian's *Europa* (the rose madder color of Europa's robe is picked up throughout the space). *Europa* is considered by most art historians to be the most important work of the Italian Renaissance in the US. Most scholars disagree with Ms. Gardner's placement of the painting, arguing that the painting was intended to be viewed at eye level and much closer-up.

The adjacent **Long Gallery** houses original manuscripts of works with a religious theme, including an original of Dante's *Divine Comedy* (make sure to lift the cloth covers off the cases to see them). The Long Gallery leads to a tiny **chapel,** tinged with stained-glass windows crafted in 1205 from over 2000 individual pieces of colored glass. Upon Ms. Gardner's request, an Anglican high mass is celebrated every year here on her birthday (April 14). Last on most tours through the house, the **Gothic Room,** where the furniture and lighting are appropriately gloomy, captures the perfect setting for Sargent's dramatic full-length portrait (completed in 1888 on the 9th try) of Ms. Gardner. The plunging neckline of her dress was considered inappropriate in her day.

SOUTH BOSTON

T: Broadway (Red). ***Discover South Boston:*** *p. 7.* ***Nightlife:*** *p. 148.*

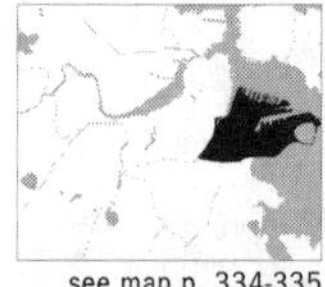

see map p. 334-335

Home to a prominent, tightly knit, and colorful working-class Irish community, "Southie" is not on many visitors' itineraries, even though it lies just across the Ft. Point Channel from Downtown. Known for being less than super-friendly toward casual visitors (particularly visitors of color, who may feel uncomfortable and out of place on the streets), Southie does offer enjoyable green spaces and historically significant spots, plus a string of authentic Irish pubs lining Broadway (see p. 148).

Though the two neighborhoods are now often violently segregated from each other, South Boston was once difficult to dissociate from nearby Dorchester (p. 97). During the early 17th-century settlement of the Shawmut Peninsula and the Greater Boston area, Southie (then known as Dorchester Neck or Great Neck) served as a cow pasture for then-independent Dorchester (Dorchester St. marks the original cowpath). In March 1776, when 3000 American troops arrived in the area to fortify Dorchester Heights (now **Thomas Park,** p. 91) against approaching British forces, only 12 families lived on the Neck. The area was eventually annexed to Boston in 1804 and renamed South Boston after the South Bridge, which spans the Ft. Point Channel coming from Downtown.

Around that time, Boston was one of the country's cheapest ports of entry for immigrants. With South Boston newly created and wide open for settlement, the neighborhood became a natural destination for newcomers, particularly the Irish, who flooded the area and built elegant brownstones on City Point, overlooking the so-called "Irish Riviera." The neighborhood remains largely Irish Catholic today, as is immediately evident from both the many green shamrock signs found throughout the neighborhood and the wild **St. Patrick's Day** parade (p. 11) held every year along W. Broadway.

CASTLE ISLAND & FORT INDEPENDENCE

William J. Day Blvd. ***T:*** *Broadway (Red), then take bus #9 (12min., every 15-30min. 6am-1am, $0.75) to the end of its route (City Point); turn right and cross Marine Park. By car, take the JFK/Columbia Rd., Exit 17 from I-93, turn left on Columbia Rd., and then right onto Day Blvd. from the rotary. Free parking.* ***Contact:*** *Run by the Metropolitan District Commission (MDC) ☎617-727-5114; www.state.ma.us/mdc.* ***Open:*** *daily 6am-11pm. Ft. Independence open in summer Th 7pm-dusk, Sa-Su and holidays noon-3:30pm.* ***Admission:*** *free. Admission to Fort Independence by 45min. guided tour only; departs when enough people gather.*

A favorite outdoor spot for residents of Southie and Greater Boston, the 22-acre Castle Island (no longer an island, but a peninsular park attached to the mainland) is great for waterfront walking and jogging. The beach may look tempting, but the water is not clean enough to swim in. Despite its name, Castle Island was joined to the mainland in 1932 by a highway that replaced the wooden bridge that had previously spanned a body of water known as Pleasure Bay. Today, the 2 mi. loop around the bay is a pleasant walk beginning at **Mariner's Park** (where the bus drops you off), past Head Island (better known as the Sugar Bowl), and on to Castle Island proper. Near Mariner's Park is **Sullivan's,** a snack bar housed in a recreated captain's quarters.

Castle Island is crowned by **Fort Independence,** a Civil War fortress that is the eighth to occupy the hilltop. The first fortification on this site was built in 1634 and remained unharmed until 1776, when retreating British troops partially destroyed it. Since then, the fort has served as training grounds for troops during the War of 1812 and the US Civil War. In addition to its defensive military function, Fort Independence was the first home of the Boston Marine Hospital (1799-1804), now the US Department of Health. The fortress opens for guided tours on the weekends and a breathtaking twilight viewing of the Boston skyline in summer every Thursday (7pm-dusk).

THOMAS PARK & DORCHESTER HEIGHTS

At the top of Telegraph St. ***Contact:*** *Boston National Historical Park ☎617-242-5642.* ***T:*** *Broadway (Red), then take bus #9 (12min., every 15-30min. 6am-1am, $0.75) to G St. By car, take the Mass. Pike (I-90) exit from I-93, bearing left at the local sign at the foot of the off-ramp. Turn left at the first set of lights onto Broadway, then right on G St. and continue for 2 blocks.* ***Open:*** *Park open sunrise-sunset. Monument open mid-June to Aug. W 4-8pm, Sa-Su 10am-4pm.*

The view of Boston from Dorchester Heights isn't quite as impressive as it was when the Minutemen stationed cannons here to drive the British troops out of Boston in March 1776, but you'll still have a lofty perspective of the spectacular "Big Dig" and Dorchester Bay from this historic landmark. The fortification of the twin hills of Dorchester Heights was an integral part of Gen. George Washington's campaign. It earned him a victory without American losses and raised Patriot morale. In the winter of 1776, 59 cannons were brought by oxen 300 mi. from Ft. Ticonderoga, New York. When they reached Roxbury, the rebels wrapped the wagon wheels in straw to deaden the sound and quietly rolled them up to the fortified summit. The British woke on March 17th to find cannons trained on their heads. They hurriedly set sail for Nova Scotia, abandoning Boston to the jubilant Patriots.

Fountain in the Gardner

The Fens

Ornate Ceiling

Troops were stationed here once more during the War of 1812, but the area lost its military significance when one of the twin hills was chopped down to fill in the tidal flats. In 1898, the General Court of Massachusetts commissioned a white marble Georgian **monument** to stand on the remaining hill in commemoration of the 1776 triumph. In 1951, Dorchester Heights was designated a National Historic Site.

SOUTH END

see map p. 336

T: Back Bay (Orange) is the nearest stop. Walk down Clarendon St. (with the T on your right) to Tremont St., the stylish main drag of the South End. ***Discover the South End:** p. 4. **Food:** p. 125. **Nightlife:** p. 149. **Shopping:** p. 172. **Accommodations:** p. 191.*

The South End has changed so many times in the last 300 years that it barely raises eyebrows to learn that the neighborhood is today experiencing another identity crisis. The streets of one of the trendiest districts in the city are the sight of a tense face-off between the wealthy and largely gay population of the South End and the less affluent residents of neighboring Roxbury, most of whom have been pushed out of their longtime homes in the South End by skyrocketing rents and creeping gentrification.

The original South End was little more than Washington St., then merely a southern road into and out of the city. When Boston's growing merchant class decided they wanted their own exclusive neighborhood like the Boston Brahmins had on Beacon Hill (p. 63), they flocked to this area, building many of the beautiful townhouses you see today. There was a mass exodus several decades later with the development of the suddenly more desirable Back Bay (p. 57), and poorer workers (many of them of African, Middle Eastern, and Eastern European descent) flooded into the South End. Throughout the 20th century, the area remained a working-class slum (even harboring a lurid red-light district for several years), until the mid-1960s attempt to renew the neglected parts of the city and scrub out its many red-light districts. Wealthier folk poured in once again; one of the first groups to move in was the city's growing queer population, and by the late 70s, the South End was Boston's gay ghetto. The neighborhood remains largely gay and, besides being one of the best (and most popular) eating and drinking destinations in the city, has some of the city's most controversial art galleries.

GALLERIES

*Most galleries are in and around the **SoWa Building,** 450 Harrison Ave., at Thayer St. **T:** E. Berkeley St. (Silver). Walk against traffic down E. Berkeley St. and turn right onto Harrison Ave. Thayer St. is the first left. **Contact:** The invaluable* Boston/New England Gallery Guide *(www.galleryguide-online.com), available free at all galleries, has a map and gallery descriptions.*

The center of the South End gallery scene, the **SoWa Building** aims for the look and feel of the hip gallery scene in NYC's SoHo ("South of Houston St.") district—the "SoWa" stands for "South of Washington St." The SoWa building is actually a giant converted warehouse filled with several small galleries devoted to contemporary art. Most of the galleries feature interesting, unusual work, and many are independently run by artists. In the past year, the building has seen a boom, and now there are at least 10 large galleries where once were only two. As construction and artistic caprice is constantly moving the galleries around, the best way to get the full experience is to wander through the building beginning on the 3rd fl. and working downwards. Since most galleries have irregular hours, try to visit on the first Friday of any month, when many are open for the "first Friday" art shows. Some of the larger galleries are listed below, but the smaller ones often have the most edge.

IN THE SOWA

Genovese/Sullivan Gallery, 23 Thayer St. (☎617-426-9738), temporarily accessible via the 2nd fl. of the SoWa Building. This cavernous space is the setting for some of the most cutting-edge multimedia art around. The owners always try and search out idiosyncratic art and pride themselves on being the antithesis of conventional Newbury St. Open Tu-Sa 10:30am-5:30pm.

Bernard Toale Gallery, SoWa Building, 450 Harrison Ave. (☎617-482-2477). Bernard Toale has been at the forefront of the Boston art scene for a decade; indeed, the gallery's 1998 move from Newbury St. (see p. 58) to SoWa gave the South End instant gallery clout. Now doubled in size and the largest gallery in Boston, Toale shows interesting but rarely provocative painting, photography, drawing, sculpture, video, etc. The gem of this gallery is the "Boston Drawing Project," a huge collection of wonderful amateur art available for viewing upon request. Open Tu-Sa 10:30am-5:30pm.

Clifford-Smith Gallery, SoWa Building, 450 Harrison Ave. (☎617-695-0255). Aiming for a younger, hipper audience than Bernard Toale, the Clifford-Smith Gallery uses its 2 rooms to show contemporary art in all media, focusing on photography, installations, and sculpture. Open Tu-Sa 11am-5:30pm.

Kayafas Gallery, SoWa Building, 450 Harrison Ave. (☎617-482-0411). Showing some of the most impressive photography in Boston, Kayafas has quickly built a name for itself in the short time it has existed, having opened in 2003. Open W-F 1-5:30pm, Sa noon-5:30pm.

Kingston Gallery, 37 Thayer St. (☎617-423-4113), temporarily accessible via the 2nd fl. of the Sowa Building. An artist-run cooperative staffed by dues-paying exhibiting artists, this is one of the friendliest, least overwhelming galleries in the South End. Open Tu-Sa noon-5pm.

OTHER GALLERIES

Qingping Gallery & Teahouse, 231 Shawmut Ave. (☎617-482-9988). This delightful Zen zone, built with the owner's own two hands, displays diverse art and occasionally screens independent films. For the food listing, see p. 128.

Mills Gallery, in the Boston Center for the Arts, 539 Tremont St. (☎617-426-5000; www.bcaonline.org), at Clarendon St. From T: Back Bay (Orange), walk with the T on your right down Clarendon St. to Tremont St. Constantly changing exhibits of works by Boston-based artists. Open Su and W-Th noon-5pm, F-Sa noon-10pm.

WATERFRONT

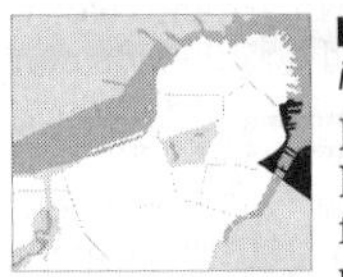

see map p. 324-325

T: *South Station (Red) or Aquarium (Blue).* ***Food:*** *p. 128.*

Despite its important place in Boston's economy, the Waterfront was for a long time a place that most Bostonians

South Boston

The Orange Line

The South End

in recent news

O Brother

Boston politics has long had a sordid flavor—just look to the Mass.-based Kennedys' sexploits, the puritanical Blue Laws regulating liquor and dancing, or the dominance of Beacon Hill and Southie by the Irish mob, which controlled Boston politics with an iron (and corrupt) fist during the 1970s and 80s.

Two of this era's most notorious characters are the Bulger brothers—former U-Mass President **Billy Bulger** and brother James Joseph, a.k.a. **Whitey Bulger.** Billy was the one with the actual government job (State Senate President 1978-96). The leader of the Southie-born Winter Hill Gang (a.k.a. Irish mafia), Whitey also has a history of extortion, racketeering, and murder, as well as Alcatraz prison time in the 1960s for bank robbery. Whitey narrowly escaped FBI arrest in 1995 (just before his indictment on 21 counts of murder) and has been on the run ever since, accompanied by local dental hygienist Catherine Elizabeth Greig. Keep an eye out for a white-haired man in his late 70s, with a fondness for animals and an ever-present pearl-handled knife.

(continued on p. 95)

avoided—a noisy, smelly industrial wasteland far from the heart of the city and seemingly always under development. In the 1960s, however, the city began renovating wharf buildings along the piers and converting them into hotels, restaurants, museums, and other attractions, transforming the Waterfront into the heavily touristed area that it is today. Bostonians know this is the best place to gorge on great seafood, and visitors come for the food, the attractions, and the ferries for the **Harbor Islands** (p. 95). Trolley tours and boat tours (see **Tours,** p. 97) also depart from the Waterfront.

BOSTON TEA PARTY SHIP & MUSEUM

Moored aside the Congress St. Bridge. ***T:*** *South Station (Red). Follow traffic up Atlantic Ave. and turn right onto Congress St.; it's just before the Hood's Milk Bottle.* ***Contact:*** *☎617-338-1773; www.bostonteapartyship.com.*

The Boston Tea Party Ship (officially named the *Beaver II*) was one of the most popular attractions in Boston, with costumed actors and visitors racing onto the deck to irreverently reenact the infamous Boston Tea Party (Dec. 16, 1773), where American patriots opposed to British tea taxes hurled a shipment of tea into Boston Harbor. Unfortunately, fire damage closed the ship in 2002, and there are currently no concrete plans for reopening the site. Call or check online for updates.

CHILDREN'S MUSEUM BOSTON

300 Congress St. ***T:*** *South Station (Red). Follow traffic up Atlantic Ave. and turn right onto Congress St.; it's across the Ft. Point Channel beyond the Hood's Milk Bottle.* ***Contact:*** *☎617-426-8855; www.BostonKids.org.* ***Open:*** *Su-Th and Sa 10am-5pm, F 10am-9pm.* ***Admission:*** *$8, seniors and ages 2-15 $7, ages 1-2 $2, under 1 free. F 5-9pm $1 for everyone.*

Designed to help children under the age of 10 understand and enjoy the world in which they live, the many floors of hands-on exhibits in the Children's Museum Boston will provide kids with endless hours of enjoyment and amusement. Every exhibit in this 4 fl. house of fun is kid-safe and interactive, designed to be jumped on, climbed over, ran around, worn, constructed, destroyed, and so on. Kids can feel free to run wild making giant bubbles, climbing walls, visiting wigwams and ancient Japanese houses, playing dress-up, weaving, and even taking part in a live performance on the KidStage. Fans of the book series or animated TV series *Arthur the Aardvark* must pay a visit to "Arthur's World," where characters and settings from the series come to life. For really little tykes (under age 3), there is the PlaySpace, and for music lovers, there's a Making America's Music exhibit until June 2004. As the kids run from exhibit to exhibit, be sure to have them glance at the walls, which have profiles of various Big Dig workers.

When walking to the Museum from the T, you'll pass the giant **Hood's Milk Bottle,** a bottle-shaped lunch stand (sponsored by Chelsea, Massachusetts-based HP Hood's dairy company) that has been a Waterfront icon for generations. The bottle was the inspiration for the recently installed "White Monster" at Fenway Park (p. 85), an electronic giant milk bottle that "splashes" milk each time the Red Sox hit a home run, make a double play, or strike out an opponent at bat.

HARPOON BREWERY

306 Northern Ave. ***T:*** *South Station (Red). From the T, follow traffic up Atlantic Ave. and turn right onto the pedestrian-only Northern Ave. Bridge. The brewery is just past the Fleet Boston Pavilion, about a 30min. walk from South Station.* ***Contact:*** *☎888-427-7666; www.harpoonbrewery.com.* ***Admission:*** *Free.* ***Tastings:*** *Free Tu-Th 3pm, F-Sa 1 and 3pm. Must be 21+ to sample.*

Founded by three Harvard graduates in 1986 and brewed at this site on the Waterfront since then, Harpoon prides itself on having the hometown advantage over rival Sam Adams, which was founded in Boston but is now brewed in remote locations across the US. (Their original brewery—now just a research and development office—is on the other side of town, in Jamaica Plain; p. 83.) Harpoon holds both the very first and the very last (well, the most recent) permit issued by the state of Massachusetts to brew and package beer commercially and is the 11th biggest seller of beer in the US and....OK, everyone knows you just came here for free beer, which you can get fresh from the brewery with explanations of the various beers—everything from their Flagship IPA to their more recent wheat beer, UFO Hefeweizen.

HARBOR ISLANDS

T: *Aquarium (Blue). Boston Harbor Cruises runs ferries to George's Island from the Long Wharf.* ***Contact:*** *Harbor Cruises ☎617-223-8666; www.bostonislands.com.* ***Open:*** *daily May-Oct. 9am-sunset (hours vary by island). Ferries daily May-June and Sept.-Oct. 10am, 2, 4pm; July-Aug. on the hr. 9am-5pm.* ***Admission:*** *round-trip ferry ticket $8, seniors $7, children $6; includes free shuttles to other islands from George's Island.*

(continued from p. 94)

Soon after Whitey went on the run, the *Boston Globe* shockingly revealed that he was actually a top FBI informant during his time as *capo,* and most likely wanted dead by other underworld figures. Now Whitey's on the FBI's Ten Most Wanted list (next to Osama Bin Laden), but in recent years, the Bulger brothers were more a punchline than a headline. All that changed in 2003 when the state legislature, investigating FBI informants, subpoenaed Billy to explain his relationship with Whitey (who called then-Senate President Billy while on the run). Though Billy said he never used his political position to aid and abet Whitey, he demanded immunity before he would speak. When he still admitted nothing on the stand, many took it as an admission that he knew more about his brother's whereabouts than he was letting onto. Joining the chorus of voices calling for Billy's resignation as U-Mass President (which had ironically hired him to overhaul its reputation). Gov. Romney actually demanded that he resign. In August 2003, Billy Bulger quietly stepped down, giving Romney no prior notice. Whitey, remains beyond the grasp of government officials. For more on the Boston mafia, try:

Boston Mafia (www.bostonmafia.com)

All Souls: A Family Story from Southie (1999). Michael Patrick MacDonald.

Black Mass: The True Story of An Unholy Alliance Between the FBI & the Irish Mob (2000). Dick Lehr & Gerard O'Neill.

Street Soldier: My Life as an Enforcer for Whitey Bulger & the Irish Mob (2003). Edward J. Mackenzie, Jr., et al.

The Big Dig

Milk

Tours

Made up of the 30-odd wooded islands floating in Boston Harbor, the Boston Harbor Islands National Park has become one of the most desirable spots for local outdoors enthusiasts. Ringed with pristine beaches and blanketed with miles of hiking trails, the Harbor Islands are a great place to escape the chaos of the city.

George's Island is the ferry hub, and few travelers venture beyond George's, which is home to **Fort Warren.** The most popular islands include Lovell's, home of the islands' best beach, and Bumpkin, a wild berry paradise. If you can't make it out to sea, try **Castle Island** (p. 90). Reclaimed from the Harbor and now attached to South Boston, the island features the same natural wonders as the others, plus the popular Ft. Independence.

NEW ENGLAND AQUARIUM

Central Wharf, at the end of State St. ***T:*** *Aquarium (Blue). Turn left out of the T onto State St. and walk until you hit water.* ***Contact:*** *☎617-973-5200; www.neaq.org.* ***Open:*** *July-Aug. M-Tu and F 9am-6pm, W-Th 9am-8pm, Sa-Su 9am-7pm; Sept.-June M-F 9am-5pm, Sa-Su 9am-6pm.* ***Admission:*** *$15.50, seniors (60+) $13.50, ages 3-11 $8.50.* ***Simons IMAX Theatre*** *tickets $8.50, seniors (60+) and ages 3-11 $6.50; Aquarium/IMAX combo admission $19, seniors (60+) $16, ages 3-11 $12.*

Though their parents may balk at the ever-rising admission fee, children of all ages will love the New England Aquarium, which uses interactive exhibits and countless creepy-crawly denizens of the deep to introduce children to aquatic life both native to New England and from all over the world. The attractive complex is built around the cylindrical 200,000 gallon, four-story **Giant Ocean Tank,** filled with sharks, sting rays, eels, Technicolor tropical fish, and three lazy sea turtles swimming in and around an artificial coral reef (follow the ramp up to the open top of the tank to see the turtles). Most popular with visitors is the ground level **Penguin Exhibit,** home to three colonies of adorable penguins from around the world; they are so beloved that the Aquarium ran an ad campaign with the slogan "No, you can't have one." Adjacent to this is the fascinating glass-walled **Animal Hospital,** where you can see in-house veterinarians tending to the Aquarium's various animals. If you want to "pet" the animals or interact with them one-on-one, check the posted schedule of daily events like the otter and seal shows and the silly "animal interviews." In 2004, the aquarium will also host a special "Living Links" exhibit, which displays the various creative and downright strange mechanisms that various animals have evolved in order to survive.

Attached to the Aquarium is the newly opened **Simons IMAX Theatre,** which shows a rotating schedule of 40-50min. giant-screen surround-sound movies, usually in 3D, on science and nature themes.

TOURS

The Freedom Trail may be Boston's most famous tour, but it isn't the only one. What follows is a list of popular and/or unique trips through Boston: by boat, by car, by foot, even by WWII amphibious attack vehicle. Each examines various historical, cultural, and social aspects of the city.

Big Dig (☎617-951-6400; www.bigdig.com). Free 2hr. underground hardhat tours of the much-maligned Central Artery/Tunnel Project (see p. 99), departing North Station (T: North Station (Green)) at very sporadic times; call for info. Map for above-ground self-guided tour can be downloaded from the website.

Black Heritage Trail. See p. 66.

Boston by Foot (☎617-367-2345, recorded tour info ☎617-367-3766; www.bostonbyfoot.com). They offer 7 walking tours of various Boston neighborhoods, including Beacon Hill, the North End, and the South End. Boston By Little Feet ($6 for everyone) is a Freedom Trail walk for kids. Departure points and times vary; see the website or call ahead. Most tours $8, under 13 $6; Boston Underground $10/$8. Tours May-Oct.

Boston Duck Tours (☎617-723-3825; www.bostonducktours.com). As much a part of tourist Boston as the Freedom Trail. Wacky condDUCKtors drive WWII-era amphibious vehicles past major historical sights before splashing down in the Charles, offering quirky facts, cheesy commentary, an endless slew of Boston "firsts," and vigorous quacking all the way. Reserve far in advance. 80min. tours depart Apr.-Nov. daily every 30min. 9am-1hr. before sunset from the Museum of Science (p. 78) and the Prudential Ctr. (Boylston

St. entrance; p. 62). $23, students and seniors $20, ages 3-11 $14. Tickets sold online and at Faneuil Hall (p. 50), the Museum of Science, and the Prudential Ctr.; selling at city locations begins daily at 8:30am.

Boston Harbor Cruises, 1 Long Wharf (☎617-227-4321; www.bostonharborcruises.com). Departs Long Wharf, near T: Aquarium (Blue). Popular operator of various history-minded sightseeing cruises (45-90min.; 3 per day; $17, students and seniors $15, under 12 $12) and whale-watching excursions (3hr.; $29, seniors $25, children $23). Operates late May to Sept. daily.

Freedom Trail. See p. 43.

Literary Trail (☎617-350-0358; www.lit-trail.org). Unique exploration of New England's impressive literary heritage, the trail visits important sights in Boston, Cambridge, and Concord. Departs Omni Parker House, 60 School St. T: State (Blue/Orange). 20 mi., 3hr. tours. Guided tours 2nd Sa of every month $30, children $26; self-guide booklet available online.

MYTOWN, 554 Columbus Ave. (☎617-536-8696; www.mytowninc.com). Innovative and informative "**M**ulticultural **Y**outh **T**ours **O**f **W**hat's **N**ow." Paid area students rigorously research and lead recent history-oriented walking tours of the South End. The focus is on community building, social activism, and civil rights–what they call "the flip side of the Freedom Trail." Tours $10. Tours May-Nov.

North End Market Tours, 6 Charter St. (☎617-523-6032; www.cucinare.com). Professional chef and 30-year North End resident Michele Topor offers phenomenal food tours of the sights, sounds, and smells of the Italian North End–past, pasta, and present. 3½hr. guided tours $42. Reservations required, limit 13 people per tour. W and Sa 10am and 2pm, F 3pm.

Old Town Trolley Tours (☎617-269-7010; www.historictours.com/boston). Dull 2hr. tours drive past 17 major Boston attractions, with unlimited boarding and disembarking at every stop. You can board at any stop, but the tours depart from New England Aquarium (p. 96) daily Apr.-Oct. every 15min. 9am-5pm; Nov.-Mar. every 30min. 9am-4pm. $25, under 12 free.

While long famous for its tumultuous tea parties and musket-blazing massacres, the chaos of present-day Boston lies far below the historical cobblestones and venerable waters that usually spring to mind. Today, Boston's making history underground, on Interstate Highways 90 and 93, the site of the infamous **Big Dig.** The Central Artery/Tunnel project, better known as the Big Dig, is the largest public works project in American history. With a price tag of almost $15 billion, it has now been 16 years since the federal legislation authorizing the project was passed, and most Bostonians have grown weary of delays detours and jackhammers.

Despite its prominence in remaking the city, not many people are aware of what the Big Dig is fixing. As the project edges toward completion, at $9 billion over budget, the problems that have plagued the city for decades are almost over.

The irony of the whole affair is that Boston's current traffic woes are entirely the result of a previously botched attempt to fix the traffic problem. After WWII, with the suburban population swelling and more and more people commuting, Boston's traffic became horrendous. Bostonians had trouble traveling within their own city, and commuters couldn't move in or out without setting aside half of their day. In an attempt to remedy these headaches, downtown Boston undertook the Central Artery Project in 1954. The plan consisted of two parts, both designed to remove cars from the winding confusing streets downtown. An elevated thoroughfare called the central artery, would allow Bostonians to quickly travel within the city, while an outer belt road routed interstate traffic on Rte. 93 around the city center. Construction was begun on the artery first, but after it forced out 20,000 residents and cut off the North End and the Waterfront from the rest of the city, Bostonians became enraged, and the project was abandoned, less than half finished. The belt road was never begun, and needing a place to put Rte. 93, planners had no choice but to funnel the heavy industrial interstate traffic onto the artery and into a space designed for light, local travel. The result was increased congestion across the board.

Like any good mob story, Boston is now hoping to remedy past mistakes by literally burying its problems. The Big Dig calls for the artery to be destroyed and a 10-lane expressway constructed underground, finally realizing the dream of keeping interstate traffic out of the city. The project hopes to return the entire metropolitan area to its past glory by tearing down the artificial neighborhood divisions that the elevated artery created and finally providing easy access to the harbor, the airport, and the regions' employment centers and neighborhoods. Boston will also be breathing easier, as the highway improvements are expected to cut carbon monoxide levels by 12% due to the decrease in traffic congestion.

Though no Bostonian thinks the Big Dig will ever be done, it is actually scheduled to be completed in 2004. As the Big Dig nears its long-awaited completion, the real debate is now about real estate. When the Big Dig is complete, 30 acres of prime land in Downtown Boston will be free for developers and architects to play with. Nearly everything has been suggested, but what will sprout will likely be "The Rose Kennedy Greenway" an expansion of the **Emerald Necklace,** (see p. 44). While everyone agrees that parkland should be part of the mix, the question remains: can Boston also use the land above the new underground expressway to spark a new residential and commercial development boom in the heart of the city?

Despite Boston's fairly aggressive attempt to remain modern with projects related to the Big Dig, like a new state of the art convention center and a high-tech subway-trolley from downtown to Logan airport, the region is still struggling to convince people to live in the city instead of its ever sprawling suburbs. While few are expecting the Big Dig to spark an urban renaissance of bustling boulevards and classy condominiums, planners and politicians still hope for a modest improvement in the atmosphere and desirability of the Hub. Unified designs of green spaces and cultural amenities should do the trick, giving a visitor another reason to spend a dollar, a commuter a place to sit outside and eat lunch, or a young professional the chance to live in a new, trendy neighborhood. The chance to turn Boston from a sleepy, Puritan city into a world-class urban playground is here, and the outcome is just a couple billion dollars and a few years away.

***Rohit Chopra** is a senior government major, with an emphasis on city planning, at Harvard University, where he also serves as President of the Undergraduate Council.*

INSIDE

Food & Drink

Once a culinary dead zone whose only claim to fame was baked beans, Boston is now a food lover's paradise. Countless trendy bistros, hot fusion restaurants, and a globetrotting array of ethnic eateries have taken their place alongside the seafood shacks, greasy-spoon diners, soul-food joints, and welcoming pubs that have been here for generations.

Bostonians (like most Americans) dine on the early side, with most establishments filling up by 7pm and shutting down by 10pm. (The only real cure for nighttime hunger pangs are the late-night eateries of Chinatown; see p. 114.) **Tipping** your server is expected; 15-20% of the total bill is a customary amount.

Throughout this chapter, Big $plurge boxes point you to phenomenal gourmet spots where the dining experience is well worth the heftier pricetag. To visit some of these spots without breaking the bank, consider **Restaurant Week,** sponsored by the Convention & Visitors Bureau (www.bostonusa.com). Every August, for one week, Boston's high-end restaurants offer discounted 3-course *prix fixe* meals at a cost commensurate with the year (e.g., in 2003, meals cost $20.03). Alternatively, pick up a copy of *Hungry? Boston* for the local scoop on the best meals under $10.

As always, *Let's Go: Boston* ranks all establishments within each neighborhood by value; the best places get a thumbs-up. At the end of each listing, you'll find a marker indicating a price range based on the average price for an entree (main dish) at dinner. Ranges are as follows:

❶	❷	❸	❹	❺
under $7	**$7-11**	**$11-16**	**$16-22**	**$22+**

BY CUISINE

AFRICAN & AFRO-CARIBBEAN

Addis Red Sea (126)	South End ❷
Asmara Ethiopian (111)	Cambridge ❸
Bob the Chef's (126)	South End ❸

BAKERIES

Bagel Rising (104)	Allston ❶
Flour (128)	South End ❶
Kupel's Bakery (109)	Brookline ❶
Bakery at Haley House (128)	South End
Bova's Bakery (124)	North End
Maria's Pastry Shop (124)	North End
Mike's Pastry (124)	North End
Modern Pastry (123)	North End
Rosie's Bakery (115)	Cambridge

BARBECUE

Jake's Boss BBQ (119)	Jamaica Plain ❷
Linwood Grill & BBQ (121)	Kenmore ❸
Redbones (124)	Somerville ❸

CAFÉS & COFFEEHOUSES

Bodhi Café (107)	Back Bay ❶
Code 10 (127)	South End ❶
Francesca's (128)	South End ❶
Panificio (107)	Beacon Hill ❶
Parish Café (104)	Back Bay ❷
1369 Coffeehouse (115)	Cambridge
Caffé dello Sport (124)	North End
Caffé Paradiso (124)	North End
Caffé Vittoria (124)	North End
CityGirl Caffé (115)	Cambridge
Diesel Café (125)	Somerville
Qingping Teahouse (128)	South End
Someday Café (125)	Somerville
Tealuxe (115)	Cambridge

CHINESE

Chau Chow City (115)	Chinatown ❷
China Pearl (115)	Chinatown ❷
Chinatown Eatery (116)	Chinatown ❷
Emperor Garden (115)	Chinatown ❷
Grand Chau Chow (117)	Chinatown ❷
Jumbo Seafood (116)	Chinatown ❷
Golden Temple (109)	Brookline ❸

DELIS & DINERS

Charlie's Sandwich (127)	South End ❶
Darwin's Ltd. (112)	Cambridge ❶
The Paramount (108)	Beacon Hill ❶
Sorella's (119)	Jamaica Plain ❶
Bartley's Burger Cottage (112)	Cambridge ❷
Grecian Yearning (105)	Allston ❷
Rosebud Diner (124)	Somerville ❷
S&S Deli (114)	Cambridge ❷
South Street Diner (117)	Downtown ❷
Zaftig's Delicatessen (109)	Brookline ❷

FRENCH

Paris Creperie	Beacon Hill ❶
1 Arrow St. Crêpes (113)	Cambridge ❷

ICE CREAM

Christina's Homemade (113)	Cambridge
Denise's Homemade (124)	Somerville
Herrell's (113)	Cambridge
J.P. Licks (119)	Jamaica Plain
Toscanini's (110)	Cambridge

INDIAN & SOUTH ASIAN

Punjabi Dhaba (113)	Cambridge ❶
India Castle (110)	Cambridge ❷
Rangoli (104)	Allston ❷
Rangzen (110)	Cambridge ❷
Bukhara (120)	Jamaica Plain ❸
Diva (124)	Somerville ❸
Kashmir (105)	Back Bay ❸
Tanjore (112)	Cambridge ❸

ITALIAN

Il Panino Express (122)	North End ❶
Anchovies (127)	South End ❷
Antonio's Cucina (108)	Beacon Hill ❷
L'Osteria (123)	North End ❷
Artú (123)	North End ❸
Dolce Vita (123)	North End ❸
Ristorante Lucia (122)	North End ❸
Trattoria Il Panino (122)	North End ❸
Caffe Umbra (127)	South End ❹
Sage (122)	North End ❺

JAPANESE & KOREA

Apollo Grille & Sushi (117)	Chinatown ❸
JP Seafood Café (119)	Jamaica Plain ❸
Korea Garden (111)	Cambridge ❸
Shabu-Zen (116)	Chinatown ❸
FuGaKyu (108)	Brookline ❹
Ginza (116)	Chinatown ❹
Gyuhama (106)	Back Bay ❹

LATIN AMERICAN

Café Belo (Brazilian) (104)	Allston ❶
Buteco (Brazilian) (120)	Kenmore ❷
Camino Real (Colombian) (104)	Allston ❷
El Oriental de Cuba (119)	Jamaica Plain ❷
Bomboa (Brazilian) (126)	South End ❺

MEXICAN

Anna's Taqueria (108)	Somerville ❶
El Pelón Taqueria (121)	Kenmore ❶
Picante (111)	Cambridge ❶
Tacos El Charro (119)	Jamaica Plain ❶
Acapulco Mexican (120)	Jamaica Plain ❷

MIDDLE EASTERN & MEDITERRANEAN

Moody's Falafel (110)	Cambridge ❶
Rami's (109)	Brookline ❶
Sultan's Kitchen (117)	Downtown ❶
Café Jaffa (107)	Back Bay ❷
Steve's Greek Cuisine (107)	Back Bay ❷
Helmand (113)	Cambridge ❸
Istanbul Café (108)	Brookline ❸
Lala Rokh (107)	Beacon Hill ❹
Oleana (112)	Cambridge ❺

NEW AMERICAN

Audubon Circle (120)	Kenmore ❷
Harvard Gardens (107)	Beacon Hill ❷
Laurel (127)	South End ❸
The Dish (126)	South End ❸
Franklin Café (127)	South End ❸
Sister Sorel (127)	South End ❸
The Blue Room (114)	Cambridge ❹
Caffé Umbra (127)	South End ❹
Henrietta's Table (112)	Cambridge ❹
Radius (118)	Downtown ❺

PAN-ASIAN

Also see Chinese, Japanese & Korean, Thai, and Vietnamese

Penang (117)	Chinatown ❷
Betty's Wok & Noodle (106)	Back Bay ❸
Island Hopper (106)	Back Bay ❸

PIZZA

Also see Italian

Pizzeria Regina (122)	North End ❶
Bella Luna (119)	Jamaica Plain ❷
Emma's Pizza (114)	Cambridge ❷
Antico Forno (123)	North End ❹

SEAFOOD

Barking Crab (129)	Waterfront ❸
The Daily Catch (123)	North End ❸
Durgin Park (118)	Downtown ❸
Jimbo's Fish Shanty (128)	Waterfront ❸
No Name (128)	Waterfront ❸
Legal Sea Foods (128)	Waterfront ❹
Ye Olde Union Oyster (118)	Downtown ❹
East Coast Grill (113)	Cambridge ❺
Summer Shack (111)	Cambridge ❺

SPANISH & PORTUGUESE

Atasca (114)	Cambridge ❹
Dalí (113)	Cambridge ❹
Tapéo (105)	Back Bay ❹

THAI

King & I (107)	Beacon Hill ❷
Spice (111)	Cambridge ❷
Wonder Spice Café (119)	Jamaica Plain ❷
Brown Sugar Café (120)	Kenmore ❸
Chilli Duck (106)	Back Bay ❸

VEGETARIAN

Buddha's Delight (116)	Chinatown ❷
Buddha's Delight Too! (109)	Brookline ❷
Country Live Vegetarian (117)	Downtown ❷
Garden of Eden (127)	South End ❷
Grasshopper (104)	Allston ❷
Centre St. Café (119)	Jamaica Plain ❸

VIETNAMESE

Pho Lemongrass (109)	Brookline ❶
V. Majestic (104)	Allston ❶
Pho Pasteur (117)	Chinatown ❷

BY NEIGHBORHOOD

ALLSTON

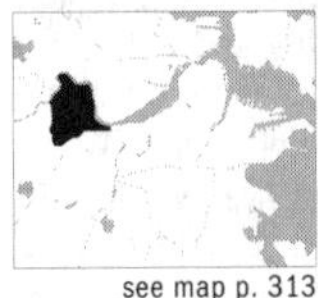

see map p. 313

T:** Harvard Ave. (Green-B; "Night Owl" Green Boston College) lets out at Commonwealth Ave. and Harvard Ave. Walk up Harvard Ave. (with McDonald's on your right) to get to the intersection with Brighton Ave. Bus #66 (p. 19; also a "Night Owl") from Harvard Sq. runs along Brighton Ave. to the intersection with Harvard Ave.* ***Discover: *p. 5.* ***Nightlife:*** *p. 134.* ***Shopping:*** *p. 172.*

Allston is home to an eclectic mix of working-class families, college students, and hipsters perennially short on cash, meaning the area is full of great bargain eateries as well as total dives. You're pretty much guaranteed a cheap, filling, tasty meal at any of the countless ethnic eateries on Brighton Ave. or Harvard Ave. Another cheap (though not particularly delicious) meal option is the 2-for-1 burgers and ½-price appetizers offered during Happy Hour (usually M-F 4-6pm) at many of the neighborhood's student-friendly bars.

Grasshopper, 1 N. Beacon St. (☎617-254-8883), at Union Sq., on the corner of Brighton Ave. and Cambridge St.; walk 5-6 blocks up Brighton Ave. (with The Kells on your right) from the Harvard Ave./Brighton Ave. intersection. The #66 bus from Harvard Sq. also stops at

Celebrity Chefs

Boston's culinary scene has come a long way from baked beans and scrod. Some of the country's top chefs now hang their toques here—the most prominent (but considered by many not actually the most talented) among them being **Todd English** (who owns Kingfish Hall in Quincy Market). Other Boston culinary maestros include **Ana Sortun** (Oleana; p. 112), **Michael Schlow** (Radius; p. 118), and **Jasper White** (Summer Shack; p. 111).

Though L.A. and New York are home to most of America's "celebrity" chefs (those flashy media hogs with their own TV shows and glossy cookbooks), Boston is arguably the birthplace of the phenomenon. Before Emeril, Bobby Flay, and Nigella, there was **Fannie Farmer,** who opened her first School of Cookery here in 1902. Until her retirement, mistress of munch **Julia Child** called Cambridge home, and did much to bring great chefs and culinary respect to the Boston area. Her favorite spot? Henrietta's Table; p. 112. And while NYC has sexy Tony Bourdain, Boston has Ken Oringer (of Back Bay's overpriced Clio), voted one of *People's* 50 most eligible bachelors.

If your budget doesn't include a gourmet blowout, try **Parish Café** (p. 105). Also worth a visit is **www.bostonchefs.com,** with droolworthy entree photos and menus from the city's best gourmet spots (including all those mentioned above).

Union Sq. Named one of the top vegetarian/vegan restaurants in the country, Grasshopper is the place "where the animals live to tell it all" (as the sign out front proclaims). Flavorful pan-Asian stir-fries ($6-8) prepared without any animal products (seitan, tofu, and root vegetables take the place of meat and fish) and delivered in soothing surroundings by a friendly staff. Lunch specials M-F 11am-3pm $5. Open Su noon-10pm, M-Th 11am-10pm, F-Sa 11am-11pm. ❷

Rangoli, 129 Brighton Ave. (☎617-562-0200). This charming rose-hued restaurant—older sister to Tanjore (p. 112)—is cheaper than most Boston curry houses and just as tasty. Lighter preparations with an emphasis on South Indian cuisine, which is even more veggie-friendly than other regional styles and uses more tropical ingredients, like tamarind and coconut. *Dosas* (lentil-and-curry crêpes) $6-9. Entrees $9-11. Open Su-Th 11:30am-3pm and 5-10:30pm, F-Sa 11:30am-3pm and 5-11pm. ❷

Pho Pasteur, 137 Brighton Ave. (☎617-783-2340). From the T, walk up Harvard Ave. and turn right at the Harvard Ave./Brighton Ave. intersection. A branch of this elegant, affordable, and delicious Vietnamese food chain, with plenty of vegetarian options. For the original Chinatown location, see p. 117. Su-Tu 11am-10pm, W-Sa 11am-10:30pm. ❷

V. Majestic, 164 Brighton Ave. (☎617-782-6088), near the Harvard Ave./Brighton Ave. intersection. The V. stands for Vietnamese, and this small deli-style eatery—with only 9 tables and 1 waiter, who is also the cashier and busboy—serves it up in huge portions at the lowest prices for Vietnamese in Boston. *Pho* (beef noodle soups) $3-5. Entrees $5-7. Open W-M noon-10:30pm. Cash only. ❶

Camino Real, 48 Harvard Ave. (☎617-254-5088). Far from their fellow countrymen in East Boston, Allston's sizeable Colombian population flocks to this somewhat sterile, family-friendly eatery that specializes in the little-known cuisine of the Colombian mountains. Hearty and meat-heavy, the simple, satisfying flavors are worth every heartburn pang. All entrees ($9) are mammoth, with rice, beans, vegetables, and fried plantains on the side and a fried egg on top. The *tostones* (twice-fried plantain chips; $2.50) are a delight. Open daily 10am-10pm. ❷

Bagel Rising, 1243 Commonwealth Ave. (☎617-789-4000), at T: Harvard Ave. (Green-B). Though clearly a yuppie breakfast mecca, Bagel Rising is also a quick, easy spot for a cheap morning snack or light lunch. Freshly baked bagels $0.65. Creative and veggie-friendly bagel sandwiches $4-5. Coffees and juices $1-2. Open Su 7am-5:30pm, M-Sa 7am-7pm. Cash only. ❶

Café Belo, 181 Brighton Ave. (☎617-783-4858), opposite Quint St., in a strip mall a few blocks up Brighton Ave. from the Harvard Ave./Brighton Ave. intersection. Authentic Brazilian food—heavy dishes with an emphasis on meat, rice, beans, and more meat—draws many local South Americans to this airy, clean restaurant. Food is served in a cafeteria-style buffet ($4.50 per lb., which is a heaping plateful). Don't miss the signature Brazilian dish *churrasco* (tasty brine-basted barbecue). Open Su 11am-10pm, M-Sa 7am-10pm. ❶

Grecian Yearning Restaurant, 174 Harvard Ave. (☎617-254-8587). Other than a few Greek twists, this is a basic diner in menu and decor. Grilled cheese ($3-5) is a house specialty, as is the breakfast, served all day (omelettes $4-6). *Moussaka* (eggplant, potato, and zucchini), *souvlaki* (cubes of meat on a skewer wrapped in pita), kebabs, and other Greek dishes $7-9. Open Su 8am-3pm, M-F 7am-8pm, Sa 7am-4pm. ❷

Posh Eating

BACK BAY

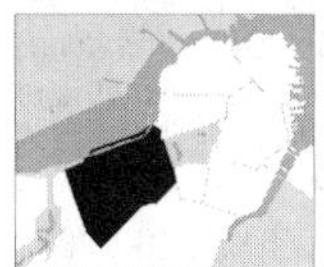
see map p. 314-315

T: *Hynes/ICA (Green-B,C,D) lets out onto Newbury St. at Massachusetts Ave.* ***Discover Back Bay:*** *p. 105.* ***Sights:*** *p. 57.* ***Nightlife:*** *p. 135.* ***Shopping:*** *p. 172.* ***Accommodations:*** *p. 184.*

The area on and around chic Newbury St. is filled with trendy cafés and fusion bistros, most of which cater to a wealthy crowd. The eateries below are the best values in the area. On warm nights, expect huge crowds and long lines for prime patio seating.

Keeping Kosher

Kashmir, 279 Newbury St. (☎617-536-1695), at Gloucester St. Though not the cheapest Indian restaurant in Boston, it is the best. The same family that runs Kashmir also owns Davis Sq.'s divine Diva (p. 124) and JP's Bukhara (p. 120). Marble floors, traditional wall hangings, and plush red seats create a setting as light and exotic as the subtly flavored curries ($12-15) and extensive vegetarian menu (entrees $11-13). All-you-can-eat buffet daily until 3pm (M-F $9, Sa-Su $12). Open M-F 11:30am-11pm, Sa-Su noon-11pm. Delivery, take-out, and catering available. ❸

Parish Café, 361 Boylston St., (☎617-247-4777), near T: Arlington (Green). With outdoor seating overlooking the green of the Public Garden, this lively bar is definitely not a secret among locals, who crowd tables and barstools to order sandwiches instead of drinks. The sandwiches ($9-17), designed by the city's hottest chefs, are one of the best gourmet deals in the city. Open Su noon-2am, M-Sa 11:30am-2am. ❷

Tapéo, 266 Newbury St. (☎617-267-4799). A bustling, fun-loving Spanish *tapas* bar, modeled on a traditional *bodega* (cozy wine bar)—complete with an

Crepes

Faneuil Hall

Copley Farner's Market

Succulent sweets

Andalusian-tiled bar and 2 fl. of romantic lighting, intimate seating, and lilting flamenco music. *Tapas* are small plates of Spanish delicacies ($5-7 each) meant to be enjoyed in groups, 3 per person is enough for a meal. The best of the over 50 *tapas* here are the garlicky sauteed shrimp, ink-drenched stuffed squid, seared duck in raspberry sauce, and the *tortilla española* (traditional potato omelette). Wash it all down with Rioja wine or sangría ($7.50 per glass), and leave room for the sticky-sweet *arroz con leche* (rice with milk and a caramelized glaze with fresh berries). Open Su noon-10pm, M-W 5:30-10pm, Th-F 5:30-11pm, Sa noon-11pm. ❹

Island Hopper, 91 Massachusetts Ave. (☎617-266-1618), at Newbury St. With its tropical decor, lightning-fast service, and exotically flavored stir-fries, noodles, and curries, affordable Island Hopper is a welcome addition to the scene surrounding Newbury St. The encyclopedic menu lives up to its name, with a country-hopping array of Chinese and pan-Southeast Asian dishes–from General Gau's Chicken to *pad thai* to Burmese Noodles. Entrees $8-16. Lunch specials $7-8. Open Su noon-11pm, M-Th 11:30am-11pm, F-Sa 11:30am-midnight. ❸

Chilli Duck, 829 Boylston St. (☎617-236-5208). With an extensive menu and incredibly fair pricing, this is the best place to get Thai food (and Thai beer) in Back Bay. One of the city's newest restaurants, their Ka Pow special sauce makes dishes dangerously spicy. If you're feeling crazy, the Chicken Madness ($8) comes highly recommended. Lunch entrees $7-9; dinner $10-13. Open daily 11:30am-11pm. ❸

Betty's Wok & Noodle Diner, 250 Huntington Ave. (☎617-424-1950), at Massachusetts Ave., opposite T: Symphony (Green). A schizophrenic diner that is neither a diner per se, nor run by a "Betty," but does serve some excellent Asian-Latino fused food. As Cuban music plays overhead, pick mix-and-match items off the menu to come up with your own personal dish. Combos involve meats, tofu, 15 vegetables, noodles, rice, wraps, and 7 sauces (including Cuban Chipotle-Citrus and Red Thai Coconut) plus spices. While freedom of creativity is a wonderful thing, be warned, it can lead to some disastrous meals. Best to get a second-opinion from the waitstaff before committing to your stir-fry. Generously portioned appetizers around $5. Stir-fries $10-16. Open Su-Th noon-10pm, F-Sa noon-11pm; hours can vary depending on business. ❸

Gyuhama, 827 Boylston St. (☎617-437-0188). Exit T: Copley (Green) onto Boylston St. and walk against traffic just past Fairfield St. Located below street level, this buzzing, festive restaurant with kimono-clad waitresses and screened-off private *tatami* booths serves super-fresh sushi at decent prices (6-pc. rolls $5-8, 30- to 40-pc. "Sushi Boat for 2" $42).

Gyuhama outshines its competitors with its "Rock 'n' Roll Sushi" (nightly 11pm-2am), when the music gets cranked up and the fruity tropical drinks like "Love Punch" (all $14 and made with 151-proof rum) flow freely. Open daily 11am-2am. ❹

Steve's Greek Cuisine, 316 Newbury St. (☎617-267-1817), at Hereford St. Amply proportioned and surprisingly light Greek food in a cozy, cafeteria-like setting. Grilled entrees don't merit their Newbury St. price tag ($10-14); stick to the hefty *gyros* and deli sandwiches ($5-7) or vegetarian classics like *tabbouleh,* hummus, and delightful vegetarian *moussaka* (eggplant, potato, and zucchini; all $6-9). Open Su 10am-10pm, M-Sa 7:30am-11pm. ❷

Legal Seafoods, Park Plaza Hotel (☎617-426-4444). T: Arlington (Green). The chicest branch of Boston's most famous seafood chain. For the original Waterfront location, see p. 128. Open Su 11:30am-10pm, M-Th 11:30am-11pm, F-Sa 11:30am-midnight. ❹

Cafe Jaffa, 48 Gloucester St. (☎617-536-0230), turn right onto Gloucester St. 2 blocks down from T: Hynes/ICA (Green-B,C,D). An Israeli eatery where patrons can grab a quick bite on the run or sit for hours. Most people opt for a falafel or chicken kebab, but the fairly standard menu leaves a little room for exploring. Sandwiches $5-7. Entrees $9-12. Open Su noon-10pm, M-Th 11am-10:30pm, F-Sa 11am-11pm. ❷

Bodhi Café, 335 Newbury St. (☎617-536-6977). Buddhism-inspired sister to the Zen Trident Booksellers & Café across the street (p. 174), Bodhi is a standard lunch deli with homemade soups ($4-6) and huge, fresh sandwiches and wraps ($6-7); the real standouts on the menu are the veggie and vegan-friendly options. Veggie Avocado sandwich $6. Open daily 8am-6pm. ❶

BEACON HILL

see map p. 317

T: *Charles/MGH (Red) lets out at the corner of Cambridge and Charles St.* ***Discover Beacon Hill:*** *p. 107.* ***Freedom Trail Sights:*** *p. 44.* ***Other Sights:*** *p. 63.* ***Shopping:*** *p. 172.* ***Accommodations:*** *p. 186.*

Snootily upper-crust Beacon Hill is actually filled with shockingly affordable restaurants drawing on all sorts of cuisines, from typically American to unforgettably exotic.

Lala Rokh, 97 Mt. Vernon St. (☎617-720-5511; www.lalarokh.com), at W. Cedar St. Walk down Charles St. and turn left onto Mt. Vernon St. Named after a Victorian version of an ancient Persian fairy tale, Lala Rokh is indeed a fantasy—a divine dining spot where everything is perfect, from the attentive, intelligent, and award-winning staff to the whimsical and unique food. Celebrating the Eastern Mediterranean cuisine of Persia and Azerbaijan (a far superior sweet-and-sour take on Indian and Middle Eastern cuisine), the kitchen at Lala Rokh turns out only the most exotic and creatively imagined stews, pilafs, and kebabs. With its romantic colors and lighting and family heirlooms on the walls, the atmosphere is almost as delightful as Lala Rokh's food. Entrees $14-18. Open M-F noon-3pm and 5:30-10pm, Sa-Su 5:30-10pm. ❹

Panificio, 144 Charles St. (☎617-227-4340). This crowded counter-service café serves up Italian-style, veggie-friendly lunchtime treats (pizza $3; sandwiches and salads $5-7) and decadent, waistline-threatening desserts ($4). Open M-F 8am-4pm and 5:30-9:30pm, Sa-Su 9am-4pm and 5:30-9:30pm. ❶

Harvard Gardens, 316 Cambridge St. (☎617-523-2727), at Grove St. Having nothing to do with Harvard or gardens, the look and feel of this restaurant is straight out of a Frank Sinatra song: killer martinis, a mahogany bar, wraparound leather booths, and jazz standards on the sound system. Calculating gold-diggers take note: by day, they cater to suited doctors on their lunch breaks; at night, this is strictly the mating ground of penniless urbane grad students and struggling young professionals. Regardless of tax bracket, everyone enjoys the high-quality, low-cost bar food standards. Pseudo-gourmet pizzas, pastas, and burgers $6-9. Open daily 11:30am-2am; food Su-W until 10pm, Th-Sa 11pm. ❷

King & I, 145 Charles St. (☎617-227-3320). This simple Thai restaurant is a serviceable, consistently reliable value. Though there is nothing attention-grabbing in the surroundings, the service is swift; the portions are large; and the prices are low (most entrees $7, nothing on the menu over $10). The menu has a seemingly endless list of seafood, noodle, and rice dishes with plenty of vegetarian options. Open Su 5-9:30pm, M-Th 11:30am-9:30pm, F 11:30am-10:30pm, Sa noon-10:30pm. ❷

The Paramount, 44 Charles St. (☎617-720-1152). By day, this convivial counter-service diner is an immensely popular breakfast and brunch spot flooded with locals. Come early in the day before the menu changes and the Paramount degenerates into a standard and overpriced American comfort food restaurant. Order and pay before sitting down. Breakfast plates $3-4; pancakes and omelettes $4-7. Breakfast served until 4:30pm. Open Su 8am-10pm, M-W 7am-10pm, Th-F 7am-11pm, Sa 8am-11pm; closed daily 4:30-5pm to change menus. ❶

Paris Creperie, 326 Cambridge St. (☎617-589-0909). A large and simple space, the creperie falls short of Paris' sophistication and elegance, but still manages to satisfy customers with reasonable prices and thicker-than-normal crepes. Serving a mostly student clientele, the most popular crepes are their sweet crepes (Brie and Apple infused with cinnamon $7), though they also have a creative lunch menu that includes the strangely named Elizabeth Goes to China (tofu, hoisin sauce, and jasmine rice $6). Different special every day of the week: M free coffee; W free smoothie. Open M-F 7am-10pm, Sa-Su 8am-10pm. ❶

Antonio's Cucina Italiana, 288 Cambridge St. (☎617-367-3310). The owners are displaced North Enders who brought their neighborhood's Italian red-sauce favorites with them when they moved this side of the Fleet Ctr. The filling, ample, but average-tasting portions at more reasonable prices than in the North End are served in a room reminiscent of a da Vinci-obsessed doctor's office (Muzak, pastels, and wan Renaissance prints). Their best bargains are on the lunch menu, which features tasty sandwiches for around $5. Pastas $8-10, chicken and veal dishes $11-12. Open M-Th 11am-10pm, F-Sa 11am-10:30pm. ❷

BROOKLINE

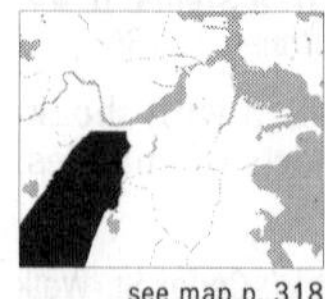
see map p. 318

T: Coolidge Corner (Green-C) lets out at Coolidge Corner, at the intersection of Harvard and Beacon St. #66 bus (p. 19) from Harvard Sq. runs along Harvard St. through Coolidge Corner. ***Discover Brookline:*** *p. 6.* ***Shopping:*** *p. 172.* ***Accommodations:*** *p. 186.*

In an area known for its sizeable Jewish population, it's no surprise to find countless great Middle Eastern eateries and kosher-style delis. Many places serving kosher food close F-Sa from sundown to sundown to observe the sabbath. The city of Brookline is also home to an ever-growing number of Japanese and pan-Asian restaurants—including the city's most inventive sushi spot.

FuGaKyu 1280 Beacon St. (☎617-734-1268). This sushi-lover's paradise is one of the most indulgent dining experiences in Boston (though dress and atmosphere are still casual). First, you're led by a kimono-clad waitress through the palatial lobby to either your private rice-screened room or the huge sushi bar (where maki rolls float by on boats). An army of servers then emerges from the wings to bring out steaming hand towels and pour your soy sauce for you, before leaving you alone to work your way through the encyclopedic menu. The sushi may not be the best in Boston (that honor goes to Ginza; p. 116), but it is the most creative, with heavy-hitting, complex flavors (and lots of fried bits), presented breathtakingly and whimsically. Specialty 4- to 6-pc. rolls $6-12, regular 6-pc. rolls $4-8. Open Su noon-3pm and 5pm-1:30am, M-Sa 11:30am-3pm and 5pm-1:30am. ❹

Anna's Taqueria, 1412 Beacon St. (☎617-739-7300). Another branch of this budget-friendly, super-tasty Mexican food chain (tacos $2, burritos $3-4). Open daily 10am-11pm. Cash only. Yet another **branch** at 446 Harvard St. (☎617-277-7111), at Thorndike St. Same hours and prices. ❶

Istanbul Café, 1414-1418 Commonwealth Ave. (☎617-232-1700). Those who know Turkish cuisine only as greasy street side *döner* sandwiches will be delightfully surprised by the real deal, a meat- and yogurt-intensive take on Middle Eastern food with myriad preparations of unique veggie-filled dishes like "swooning imam" (pepper-stuffed eggplants) and *lahmacun* (a special flatbread pizza; $7). Though their emphasis is on Turkish fish and veggie dishes, they also have a few mouth-watering kebabs on the menu. Entrees $11-14. Open daily 11am-midnight. ❸

Zaftig's Delicatessen, 335 Harvard St. (☎617-975-0075), at Babcock St. Perhaps the best deli in Boston, yet it's not kosher, not technically in Boston and not deli-like (with swank leather and jazz music?). It remains a Brookline favorite nonetheless. The tastiest and happily most affordable eats are the kosher-style starters (*kasha varnishka, knishes, gefilte* fish, etc.; $4-6) and the hearty all-day breakfast options ($4). If you can stomach the idea of spending $10 on a sandwich, try the pastrami or the corned beef, both well worth the money. Open daily 8am-10pm. ❷

Rami's, 324 Harvard St. (☎617-738-3577), at Babcock St. This no-frills, counter-service kosher eatery serves the second-best falafel in Boston (the best is Moody's Falafel Palace in Central Sq., see p. 110), plus other Middle Eastern fare like hummus and shawerma, crammed into overstuffed pita sandwiches ($4-6). Open Su-Th 10am-10pm, F 10am-3pm. Cash only. ❶

Kupel's Bakery, 421 Harvard St. (☎617-566-9528). Undoubtedly the best bagels in the Boston area, by people who know how to do them right—crunchy on the outside, chewy on the inside, and always piping hot and fresh. Baker's dozen $5.50. Open Su-Th 6am-10pm, F 6am-6pm. ❶

Pho Lemongrass, 239 Harvard St. (☎617-731-8600). Recently voted best Vietnamese restaurant in Boston, Pho Lemongrass ladles up its cheap, filling namesake *pho* (a beef noodle soup; $5-7), rice and noodle dishes ($7), and the light and popular *bun* (mint- and meat-filled vermicelli salads; $6-7). Open Su-Th 11:30am-10:30pm, F-Sa 11:30am-midnight. ❶

Golden Temple, 1651 Beacon St. (☎617-277-9722), at T: Washington Sq. (Green-C), 4 stops past T: Coolidge Corner. This temple to suburban American-Chinese food serves non-greasy takes on typical Chinese dishes in portions as monumental as the airy dining hall. Entrees get pricey ($12-20), but 1 dish is big enough for 2 people when paired with an appetizers ($6-7), which include dim sum favorites (for more on dim sum, see p. 115) and a novel take on crab rangoon. Popular with area families, who don't mind the inattentive service. Open Su-Th 11:30am-1:30am, F-Sa 11:30am-2am. ❸

Buddha's Delight Too!, 404 Harvard St. (☎617-739-8830), at Naples Rd. The smaller, cozier little sister to Chinatown's Buddha's Delight (see p. 116) will convert diehard carnivores with tofu-based, pan-Asian food. Dishes are spiced to taste like their meat-filled incarnations. Most entrees around $8, nothing over $10. Open Su-Th noon-9:30pm, F-Sa 11am-10:30pm. ❷

Shays

Au Bon Pain

Bartley's

ON THE MENU

Indian Buffets

Harvard, M.I.T....Cambridge has many hallowed institutions, but most cherished among them is the all-you-can-eat lunch buffet (M-F 11:30am-3pm) offered by the city's countless Indian restaurants. For less than $10, you get to gorge on an endless supply of rice, fried appetizers, *naan* flatbread, meat and veggie curries, and *kheer* (a sweet rice pudding).

Dishes are mostly the same from place to place, so deciding on which restaurant to eat at—most line Mass. Ave. from Harvard Sq. to Central Sq.—is just a question of price. The buffets in Harvard Sq. are the most expensive ($8-9), getting cheaper as you head down Mass. Ave. to the dingier Central Sq. eateries ($5-6).

This is not haute cuisine, of course: everything's delicious, but it's all cooked in bulk early in the day and kept on warming plates through the afternoon. The exception is **India Castle** ❷, 982 Mass. Ave. (☎617-864-8100), between Harvard and Central. They serve the best buffet in the city ($7), with the freshest *naan* flatbread and the largest and most inventive selection of dishes.

CAMBRIDGE

see map p. 320-321

CENTRAL SQ.

***T:** Central (Red) lets out onto Massachusetts Ave.* ***Discover Cambridge:** p. 7.* ***Sights:** p. 70.* ***Nightlife:** p. 137.* ***Shopping:** p. 172.* ***Accommodations:** p. 187.*

Central Sq. is a veritable UNsanctioned gathering of affordable ethnic eateries, with restaurants serving everything from Mexican to Tibetan. This makes it the perfect place for a lunch break from sightseeing in nearby (and overpriced) Harvard Sq. or a handy spot for grabbing dinner before a night out pubbing in Cambridge. The neighborhood is also home to many Bohemian coffeeshops: on one of the city's frequent rainy afternoons, nothing says Cantabrigian quite like curling up in a Central Sq. café with a stiff latté and a dog-eared paperback from one of Harvard Sq.'s many new and used bookstores (see p. 173).

Moody's Falafal Palace, 25 Central Sq. (☎617-864-0827). From Mass. Ave., turn left down Western Ave.; it's on the right. Hardly palatial, this family-run hidden takeout counter, with 2 small tables, serves the best (and cheapest) falafel that can be found outside of Jerusalem, plus other Syrian/Middle Eastern favorites. Roll-up sandwiches (with falafel, shawerma, hummus, etc.) $3.75; combo plates $5-6. Nothing over $6. Open daily 11am-midnight. Cash only. ❶

Toscanini's, 899 Main St. (☎617-491-5877) From the T, walk down Mass. Ave. (with Starbucks on your left), it's at the corner of Main St. and Mass. Ave. Probably the best ice cream in Cambridge, Toscanini's has been making their unusual flavors in small batches since 1981. While Christina's boasts variety, Toscanini's features the bizarre—try Guiness or whiskey ice cream. Exquisite taste so silky-smooth, it's probably illegal. Open Su 9am-11pm, M-Th 8am-11pm, F 8am-midnight, Sa 9am-midnight. **Harvard Sq.** branch at 1310 Massachusetts Ave. Open Su-Th 8am-10pm, F-Sa 8am-11pm.

Rangzen, 24 Pearl St. (☎617-354-8881). From the T, walk down Mass. Ave. (with Starbucks on your left) and take the 1st right onto Pearl St. Mostly unknown (even to locals), Rangzen (Tibetan for "Independence") is one of Cambridge and Boston's only Tibetan restaurants—and perhaps the most soothing dining spot in the area, with a wall-length shot of the Himalayas, calm music, and an appropriate Zen vibe. Tibetan is a subdued, simpler mix of Chinese and Indian flavors and preparations (appropriate given Tibet's location), with thick mountain stews and meat dishes ($7-10) preceded by fried appetizers ($5-7).

Sample all the representative dishes in the vast all-you-can-eat lunch buffet ($7; M-F 11:45am-3pm). Open M-Sa 11:45am-3pm and 5:30-10pm. ❷

Asmara Ethiopian, 739 Massachusetts Ave. (☎617-864-7447). Though not as cheap as its main competition, Addis Red Sea (p. 126), Asmara still presents a strong and satisfying argument for the spicy, curry- and veggie-heavy cuisine of Eritrea and Ethiopia. With all the dishes served on traditional *mesob* tables—utensil-free and meant to be scooped up with spongy, slightly sour *injera* bread—a meal here is a unique and enjoyable dining experience, upset only by the hotel lobby-like decor. Entrees $10-12. Open Su-Th 11:30am-10:30pm, F-Sa 11:30am-11:30pm. ❸

Korea Garden, 20 Pearl St. (☎617-492-9643). From the T, walk down Mass. Ave. (with Starbucks on your left) and take the 1st right onto Pearl St. This small, family-run restaurant—popular with locals and Korean immigrants—serves up traditional Korean comfort food ($9-10), like tofu-heavy "Korean Home Dishes" and complex stews and soups (*ji gae*). Those dishes familiar to Westerners—like *bulgogi* (barbecue) and *bi bim bap* (a sizzling pot of veggies, rice, beef, and chili paste)—are pricier ($12-16) here than elsewhere, but just as delicious as everything else coming out of the kitchen. Open M-Th noon-10pm, F-Sa noon-10:30pm. ❸

Picante, 735 Massachusetts Ave. (☎617-576-6394), at Pleasant St. A taste of California in Central Sq., this cheap, quirkily decorated Cali-Tex-Mex joint lays out that sweet, pseudo-fresh food that the west coast has embraced for years. If Anna's Taqueria (p. 124) isn't nearby, and it's fast Mexican food with plenty of veggie options that you crave, head here and order some quesadillas ($3-4), a giant burrito ($5-7), or a heaping combo plate ($8). Most dishes big enough for 2 people. Another branch in Davis Sq. (see p. 125). Open M-F 11am-11pm, Sa-Su 10am-11pm. ❶

HARVARD SQ.

T: Harvard (Red) lets out into the heart of Harvard Sq., at the chaotic intersection of Massachusetts Ave., Brattle St., JFK St., and Dunster St.

Despite the large number of students in the area, there are few affordable values in Harvard Sq., with chains (there are currently four Starbucks) having slowly ousted beloved student dives. There are still a few places to eat well for less, though, and more budget-friendly Central Sq. (see above) is just a 15min. walk (or 5min. T ride) away.

Spice, 24 Holyoke St. (☎617-868-9560), at Mt. Auburn St. From the T, walk up Massachusetts Ave. (against traffic) and turn right onto Holyoke St. Defying the seeming curse on their location (which has

the BIG $plurge

Jasper White's Summer Shack

***Cambridge:** 149 Alewife Brook Pkwy. Opposite **T:** Alewife (Red). **Contact:** ☎617-520-9500; www.summershackrestaurant.com. **Open:** Su 3-9pm, M-F 11:30am-10pm, Sa 1-11pm. Lobster from $17, other seafood $15-22.* ❹

Voted one of the 5 best new restaurants in the *country* in 2001, this rambunctious gourmet spot lives up to its downtrodden name, with tin walls and picnic benches that recreate the look and feel of an authentic New England seafood shanty.

There's nothing shabby about the food, though. The eats here are very fresh and very simple—mostly seafood boiled, grilled, or fried to perfection—and they're nothing short of divine. Jasper White is one of the city's best (and best-loved) chefs, and he knows how to do it right, lavishing as much care and finesse on corndogs ($3-4) as on sophisticated lobster dishes. (The "Jasper's Pan-Seared Lobster" is easily the best thing on the menu.)

Despite its imposing warehouse exterior (it's guarded by a frightening 2-story statue of a fisherman), the Summer Shack is a casual, lighthearted spot that's especially great for families and groups.

the BIG $plurge

Oleana

***Cambridge:** 134 Hampshire St., Inman Sq. From **T:** Harvard (Red), walk or take bus #69 up Cambridge St. and turn right onto Hampshire St. **Contact:** ☎617-661-0505. **Open:** Su-Th 5:30-10pm, F-Sa 5:30-11pm. Entrees $19-26.* ❺

If you can only splurge once in Boston, make it Oleana.

Recently named one of the 5 best new restaurants in the *country*, Oleana seems like nothing special at first–just a few simple beige rooms (with exotic accents) tucked away on an unassuming residential street. But just one taste and you'll realize what all the fuss is about. Fresh from her years at Casablanca (p. 139), Ana Sortun's note-perfect Mediterranean menu (think Turkish, Greek, and Middle Eastern favorites with a few intelligent French flourishes) is exquisite but simple, with light grilling the technique of choice and complex, tongue-tingling spices dusting everything. The crowning achievement? Sortun's signature lamb, grilled with Turkish spices and served with a divine fava bean *moussaka*.

And then there's Maureen Kilpatrick's dessert menu. Your trip to Boston isn't complete without a taste of the dramatically plated baked Alaska–a macaroon and coconut confection with passionfruit caramel–the perfect ending to a perfect meal.

seen 3 restaurants in as many years), Spice is thriving, thanks to their swift service and epic portions of various high-quality Thai dishes (entrees $8-12) with lots of veggie options and excellent soups. Open M-F 11:30am-3pm and 5-10pm, Sa-Su noon-10pm. ❷

Darwin's Ltd., 148 Mt. Auburn St. (☎617-354-5233). A 5min. walk from Harvard Sq. proper: exit the T onto Brattle St. and turn right at the Harvard Sq. Hotel onto Mt. Auburn St.; it's 6-7 blocks up on the left. The attractive, Bohemian staff at this busy deli counter with a quiet attached café craft Boston's best gourmet sandwiches ($5-6.25), all served on fresh bread and named after nearby streets. Try the "Longfellow" (ham, apples, cheddar, and dijon mustard). Open Su 7am-7pm, M-Sa 6:30am-9pm. Cash only. ❶

Pho Pasteur, 35 Dunster St. (☎617-864-4100). A branch of this elegant, affordable, and delicious Vietnamese food chain, with plenty of vegetarian options. For their original Chinatown location, see p. 117. ❷

Bartley's Burger Cottage, 1246 Massachusetts Ave. (☎617-354-6559). For over 40 years, this tiny, kitschy joint has been serving some of Boston's biggest and juiciest burgers, not too mention the thickest frappes (milkshakes, to most people) in Boston. The ever-changing selection of burgers, topped with everything from bacon to brie, are named after American politicians and celebrities; the Ted Kennedy is a "plump liberal" burger. Be ready for a long wait and company at one of the group picnic-style tables. Burgers $8-12. Open M-Tu, Sa 11am-9pm; W-F 11am-10pm. Cash only. ❷

Henrietta's Table, Charles Hotel, 1 Bennett St. (☎617-661-5005). From JFK St., turn right on Eliot St.; the Charles is at the end of the street. The favorite restaurant of longtime Cambridge resident and mistress of munch Dame Julia Child, airy Henrietta's emphasizes farm-fresh ingredients and inventive preparations in their small country kitchen menu (pork chops, poached fish, chicken, etc.). All entrees ($13-22) are à la carte, but the hearty side dishes ($4-5) are enough to supplement the entire table. The same delicious breakfast food served at the exorbitant Su buffet brunch ($42) is available cheaper ($7-12) M-Sa until 11am. Open Su 7am-10pm, M-Th 6:30am-10pm, F-Sa 7am-11pm. ❹

Tanjore, 18 Eliot St. (☎617-868-1900). Exit the T onto JFK St. and turn right onto Eliot St. The best of Harvard Sq.'s countless Indian restaurants, with a menu that spans the entire subcontinent (each carefully prepared dish is labeled with its region of origin). Unique among area Indian restaurants is the *xacuti*, a sweet and sour coconut-tamarind curry. Entrees (many vegetarian) $10-12. All-you-can-eat lunch buffet ($8) daily 11:30am-3pm. Open daily 11:30am-3pm and 5-11pm. ❸

1 Arrow St. Crêpes, 1 Arrow St. (☎617-661-2737), at Massachusetts Ave. Walk up Mass. Ave. against traffic to the Inn at Harvard, turn right onto Dewolfe St., then left onto Arrow St. Aiming for the très cool feel of a Left Bank café, this breezy corner *crêperie* throbs with the sounds of Europop, while the staff concocts unusually thick crêpes, both savory ($5-7) and sweet ($3-8). Try the lamb and minted cucumber crepe, it's a decadent lunch for under $10. 15% discount with student ID. Open Su 10am-10pm, M-Th 11am-11pm, F-Sa 11am-midnight. $8 min. for credit cards. ❷

Herrell's Ice Cream, 15 Dunster St., (☎617-497-2179). Founded a year before rival Toscanini's moved into town, Herrell's has cornered the Harvard Sq. market on good, but overpriced ice cream. Decide for yourself if it's worth the extra money. Small $3.25, large $4. Open in summer Su-Th 10am-midnight, F-Sa 10am-1am; in winter daily 11am-midnight.

INMAN SQ.

At the junction of Cambridge and Hampshire St., a pleasant 15min. walk up Cambridge St. from Harvard Sq. Alternatively, the #69 bus *(p. 19)* *runs from T: Harvard (Red) up Cambridge St.*

Centered on half-hippie, half-yuppie **Inman Sq.,** East Cambridge is an off-the-beaten-path hodgepodge of phenomenal ethnic restaurants and traditional American food spots. **Cambridge St.,** which runs through Inman Sq., is lined with countless identical, delicious Portuguese and Brazilian restaurants that cater to the neighborhood's strong Portuguese-speaking community. The large number of professionals and academics who live in East Cambridge mean prices are sometimes higher than they are elsewhere, but all the higher-end eateries listed below are well worth their heftier pricetag.

Punjabi Dhaba, 225 Hampshire St. (☎617-547-8272). Indian restaurants are a rupee a dozen in Cambridge, but the Dhaba stands head and shoulders above the rest with its incredibly cheap, incredibly spicy menu. In recreating the sights, sounds, and tastes of a traditional *dhaba* (roadside truck stop), the restaurant offers no-frills dining (order at the open kitchen counter and take a number), with 2 fl. of bench seating, tacky posters, Hindi music, and the occasional Bollywood film. Thankfully, the tastes more than make up for the tasteless decor. Veggie dishes $5; huge combos (a light meal for 2, with curry, *naan* flatbread, rice, samosa, chutney, and yogurty *raita*) $8. Open daily noon-midnight. Cash only. ❶

Helmand Restaurant, 143 First St. (☎617-492-4646). T: Lechmere (Green); the #69 bus from T: Harvard (Red) through Inman Sq. runs to T: Lechmere (Green). From the T, walk across Cambridge St. onto First St. (with Monitor Co. on your left); after about 6 blocks, it's on the right. Owned by members of the Karzai family, whose scion Hamid is busy rebuilding war-torn Afghanistan. Luxurious, romantic Helmand is one of the best values in Boston, offering note-perfect, exquisitely flavored gourmet dishes at a fraction of the price you'd expect them to cost (entrees $10-16). Unknown Afghani cuisine is a far superior and more deftly seasoned take on Middle Eastern, with marinated and roasted lamb and beef and a love of harvest vegetables, like pumpkin and eggplant. No Helmand experience is complete without *kaddo borawni* ($4), sugar-dusted, twice-cooked baby pumpkin in a garlic-yogurt sauce. Open Su-Th 5-10pm, F-Sa 5-11pm. ❸

Dalí, 415 Washington St. (☎617-661-3254), at Beacon St. From Inman Sq., walk up Hampshire St. (with the Punjabi Dhaba on your right), which becomes Beacon St. From Harvard Sq., walk up Kirkland St., which becomes Washington St. in front of Dalí. A bustling, fun-loving Spanish *tapas* joint with the same exact menu and owners as the Back Bay's Tapéo (for prices and options, see p. 105). The surreal decor (inspired by their flamboyant artist namesake) doesn't deter Dalí from being the most romantic spot near Inman Sq. Open daily 5:30-11pm; bar area until midnight. ❹

Christina's Homemade Ice Cream, 1255 Cambridge St. (☎617-492-7021), Vying with Toscanini's for the title of "Best Ice Cream in Cambridge," Christina's strong suit is variety, offering the most unique flavors around, from vanilla to verbena. Most customers swear by Mexican Chocolate. Open M-W 1:30am-10:30pm, Th and Su 11:30am-11pm, F-Sa 11:30am-11:30pm.

East Coast Grill & Raw Bar, 1271 Cambridge St. (☎617-491-6568; www.eastcoastgrill.net). Some of the city's best chefs started out under East Coast Grill's award-winning Chris Schlesinger, and he's still the man behind the tongue-scorchingly hot, deep South

BBQ-meets-seafood bar menu at this always busy Inman Sq. institution (done up with tropical touches like a faux volcano and tiki-style drinks). Skip the BBQ and concentrate on the masterfully prepared seafood; the white pepper tuna is about as good as tuna gets. A popular and affordable option is ECG's festive Su soul brunch (11am-2:30pm). Raw bar $3-20. Seafood entrees $20-25; BBQ entrees $15-20. Open Su 11am-2:30pm and 5:30-10pm, M-Th 5:30-10pm, F-Sa 5:30-10:30pm. ❺

S&S Deli, 1334 Cambridge St. (☎617-354-0777). As the lines out the door on weekends attest, this Cambridge landmark has cured over 4 generations of hangovers with its unending menu of kosher-style breakfast food (served all day). Skip the overpriced entrees and uncharacteristically mediocre sandwiches and head straight for the omelettes ($7-9—avoid any with pesto) and other breakfast items ($7-8), including an amazingly fluffy Quiche Lorraine. On Su, avoid the wait at nearby **Ryles** (p. 140); their hopping Jazz Brunch (Su 10am-3pm) has the same food (though there are fewer options). Open Su 8am-10pm, M-W 7am-11pm, Th-Sa 7am-midnight. ❷

KENDALL SQ.

All listings below are near the 1 Kendall Sq. complex, which is not near T: Kendall (Red). From the T, walk through the Marriott Hotel (they're OK with it), turn left onto Broadway, and cross the railroad tracks; you'll see the complex on your right, when the road splits into Broadway (to the left) and Hampshire St. (to the right). "The Wave" shuttle bus (free, every 20min. until 6pm) runs from T: Kendall/MIT (Red) to the Kendall Sq. Cinema (p. 166), which is behind 1 Kendall Sq.

Emma's Pizza, 40 Hampshire St. (☎617-864-8534), opposite the 1 Kendall Sq. complex. Intimate Emma's dishes up the best gourmet pizza in Boston. Have your choice of unique toppings—everything from capers to cranberries—heaped high on the perfectly crisp crusts. Of the tried and true combos ($15-20), roasted pumpkin and goat cheese is the surprise favorite. 6-slice 12" pies ($8) and 8-slice 16" pies ($11) are each big enough for 2. Open Tu-F 11:30am-10pm, Sa 4-10pm. ❷

The Blue Room, 1 Kendall Sq. (☎617-494-9034). One of the most reliable high-end restaurants in a city where high prices don't always mean high quality. Neither blue (it's gold and purple) nor a room (it's a former warehouse, cut up into several dining areas), the Blue Room is consistent where it matters—in the kitchen. Recently voted best chef in Boston, chef/owner Steve Johnson dreams up flavorful Asian- and Mediterranean-influenced takes on traditional American cuisine. Entrees (around $20) are inventive and tasty, but the real highlights are the appetizers ($8-9) and heavenly desserts ($6), making this a perfect spot for a pre-film snack or post-film treat (the Kendall Sq. Cinema (p. 166) is just steps away). Su brunch 11am-2:30pm. Open Su 11am-2:30pm and 5:30-10pm, M-Th 5:30-10pm, F-Sa 5:30-11pm. ❹

Atasca, 50 Hampshire St. (☎617-621-6991), a block up from the 1 Kendall Sq. complex (walk with the complex on your right); next to Emma's Pizza. One of the most romantic Portuguese restaurants in the city, Atasca is the comfy parlor of that Portuguese grandmother you never had, complete with warm lights and beautiful tableware. The food has equally homespun tastes from all over Portugal, a country with a hearty, mildly spiced cuisine and an emphasis on meat and salty seafood. Portions aren't cheap (entrees $14-20), but they are huge: the popular *cataplana* (copper steamer filled with seafood; $15) is nearly unconquerable. Open Su noon-10pm, M-Sa 11:30am-11pm. Tiny original **branch,** even more charming than it's younger sister, at 279a Broadway (☎617-354-4355). Head 7 blocks up Broadway from 1 Kendall Sq. (with the complex on your right). Open Su 5-10pm, Tu-Sa 5-11pm. ❹

Legal Sea Foods, 5 Cambridge Ctr. (☎617-864-3400), on Main St., at 6th St. T: Kendall (Red) lets out onto Main St. Another branch of this delicious, though pricey seafood restaurant. For the Waterfront location, see p. 128. Open Su noon-9pm, M-F 11am-10pm, Sa noon-10:30pm. ❹

CAFÉS & COFFEEHOUSES

The Cantabrigian intelligentsia keeps a slew of comfy cafés and coffeehouses in business all over the city. **Central Sq.** has the city's highest concentration of spots where you can sit, read, and sip.

1369 Coffee House, 1369 Cambridge St. (☎617-576-1369). **Inman Sq.** A 15min. walk up Cambridge St. from T: Harvard (Red); also accessible from Harvard Sq. by the #69 bus. Every hip, studious resident of Inman Sq. makes the inviting and quietly cozy 1369 their home away from home. Perfect for wasting away an afternoon poring over the free newspapers with a mug of coffee ($1-2) and their note-perfect lemon bar ($2). Open Su 8am-10pm, M-Th 7am-10pm, F 7am-11pm, Sa 8am-11pm. **Central Sq. branch,** at 757 Massachusetts Ave. (☎617-576-4600). T: Central (Red). Open M-F 7am-11pm, Sa-Su 8am-11pm.

Tealuxe, 0 Brattle St. (☎617-441-0077). **Harvard Sq.** This peaceful, copper- and chrome-plated tea room is a soothing haven of calm amidst the chaos of Harvard Sq. Settle in to one of the few chairs with a book and a personal pot ($3-4) of one of their over 100 tea varieties, from Earl Grey to Superfine Cherrybana Big Fruit. Open Su 8am-10pm, M-Sa 8am-11pm. Second location with outdoor seating, 108 Newbury St. (☎617-927-0400). **Back Bay.** Open Su 9am-10pm, M-Th 8am-10pm, F 8am-11pm, Sa 9am-11pm.

Rosie's Bakery, 243 Hampshire St. (☎617-491-9488), a block up Hampshire St. (walk with the Punjabi Dhaba on your right). **Inman Sq.** Rosie's fresh-from-the-oven goodies (most $2) are the perfect ending to an evening out in Inman Sq. Try the "Harvard Square;" it's the best brownie in Boston. Also serves Herrell's ice cream (p. 113). Open Su 8:30am-6pm, M-Th 7:30am-7pm, F 7:30am-7:30pm, Sa 8am-7:30pm.

CityGirl Caffé, 204 Hampshire St. (☎617-864-2809). **Inman Sq.** This queer-owned and frequented eatery serves vegetarian pizzas, sandwiches, and salads ($4-8) in a funky atmosphere. Not quite the scene that Diesel (p. 125) represents, CityGirl is more subdued. Open Su 11am-7pm, Tu-F 11am-9pm, Sa 10am-9pm. ❷

CHINATOWN

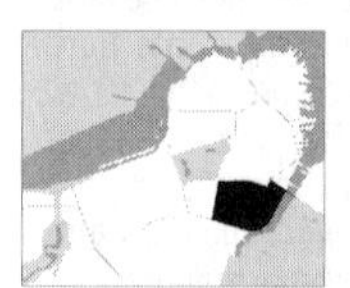

see map p. 322

T: Chinatown (Orange; "Night Owl" Orange Forest Hills) lets out onto Essex St. at Washington St., 1 block north of Chinatown's heart, at Beach St. and Harrison Ave. ***Sights:*** *p. 78.*

Chinatown is *the* place to go for great Asian food (and not just Chinese) anytime. The eateries here may not be the classiest or cleanest in the city, but for delicious, cheap, filling food from myriad ethnic cuisines—everything from traditional Cantonese to exotic Filipino—you can't go wrong. This is also the one neighborhood in Boston where eateries are open late (most until 3-4am). Just steps from the clubs and bars of the Theatre District (p. 151) and the watering holes of Downtown (p. 141), Chinatown is the perfect place to chow

Dim Sum

Cantonese for "little bits of the heart," dim sum are the foods traditionally eaten at a Chinese *yum cha* (tea lunch), a meal of dumplings and small dishes typically served for brunch on weekends in various restaurants in Chinatown. If you've never had dim sum before, the experience can be intimidating and a little overwhelming. But when everything's so cheap, there's no harm in experimenting.

Waitresses walk around the restaurant pushing carts laden with all sorts of steamed and fried Chinese "finger foods" (mostly rice dishes and meat- and seafood-filled dumplings, but including everything from tapioca to chicken feet). When she stops at your table, point to whatever looks good. The waitress will then stamp the card given to you at the door to charge you by the dish (they average $2-3; 3-4 per person will stuff you silly).

Popular dim sum spots include the following, all near T: Chinatown (Orange):

Emperor Garden, 690 Washington St. (☎617-482-8898), at Beach St. A former burlesque house. Dim sum daily 9am-3pm.

China Pearl, 9 Tyler St. (☎617-426-4338), at Beach St. Head down Washington St. then left on Beach St. Dim sum daily 8:30am-3pm.

Chau Chow City, 83 Essex St. (☎617-338-8158), 5 blocks down Essex St. Dim Sum M-F 8:30am-3pm, Sa-Su 8:30am-4pm.

the hidden deal

Chinatown Eatery & Juice Bar

Chinatown: 44-46 Beach St., 2nd fl. **T:** Chinatown (Orange). From the T, walk against traffic down Washington St. and turn left onto Beach St. At Harrison Ave. is a mall: enter and walk up the winding staircase; this food court is on the 2nd fl. **Open:** Food court daily until 2am. Juice bar Su-Th 11am-11pm, F-Sa 11am-2am. Cash only. ❶

As the clientele gobbling up food on styrofoam plates and chattering in Cantonese attests, this hidden food court has some of the most authentic Asian food in Chinatown, with regional spins on traditional Chinese food–like Shanghainese and Swatowese– plus a Thai place (rice plates $5-6, meat entrees $8-9).

The most popular spot here, though, is the Juice Bar in the corner. Don't even think about coming here without stopping in at this counter, popular with second-generation kids and adventurous yuppies. The mother-daughter team behind the counter sells super-sweet traditional fruit shakes and pearl teas ($2-3.50), served up with oversized straws–perfect for sucking up the wonderfully textured black pearls (tapioca balls) stirred in to every drink for an extra $0.75.

down after a night out on the town. Moreover, even though Boston's blue laws dictate that alcohol cannot be served after 2am, it is rumored that if you ask for "cold tea" at a late-night Chinatown eatery, you'll be served a cold, frosty teapot filled with something that's brewed, but not from tea leaves. If you do head to Chinatown in the wee hours, exercise caution, as some areas are deserted at night.

Shabu-Zen, 16 Tyler St. (☎617-292-8828; www.shabuzen.com), off Beach St. Spacious and spartan Shabu-Zen (a rarity in cramped Chinatown) is named for its signature do-it-yourself dish *shabu-shabu,* the delicious Japanese version of Chinese hotpot (akin to Western fondue). Waitresses offer plates of thinly sliced meats and vegetables that can then be cooked in the provided pots of boiling water. The broth becomes more and more flavorful as more items are added, so if you wait until the end to cook the udon noodles or rice, the taste is transcendent. The waitstaff isn't very helpful with instructing first-timers, but half the fun is experimenting. 2-person combo plates $12-16, à la carte $5-8. Open Su-W 11:30am-midnight, Th-Sa 11:30am-1am. ❸

Jumbo Seafood Restaurant, 5-7-9 Hudson St. (☎617-542-2823). Walk against traffic down Washington St., turn left at the parking lot onto Beach St., and head several blocks down to Hudson St. Named after an unrelated Hong Kong chain (note the velvet mural of the HK skyline on the wall), this is the best of Chinatown's many Cantonese-style seafood spots, featuring huge plates and a light touch. Feel free to sadistically greet your dinner swimming in the tanks by the entrance. Dinner entrees $9-13; vegetarian entrees $7-9; lunch specials $5-6. Open Su-Th 11am-1am, F-Sa 11am-2am. $10 min. for credit cards. ❷

Ginza, 16 Hudson St. (☎617-338-2261). From the T, walk against traffic down Washington St., turn left at the parking lot onto Beach St., head several blocks down to Hudson St., and turn right onto Hudson St.; it's on the left. Rolling up some of the freshest sushi in Boston, Ginza is a must for fans of Japanese cuisine. The minimalist dining room (the coziest in Chinatown) is crowded with hipsters and businessmen late into the night, so be prepared for a wait (reservations only for parties of 6+ people). Ginza's sushi doesn't come cheap ($3-10–trust us, it's worth it), but their full lineup of sake bombs will ease whatever pain your bill might inflict. Open Su-M 11:30am-2am, Tu-Sa 11:30am-4am; closed M-F 2:30-5pm, Sa-Su 4-5pm. ❹

Buddha's Delight, 5 Beach St. (☎617-451-2395). Filled with huge windows and fat buddhas smiling benevolently down on patrons, vegetarian-friendly Buddha's Delight is soothing to both the stomach and the soul; there are no animal products in their tofu-based entrees, flavored to taste like meat and seafood. Though they offer meat entrees, their vegetarian options are hands-down the reason to eat here. Entrees $6-10. Open Su-Th 11am-10pm, F-Sa 11am-11pm. ❷

Pho Pasteur, 682 Washington St. (☎617-482-7467), at Beach St. The original outpost of this elegant, affordable Vietnamese food chain, with plenty of veggie options. All branches share similar prices and hours: *pho* (beef noodle soups) and *bun* (vermicelli plates) $5-7; rice and meat dishes $7-10. Open Su 8am-10:45pm, M-Sa 9am-10:45pm. ❷

Grand Chau Chow, 41-45 Beach St. (☎617-292-5166). Despite its ritzy name, this dimly lit (but clean) spot is one of the cheapest eateries in Chinatown and an absolute favorite with the post-clubbing chowhounds. Rice and noodle dishes $5-7, meat and seafood $8-11. Open Su-Th 10am-3am, F-Sa 10am-4am. ❷

Penang, 685-691 Washington St. (☎617-451-6373; www.penangboston.com), at La Grange St., opposite Beach St. A NYC-based chain dishing up hearty and spicy Malaysian food (an amalgam of Indian, Cantonese, Middle Eastern, and Thai). The atypical-for-Chinatown tropical decor (including individual bamboo huts!) complements the tropical flair of the dishes, which are often served up in halved coconuts and mangos. Divine *roti canai* (flatbread with curry dipping sauce; $3.25) is now a Boston appetizer legend, and the noodle dishes ($6-7) and myriad veggie options ($7-10) are perfect for those with large appetites and small wallets (other entrees $10-15). Brusque service is the only drawback. Open Su-Th 11:30am-11:30pm, F-Sa 11:30am-midnight. $12 min. for credit cards. Another location in **Cambridge (Harvard Sq.),** at 57 JFK St. (☎617-491-1160). Same hours and prices. ❷

Apollo Grille & Sushi, 84-86 Harrison Ave. (☎617-423-3888 or 617-426-7888). Specializing in both Japanese and Korean cuisine, the tastefully decorated Apollo offers a balance between subtle, delicate sushi and robust, flavorful Korean specialties like Korean barbecue ($12-17) and *bi bim bap* (a sizzling pot of veggies, rice, beef, and cold chili paste; $11). Popular with the wee hour crowd, who down fried appetizers ($4-7) and sushi platters (15- to 18-pc. $15-20) after a night out dancing. Lunch, when everything is about ½-price, is much more affordable. Open M-F 11:30am-2:30pm and 5pm-4am, Sa-Su 5pm-4am. ❸

DOWNTOWN

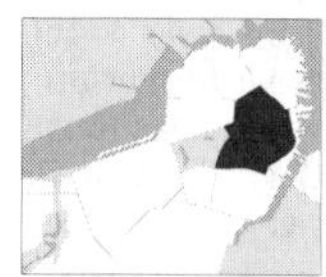

see map p. 324-325

T: Park St. (Green/Red), Downtown Crossing (Orange/Red), and Government Ctr. (Blue/Green) all serve Downtown. ***Discover Downtown:*** *p. 3.* ***Freedom Trail Sights:*** *p. 43.* ***Other Sights:*** *p. 80.* ***Nightlife:*** *p. 141.* ***Shopping:*** *p. 173.* ***Accommodations:*** *p. 117.*

Because the Freedom Trail runs through it, Downtown is the most heavily touristed part of Boston. Expect mediocre food, big crowds, and high prices. A better culinary experience awaits you in the delicious Italian-American North End (p. 121) and dirt-cheap Chinatown (p. 114), just steps away. If you're on the Trail and don't want to wander off the path to those neighborhoods, the most affordable food options in Downtown proper are the identical sandwich shops (sandwiches $5-7) in the **Financial District** and the more diverse fare in the food court inside **Quincy Market** (p. 51; most dishes $5-7).

Sultan's Kitchen, 72 Broad St. (☎617-338-7819), at Custom House St. From T: State (Blue/Orange), walk against traffic down State St. and turn right onto Broad St. The most popular lunch-to-go spot in the Financial District, with long lines of suits queuing for savory Middle Eastern and Turkish delights ($2-5)—everything from falafel and hummus to more exotic fare like *taramasalata* (fish roe dip). The gourmet touch of Cordon Bleu-trained owner Ozcan Ozan places the Sultan far above your typical greasy falafel joint. Salads $2.75. Open M-F 11am-5pm, Sa 11am-3pm. $10 min. for credit cards. ❶

South Street Diner, 178 Kneeland St. (☎617-350-0028), at South St. From T: Chinatown (Orange), walk against traffic down Washington St. and turn left onto Kneeland St. The classic American greasy spoon (burgers, fries, omelettes, etc.) housed in a funky little train car. Incredibly popular with the late-night party crowd. Coffee $1. Everything under $10. Open 24hr. ❷

the BIG $plurge

Radius

Downtown: *8 High St., at Summer St.* ***T:*** *South Station (Red). Follow traffic up Summer St. and turn right onto High St.* ***Contact:*** *☎617-426-1234.* ***Open:*** *lunch M-F 11:30am-2:30pm; dinner M-Th 5:30-10pm, F-Sa 5:30-11pm. Entrees $28-40.* ❺

If you're going to splurge, you might as well go all the way—and Radius can take you there. With a list of prestigious culinary awards too numerous to mention, posh, stylish Radius has everything most of its upscale competitors lack: sophisticated but hip style; enthusiastic, unpretentious service; and breathtakingly original food, courtesy of Michael Schlow.

Radius restlessly reinvents its menu every month, with Schlow's hyper-modern French cuisine (with a touch of pure Tuscany running through it) constantly juxtaposing unusual tastes in such dishes as *foie gras*-suffused pheasant with kumquats and rabbit-, apple-, and sage-stuffed tortellini.

The crowd is mostly power suits, and the dishes tend to be small, especially for the astronomical price (the emphasis is on presentation and conversation-stopping flavors), but the experience of eating at Radius is pleasing from beginning to end.

Country Life Vegetarian, 200 High St. (☎617-951-2534, menu ☎617-951-2685). Entrance on Broad St. From T: State (Blue/Orange), walk against traffic down State St. and turn right onto Broad St. It's a chain, it's far away, it's dreary, and it feels like a high school cafeteria, but it also happens to serves the best vegan deal in Boston: $7 ($8 at dinner) gets you an all-you-can-eat buffet of animal product-free fare, plus a huge salad bar. Popular vegan Su brunch 10am-3pm ($9). Open Su 10am-8pm, M and F 11:30am-3pm, Tu-Th 11:30am-8pm; closed Su and Tu-Th 3-5pm. ❷

Durgin Park, Quincy Market, 340 North Market (☎617-227-2038; www.durginpark.citysearch.com). T: Government Ctr. (Blue/Green). The most touristed restaurant in Boston, Durgin Park has been serving traditional New England dishes since 1827—and the menu hasn't changed since. Expect rare old fare like Yankee pot roast, Boston Baked Beans, Indian pudding, and fried seafood and lobster. The waitresses are no longer as rude as they were once known for being (though their pantsless outfits remain), and the communal tables keep the Hawaiian shirt-clad atmosphere friendly. Meat entrees $9-13; seafood entrees $14-17 (lobster at market price). Open Su-Th 11:30am-midnight, F-Sa 11:30am-1am. ❸

Ye Olde Union Oyster House, 41 Union St. (☎617-227-2750). T: Government Ctr. (Blue/Green), just past Faneuil Hall/Quincy Market. This always packed tourist trap was JFK's favorite seafood spot in Boston and remains America's oldest continuously operating restaurant (it opened in 1826, beating Durgin Park (see above) by 1 year). The seafood is fresh but too expensive (appetizers $8.50-10; entrees $17-30)—skip it and head to the cheaper, better Waterfront (p. 128). Open Su-Th 11am-9:30pm, F-Sa 11am-10pm. ❹

JAMAICA PLAIN

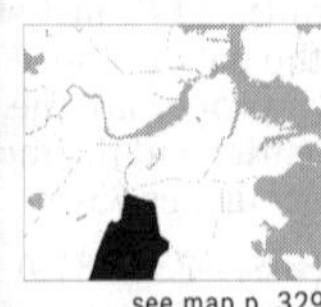

see map p. 329

T: *The Orange Line runs through JP 5-6 blocks east of Centre St., JP's main thoroughfare. To get there from the T, exit left out T: Green St. or right out of T: Stony Brook and walk 5-6 blocks.* ***Discover Jamaica Plain:*** *p. 6.* ***Sights:*** *p. 82.* ***Nightlife:*** *p. 144.* ***Shopping:*** *p. 172.*

After a hard day of running around outdoors or beating back the crowds in Downtown Boston, there's no better escape than the eateries of leisurely Jamaica Plain. Almost all the restaurants in the neighborhood are great bargains, featuring a variety of ethnic cuisines at hard-to-beat prices. Authentic and dirt-cheap Latin American establishments (a rarity in Boston) are everywhere, with the highest concentration around the less safe stretch of Centre St. from T: Jackson Sq. (Orange) to Perkins St. Most non-Latin restaurants in the neighborhood are geared toward JP's huge vegetarian population. Dress everywhere is casual.

Bella Luna, 405 Centre St. (☎617-524-6060). Turn right out of T: Stony Brook (Orange), upstairs from the **Milky Way Lounge & Lanes** (p. 144), a bowling alley-*cum*-karaoke bar. One of Boston's premier values, Bella Luna serves the city's best gourmet pizza (after Emma's; p. 114) in a fun and funky setting–with hand-decorated plates, local art on the walls, and crayons at the tables. The toppings are mostly vegetarian, with everything from asparagus to zabaglione. You *must* save room for their super-sweet desserts ($5.50-6.50), especially the rich peanut butter pie. 6-slice 8" pies $5-10, 6-slice 12" pies $7-14 (either one big enough for 2), 8-slice 16" pies $9-18. Open Su noon-10pm, M-W 11am-3pm and 5-10pm, Th-F 11am-3pm and 5-11pm, Sa 11am-11pm. ❷

J.P. Licks, 659 Centre St. (☎617-236-1666). T: Green St. (Orange). The original home of this Boston chain scoops both hard and soft yogurt as well as ice cream in deliciously large portions (small $3, large $4). 4 other locations around the city, including 352 Newbury St., **Back Bay.** Jamaica Plain location open in summer daily 6am-midnight. Otherwise, chains are open Su-Th 11:30am-11pm, F-Sa 11:30am-midnight.

Tacos el Charro, 349 Centre St. (☎617-522-2578), at Westerly St. Turn right out of T: Jackson Sq. (Orange). Delicious tacos, burritos, tostadas, and quesadillas ($1.50-5) dished up amidst sombreros, piñatas, and *musica mexicana* to locals and gringos alike. Wash it all down with your choice of imported beers–Sol, Tecate, Bohemia, Corona, and Dos Equis ($3.50)–or Mexican sodas ($1.25-1.75). **Live mariachi music** F-Su 7-10pm ($1 cover). Open M-Th 5-11pm, F-Su 11am-midnight. ❶

El Oriental de Cuba, 416 Centre St. (☎617-524-6464). Turn right out of T: Stony Brook (Orange). No Asian food here–the Oriental of this divey, diner-like restaurant's name is the Cuban Orient, home to a hearty, plantain-loving, meat-heavy cuisine. Long a weekly pilgrimage for local Cuban and Dominican immigrants, El Oriental specializes in divine Cuban sandwiches ($5) and other tropically influenced, succulently authentic Latin/Caribbean fare, like plantains and beans and Puerto Rican *mofongo* (fried and mashed garlicky plantains). Entrees $7-10. Open Su 8am-8pm, M-Sa 8am-9pm. ❷

Sorella's, 386-388 Centre St. (☎617-524-2016), turn right out of T: Stony Brook (Orange). A JP institution, homey Sorella's has been serving breakfast all day, every day for 15 years. Their giant breakfast plates and gourmet omelettes are Boston's cheapest jump-start ($3-6), but don't overlook their French toast and inventive pancakes (try Pumpkin Cranberry Walnut or Raspberry Butterscotch; $4-7). Open daily 7am-2pm. Cash only. ❶

Jake's Boss BBQ, 3492 Washington St. (☎617-983-3701). Turn right out of T: Green St. (Orange), then right again onto Washington St. The first solo effort by Boston's most respected pit-master, Kenton Jacobs (the "Jake" of the name), brings real down-home Texas smoked ribs and brisket to these cold northern reaches. Hefty sandwiches around $5.50, Boss dinners $7.50-9.50. Open Su-W 11am-10pm, Th-Sa 11am-11pm. ❷

Centre St. Café, 669 Centre St. (☎617-524-9217), opposite Seaverns St. Turn left out of T: Green St. (Orange). At the forefront of Jamaica Plain's artsy/crunchy revival, the tastefully bohemian Centre St. Café dishes up an always changing, always creative menu that works miracles with locally grown organic ingredients. Vegetarians and carnivores alike will rejoice at the healthful, fresh dishes (around $10; seafood $15), which are unusually named (Danno's Szechwan Shaboom?) but simply flavored. Open Su 9am-3pm, M-F 11:30am-10pm, Sa 9am-10pm; closed daily 3-5pm. ❸

Wonder Spice Café, 697 Centre St. (☎617-522-0200). Turn left out of T: Green St. (Orange). Serving up a cross between Thai and Cambodian cuisine, Wonder Spice specializes in elegant food in a low-key, small café setting. Customers with a creative streak can design their own entrees ($9-12) by selecting from a set list of noodle, meat, and vegetable options. Regular noodle dishes $7.50-9. Open Su noon-10pm, M-Th 11:30am-10pm, F 11:30am-10:30pm, Sa noon-10:30pm; closed daily 3:30-5pm. ❷

JP Seafood Café, 730 Centre St. (☎617-983-5177; www.jpseafoodcafe), at Harris Ave. Turn left out of T: Green St. (Orange). Initially part of a seafood shop, it's no surprise that this sleek Asian eatery has some of the freshest, most deftly prepared sushi in town (and for cheap—6-pc. rolls from $6). What *is* surprising is the separate chef who prepares great Korean food (entrees $9-13), including favorites like *bulgogi* (barbecue) and *bi bim bap* (a sizzling pot of veggies, rice, beef, and chili paste). Economical lunch boxes (with miso soup, sushi, and an entree) are a steal at $8-10. Open Su 4:30-10pm, Tu-Th 11:30am-10pm, F-Sa 11:30am-10:30pm; closed Tu-Sa 2:30-5pm. ❸

Acapulco Mexican Restaurant, 464 Centre St. (☎617-524-4328). Turn right out of T: Stony Brook (Orange). Acapulco manages to stand out from the area's many cheap Mexican eateries with its romantic, upmarket atmosphere and downmarket-priced food. Choose from authentic and hearty Mexican standbys like tacos and burritos ($7-10), or if you're feeling more daring, try one of their house specialties, like *chiles rellenos* (stuffed peppers; $8.50) or *mole poblano* (a spicy sauce of roasted chilis, chocolate, and peanuts; $10.25). Open M-W 4-10pm, Th noon-10pm, F noon-11pm, Sa-Su 1-11pm. ❷

Bukhara, 701 Centre St. (☎617-522-2195), at Burroughs St. Turn left out of T: Green St. (Orange). Owned by the same family that runs Kashmir (p. 105) and Diva (p. 124), this quiet, quality Indian restaurant doesn't quite live up to the standard set by its brethren, but still satisfies. Expect the typical array of spicy, veggie-friendly curries (entrees $12-13), served quickly and efficiently. All-you-can-eat buffet daily 11:30am-3pm (M-F $8, Sa-Su $10). Open Su-Th 3-11pm, F-Sa 3-midnight. ❸

KENMORE SQ. & THE FENWAY

see map p. 330-331

T: Kenmore (Green-B,C,D). The B and E Green Lines run through the area. ***Discover Kenmore Sq. & the Fenway:*** *p. 4.* ***Sights:*** *p. 84.* ***Nightlife:*** *p. 145.* ***Shopping:*** *p. 172.* ***Accommodations:*** *p. 190.*

Huntington Ave. is lined with cheap but low-quality eateries to satisfy the area's large student population, while the rest of the neighborhood is dotted with a few truly remarkable (and remarkably well-hidden) finds. For a quick bite before a game at Fenway Park, join all the Sox fans lining up for the traditional pre-game sausage from the vendors on **Yawkey Way.** Any of the following will happily satisfy your pre-clubbing or post-museum hunger pangs.

Brown Sugar Café, 129 Jersey St. (☎617-266-2928; www.brownsugarcafe.com). Walk down Brookline Ave. (with Hotel Buckminster on your right) and turn left onto Yawkey Way, which becomes Jersey St. Unquestionably the best Thai restaurant in Boston. Peruse the dizzying 12-page menu of fresh, veggie-friendly, sweetly spiced dishes—many with bizarre names like "Old Lady Spicy" and "Avocado Dancing"—livened up by such exotic ingredients as papaya and mango. Service is lightning-quick, and many meals come to the table on fire or dished up in halved tropical fruits. Entrees $8-15. Larger, equally intimate **branch** at 1033 Commonwealth Ave. (☎617-787-4242). T: Babcock St. (Green-B). Both open Su-Th 11am-10pm, F-Sa noon-11pm. ❸

Buteco, 130 Jersey St. (☎617-247-9508). Walk down Brookline Ave. (with Hotel Buckminster on your right) and turn left onto Yawkey Way, which becomes Jersey St. This homey, tiny restaurant is the oldest Brazilian eatery in town, offering gigantic portions (each entree takes up 2 plates) of hearty Brazilian food—a simple, meat-heavy cuisine with a love of coconut milk and garlic. The *mandioca* (fried cassava with tangy carrot sauce; $3-4) is a must-have prelude to the unique preparations of fish, beef, chicken, pork, or lamb. Confused? Be sure to ask the owner for her recommendations. Entrees $9-11. Open Su 3-10pm, M-Th noon-10pm, F noon-11pm, Sa 3-11pm. $10 min. for credit cards. ❸

Audubon Circle, 838 Beacon St. (☎617-421-1910). At night, this sleek, chic bar-restaurant is a favorite hangout of equally sleek, chic 20-somethings, but the inventive American food, one of the city's best cheeseburgers ($7), and an exhaustive jazz record collection makes it worth a visit before sundown. Everything here is quality, from the adorable potstickers ($7; served in an oversized takeout box) to the phenomenal grilled items (like hoisin-seared tuna with banana salsa; $13). Entrees $7-13. Open M-F 11:30am-1am, Sa-Su 11am-1am; food served until 11pm. ❷

El Pelón Taqueria, 92 Peterborough St. (☎617-262-9090; www.elpelon.com). Walk down Brookline Ave. (with Hotel Buckminster on your right), turn left onto Yawkey Way, then right onto Peterborough St. More authentically Californian than authentically Mexican, informal El Pelón is a breezy West Coast-style spot that's a great place for a filling and cheap meal of burritos ($4-5), quesadillas ($3-4), or tacos ($4). Nothing over $6. Open daily 11:30am-11pm. ❶

Linwood Grill & Barbecue, 81 Kilmarnock St. (☎617-247-8099). Walk down Brookline Ave. (with Hotel Buckminster on your right), turn left onto Yawkey Way, right onto Peterborough St., then left onto Kilmarnock St. Gaining instant street credibility through its attachment to a local dive bar, the restaurant proves to be far from a dive; it's a lively, well-scrubbed, Texas-style smoked BBQ joint with some sweet Caribbean influences. The lineup here is surprisingly non-spicy and diverse, from classics like pulled pork, dry-rubbed ribs, and ribeye steak to more exotic fare like lamb and andouille sausage. Appetizers ($7-10) are big enough to be light meals. Proper entrees $13-17. Open Su 11:30am-9pm, M-Th 11:30am-10pm, F-Sa 11:30am-11pm. ❸

Chinatown

NORTH END

see map p. 332

T: Haymarket (Green/Orange). Follow signs through construction and over the Fitzgerald Expwy. (I-93). Turn right onto Cross St. (parallel to the Expwy.), then left up Hanover St., the North End's main street. ***Discover the North End:*** *p. 4.* ***Freedom Trail Sights:*** *p. 43.* ***Other Sights:*** *p. 52.* ***Food:*** *p. 121.* ***Shopping:*** *p. 173.*

An overwhelming sense of community coupled with the old buildings has led many to call the North End the most old-world "European" of Boston's quarters. A charming respite far removed from the industrial hustle of downtown Boston, nearly every business is family-owned, and the lack of large supermarkets perpetuates the old country custom of shopping in small *salumerias* and bakeries (not to mention the popular outdoor **Haymarket;** see p. 81). On sunny days, older residents set out chairs on the sidewalks, and everyone greets each other by name on the streets. As you wander around the North End (and wander you will, until you decipher the street layout), you'll see signposts pointing you toward Genoa and Naples. The quickest way there, though, may be through the doors of one of the countless Italian eateries that line the streets of this charming Italian-American enclave.

Haymarket

JP Licks

the BIG $plurge

Sage

North End: 69 Prince St. **T:** *Haymarket (Green/Orange). Follow pedestrian signs through the construction work, cross the Fitzgerald Expwy. and Cross St. (which run parallel to each other), and continue up Salem St. Sage is at the corner of Salem and Prince St.* **Contact:** ☎*617-248-8814.* **Open:** *M-Sa 5:30-10:30pm.* **Menu:** *Pastas $16-18, entrees $25-30. 3-course* prix-fixe *$45.* ❺

North End native Tony Susi (son of the local butcher) is garnering national attention as the chef/owner of this tiny but elegant new bistro, a gourmet fusion spot for those sick of the North End's identically quaint red sauce-slinging *trattorie.*

The menu (which changes monthly and has only 15 options) features inventive interpretations of traditional Italian and American dishes (many with rich and luxurious French and Franco-African touches), yielding such sophisticated delights as hand-rolled *gnocchi* (potato dumplings) with pulled rabbit and fava beans and duck confit with harissa-spiced couscous and olives. Susi's globe-hopping culinary exploits are all on display—dishes show the mark of everywhere from Algeria to the American South—but his strongest suit is his highly flavored pastas and *risotti.*

With over 100 restaurants packed into a single square mile, there's something to please every palate in the North End. Neighborhood menus are similar, offering different types of pasta and meat (usually chicken or veal) and your choice of a variety of Italian regional preparations and sauces (red sauces dominate). Quality doesn't vary too drastically from place to place, but price does (the restaurants below are standouts either for their low price or their value). Your best bet is to walk around and find the place with the shortest wait and the menu that best fits your wallet. Just bear in mind that fancy decor isn't necessarily an indicator of good food. Stop by on a weekday and get equally delicious food with fewer crowds, more locals, and more time to linger over a post-dinner pastry or two.

RESTAURANTS

Trattoria Il Panino, 11 Parmenter St. (☎617-720-1336). Turn left off Hanover St. onto Parmenter St. The classic romantic North End *trattoria:* soft music, warm lighting, exposed brick, jovial staff, and intimate seating—perfect for a dinnertime seduction. The food is just as classic and heartwarming and comes in gigantic proportions. *Antipasti* $11-13; pastas $10-15, chicken dishes $16-17). Open Su-Th 11am-11pm, F-Sa 11am-midnight. ❸

Ristorante Lucia, 415 Hanover St. (☎617-367-2353), next to St. Stephen's Church. Tucked into the northeast corner of the North End, Lucia's provides a quiet environment away from the lines queuing for meals at restaurants deeper in the neighborhood. The service is attentive; the environment is soothing; and the food is classic Italian perfection. Entrees from $12; vegetarian dishes from $8.50. Open Su 1-11pm, M-Th 4:30-11pm, F-Sa 11:45am-11pm. Another location in Charlestown at 5-13 Mt. Vernon St. (☎617-729-0515). Open same hours, except Su 2-10pm. ❸

Il Panino Express, 264 Hanover St. (☎617-720-5720), at Parmenter St. This charming lunch counter and café—the cheaper offspring of Trattoria Il Panino—serves hearty and huge lunch favorites (giant calzones and 1-ft. subs $6-8; mammoth soups and salads $5-7). Open daily 11am-11pm. Cash only. ❶

Pizzeria Regina, 11 Thatcher St. (☎617-227-0765). Turn left off Hanover St. onto Prince St., then left again onto Thatcher St. Since 1926, the North End's best pizza (and sassiest waitresses)—gooey, greasy, and always piping hot. Even lifetime residents have trouble navigating the North End's maze of streets to this dark little dive, but the trip (and the wait) is well worth it. Small pizzas $7-9. Open Su-Th 11am-11pm, F-Sa 11am-midnight. Cash only. ❶

L'Osteria, 104 Salem St. (☎617-723-7847). Turn left off Hanover St. onto Parmenter St., then right onto Salem St. A simple, reliable *trattoria* that serves all the robust Italian favorites found on Hanover St., but at much lower prices (*antipasti* $7-10; pastas around $10, chicken dishes $14-15). The roomy pastel interior is a welcome relief from the dark brick of the rest of the neighborhood. Open Su-Th noon-10pm, F-Sa noon-11pm. ❷

Dolce Vita, 221 Hanover St. (☎617-720-0422; www.dolcevitaristorante.com). Dolce Vita's menu is similar to those of its Hanover St. brethren in price and quality (*antipasti* $5-10; pastas $11-13, meat dishes $14-18); the real reason to visit is chatty owner Franco Graceffa, who works the dining room nightly and spontaneously bursts into love songs from the Old Country (accompanied by his brothers) on weekends (F-Sa). Open daily 11am-11pm. ❸

Antico Forno, 93 Salem St. (☎617-723-6733). Turn left off Hanover St. onto Parmenter St., then left onto Salem St. As its name ("old oven") suggests, Antico Forno works wonders with its brick oven, offering crispy thin-crust pizza ($10-15) and rustic baked dishes from Southern Italy ($13-20; try snapper, peppers, olives, and herbs baked in a terra cotta pot, $19). Less romantic than other spots. Open Su-Th 11:30am-10pm, F-Sa 11:30am-10:30pm. ❹

The Daily Catch, 323 Hanover St. (☎617-523-8567). With a name like The Daily Catch, the menu at this cramped, diner-like seafood shack should come as no surprise—just ultra-fresh seafood in various Italian preparations, and lots of it. Highlights include their signature fried calamari and the black pasta entrees, dyed with squid ink ($16). Entrees $12.50-19. Open Su 11:30am-10pm, M-Th 11am-10pm, F-Sa 11am-11pm. Another location at 441 Harvard St. (☎617-734-5696), in **Brookline.** Open daily 5-10pm. ❸

Artú, 6 Prince St. (☎617-742-4336). Turn right off Hanover St. onto Prince St. The Italian standards at Artú may be slightly greasier than normal, but it's hard to complain given the cheaper pricetag (*antipasti* $8.50-10.50; pastas and chicken dishes $10-13, veal $18) and the swanky decor. Surrounded by vintage posters, light jazz, sleek furnishings, and black-clad (but incredibly friendly) waiters, you might mistakenly think you're having dinner at the latest Downtown hotspot. Open daily 11am-11pm. ❸

PASTRY SHOPS

Modern Pastry, 257 Hanover St. (☎617-523-3783), is flat-out the best *cannoli* ($2.50) to be found in the North End. The staff is like family, and the baked goods are better than home-made. Pastries $1.75-3.50. Open M-Th 8am-9pm, F-Su 8am-10pm.

Trattories

Pastries

North End Signs

Caffé Paradiso, 255 Hanover St. (☎617-742-1768). Slightly overpriced, Paradiso still has authentic baked goods and the *gelato* ($3 per scoop) to satisfy on a sweltering summer day. Open daily 6:30am-2am. Second branch in **Cambridge (Harvard Sq.),** 1 Eliot Sq. (☎617-868-3240), off JFK St. Open daily 7am-midnight.

Mike's Pastry, 300 Hanover St. (☎617-742-3050). Definitely not a secret, the lines to get to the pastries are always long, but the wait and hassle is worth it. *Cannolis* $2.25-2.50. Open Su 8am-9:30pm, M and W-Th 8am-9pm, Tu 9am-8pm, F 8am-10:30pm, Sa 8am-11pm.

Maria's Pastry Shop, 46 Cross St. (☎617-523-1196), to the left after exiting the pedestrian walkway that crosses the expressway. A small shop, Maria's offers freshly baked pastries without the showy storefront facade that is common in the rest of the neighborhood. Pastries $1.75-2.50. Open daily 7am-6pm.

Caffé dello Sport, 308 Hanover St. (☎617-522-5063). Perhaps the most elegant place in the North End to grab a *cannoli* ($3) or sip a cappucino (around $3). Open Su-Th 7am-midnight, F-Sa 7am-1am.

Caffé Vittoria, 296 Hanover St. (☎617-227-7606). One of the busiest caffès on the North End, Vittoria is a run-of-the-mill pastry shop. Pastries $2.50-3. Open daily 8am-midnight.

Bova's Bakery, 34 Salem St. (☎617-523-5601). If you're craving some Italian pastry in the wee hours, Bova's is the place to go. Open 24hr., they serve up cheap baked goods ($1-2.25; bread $2-4.50), whenever the urge strikes.

SOMERVILLE

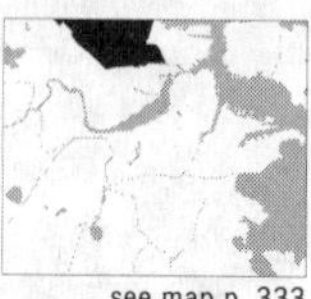

see map p. 333

T: *Davis (Red) lets out onto Holland St., which splits into Highland Ave. (to the left) and Elm St. (to the right) several blocks later.* ***Discover:*** *p. 8.* ***Nightlife:*** *p. 147.* ***Shopping:*** *p. 172.*

The diverse array of affordable restaurants in Davis Sq. makes it a tasty spot to grab dinner before a night out in Davis or nearby Harvard Sq. (just a 5min. T ride away; for nightlife options in Harvard, see p. 139).

RESTAURANTS

Anna's Taqueria, 236a Elm St. (☎617-666-3900). The largest and best branch of this budget-friendly, no-frills, super-tasty Mexican chain (tacos $2, burritos $3-4). For 2 other Anna's, both in **Brookline,** see p. 108. Open daily 10am-11pm. ❶

Rosebud Diner, 381 Summer St. (☎617-666-6015). Summer St. forks off Elm St. a few blocks south of the T. A greasy-spoon diner, housed in an old boxcar, where the waitresses still call you "hon" and mean it. Omelettes ($5-7), pancakes ($4-6), and other cheap breakfast specials are served until 3pm, when pricier American dinner fare (around $12) takes over. Expect long lines for weekend brunches. Open daily 8am-midnight. ❷

Denise's Homemade Ice Cream, 4 College Ave., opposite T: Davis (Red). The drab decor in this tiny shop belies the rich color of the flavors. Perfect for an ice cream after a movie and before heading to Johnny D's (p. 147), try the best of their ultra-rich flavors, blood peach.

Diva, 246 Elm St. (☎617-629-4963). A "bistro" twist on Cambridge-style Indian cuisine: the same thick curries and sauces, but with fresher ingredients and more dramatic decor. After the waiter trots out the très French *amuse-bouches* (complimentary miniature appetizers), skip the over-fried regular appetizers and average entrees ($11-15). The saving grace of this institution is the divine—and dramatically plated—*dosas* ($8-10), south India's lentil-and-curry take on crêpes. Full bar (cocktails $5-6). Average-tasting all-you-can-eat buffet (M-F $8, Sa-Su $10) daily 11:30am-3pm. Open daily 11am-11pm. ❸

Redbones, 55 Chester St. (☎617-628-2200; www.redbones.com). From Elm St., turn right onto Chester St. at Diva restaurant. Blues music, bench seating, drinks in Bell jars, and mediocre BBQ dished up in nearly unconquerable portions (ribs $10-16; over-stuffed barbecue sandwiches $7) complete the picnic feel of this casual, festive spot. Sure the food isn't that great, but it's so much fun to eat it. Popular all-you-can-eat ribs and chicken lunch special $9. Open daily

11:30am-11pm. The raucous downstairs bar **Underbones** serves booze (beer $3-4) and a smaller barbecue-heavy menu daily until 12:30am. Cash only. ❸

Picante, 217 Elm St. (☎617-628-6394). The other branch of this quirkily decorated, cheap Cali-Tex-Mex chain, popular for their quesadillas ($3-4), giant burritos ($5-7), and heaping combo plates ($8). Most entrees are big enough for 2 people. Open M-F 11am-11pm, Sa-Su 10am-11pm. For the nearby **Central Sq. branch,** see p. 111. ❶

CAFÉS

Diesel Café, 257 Elm St. (☎617-629-8717). Industrial but inviting Diesel is the mecca of Davis' strong (largely female) queer community, who gather nightly to shoot pool, flirt with the hip staff, and play R-rated Scrabble. Breeders and Bohos alike shun the neighboring Starbucks (hiss!) in favor of Diesel's myriad coffees, teas, and chais ($1-4), veggie sandwiches ($3-5), and decadent desserts ($1-2). Queer events and resources posted in back. Open Su 8am-midnight, M-Th 7am-midnight, F 7am-1am, Sa 8am-1am. Cash only. ❶

Someday Café, 51 Davis Sq. (☎617-623-3323), a quick right out of the T station. The funkier, cozier, and straighter sister to Diesel, with mismatched furniture, an alt-rocker staff and clientele, and local artists' work on the walls. Coffees and teas $1.50-3. So-so baked goods $1-2. Open Su 8am-11pm, M-Th 7am-11pm, F 7am-midnight, Sa 8am-midnight. Cash only.

Bob the Chef's

Diesel Café

SOUTH END

see map p. 336

T: *Back Bay (Orange) or Newton St. (Silver). Eateries line trendy Tremont St. or quiet Washington St. To get to* ***Tremont St.,*** *exit T: Back Bay (Orange) onto Clarendon St. and walk 4 blocks south (with the T on your right).* ***Washington St.*** *is parallel to Tremont St., 2 blocks south (follow any Tremont side street that begins with "W," like Waltham or W. Brookline St.). The Silver Line runs above ground along Washington St., with T: Newton St. (Silver) being the most central.* ***Discover the South End:*** *p. 4.* ***Sights:*** *p. 92.* ***Nightlife:*** *p. 149.* ***Shopping:*** *p. 172.* ***Accommodations:*** *p. 191.*

Despite its intense trendiness and its popularity as a dining destination, the South End retains much of its charming neighborhood feel, with lots of intimate bistros, outdoor cafés, and crowds of locals chatting happily together. Prices continue to rise, and lines grow ever longer, but the wait and the hefty bill are usually worth it. The South End has a lion's share of Boston's best eateries, which

Francesca's

the BIG $plurge

Bomboa

South End: *35 Stanhope St.* ***Contact:*** *☎617-236-6363; www.bomboa.com.* ***T:*** *Back Bay (Orange). Walk 1 block up Clarendon St. (with the T on your left), then right onto Stanhope St.* ***Open:*** *daily 5:30-2am; food until midnight. Entrees $22-28; 3-course* prix-fixe *Su-Th $30.* ❺

With food as scandalous, sensual, and unique as its decor (complete with a zinc bar, bright clashing colors, and zebra-striped seats) Bomboa is a breath of fresh Caribbean air in the often too similar and too mediocre high-end Boston dining scene. The orchestration of flavors, techniques, and colors on the plate will delight all your senses.

Most importantly, Felino Samson's tropical, Franco-Brazilian and Latin fusion cuisine will awaken tastebuds tired of French bistro knock-offs with such delights as prawns and honey-braised rutabagas in a spicy coconut crab broth or mackerel *ceviche* with avocados, popcorn, and pineapple wasabi. Even the *feijoada*—a traditional Brazilian black bean dish—gets the celebrity chef treatment thanks to crispy yucca and the aptly-termed "papaya mojo."

Bomboa is also one of the city's hottest drinking destinations.

creatively meld flavors and techniques from around the world to create amazing meals. **Washington St.** in particular has recently become one of the city's hottest culinary outposts, with excellent restaurants opening up along the street every month.

The line between restaurant and bar in the South End is blurry. The hip crowd here dines late; on weekends (Th-Sa), eating almost always segues into drinking. So when you're looking for a place to dine, don't ignore the bar-restaurants under **Nightlife** (p. 149); the food at watering holes Bomboa (p. 126), Pho Republique (p. 150), and Red Fez (p. 150) is particularly amazing.

Addis Red Sea, 544 Tremont St. (☎617-426-8727). Simply not to be missed. The best of Boston's many Ethiopian restaurants (a mild curry based cuisine), Addis is also one of the city's best places to take a group of friends. Trying to sit at the short wicker *mesob* tables on the three legged stools requires almost as much skill as actually eating the food—all entrees are served utensil-free to be scooped up with spongy, slightly sour *injera* bread. Highlights include buttery *kitfo* (steak tartare; $10), exotic *zilzi-tibs* (beef and onion curry), and *atakilt* (spicy veggie curry; $9). Entrees $8-10, 2-person combos $11-17. Open Su noon-10pm, M-F 5-10:30pm, Sa noon-11pm. ❷

The Dish, 253 Shawmut Ave. (☎617-426-7866), at Milford St. Turn right off Tremont St. onto Milford St. Alternatively, turn left onto Shawmut Ave. off E. Berkeley St. coming out of T: E. Berkeley (Silver). Alternatively, look in the dictionary under "perfect neighborhood bistro." The Dish attains the culinary and atmospheric perfection all casual neighborhood eateries aspire to. Upscale decor meets a low-key local clientele and a uniformly delicious menu of gourmet and/or pseudo-Mediterranean updates on classic Americana (Cajun-style meatloaf, pork chops with pistachio and goat cheese, etc.). Entrees $11-17. Open daily 5pm-midnight. ❸

Bob the Chef's, 604 Columbus Ave. (☎617-536-6204; www.bobthechefs.com), at Northampton St. Turn right out of T: Mass. Ave. (Orange) and right again onto Columbus Ave. The #1 bus (p. 20) from Harvard Sq. and Newbury St. runs along Mass. Ave. to Columbus Ave. Boston's best place for stick-to-your-ribs soul food and down-home Southern favorites. Skip the BBQ and head straight for the meatloaf or the "glorifried" chicken, either with a side of collard greens. Huge entrees $11-15. **Live jazz** Th-Sa 7:30pm-midnight (cover $3-7). Su all-you-can-eat gospel and jazz brunch (10am-3pm) $16. Open Su 10am-9pm, Tu-W 11:30am-10pm, Th-Sa 11:30am-midnight. ❸

Franklin Café, 278 Shawmut Ave. (☎617-350-0010), opposite Hanson St., a block south of Tremont St., look for the neon martini glass. One of the neighborhood's most beloved eateries, featuring gourmet American food prepared by a world-class chef and served in a tiny, dark room. Also an incredibly popular nighttime spot. Appetizers/bar food $4-8; entrees $11-18 Open daily 5pm-2am; food until 1:30am. ❸

Caffé Umbra, 1395 Washington St. (☎617-867-0707). Laura Brennan emerged triumphantly from second banana chefdom to open her own place—and what a debut. Named for its location in the shadow (*umbra* in Latin) of the Cathedral of the Holy Cross, this stately room put Washington St. on the gourmet map with its winning selection of rustic French and Italian favorites. The emphasis is on thick cuts of meat, hearty sauces, and heady flavors. Entrees $15-22. Open Su and Tu-Th 5:30-10pm, F-Sa 5:30-11pm. ❹

Code 10, 1638 Washington St. (☎617-375-6333), at E Concord St. T: Newton St. (Silver). Named for the police radio signal for "lunch break," this sunny, modern-looking café brings you simple deli food (mostly sandwiches, soups, and hot dogs) at great prices. The juicy gourmet hot dogs (2 "naked" for $4.25, with fixins $3.50 each) are the best in the city and go perfectly with nostalgic fountain drinks like "Brown Cow" (ginger ale and chocolate ice cream; $3.50). Open daily 11am-9pm. ❶

Garden of Eden, 571 Tremont St. (☎617-247-8377). As much a people-watching scene as an eatery, crowded, noisy Garden of Eden serves light, veggie-friendly fare like sandwiches (that are big enough for two), salads, and pastas ($5-8), plus a dinner menu of French- and Italian-influenced entrees ($8-12). Go for lunch and sit outside for the full experience. Open Su 7:30am-10pm, M-W 7am-10:30pm, Th-Sa 7am-11pm. ❷

Anchovies, 433 Columbus Ave. (☎617-266-5088), opposite Pembroke St. From Tremont St., turn right onto Pembroke St.; Columbus Ave. is 2 blocks up. Not needing a sign is a pretty cocky statement, and Anchovies has every reason to be. Huge portions meet low prices at this boisterous, dimly lit Italian eatery (pastas $8-11; pizzas and calzones $6, plus $1 per topping). Voted Boston's best late-night spot last year, the South End's best-kept secret is now out (like everything else in the neighborhood). Waits get longer as the night progresses. Bar open daily 4pm-2am; food starts at 5pm. ❷

Charlie's Sandwich Shoppe, 429 Columbus Ave. (☎617-536-7669). From Tremont St., turn right onto Pembroke St.; Columbus Ave. is 2 blocks up. This dingy diner has been curing South End hangovers for decades. Breakfast ($6-7) served all day. Lunch is also served, but no one seems to notice. Signature turkey hash and eggs $7. Open M-F 6am-2:30pm, Sa 7:30am-1pm. Cash only. ❶

the hidden deal

Budget Gourmet

T: Back Bay (Orange). ***Open:*** *both open daily 5:30-10pm, F-Sa 5:30-10:30pm, Su 10:30am-3pm and 5:30-10pm.*

The South End is home to some of the best, most inventive food in Boston—but high quality usually comes at a high price. But fear not! For full-blown gourmet flavors at deflated prices, try:

Laurel, 142 Berkeley St. (☎617-424-6711). Atmosphere at Laurel is lacking, but all entrees ($10-14) are half the price they'd be anywhere else with this quality. Artfully crafted culinary masterpieces, like duck confit with sweet potatoes or shrimp and prosciutto ravioli, come in gigantic proportions. Lunch: Su 11am-3pm, M-Sa 11:30am-2:30pm. Dinner: M-Th 5:30-10pm, F-Sa 5:30-11pm. ❸

Sister Sorel, 645 Tremont St. (☎617-266-4600), is a phenom American bistro with intense flavors and grilling panache. Sorel capitalizes on Tremont 647 (a ridiculously priced restaurant with an even more ridiculous wait) by offering a menu of ½-sized Tremont 647 entrees at ½ price ($9-13) and without the wait. Sister Sorel also has all the to-die-for 647 appetizers and desserts, plus 647's legendary complimentary bread basket. ❸

CAFÉS & BAKERIES

Flour, 1595 Washington St. (☎617-267-4300), at Rutland St. After pastry chef stints at several of Boston's top gourmet restaurants, Harvard-educated chef/owner Joanne Chang (who left a high-paying corporate job to become a cook) opened up the cheerful, cornflower-blue Flour, undoubtedly the best bakery in the city. The mouth-watering cakes, cookies, and pastries ($1-3) lined up on the counter are nothing short of transcendent, and everything—from the meringue clouds to the lemon-raspberry cake—is perfectly sweetened and flaky. Take your sweets or one of the gourmet sandwiches ($6-7) to the outdoor cafe for some great people-watching. Open Su 9am-3pm, M-F 7am-7pm, Sa 8am-6pm. ❶

Qingping Gallery & Teahouse, 231 Shawmut Ave. (☎617-482-9988), at Dwight St., a block south of Tremont St. Unwind after a long day of sightseeing at this delightfully cozy spot, which was built with the owner's own 2 hands. Opt for one of the several types of traditional Chinese tea (cups $3-9, pots $6-18) in a soothing, plant-filled Zen setting. Open daily noon-midnight.

Bakery at Haley House, 23 Dartmouth St. (☎617-236-8132), at Montgomery St. Exit T: Back Bay (Orange) onto Dartmouth St. In their ongoing efforts to rehabilitate the homeless, the Haley House offers basic skills training programs for underemployed individuals. The result is tasty, oversized goods for dirt cheap (loaves and foccaccia rounds $3-4; jumbo cookies $1). Open Su 8:30am-3:30pm, Tu-W 6:30-9:30am and 2:30-7pm, Th-F 6:30am-7pm, Sa 8:30am-6pm. Cash only.

Francesca's, 564 Tremont St. (☎617-482-9026), at Union Park. A gay-friendly local hangout with a sleek espresso bar that whips up steamed milk and coffee drinks ($2-4) with suggestive names like "Sex on the Counter" and "Boston Bare Naked." Gourmet sandwiches $5-7. Open Su 9am-11pm, M-Th 8am-11pm, F-Sa 8am-midnight. Cash only. ❶

WATERFRONT

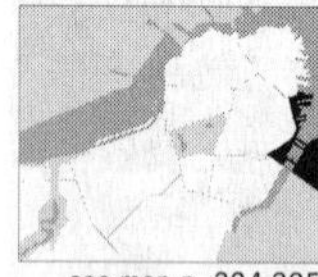

see map p. 324-325

Eateries are on or around the piers lining Seaport Blvd; Northern Ave. becomes Seaport Blvd. after crossing the Ft. Point Channel. ***T:*** *South Station (Red). Follow traffic up Atlantic Ave., turn right onto the Northern Ave. Bridge, and cross the Ft. Point Channel to get to the Waterfront. Alternatively, you can take the free shuttle (5-7min., M-F 6am-12:30am) that runs along Northern Ave. from South Station to the World Trade Ctr., which is on one of the Waterfront piers.* ***Discover the Waterfront:*** *p. 128.* ***Sights:*** *p. 93.*

The Waterfront is naturally the best place in the city for seafood. Although most places here cater to tourists, prices are more reasonable than tourist-heavy Downtown, and the experience is unforgettable—just you, an ocean breeze, a view of the Harbor, and big, messy buckets of clams fresh from the water.

No Name, 15½ Fish Pier (☎617-338-7539), at D St.; the next pier over from the World Trade Ctr. What began as a shack for local fishermen to eat the morning's catch has expanded to a top-notch seafood restaurant, which sends all manner of sea creatures fin-flapping fresh from the nearby boats to your table. Add a view of the harbor and the most happy-go-lucky service in Boston and No Name emerges as, hands-down, the best seafood restaurant in Boston. Entrees $8-12. Open Su 11am-9pm, M-Sa 11am-10pm. Cash only. ❸

Legal Sea Foods, 255 State St. (☎617-227-3115; www.legalseafoods.com), opposite the New England Aquarium (p. 96). Turn left out of T: Aquarium (Blue). Now with branches from West Palm Beach to Paramus, New Jersey, Legal Sea Foods remains Boston's finest seafood restaurant (their motto: "If it isn't fresh, it isn't Legal"). Expect high-quality cuisine—perfectly seared seafood, smooth bisques and chowders—at high prices (raw bar $8-9; entrees $18-30, lunch $9-20). Their clam chowder ($3.75-4.50) is revered as the best in the city, if not the world. Open Su noon-10pm, M-Th 11am-10pm, F-Sa 11am-11pm. ❹

Jimbo's Fish Shanty, 242 Northern Ave. (☎617-542-5600). The Doulos family opened Jimbo's as a more festive and affordable alternative to the upscale, ultra-expensive Jimmy's Harborside Restaurant, just a cod's-throw away on the Waterfront. Quality doesn't drop with price, as the seafood here ($10-17) is delightful—especially the signature crab cakes ($9). Open Su noon-8pm, M-Sa 11:30am-9pm. ❸

Barking Crab, 88 Sleeper St. (☎617-426-2722), at the Northern Ave. Bridge, just across the Ft. Point Channel. A festive, down-and-dirty seafood shanty—picnic tables, entrees in buckets, ceiling lights made of crab traps, a tent over your head, etc.—with a phenomenal view of the skyline and Boston Harbor. Choose from huge tubs of steamers, crab claws, mussels, and the like ($7-22), or go with lobster (market price; usually around $19 per lb.) smashed to pieces with the big stone at your table. Restaurant open Su-Tu 11:30am-9:30pm, W-Sa 11:30am-10pm; bar stays open Th-Su until 1:30am. ❸

GROCERS & SPECIALTY FOODS

Cardullo's, 6 Brattle Sq. (☎617-491-8888), across Brattle St. from T: Harvard (Red). **Cambridge (Harvard Sq.).** Over 50 years old, this gourmet grocer is one of the last "old Harvard Sq." institutions still standing. Though they feature imported cheeses and meats $8-12 per lb. and a globe-trotting wine selection under $20, they are better known for their selection of imported sweets and candies. Whether you're craving Haribo jellies ($2 per bag), nutty *Baci* balls (90¢ per piece), pistachio-and-marzipan *Mozart Kugeln* ($20 per box), or even Turkish Delight ($2.50 for 3oz.), Cardullo's is the place for you. They also create some of Cambridge's best gourmet sandwiches (around $6.50). Open Su 11am-7pm, M-F 8am-8pm, Sa 9am-9pm. $20 min. for credit cards.

Chung Wah Hong Co., 55 Beach St. (☎617-426-3619), at Tyler St. **Chinatown.** From T: Chinatown (Orange), walk against traffic down Washington St. and turn left onto Beach St. The large selection at this Chinatown grocer includes everything from Asian vegetables and exotic fresh fish to kitschy trinkets and imported groceries. Open daily 8:30am-7:30pm.

Harvest Co-op Supermarket, 581 Massachusetts Ave. (☎617-661-1580; www.harvestcoop.com). **Cambridge (Central Sq.).** T: Central (Red) lets out onto Mass. Ave. A socially conscious grocery store that sells organic produce and beauty products and high-quality meat and fish at affordable prices. Large selection of pre-made vegan food. Open daily 9am-9pm. Smaller **Jamaica Plain** branch, 57 South St. (☎617-524-1667), at Carolina Ave. Head up South St. from T: Forest Hills (Orange). Open daily 8am-10pm.

Salumeria Italiana, 151 Richmond St. (☎617-523-8743; www.salumeriaitaliana.com), at Hanover St. **North End.** From T: Haymarket (Green/

GIVING BACK

Soup for the Soul

It was 8am on a rainy Saturday, so naturally I was wearing latex. That's right. With latex gloves, a great big apron, and a hair net, I cut pies in the kitchen of **Community Servings** (for more on volunteering, see p. 272).

It was late November, so Community Servings had kicked into high gear to do what they do best: provide meals to people affected by AIDS. Every day, they deliver 3-course meals (plus snacks) to 465 homes. For families, this non-profit packs enough food for every member.

Now, I am used to eating in a dining hall every day with 300 university students, so I know my mass-produced meals. The chefs at Community Servings put Julia Child to shame. More importantly, they also make sure they exceed nutrition recommendations for AIDS patients and cater to all other dietary needs and requests.

And it's all done with a smile bigger than the vat of apples I reached into hundreds of times that morning. Even as a certified cynic, I can safely say that the folks who work there are downright inspiring. Always ready with a joke, friendly in the face of such suffering; the volunteers aren't so bad either, if I do say so myself.

So if you have a few hours to donate, go now! They need you.

—Lauren Bonner, 2003

Fresh Fish?

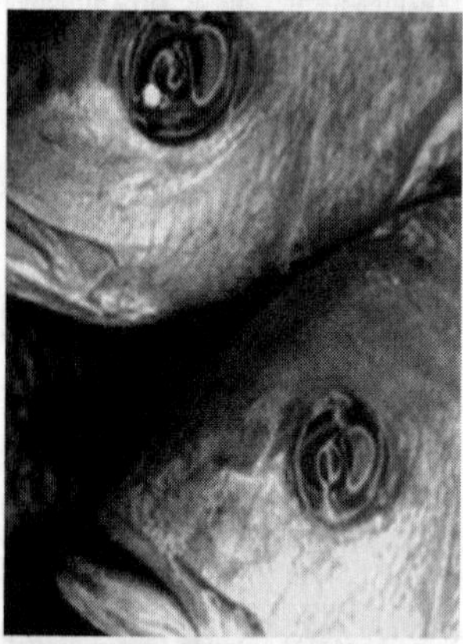
Yeah!

Quinping teahouse

Orange), follow pedestrian signs through the construction on the Fitzgerald Expwy. (I-93), turn right onto Cross St. (which runs parallel to the Expwy.), then left up Hanover St. Repeatedly voted the city's best Italian grocery, this mid-sized *salumeria* has just about any Italian product your heart could desire, from pre-made *antipasti* ($8 per lb.) to 12 kinds of olive oil, plus a vast array of pastas, cheeses, meats, and breads. Open M-Sa 8am-6pm. $10 min. for credit cards.

Savenor's Market, 160 Charles St. (☎617-723-6328). **Beacon Hill.** T: Charles/MGH (Red). A popular local grocery with incredibly fresh produce and a gourmet flair—a perfect pre-Esplanade picnic stop (for more on the Esplanade, see p. 69). Cheeses are overpriced, but the meat, game (pâté $4-6), and meals-to-go are a gourmet steal. Open Su noon-7pm, M-F 9am-8:30pm, Sa 9am-8pm.

Shalimar Indian Food & Spices, 571 Massachusetts Ave. (☎617-868-8311). **Cambridge (Central Sq.).** T: Central (Red) lets out onto Mass. Ave. A tiny Indian grocery crammed full of everything you need for a feast fit for a maharajah: spices ($1 per lb.), sauces ($3-4), imported canned goods, heat-and-serve appetizers, breads, and Indian sweets ($1 per piece). Also has Hindi video rental, a sari and *salwar kameez* fabric store, a selection of Bollywood fillum magazines, and a small counter-service restaurant in the back (entrees $4; sweets $5 per lb.). Open Su 11am-8pm, M-Sa 10am-9pm.

Star Market, 800 Boylston St., Prudential Ctr. (☎617-262-4688). T: Prudential (Green-E). **Back Bay.** A cheap chain supermarket (found all over Massachusetts) with low-priced generic brand and discounted name-brand goods. Open daily 6am-midnight. **Brookline,** 1717 Beacon St. (☎617-566-1802), at T: Tappan St. (Green-C). Open daily 7am-midnight. Two **Cambridge** branches: **Porter Sq.,** 49 White St. (☎617-492-5566), at T: Porter (Red). Open daily 6am-midnight. **Central/Kendall Sq.,** 20 Sidney St. (☎617-494-5250), off Mass. Ave. From T: Central (Red), walk several blocks down Mass. Ave. (with Starbucks on your left) until you see the sign. Open daily 7am-midnight. **Fenway,** 33 Kilmarnock St. (☎617-267-4684). From T: Kenmore (Green-B,C,D), walk down Brookline Ave. (with Hotel Buckminster on your right), turn left onto Yawkey Way, right onto Peterborough St., then right onto Kilmarnock St. Open 24hr. **Kenmore Sq.,** 1065 Commonwealth Ave. (☎617-783-5878), at T: Brighton Ave. (Green-B). Open 6am-midnight.

Syrian Grocery, 270 Shawmut Ave. (☎617-426-1458). **South End.** From T: E. Berkeley St. (Silver), follow traffic up E. Berkeley St. and turn left onto Shawmut Ave. The only reminder of the neighborhood's once large Middle Eastern community (Lebanese poet/mystic Kahlil Gibran lived nearby), the Syrian Grocery stocks authentic sweets (like *halvah* and baklava, $5 for 6) and lots of Mediterranean spices, olives, and imported pastas. Open Tu-F 11:30am-6:30pm, Sa 11am-6pm.

Trader Joe's, 899 Boylston St. (☎617-262-6505; www.traderjoes.com). **Back Bay.** T: Copley (Green) lets out onto Boylston St. A fantastic Los Angeles-born alternative grocery store for the health- and budget-conscious, selling their own, eminently affordable brand of everything from dry pastas and pre-made entrees to fresh cheeses, wines, and baked goods. **Cambridge (Central Sq.)** branch, 727 Memorial Dr. (☎617-491-8582). From T: Central (Red), walk up Mass. Ave. (with Starbucks on your right), turn left onto Pleasant St., and follow it for 10-15min. until it hits Memorial Dr. **Brookline** branch, 1317 Beacon St. (☎617-278-9997), at T: Coolidge Corner (Green-C). All open daily 9am-10pm.

Yoshinoya, 36 Prospect St. (☎617-491-8221). **Cambridge (Central Sq.).** From T: Central (Red), turn right off Mass. Ave. onto Prospect St. Huge Japanese grocer with ingredients for making sushi–rice in bulk (20lb. for $9), pre-sliced fish ($2-8 per lb.), and *nori* (seaweed; $1-2). Heat-and-serve Japanese finger foods (*mochi* 6 for $3, *gyoza* 50 for $6). Open Su 2-5pm, Tu-F 10:30am-7pm, Sa 9am-7pm. $10 min. for credit cards.

Lite
Corona
No Smoking

INSIDE

Nightlife

Boston is a town for pubbers, not clubbers. The city and its environs of Cambridge and Somerville have more than their fair share of quality drinking spots, from dingy neighborhood dives and raucous college pick-up spots to chic martini lounges and quiet Irish pubs. The live music scene in Boston is also impressive, having given birth to such rockin' acts as Aerosmith, Tracy Chapman, the Mighty Mighty Bosstones, and of course prog rock superstars Boston. Nightspots that happen to feature live music are listed in this chapter; establishments where the focus is primarily on live music are in **Entertainment** (p. 156). Those looking for megawatt dance clubs and flashy discos should hop the first plane to New York or London. Boston's few clubs—most of which are on **Lansdowne St.** (near Kenmore Sq.; p. 145) and in the **Theatre District** (p. 151)—are great for a night of dancing to Top-40 hits or indiscriminate house music with throngs of college students, but most clubs' big-city prices and attitude belie rather provincial tastes in music and dancing.

Bars and clubs in Boston are notoriously strict about minimum age requirements. Every establishment below requires **21+** photo ID for entrance, unless indicated otherwise. If you don't present a passport or Massachusetts-issued ID, be prepared to show back-up (like student IDs, credit cards, etc.). Arcane zoning laws require that all nightlife in Boston shut down by **2am**—so there's no after-hours scene, unless you count the exhausted crowds who flood Chinatown's late-night eateries (most stay open until 3-4am; p. 114) after last call. The **T** stops running at 1am, so bring extra cash for the taxi ride home. The MBTA late-night weekend bus service, the "Night Owl" runs F-Sa 12:30-2:30am (see p. 21).

ALLSTON

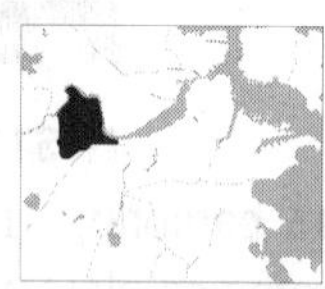

see map p. 313

T: Harvard Ave. (Green-B; "Night Owl" Green Boston College) lets out at Commonwealth Ave. and Harvard Ave. Walk up Harvard Ave. (with McDonald's on your right) to the intersection with Brighton Ave. Bus #66 (p. 21; also a "Night Owl") from Harvard Sq. runs along Brighton Ave. to the intersection with Harvard Ave. ***Discover Allston:*** *p. 5.* ***Food:*** *p. 103.* ***Shopping:*** *p. 172.*

Allston is *the* place for a cheap, sweaty, fun night out. Dreary and deserted by day, the neighborhood comes alive at night, as the area's college students and angst-ridden hipsters flock to countless bars, pubs, and live music venues (there's even a bacchanalian dance club). The crowd is casual, friendly, and almost exclusively college-aged (anyone over 27 years old might feel out of place). On weekends (Th-Sa), expect covers and big crowds—though little waiting in line.

The Kells, 161 Brighton Ave. (☎617-782-9082), at the intersection of Brighton and Harvard Ave. The reason why most people come to Allston. Don't be fooled by the more respectable bar out front (which offers very respectable $1 beers on W nights and open air seating in the summer): The Kells is a massive, Top-40 dance club disguised as an Irish pub. In back is a raging, sweaty disco where everyone has just one thing on their mind: getting it on to the beat of the latest R. Kelly remix. Brutal bouncers here almost always demand back-up ID. 21+. Cover F $5, Sa $7; cover-free Th is just as wild as the weekend. Open daily until 2am.

Our House, 1275 Commonwealth Ave. (☎617-782-3228). Not in the middle of the street, but a 5min. walk (with Bagel Rising on your right) down Comm. Ave. Despite the frat house feel of this maze-like bar and restaurant (couches, dim lights, large-screen TVs, foosball tables), the crowd and atmosphere here are less preppy and more sedate than elsewhere in Allston. Comfy and not too crowded, this house is a great place to stay for the night. 2-for-1 burgers and appetizers M-F 4-7pm. Tu also features rowdy *Simpsons* marathons. Beer and cocktails $3.75. No cover. Open M-F 4pm-2am, Sa-Su noon-2am.

Model Café, 7 N. Beacon St. (☎617-254-9365), at Union Sq. (corner of Brighton Ave. and Cambridge St.); walk 5-6 blocks up Brighton Ave. (with The Kells on your right) from the Harvard Ave./Brighton Ave. intersection. The #66 bus from Harvard Sq. also stops at Union Sq. This dark, diner-like dive draws an alt-rocking crowd from all over the city with its legendary jukebox and cheap, cheap booze (beer $2-3.50, mixed drinks $3-4). No cover. Open daily 4pm-2am. Cash only.

The Avenue Bar & Grill, 1249 Commonwealth Ave. (☎617-782-9508). A popular student hangout, The Avenue proudly boasts some of the most fun-loving (not to mention attractive) bartenders in Allston, who serve cheap mugs ($2) of decent beer from the massive wall of taps that towers over the bar. A great place to chill on weekdays, the narrow bar area becomes so jam-packed on weekends that it's best to down a shot ($3) or 3 and head somewhere less crowded. 21+ after 8pm. No cover. Open daily 11am-1am.

White Horse Tavern, 116 Brighton Ave. (☎617-254-6633). This always buzzing, non-cruisy warehouse of a nightspot is popular with college students, pool sharks, and fun-loving locals alike. Beer $3-3.75. No cover. Open daily 11:30am-2am.

Sunset Grill & Tap, 130 Brighton Ave. (☎617-254-1331). At the Harvard Ave./Brighton Ave. intersection. A malt-head's wet dream: 112 beers on tap, over 400 more in bottles, and a selection that changes every 2 weeks (pints start at $3.50). Though its popularity as a restaurant keeps the bar uncrowded, it also keeps the pub scene from fully developing. Stop in for a bizarre draught with a name you can't pronounce, then move on. If you do decide to tough it out, you may be rewarded with "Midnight Madness" (free buffet with two drink min.) Su-Tu midnight-1am. No cover. Open daily 11:30am-1:30am.

Common Ground Bar & Grill, 85 Harvard Ave. (☎617-783-2071), at the Harvard Ave./Brighton Ave. intersection. A raucous, busy, run-of-the-mill Boston pub, with dark wood, thickly drawn pints ($3.75), lots of regulars, and footie (otherwise known as soccer) on the telly. Nightly music W-Sa. 21+ after 11pm. Cover W $3, Th-Sa $2-5. Open daily noon-2am.

Wonder Bar, 186 Harvard Ave. (☎617-351-2665). You know that really thin girl in a clingy black designer dress talking on her cell phone while simultaneously smoking a cigarette and blowing you off? This is where she hangs out every night. How she found her way here from the Boylston St.

scene (see p. 135) is beyond us. With its unspoken all-black dress code (and overt "no sneakers" policy), sleek bar, nouveau-trendy crowd, and nightly live jazz (9:30pm), this swank and slightly pretentious spot draws patrons who seem out of place in dive-loving Allston. The high life brings high prices: beer $4-5; mixed drinks $5-6. No cover. Open until 2am.

The Kinvara, 34 Harvard Ave. (☎617-783-9400). The epitome of everything cliché about college nightlife: flushed coeds and overeager frat boys cram shoulder-to-shoulder on the beer-slicked floor, swapping spit in rhythm to the 80s-90s rock and R&B blasting on the sound systems. W trivia contest and Th dollar beers are the saving graces. Beer $5. Cover F-Su $3-5. Open daily until 2am.

Beer!

BACK BAY

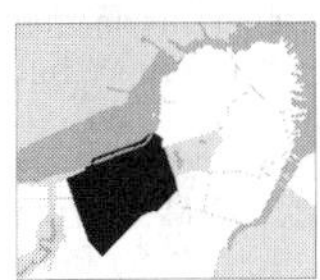

see map p. 314-315

T: Hynes/ICA (Green-B,C,D; all "Night Owl" Green Lines except Green Forest Hills) and the #1 bus from Harvard Sq. (p. 21; also a "Night Owl") both let out onto Newbury St. at Massachusetts Ave. To get to Boylston St. (the heart of the action), walk 1 block south with the Virgin Megastore on your left, then turn left onto Boylston St. ***Discover Back Bay:*** *p. 2.* ***Sights:*** *p. 57.* ***Food:*** *p. 105.* ***Shopping:*** *p. 172.* ***Accommodations:*** *p. 184.*

One of the city's more popular nightlife spots, chic Boylston St. is lined with many noisy, yuppie-filled bars. To survive this ruthless and affluent singles scene, cop an attitude, dress well (the tighter and blacker, the better), and down a few overpriced drinks (beers start at $5, cocktails run $6-10) to steel your resolve.

Overpriced touristy Beer

Bukowski's Tavern, 50 Dalton St. (☎617-437-9999). From Boylston St. turn right onto Dalton St., between Hynes Convention Ctr. and Berklee Performance Ctr. Named after boozer-poet Charles Bukowski, this fantastic dive bar is the perfect antidote to Boylston St., with a casual atmosphere, alternative crowd, hard-rocking music, and a 5-page menu of traditional and eclectic beers from around the world (15 or so on tap and 99+ bottles on the wall; $3-20). Open daily until 2am. Leave your gold card at Barcode (p. 136): Bukowski's is cash only.

Whiskey Park, Park Plaza Hotel, 64 Arlington St. (☎617-542-1483). Walk with traffic down Arlington St. from T: Arlington (Green); it's on the left at the corner of St. James and Arlington St. Owned by Mr. Cindy Crawford (a.k.a. Rande Gerber, the millionaire behind L.A.'s celebrity-frequented Sky Bar), the ultra-hip, too sexy Whiskey Park is the scene to end all scenes. Sensual lighting, scantily-clad waitresses, and luxe faux mink and leather couches are the perfect setting to

Little Joe Cook

in recent news

Kicked to the Curb

Smokers beware, you will have to start keeping those lighters holstered in Boston. As of May 5, 2003, smoking is banned citywide in all public establishments, including bars and restaurants. Despite some public support, local establishments aren't looking forward to enforcing the ban. Many owners are expressing economic concerns linking smoking to private consumption. They argue that by restricting smoking, especially at bars, patrons will spend less time at establishments and not consume as much (say, alcohol) as they would have otherwise.

Across the Charles River, the city of Cambridge tried to capitalize on the Boston smoking ban, since the ban did not include provisions for Cambridge. Restaurants and bars tried to draw patrons away from Boston with a "We're Still Smoking" campaign. That campaign, however, ended on June 9, 2003, when a new piece of legislation was passed extending the smoking ban to Cambridge. With Cambridge smoke-free, the prediction is that soon all of Massachusetts will implement bans, and smokers visiting Boston and environs will have to take their habit curbside before lighting up.

find the "in crowd." Dress like money is no object—and it better not be, given the cost of drinks ($6-14, martinis $9-13). Open daily 4pm-2am.

The Cactus Club, 939 Boylston St. (☎617-236-0200). The always crowded Cactus Club is one of Boylston St.'s most lighthearted and least pretentious options, with a fun-loving, younger crowd, some of the biggest and baddest margaritas in Boston ($6+), and a boisterous, Tex-Mex influenced atmosphere. A great place to meet up with friends to start a Boylston St. pub crawl. In addition to their margaritas, they serve up standard Southwestern food: the bartender recommends the Tequila Sunrise (tequila marinated grilled chicken with citrus and mango salsa; $12). Happy hour ½-price appetizers M-Th 4-7pm. Open May-Sept. daily 11:30am-2am; Oct.-Apr. M-Tu 4pm-2am, W-Su 11:30am-2am.

Whiskey's, 885 Boylston St. (☎617-262-5551). There are no Armani-clad social climbers in this noisy, crowded bar whose crowd is cruisy but casual. They have countless cheap beers on tap ($3.75-4.50) and also serve big (if weak) cocktails ($4.50+). All appetizers drop to $2.50 M-F 4-7pm and Sa-Su noon-6pm; 10¢ chicken wings Su-Th 4-11pm. Open daily 11:30am-2am.

Vox Populi, 755 Boylston St. (☎617-424-8300). Stylishly chic Vox may look exclusive and snobby, but this dim yuppie watering hole with the best patio seating on Boylston St. is surprisingly inviting even if the dress code is strict. Inventive, pricey gourmet American food (served Su-Tu until 10pm, W-Th 11pm, F-Sa 11:30pm) cushions the blow of the popular killer martinis, which rotate on a seasonal menu. Dreamsicle martini $9. Open daily 11:30am-1am.

Barcode, 955 Boylston St. (☎617-421-1818). Unmarked save a UPC code above the door, this dark, super-exclusive bar is the favorite spot of the Newbury St. elite—that snotty, well-dressed mix of fashionistas, international students, and *nouveau riche* yuppies that rule Newbury and Boylston St. If you're looking to pair up with someone, skip this subdued spot and head to the crowd's other favorite hangout, Sonsie. Beer $4-5; martinis $7.50-9. Open daily until 2am.

Daisy Buchanan's, 240 Newbury St. (☎617-247-8516), at Fairfield St. The term "meat market" doesn't begin to do justice to this packed sports bar-*cum*-pick-up spot, featuring a crowd that's younger, rowdier, and friskier than most on Boylston St. Dress is as casual as the sex. Beer $3-5. Open daily until 2am.

Sonsie, 327 Newbury St. (☎617-351-2500). Technically a breezy café-bistro (standard American fare $15-25), Sonsie is better known as one of the premier nighttime hangouts of the slick, international

Newbury St. elite. Upstairs is surprisingly low-key, while the downstairs "Red Room" (open W 8pm-1am, Th-Sa 7pm-1am) is a sweaty make-out lounge bathed in a lurid red glow. Martinis $8-10. Open daily until 1am.

CAMBRIDGE

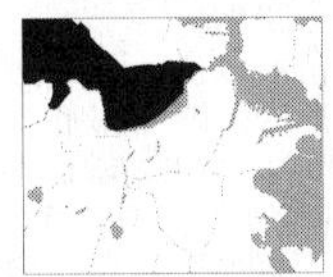

see map p. 320-321

CENTRAL SQ.

T: *Central (Red; "Night Owl" Red Alewife) lets out onto Mass. Ave.* **Discover Cambridge:** p. 7. **Food:** p. 110. **Shopping:** p. 172.

Think of Central Sq. as Harvard Sq. with balls. The bars are dark and dingy; the people are real; and the beer is cheap. One of the best nightlife spots in Boston, Central Sq. features something for everyone, as long as everyone is looking to drink. There's a hot dance club, an enviable live music scene, and countless watering holes of all stripes. Best of all, the neighborhood's scruffy young residents have resisted the ever-encroaching, upwardly-mobile yuppification threatening almost every other nightlife enclave in the city.

BARS & PUBS

The People's Republik, 878-880 Massachusetts Ave. (☎617-491-6969), at the outskirts of Central Sq. (walk up Mass. Ave. with the Starbucks on your right). Cheeky chalkboards outside entice passersby to drop in for a drink ("Drink beer—It's cheaper than gasoline"), and proletarians do indeed choose beer over vodka at this Communist-themed dive. A typical Central Sq. mix of students, alt-rockers, and older locals gather together amidst Cold War-era posters, a hanging bomb, and exit signs labeled "Exile" (to remind you of the crushing capitalist machine awaiting without). Possibly the best bar in Boston for its laid back attitude, cheap beer, competitive darts, and the omnipresent camaraderie that inexplicably forms every night. Beer $2-4; cocktails $4-4.50. No cover. Open Su-W noon-1am, Th-Sa noon-2am. Cash only.

The Field, 20 Prospect St. (☎617-354-7345). From the T, turn right onto Prospect St. (with Starbucks on your right). This buzzing, convivial spot is the best of the neighborhood's many faux Irish pubs. A carefree, young, and very attractive crowd gathers in 3 warmly and eclectically decorated rooms (1 a pool hall-*cum*-TV lounge) to linger for hours over pints ($3.75) and mixed drinks ($4.50). No cover. Open daily until 1am.

The Enormous Room, 567 Massachusetts Ave. (☎617-491-5550), next to Central Kitchen. Unmarked save an outline of an elephant on the window. With no sign or announcement of its opening (one night, it was just *there*), the Enormous Room cultivates an air of exclusivity that belies this neighborhood hangout's casual but fabulous atmosphere. Exposed brick, dim arabesque lighting, comfy floor pillows, and a well-scrubbed mixed crowd make it feel like you're hanging out with your best friends in their cozy West Village loft—of course, this loft has hipster waitresses, expensive Moroccan-influenced *mezze* plates ($14 per person), and a hidden DJ spinning old-school rap and hip-hop. No cover. Open daily until 1am; lines form around 11pm. Cash only.

Cantab Lounge, 738 Massachusetts Ave. (☎617-354-2685). The ultimate Central Sq. dive bar: dim lighting, creaky chairs, sassy barmaids, and lots of local barflies. With their long-time headliner Little Joe Cook, the Cantab can easily boast the best music show in Cambridge—the legendary bluesman is so beloved that the city renamed the area in front of the club "Little Joe Cook Sq." When Cook is not playing, an ever-changing line-up of local roots musicians (folk, blues, etc.) take the stage. The phenomenal and carefree weekly bluegrass jams (no cover; Tu 8pm-1am) are a hidden local secret quickly gaining popularity. Weekly poetry slam W 8pm-1am. Cover $3-8. Open Su-W until 1am, Th-Sa until 2am. Cash only.

The Miracle of Science, 321 Massachusetts Ave. (☎617-868-2866). The ultimate nerd bar, next to the ultimate nerd school (the bar menu is shaped like a periodic table). Sporting friendly patrons, amiable bartenders, and the best cheeseburger in Boston (in a dead heat

Boys' Night Out

You're queer, you're here, and you want a good time. Where to go? You can always head to the **South End's** bars and late-night restaurants (p. 149), all gay-friendly; the sports bar Fritz (p. 151) and divey Eagle (p. 150) are exclusively gay, while Jacque's (p. 150) caters to a transgendered crowd. Boston's other major exclusively gay bar/clubs are **Vapor** (p. 152), **Machine/Ramrod** (p. 146), and stripper-filled **Paradise** (p. 139; in Cambridge's Central Sq.).

Outside of the South End, you'll have to stick to gay nights at breeder clubs—but fear not, these are some of Boston's hottest gay dance parties. Here's a rundown:

Sunday: Every gay man in Boston sashays from Vapor's evening "T-Dance" (p. 152) to the legendary gay night at Avalon (p. 145).

Monday: Axis (p. 146)—complete with fantastic live drag shows—is the place to be.

Thursday: Everyone starts the evening at Club Café/Moonshine (p. 150); most make it across the river to ultra-fun ManRay/Campus (p. 138).

Friday: Raging Machine (p. 146) is busiest on Fridays.

Saturday: The best night to visit any of the gay clubs, but nobody beats Buzz (p. 151).

with sister bar Audubon Circle), Miracle of Science is a fun "all-day" kind of bar. Packed with MIT students and professors most of the time, the bar grooves at night and is about as far from a threatening meat market as you'll find. Transforms into a breakfast joint before noon. Beer $3.75, Cocktails $4.50. Open M-F 7am-1pm. Sa-Su 9am-1pm

The Phoenix Landing, 512 Massachusetts Ave. (☎617-576-6260). It may look like a subdued pub on the outside, but inside this dark, grungy, and cavernous "alternative Irish bar" literally throbs with the sounds of some of the city's best electric grooves (think low-key rave). Local and international DJs spin deep house, trance, trip-hop, and the like (nightly 10pm). The alterna-crowd is not unfriendly, but keeps to itself—you may get funny looks if you decide to join their spontaneous trance-dancing. Beer $3.75; cocktails $4.25. Su and W-Th 19+, M-Tu and F-Sa 21+. Cover $3-5. Open daily until 1am.

Green St. Grill, 280 Green St. (☎617-876-1655; www.greenstreetgrill.com). From the T, walk down Mass. Ave. (with Starbucks on your left), take the 1st right onto Pearl St., then another right onto Green St. Once a rowdy neighborhood dive, the former Charlie's Tap Jazz Club has been transformed into a dark, mellow Latin jazz club with an international flair and a tasty Franco-Caribbean bar menu. Live jazz, Latin, international, and rock Tu-Su; mambo Sa is the best. Music starts around 10pm; check the website for specific acts. No cover. Open Su-W 3pm-1am, Th-Sa 3pm-2am.

The Good Life, 720 Massachusetts Ave. (☎617-868-8800). With branches popping up all over the city, the snazzy, Rat Pack-inspired Good Life is fast becoming the favorite nightspot of young professionals—and this in a neighborhood where yuppies still fear to tread. The high-class atmosphere: smooth jazz, dark wood, plush booths, and 50s-era cocktails (like sidecars and Old Fashioneds) is thoroughly misleading. The crowd here is affluent but completely casual, basking in the glow of the bar's lurid red lighting and enjoying tasty (but fattening) bar food ($6-8). Beer $4-5; cocktails $5-7; martinis $7+. No cover. Open daily 5pm-1am. Branch **Downtown,** 28 Kingston St. (☎617-451-2622). T: Downtown Crossing (Orange/Red). Open daily until 2am.

DANCE CLUBS

ManRay, 21 Brookline St. (☎617-864-0400; www.manrayclub.com). Walk down Mass. Ave. (with Starbucks on your left) and turn right onto Brookline St. Goth Night (W) and Industrial/Fetish F have their own cult followings, but by far the most popular night at ManRay is "Campus" Th, when a mostly college crowd descends in their tiny tees for one of Boston's best gay dance nights. Two sweaty dance floors and a cage fill with topless go-go boys and the sounds of disco and Top-40 gay anthems, while a dyke crowd sticks to the 2 lounge areas and averts their eyes from the TVs showing gay male porn. Voted best dance club in Boston last year, it is one of the least cruisy and sketchy gay nights in the city. Sa mixed gay/straight crowd flocks here for disco/80s. No dress code Th and Sa; strict goth/fetish dress required W and F. W 18+, Th and Sa 19+; F 21+. Open W 9pm-1am, Th-F 9pm-2am, Sa 10pm-2am.

Paradise, 180 Massachusetts Ave. (☎617-494-0700; www.paradisecambridge.com). Cambridge's only full-time gay bar and club, this hidden warehouse features a crowded Top-40 dance floor downstairs and sexy male strippers upstairs. The all-male crowd is cruisy and much older than at neighboring ManRay (mostly late 20s/early 30s). No cover. Open Su-W 7pm-1am, Th-Sa 7pm-2am.

Mix master, cut faster

HARVARD SQ.

T: Harvard (Red; "Night Owl" Red Alewife) lets out at the intersection of Massachusetts Ave., Brattle St., JFK St., and Dunster St.—the same chaotic intersection in the photograph that opens this chapter. ***Discover Cambridge:*** *p. 7.* ***Sights:*** *p. 71.* ***Food:*** *p. 111.* ***Shopping:*** *p. 172.* ***Accommodations:*** *p. 139.*

For such an upwardly mobile place, Harvard Sq. nightlife is surprisingly casual—but unsurprisingly, quite uniformly yuppie-filled. (Head to nearby Central Sq., a 15min. walk or 5min. T ride, for more diverse options.) If you're bar crawling here, keep your head down; for some reason, most Harvard Sq. nightspots are below ground. None of the following charge cover.

The Cellar

Charlie's Kitchen, 10 Eliot St. (☎617-492-9646). From JFK St., turn right onto Eliot St. A smoky, raucous 2 fl. dive bar (done up like a diner from hell) that's indescribably popular with slumming students and tattooed locals. There's nothing in this world better than a few greasy double cheeseburger specials ($5) and a pitcher of Sam Adams ($10-12)—except perhaps Charlie's jukebox, which plays everyone from Björk to Bruce Springsteen. Open daily until 2am.

Casablanca, 40 Brattle St. (☎617-876-0999). Exit the T onto Brattle St. and follow it as it veers right in front of HMV music store; Casablanca is downstairs from the Algiers coffeehouse. The most sophisticated bar in Harvard Sq. is straight out of its namesake movie, which is commemorated by a giant wall mural. Bogie and Bacall would be right at home with the world-weary, well-heeled crowd sipping *de rigueur* martinis ($6-9) in a romantic, vaguely Mediterranean atmosphere. Entrees $18-22. Open Su-Th until 1am, F-Sa until 2am.

Cantab Lounge

Grafton St., 1230 Massachusetts Ave. (☎617-497-0400). This sprawling, upscale pub, decorated in plush leather and dark colors, is packed all hours of the day and night with students and local professionals. Things get cruisier as the night wears on. Pricey drinks (beer $4-5) to match the affluent atmosphere. Open daily until 1am; Irish pub fare ($8-15) until midnight.

Grendel's Den, 89 Winthrop St. (☎617-491-1160). An underground watering hole with the best dinner-and-drinks deal in town: during their eternal dinnertime Happy Hour (daily 5-7:30pm and Su-Th 9-11:30pm), everything on their surprisingly diverse–if rather greasy–menu is ½-price with $3 worth of drinks (that's a beer or 2 soft drinks). Open daily until 1am.

The Cellar, 991 Massachusetts Ave. (☎617-876-2580). Walk 5min. (against traffic) up Mass. Ave. Though populated entirely by pseudo-intellectual thirty-somethings, grad students, and those who wish they were one of the two, this subterranean haunt is a surprisingly nice place to warm up on a cold Cambridge night. With their mammoth-sized mixed drinks ($4-5), how could you resist? Stick to the downstairs; the only time worth venturing upstairs is when they have occasional live music. Beer $4. Open daily until 1am.

Shay's, 58 JFK St. (☎617-864-9161), at South St. Below ground level, this unassuming wine and beer bar is nothing special–except in the summertime, when their sunken outdoor patio (the only outdoor boozing spot in the square) becomes the most coveted patch of sunlight in Cambridge. Beer $4; wine $6. Open daily until 1am.

John Harvard's Brew House, 33 Dunster St. (☎617-868-3585). Bustling, super-sized pub full of fun-loving yuppies downing pints ($4) and pitchers ($11-12) of the low-quality house brews. There's also a hearty and diverse menu (everything from light salads to the "legendary" chicken pot pie; $10-15) of mediocre food to kill the taste. John Harvard's is saved only by M night when students and locals flock to the ½-price appetizers served after 10pm. Full menu Th-Sa until 11pm, Su-W 10pm; pub fare daily until midnight. Open Su until midnight, M-W 1am, Th-Sa 2am.

INMAN SQ.

Discover Cambridge: p. 7. *Food:* p. 113. *Shopping:* p. 172.

B-Side Lounge, 92 Hampshire St. (☎617-354-0766), at Windsor St. From T: Kendall (Red), walk through the Marriott (they're OK with it), turn left onto Broadway, and veer right onto Hampshire St. A laid-back lounge that has quickly become Cambridge's favorite neighborhood hangout, despite its antisocial location in the middle of nowhere. Timeless, quirky, and classy, with diner decor, a soul food menu, strong martinis ($7+), and free hard-boiled eggs at the bar. No cover. Open Su-W until 1am, Th-Sa 2am.

Ryles, 212 Hampshire St. (☎617-876-9330; www.rylesjazz.com). Take the #69 bus from Harvard Sq. (p. 20) up Cambridge St. to Hampshire St. Casual Ryles is a neighborhood jazz and international music joint that's cheaper and more fun-loving than the area's pretentious hotel jazz clubs. The downstairs room hosts live music (usually all ages; nightly 9pm; cover $7-12), while upstairs is all dancing (usually 21+; Th-Sa 9pm; cover $10). Th salsa and merengue (lessons 8:30pm), F Brazilian dance party, Sa all-genre "Ryles Dance Hall." Open Tu-Th until 1am, F-Sa until 2am.

PORTER SQ.

T Porter (Red; "Night Owl" Red Alewife) lets out onto Mass. Ave.

A short walk along Massachusetts Ave. from Harvard Sq., Porter Sq. is essentially the holding tank for everything the preppier square to the south shuns, but still wants to have nearby. From fast food to grocery stores to fun bars, Porter is a place to unwind and indulge in some of life's guilty pleasures.

Cambridge Common, 1667 Massachusetts Ave. (☎617-547-1228). Follow traffic down-Mass. Ave. towards Harvard for 5-7min. This casual neighborhood bar is the best nightspot in Porter. A convivial, low-key vibe, 25 interesting beers on tap (including robust Magic Hat Humble Patience), and the best bar food for miles around (American comfort food $8-12), mean that Cambridge Common is a sweet late-night spot to relax with friends and booze. Open Su-W until 1am, Th-Sa until 2am; dinner served until 1hr. before closing. **Lizard Lounge,** a funky music club, is in the basement of Cambridge Common., see p. 159 for more details.

Toad, 1920 Massachusetts Ave. (☎617-497-4950). From T: Porter (Red), walk straight across Massachusetts Ave. Tiny hole-in-the-wall Toad boasts live music every night and no cover. Artists range from hardcore bluegrass to folky singer songwriters to straight-up bar rock. Generally populated by locals and students, Toad is casual to a fault. Those with Gucci may feel a bit out of place, but most people will feel like they're drinking in a friend's basement. Open daily until 1am.

Temple Bar, 1688 Massachusetts Ave. (☎617-547-5055). Walk from T: Porter (Red), towards Harvard, and the bar is 4-5 blocks up on the right. Temple is the classier option in Porter Sq. Come early and enjoy fondue, and then stay for a few drinks. Especially popular on the low-key nights early in the week (Su-M), when locals try to ease the pain of beginning a new week of work (or classes). Beer $3.50-4; mixed drinks $5.50-6.50. Open daily until 1am; food until 10:30pm.

Communist bars

DOWNTOWN

see map p. 324-325

Discover Downtown: *p. 3.* **Sights:** *p. 80.* **Food:** *p. 141.* **Shopping:** *p. 173.* **Accommodations:** *p. 189.*

Downtown nightlife comes in three forms. The area around **Faneuil Hall & Quincy Market** features mid-sized pubs catering to an after-work crowd of casual professionals and curious tourists. Farther back on the Freedom Trail, the blocks between Tremont and Washington St. (just off Boston Common in **Downtown Crossing**) were recently rechristened the "Ladder District" in an attempt to market the lounge-heavy area as a trendy, exclusive, and upscale nightlife destination. For sports fanatics, there's no shortage of bars surrounding the Fleet Ctr. at **North Station**—each complete with multiple televisions covering everything from Patriot football to Wimbledon tennis.

Wherever you decide to go Downtown, there's only one place to go after 2am. Follow the crowds to nearby **Chinatown** to feed your late-night cravings (and maybe even score an after-hours beer; see p. 115).

Irish bars

DOWNTOWN CROSSING (THE "LADDER DISTRICT")

T: Park St. (Green/Red; "Night Owl" Red Ashmont) lets out onto Tremont St. T: Downtown Crossing (Orange/Red; "Night Owl" Orange Forest Hills) lets out onto Washington St. All streets listed below are in the 1 block-wide area between Tremont and Washington St.

Packed to the gills with industrious shoppers by day, Downtown Crossing was once completely deserted and not entirely safe after

Trendy bars

dark. In the past year, however, the neighborhood has been transforming itself from deserted commercial district into ultra-chic playground for the rich and fashion-forward. Public relations wonks went as far as to rechristen the area the "Ladder District," for the vague ladder shape of the rung-like streets running between Tremont and Washington St. Downtown hasn't completely scrubbed out its unsafe parts, but the area's newly opened lounges and bar/clubs are some of the most creative and unique nightspots in the city, and are quickly becoming the hottest places to see and be seen, so dress to impress.

All establishments below are 21+ and (except for Emily's) do not charge cover.

Mantra/OmBar, 52 Temple Pl. (☎617-542-8111). Temple Pl. runs between Tremont and Washington St.; accessible from T: Temple Pl. (Silver). Seductive. Scandalous. Incomprehensible...and that's just the bathroom (which features 1-way mirrored stalls and ice cubes in the urinals). Few can afford Mantra's of-the-moment, award-winning French-Indian fusion cuisine (entrees $25-40), but all are welcome after dark, when the thumping, global dance-spinning OmBar opens in the bank vault downstairs, while the upstairs becomes the favored haunt of the international elite. Skip their pricey cocktails ($9) and head straight for the surreal "hookah den," a genie bottle-esque hideaway with plush couches, but—in smoke-free Boston—no hookah. Open M-Sa 5:30pm-2am.

Emily's/SW1, 48 Winter St. (☎617-423-3649), enter the building and the club's downstairs. A fun college crowd throngs to this hopping, nearly pitch-black Top-40 dance club that was catapulted to fame as the hangout of choice for the cast of MTV's *Real World: Boston,* who lived across the Common in Beacon Hill. Beer $4. Live acoustic music Tu 8pm; DJ spins F-Sa 9pm. Most nights cover $5; W no cover. Open Tu-Th until midnight, F-Sa until 2am.

The Littlest Bar, 47 Province St. (☎617-523-9766). Turn right off Tremont St. onto Bromfield St., then left again onto Province St. Be prepared to get friendly: this (very) cozy, predominantly local watering hole also draws curious tourists and celebrities (note the "Seamus Heaney peed here" sign) hoping for a spot inside what is, in fact, the littlest bar in Boston (it measures just 16ft. from end to end). Don't even think of mentioning the words "Ladder District" here. Open daily 8:30am-2am. Cash only.

Felt, 533 Washington St. (☎617-350-5555; www.feltboston.com). A space-age 3 fl. chill lounge and billiard hall that tries to draw the trendiest crowd in the city with its appealingly futuristic decor, ultra-picky bouncers, and expensive and exotic drink selection (beer $5, *ouzo* $6-7). Though it doesn't quite live up to the attitude or the hype, Felt is still an enjoyable place to start or end the night. DJ spins F-Sa. Open daily 5pm-2am.

NEAR FANEUIL HALL & QUINCY MARKET

T: Government Ctr. (Blue/Green; all "Night Owl" routes) or T: State (Blue/Orange).

The streets around Boston's tourist central are filled with friendly but nearly identical faux Irish pubs, popular with an after-work crowd who eventually give way to throngs of tourists looking for an "authentic" Boston pub experience. Most places feature live music of so-so quality—meaning most places also feature a cover charge on weekends (usually $5); hang with the after-work crowd on weekdays or arrive early to avoid these. All establishments below are 21+.

Black Rhino 21 Broad St. (☎617-263-0101) and **Aqua,** 120 Water St. (☎617-720-4900). From either T, walk against traffic up State St. and turn right onto Broad St. For Aqua turn onto Water St. Though the two bars are technically connected, they have separate entrances and covers. These two bars epitomize the Financial District scene; voted best after hours bar and best singles scene, area lawyers flock here after work. With Djs spinning Top 40 hits on all 3 fl. Th-Sa and a rooftop bar deck, both bars pack it in; lines form as early as 6pm on F. Black Rhino has a younger clientele than Aqua, but both bars get rowdy when the music starts. Separate covers; each bar F-Sa $5-10. Open M-F 11:30am-2am, Sa 3pm-2am.

Bell in Hand Tavern, 45-55 Union St. (☎617-227-2098). From either T, walk through City Hall Plaza to Congress St., parallel to Union St. Although it's supposedly the oldest tavern in the US (built in 1795), this busy joint remains young at heart. 3 bars, an attractive, fun-loving crowd, nightly live music, and even their own signature beer (courtesy of Sam Adams; $6) make the Bell in Hand incredibly popular with tourists and locals alike. Cover Th-Sa $5. Open daily 11:30am-2am.

Green Dragon Tavern, 11 Marshall St. (☎617-367-0055), at Union St. From either T, walk through City Hall Plaza to Congress St., parallel to Union St. Opposite the Bell in Hand, and identical to it in atmosphere and crowd (although it's much smaller and a bit more sedate). Though the books, candles, and colonial artifacts may lead you to mistake it for a library, this has been a neighborhood bar for a long time: 18th-century patriot rebels used to meet here to plot revolution. Cover F-Sa $5. Beer $2-4.50. Open daily 11:30am-2am.

Purple Shamrock, 1 Union St. (☎617-227-2060; www.irishconnection.com). From either T, walk through City Hall Plaza to Congress St., parallel to Union St. Named after infamously corrupt former mayor James Michael Curley (those are his twin statues in the courtyard outside), this faux pub stands out from its neighbors as the spot most popular with college kids. A young crowd packs it in all nights of the week, especially Karaoke Tu (beginning around 9-10pm). 21+. Cover Th-Sa $5. Open daily until 2am.

The Black Rose, 160 State St. (☎617-742-2286; www.irishconnection.com). T: State (Blue/Orange). Considered by many to be the most "authentically" Irish of the many pseudo-Irish pubs owned by the Glynn Group (who also run the Purple Shamrock and Jose McIntyre's). Live Irish music nightly. 21+ after 9pm. Cover F-Sa after 9pm $5. Open M-F 11:30am-2am, Sa-Su 9am-2am.

The Rack, 24 Clinton St. (☎617-725-1051), across the street from Quincy Market. Racks—pool racks and otherwise—are indeed the focus of the action at Boston's premier meat market, an always crowded spot with 2 bars (including a signature martini bar), 22 pool tables, a flirty patio, and live music nightly. *The* place to find visiting celebrities and local sports figures, not to mention an affluent, yuppie-filled, testosterone-soaked atmosphere of cigars, martinis, and Red Sox chit-chat. Dress to impress; after 5pm: no sneakers, no t-shirts, and no hats. Sa, no jeans. 21+. Open daily 11:30am-2am.

NORTH STATION

Referred to only by city planners as "Bulfinch Triangle", most locals call this area North Station, and if you're looking for a rowdier or more local scene, this is the place. For the most concentrated nightlife, head to the sports bars and Irish pubs—the most authentic outside of Southie—around the Fleet Ctr (T: North Station (Green/Orange.)) Before and after Celtics or Bruins games, the bars are packed with locals looking to celebrate victory or drown their sorrows, depending on the game's outcome. Single women may feel uncomfortable here, especially on less busy nights.

McGann's, 197 Portland St. (☎617-227-4059). Exit T: North Station onto Causeway St. With the Fleet Ctr. on your right, head down Causeway St., and turn left on Portland St. Come prepared to down a pint and get crazy after a Celtics victory. Rotating special on drafts $1.75, otherwise a pint runs $3.25-4.25. Open daily until 2am.

Paddy Burke's, 132 Portland St. (☎617-367-8370), at the intersection of Merrimac and Portland St. Exit T: North Station onto Causeway St., and turn left on Portland St. With 4 fl. of bars and live music Th-Sa, this oddly-shaped building gets raucous quickly. 20oz. beer $4-4.25, domestic $3. Open M-F 11:30am-2am, Sa-Su 12:30pm-2am.

Irish Embassy Pub, 234 Friend St. (☎617-742-6618), downstairs from the Irish Embassy Hostel. Exit T: North Station (Green/Orange onto Causeway St. With the Fleet Ctr. on your right, head down Causeway St. and turn left onto Friend St. Filled with expats, the pub is wildly popular after a victorious showing at the Fleet. Beer around $4. 21+ after 8:30pm. No cover. Open daily 11:30am-2am

Girls' Night Out

You're queer, you're here, and you want to meet other like-minded women. Where to go? The **South End** (see p. 149) is where gay boys (and increasingly more girls) are, and most places there feature a mixed crowd all nights of the week (and did we mention the phenomenal food?).

However, the most popular dyke nightspots are farther out. **Somerville's** late-night cafés (p. 124)—like the queer-owned and -operated Diesel Café (p. 125)—feature a young, friendly crowd. True dyke heaven awaits everywhere in **Jamaica Plain's** bookstores and cafés (p. 6). On Thursdays, the grrrls all trek out to JP's **Midway Café** (p. 144) for the phenomenally popular (and very cruisy) **Dyke Night.** On Fridays, queer women flock to **"Circuit Girl"** at Europa/Buzz (p. 151), undoubtedly Boston's hottest lesbian night. Take a breather on Saturday, because Sunday means **"Trix"** lesbian night at Machine (p. 146).

JAMAICA PLAIN

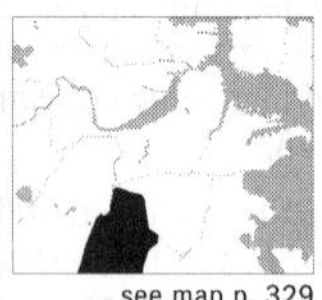

see map p. 329

T: The Orange Line ("Night Owl" Orange Forest Hills) runs through JP 5-6 blocks east of Centre St. and 1 block west of Washington St. ***Discover Jamaica Plain:*** *p. 6.* ***Sights:*** *p. 82.* ***Food:*** *p. 118.* ***Shopping:*** *p. 172.*

JP is no Southie (see p. 148), but Centre St. and the tail end of Washington St. are lined with countless dark, smoky corner pubs. Visitors (especially lone female visitors) may feel slightly out of place at these mostly local watering holes, but most will be warmly welcomed.

Milky Way Lounge & Lanes, 405 Centre St. (☎617-524-3740), downstairs from **Bella Luna** (see p. 119). Turn right out of T: Stony Brook (Orange). A cheeky retro bowling alley with pool tables, gumball machines, and a full dance and bar area that draws both long-time JP residents and area hipsters looking for a lighthearted, fun night out. Live music and dancing most nights: "Mango's Latin Dance Club" (Sa 10pm, lessons 8:30pm; cover women $5, men $10; ladies free before 10:30pm,) features local Latin couples strutting their stuff, but by far the most popular night is the insane and R-rated "Mary Mary's All-Star Karaoke" (Tu 9pm; cover $3). 21+. Covers run up to $10, but average around $6. Open daily 6pm-1am.

Brendan Behan Pub, 378 Centre St. (☎617-522-5386). Turn right out of T: Jackson Sq. (Orange). No TVs, DJs, Irish *seisiun,* or other such gimmicks like you find at most "traditional" Irish pubs in Boston. The Behan (BAY-hen, named after Irish boozer playwright Brendan Behan) is the real McCoy, with dark wood, surly bartenders, a local clientele, and pints so breathtaking they earned a Perfect Pint Award from Guinness. Single women may feel uncomfortable here. Beer $2.50-4. Open daily noon-1am. Cash only.

Midway Café, 3496 Washington St. (☎617-524-9038; www.midwaycafe.com). Turn right out of T: Green St. (Orange), then right again onto Washington St. This grungy neighborhood bar features live music and a laid-back atmosphere most nights. What really brings in the crowds is Kristen Porter's legendary **Dyke Night** (www.dykenight.com; every Th; cover $5), *the* place to meet lesbian women in Boston. Beer $3-4; mixed drinks $3-6. 21+. Cover varies, usually around $5; M night free. Open daily 4pm-2am.

F.J. Doyle & Co., 3484 Washington St. (☎617-524-2345; www.doylescafe.com), at Williams St. Turn right out of T: Green St. (Orange), then turn right again onto Washington St. Founded in 1882, Doyle's is one of the oldest Irish pubs in America and was called the best pub outside Galway, Ireland by the mayor of Galway. With the addition of two dining rooms, the atmosphere has become more family-oriented in recent years, but they still stock over 100 single-malt scotches, plus nearly as much Sam Adams as the brewery (p. 83) up the street. While on the campaign trail, almost every Boston mayorial candidate stops by for a pint and photo op. Past mayors' photos line the walls; Curley is on the left. Entrees $8-13; more importantly, beer $2.75-5.25. Open daily 9am-1am. Cash only.

Triple D's Fine Food and Drink, 435 S. Huntington Ave. (☎617-522-4966), at Centre St. Turn right out of T: Stony Brook (Orange). Lacking the character of other neighborhood bars, Triple D's is a brooding sports bar-*cum*-Irish pub, with 4 TVs and photos of legendary sports figures on the walls. Single women may feel out-of-place. Open M-Sa 8am-1am. Cash only.

KENMORE SQ. AND THE FENWAY

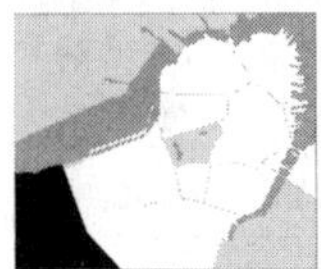

see map p. 330-331

***T:** Kenmore (Green-B,C,D; any Green "Night Owl" except Green Forest Hills). Most nightlife lines Lansdowne St. Take the left exit out of the T (follow signs for Fenway Park) onto Commonwealth Ave., veer left down Brookline Ave. (with the Hotel Buckminster on your right), then take a sharp left onto Lansdowne St. at the Cask & Flagon pub. **Discover Kenmore Sq. & the Fenway:** p. 4. **Sights:** p. 84. **Food:** p. 120. **Shopping:** p. 172. **Accommodations:** p. 190.*

You haven't really experienced Boston until you've downed some pints with rowdy Sox fans before and/or after a Fenway home game. Just follow the crowds to all their favorite pre- and post-game sports bars, all of which are on or around **Yawkey Way,** or **Lansdowne Street.** Also on Lansdowne St. are a slew of identical Euro/house dance clubs that have given Kenmore Sq. and the Fenway the distinction of being Boston's clubbing mecca. Leave torn jeans, T-shirts, and athletic shoes at home, but don't forget your tight black pants, knee-high boots (that work better than any pick-up line), and back-up ID.

Cask & Flagon 62 Brookline Ave. (☎617-536-4840) at the corner of Lansdowne St. The only real place to get a beer before or after a Sox game. The crowd is as rowdy as they come, and win or lose there's always a reason to get tanked (especially with the inexpensive 22oz. beers on special). Bouncers expect back up ID and are famous for not taking any crap from wanna-be fans or wanna-be drinkers. Sport a Sox jersey to fit in or a Yankee jersey to start trouble. Open M-Sa 11:30am-2am, Su 10:30am-9pm.

Avalon, 15 Lansdowne St. (☎617-262-2424; www.avalonboston.com). The biggest, baddest spot on Lansdowne St., Avalon is the flashy, trashy grand dame of Boston's discotheque scene (and the closest Puritan Boston gets to Ibiza), with world-class DJs, amazing light shows, gender-bending cage dancers, and throngs of pretty young things packing the giant dance floor every night. Avalon and Embassy jointly host an older, more upscale crowd for hip-hop Th "International Night" (19+; cover $15); F is Paul Oakenfold's favorite, the extravagant, big-name DJed bang-up "Avaland" (19+; cover $20), which is co-hosted by most of the other Lansdowne St. clubs; Sa is a tamer, Avalon-only version of Avaland, with big DJs (19+; cover $15); and Su (21+; cover $15) is Boston's biggest gay night—*every* gay go-go boy in Boston will be there. Open Th-Su 10pm-2am.

Jake Ivory's, 9 Lansdowne St. (☎617-247-1222; www.jakeivorys.com). Completely different from anything else on the strip, Jake Ivory's is a "dueling piano bar," a crowd-pleasing rock sing-along spot that you'll either love or loathe—but which you have to see to believe. Two very talented pianists face off on stage, while the rowdiest, most drunken revelers on Lansdowne St. shout out requests for everything from the Beatles to Bob Marley. Not for introverts—things get really crazy by the end of the night. 21+. Cover Th $6, F-Sa $8. Open Th-Sa 7:30pm-2am; show starts at 9pm.

Tiki Room, 1 Lansdowne St. (☎617-351-2580; www.tikiroomboston.com). Cross a Polynesian restaurant with a swinging bar, place it in the trance-party capital of Boston, eliminate the sleazy guys and the result is this refreshingly casual night spot. The antidote to the rest of

Lansdowne St., head to the Tiki Room to avoid that guy in the FCUK t-shirt with the badly gelled hair who was eyeing you on the T ride over. He's going to Avalon. Beware, plastic trees and bamboo bars do not come cheap—drinks can get pretty pricey. Open Tu-Sa 5pm-2am.

Machine/Ramrod, 1256 Boylston St. (☎617-266-2986; www.ramrodboston.com, website is 18+). T: Kenmore (Green-B, C, D; all "Night Owl" Green lines except Green Forest Hills). Walk down Brookline Ave. (with Hotel Buckminster on your right), turn left onto Yawkey Way, then right onto Boylston St. The city's only gay leather and fetish club. Frequented mostly by an older Leather and Levis crowd, leather attire is required for the back room. Downstairs from Ramrod is a non-fetish gay dance club and lounge, where DJs usually spin techno hits. 21+. Cover usually $6-8; no cover at Ramrod F-Sa. Ramrod open daily until 2am; Machine M-Tu and F-Sa 10pm-2am.

Sophia's, 1270 Boylston St. (☎617-351-7001; www.sophiasboston.net). Walk down Brookline Ave. (with Hotel Buckminster on your right), turn left onto Yawkey Way, then right onto Boylston St. Far from Lansdowne St. in both distance and style, Sophia's is fast becoming one of Boston's best and most popular nightspots. This fiery Latin dance club features fun dance hits in the basement, hot salsa and merengue bands (starting at 10pm) in the 1st fl. bar-restaurant, a swank lounge with harder Latin house on the 2nd fl., and an amazing rooftop bar-club with a beautiful view of Boston. The crowd is trendy and international, but thankfully unpretentious. Dress smartly and sharply (no jeans or sneakers), and get there before 10:30pm to avoid the interminable lines (each floor also has a separate entrance line). 21+. Cover $10; no cover before 9:30pm W-Th and Sa). Open W-Sa 5pm-2am; food until 11pm.

An Tua Nua, 835 Beacon St. (☎617-262-2121), opposite Audubon Circle (p. 120). Long-forgotten as the site of cozy pub Rí~Rá, An Tua Nua (Gaelic for "The New Beginning") still looks like an Irish pub, but now sounds and feels like a Top-40 dance club. Always crowded and catering mostly to the college pick-up scene. 21+. Cover $3-5. Open daily until 2am.

Bill's Bar, 5½ Lansdowne St. (☎617-421-9678; www.billsbar.com). A rambunctious, divey live music venue and pseudo-dance club with a nightly lineup of DJs and live bands playing all sorts of hard-rocking music, from reggae to hip-hop to punk. Less pretentious than other Lansdowne scenes. M heavy metal gets wild, while Sa cover bands are just a throw-your-head-back-and-sing good time. M-Th 19+, F-Su 21+. Cover around $8. Open daily 9pm-2am.

Axis, 13 Lansdowne St. (☎617-262-2437). Smaller, less popular version of Avalon, with a similar techno beat and identical sweaty college crowd. The exception is their fun-loving and incredibly popular M "static" night, where every other week a mixed gay and straight crowd dances to club tunes until 12:30am, when sassy 6-ft. drag diva Mizery trots out to host her amateur drag revue. M 18+, Th-Sa 19+. Cover M $7, Th $5, F $20, Sa $10. Open M and Th-Sa 10pm-2am. Upstairs from Axis is a new club called **ID.** 19+. Cover $15. Open Th-Sa same hours as Axis.

The Modern/Embassy, 36 Lansdowne St. (☎617-536-2100). If dancing isn't your thing, you shouldn't really be on Lansdowne St., but thankfully there's The Modern, an ultra-cool lounge with an emphasis on kicking back, flirting, seeing, and being seen. If air kisses and pricey wine cocktails ($9-11) aren't your thing, head upstairs to Embassy, a standard but swanky Euro/house dance club with a small balcony for catching your breath (Sa is the best night). 19+. Cover Th-Sa $15; covers entrance to both. Both open Th-Sa 10pm-2am, The Modern also open Tu 10pm-2am (no cover).

Jillian's, 145 Ipswich St. (☎617-437-0300; www.jilliansboston.com), at the end of Lansdowne St. All-ages Jillian's is the slightly cheesy alternative to the serious attitude and indiscriminate house music of the rest of Lansdowne St. The 1st fl. is a video bar and dance area that becomes the Top-40 club **Atlas Dance** F-Sa 10:30pm-2am (21+; cover $7), with jeans-clad college kids dancing in the glow of a giant video wall. The 2nd fl. is a high-tech arcade (don't miss the virtual bowling!), while the 3rd fl. is a pool hall and bar with an older crowd pretending they're at The Rack (p. 143). 18+ after 8pm; Atlas Dance 21+. No cover, except $7 for Atlas Dance F-Sa 10:30pm-2am. Open daily until 2am.

SOMERVILLE

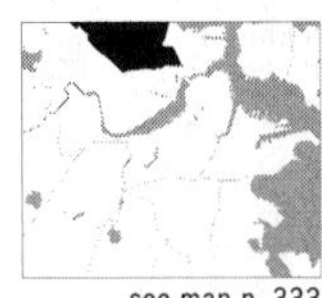

see map p. 333

T: Davis (Red). There is no "Night Owl" in Davis Sq., so you'll need to hop in a taxi. Nightlife is centered on Elm St. Turn right out of the T onto Holland St., which becomes Elm St. ***Discover Somerville:*** *p. 8.* ***Food:*** *p. 124.* ***Shopping:*** *p. 172.*

Though far from Boston proper, Somerville's Davis Sq. is a great place for a chill night out, as the students and other hipsters who live and play in the area demand cheap booze and lots of impressive live music—everything from bluegrass to Irish traditional. The downside: long lines and cover charges on weekends. Don't miss the **Somerville Theatre** (p. 160) in the heart of the square—a second-run/indie movie palace by day and a folk- and rock-music venue by night.

The Burren, 247 Elm St. (☎617-776-6896). The most popular nightspot in Davis, for locals and visitors alike, brings a touch of the Emerald Isle to Boston. The chill, dimly lit front room of this charming Irish pub basks in the glow of enchanting **Irish traditional** in the round (including bagpipes!) M-Sa 10pm-1am, Su 2pm-1am. Live acts of more unreliable quality rock hard in the grungier back room. Traditional Irish breakfast (bangers and mash, cabbage, etc.) Su 10am-3pm. Guinness $4. Cover Th-Sa $3. Open M-Sa 10pm-1am, Su 2pm-1am.

Sligo Pub, 237 Elm St. (☎617-623-9651). There's nothing particularly Irish about this "pub" except its name and the Guinness on tap, but who cares? With its cheap drinks (pints $3; mixed drinks $2.75), eclectic jukebox, and friendly local folk, this crowded hole-in-the-wall has all the good things about a dive bar and none of the bad. Open daily until 1am.

Johnny D's Uptown, 17 Holland St. (☎617-776-2004; www.johnnyds.com). The Boston area's premier blues, funk, and roots music venue, with a consistently great nightly lineup of acts. If you come for dinner, keep your table and enjoy the performance (nightly 9pm) cover-free. Italian bistro-influenced entrees $8-13. 21+. Cover averages $6-10. Open daily until 1am; food served Tu-Sa 4:30-9:30pm.

Joshua Tree Bar & Grill, 256 Elm St. (☎617-623-9910). Trendy yuppies and collegiate yuppies-in-training are packed shoulder-to-shoulder in this sleek, noisy bar that aims for the black-clad cool of Boylston St. (p. 135). Average pseudo-southwestern bar food ($8-12) until 10pm. Beer (26 on tap) $4; mixed drinks $5. Open M-Sa 11:30am-1am, Su 10:30am-1am.

Axis

Knock one back

South Boston

the insider's CITY

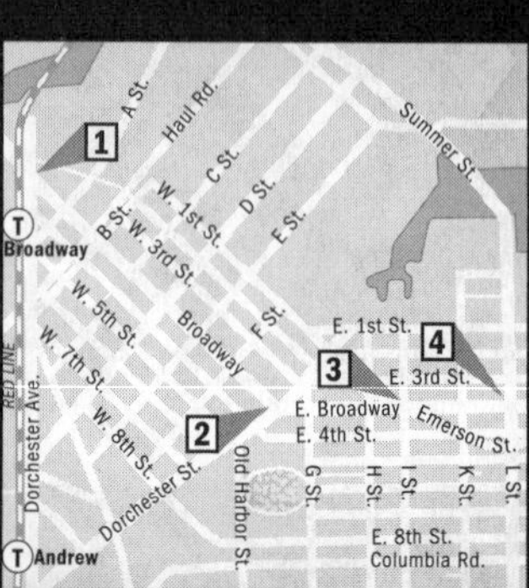

Southie Pub Crawl Competition

If you have a strong liver, a taste for grungy dive bars, and a desire to compete at the highest level of drinking sport, then the Southie Pub Crawl Competition is your Xanadu. Cheap beer, real Boston accents, and people with a hard-core love of the sauce make this an experience that is truly representative of the city (unlike the boring Freedom Trail). The pub crawl is arranged in order and scored in points, 5 points is respectable; most points wins.

Take the T to Broadway and head across the street to **1 The Cornerstone Pub.** Go inside, have a cheap bottled domestic beer (1 point), and play a round of Keno (1 point, 2 if you win), then move on down Broadway.

(continued on next page)

SOUTH BOSTON

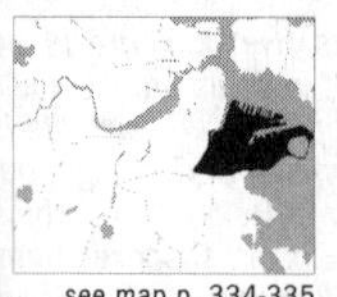
see map p. 334-335

T: *Broadway (Red; "Night Owl" Red Ashmont). Turn right out of the T onto W. Broadway, which becomes E. Broadway at Dorchester St. Alphabetical streets (from A St. to P St.) intersect Broadway.* ***Discover Southie:*** *p. 7.* ***Sights:*** *p. 97.*

South Boston doesn't offer the sleek clubs of Lansdowne St. or the funky student bars of Cambridge, but if you want a real Irish pub (*nothing* like the faux yuppie "pubs" found Downtown), this is the place to go. Although Southie doesn't see too many outsiders, the flashier establishments can really swing (especially later in the week)—and it's an excellent place for taking in a little local color (albeit of a very white hue). The liveliest nightlife is on E. Broadway, near L and M St., though this area is more gentrified than the rest of the neighborhood. Non-white visitors will most likely feel out of place, though they will probably not be unwelcome.

Lucky's, 355 Congress St. (☎617-357-5825). From the South Station T, walk down Summer St. (towards the bridge), take a left on Dorchester Ave., then a right onto Congress St. When you hit 355, walk through the unmarked doorway and pretend that you knew it was a bar and not another warehouse. Follow the sounds of raucous music down the stairs to this effortlessly cool bar. Great live jazz, attractive people, and hip bartenders abound. The patrons here are as cool as the decor, a mix of students, 20-somethings, and old Boston natives. The setting is down-to-earth, so grab a beer and mingle, or if you're not feeling social just sit at the bar and watch the Red Sox. Lucky's is most famous for its Frank Sinatra impersonator, who bears an astonishing (vocal) resemblance to Old Blue Eyes himself. Live Music Tu-Su. Tu R&B, Su Strictly Sinatra (8-10pm). Beer $4+; mixed drinks $6+. Open M-F 11:30am-2am, Sa-Su 6pm-2am; kitchen Th-Sa until midnight.

Playwright Bar & Café, 658 E. Broadway (☎617-269-2537), at K St. Formerly Molly Darcy's, this location has hosted a bar for the last 25 years and the same bartender for almost as long. This incarnation is a simple, stylish bar boasting black tables, dim lighting, and wood paneling. The Playwright also serves dinner, though judging by price and quality, the patrons are here for other reasons. It's a bit pretentious for Southie, though nothing up to Theatre District snobbery standards, and not quite the meat market that some Southie bars have become. Beer $3.50; mixed drinks $4.75. Open M-F 10:30am-1am, Sa-Su 11:30am-1am.

The Black Thorn, 471 W. Broadway (☎617-269-1159), at D St. Don a white T-shirt and warm-up pants to fit in–Southie's softball crowd has made this spot their own. The extensive selection of tropical frozen drinks ($5.50) really fit right in with all the Irish soccer paraphernalia. Su hosts *the* afternoon party of the neighborhood, with live bands "when they show up" and an open mic starting a 4pm. DJs spin Top 40 Th-Sa after 9pm. Beer $2.50; mixed drinks $4. Open M-Sa 8am-1am, Su noon-1am. Cash only.

Tom English's Cottage, 118 Emerson St. (☎617-269-9805), veer right off E. Broadway just past I St. Don't be fooled by the name, Tom's is about as Irish as it gets and is probably the most authentic of the bars in Southie (at least of those with signs). If you've ever wanted to see a living example of the local phrase "Masshole," try chatting it up with the staff. Two pool tables, darts, and low prices prove an inevitable lure for some. Beer and mixed drinks $3. Open M-Sa 8am-1am, Su noon-1am. Cash only.

The Cornerstone Pub, 16 W. Broadway (☎617-268-7158), at the T. The ideal starting point for a Southie pub crawl, the laid-back, blue-collar Cornerstone is at its liveliest F-Sa nights, when various musical acts from blues to rock take the stage. The patrons aren't flashy, but they're an amiable bunch. During the week, a crowd of locals quietly enjoys the Sox or Bruins on TV. Beer from $2.50; mixed drinks $3.75. Open daily 10am-2am.

Boston Beer Garden, 732 E. Broadway (☎617-269-0990; www.bostonbeergarden.com), past L St. Like a horny Irish Phoenix in his late 20s, Boston Beer Garden has risen from the ashes to become Southie's premiere meat market. Just renovated, the Beer Garden offers a bar that is too big for the room, a TV that is too big for the bar, and patrons that are too yuppie for Southie. This is balanced by loud music and the largest selection of beers in the neighborhood. Bottled beers from $3; mixed drinks $4.75. Open M-F 11am-1am, Sa-Su 10am-1am.

SOUTH END

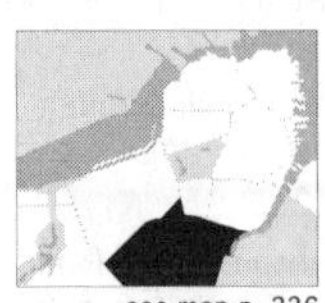

see map p. 336

T: *Back Bay (Orange; "Night Owl" Orange Forest Hills). Washington St. is better served by T: Newton St. (Silver).* ***Discover the South End:*** *p. 4.* ***Sights:*** *p. 92.* ***Food:*** *p. 125.* ***Shopping:*** *p. 172.* ***Accommodations:*** *p. 191.*

There are no dance clubs in the South End, but there are plenty of hopping bars—some exclusively gay, most featuring a

(continued from p. 148)

The next stop is **2 Black Thorne,** order a Guinness, try to use the phrase "wicked pissah" when ordering (1 point). Have a conversation entirely about the Red Sox with a local (1 point, -1 point if "the curse" is mentioned by either of you). Move on, next stop **3 Tom English's Cottage.** Settle in here and play at least one game of pool or darts, loser buys shots of Irish whiskey (1 point if you play a local, 2 points if you beat him). Continue on Broadway to your last stop, **4 Boston Beer Garden;** here's your chance to use the accumulated liquid courage on Southie's hottest residents (1 point per phone number, 2 points per real phone number.)

You're done, but if you have the balls, try one of the unnamed unmarked storefront pubs on your way back to the T (10 points for getting into one, another 10 for not getting your ass kicked.) Now walk back to the T (1 point.), and find your way home (1 point).

Miscellaneous points available at any bar include: 2 points for ordering a frozen drink with a straight face, 5 points for complaining if it doesn't come with an umbrella, 1 point for starting a chugging contest, 5 points for winning a chugging contest, 10 points if more than 5 people that you don't know enter your chugging contest, and 20 points if that chugging contest is undertaken with pina coladas.

gay-friendly mixed crowd. Most nightspots here are expensive but still casual, and several double as fantastic restaurants (which means plenty of seating—rare in this cramped city). With a lion's share of the city's great nightlife and food, the South End is a great place to take a big group for drinks and a late dinner. For other potential nightlife spots, check out the restaurant listings (p. 125).

Delux Café, 100 Chandler St. (☎617-338-5258), at Clarendon St. 1 block south of T: Back Bay (Orange). Funky and eclectic describe the food and atmosphere at this busy dive bar-*cum*-restaurant. Despite such decorative distractions as Elvis shrines, blinking Christmas trees, and continuously looped cartoons on the TV, you'll be transfixed by the inventive international menu (entrees $6-10), which changes every 6 weeks and has featured everything from seafood tamales to jasmine rice crêpes. Diverse crowd–from bike messengers to businessmen. Cocktails $4-5. Open M-Sa 5pm-1am; food until 11:30pm. Cash only.

Wally's Café, 427 Massachusetts Ave. (☎617-424-1408; www.wallyscafe.com), at Columbus Ave.; turn right out of T: Massachusetts Ave. (Orange) or T: Symphony (Green). Established in 1947 and nothing like its trendy South End brethren, Wally's is Boston's longest-standing jazz joint, and it's only improved with age. Jazz lovers from all over cram into this divey, cozy neighborhood joint for nightly live music, from classic jazz to Latin-fusion beats. Beer $3-4; mixed drinks $6. 21+. No cover. Open daily 9pm-2am. Cash only.

Red Fez, 1222 Washington St. (☎617-338-6060). T: Newton St. (Silver). This lively, convivial spot–hung with exotic rugs and intricate arabesque lamps–has quickly become one of the most popular spots in the South End for a light meal and drinks, frequented by everyone from construction workers to affluent local "guppies" (gay yuppies). Forgo the overpriced, average-quality entrees and stick to the delightful *mezze* ($4 each, 3 for $10, 6 for $18), delicately spiced Middle Eastern appetizers (like hummus, olives, lamb, etc.) best enjoyed with a few drinks and a lot of friends late into the night. Open daily M-Sa 4pm-2am, Su 11am-3pm; food M-Sa until 12:30am.

Jacque's, 77-79 Broadway (☎617-426-8902; www.jacquescabaret.com), at Piedmont St. From T: Arlington (Green), walk with traffic down Arlington St. and turn left onto Piedmont St. A South End bar only in temperament (it's technically in the Theatre District), red-drenched Jacque's is home to the most diverse, gender-bending crowd in Boston. Trannies, tourists, and everyone else (gay, straight, or whatever) takes in the boisterous party scene, which features a hard rock venue and luscious **drag shows** every night. 21+. Cover $5-8 after 8pm. Open M-Sa 10am-midnight, Su noon-midnight. Cash only.

Pho Republique, 1415 Washington St. (☎617-262-0005), at Pelham St. T: Newton St. (Silver). This Franco-Vietnamese fusion restaurant, which turns into a hopping bar at night, boasts a lavish cocktail menu ($7-9) and a wide-ranging crowd, from the young and hip to the old and sleazy. Last year, Bostonians voted bartender Pete Cipriani the best bartender in the city. Th "Sting of the Scorpion Bowl" nights mean 2-person Scorpion Bowl cocktails ($16) and an in-house DJ. No cover. Open daily 5:30pm-1am.

The Eagle, 520 Tremont St. (☎617-542-4494), at Dwight St. From the T, walk down Clarendon St. (with the T on your right) to Tremont St. Most every major city in North America and Europe has a smoky, divey gay bar called The Eagle, and Boston is no exception. The South End's version is a little more upscale, and all Boston bars are smoke-free, but the idea is the same. The crowd here is older, exclusively male, and very cruisy, though vibe and dress are casual. The favorite spot of Boston's Leather & Levis contingent, after Ramrod (p. 146). Mixed drinks $3-5. 21+. No cover. Open daily until 2am. Cash only.

Franklin Café, 278 Shawmut Ave. (☎617-350-0010). This tiny, always busy New American restaurant (see p. 127) is also one of the neighborhood's favorite watering holes, with food until last call. Open daily 5pm-2am; food until 1:30am.

Club Café/Moonshine, 209 Columbus Ave. (☎617-536-0966; www.clubcafe.com). From the T, walk down Clarendon St. (with the T on your right) and turn immediately left onto Columbus Ave. The right hallway at the entrance to the gourmet restaurant Club Café leads to the back video lounges **Moonshine** and **Satellite Lounge.** Well-dressed, though still casual, male and female guppies (gay yuppies) sip signature martinis ($8) and mingle amid big-screen TVs playing the latest dance music videos. Things get *wild* on the weekends (Th-Sa), with live DJs in the 2 back lounges and a cabaret show out front. Mixed drinks $4-5. 21+. No cover. Open M-F 11:30am-2am, Sa 2pm-2am, Su 11am-2am.

Fritz, 26 Chandler St. (☎617-482-4428), at Berkeley St. From the T, walk down Clarendon St. (with the T on your right) and turn left onto Chandler St. Beneath the Chandler Inn (see p. 189). The game's always on (and we don't just mean on the TV) at this local gay sports bar, frequented by a friendly neighborhood crowd of all ages and types. Mixed drinks $3-6. 21+. No cover. Open daily noon-2am. Cash only.

Dance!

THEATRE DISTRICT

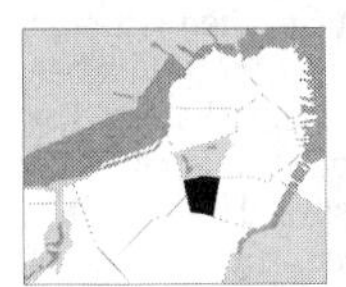

see map p. 322

T: Boylston (Green; all "Night Owl" Green lines) lets out at the corner of Boylston St. and Tremont St. All clubs are within 1-2 blocks. ***Discover the Theatre District:*** *p. 5.*

Aside from the obvious, the Theatre District's main attraction is its chi-chi bars and clubs. Except for the yuppie-filled **Alley,** which seems to have found its way here from nearby Boylston St. (p. 135), most of the sweaty venues in this neighborhood throb with the sounds of indiscriminate international house music and cater to a well-dressed, well-funded international crowd. Those looking for a casual night out should look elsewhere, and those seeking scene-free dancing will have to stick to the popular gay/mixed clubs **Europa/Buzz** and **Vapor.**

After a night out in the Theatre District, follow the crowds to neighboring **Chinatown** and indulge in food you'll either regret or won't remember having eaten the next morning. You might even be able to score an after-hours beer (see p. 115).

Or go to a laid back pub

Pravda 116, 116 Boylston St. (☎617-482-7799). The caviar, red interior, long lines, and 116 brands of vodka may recall Mother Russia, but capitalism reigns supreme at commie-chic Pravda, one of the city's most popular gathering spots for trendy, upwardly-mobile 20-somethings. Full house/Top-40 dance club and 2 bars (1 made of ice!). Dress to impress. 21+. W Latin night, cover $15, F-Sa $10. Bars open W-Sa 5pm-2am; club open W and F-Sa 10pm-2am.

Europa/Buzz, 51 and 67 Stuart St. (Europa ☎617-482-3939, Buzz ☎617-267-8969; www.buzzboston.com or www.circuitgirl.com). 2 fl., a gilded pool room, a martini lounge, and 2 of the best and biggest gay nights in Boston: what more could you want? F is

and hang out with these guys

Buy yourself something nice

Pull up on one of these

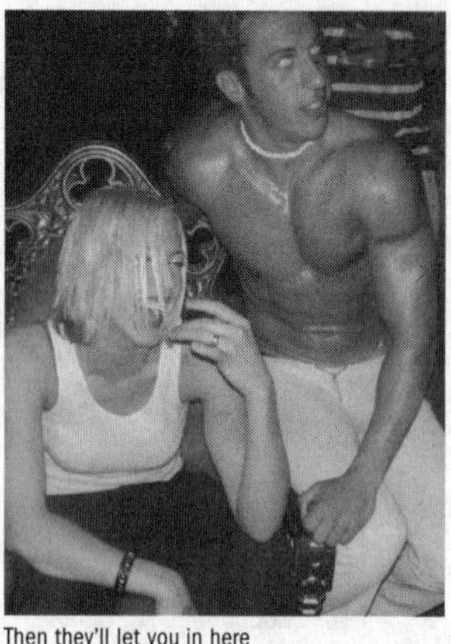
Then they'll let you in here

"Circuit Girl"—the city's hottest lesbian night—while Sa is sweaty, cruisy "Buzz," a gay, mixed-age night. 21+. Cover $10. Open Th-Sa 10pm-2am.

Aria, 246 Tremont St. (☎617-338-7080; wwww.aria-boston.com), at Stuart St. (downstairs from the Wilbur Theatre). The beautiful people come out to play and show off for each other at this upscale, luxe club—complete with velvet rope and red-velvet-and-chandeliers decor. Dress to kill (black is best, and less is more). Tu hip-hop night caters to those more interested in dancing than throwing their money around. Sa Classic 80s funk. 21+ for men, ladies under 21 with valid college ID. Cover Tu and Th-Sa $15, W $5. Open Tu and Th-Sa 11pm-2am, W 10pm-2am.

Venu, 100 Warrenton St. (☎617-338-8061). From the T, walk down Tremont St. (with the Common on your right), turn right onto Stuart St., then left onto Warrenton St. Venu is the latest Theatre District see and be scene (they make even Aria look shabby). The Art Deco interior, black-clad international clientele (fairly young and student-heavy, especially for the Theatre District), and big bouncers with bigger attitudes are the closest Boston gets to Miami. International music Tu and F-Sa. Th hip-hop. Su Brazilian night. 19+. Cover $15. Open Tu and Th-Su 11pm-2am.

Upstairs at Dedo, 69 Church St. (☎617-338-9999), look for the rainbow flag and sign for Mario's until it is replaced with one for Dedo. This newly opened bar and New American-style restaurant offers a refreshingly welcoming and relaxed space to spend a night in the Theater District. A predominantly gay and lesbian clientele, reasonably-priced drinks (beer $3-4; cocktails from $4.50), friendly staff, classy decor, and rousing renditions of show tunes around the baby grand on Tu, Th, F, and Sa nights would make Dedo, the mythical mischievous gargoyle and namesake, proud. Don't miss Tu "Stand and Screen" party. Open daily 5pm-1am.

Vapor/Chaps, 100 Warrenton St. (☎617-422-0862, recording ☎617-695-9500; www.vaporboston.com or www.chapsofboston.com). From the T, walk down Tremont St. (with the Common on your right), turn right onto Stuart St., then left onto Warrenton St. Sleek Vapor is the latest high-tech reincarnation of Chaps, the granddaddy of Boston gay bars (regulars still refer to the bar as "Chaps" during the day). A mostly gay, mostly male crowd dances the night away to the hottest, sweatiest techno. Popular Sa "Vortex/crosswalk" is a wild gender-bending club night. Su "T-Dance" (6-11:30pm) is where the gay go-go boys warm up for Avalon's legendary gay Su (see p. 145). W Latino night; F straight night. No official dress code. 21+ (W 19+). Cover $5-10. Open until 2am. Cash only.

The Alley, 1 Boylston Pl. (☎617-351-7000; www.alleyboston.com), off Boylston St. (next to Pravda 116). This small courtyard/street is lined with several fun-loving clubs that differ only in name and cover charge and cater to a more casual, raucous crowd than most of the swankier Theatre District clubs. The most popular of the Alley clubs are the Mardi Gras-themed **Big Easy** and bubble-filled **Sugar Shack** (they're connected to each other), both rowdy spots popular with local professionals looking to loosen their ties, drink hard, and party harder. In the alley, though technically not part of "the Alley," **La Boom,** 25 Boylston Pl. (☎617-357-6800; www.laboomboston.com), is more typical of the Theatre District scene, with well-dressed patrons slinking along to high-energy dance music in a chic modern setting. 21+, unless noted otherwise. Dress neat casual. Cover $8, La Boom $10; join the free online guest list and party wait-free. Open F-Sa 9pm or 10pm-2am; Sugar Shack also open W-Th 10:30pm-2am.

The Roxy, 279 Tremont St. (☎617-338-7699; www.roxyboston.com). Lavish, spacious 2-fl. ballroom where the look is classy and exclusive and the emphasis is on wild dancing. The lines out the door can attest to its popularity with local students. "Legendary Sa" is house music night (21+, cover $15), expect a long wait after 11pm. Cover $10-15. Open Th-Sa 10pm-2am.

INSIDE

Entertainment & Sports

From the low-brow to the high-brow, the following is a brief compilation of Boston's best entertainment options. For a complete listing of what's going on any given night, check one of the city's entertainment publications (listed on p. 26); the best are the *Phoenix*'s "8 Days A Week" (free at streetside boxes; www.bostonphoenix.com) and the *Globe*'s "Calendar" section (published every Th with the *Globe*; $0.50 at newsstands and streetside boxes; www.boston.com/globe/calendar).

TICKETS

Tickets to shows at Boston's many small venues—both theatrical and musical performances—often sell out, so try to buy them ahead of time from the venue's box office. Purchasing tickets from the box office also means you'll save the $6+ service charge levied by ticketing agencies like **Ticketmaster** (☎617-931-2000; www.ticketmaster.com) or **NEXT Ticketing** (☎617-423-6398, operator ☎617-423-6000; www.nextticketing.com). For discount tickets or tickets to events that are sold out, try the following options:

Bostix (☎617-723-5181; www.artsboston.org). At 11am every day, Bostix (a Ticketmaster outlet) sells ½-price day-of-show tickets to select **theater** shows (cash only); the booths post which shows they offer tickets to each day (also listed on the website). **Faneuil Hall** branch, at T: Government Ctr. (Blue/Green). Open Tu-Sa 10am-6pm, Su 11am-4pm. **Copley Sq.** branch, at Boylston and Dartmouth St., T: Copley Sq. (Green). Open M-Sa 10am-6pm, Su 11am-4pm.

Alternative@rt

Boston theatre may have been slow getting started, due in large part to its puritanical beginnings, but it is now thriving as a hip starting ground for many artists and musicians. As America's largest college town, Boston is a great place to see the best while they are still learning the craft and honing their skills. Boston's edgy collegians often have little to do but stick around after graduation, meaning the city is filled with many unemployed artists and musicians who strive to entertain themselves and their peers. Many spend their days dreaming up wild underground entertainment and performance art.

The king of these underground happenings—and without question the wildest— is the wacky **Kaiju Big Battel** (www.kaiju.com), billed as "the world's only live monster wrestling spectacle event." Taking their cue from B-grade Japanese monster movies like *Godzilla vs. Mothra*, the Kaiju folk dress up in elaborate costumes, and stage matches where space-age villains like Hell Monkey and Evil Dr. Cube wrestle live against beloved heroes like Space Potato and Kung Fu Chicken Noodle, all amidst lavish cityscapes.

Kaiju Big Battel, like most underground entertainment, has no regular schedule. Check the website for the latest times, and to find bios of your favorite characters—so you'll have someone to root for.

Hub Tickets, 240 Tremont St. (☎617-426-8340). **Theatre District.** T: Boylston (Green). The white trailer next to the Wilbur Theater (see p. 162). Since 1975, the best spot for discounted **theater** and **sports** tickets. Open M-F 9am-5pm, Sa 10am-noon.

Ticket City, 128 Harvard Ave. (☎617-787-2370; www.tixboston.com), inside Mr. Music record store. **Allston.** T: Harvard Ave. (Green-B). The best place in the city to find tickets to sold-out **music** (and some sports) events. Open M-F 10:30am-7pm, Sa 10:30am-6pm, Su noon-5pm.

MUSIC

Although Boston is a common stop for touring dance and theater groups, live music is where the city really shines, with rock superstars like Aerosmith and classical masters like the Boston Symphony Orchestra. Most nightlife establishments feature occasional or regular live music (of varying quality), and all the venues below stay busy every night of the week. Nightspots where the focus is less on the music and more on drinking and hanging out are listed in the **Nightlife** chapter (see p. 133).

CLASSICAL MUSIC

ORCHESTRAS

Boston Symphony Orchestra (www.bso.org). The august BSO is one of the most respected and talented symphonies in the world, although it has dropped in quality since its pitch-perfect mid-1900s heyday under the legendary Sergei Koussevitzky (who commissioned Bartók's *Concerto for Orchestra* and founded Tanglewood). Beloved Seiji Ozawa left the BSO's podium amid much fanfare in April 2002 to conduct the equally august Vienna Staatsoper, and the NYC Met's James Levine took over in 2003. The BSO's summer home is at gorgeous Tanglewood (p. 249), in the Berkshires. All other concerts are at Symphony Hall (see below). Season Oct.-Apr.

Boston Pops (www.bso.org). The light-hearted younger sibling of the stuffy BSO performs popular classical works, as well as more mainstream fare like movie soundtracks, musicals, and Americana standards, throughout the year. Dreamy Keith Lockhart is the latest in a line of well-known Pops conductors that has included Arthur Fiedler and *West Side Story* composer Leonard Bernstein. The Pops' winter holiday concerts and spring series (both at Symphony Hall; p. 86) sell out quickly, but during the summer they give free outdoor concerts throughout the Bay State. On Independence Day (4th of July), the Pops form the centerpiece of an amazing free nighttime concert at the Charles River Esplanade's Hatch Shell (p. 69) that includes Tschaikovsky's *1812 Overture* (with real cannons) and a several-ton fireworks display. This concert is incredibly popular, so get to the Hatch Shell early if you want a seat. If you don't get a seat at the Hatch Shell, head to the nearest rooftop; fireworks can be seen from all over the city, and the concert is broadcast live on the radio (WCRB 102.5 FM). Season May-July.

Boston Camerata (☎617-262-2092; www.bostoncamerata.com). A gifted group dedicated to performing early choral and orchestral music, with an emphasis on French Baroque and Renaissance works, all over Boston and the world. Check the website for events. The gorgeous music is almost overshadowed by the camertata's perennial choice of beautiful performance spaces; past venues have included the courtyard of the Gardner Museum (p. 88) and a medieval cloister.

Boston Philharmonic (☎617-236-0999; www.bostonphil.org). Thanks largely to the brilliant work of director Benjamin Zander, the young (24-year-old) Boston Phil is rapidly growing in area musicians' esteem, often surpassing the stodgier BSO's concerts in style, quality, and musicianship. Performs at Jordan Hall and Sanders Theatre (see below). Tickets $17-60.

Handel & Haydn Society (☎617-266-3605; www.handelandhaydn.org). Since giving the American premiere of Handel's monumentally popular *Messiah* in 1818, the orchestra and chorus of the H&H have been performing classical works (not just by Handel or Haydn) on period instruments and in period-appropriate musical style. Their early Dec. performances of Handel's *Messiah* at Symphony Hall sell out quickly. Performances at Symphony Hall, Jordan Hall, and Sanders Theatre. Tickets $21-72.

VENUES

Jordan Hall, 290 Huntington Ave. (☎617-536-2412; www.newenglandconservatory.edu/jordanhall/about.html), at Gainsborough St. **Fenway.** T: Symphony (Green-E) lets out onto Huntington Ave. Run by the prestigious New England Conservatory (NEC), NEC concerts are always free and usually high quality; non-NEC concerts vary in price, but the gilded interior alone is worth the price of admission. Box office (see p) open M-F 10am-6pm, Sa noon-6pm; always opens 90min. before showtime.

Sanders Theatre, Memorial Hall, 45 Quincy St. (☎617-496-2222). **Cambridge (Harvard Sq.).** Exit T: Harvard (Red) onto Mass. Ave. and follow the sidewalk as it curves, with Harvard Yard on your right; it's the cathedral-looking building up ahead (half of which serves as a cafeteria for Harvard freshman). Box office located in the Holyoke Ctr., enter on Mass. Ave., across from Harvard Yard, next to Au Bon Pain. Eclectic line-up of national and international acts (and excruciatingly painful Harvard *a cappella* groups), from throat-singing monks to performance artist Laurie Anderson. Box office open daily noon-6pm.

Symphony Hall, 301 Massachusetts Ave. (☎617-266-1200 or 888-266-1200; www.bso.org), at Huntington Ave. **Fenway.** T: Symphony (Green-E). For more info, see p. 86. This spare but acoustically amazing building is modeled on the most acoustically perfect hall in the world (the Gewandhaus in Leipzig, Germany). **BSO** (season Oct.-Apr.) $25-90. General seating at fascinating open rehearsals (W night and Th morning) $16. Rush tickets (Tu and Th 5pm, F 9am) $8. **Boston Pops** (season May-July) $15-67. Box office open daily 10am-6pm.

ROCK, POP & HIP-HOP

The live music scene in Boston is always hopping, thanks to the insatiable musical appetite of the city's large collegiate population. To satisfy those adoring college-aged fans, most major rock and pop groups make a tour stop in Boston. Megawatt headliners, like Madonna and U2, perform at the city's giant sports arenas and outdoor venues. Many acts—big and small—have also begun performing at major nightclubs (**Avalon**, (see p. 145) is especially popular).

To see acts before they get million-dollar record deals, there are several smaller, high-quality venues for live rock, pop, and hip-hop throughout the city. Cambridge—particularly Central Sq. and Kendall Sq. (p. 7)—is the Boston area's live music mecca; most of the venues in the city are safe bets on any night of the week. Check the "8 Days A Week" section of the *Boston Phoenix* (available free in streetside boxes; see p. 27) for comprehensive listings. Here are the most popular:

Harper's Ferry, 158 Brighton Ave. (☎617-254-9743, box office ☎617-254-7380; www.harpersferryboston.com). **Allston.** One of the Boston area's premier blues and roots rock joints, as well as Bo Diddley's favorite local spot, they have live acts (nightly 9:30pm) in a relaxed atmosphere that feels slightly older and less sleazy than Allston's typical college pick-up scene. Beer and mixed drinks $3-4. Su-M and W-Th 18+, Tu and F-Sa 21+. Cover $3-12. Open daily 1pm-2am. Cash only.

Kendall Café, 233 Cardinal Medeiros Ave. (☎617-661-0993; www.thekendall.com). **Cambridge (Kendall Sq.),** opposite the Kendall Sq. Cinema (p. 166). From T: Kendall (Red), walk through the Marriott (they're OK with it), turn left onto Broadway, and turn right onto Cardinal Medeiros Ave. 3½ blocks later. This small faux-Irish pub—which has hosted the likes of Elvis Costello, Jewel, and Ben Harper—is currently the hottest spot in town to hear up-and-coming local indie rockers. 21+. Cover Tu $3, W-Sa $5. Open daily until 1am.

Lizard Lounge, 1667 Massachusetts Ave. (☎617-547-0759) **Cambridge (Porter Sq.).** Follow traffic down Mass. Ave. towards Harvard for 5-7min., it's in the basement of Cambridge Common. A dark music club with intimate tables and usually excellent music. Genres vary from trip-hop to Jazz, call for the week's line up. Su Poetry Jam. 21+. Cover varies depending on night and performer. Open daily until 2am.

The Middle East, 472-480 Massachusetts Ave. (☎617-864-3278; www.mideastclub.com), at Brookline St. **Cambridge (Central Sq.).** T: Central (Red). The hippest hipsters flock to the grungy, 2-floor Middle East to hear indie rock and hip-hop (both national and international acts). 3-4 rock acts play nightly at the 200-person capacity **Upstairs,** while better-known performers play nightly at the 575-person **Downstairs.** Also popular is the amateur and professional **belly dancing,** held in the tiny "Corner" venue, part of the Middle East restaurant attached to the club (W 10pm; cover $2-3). Upstairs/Downstairs 18+. Cover $9-12, includes admission to both Upstairs and Downstairs. Box office (no service charge) open daily 1-7pm.

Paradise Rock Club, 969 Commonwealth Ave. (☎617-562-8800). **Kenmore Sq.** Visible from T: Pleasant St. (Green-B), which runs along Commonwealth Ave. This smoky, spacious, Asian fetish-themed venue hosts fairly well-known national and international rock acts; past acts have included U2 and Soul Asylum. 18+. Cover $10-20 Tickets available in person or through NEXT ticketing (see p. 155).

T.T. the Bear's Place, 10 Brookline St. (☎617-492-2327; www.ttthebears.com), next to the Middle East. **Cambridge (Central Sq.).** From T: Central (Red), walk 2 blocks down Mass. Ave. (with Starbucks on your left) and turn right onto Brookline St. The Middle East's dingier little sister is Boston's leading venue for (very) alternative rock. A tiny performance area ensures that the crowd gets up close and personal with local and national acts. 18+. Cover $5-8. Box office open Su-M 7pm-midnight, Tu-Sa 6pm-midnight. Cash only.

FOLK

Cambridge was the epicenter of the American folk and acoustic music boom of the 1950-60s, when area university students sought intellectual stimulation outside the ivory tower and began to gather in coffeehouses and bars to enjoy live music with a political edge. Cambridge is still the best place in the area for folk music and is filled nightly with numerous folk acts. Probably the most famous of these is neo-folkie Tracy Chapman, who spent the time between classes at nearby Tufts University playing in the Harvard Sq. T stop, which is still a popular venue for musical hopefuls. Flyers for folk acts are posted everywhere in Boston and Cambridge; check www.wumb.org for complete listings.

Boston is home to the only all-folk radio station in the US (WUMB 91.9 FM), which hosts the popular **Boston Folk Festival** (☎617-287-6911; www.bostonfolkfestival.org) at UMass-Boston every fall. In addition, the largest free folk festival in the US is held in nearby Lowell, MA in July, the **Lowell Folk Festival** (☎978-970-5000; www.lowellfolkfestival.org). For those who miss the festivals, here are some popular folk music venues:

Club Passim, 47 Palmer St. (reservations ☎617-492-7679, info ☎617-492-5300; www.clubpassim.org), at Church St. **Cambridge (Harvard Sq.).** T: Harvard (Red). A 17-year-old Joan Baez premiered here, Dylan played between sets, and countless acoustic

Wang Ctr.

Fenway

The Hasty Pudding

acts from Tom Rush to Suzanne Vega hit this intimate 125-seat venue before making it big. During the performance, listeners can eat at Veggie Planet, the in-house restaurant specializing in creative twists on standard dishes, like pizza. Popular open mic night Tu 7pm. Cover $10-20. Box office open daily 6:30-10pm. Reservations suggested.

Nameless Coffeehouse, 3 Church St. (☎617-864-1630; www.namelesscoffeehouse.org). **Cambridge (Harvard Sq.).** T: Harvard (Red). Tiny, volunteer-run folk venue with monthly performances (usually 1st Sa of the month at 8pm: check website for schedule). Suggested donation $6.

Somerville Theatre, 55 Davis Sq. (☎617-625-4088; www.somervilletheatreonline.com). **Davis Sq.** T: Davis (Red). This second-run and indie movie theater is the area's funkiest venue and occasionally features folk acts. For more on the theatre, see p. 166.

JAZZ & BLUES

Jazz, blues, and other American roots music all have a decent following in Boston, although the city is nowhere near as fanatical about jazz as global hotspots like Chicago or Paris. The following is a list of venues where the focus is mostly on jazz or blues. Much of the live music promised at smaller bars and pubs is also of the jazz persuasion, though usually provided by lesser-known combos:

Green St. Grill, 280 Green St. (☎617-876-1655; www.greenstreetgrill.com). **Cambridge (Central Sq.).** For more info, see p. 138.

Harper's Ferry, 158 Brighton Ave. (☎617-254-9743, box office ☎617-254-7380; www.harpersferryboston.com). **Allston.** For more info, see p. 159.

House of Blues, 96 Winthrop St. (☎617-497-2229; www.hob.com/venues/clubvenues/cambridge/). **Cambridge (Harvard Sq.).** T: Harvard (Red). From JFK St., turn right onto Winthrop St. This cramped restaurant/bar is the original HOB, now a Dan Aykroyd-fronted chain with branches from Orlando to Las Vegas. Nightly lineup of live acts (Su-W 9pm, Th-Sa 10pm) is broader than the name implies, featuring popular blues, funk, and folk acts from all over the world. Su-W 18+, Th-Sa 21+. Tickets $6-35. Box office open daily noon-midnight.

Johnny D's Uptown, 17 Holland St. (☎617-776-2004; www.johnnyds.com). **Davis Sq.** The city's premier roots music venue also features bop and contemporary jazz, hip-hop and funk. For more info, see p. 147.

Regattabar, Charles Hotel, 1 Bennett St., 3rd fl. (info and reservations ☎617-876-7777; www.regattabar.com). **Cambridge (Harvard Sq.).** T: Harvard (Red). From JFK St., turn right on Eliot St.; the Charles is on the left. This swanky jazz venue features big-name acts, like Wynton Marsalis and Norah Jones, on its small stage. Sedate, upscale crowd washes down expensive tidbits with even more expensive martinis. Shows W-Sa (usually 2 per night, 7:30 and 10pm). Tickets $12-20. Dress semi-formal. Reservation line open M-F 10am-5pm, Sa 11am-3pm.

Ryles, 212 Hampshire St. (☎617-876-9330; www.rylesjazz.com). **Cambridge (Inman Sq.).** Mostly really cool jazz in a laid back atmosphere. For more info, see p. 140.

Wally's Café, 427 Massachusetts Ave. (☎617-424-1408; www.wallyscafe.com). **South End.** Mostly underground jazz and funk. No cover. For more info, see p. 150.

Western Front, 343 Western Ave. (☎617-492-7772). **Cambridge (Central Sq.).** T: Central (Red). From the T, take Western Ave. 8 blocks to Putnam Ave.; it's on the right. Boston's premier (OK, only) reggae club still looks the same as it did when it opened during Bob Marley's reefer-tinged heyday, with table-top Pac-Man and vintage cigarette machines. W extreme jazz, Th funk, F-Sa reggae. Cover $3-10. Open Su-Th 5pm-1am, F-Sa 5pm-2am. Cash only.

Wonder Bar, 186 Harvard Ave. (☎617-351-2665). **Allston.** Live jazz nightly. For more info, see p. 134.

THEATER

The Puritans who first settled Boston in 1630 believed that theater was sinful and immoral, so America's first theatrical venue was built illegally in 1792 inside a barn on now-extinct Hawley St. (near Filene's in Downtown Crossing). Then-governor John Hancock (of signature fame) quickly had the place shut down, and it was another 100 years before Boston came to theatrical prominence. In the early 20th century, the Theatre District (p. 5) was the prime try-out spot for productions headed for Broadway. Until the mid-1940s, there were as many as 55 theaters in the city, many also specializing in vaudeville, a style some claim first came to America via Boston. With the birth of film (and later TV) and the rise of New Haven, Connecticut as a more desirable pre-Broadway tryout spot, Boston's theater count has plummeted: there are now roughly 15 theaters in the entire city, most in the tiny **Theatre District,** two blocks south of Boston Common. Almost all of these feature touring productions of Broadway fare, with occasional original works or productions.

Boston's large student population ensures that most every venue offers **rush tickets,** deeply discounted tickets available from the box office 30min.-2hr. before showtime (sometimes rush tickets are only available to students). **Bostix** (p. 155) also has ½-price tickets on the day of the show. Most of the theatres below offer ticketing through **Telecharge** (☎800-447-7400). For more info on Boston's theatre scene, check out the Broadway in Boston pamphlets (available at most theaters) or look online at www.broadwayinboston.com.

DRAMATIC THEATER

Boston is nowhere near New York or London as far as dramatic theater goes, but drama fans will find some world and area premieres and a few imaginative reinventions of theater classics.

American Repertory Theatre (ART), Loeb Drama Ctr., 64 Brattle St. (☎617-547-8300; www.amrep.org). **Cambridge (Harvard Sq.).** Exit T: Harvard (Red) onto Church St. and follow Church St. until it hits Brattle St.; the ART is a block down on the left. Named the third best regional theatre in the country by *Time* Magazine, the A.R.T showcases a varied selection of classics and avant garde American premieres in repertory on the 556-seat Mainstage, designed so all seats have a great view. Student rush tickets (30min. before curtain) $12. Box office open M 10am-5pm, Tu-Sa 10am-7pm, Su noon-5pm (tickets $5-10 cheaper when ordered online); closes 30min. before showtime. **Experimental Black Box Theater** within the Loeb Drama Center is home to (usually free) experimental productions by Harvard students.

Boston Center for the Arts, 539 Tremont St. (☎617-426-2787; www.bcaonline.org). **South End.** From T: Back Bay (Orange), walk down Dartmouth St. (with the T on your right) to Tremont St. A contemporary arts compound of theaters and visual art exhibition

the local story

Life's a Drag....

Since 1795, the Hasty Pudding has thrilled audiences with their all-male student-written camp comedy show and annual Man and Woman of the Year awards. Daniel Hoyos is a 3-year veteran of the show and an Associate Editor for Let's Go: India and Nepal.

LG: What's the best part about performing?

A: Certainly not the high heels! I think what I love most is hearing the cheers from the audience at the end of the night. Sometimes they just can't get enough, and we have three curtain calls. An average day with the Pudding can consist of anything from riding mopeds across a tropical island to partying with Hollywood celebrities. Even so, the roar of the crowd, more than anything else, is really what makes it worth it.

LG: What celebrities have you had the chance to meet?

A: Every year in February we throw a big parade for the Woman of the Year; past winners included Drew Barrymore, Anjelica Huston, and Sarah Jessica Parker, all of whom I got to meet. They were all so happy to be getting the award.

spaces. Artwork and performances by the queer-oriented **Theater Offensive** and the Irish/Celtic **Sugan Theater Company.** Also houses the Mills Gallery (p. 93) and the large historic cyclorama, built in 1884 to display a single painting. No student rush. Box office open Tu-Sa noon-5pm or until 15min. after showtime; closed Tu June-Aug.

Huntington Theater Company, 264 Huntington Ave. (☎617-266-0800; www.bu.edu/huntington). **Fenway.** T: Symphony (Green-E), opposite Symphony Hall. The 890-seat Huntington is Boston's premier venue for professional dramatic theater and also home to professional-quality Boston University productions. Tickets \$36-65 (special last row balcony seats \$14); \$5 discount for students and seniors (65+). ½-price rush (2hr. before showtime) for those under 25. Box office open Tu 11am-5pm, W-Th 11am-7:30pm, F 11am-8pm, Sa noon-8pm, Su noon-7pm.

Lyric Stage Company of Boston, 140 Clarendon St. (☎617-437-7172; www.lyricstage.com), on the 2nd fl. of the YWCA building. **Back Bay.** Exit onto Boylston St. from T: Copley (Green-E) and follow traffic to Clarendon St.; turn right and follow Clarendon St. until it hits Stuart St. Home to Boston's lesser-known Broadway and off-Broadway musical productions. \$17 student rush tickets 30min. before showtime, based on availability. Tickets \$20-40; \$5 senior discount. Box office open Su and Tu noon-5pm, W-Sa noon-7pm.

Wilbur Theater, 246 Tremont St. (☎617-423-4008). **Theatre District.** From T: Boylston St. (Green), head down Tremont St. (away from Boston Common) 2 blocks; it's on the left, past Stuart St. Intimate 1200-seat theater featuring mostly hit Broadway dramas and comedies; in spring of 2004, they will show the Irish-set drama *The Plough and the Stars* and Shakespeare's *As You Like It*. Student and senior (65+) rush tickets \$25 (Su-F 1hr. before showtime), availability permitting. Box office open M-Sa 10am-6pm or until 30min. after showtime, Su noon-30min. after showtime; closed Su on non-performance days.

MUSICAL THEATER

Few of the professional musical productions in Boston are original; most are touring productions of Broadway/West End favorites. Venues include:

Charles Playhouse, 74 Warrenton St. (Blue Man: ticketing ☎617-931-2787, student rush info ☎617-426-6912; www.blueman.com. Shear Madness: ☎617-426-5225; www.shearmadness.com). **Theatre District.** From T: Boylston (Green), follow traffic down Tremont St., turn right onto Stuart St., then left on Warrenton St.; it's on the right. Boston's longest-running and most popular productions—Blue Man Group and Shear Madness—both play at the Charles. Tickets are a bit of a splurge, but both shows are worth it. Blue Man dazzles as interactive performance art, and Shear Madness (a wacky whodunit set in a hair salon) premiered in Boston in 1980 and is the longest-running play in America. Volunteer to usher for Blue Man Group and see the show for free. Tickets for Blue Man $43-53; Shear Madness $34.

Colonial Theater, 106 Boylston St. (☎617-426-9366). **Theatre District.** From T: Boylston (Green), turn right on Boylston St.; it's on the left. Boston's oldest continuously operating theater is now home to touring Broadway and off-Broadway productions. In their 2003-2004 season (Sept.-June), they will host *Movin' Out, Urinetown, Def Poetry Jam,* and *Oklahoma*. Student and senior (65+) rush tickets $25 (1hr. before showtime), availability permitting. Box office open M-Sa 10am-6pm, Su noon-30min. after showtime; closed Su on non-performance days.

Cutler Majestic Theatre, 219 Tremont St. (☎617-824-8000; www.maj.org). **Theatre District.** From T: Boylston (Green), follow traffic down Tremont St.; it's down 1 block on the right. Affiliated with Emerson College and built in 1903 as an opera-only venue, the 976-seat Majestic now books modern dance, musicals, and plays (most shows stay for a week). Reopened in Sept. 2003 after renovations, the Majestic's 100th season will feature productions of *Don Giovanni*, *La Traviatti*, *Rigoletto*, and Gershwin's *Porgy and Bess*.

Stuart Street Playhouse, 200 Stuart St. (☎617-426-4499; www.stuartstreetplayhouse.com). **Theatre District.** From T: Boylston (Green), turn right onto Boylston St., then left onto Charles St. South; it's just past the Radisson Hotel Boston at Charles St. South and Stuart St. Features just 1 off-Broadway musical for a year or so at a time (next year's feature will be the dynamic *Stomp*) at more affordable rates than its Broadway-peddling Theatre District neighbors. Tickets $45-55. Show W-Th 8pm, F 7 and 10pm, Sa 5 and 9pm, Su 3 and 7pm; in fall and winter, additional Tu performance. Box office open M-Tu 10am-6pm, W-Sa 10am-showtime, Su noon-showtime.

Wang Center, 270 Tremont St. (☎617-482-9393, toll-free ticketing ☎800-447-7400; www.wangcenter.org). **Theatre District.** From T: Boylston (Green), head down Tremont St. (away from Boston Common) 2 blocks. Boston's largest theater (seating 3700), the huge Wang Ctr. is the favorite tour stop of most blockbuster musicals that pass through the city. Broadway hits also run at the Wang-owned **Shubert Theater,** 265 Tremont St., across the street, though it has less than half the seating capacity. Both box offices open M-Sa 10am-6pm; Shubert box office closed in summer.

(continued from p. 162)

Just before Valentine's Day, we have our roast for Man of the Year. A roast means that we get to stand around making jokes about the celeb's career. You should have seen Bruce Willis squirm.

LG: Describe a typical show.

A: The show changes a little bit every night, but the all-male cast of around 14-or-so Harvard students is consistent. I think the audience is always a little surprised by the crazy characters and costumes, not to mention that around half of the cast are playing women! In past years people have played camels, clouds, vampires, and abominable snowmen. Watching the show is a bit like watching a cartoon; everything is that exaggerated. There's always a few lively group dance numbers, usually including a love song or two, and we always make fun of Yale, Harvard Business School, and Wellesley any chance we get.

LG: What is Hasty Pudding tour like?

A: For the past 30 years we've taken the show to New York and Bermuda for spring break. On Bermuda, we always ride mopeds around the island, and when we have a show, we ride them around the theater during intermission. On the whole the tour is great, though wearing that much make-up when you're sunburned from a day at the beach is not a good idea, I can tell you that.

HPT Performs Feb.-Mar. at 12 Holyoke Street, in Cambridge. (☎617-495-5205; www.hastypudding.org)

DANCE

There are no major dance-only venues in Boston, but the area's companies and choreographers are not deterred by the lack of an exclusive performance space. The **Boston Dance Alliance** (☎617-482-4588; www.bostondancealliance.org) has a comprehensive listing of all the dance events going on around town. Every July, the nearby Berkshires (p. 248) play host to the oldest contemporary dance festival in the country, **Jacob's Pillow** (☎413-637-1322; www.jacobspillow.org), held in Lee, MA.

Boston Ballet (☎617-695-6950; www.bostonballet.org). Most famous for their 6-week run of Tschaikovsky's Christmastime favorite *The Nutcracker,* which draws over 140,000 people (making it the most widely attended ballet performance in the world), the ballet dances 4-5 shows Oct.-May. All performances at the Wang Ctr. (p. 163).

Nicola Hawkins Dance Co. (☎617-666-5372; www.nicolahawkinsdanceco.org). Contemporary dance troupe that performs throughout Boston.

Prometheus Dance (☎617-576-5336; www.prometheusdance.org). Founded in 1986 Prometheus is an ensemble of ten dancers that performs all over the city and the world.

CINEMA

Theaters showing American blockbuster movies are very easy to find: just check any newspaper (see p. 26 for a list) or **Fandango** (☎800-555-8355; www.fandango.com) for showtimes and directions. The following are second-run, indie, and revival theaters:

Bombay Cinemas @ Regent Theater, 7 Medford St., Arlington (info line ☎978-671-9212, box office ☎781-646-4849), at Massachusetts Ave. North of **Cambridge.** From T: Harvard (Red), take bus #77 (20min., daily every 10-20min.) up Mass. Ave. to Medford St. On weekdays, the Regent screens the latest Bollywood hits—India's patently gaudy, preposterously plotted 3-4hr. movie musicals (in Hindi, with occasional English subtitles). Rowdy all-immigrant crowds perfectly recreate the unique and unforgettable experience of a trip to the movies in the subcontinent.

Boston Public Library, 700 Boylston St. (☎617-536-5400; www.bpl.org). T: Copley (Green-E). Screens diverse weekly film series, everything from classics to recent releases, both American and foreign. The best part: they're always free! For more info, see p. 61.

Brattle Theater, 40 Brattle St. (recorded info ☎617-876-6837, box office ☎617-876-6838; www.brattlefilm.org). **Cambridge (Harvard Sq.).** The theater in the full-page photo at the start of this chapter. Exit T: Harvard (Red) onto Brattle St. and follow it as it veers right in front of HMV music store; the theater is downstairs from the Algiers coffeehouse. A Cambridge institution, the Brattle's amazing lineup of films is an always interesting array of well-chosen cult flicks, art-house darlings, and American and foreign classics (they *love* Hitchcock). Annual traditions like the Harvard exam week Bogart blitz or the Valentine's Day *Casablanca* showing are almost as popular as the W series "Recent Raves" (critically acclaimed films from the past year). 2 films daily (usually 2-for-1 double billings). Admission $8, seniors (65+) and children $5; matinees (M-F before 5pm) $7.

Coolidge Corner Moviehouse, 290 Harvard St. (recorded info ☎617-734-2500, box office ☎617-734-2501; www.coolidge.org). **Brookline.** T: Coolidge Corner (Green-C) lets out at Beacon and Harvard St.; it's immediately up Harvard St. on the left. Although Brookline residents protested its opening in 1931, the Art Deco Coolidge Corner is now one of the jewels of the city, complete with recently unveiled period-appropriate marquee. 2 theaters show 2-3 recent indie or limited-release films; schedules change every 1-3 months. So-bad-they're-good cult classics screen at "Midnight Movies" (F-Sa midnight). Admission $8.50, seniors (62+) and children $5.50; matinees (M-Sa before 4pm, Su before 2pm) $6.

Harvard Film Archive, 24 Quincy St. (☎617-495-4700; www.harvardfilmarchive.org). **Cambridge (Harvard Sq.).** Exit T: Harvard (Red) onto Mass. Ave., walk against traffic, and turn left on Quincy St.; it's in the basement of the Carpenter Ctr. (p. 75). The Archive screens one of the country's most intelligently chosen and consistently fantastic lineups of popular and lesser-known foreign films. Films are organized in weekly and biweekly series devoted to specific directors, themes, or movements (their fetish for the French New Wave is remarkable), with special premieres and director visits interspersed throughout. Admission $7, students and seniors $5.

Kendall Square Cinema, 1 Kendall Sq. (☎617-494-9800; www.landmarktheatres.com). **Cambridge (Kendall Sq.).** From T: Kendall/MIT (Red), walk through the Marriott (they're OK with it), turn left onto Broadway, and after you cross the railroad tracks, turn right into the 1 Kendall Sq. complex; the movie theater is out back. Alternatively, you can catch "The Wave" shuttle bus (free, every 20min. until 6pm) from T: Kendall (Red). Boston's classiest "art-house"–large screens, validated parking, spacious seating, and a gourmet concession stand–shows current, well-known foreign and independent films as well as mainstream films in limited release. Admission $9, 1st show of the day $6.50.

Museum of Fine Arts, 465 Huntington Ave. (☎617-267-9300, box office ☎617-369-3306; www.mfa.org/film or tickets.mfa.org). **Fenway.** T: Museum (Green-E). The MFA Film Program specializes in series about groups typically underrepresented in film (like the Gay & Lesbian and Jewish Film Festivals). For more info, see p. 86.

Somerville Theatre, 55 Davis Sq. (☎617-625-5700; www.somervilletheatreonline.com). **Davis Sq.** T: Davis (Red). Revives popular indie flicks and shows limited-run mainstream films weeks or months after they open. Also a great live music venue, with mostly alt-rock and folk acts. Film admission $6. Live music tickets generally $20-25.

SPORTS

Recently voted the best sports city in the country, Boston takes sports seriously—and with good reason. The franchises headquartered in the city are some of the most storied in America. If you really want to understand the city's obsession with sports—or if you just want to see Larry Bird's giant shoes—visit the **Sports Museum of New England,** on the 5th and 6th fl. of the Fleet Ctr. For more info, see p. 81.

MAJOR SPORTS TEAMS

BASEBALL

The Sox play at Fenway Park. ***Fenway Ticket Office,*** *4 Yawkey Way (☎617-482-4769; www.redsox.com). From T: Kenmore (Green-B,C,D), walk down Brookline Ave. (with Hotel Buckminster on your right), then turn left onto Yawkey Way.* *For info on getting affordable tickets, see p. 167.*

The Boston American League Base Ball Club, popularly known as the Pilgrims, formed in 1901 (they donned red hosiery in 1907, hence "Red Sox"). Led by famed pitcher **Cy Young,** the team won the first World Series ever played in 1903. The Sox acquired pitcher **George Herman "Babe" Ruth** after the 1914 campaign, and the move portended great success, as the squad won championships in 1915, 1916, and 1918.

Owner Harry Frazee gutted the core of his baseball superpower in 1920, selling most of his best players, including Ruth, to the previously meager New York Yankees. Frazee wanted the money to finance the musical "No No Nanette," which (like the Red Sox) quickly bombed. The move still rankles loyalists and sports writers, some of whom continue to bemoan the so-called "Curse of the Bambino." (For more on the curse, see p. 169.) Curse or no, Boston hasn't captured a World Series since Ruth left, while the Yankees have snagged 26 titles.

Tom Yawkey bought the team in 1934 and purchased the best players from cash-starved, Depression-era rivals, but couldn't assemble enough talent to unseat New York's juggernaut. Larger-than-life **Ted Williams** arrived in Boston in 1939, but his epic exploits—including being the last player to hit .400 in a season (in 1941)—led to just one World Series appearance in 1946. The team returned to baseball's highest stage in 1967, when Carl Yastrzemski's squad realized an "Impossible Dream" season. A 1986 team sparked by the meteoric rise of **Roger "The Rocket" Clemens** came within one strike of World Series victory, but after a ground ball slipped through the legs of injured first-baseman Bill Buckner (his name still inspires profane utterances in New England), devastation followed.

Recently, with a luminous squad that includes Cy Young-esque hurler **Pedro Martinez,** extraordinaire shortstop **Nomar Garciaparra,** and batting champ **Manny Ramirez,** the Sox continue to inspire hope at the season's outset and snuff it out by autumn, as chants of "Yankees Suck" transform from arrogant insistence to irrelevant truth. Fans seem resigned to a melancholic mix of self-pity and self-loathing, following their team with a desperate passion in anticipation of its annual failures—except for this year, the year they're going to turn it around.

BASKETBALL

The Celtics play at Downtown's ***Fleet Ctr.*** *(☎617-624-1750; www.nba.com/celtics). T: North Station (Green/Orange). Tickets also available from Ticketmaster (☎617-931-2000; www.ticketmaster.com).*

The **Boston Celtics** have one hell of a legacy. With 28 Hall of Famers and 16 World Championships, they are the winningest team in NBA history. Big names like Bill Russell, John Havlicek, Tom Heinsohn, Bob Cousy, Kevin McHale, Robert Parish, and legendary **Larry Bird** once graced the parquet floor of Boston Garden with some of the greatest moments in sports history.

Unfortunately, a legacy can't put on a uniform and win games. The Celtics suffered horribly throughout the 90s, as their aging superstars retired without replacement. The same era saw the deaths of promising young prospects **Len Bias** and **Reggie Lewis,** leading some Bostonians to believe that a curse similar to the Red Sox's had also been cast on their beloved Celtics. The last years have seen a turnaround as the Celtics made it into the playoffs under the leadership of flashy **Antione Walker** and all-star **Paul Pierce**, but the team is still rebuilding.

FOOTBALL

The Pats play at ***Gillette Stadium,*** *1 Patriot Pl., Foxborough, MA (☎800-543-1776; www.patriots.com), 30 mi. south of Boston. Tickets also available from Ticketmaster (☎617-931-2000; www.ticketmaster.com).*

The **New England Patriots** were for many years the laughingstock of the NFL (National Football League). They were trounced 46-10 in their first appearance in the Super Bowl in 1985 and garnered little attention, save when sports-starved Bostonians turned to them during other franchises' off-seasons.

All that changed in the early 90s, when the Pats acquired head coach **Bill Parcells,** quarterback **Drew Bledsoe,** and new owner **Robert Kraft.**

the hidden deal

Take Me Out to the Ball Game

Tiny Fenway Park sells out almost every night, and tickets—the most expensive in baseball—remain hard to come by. Illegal scalpers hawk billets at up to a 500% markup (though after games start, prices plummet).

But fear not: there *are* options for snagging choice seats without parting with a first-born. On game days, the box office sells obstructed-view ($25) and standing-room ($18) tickets beginning at 9am (line up early, especially for Sox-Yankees games). Obstructed-view seats in the infield are excellent, while standing-room seats offer tremendous views of the field. Risktakers can wait until just a few hours before a game, hoping the team will release the superb seats held for players' friends and families.

When purchasing, know that seat quality varies widely. Avoid sections 1-7, unless you enjoy craning your neck for 3hr. The best "cheap" seats are sections 32-36 (32-33 are down the left-field line in the outfield grandstand, close enough to touch the famed Green Monster). Bleacher sections 34-36 have perfect sightlines for watching pitches, but most fans emerge lobster-red from three hours of direct sunlight.

The team started winning games and getting noticed, as no-nonsense Parcells transformed them into disciplined and successful gridiron giants. Unfortunately, Parcells didn't lead the Patriots to Super Bowl victory as he was expected to; the closest they got was a loss to the Green Bay Packers in Super Bowl XXXI.

In 2000, another Bill—**Bill Belichick**—assumed the position of head coach. He led the team to victory in 2002's Super Bowl XXXVI, considered by many to be one of the best Super Bowl games in history. The Pats breathtaking path to victory began with Belichick's decision to replace starter QB Bledsoe (since traded to the Buffalo Bills) with newbie **Tom Brady** (now the Pats' starter) and ended with a last-minute field goal—known fittingly as "the kick heard 'round the world"—by stud **Adam Vinatieri.**

HOCKEY

The Bruins play at the ***Fleet Ctr.*** *(☎617-624-1750; www.bostonbruins.com). T: North Station (Green/Orange). Tickets available from Ticketmaster (☎617-931-2000; www.ticketmaster.com).*

Like the Celtics and Red Sox, the **Boston Bruins** have a long and winning history, having attracted national attention since 1924, thanks to the such legends as Bobby Orr, Phil Esposito, Cam Neely, and Ray Bourque. Not as strong as they once were—though their rivalry with the Montréal Canadiens (a.k.a. the "Habs") remains quite healthy—the Bruins fight every year to return a sixth Stanley Cup to Boston.

The Fleet Ctr. is also the stage for the city's fiercest college hockey rivalry. Every February, Boston University, Boston College, Harvard, and Northeastern vie for the coveted silver beanpot at the annual **Beanpot Hockey Tournament.**

ANNUAL SPORTS EVENTS

BOSTON MARATHON

26.2 mi. ***Start:*** *Hopkinton, MA (to the west of Boston).* ***Finish:*** *Copley Sq., in Back Bay.* ***Contact:*** *www.bostonmarathon.org.* ***Date:*** *Patriot's Day; the 3rd M in Apr.* *(see p. 38).*

The world's most respected foot race attracts hundreds of thousands of runners and spectators from all over the world. The best places to watch the race are: "Heartbreak Hill" (between mile 20 and 21), in Newton; near T: Cleveland Circle (Green-C), where many colleges hold tailgates; under the Citgo sign at Kenmore Sq. (the mile-to-go marker), where you'll be joined by Sox fans leaving the traditional morning game at Fenway Park; and at the finish line at Copley Sq.

HEAD OF THE CHARLES

Contact: *www.hocr.org.*

Since 1965, this fall regatta—the world's largest two-day crew race (occurring every year in mid-Oct.)—has drawn preppies past and present to the Charles River. The 3-mile row begins at the BU boathouse and heats up beneath Harvard's Weeks Footbridge and Anderson Bridge (the best places to view the race; see p. 54), where oars often crash and sometimes boats even collide. The boats that escape the bridge entanglements finish the race a mile beyond the Harvard boathouses.

Can science reverse the curse?

In a city marked by unsurety, clinging strongly to its history while pushing the bounds of futuristic technological innovation, one thing remains constant: the almost-winning ways of the Boston Red Sox. The baseball club has not won a World Championship since 1918, and despite the scientific sensibilities of this highly educated locale, most Bostonians are content to place the blame squarely upon the local superstition known as "the Curse of the Bambino". Not happy to have paid $660 million for a cursed team, the new Red Sox ownership and management regime is attempting to appeal to the scientific community and apply statistical methods to exorcise the demons. The Sox are quickly finding that the application of social science to real life will invariably wage an arduous battle with human behavior and its many curses.

The Curse of the Bambino was born in 1920 when Red Sox owner Harry Frazee sold oft-nicknamed George Herman "Babe" Ruth—a.k.a. "the Bambino," perhaps the greatest player in baseball history—to the New York Yankees for $100,000 and a $300,000 loan to help pay the lease on Fenway Park. Allegedly, Frazee was short on cash from financing the awful musical *No, No Nanette*. The Sox finished last in the American League nine times in the 13 seasons after the Babe was sold and did not win the pennant again until 1946. They have been to the World Series four times since the sale and have lost each time in seven games.

Enter John Henry, leader of a new ownership group that purchased the Sox in 2002. Already their public-relations savvy and ballpark improvements seem to have assuaged some of Boston's bitterness, at least superficially. While the bleacher creeps may seem tamer than many can ever recall, it will take a lot more than smiles, handshakes, and fresher hot dogs to convince Boston that the curse is gone. The Sox need a championship.

Looking for inspiration, John Henry and team president Larry Lucchino lit upon the rise of the Oakland Athletics. One of the poorest teams in baseball, the "A"s became one of baseball's best teams—and certainly its most efficient—by throwing out "the book" and treating the business of baseball as a social science. Following their lead, Henry and Lucchino have built a management team to implement these more objective decision-making methods and depart from the traditional ways, which are based on conventional wisdom propagated by lifetime "baseball men." They hired Bill James, baseball's preeminent statistician and the founding father of contemporary baseball's intelligentsia class—most of whom remain on the game's periphery—to churn out objective research known as "sabermetrics." James brought with him the supermodern stat "Win Share," which measures the total sum of a player's contribution to his team, comparing players across positions, teams, and eras. The Sox are now making decisions and trades based upon his input and are hoping it will be enough to overcome an 83 year old curse.

While the fans seem willing to give it a try, some in the media and certainly those lodged in the old baseball establishment are resistant and fearful. Boston Globe writer Dan Shaughnessy has been one of the most ardent critics of the new school in Boston, throwing out some choice lines calling the approach too drastic and claiming that "It wouldn't be quite as ridiculous if the Sox hadn't spent the off-season telling us how they were going to reinvent baseball."

It comes as no surprise, then, that Shaughnessy also penned the Red Sox classic *The Curse of the Bambino*, the definitive volume chronicling the legacy of the Babe's trade. Even in "no bull" Boston, a well-respected journalist, while advancing a business that seeks objectivity against human odds, can find comfort in the preternatural when logic seems to fail. Time will tell whether superstition will succumb to science in Red Sox Nation—so keep your fingers crossed, but don't hold your breath.

***Derek Glanz** is currently earning a Ph.D. in political science and is a freelance writer covering the St. Louis Cardinals.*

FAMOUS
PILE OF
Clothing $1

INSIDE

Shopping

Most visitors don't come to Boston to shop; tastes are rather conservative, and chain superstores are quickly taking over every corner of the city. However, for new and used **books** (p. 173), Boston's selection is unmatched in North America if not the world. The city's large college population also ensures that Boston has a great selection of new and used **music** stores (p. 179). Below we list the gamut of bookstores and music stores, as well as the best, most intriguing, or cheapest of everything else.

Below is a brief breakdown of the best neighborhoods to (literally) spend an afternoon shopping, followed by a run-down of individual stores, organized by their wares.

BY NEIGHBORHOOD

BACK BAY. The exception to the Puritan rule, chic **Newbury St.** (p. 58) is an 8-block parade of everything fashionable, form-fitting, and fabulous. The high-priced attitude belies what is actually quite a diverse lineup of shops, with everything from sleek luxury boutiques to musty used bookstores. Most major European and American fashion houses have stores here, and in case of rain, there's always a high-priced mall nearby (p. 179).

BEACON HILL. The antique shops and conservative clothing shops lining Beacon Hill's **Charles St.** have long been popular with Cambridge blue-bloods, as the exorbitant price-tags everywhere demonstrate. In the past few years, Charles St. has also become *the* place to find high-end, yuppie-friendly boutiques and houseware stores. It's as pricey and high-quality as the Back Bay's Newbury St., but not as trendy or trashy.

ALLSTON

Flyrabbit (178)	Gifts

BACK BAY

Anthropologie (175)	Clothing
Ave. Victor Hugo Bookshop (174)	Books
CD Spins (180)	Music
Copley Place Mall (179)	Malls
Dorothy's Boutique (175)	Clothing
FAO Schwartz (178)	Gifts
fresh (178)	Gifts
Louis Boston (176)	Clothing
Matsu (176)	Clothing
Newbury Comics (180)	Music
Planet Aid (176)	Clothing
Satellite Records (180)	Music
Second Time Around (176)	Clothing
Shops at Prudential Ctr. (179)	Malls
Smash City Records (180)	Music
Spenser's Mystery Book Shop (174)	Books
Star Market (130)	Grocers
Sweet 'n' Nasty (177)	Erotica
Trader Joe's (131)	Grocers
Trident Booksellers (174)	Books
Urban Outfitters (179)	Gifts

BEACON HILL

Black Ink (178)	Gifts
Koo de Kir (179)	Gifts
Savenor's Market (130)	Grocers

BROOKLINE

Brookline Booksmith (173)	Books
Grand Opening! (177)	Erotica
Star Market (130)	Grocers
Trader Joe's (131)	Grocers

CAMBRIDGE

Black Ink (178)	Gifts
Buckaroo's Mercantile (178)	Gifts
CambridgeSide Galleria (179)	Malls
Cardullo's (129)	Grocers
CD Spins (180)	Music
Cheapo Records (180)	Music
Curious George (174)	Books
The Garment District (176)	Clothing
Globe Corner Bookstore (173)	Books
Grolier Poetry Bookshop (173)	Books
Harvard Book Store (174)	Books
Harvest Co-op Supermarket (129)	Grocers
Hootenanny (175)	Clothing
Hubba Hubba (177)	Erotica
Newbury Comics (180)	Music

CAMBRIDGE (CONTINUED)

Nuggets (180)	Music
Oona's (176)	Clothing
Planet Aid (176)	Clothing
Planet Records (180)	Music
Revolution Books (174)	Books
Schoenhof's Foreign Books (174)	Books
Second Time Around (176)	Clothing
Shalimar Indian (130)	Grocers
Skippy White's (180)	Music
Star Market (130)	Grocers
Trader Joe's (131)	Grocers
Urban Outfitters (179)	Gifts
WordsWorth Books (174)	Books
Yoshinoya (131)	Grocers

CHINATOWN

Chung Wah Hong Co. (129)	Grocers

DOWNTOWN

Brattle Book Shop (174)	Books
CD Spins (180)	Music
DSW (175)	Clothing
Filene's Basement (175)	Clothing
H&M (175)	Clothing
Hip Zepi USA (175)	Clothing
Marquis (177)	Erotica
Newbury Comics (180)	Music

KENMORE SQ. & THE FENWAY

Nuggets (180)	Music
Star Market (130)	Grocers
Sugardaddy's Smokeshop (179)	Gifts

JAMAICA PLAIN

Boomerangs (176)	Clothing
CD Spins (180)	Music
Harvest Co-op Supermarket (129)	Grocers

NORTH END

Salumeria Italiana (129)	Grocers

SOMERVILLE

Black & Blues (175)	Clothing
CD Spins (180)	Music
Disc Diggers (180)	Music
Kate's Mystery Bookstore (173)	Books

SOUTH END

Lucy Parsons Center (174)	Books
Market (176)	Clothing
Eros (177)	Erotica
Syrian Grocery (130)	Grocers
We Think the World of You (174)	Books

CAMBRIDGE. Boston's "Left Bank" features an appropriately Boho array of cheap and eclectic stores of all stripes. While much of **Harvard Sq.** now resembles a giant corporate-sponsored mall, the area still boasts the world's highest density of **bookstores** per square mi. Harvard and **Central Sq.** will satisfy all your music store cravings, from the "wicked cheap" to the international and esoteric.

CHINATOWN. The shopping selection in Chinatown is as chaotic as its streets, with countless Asian grocers, fabric stores (left over from the neighborhood's industrial days), and gift and toy shops selling the hottest imported trinkets, from Hello Kitty pencil sharpeners to Coco Lee Karaoke DVDs.

DOWNTOWN. Crowded **Downtown Crossing** is a giant open-air mall filled mostly with chains and generic stores and one of the cheapest shopping districts in the city. Famed as the site of the legendary Filene's Basement (p. 175), where designer clothes are criminally cheap, Downtown Crossing also has the highest concentration of shoe stores (of all price ranges) in Boston.

NORTH END. The *salumerias* (corner stores) and bakeries of the Italian-American North End are sure to satisfy your sweet tooth or your craving for pasta, while the open-air **Haymarket** (p. 81) is the best spot in Boston for super-cheap, super-fresh fruits and vegetables.

SOUTH END. Where the boys are. Busy Tremont St., the heart of the increasingly trendy (and increasingly gentrified) South End, is home to countless high-end men's boutiques and upscale home furnishing shops, with an unusual mix of alternative bookstores in the surrounding area.

BY TYPE

BOOKS

With over 20 bookstores in just a few blocks, the best place to find new and used books in Boston (if not the world) is Cambridge's **Harvard Sq.** (p. 7).

NEW

Brookline Booksmith, 279 Harvard St. (☎617-566-6660; www.brooklinebooksmith.com). **Brookline.** T: Coolidge Corner (Green-C) lets out onto Harvard St. The #66 bus from Harvard Sq. also passes by it. A phenomenal independent bookstore with a huge fiction collection and an impressive array of film and art books. Their frequent author signings and readings ($2) are the best in Boston. Open Su 10am-8pm, M-F 8:30am-11pm, Sa 9am-11pm.

Curious George Goes to WordsWorth, 1 JFK St. (☎617-498-0062), at the corner of Mass. Ave. and JFK St. **Cambridge (Harvard Sq.),** houses discounted children's books and adorable book-related gifts and toys, including countless trinkets featuring their namesake monkey. Open Su 10am-8pm, M-Sa 9am-9pm.

Globe Corner Bookstore, 28 Church St. (☎617-497-6277; www.globecorner.com). **Cambridge (Harvard Sq.).** T: Harvard (Red). A huge selection of travel guides and travel-related books and maps, from glossy coffee table books ($25 and up) to detailed hiking and bicycling maps. Open Su 11am-6pm, M-Sa 9:30am-9pm.

Grolier Poetry Bookshop, 6 Plympton St. (☎617-547-4648). **Cambridge (Harvard Sq.).** Walk against traffic up Mass. Ave. from T: Harvard (Red) and turn right onto Plympton St. One of the only bookstores in the Western Hemisphere devoted solely to poetry, with over 15,000 volumes of verse (all guarded by a poetically bedraggled pooch). Owner Louisa Solano is as much a Cambridge legend as her little shop. Open M-Sa noon-6:30pm.

Kate's Mystery Bookstore, 2211 Massachusetts Ave. (☎617-491-2660; www.katesmysterybooks.com), near Davis Sq. **Somerville.** Turn right out T: Davis (Red) onto Holland St., right again onto Day St., walk 3 blocks, and turn left onto Mass. Ave. This supposedly haunted red mansion houses a comprehensive mystery-only bookstore of over 10,000 new and used titles, many of them autographed. The biggest mystery may be the store's incomprehensible organization system; ask the very knowledgeable staff for help or recommendations. Open Su noon-5pm, M-F noon-7pm, Sa 11am-5pm.

Lucy Parsons Center, 549 Columbus Ave. (☎617-267-6272). **South End.** Turn right out of T: Mass. Ave. (Orange), then left onto Columbus Ave. Stocks books, newspapers, pamphlets, and posters on social issues, including environmentalism, feminism, queer rights, and immigration. **Free internet access,** and a helpful staff make this a must for the net-savvy Marxist. Open Su noon-6pm, M-Sa noon-9pm.

Revolution Books, 1156 Massachusetts Ave. (☎617-492-5443). **Cambridge (Harvard Sq.).** T: Harvard (Red). The People's bookstore, non-profit and dedicated to bringing about a Communist America, they stock independently published pamphlets, manifestos, and historical/theoretical books on a range of radical and revolutionary topics. "People's Republic of Cambridge" T-shirt $14-16. Open Su 2-6pm, Tu-F 2-8pm, Sa noon-8pm.

Schoenhof's Foreign Books, 76a Mt. Auburn St. (☎617-547-8855). **Cambridge (Harvard Sq.).** Exit T: Harvard (Red) onto Dunster St. and turn left onto Mt. Auburn St. The largest assortment of foreign language novels and poems, reference books, and language instruction tapes in North America. Their emphasis is on Classical and Western European languages and all their attendant dialects, like Quebecois French and Brazilian Portuguese. Titles get expensive (novels up to $30), but where else can you find *Harry Potter* in Korean *and* Bulgarian? Open M-W and F-Sa 10am-6pm, Th 10am-8pm.

Spenser's Mystery Book Shop, 223 Newbury St. (☎617-262-0880). **Back Bay.** T: Hynes/ICA (Green-B,C,D). Named for Robert B. Parker's fictional Boston-based sleuth (of "For Hire" fame), Spenser's stocks a comprehensive selection of new, used, and rare mysteries. Nice collection of used paperbacks (10 for $5) in the back of the store. Open M-W, F-Sa 10:30am-5:30pm; Th 11:30am-6:30pm.

Trident Booksellers and Café, 338 Newbury St. (☎617-267-8688). **Back Bay.** T: Hynes/ICA (Green-B,C,D). This relaxed bookstore and café is the perfect place to escape the flashy pretension of Newbury St. Relax with a cup of coffee or tea ($1.50-2) or even a smoothie ($4) while reading an obscure magazine or book. New and used titles with an emphasis on health, philosophy, and religion, plus the best selection of magazines in the city—everything from the Russian-language *GQ* to *Vogue Bambini* (Italian Vogue for children). Open daily 9am-midnight.

We Think the World of You, 540 Tremont St. (☎ 617-574-5000). **South End.** Exit T: Back Bay (Orange) onto Clarendon St. and walk 4 blocks south (with the T on your right) to Tremont St. A friendly gay bookstore (catering almost exclusively to gay men) with a diverse collection of fiction by and about queers, lots of gay community info, and a beefy selection of soft- and hard-core gay porn all sharing the same racks. Open Su 11:30am-5:30pm, M-F 10am-7pm, Sa 10am-6:30pm.

WordsWorth Books, 30 Brattle St. (☎617-354-5201; www.wordsworth.com), at Mt. Auburn St. **Cambridge (Harvard Sq.).** T: Harvard (Red). 2 fl. independent bookseller where "every book is discounted, every day" (discount after tax 10-15%). Open Su 10am-10:15pm, M-Sa 9am-11:15pm.

USED

Ave. Victor Hugo Bookshop, 353 Newbury St. (☎617-266-7746). **Back Bay.** T: Hynes/ICA (Green-B,C,D). Though in the process of settling into a smaller location, Victor Hugo is still everything a good used bookstore should be: mysterious, musty, and dark. Miles of floor-to-ceiling bookshelves (75,000 titles) are guarded by a feisty black cat and the most knowledgeable staff in Boston. Mostly discounted hardcovers, with an emphasis on science-fiction and mystery. Open Su noon-8pm, M-Sa 10am-8pm.

Brattle Book Shop, 9 West St. (☎617-542-0210; www.brattlebookshop.com). **Downtown.** From T: Park St. (Green/Red), follow traffic down Park St. and turn left onto West St. The best used bookstore in Boston (after the Harvard Book Store; see below) and the country's oldest continuously operating bookstore (since 1825), they have 3 fl. and a parking lot full of books from every genre (all ½ off the cover price or cheaper), with non-fiction upstairs and an amazing literary fiction collection downstairs. Rare book room on the 3rd fl. is great for out-of-print or hard-to-find titles. Open M-Sa 9am-5:30pm.

Harvard Book Store, 1256 Massachusetts Ave. (☎617-661-1515; www.harvard.com). **Cambridge (Harvard Sq.).** T: Harvard (Red). Named Bookseller of the Year by prestigious *Publisher's Weekly* in 2002, HBS is the best bookstore in Boston, thanks largely to the discerning tastes of its intelligent and accommodating staff. Even more impressive than the upstairs' new books selection is the basement's vast holdings of recent and classic works of fiction and non-fiction, most at 40-50% off the cover price. If you're browsing for more than just books, HBS becomes a notorious Cantabrigian pick-up spot on weekend evenings. Open Su 10am-10pm, M-Th 9am-11pm, F-Sa 9am-midnight.

CLOTHING & SHOES

Fashionistas flock to the Back Bay's chic **Newbury St.**, where fashionable boutiques line the street from one end to the other. For thriftier shoppers, several funky (but quality) used clothing stores are scattered throughout **Cambridge.**

NEW

Anthropologie, 799 Boylston St. (☎617-262-0545). **Back Bay.** T: Copley (Green). Bohemian cool meets too-cute French countryside chic in this yuppier, grown-up version of Urban Outfitters (p. 179). Floral dresses, chunky jewelry, and cheery vintage housewares (the highlight of the store) range in price from the sublime (furnishings $10-20, upstairs clearance tops and bottoms $30-40) to the ridiculous (skirts $100-200). Open Su noon-6pm, M-F 10am-8pm, Sa 10am-8pm.

Black & Blues, 89 Holland St. (☎617-628-0046). **Somerville (Davis Sq.).** T: Davis (Red). What sets this Newbury St.-like men's and women's clothing boutique apart is its unique and affordable selection of vintage Levi's ($20-30). Open Su noon-6pm, M-F 11am-7pm, Sa 10am-6pm.

Dorothy's Boutique, 190 Massachusetts Ave. (☎617-262-9255). **Back Bay.** T: Hynes/ICA (Green-B,C,D). Credit Dorothy's with tarting up Boston's drag scene with their 200+ theatrical wigs ($12+), flamboyant high heels ($14), and glittery accessories—everything from feather boas to fake eyelashes. Open M-Sa 9:30am-6:30pm, Su noon-5pm.

DSW: Designer Shoe Warehouse, 385 Washington St. (☎617-556-0052). **Downtown.** Exit T: Downtown crossing onto Washington St. and ascend the escalator to this shoe-lovers' Nirvana. A 2 fl., no-frills warehouse filled with over 43,000 styles of men's and women's designer shoes, all organized by style (for ease of comparison shopping) and all discounted 30-70% (pairs average $40-50). Their widest variety is in mid-range brands like Skechers, Chinese Laundry, and Liz Claiborne. Great selection of hard-to-find sizes. Open Su 11am-6pm, M-Sa 10am-8pm.

Filene's Basement, 426 Washington St. (☎617-542-2011; www.filenesbasement.com). **Downtown.** T: Downtown Crossing (Orange/Red). A bargain hunter's dream and a neat freak's worst nightmare, Filene's Basement is where the overstocked and unsold designer and brand-name goods from department stores end up—only to be turned around and sold to you at a deep, deep discount (10-75% off). Fights have broken out here (especially during the wedding dress and prom dress sales), but it's worth braving the open dressing rooms and crowds of ruthless clotheshorses for that $50 wool coat (originally $300) or a few dirt-cheap Ralph Lauren dress shirts (under $30). Open Su 11am-7pm, M-F 9:30am-8pm, Sa 9am-8pm.

H&M, 350 Washington St. (☎617-482-7081; www.hm.com). **Downtown.** Exit T: Downtown Crossing onto Washington St. Sweden's biggest export since ABBA, H&M peddles disposable clothing for the fashion- and budget-conscious—tight ripped jeans, racy clubwear, flirty Boho skirts, and more, all at shockingly low prices. Style and quality won't last longer than a weekend on Lansdowne St. (where everyone's wearing H&M these days), but at less than $25 for pants and $15 for dress shirts and tops, can you really complain? Open Su 11am-7pm, M-Sa 10am-8pm.

Hip Zepi USA, 31 Winter St. (☎617-350-6174 or 617-350-6870). **Downtown.** T: Park St. (Green/Red). This local legend is a requisite stop for those in search of the latest hip-hop fashions and accessories. All the fabulous brand names you'd expect—FUBU, Varcity, Phat Farm, M+FG—at equally fabulous prices (shirts $20-30; jeans $50). Prices drop 50-70% during frequent sales. Open Su 11am-7pm, M-Sa 9am-8pm.

Hootenanny, 36 JFK St. (☎617-864-6623), at Mt. Auburn St., inside "The Garage" mall. **Cambridge (Harvard Sq.).** Intimidating clothing sold by an unintimidating and ultra-friendly staff. Rock, goth, and punk fashion for the discerning (or vinyl-loving) urban hipster, from cutesy baby tees to hardcore fetishwear. Skip the snooze-worthy men's section and head straight for the novelty accessories (doll-head belt $20) or the eternal clearance racks (tops $15-20; pants $30-40). Where else will you find glittering lycra spiderweb pants for $20? Open Su noon-6pm, M-Th 11am-8pm, F-Sa 11am-9pm.

Louis Boston, 234 Berkeley St. (☎800-225-5135), at Newbury St. **Back Bay.** T: Hynes/ICA (Green-B,C,D), or walk against traffic up Arlington St. from T: Arlington (Green) and turn left onto Newbury St. A Newbury St. legend. Forget Aria (p. 152), Barcode (p. 136), or Whiskey Park (p. 135): *this* is Boston's most fashion-forward, cooler-than-thou spot. It's housed in a former museum, which explains its look-but-don't-touch feel. With frequently rotating designers only the trendiest, most exorbitantly priced designers are on display in this 4-story palace of Eurotrash couture, with gourmet restaurant, in-house DJ and salon, and requisite surly staff. Jan. and June clearance. T-shirts from $75. Open M-Tu and F-Sa 10am-6pm, W-Th 10am-7pm.

Market, 558 Tremont St. (☎617-338-4500), opposite Clarendon St. **South End.** Exit T: Back Bay (Orange) onto Clarendon St. and walk 4 blocks south (with the T on your right) to Tremont St. The pretty boys are flocking to this hot new high-end boutique, which features the tightest, trendiest clothes (from tiny tees to fitted car coats) by popular designers—Gaultier, Dolce & Gabbana, Paul Frank, and Versace. Sale racks throughout the store bring prices down from the stratosphere. Open Su 11am-6pm, M-Th 11am-7pm, F-Sa 11am-8pm.

Matsu, 259 Newbury St. (☎617-266-9707). **Back Bay.** T: Hynes/ICA (Green-B,C,D). This Zen-influenced, offbeat boutique promises "life-enriching clothes and gifts," and its unique stock, hand-picked by stylish owner Dava Muramatsu, never disappoints. Out front is a wide variety of subdued but elegant jewelry (from $20) and hip housewares. The back half is filled with pricey but stylish women's clothing from such big names as Comme des Garçons and Rozae Nichols. Open in summer Su 1-5pm, M-Th 11am-6pm, F-Sa 11am-7pm; off-season Su 1-5pm, M-Sa 11am-6pm.

USED & VINTAGE

Boomerangs, 716 Centre St. (☎617-524-5120), at Harrison Ave. **Jamaica Plain.** Turn left out of T: Green St. (Orange) onto Green St. and left again onto Centre St. This thrift store's collection of high-quality clothes, jewelry, housewares, and more is donated by everyone from mid-range national chains to hip Newbury St. shops. All proceeds benefit Boston's AIDS Action Committee. Pants $5; skirts $5; shorts $3. Open Su noon-6pm, M-Sa 10:30am-7pm.

The Garment District, 200 Broadway (☎617-876-5230; www.garment-district.com). **Cambridge (Kendall Sq.).** From T: Kendall/MIT (Red), walk through the Marriott (they're OK with it), turn left onto Broadway, and cross the railroad tracks. This funky warehouse is filled with rows of gently used and eternally stylish vintage duds (emphasis on swingin' 60s- and 70s-era threads) and room after room of discounted shoes and accessories, from sensible Mary Janes to fluorescent feather boas. Check downstairs for giant-pile clothing sold at $1.50 a pound and some great cheap CDs. Most clothes $8-15. Open Su-Tu 11am-7pm, W-F 11am-8pm, Sa 9am-7pm.

Oona's, 1210 Massachusetts Ave. (☎617-491-2654). **Cambridge (Harvard Sq.).** T: Harvard (Red). Boasting a celebrity clientele that has ranged from John and Yoko to Pearl Jam, shopping at Oona's is like raiding your funky aunt's attic, only much, much cooler. This tiny store is crammed full of costume jewelry, wild polyester shirts and skirts ($12-15), vintage cords and slacks ($15-20), and leather and wool coats (most 50% off). Also stocks a large selection of costume ball musts like fright wigs and late-80s prom dresses. Open Su noon-6pm, M-Sa 11am-7pm.

Planet Aid, 30 JFK St. (☎617-354-6413). **Cambridge (Harvard Sq.).** T: Harvard (Red). Aside from the thrift store standards like flamboyant polyester shirts and worn-in jeans and cords (around $12), Planet Aid's strongest suit is its many sturdy and stylish vintage coats ($20-40). Proceeds from the sale of Planet Aid's donated duds fund grassroots programs in developing countries. Open Su noon-7pm, M-Sa 11am-8pm. **Back Bay** branch, 306 Newbury St. (☎617-262-9337). T: Hynes/ICA (Green-B,C,D). Lots of mint-condition goods from mid-range American chains like Gap and Banana Republic. Open Su noon-7pm, M-F noon-8pm, Sa 11am-8pm.

Second Time Around, 176 Newbury St. (☎617-247-3504). **Back Bay.** T: Hynes/ICA (Green-B,C,D). Thanks to a rigorous admissions process everything at this recently expanded consignment shop is designer label, less than 2 years old, and in close-to-perfect condition. Pair discounted cocktail dresses and slacks (Michael Kors sequined sheath $100, Prada tuxedo pants $40–the older the clothes, the bigger the discount) with something from a stash of extensive, chic shoes–Manolos, Miu Mius, Jimmy Choos, and more (most about $50 per pair). Open Su noon-6pm, M-F 11am-8pm, Sa 10am-7pm. Smaller **Cambridge (Harvard Sq.)** branch at 8 Eliot St. (☎617-491-7185). T: Harvard (Red). Open Su noon-7pm, M-W 11am-7pm, Th-F 11am-8pm, Sa 10am-8pm.

Newbury St.

EROTICA

Grand Opening!, 318 Harvard St., 2nd fl. #32 (☎877-731-2626; www.grandopening.com), in the "Coolidge Corner Arcade." **Brookline.** T: Coolidge Corner (Green-C). The #66 bus from Harvard Sq. also passes by it. The most unintimidating, honest sex shop in Boston (no giggling thrill-seekers, please). Owner Kim Airs, who apprenticed at SF's infamous Good Vibrations, designed this "sexuality boutique" especially (thought not exclusively) for women. The helpful all-female staff will guide you through their vast array of erotica and sex toys (items from the wall of dildos $20+) or sign you up for one of their frequent how-to classes. Sponsors annual amateur porn festival ("You Ought to Be in Pictures") at Coolidge Corner Moviehouse (p. 165). Open Su noon-6pm, M-W 10am-7pm, Th-Sa 10am-9pm.

Filene's Basement

Hubba Hubba, 534 Massachusetts Ave. (☎617-492-9082). **Cambridge (Central Sq.).** T: Central (Red) lets out onto Mass. Ave. The most tongue-in-cheek of the city's erotica shops, with humorous dildos, kitschy toys, and provocative lingerie. Hubba Hubba is also *the* place for bondage and dominatrix accessories and gear, with a huge selection of ball-gags, riding crops, and handcuffs. Crotch high red boots with spike heels run $120, a steal for such versatile footwear. Open M-Sa noon-8pm.

Marquis, 92 South St. (☎617-426-2120), **Downtown.** T: South Station (Red). Walk south on Atlantic Ave. and take a left onto East St.; it's on the corner of East and South St. Fittingly re-located to Boston's leather district, this gay male-oriented sex shop is well hung with a full array of both serious and gag leather goods and toys (from playful dildos to spanking bats to full harnesses), plus the city's most impressive adult video and magazine section. Open daily 10am-11pm. Equally diverse sister store **Eros,** 581 Tremont St. (☎617-425-0345), in the **South End,** stocks similar gear for both gay and straight, male and female clientele. Open daily 10am-10pm.

Erotica!

Sweet 'n Nasty, 90 Massachusetts Ave. (☎617-266-7171). **Back Bay.** T: Hynes/ICA (Green-B,C,D). Boston's best (OK, only) erotic bakery. Adult novelty cards and gag sex toys pale in comparison to the vast array of cream-filled chocolate "cock pops" ($1-5) or the homemade, anatomically correct cakes (10" cakes $26; "Breast Wishes" is by far the most popular). Open Su noon-5pm, M-F 10am-7pm, Sa 11am-6pm.

the BIG $plurge

Teuscher Chocolatier

Back Bay: 230 Newbury St. T: Hynes Convention Ctr. The #1 bus also lets out at the end of Newbury St., at Massachusetts Ave. Contact: ☎617-536-1922. Open: Su noon-5pm, M-Sa 11am-7pm. Prices: 4-pc. champagne truffles $7.90.

Amidst the trendy boutiques of Newbury St., Teuscher stands out as an experience worth its expensive price tag. Dolf Teuscher began making world-class chocolates sixty years ago in the Swiss Alps. Today, his chocolates are world-renowned, as the Teuscher recipe has travelled across the Atlantic to become the best chocolate in the city of Boston.

Even those who can't afford the chocolates have reason to pause at the storefront, as the overflowing pastel of fresh flowers, stands out (even on Newbury St.). Upon entering, creative cocoa concoctions allude to the movie *Chocolat*, as does the full-size poster hanging over the cash register. For those willing to splurge, the champagne truffles are a memorable (and hangover free) indulgence.

GIFTS

Black Ink, 101 Charles St. (☎617-723-3883; www.themut.com). **Beacon Hill.** T: Charles/MGH (Red). A quirky gift store crammed full of mid-range "useless necessities" ($5-20)—cards, toys, trinkets, and housewares, from the cool to the nostalgically kitschy. Open Su noon-6pm, M-F 10am-7pm. **Cambridge (Harvard Sq.)** branch, 5 Brattle St. (☎617-497-1221), opposite T: Harvard (Red), has an unsettling obsession with sushi and sushi-adorned paraphernalia. Open Su 11am-7pm, M-Sa 10am-8pm. **Central Sq.** branch at 370 Broadway (☎617-576-0707). Open Su noon-6pm, M-F 11am-7pm, Sa 10am-6pm.

Buckaroo's Mercantile, 1297 Cambridge St. (☎617-492-4792). **Cambridge (Inman Sq.).** Bus #69 runs up Cambridge St. from T: Harvard (Red); alternatively, walk 15min. up Prospect St. to Cambridge St. from T: Central (Red). Everything here is a conversation piece. Recently displaced from Central Sq., this flamboyant toy store-*cum*-boutique sells campy, 50s-inspired housewares (velvet Elvis wall hangings $3; wrestling lesbians clock $15) and expensive handmade clothing and accessories (cereal box handbag $35). Open Su noon-7pm, M-W noon-9pm, Th-F noon-10pm, Sa 11am-10pm.

FAO Schwartz, 440 Boylston St. (☎617-262-5900). **Back Bay.** T: Arlington (Green) or Copley (Green). This world famous toyland allows visitors of all ages to feel like children as they wander in a wonderland of stuffed animals, board games, and action figures that would make Willy Wonka jealous. Open June-Aug. Su 11am-7pm, M-Sa 10am-8pm; Sept.-May Su 11am-6pm, M-Sa 10am-7pm.

Flyrabbit, 155 Harvard Ave. (☎617-782-1313). **Allston.** T: Harvard Ave. (Green-B). Alternative gift store crammed full of items that are funky, bordering on freaky—vintage postcards, pink flamingo lamps, cat skeletons, clown-head bustiers, etc. Don't overlook the impressive collection of bizarre greeting cards including oft overlooked sentiments like "I know you've been cheating on me" and "I'm breaking up with you." Open Su noon-5pm, M-W and F-Sa 11am-7pm, Th 11am-9pm.

fresh, 121 Newbury St. (☎617-421-1212; www.fresh.com). **Back Bay.** T: Hynes/ICA (Green-B,C,D). This high-end skin care shop started in the South End in 1990 and hit it big when media maven Oprah began gushing over their wares on TV. Now with outposts in every trendy corner of the country, most of their products ask customers to dig deep in their pockets (facial cream as much as $250). Luckily, fresh continues to produce the planet's most luscious array of "gourmet" soaps at reasonable prices ($8-12 per bar). Decide whether to nibble on or lather up with soap flavors like orange cranberry, honey plum, pomegranate anise, and Moroccan tea—all wrapped in too-beautiful-to-open jeweled packaging. Open Su noon-6pm, M-Sa 10am-7pm.

Koo de Kir, 65 Chestnut St. (☎617-723-8111; www.koodekir.com). **Beacon Hill.** T: Charles/MGH (Red). The name is a play on the French *coup de coeur*, literally "take the breath away," and this sleek shop doesn't disappoint with its well-designed contemporary home furnishings and accessories at correspondingly high prices. For the customer with a taste for "Asian-inspired minimalism," the ceramics (from $12) are the highlight of the store. One corner of the store is often set aside for shoppers to field-test the latest trends in home decor. Open Tu-F 10am-7pm, Sa 10am-6pm.

Sugardaddy's Smokeshop, 472 Commonwealth Ave. (☎617-537-6922; www.sugardaddys.com). **Kenmore Sq.** T: Kenmore (Green-B,C,D). Boston's only head shop sells a bewildering array of paraphernalia for smoking (um) tobacco—everything from wooden pocket-sized pipes ($8-10) to rainbow-colored pyrex bowls (most $25-30, some up to $500). If you don't see an item, ask, they probably have it somewhere out back. 18+ ID required to enter the store (because "that's how the man is"); mention anything other than tobacco and you'll be out on the street. Open Su noon-6pm, M-Th noon-7pm, F-Sa noon-8pm.

Urban Outfitters, 11 JFK St. (☎617-864-0070). **Cambridge (Harvard Sq.).** T: Harvard (Red). With branches from Houston, Texas to Dublin, Ireland, Urban Outfitters is the mecca of mass-produced, "alternative" street style. Upstairs features overpriced, low-quality clothes and hilarious gag gifts and housewares (*Messiah*-singing Bible clock $12). In the "Bargain Basement," clothes are just as shoddy, but with prices so low (most items $2-15) and trendiness so fleeting, who cares? **Back Bay** branch, 361 Newbury St. (☎617-236-0088). T: Hynes/ICA (Green-B,C,D). Both open Su noon-8pm, M-Th 10am-10pm, F-Sa 10am-11pm.

MALLS

CambridgeSide Galleria, 100 CambridgeSide Pl. (☎617-621-8666). **Cambridge.** Follow signs from T: Lechmere (Green); the #69 bus from Harvard Sq. also terminates at Lechmere. Alternatively, you can catch "The Wave" shuttle bus (free, every 20min. until 6pm) from T: Kendall (Red). A standard 3-story, 90-store suburban shopping mall, with a food court and such exotic fare as the Gap and Radio Shack. Open Su 11am-7pm, M-Sa 10am-9:30pm.

Copley Place Mall (☎617-369-5000), at Huntington and Dartmouth St. **Back Bay.** From T: Copley (Green), walk down Dartmouth St. 2 blocks (with Copley Sq. on your left). This temple to excess, once referred to in a novel by Boston-based author Dennis Lehane as what would come out "if Donald Trump puked," is Boston's most upscale mall, with expensive chain boutiques (Armani, Gucci, Pink, Tiffany's, etc.) and swanky department stores (Neiman Marcus, etc.). Stores open Su noon-6pm, M-Sa 10am-8pm.

Shops at Prudential Center, 800 Boylston St. (☎800-746-7778 www.prudentialcenter.com). **Back Bay.** See p. 62. T: Prudential (Green); also accessible by a covered walkway from Copley Place. The cheaper sister to upscale Copley Place, with trinket carts and generic mid-range mall stores like Structure, Levi's, Ann Taylor, and Lord & Taylor. The information center in the mall's Center Court is a terrific resource for visitors to the city. Mall open Su 11am-6pm, M-Sa 10am-8pm.

MUSIC

Harvard Sq. and Central Sq. in **Cambridge** have the very best selection of new and used CDs and vinyl.

NEW

Satellite Records, 49 Massachusetts Ave. (☎617-536-5482), at Marlborough St. **Back Bay.** T: Hynes/ICA (Green-B,C,D). Boston outpost of NYC's hottest DJ shop. Countless bins of the latest trance, trip-hop, and electronica LPs (most $10), plus in-store turntables to take them for a spin. Flyers on after-hours events. Open Su 1-7pm, M-Tu and Th-Sa noon-8pm, W noon-9pm.

Newbury Comics, 332 Newbury St. (☎617-236-4930). **Back Bay.** T: Hynes/ICA (Green-B,C,D). The original of the 23-store New England chain known for some of the lowest new music prices. Started as a spot for underground music, they now carry everything from obscure indies to Billboard chart-toppers. Open Su 11am-8pm, M-Th 10am-10:30pm, F-Sa 10am-11pm. **Cambridge (Harvard Sq.)** branch, 36 JFK St. (☎617-491-0337), in "The Garage" mall. T: Harvard (Red). Open Su 11am-8pm, M-Sa 10am-10pm. **Downtown** branch, 1 Washington Mall, Government Ctr. (☎617-248-9992). T: Government Ctr. (Blue/Green).

USED

CD Spins, 324 Newbury St. (☎617-267-5955; www.cdspins.com). **Back Bay.** T: Hynes/ICA (Green-B,C,D). Their constantly replenished stock of CDs from every genre clinches their title as Boston's best used music store. Most CDs $5-10. Open Su noon-8pm, M-W 11am-8pm, Th-F 11am-9pm, Sa 11am-10pm. **Downtown** branch, 58 Winter St. (☎617-357-0525). T: Park St. (Green/Red). Open Su 11am-7pm, M-F 11am-8pm, Sa 10am-8pm. **Jamaica Plain** branch, 668 Centre St. (☎617-524-4800). T: Green St. (Orange). Open M-W 11am-8pm, Th-Sa 11am-9pm, Su noon-8pm. **Cambridge (Harvard Sq.)** branch, 54 Church St. (☎617-497-7070). T: Harvard (Red). Open Su noon-8pm, M-W 11am-8pm, Th-F 11am-9pm, Sa 11am-10pm. **Somerville (Davis Sq.)** branch, 235 Elm St. (☎617-666-8080). T: Davis (Red). Open Su noon-8pm, M-F 11am-8pm, Sa 11am-9pm.

Cheapo Records, 645 Massachusetts Ave. (☎617-354-4455). **Cambridge (Central Sq.).** T: Central (Red) lets out onto Mass. Ave. An underground room bursting at the seams with a dizzying array of used vinyl and CDs ($10-15) from all eras and genres with lots of very recent releases. The reggae section is particularly impressive. Open Su 11am-5pm, M-W and Sa 10am-6pm, Th-F 10am-9pm. $10 min. for credit cards.

Disc Diggers, 401 Highland Ave. (☎617-776-7560). **Somerville (Davis Sq.).** Turn right out of T: Davis (Red) and take the left fork in the road (Highland Ave.). The alternative staff and musical fetishism may remind you of a record store, but you'll only find used CDs here (most $10). Their overwhelming selection is the largest in New England, with an emphasis on rock, soundtracks, and jazz. Open daily 11am-7pm.

Nuggets, 486 Commonwealth Ave. (☎617-536-0679). **Kenmore Sq.** T: Kenmore (Green-B,C,D). With a nerdy feel, Nuggets is home to thousands of used CDs and records ($6-10) with an emphasis on rock and jazz/blues. Clerks are helpful, but sport a serious AC/DC fetish (those who do not appreciate AC/DC are probably better off keeping it to themselves while in here). Open Su noon-7pm, M-Sa 11:30am-8pm. **Cambridge** branch, 46 White St. (☎617-623-1001), opposite the Star Market supermarket at T: Porter (Red).

Planet Records, 54b JFK St. (☎617-492-0693; www.planet-records.com). **Cambridge (Harvard Sq.).** T: Harvard (Red). They stock lots of imported and hard-to-find CDs ($15-20). Open M-Sa 10am-10pm, Su 11am-8pm.

Skippy White's, 538 Massachusetts Ave. (☎617-491-3345). **Cambridge (Central Sq.).** T: Central (Red) lets out onto Mass. Ave. Focuses almost exclusively on music by black artists from all genres. Skip (ahem) the latest releases out front ($15-18) and wade through the back area's disorganized used old-school CDs. Open M-W and Sa 10am-6pm, Th-F 10am-8pm.

Smash City Records, 304 Newbury St. (☎617-536-0216). **Back Bay.** T: Hynes/ICA (Green-B,C,D). Spotty used CD selection ($8-10) consists mostly of concert bootlegs. Their saving grace are their oddball vinyl cuts ($6-8), like *The Travel Agent's Serenade*. Groan-worthy collection of B-movie videos and DVDs (3 for $15). Open Su 10:30am-8pm, M-Th 10:30am-9pm, F-Sa 10:30am-10pm.

INSIDE

Accommodations

The outlook is not bright for those seeking accommodations in Boston: there are few places to stay at any price range, and there are hardly any inexpensive options. The cheapest bed is $25, and prices skyrocket from there. Rates and bookings are highest in summer when most tourists visit the city, as well as in September, late May, and early June, when parents flock to Boston's many colleges to drop off anxious freshmen or celebrate with graduating seniors.

Boston has only four dormitory-style hostels, two private and two affiliated with HI-AYH, all with beds just under $35 per night. Most affordable accommodations in the city are elegant brownstones or old Victorian mansions that have been carved up into mid-range (under $75) guest houses, most with bed and breakfast-like amenities (complimentary breakfast, friendly owners, etc.). Student dorms at Boston's many universities empty out in summer (June-Aug.), but most are used by students attending summer programs. Smokers take note: most places have strict no smoking policies.

BY PRICE

Price categories below are per person, per night, based on double occupancy.

BY NEIGHBORHOOD

The accommodations listed below are ranked by value within each neighborhood. Boston is very small and relatively safe and everywhere in the city is easily accessible by public transportation and close to the action. Wherever you do end up, book far in advance, as places fill up quickly year-round. Prices below do not include the 12.45% room tax.

BACK BAY

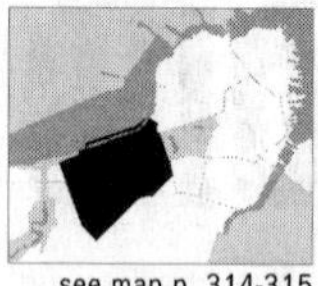

see map p. 314-315

***Discover Back Bay:** p. 2. **Sights:** p. 57. **Food:** p. 105. **Nightlife:** p. 135. **Shopping:** p. 172.*

Staying in the well-manicured **Back Bay** (or nearby Beacon Hill; see p. 186) puts you in the heart of it all—whether it's shopping, eating, or sightseeing that you desire. As a result, accommodations in this area tend to fill up the fastest.

Newbury Guest House, 261 Newbury St. (☎617-437-7666 or 800-437-7668; www.hagopianhotels.com), between Gloucester and Fairfield St. T: Hynes/ICA (Green-B,C,D). In a to-die-for central location, their 32 immaculately clean, bright, and tastefully decorated double rooms have some of the best amenities in the city; all rooms come with private bath and digital cable. Full complimentary breakfast daily 7:30-10:30am. Two smoking rooms available. Reception 24hr. Check-in 3pm; check-out noon. Doubles Apr.-Oct. $125-190; Nov.-Mar. $99-125. ❹

Hostelling International—Boston (HI-AYH), 12 Hemenway St. (☎617-536-1027; www.bostonhostel.org, online reservations www.hostel-booking.com). From T: Hynes/ICA (Green-B,C,D), walk down Massachusetts Ave., with the Virgin Megastore on your left, turn right onto Boylston St., then left onto Hemenway St. Sure, the location—central, near the T, in the middle of everything—can't be beat. Sure, the dorm rooms (co-ed and single sex; 234 beds) and bathrooms are spotless and quiet. But the real reason to stay here is the amazing lineup of nightly events, including free entrance to museums, comedy clubs, and dance clubs around Boston and countless free movie screenings (even some private screenings with the stars of the film). Free linen, lockers, and kitchen use. Laundry $1.25 per cycle. Internet available on 4 terminals $1 per 5min. Check-in noon; check-out 11am. Dorms $32 for members, $35 for nonmembers; private rooms Su-Th $69/$72, F-Sa $87/$90. Reservations recommended up to 1 month in advance. ❶

463 Beacon St. Guest House, 463 Beacon St. (☎617-536-1302; www.463beacon.com). From T: Hynes/ICA (Green-B,C,D), walk up Massachusetts Ave., with the Virgin Megastore on your right, and turn right onto Beacon St. Claiming to be the city's "best slept secret," this clean, calm old townhouse in the heart of the Back Bay has 20 spacious, high-ceilinged rooms (singles and doubles), most with private bath, cable TV, telephone (free local calls and voice mail), A/C, and kitchenette. The homey, quiet atmosphere makes this an ideal home away from home in Boston. In addition to nightly rooms, they have 20 small to medium-sized apartments available fully furnished $1500-2600 per month. Check-in after 1pm; check-out noon. Rooms $69-129, lower off-season. ❷

Copley Inn, 19 Garrison St. (☎617-236-0300; www.copleyinn.com). From T: Prudential (Green-E), walk up Huntington Ave., with the Prudential Colonnade on your left, and turn right onto Garrison St. More like a cozy B&B than an urban budget hotel, this homey, smoke-free inn features 21 intimate, fully furnished double rooms, all with daily housekeeping service, private bath, cable TV, phone with voicemail, A/C, and full kitchenette. Doubles $75-145, rates vary seasonally. ❸

Copley House, 239 W. Newton St. (☎617-236-8300 or 800-331-1318; www.copleyhouse.com). Exit T: Prudential (Green-E) onto Huntington Ave. and turn immediately left onto W. Newton St. Copley House is actually a series of 6 buildings throughout the Back Bay with a total of 48 beautiful, modern, fully furnished studios and single bedroom units available for daily, weekly, or monthly stays. All rooms include private bath, cable TV, free local phone service, A/C, and kitchenette. Check-out noon. Studios and 1-bedrooms $425-800 per week or $75-125 per person per night, lower rates may be available off-season. ❹

The College Club, 44 Commonwealth Ave. (☎617-536-9510; www.thecollegeclubofboston.com), at Berkeley St. Exit T: Arlington (Green) onto Arlington St., walk with the Public Garden on your right, and turn left onto Comm. Ave. Established in 1890 as a private educational society, the College Club has 11 airy rooms, which feel more like a country retreat than city lodging. The relaxed feel is due in part to the fact that none of the rooms have television, though all of them have a full bookshelf and A/C. Check-in 1pm; check-out 11am. Singles with shared bath $75-90; doubles with private bath $120-150; rates vary seasonally. ❸

Commonwealth Court Guest House, 284 Commonwealth Ave. (☎617-424-1230 or 888-424-1230; www.commonwealthcourt.com), at Gloucester St. From T: Hynes/ICA (Green-B,C,D), walk up Massachusetts Ave., with the Virgin Megastore on your right, and turn right onto Comm. Ave. Similar in setup to the Copley House, with tidily decorated, fully furnished double rooms with either queen bed or 2 twin beds, available for nightly, weekly, or monthly rentals. Though the staff is not the most attentive, the location is delightful. All rooms include private bath, cable TV, telephone, A/C, and full kitchenette. Nightly rates: Apr.-Oct. $99-140; Nov.-Mar. $75-110. Weekly rates Apr.-Oct. $500-750; Nov.-Mar. $350-550. ❸

MidTown Hotel, 220 Huntington Ave. (☎617-262-1000 or 800-343-1177; www.midtown-hotel.com), at Cumberland St., opposite Christian Science Plaza. Exit T: Prudential (Green-E) onto Huntington Ave. and walk with the Prudential Colonnade on your right. A typical mid-range hotel of mid-range quality. Perks include free toiletries, daily housekeeping service, free parking, and a pool. All rooms have private bath, TV, phone, and A/C. Check-in 3pm;

ESSENTIAL INFORMATION

RESERVATION SERVICES

One of the cheapest and easiest ways to ensure a bed for a night is by reserving online. Our website features the **Hostelworld** booking engine; access it at **www.letsgo.com/resources/accommodations.** Hostelworld offers bargain accommodations everywhere from Argentina to Zimbabwe with no added commission.

Other reservation services (a.k.a. "hotel brokers") include those below. Even during full vacancy periods, these services can find rooms in high-end hotels at discounted, mid-range prices (averaging around $100-200 per night, double occupancy). Many travel websites also have similar services.

Accommodations Express (☎800-277-1064; www.accommodationsexpress.com)

Boston Reservations (☎617-332-4199)

Central Reservation Service (☎800-332-3026 or 617-569-3800; www.bostonhotels.net)

Citywide Reservation Services (☎617-267-7424 or 800-468-3593; www.cityres.com)

Hotel Reservations Network (US toll-free ☎800-715-7666, Europe toll-free ☎00800 1066 1066; www.hoteldiscount.com)

the hidden deal

Oasis Guest House

Back Bay: ***22 Edgerly Rd., at Stoneholm St. T: Hynes/ICA (Green-B,C,D). Exit onto Mass. Ave. Walking with the Virgin Megastore on your left, cross Boylston St. and turn right onto Haviland St.; the next left is Edgerly Rd.*** **Contact:** *☎617-267-2262; www.oasisgh.com.* **Room rates:** *Apr. to mid-Nov. singles $59; doubles with shared bath $69, with private bath $89. Mid-Nov. to Mar. singles $80; doubles with shared bath $90, with private bath $125.* ❷

The accommodation of choice for relatives visiting students at nearby Berklee School of Music and Boston University, this rambling 30-room guest house tucked into a residential corner of the Back Bay is truly an oasis—a calm, quiet respite from the traffic and noise of bustling Mass. Ave. The bedrooms and bathrooms are small but sparkling clean, and the chatty staff is incredibly knowledgeable and always helpful to first-timers. Continental breakfast is served daily 8-11am, and a common kitchen area with microwave and fridge is provided. Reservations recommended up to 2 months in advance.

Note that the Oasis is a popular temporary home-base for apartment-hunting new arrivals to the city, who make good use of the free voicemail and data ports found in every room.

check-out noon. Doubles (2 double beds) $109-239; $15 each additional person (max. 4 people per room). Rates vary greatly by season. ❸

YMCA of Greater Boston, 316 Huntington Ave. (☎617-927-8040 or 617-536-7800). T: Northeastern (Green-E) lets out onto Huntington Ave. Near Symphony Hall and the MFA, this full-service YMCA provides easy access to world-class athletic facilities and Boston's most important cultural attractions. A long-term men-only residence during the summer, the YMCA becomes co-ed Sept. to mid-June. and opens up its 2 fl. of sterile but serviceable rooms with shared hallway bathrooms to short-term visitors. Breakfast included. 24hr. reception. Check-out 11am. Must be 18+. Singles $45; doubles $65. ❶

BEACON HILL

see map p. 317

Discover Beacon Hill: *p. 3.* ***Sights:*** *p. 63.* ***Food:*** *p. 107.* ***Shopping:*** *p. 44.*

John Jeffries House, 14 David G. Mugar Way (☎617-367-1866; www.johnjeffrieshouse.com), at the corner of Charles and Cambridge St. From T: Charles/MGH (Red), head down the stairs to Charles St. and turn right onto tiny Mugar Way; signs point to the entrance around the corner. Built in 1824 as a hospital annex and later used as nurses' dormitories, this renovated B&B now resembles a nice mid-range hotel—spotless, tidy, quiet, and safe. The real draw is its ideal location, just minutes from Boston Common. All 46 rooms have kitchenettes, TV, and private baths. Continental breakfast. Singles $95; doubles $125; 3-person suites $150-175; Dec.-Mar. $15-20 cheaper; each additional person $10. ❸

BROOKLINE

see map p. 318

Discover Brookline: *p. 6.* ***Food:*** *p. 108.* ***Shopping:*** *p. 172.*

Though a good 30-40min. T ride from Boston proper, Brookline's Coolidge Corner is a thriving urban center with unique eateries and attractions. All of the following are B&B-style converted brownstones, located at or around Coolidge Corner and varying little in quality.

Beech Tree Inn, 83 Longwood Ave. (☎617-277-1620 or 800-544-9660). From T: Saint Paul St. (Green-C), head down St. Paul St. and turn left onto Longwood Ave. This quiet, charming B&B may be

Brookline's best accommodation and the closest one to Coolidge Corner. Features wireless Internet, a beautiful garden, well-appointed rooms, and fresh cookies every afternoon. Singles $79; doubles $95-135; triples with private bath $150. ❸

Beacon Townhouse Inn II, 1023 Beacon St. (☎617-232-2422 or 888-714-7779; www.beacontownhouseinn.com). T: St. Mary's St. (Green-C). Combining the anonymity of a professional hotel with the attention of a B&B this brand-new townhouse offers 16 spacious, well decorated rooms all with cable TV, phone, and kitchenette. Doubles $135-155. ❹

Beacon Inn, 1087 Beacon St. (☎888-575-0088; www.beaconinn.com). T: Hawes St. (Green-C). This renovated 19th-century brownstone has charming, spacious rooms done up in elegant hardwood and soft colors. All rooms include bath, cable TV, and phone. Doubles $99-129. Slightly larger location at **1750 Beacon St.,** opposite T: Dean Rd. (Green-C). Same rates and amenities. ❸

Anthony's Town House, 1085 Beacon St. (☎617-566-3972; www.anthonystownhouse.com). T: Hawes St. (Green-C). A decent value for the price, the comfortable rooms all come with shared baths, cable TV, and A/C. Fake flowers and European-style furniture add to the feeling that you are staying in someone's house. Singles and doubles $50-90; sometimes lower. ❷

CAMBRIDGE

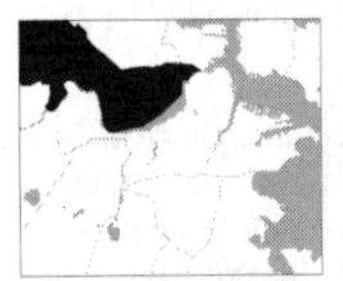
see map p. 320-321

Discover Cambridge: *p. 7.* ***Sights:*** *p. 97.* ***Food:*** *p. 110.* ***Nightlife:*** *p. 137.* ***Shopping:*** *p. 172.*

Just across the river from Boston (a 10-15min. T ride) but worlds away in temperament, bohemian Cambridge is a vibrant, low-key destination of its own, with countless dining and nightlife options. Harvard and MIT both hold commencement ceremonies and class reunions in Cambridge in late May and early June: rates often double during this time, and most people book a year or more in advance.

A Friendly Inn, 1673 Cambridge St. (☎617-547-7851; www.afinow.com/afi), at Fuller St. **Harvard Sq.** From T: Harvard (Red), follow Mass. Ave. along the perimeter of Harvard Yard until it runs into Cambridge St. in front of the Harvard Science Center. Follow Cambridge St. for about 2 blocks; the inn is on your left. This old red Victorian is now a very basic B&B with 18 tidily kept rooms, all with clean private bath, cable TV, and A/C. The best deal in town except in June (Harvard graduation), when rates go through the roof. Doubles Dec.-Apr. $77-117; May-Nov. $97-117. ❸

A Cambridge House, 2218 Mass. Ave. (☎800-232-9989; www.acambridgehouse.com), near **Davis Sq.** Turn right out of T: Davis (Red) onto Holland St., right again onto Day St., walk 3 blocks, and turn left onto Mass. Ave. An immaculate, upscale 15-room B&B popular with businessmen and international travelers. Living up to Both "B"s, a spectacular made to order breakfast meets lavishly appointed rooms (with period antiques, working fireplaces, and canopy beds). All have private bath, cable TV, and A/C. Reception 6:30am-midnight. Singles $99-209; doubles $109-290. Beware, prices become ridiculous during graduation (May-June). ❺

Mary Prentiss Inn, 6 Prentiss St. (☎617-661-2929; www.maryprentissinn.com). **Porter Sq.** From T: Porter (Red), walk down Mass. Ave. (with the T stop on your left) and turn left onto Prentiss St. A gorgeous inn with 20 tastefully furnished double rooms (all with TV, telephones, and A/C), some with wood-burning fireplaces and jacuzzis. Check-in 3-9pm; check-out 11am. Doubles in winter $129-209, in summer $169-259. ❹

Harding House, 288 Harvard St. (☎617-876-2888; www.irvinghouse.com). **Central Sq.** From T: Central (Red), turn right onto Prospect St. (at Starbucks), then left onto Harvard St.; it's 2 blocks up on your left. All the same amenities as Irving House (see below), with larger rooms (though there are only 14 of them) and the same rates. Rooms Dec.-Apr. with shared bath $85-105, private bath $99-180. May-Nov. $99-115/$140-215. Peak rates around graduation and other special events as high as $325. ❷

Irving House, 24 Irving St. (☎877-547-4600; www.irvinghouse.com). **Harvard Sq.** From T: Harvard (Red), follow Mass. Ave. along the perimeter of Harvard Yard until it runs into Cambridge St. in front of the Harvard Science Center. Follow Cambridge St. for about 2 blocks and turn left onto Irving St. A large, comfortable B&B with 44 charming but small rooms, all with antique furniture and books. Rooms Dec.-Apr. with shared bath $85-105, private bath $99-180; May-Nov. $99-115/$140-215. Peak rates around graduation and other special events as high as $325. ❷

DOWNTOWN

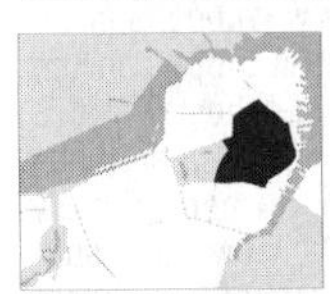

see map p. 324-325

Discover Downtown: *p. 3.* ***Sights:*** *p. 80.* ***Food:*** *p. 117.* ***Nightlife:*** *p. 141.* ***Shopping:*** *p. 173.*

Downtown is home to most of Boston's major sights, including the famed Freedom Trail (see p. 43). The after-work crowd keeps early nightlife here hopping, while the tragically hip flock to the newly chic Ladder District later in the evening (see p. 141). For quality food, you'll have to hoof it to nearby Chinatown (see p. 115) or the North End (see p. 121). Most accommodations are near the Fleet Ctr. and, though fairly safe, exercise caution in the area at night, especially when the Fleet Ctr. isn't hosting an event.

Beantown Hostel & Irish Embassy Hostel, 222 Friend St., 3rd Fl. (☎617-723-0800). Exit T: North Station (Green/Orange) onto Causeway St. With the Fleet Center on your right, head down Causeway St. and turn left onto Friend St.; entrance is next door to Hooters. Those used to the free-wheeling, party-hardy camaraderie of European youth hostels will feel right at home at these 2 fun-loving, connected hostels. These are some of Boston's cheapest but more dilapidated accommodations, with dimly lit dorms (co-ed and single sex; 110 beds), musty furnishings, and fairly clean common bathrooms. Both employ incredibly helpful, super-friendly staff. Quieter Beantown has a 1:45am curfew; Irish Embassy (above a pub) is rowdier and curfew-free. Check-in for both at Beantown; enter Irish Embassy thereafter at 232 Friend St. (☎617-973-4841). Free linen, free lockers (bring your own lock). Beantown has A/C, while the Irish Embassy has a kitchen for guests to use. **Free buffet** in summer Tu, Th 8pm. Laundry (wash/dry) $3.50. Check-out 10am. Dorms $25. Cash or traveler's checks only. ❶

Shawmut Inn, 280 Friend St., 2nd Fl. (☎617-720-5544 or 800-350-7784; www.shawmutinn.com). Exit T: North Station (Green/Orange) onto Causeway St.; with the Fleet Ctr. on your right, head down Causeway St., then left on Friend St. A quiet refuge just steps

Chandler Inn Hotel

South End: *26 Chandler St., at Berkeley St.* ***T:*** *Back Bay (Orange). From the T, follow traffic down Clarendon St. and turn left onto Chandler St.* ***Contact:*** *☎617-482-3450 or 800-842-3450; www.chandlerinn.com.* ***Room rates:*** *Singles or doubles Dec.-Mar. $129, Apr.-Nov. $149-159.* ❸

The Chandler Inn is a charming and gay-friendly budget hotel right in the heart of the South End scene. Just a quick sashay away from the phenomenal gourmet restaurants and mixed-crowd bars of trendy Tremont St., the Chandler can also accommodate those who don't like to go far for fun: downstairs from the hotel is the popular gay sports bar Fritz (p. 151), a hopping neighborhood spot.

The hostel typically draws a mixed crowd to its 56 tidy but rather small and sparsely decorated rooms (it used to be a coast guard dormitory), all with private bath, cable TV, and phones with voicemail. Reserve in advance, as spots tend to fill up quickly.

from the Fleet Ctr. and the chaos of the Big Dig. Basic, spacious rooms with kitchenettes, cable TV, A/C, and continental breakfast (daily 7-11am). Young international clientele. Key deposit $10. Check-in 3pm; check-out 11am. Doubles, Apr.-Nov. $130-160; Dec.-Mar. $100-130. ❸

KENMORE SQ. & THE FENWAY

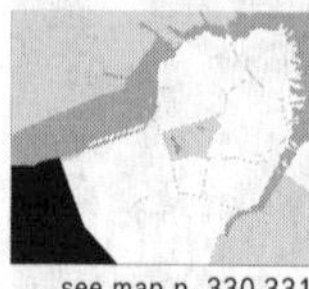

see map p. 330-331

***Discover Kenmore Sq. & the Fenway:** p. 4. **Sights:** p. 84. **Food:** p. 120. **Nightlife:** p. 145. **Shopping:** p. 172.*

Kenmore Sq. is a bit farther from major attractions (about a 20min. T ride or 30min. walk), but this club- and pub-filled neighborhood in the shadow of storied Fenway Park (p. 85) is popular with Boston's many college students.

Hosteling International—Boston Fenway (HI-AYH), 575 Commonwealth Ave. (☎617-267-8599; www.bostonhostel.org, online reservations www.hostel-booking.com). T: Kenmore (Green-B,C,D) lets out onto Comm. Ave. Though it's open in the **summer only,** it remains the best hostel in Boston. You'll forget you're in a hostel at this former Howard Johnson hotel, which serves as student housing during the school year. It has 155 bright and airy 3-bed dorm rooms (each room comes with private bath and privately controlled A/C) and a gorgeous penthouse common area with a 360° view of Boston (including a bird's-eye view of Fenway Park). Guests here get the same lineup of free private movie screenings and free museum, comedy club, and dance club entrance offered at HI-Boston (see p. 184). Free linen. Check-out 11am. Individual dorm bed $35 for members, $38 for nonmembers; $99 per 3-bed room. Open June-Aug. ❶

Hotel Buckminster, 645 Beacon St. (☎617-236-7050 or 800-727-2825), sign visible from T: Kenmore (Green-B,C,D). Built in 1903, the musty Buckminster features a lavish, gilded lobby and grand hallways leading to—surprise!—very small, very basic hotel rooms. All rooms with TV, telephone, A/C, and the cleanest bathrooms in Boston. Check-in 3pm; check-out 11am. Singles $109; doubles $139-169; larger-occupancy rooms (quads, suites, etc.) average $50 per person per night. ❹

SOUTH END

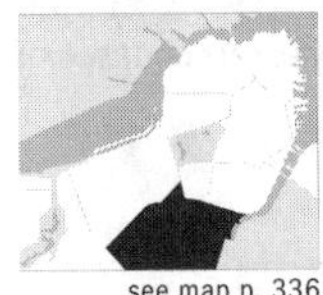

see map p. 336

Discover the South End: *p. 4.* **Sights:** *p. 92.* **Food:** *p. 125.* **Nightlife:** *p. 149.* **Shopping:** *p. 172.*

The South End is 15min. from the nearest public transportation (about a 30min. walk to downtown Boston), but the beautiful neighborhood has a lion's share of the city's phenomenal restaurants, shopping, and nightlife, as well as being the cultural heart of Boston's gay community.

Milner Hotel, 78 Charles St. South (☎617-426-6220, toll-free reservations ☎877-645-6377; www.milner-hotels.com/milnerboston.html), at Warrenton St. Though close to the South End, Milner House is actually in the **Theatre District.** From T: Boylston (Green), turn right onto Boylston St., then left on Charles St. South. The Milner's basic, neat rooms are definitely more about utility than luxury. A 5min. walk from the Theatre District's playhouses and upscale nightlife, they are very quiet at night. Continental breakfast, TV, A/C. Reception 24hr. Check-in 2:30pm; check-out 11am. Singles $99-129; doubles (2-4 people) $149-179. ❹

YWCA Berkeley Residence, 40 Berkeley St. (☎617-375-2524; www.ywcaboston.org), at Appleton St. From T: Back Bay (Orange), follow traffic down Clarendon St. and turn left onto Appleton St. Hostel-style accommodations for **women only,** with cramped but spotless quarters and 2 spacious communal bathrooms on each fl. Breakfast included. Reception 24hr. Singles $56; doubles $86; triples $99 (discounts for stays longer than 14 days). ❷

LONG-TERM HOUSING

Long-term housing in Boston is as exorbitantly priced and as difficult to find as short-term housing. Boston has one of the highest costs of living in the country (third behind New York City and San Francisco); rents lower than $600 per person per month are hard to come by, and most places run $700-1000 per month. The city's constant influx of college students means the housing market is always incredibly tight. Moreover, the cheapest rentals are often passed from one student to another. Accommodations on websites and in newspapers are more expensive and are usually owned by rental agencies, which sometimes charge steep fees.

If you are coming to the Boston area to go to school, your college or university is your best housing resource: university housing offices always have roommate referral services and listings of apartments on or near campus.

RESOURCES

If you won't be looking for housing until you get to Boston, you'll need to make reservations at a local hotel or hostel and use it as a home base. If you don't plan on getting a cell phone (mobile phone), make reservations at an establishment with free local phone service and voicemail, as you'll be placing calls to agents and landlords and won't always be around to take the call. Most establishments offer discounts for extended stays or have lower weekly rates.

The best places to start any search for long-term housing are the classified ads in the print and online versions of city and neighborhood newspapers (see p. 26 for a list). Particularly useful are the listings in the *Boston Globe* (www.boston.com/globe; $0.50 at streetside boxes or newsstands), those online at www.boston.craigslist.com, and the listings in the various housing publications available for free throughout the city.

You'll quickly find that most apartment rental ads are not placed by the owner but by rental agencies or real estate brokers (see below for more on these). If you don't want to deal with a broker, note that most private landlords post "for rent" flyers in high-traffic areas, such as local coffeeshops, bookstores, and grocery stores—not to mention all over the city's many college campuses. There are also flyers posted in student-filled areas such as Kenmore Sq. (p. 4) and the intersection of Boylston St. and Massachusetts Ave., near Berklee College of Music in the Back Bay (p. 2). Outside Boston proper, try Allston (p. 5), Jamaica Plain (p. 6), and the various squares of Cambridge (p. 7) and Somerville (p. 8).

LANDLORDS & AGENTS

Affordable long-term housing in Boston means either leasing/renting an apartment from a landlord or subletting a place from a current tenant. Housing in Boston is at a premium, so landlords can and will demand a lot before you can sign on the dotted line. Aside from the exorbitant rent they'll be charging you, don't be surprised to find them requiring year-long leases, the first and last month's rent up front, and even interviews and background checks. If you are subletting, always double check that the landlord is aware of the arrangement and its terms.

Most available apartments in the city are listed with a rental agent (a.k.a. real estate broker). The advantage of going through an agent is that they have more listings than you do, meaning they'll probably have better luck finding a place that suits your needs. The disadvantage is that some agents charge fees totaling up to an entire month's rent. Although fees are rare among Boston real estate brokers, ask up front. Real estate agencies in Boston are usually more hassle-free than those found in larger cities, like New York. As noted before, whether you go through an agent or not, your landlord will most likely ask for the first month's rent, last month's rent, and occasionally a security deposit before you can move in.

COST

Studios and one-bedroom apartments in Boston proper rarely rent for lower than $1000 per month (not including utilities), making roommates a must. Look online at www.roommateconnection.com or www.bostonroommates.com. Apartments for two or more people in the city start at $700-900 per person per month. Rent rarely includes utilities—heat, hot water, electricity, etc.—which usually run another $50 per month. The amount charged is not always related to the quality of the place—always visit an apartment before agreeing to sign a lease. The farther you live from downtown Boston and the T (local T buses run through every neighborhood), the cheaper rent will be. Thankfully, the Greater Boston area is so small and so well-connected by public transportation that no matter where you live, the rest of the city will be easily accessible.

LOCATION

Rent anywhere in the city of Boston is incredibly high. As the millions who watch *Ally McBeal* and her fellow lawyers on *The Practice* know, the **Back Bay** (p. 2) and the **North End** (p. 4) are by far the most popular places for young professionals to live. Artists and queer folk have long flocked to the trendy, gay-friendly **South End** (p. 4) and recently so have affluent yuppies who have driven rents sky-high. Despite the neighborhood's tight-knit feel and phenomenal shopping, food, and nightlife options, its distance from public transportation makes it a less than ideal choice for those working or studying in Boston proper.

Affordable housing is really only available outside of Boston proper, especially across the river in Cambridge and Somerville. Gentrification is jacking up rents in **Cambridge** (p. 7), although Central Sq. remains fairly affordable. Most places in Cambridge are passed on from student to student anyway, leaving a newcomer out of luck. Many young people and students live in **Somerville** (p. 8) and **Allston** (just west of Kenmore Sq., popular with Boston University students; see p. 5). Funky **Jamaica Plain** (p. 6), a residential neighborhood in the southwest corner of Boston, has also begun drawing in young people. Expect to pay about $500-700 per person per month if you live in one of these neighborhoods' multi-bedroom apartments, which are mostly old Victorians or three-family houses that have been carved up into tiny flats, usually some configuration of kitchen, living room, three bedrooms, and a bath. Studios and one-bedroom apartments are also rare here, so you'll need roommates. All these places are about a 30min. commute (by T) from Boston proper, but all are relatively safe and filled with families (meaning lots of family-friendly amenities like supermarkets and on-street parking) and have lively commercial centers, with plenty of food, shopping, and nightlife.

INSIDE

Daytrips from Boston

THE GREAT OUTDOORS

While Boston's Emerald Necklace (p. 44) makes the city one of the greener urban spots in the country, sometimes you need to escape the chaos of city life by finding a beach or tide pool or hiking around some place where you can't see the John Hancock Tower. Thankfully, the Greater Boston area is blanketed with rolling hills and lined with rocky beaches—offering endless opportunities for exploring the lesser-known gems of the area. The following are our favorite options for getting out and about.

BEACHES

It's well worth the 45min. trip north to the beautiful, well-kept beaches on and around Cape Ann, on the North Shore. The water is cold ("invigorating") and relatively calm, and best of all, most spots are accessible by commuter rail from Boston. (Trains depart North Station, at T: North Station (Green/Orange). Schedules are complicated and change frequently, so ask at the station or check www.mbta.com.) Remember your insect repellent, as greenheaded horseflies swarm to these shores.

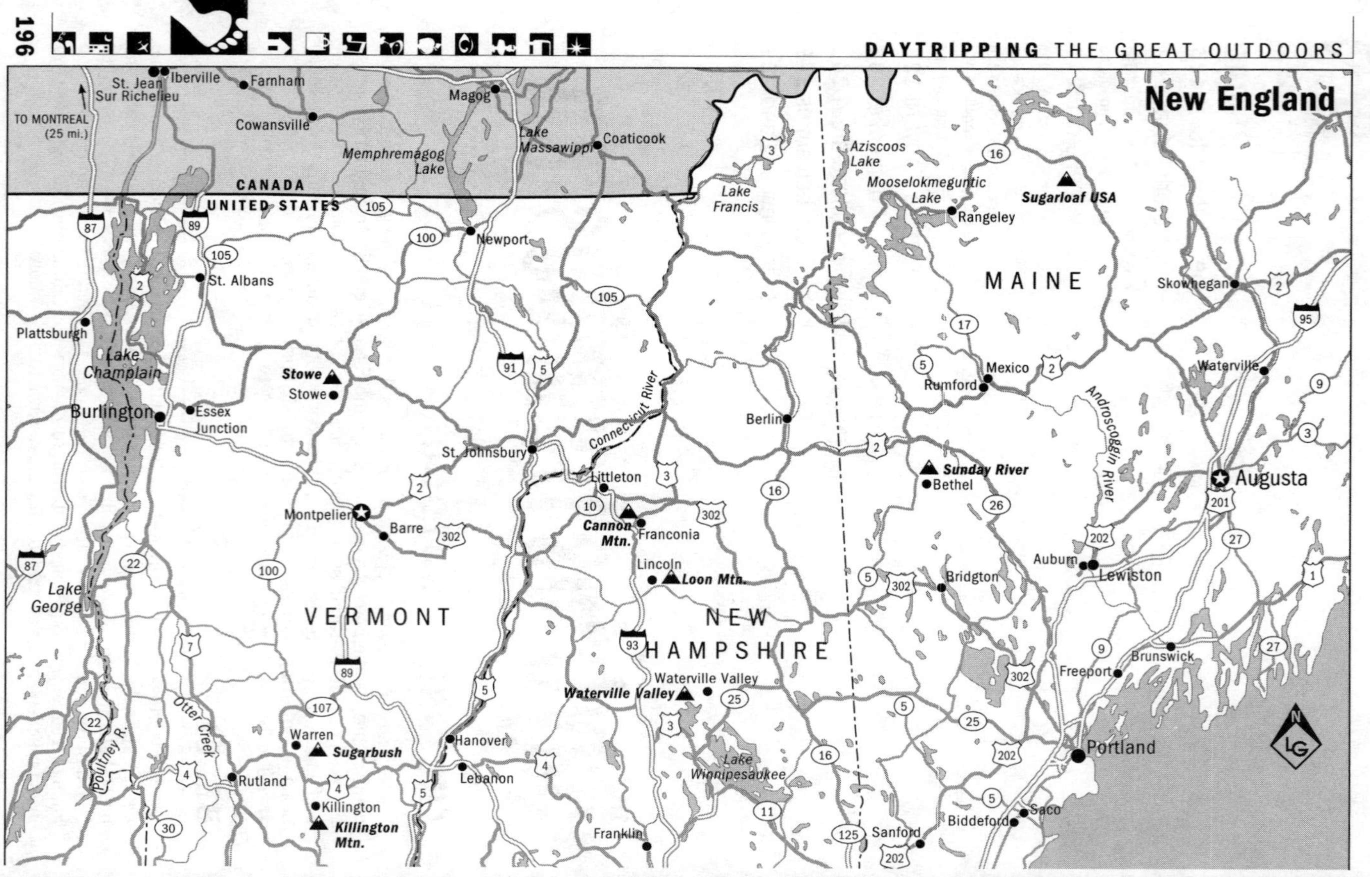

New England
TO MONTREAL (25 mi.)
St. Jean Sur Richelieu
Iberville
Farnham
Cowansville
Magog
Memphremagog Lake
Lake Massawippi
Coaticook
CANADA
UNITED STATES
Aziscoos Lake
Mooselokmeguntic Lake
Rangeley
Sugarloaf USA
Lake Francis
MAINE
Skowhegan
Waterville
Augusta
Mexico
Rumford
Androscoggin River
Sunday River
Bethel
Berlin
Connecticut River
Newport
St. Albans
Plattsburgh
Lake Champlain
Burlington
Essex Junction
Stowe
St. Johnsbury
Littleton
Cannon Mtn.
Franconia
Montpelier
Barre
Lincoln
Loon Mtn.
Auburn
Lewiston
Bridgton
Lake George
VERMONT
NEW HAMPSHIRE
Waterville Valley
Brunswick
Freeport
Portland
Warren
Sugarbush
Hanover
Lebanon
Rutland
Otter Creek
Poultney R.
Killington
Killington Mtn.
Lake Winnipesaukee
Franklin
Sanford
Biddeford
Saco

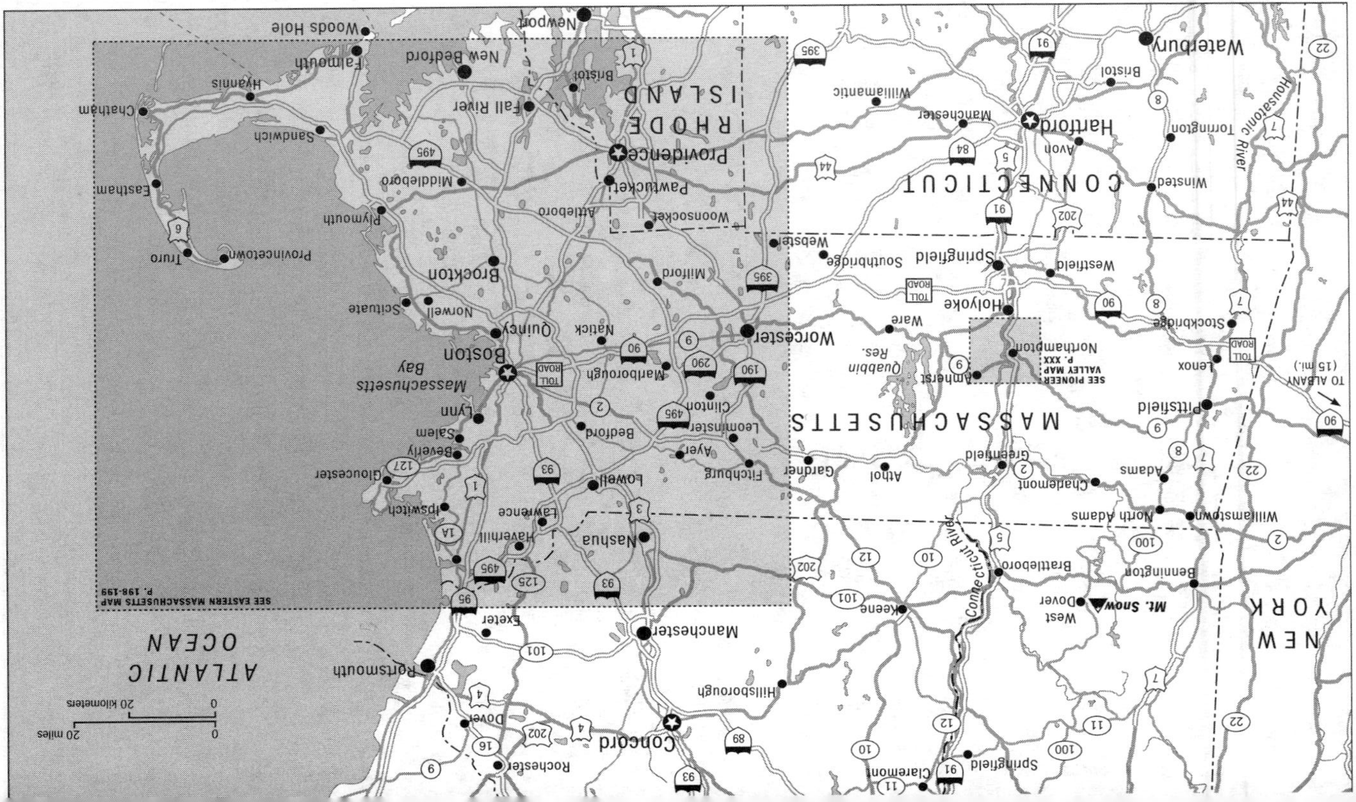

ATLANTIC OCEAN

0 20 miles
0 20 kilometers

SEE EASTERN MASSACHUSETTS MAP P. 198-199

SEE PIONEER VALLEY MAP P. XXX

NEW YORK

MASSACHUSETTS

CONNECTICUT

RHODE ISLAND

Massachusetts Bay

Quabbin Res.

Connecticut River

Housatonic River

TO ALBANY (15 mi.)

TOLL ROAD

Mt. Snow

Springfield
Claremont
Concord
Rochester
Dover
Portsmouth
Hillsborough
Manchester
Exeter
West Dover
Keene
Bennington
Brattleboro
Nashua
Haverhill
Lawrence
Ipswitch
Williamstown
North Adams
Charlemont
Adams
Greenfield
Athol
Gardner
Fitchburg
Lowell
Gloucester
Ayer
Bedford
Beverly
Salem
Leominster
Lynn
Pittsfield
Clinton
Amherst
Marlborough
Boston
Lenox
Northampton
Worcester
Natick
Quincy
Stockbridge
Ware
Holyoke
Norwell
Scituate
Westfield
Springfield
Southbridge
Milford
Brockton
Webster
Provincetown
Truro
Woonsocket
Attleboro
Plymouth
Winsted
Pawtucket
Middleboro
Eastham
Avon
Providence
Torrington
Hartford
Manchester
Sandwich
Fall River
Chatham
Williamantic
Hyannis
Bristol
Bristol
Falmouth
Waterbury
New Bedford
Woods Hole
Newport

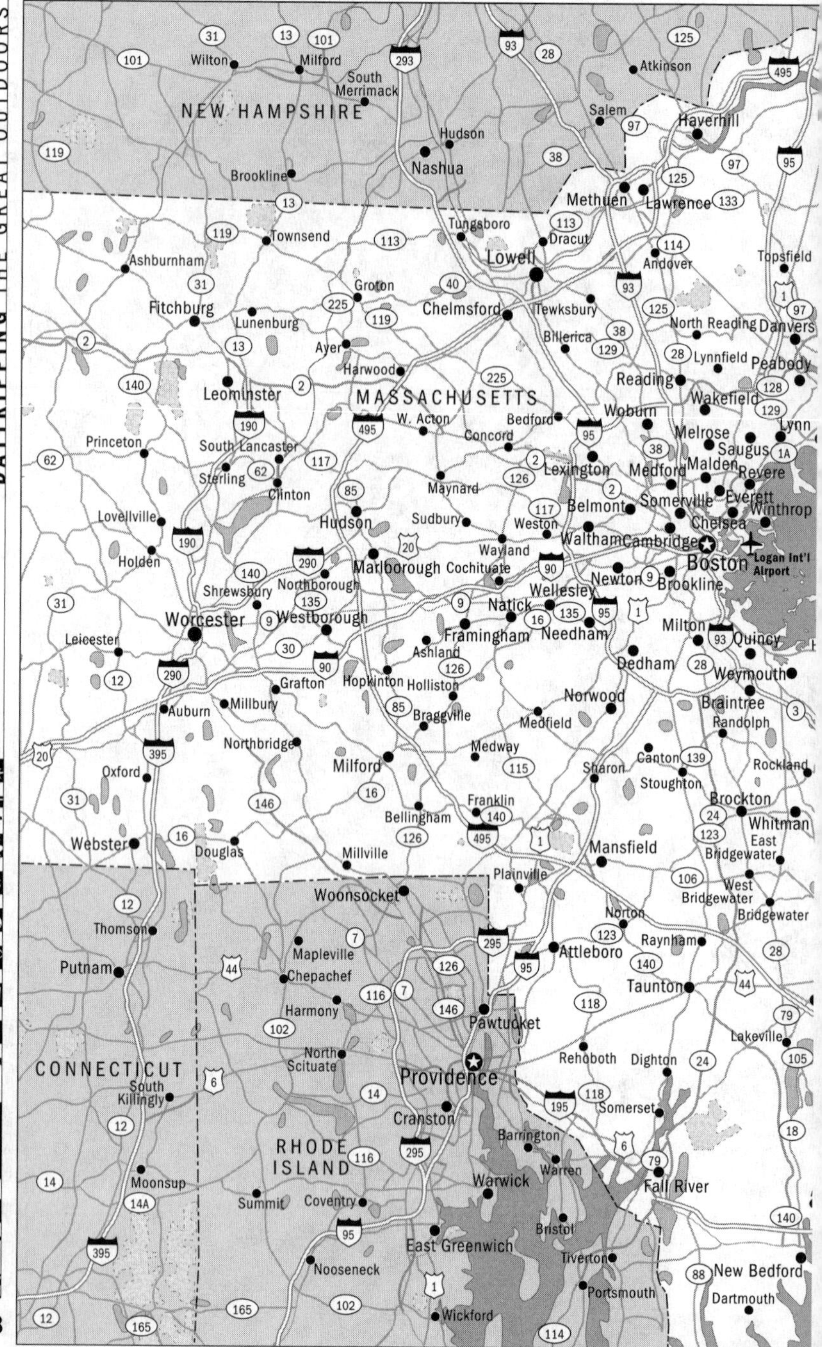
NEW HAMPSHIRE
MASSACHUSETTS
CONNECTICUT
RHODE ISLAND
Wilton
Milford
South Merrimack
Atkinson
Salem
Haverhill
Hudson
Nashua
Brookline
Methuen
Lawrence
Tungsboro
Townsend
Dracut
Lowell
Andover
Topsfield
Ashburnham
Groton
Fitchburg
Lunenburg
Chelmsford
Tewksbury
North Reading
Danvers
Billerica
Lynnfield
Peabody
Ayer
Harwood
Reading
Wakefield
Leominster
W. Acton
Bedford
Woburn
Lynn
Princeton
South Lancaster
Concord
Melrose
Saugus
Sterling
Clinton
Maynard
Lexington
Medford
Malden
Revere
Everett
Belmont
Somerville
Winthrop
Chelsea
Lovellville
Hudson
Sudbury
Weston
Waltham
Cambridge
Boston
Logan Int'l Airport
Holden
Marlborough
Cochituate
Wayland
Newton
Brookline
Shrewsbury
Northborough
Wellesley
Worcester
Westborough
Natick
Needham
Milton
Quincy
Leicester
Framingham
Ashland
Dedham
Weymouth
Hopkinton
Holliston
Grafton
Norwood
Braintree
Auburn
Millbury
Braggville
Medfield
Randolph
Northbridge
Medway
Canton
Rockland
Oxford
Milford
Sharon
Stoughton
Franklin
Brockton
Bellingham
Whitman
Webster
Douglas
Millville
Mansfield
East Bridgewater
Plainville
West Bridgewater
Bridgewater
Woonsocket
Norton
Thomson
Raynham
Mapleville
Attleboro
Putnam
Chepachet
Taunton
Harmony
Pawtucket
Lakeville
North Scituate
Rehoboth
Dighton
Providence
South Killingly
Somerset
Cranston
Barrington
Warren
Warwick
Fall River
Moonsup
Summit
Coventry
Bristol
East Greenwich
Tiverton
New Bedford
Nooseneck
Portsmouth
Dartmouth
Wickford

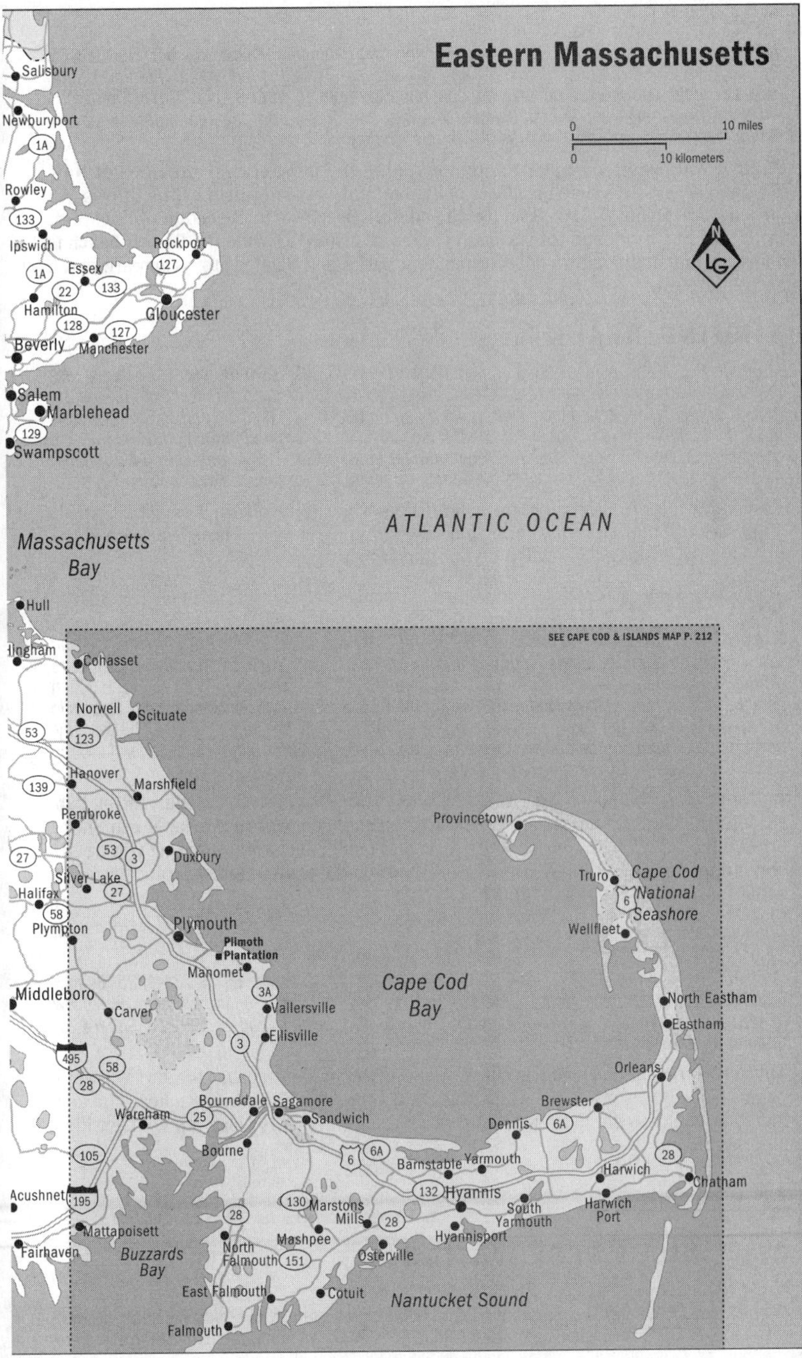

Eastern Massachusetts

0 10 miles
0 10 kilometers

Salisbury
Newburyport
1A
Rowley
133
Ipswich
Rockport
127
1A
Essex
22
133
Hamilton
Gloucester
128
127
Beverly
Manchester
Salem
Marblehead
129
Swampscott

ATLANTIC OCEAN

Massachusetts Bay

Hull
Hingham
Cohasset

SEE CAPE COD & ISLANDS MAP P. 212

Norwell
Scituate
53
123
Hanover
Marshfield
139
Pembroke
Provincetown
53
3
Duxbury
27
Truro
Cape Cod National Seashore
6
Silver Lake
27
Halifax
58
Plympton
Plymouth
Wellfleet
Plimoth Plantation
Manomet
Cape Cod Bay
3A
Middleboro
Vallersville
Carver
North Eastham
Eastham
Ellisville
3
495
58
28
Orleans
Bournedale
Sagamore
Brewster
Wareham
25
Sandwich
Dennis
6A
Bourne
6
6A
28
105
Barnstable
Yarmouth
Harwich
Chatham
Acushnet
195
130
Marstons Mills
132
Hyannis
South Yarmouth
Harwich Port
28
28
Mattapoisett
Hyannisport
Mashpee
Fairhaven
Buzzards Bay
North Falmouth
151
Osterville
East Falmouth
Cotuit
Nantucket Sound
Falmouth

ROCKPORT

Just past Gloucester on Rte. 127A. ***Contact:*** *Rockport Chamber of Commerce ☎ 978-546-6575.* ***By car:*** *Take Rte. 127A past Gloucester and follow signs. Parking is metered in downtown Rockport.* ***By public transportation:*** *Take the commuter rail from T: North Station (Green/Orange) to Rockport (Rockport Line; $5). All beaches are less than ½ mi. from the commuter rail station.* ***Open:*** *daily sunrise-sunset; lifeguards at Front Beach only.*

Right on the edge of Cape Ann, this is one of the most scenic stretches of New England shore. The beach is quite rocky, but still draws tourists by the droves. All beaches are on Sandy Bay. **Front Beach** and **Back Beach** are in the center of Rockport, with parking, food, and toilets within walking distance, while **Old Garden Beach** is more secluded and allows only for resident parking, though visitors can park in the town and walk.

SINGING BEACH

Beach Rd., Manchester-by-the-Sea, MA. ***Contact:*** *☎ 978-526-2000.* ***By car:*** *It's actually less preferable to go by car, as parking is difficult. Take I-95N to Rte. 128 and get off at Exit 16, Pine St.; go to the end of Pine St. and take a left; you are now on Beach Rd. You must park in town and walk the ½ mi. to the beach (pick-up and drop-off at beach allowed).* ***By public transportation:*** *Take the commuter rail from T: North Station (Green/Orange) to Manchester (Rockport Line; $4.25). From the station, it's an easy ½ mi. walk to the beach.* ***Open:*** *daily 8am-sunset.* ***Fees:*** *walk-on $2.*

Named for the squeaky sound the sand makes when you walk on it, Singing Beach's soft sand will massage your feet, while the stunning view—of both the sea and the mansions overlooking it—will put your mind at ease.

CRANE BEACH

Argilla Rd., Ipswich, MA. ***Contact:*** *☎ 978-356-4354.* ***By car:*** *Take I-95N to Exit 20A (Rte. 1A) and follow north for 8 mi. to Ipswich. Turn right onto Rte. 133E and follow for 1½ mi. Turn left onto Northgate Rd. and follow for ½ mi. Turn right onto Argilla Rd. and follow for 2½ mi. to Crane Beach gatehouse at the end of the paved road. Parking M-F $15, Sa-Su $20; ½-price after 3pm.* ***By public transportation:*** *Take the commuter rail from T: North Station (Green/Orange) to Ipswich (Newburyport Line; $4.25). From the station, take a taxi (☎ 978-356-7238) or bring your bike for the 5 mi. ride to Crane Beach.* ***Open:*** *daily 8am-sunset.*

Buffering the grounds of the Crane family mansion from the ocean, this 4½ mi. barrier beach offers the classic New England coastal scene with typical North Shore attractions—a wide stretch of white sand and cold, calm water bursting with teens and families in the summer. The acres of dunes and maritime forest protect a fragile ecosystem, so look, but don't touch.

WINGAERSHEEK BEACH

Atlantic Rd. (off Rte. 128) on Ipswich Bay, Gloucester, MA. ***Contact:*** *☎ 978-281-9785.* ***By car:*** *Take I-95N to Rte. 128 and get off at Exit 13. Turn left onto Concord St. off the exit ramp and follow to Atlantic Ave. Turn right; the beach is about 1 mi. down to the right. Parking M-F $15, Sa-Su $20.* ***Open:*** *daily 8am-sunset.*

This wide, soft-sanded beach is very popular with families because the surf is always calm, and the water is a bit warmer than at other North Shore beaches. The salt marshes, rocks to climb all over, and fascinating tide pools will keep younger kids entertained.

TRAILS

BLUE HILLS RESERVATION

Metropolitan District Commission Blue Hills Park Headquarters, off Hillside St. in Milton, MA. ***Contact:*** *☎ 617-698-1802, museum ☎ 617-333-0690; www.state.ma.us/mdc/blue.htm.* ***By car:*** *Take I-93S to Exit 3, follow the signs toward Houghtons Pond, and turn right at the stop sign onto*

Hillside St. A parking lot will be on your right, next to Houghtons Pond. To reach park headquarters, continue past the parking lot 500 yards; the headquarters are on the left. **By public transportation:** *While the Blue Hills are not close to any major public transportation, a 15min. bike ride down Randolph Ave. from the "Milton" trolley stop, after T: Ashmont (Red), will take you to a few trails.* **Open:** *Reservation dawn-dusk; museum W-Su 10am-5pm.* **Admission:** *Reservation free; museum $3, seniors $2, ages 3-15 $1.50, under 2 free.*

This 7000 acre park is only 8 mi. from Boston and stretches across five towns, offering 125 mi. of hiking and mountain bike trails as well as swimming, fishing, skiing, ice-skating, horseback riding, and golfing. At the summit of Great Blue Hill, you'll find the **Blue Hill Weather Observatory** in Eliot Tower, one of two stone observation towers constructed by President Roosevelt's Civilian Conservation Corps (CCC) during the 1930s—it's still in use as a weather center.

The **Blue Hills Trailside Museum Visitors Center,** at the foot of the Great Blue Hill, has exhibits with live native animals and their habitats in the Blue Hills. Young-at-heart visitors can climb the lookout tower, feed ducks and deer, and participate on weekends in educational and instructional programs, such as storytime (11am), a live "mystery animal" presentation (12:30pm), family hour (2pm), and Naturalist's Choice (3:30pm). Don't miss the special seasonal events, such as owl prowls in winter, maple sugaring in the spring, and the honey harvest in the fall. The museum is run by the Massachusetts Audubon Society.

MIDDLESEX FELLS RESERVATION

4 Woodland Rd., Stoneham, MA. Botume House is home to the Visitors Ctr. **Contact:** *☎781-662-5230; www.state.ma.us/mdc/fells.htm.* **By car:** *Take I-93N to Exit 33 (Rte. 28N); the parking lot turnoff is about 1½ mi. down. To get to the Botume House, turn right off Rte. 28 onto Elm St. and pass through a rotary onto Woodland Rd. To reach the Bellevue Pond parking lot, take Exit 33 and turn right onto S. Border Rd. at the Roosevelt Circle rotary.* **By public transportation:** *T: Wellington (Orange), then catch a bus ($0.75). For Botume House, take bus #99 to Boston Regional Medical Ctr. For Sheepfold, take bus #100 to Elm St., then continue along Rte. 28, crossing under I-93. For Bellevue Pond, get off bus #100 at Roosevelt Circle and turn onto S. Border Rd. at the Roosevelt rotary.* **Open:** *Reservation daily dawn-dusk; office M-F 9am-5pm, Sa 9am-3pm.*

Spanning parts of Medford, Winchester, Stoneham, Melrose, and Malden, the 2020 acres of the Fells straddle I-93, granting stressed Bostonians a wild backyard only 8 mi. from the city's center. Criss-crossed by old logging roads, hiking trails, and a specially designated mountain biking loop (one of the best in the country), the terrain of the Fells varies from rocky outcroppings sparsely dotted with pine trees to lush marshes awash in lilies.

Created shortly after the inception of the Metropolitan Parks Commission (now the Metropolitan District Commission) in 1892, the Fells have weathered almost 100 years of human use, including the grazing of sheep at the sheepfold parking area in an attempt to create a "pastoral" environment. A noteworthy remnant from this checkered past is **Wright's Tower,** built atop Pine Hill in the 1930s by the Works Progress Administration (WPA). Intended to commemorate Elizur Wright, a successful founder of the life insurance industry who began lobbying for the creation of the park in 1869, it also offers not-to-be-missed views of the city, despite the sad abundance of broken beer bottles.

Thankfully, most of the park shows far fewer signs of human use; the trails and overgrown roads wind undisturbed through airy woods dotted with lakes, making for perfect hiking, biking, and even cross-country skiing. The **Spot Pond Boating Center** (next to the Botume House) loans out kayaks, canoes, rowboats, sailboats, and two-person bicycles. (Must be 18+ with valid photo ID to rent. Open July-Aug. or Sept. W-Su 9:30am-4pm.) However you choose to tackle the Fells, take along a copy of the indispensable *Middlesex Fells Reservation Trail Map* (available for $5 by contacting Friends of the Fells); they're somewhat difficult to obtain, but well worth the effort. For more information on the history of the Fells and current conservation efforts, contact **Friends of the Fells** (☎781-662-2340; www.fells.org). To find out about current goings-on, contact the Botume House Visitors Center.

HISTORIC TOWNS

LEXINGTON

6 mi. northwest of Cambridge and 9 mi. northwest of Boston. ***By car:*** *Follow signs from Rte. 2, Rte. 2A, Rte. 128, or Mass. Ave. Metered parking available on streets surrounding Battle Green.* ***By public transportation:*** *From T: Alewife (Red), take bus #62/76 to Lexington Ctr. (M-Sa only; see www.mbta.com for schedules).* ***By bike:*** *The excellent "Minuteman Trail" runs parallel to Mass. Ave. from Cambridge to New Bedford, passing Lexington en route.* ***Visitors Center:*** *1875 Mass. Ave. (☎781-862-1450), opposite Battle Green. Open daily May-Oct. 9am-5pm, Nov.-Apr. 10am-4pm.*

The famous "shot heard round the world"—the official start of the American Revolution—was fired on Lexington's Battle Green, the destination of famed midnight riders Paul Revere and William Dawes, who raced here on horseback after a signal lantern calling rebel troops to arms was hung at Boston's Old North Church (see p. 53). British troops had hoped to advance secretly on a store of munitions the patriots had gathered at Lexington, but thanks to Revere and Dawes, in the early morning of April 19, 1775, about 77 Minutemen (a moniker bestowed on patriot soldiers because they could be ready in minutes) met the 700 advancing British regulars and kept them at bay. The now famous—though unsubstantiated—words of Capt. John Parker are engraved on a stone at the edge of the Green: "Stand your ground. Don't fire unless fired upon, but if they mean to have a war, let it begin here!"

That frantic late-night battle is still the most important thing that ever happened in Lexington. Now an upscale residential community, the town's layout—and its tourism trade—revolve around the Battle Green and the fateful event that took place one April over 200 years ago.

BATTLE GREEN

You can't miss it. ***Open:*** *24hr.* ***Admission:*** *Free.*

Presided over by a statue of a Lexington Minuteman, the Battle Green is where it all took place on April 19, 1775. A boulder on this expanse of green in the middle of the town bears a plaque that marks the site of the **Old Belfry,** which rang the alarm to the Minutemen. The **Revolutionary Battle Monument,** a granite obelisk erected in 1799 on the west side of the Green, has a tomb with the remains of the slain Minutemen from Lexington. The cemetery behind the large white church on the Green is filled with the well-preserved slate gravestones of other victims of the battle. The enormous mural "The Birth of Liberty" decorates **Cary Memorial Library,** 1874 Mass. Ave., off the Green. Enthusiasts reenact the Battle of Lexington each year at 6am on Patriot's Day (see p. 11).

BUCKMAN TAVERN

1 Bedford St. ***Contact:*** *☎781-862-5598.* ***Open:*** *Mar.-Nov. Su 1-5pm, M-Sa 10am-5pm; hours may change, call ahead.* ***Admission:*** *$5, ages 6-16 $3, under 6 free. Lexington Historical Society offers combo tickets to visit here in conjunction with the Hancock-Clarke House and/or the Munroe Tavern: any 2 houses $8, seniors $7, children $5; all 3 houses $12, seniors $11, children $7.*

Located in Lexington's city center, this tavern is best known as the place where the Minutemen gathered in the pre-dawn darkness to await the arrival of the British troops. When the Redcoats were sighted, Capt. John Parker and his company left the security of the tavern and formed two long lines on the Green. After the fighting was over, the dining table in the kitchen became an operating table for both the Minutemen and the Redcoats. The tavern was popular with colonial travelers passing through the area and remains the most visited of Lexington's historical buildings.

HANCOCK-CLARKE HOUSE

36 Hancock St., ½ mi. from the Visitors Center. **Contact:** *☎ 781-861-0928.* **Open:** *Apr.-May Sa 10am-5pm, Su 1-5pm; June-Oct. Su 1-5pm, M-Sa 10am-5pm; hours may change, call ahead.* **Admission:** *$5, ages 6-16 $3, under 6 free. Admission by guided tour only. Lexington Historical Society offers combo tickets to visit here in conjunction with the Buckman Tavern and/or the Munroe Tavern; for prices, see Buckman Tavern info p. 202.* **Tours:** *30min. tours depart every ½hr. 10am-4:30pm.*

Where's Ralph Waldo Emerson?

Reverend John Hancock, grandfather of the patriot of the same name, came to Lexington in 1698 to serve as the parish priest. He built a small parsonage on this site with a view of the cow pasture that served as Lexington Common. Famed signatory **John Hancock** and fellow rebel **Samuel Adams** were staying the night here (they shared a bed, on display in the house), when **Paul Revere** came pounding on the door around midnight. Hancock wanted to grab a musket and join the Minutemen on the Green, but was persuaded to leave town with Adams and the important papers the men were guarding. Today, the beautifully restored house is full of things that belonged to the Hancocks (and the Clarkes who succeeded them), as well as several unusual colonial war artifacts.

MUNROE TAVERN

Minuteman

1332 Massachusetts Ave., 1 mi. east of Lexington Common. **Contact:** *☎ 781-862-1703 or 781-674-9238.* **Open:** *Apr.-Oct. Sa 10:30am-4:30pm, Su 1-4:30pm; hours may change, call ahead.* **Admission:** *$5, ages 6-16 $3, under 6 free. Admission by guided tour only. Lexington Historical Society offers combo tickets in conjunction with the Buckman Tavern and/or the Hancock-Clarke House; for prices, see Buckman Tavern info p. 202.* **Tours:** *30min. tours depart every ½hr. 10am-4:30pm.*

The man in charge of guarding the Hancock-Clarke house was Orderly Sergeant William Munroe, who ran the Munroe Tavern. Sergeant Munroe fought with 10 of his kinsmen on Battle Green the next morning. Three of them were killed, but he received little thanks for his faithful service. Instead, his tavern was stormed and occupied by Lord Percy and the British regulars retreating from the battle at Concord, who broke into his wine cellar and shot his neighbor John Raymond. Munroe eventually got his tavern back and served as proprietor until 1827, during which time **George Washington** came to dine here (in 1789); an upstairs room preserves any and all items he encountered during the stay. The tavern is also the headquarters of the **Lexington Historical Society** (☎ 781-862-1703), which has a small garden of colonial wildflowers.

Old North Bridge

Minuteman Historical Park

Off Rte. 2A, between Concord and Lexington. ***Contact:*** *Visitors Center ☎ 781-862-7753.* ***Open:*** *Visitors Center daily Apr.-Nov. 9am-5pm; Dec.-Mar. 9am-4pm. Park daily sunrise-sunset. Pick up a copy of the Park's free* Minuteman Messenger *for details on park events and programs.*

The impressive Visitor Center is the best starting point for a trip to this area, as it offers plentiful historical background on the area (including the moving "Road to Revolution" and info on battle reenactments, lectures, and programs year-round).

Battle Road Trail is the true center of this sprawling park's 900 acres. The Trail traces the road on which local militiamen traveled on April 19, 1775 as they confronted the British Regulars in a series of unplanned skirmishes (known as the Battles of Lexington and Concord) that marked the official beginning of the Revolutionary War. (In Lexington (p. 202) and Concord (p. 204), these skirmishes are appropriately the focus of the sights.) The park preserves and protects the sites associated with the battles and interprets the colonists' motivation for revolting against the British

MUSEUM OF OUR NATIONAL HERITAGE

33 Marrett Rd. (Rte. 2A). ***Contact:*** *☎ 781-861-6559; www.monh.org.* ***Open:*** *Su noon-5pm, M-Sa 10am-5pm.* ***Admission:*** *Free.*

This excellent museum (surprisingly under-touristed, considering the quality of its exhibits) is dedicated to the thoughtful exploration of American history through cultural artifacts. In addition to several unusual temporary exhibitions, there are many interesting permanent exhibits that explore life in colonial Lexington. The complex includes a small, non-circulating library of books on American history.

CONCORD

18 mi. northwest of Boston and 6 mi. west of Lexington. ***By car:*** *Take Rte. 2 from Boston or Rte. 2A from Lexington.* ***By public transportation:*** *Commuter rail trains from T: North Station (Green/Orange) run to Concord (Fitchburg Line; $4).* ***Concord Chamber of Commerce:*** *58 Main St. (☎ 978-369-3120; www.concordmachamber.org). Open Apr.-Oct. M-F 9:30am-4:30pm.*

Concord is famous as the site of the second conflict of the American Revolution, and for its status as a 19th-century haven for authors and Transcendentalist philosophers. Today an affluent New England town, Concord is also near both the sprawling **Great Meadows National Wildlife Refuge** (p. 206), one of the best bird-watching spots in Massachusetts, and famed **Walden Pond** (p. 205), popular with nature lovers eager to discover for themselves the wonders Thoreau described in his book *Walden*.

ORCHARD HOUSE & THE WAYSIDE

Lexington Rd., on the Cambridge Turnpike. ***Contact:*** *Orchard House ☎ 978-369-4118; www.louisamayalcott.org. Wayside ☎ 978-369-6975; www.nps.gov/mima/wayside.* ***Open:*** *Orchard House open Apr.-Oct. Su 1-4:30pm, M-Sa 10am-4:30pm; Nov.-Mar. Su 1-4:30pm, M-F 11am-3pm, Sa 10am-4:30pm. Wayside open May-Oct. Th-Tu 10am-5pm.* ***Admission:*** *Orchard House $8, students and seniors $7, ages 6-17 $5; families $20. Wayside $4, under 17 free.* ***Tours:*** *Hourly; admission to both by guided tour only.*

The **Orchard House** was the home of the multi-talented Alcott family. It was here that Alcott daughter Louisa wrote *Little Women*. The tours provide wonderful insight into her life as well as the life of her father Bronson Alcott, a great thinker. **The Wayside,** down the street, was the home of the Alcotts prior to their move to Orchard House and was later occupied by the

Hawthornes, another literary family. Its eclectic architectural styles are somewhat more enticing than the rambling tours within. Louisa May Alcott, Nathaniel Hawthorne, and fellow American writers Ralph Waldo Emerson and Henry David Thoreau have taken up their final residences on "Author's Ridge" in **Sleepy Hollow Cemetery,** on Rte. 62 (three blocks from the town center).

THE OLD MANSE

269 Monument St., ½ mi. from the town center, before the Old North Bridge. ***Contact:*** *☎978-369-3909.* ***Open:*** *Apr.-Oct. Su noon-5pm, M-Sa 10am-5pm.* ***Admission:*** *$7.50, students and seniors $6.50, ages 6-12 $5; families $22.* ***Tours:*** *30min. guided tours every ½hr.; last tour 4:30pm. Admission by guided tour only.*

The Old Manse has changed little since its 18th-century construction and contains many of its original pieces. Most notably, the house was where Nathaniel Hawthorne (of *Scarlet Letter* fame) and his wife Sophia spent their first three years of marriage. The garden outside is based on one planted for Hawthorne by Thoreau. Messages that the Hawthornes etched on windowpanes can still be seen in the house.

CONCORD MUSEUM AND EMERSON HOUSE

Lexington Rd. ***Contact:*** *Museum ☎978-369-9609; www.concordmuseum.org. Emerson House ☎978-369-2236.* ***Open:*** *Museum open Apr.-Dec. Su noon-5pm, M-Sa 9am-5pm; Jan.-Mar. Su 1-4pm, M-Sa 11am-4pm. Emerson House open Apr.-Oct. Su noon-4:30pm, W-Sa 10am-4:30pm.* ***Admission:*** *Museum $7, students and seniors $6, ages 5-18 $3, under 5 free; families $16. Emerson House by 30min. guided tour only. Tours $6, seniors and ages 7-17 $4.*

The Concord Museum's period rooms walk you through Concord's history, starting with the Native Americans and the Puritans. Highlights include the original lamp from Paul Revere's midnight ride and an exhibit of Emerson's study, which is curiously missing from his well-preserved home across the street.

JONATHAN BALL HOUSE

37 Lexington Rd., past the Concord Museum. ***Contact:*** *☎978-369-2578.* ***Open:*** *Su noon-4pm, Tu-Sa 10am-4:30pm.* ***Admission:*** *Free.*

The Concord Art Association, in the Jonathan Ball House, has supported the arts in Concord ever since its founding by American Impressionist painter Elizabeth Wentworth Roberts in 1917. One of the country's oldest non-profit organizations, the Concord Art Association holds 10 exhibitions throughout the year that show the work of promising local artists.

WALDEN POND

915 Walden St., off Rte. 126. ***Contact:*** *☎978-369-3254.* ***By car:*** *Take Rte. 2E to Rte. 126 and follow signs.* ***Open:*** *daily dawn-dusk.* ***Admission:*** *Free. No dogs, fires, camping, bikes on trails, alcoholic beverages, gasoline engines, wind-powered sail craft, novelty inflation devices, or parking on-street.* ***Parking:*** *$5, season pass $35 for the lot off Rte. 126.*

Walden Pond is a "kettle hole," a deep (103 ft.) pond formed over 12,000 years ago by melting glacial ice. When Henry David Thoreau, a devout nature-lover, came to live on Emerson's woodlot on Walden Pond in 1845, he mused: "My friends ask what I will do when I get there. Will it not be employment enough to watch the progress of the seasons?" He built himself a one-room cabin here and did just that—while also studying natural history, gardening, reading, making the first accurate survey of the pond, and drafting his first book. Thoreau occasionally walked into the village and entertained visitors at his house, but spent most of his two years wandering through the forest around Walden Pond. During this time, he kept a journal of his thoughts and encounters that he published in 1845 under the title *Walden*—considered one of the important works of the Transcendentalist movement.

DeCordova Museum & Sculpture Park

Lincoln, MA: 51 Sandy Pond Rd., 16 mi. northwest of Boston. ***Contact:*** *781-259-8355; www.decordova.org.* ***By car:*** *From Rte. 2W, take Rte. 128S, then the Trapelo Rd./Lincoln exit. Turn right onto Trapelo Rd., continue 3 mi. to the Lincoln Ctr. 5-road intersection, and continue ahead onto Sandy Pond Rd.* ***Open:*** *Museum open Tu-Su 11am-5pm. Sculpture Park open sunrise-sunset.* ***Admission:*** *Museum $6; students, seniors, and under 12 $4. Sculpture Park free.*

Named for Julian DeCordova, this museum was one of the first solely devoted to modern art to open in the area. Though now there are several spaces exhibiting contemporary art in the Bay State, few match the depth and breadth of the works shown at the DeCordova—which has shown everything from color photography (its strongest suit) to looped video art.

The true highlight of the DeCordova, however, is not the museum, but its adjacent **Sculpture Park.** Covering the nearly 35 acres of woodlands surrounding the main museum building, the park exhibits an ever-rotating collection of large-scale, outdoor contemporary sculpture by American artists (over 70 works are on display at any time). Most of the works are taken from the permanent collections of museums across the globe, but a handful are site-specific works commissioned by the DeCordova and created with its location in the park in mind.

Due in large part to Thoreau's efforts to preserve Walden for human enjoyment, Walden Pond became a state reservation in 1922. It encompasses 411 acres, where visitors are welcome to swim, hike, picnic, canoe, fish, cross-country ski, and snowshoe—trail activities are limited to foot traffic. Reservation staff conduct guided walking tours by prior arrangement, as well as craft making, poetry readings, stargazing, and storytelling. Although visiting after the pond closes is forbidden, it has become something of a rite of passage for local college students to slip in after dark and skinny-dip.

GREAT MEADOWS

Accessible by Weir Hill Rd. (Sudbury) and Monson Rd. (Concord). ***Contact:*** *Visitors Center, Weir Hill Unit, Weil Hill Rd. 978-443-4661.* ***By car:*** *Take Rte. 2W to Sudbury Rd., turn left on Concord Rd., then left on Lincoln Rd. after Lincoln-Sudbury High School, then left on Weir Hill Rd.* ***Open:*** *Reservation dawn-dusk; Visitors Center M-F 8am-4pm.* ***Admission:*** *Free. No horses, motorized vehicles, hunting, campfires, or swimming.*

This 3400 acre national fish and wildlife refuge is composed of freshwater wetlands and upland areas that provide some of the best inland birding sites in Massachusetts. The area is also crisscrossed with trails for wildlife observation, hiking, cross-country skiing, photography, and environmental education programs.

SALEM

16 mi. northeast of Boston. ***By car:*** *Take Rte. 1A or Rte. 107N through Lynn and Swampscott. Alternatively, take I-95 or Rte. 1N to Rte. 128, then follow Rte. 114 into the center of Salem. Color-coded signs will direct you to the Visitors Center (brown), museums and historic sites (green), and parking garages (blue). Parking is free on streets around the Salem Common.* ***By public transportation:*** *Commuter rail trains run from T: North Station (Green/Orange) to Salem (Newburyport/Rockport Line; 30min., $3). MBTA Buses #450 and 455 from T: Haymarket (Green/Orange) also run to Salem (45min., $0.75; see www.mbta.com for schedules).* ***Salem Visitors Center:*** *2 New Liberty St. (978-740-1650), sells tickets for Salem Trolley Tours ($10, seniors $9, under 12 $5), which stop at all the historic sites. Open daily 9am-5pm. The trolleys are somewhat unnecessary, since most of the tourist sites are in the northeast corner of this entirely walkable city.*

Founded in 1626 by Puritans from Plymouth Colony, Salem is infamous for its **witch trials** of 1692, which resulted in the deaths of 19 innocent victims and the imprisonment of over 150 more. (The names of those hanged are inscribed on a pile of stone blocks known as the Witch Memorial, at the corner of Charter and Liberty St., in the Old Burying Ground. The cemetery is also where John Hathorne, one of the most notorious witch trial judges, is buried.) Almost as frightening as the actual trials, however, is the way commercialized witch kitsch has nearly taken over this pleasant waterfront city and the plethora of "witching" sites threatens to obscure Salem's quintessentially New England character.

In its shipping heyday in the 19th century, the "Venice of the New World" had the fifth-busiest seaport in the country and was the richest city in the country per capita. At one point, Salem sent so many ships to China that the Chinese Emperor mistakenly believed Salem to be a sovereign nation. The Peabody Essex Museum, established in 1799 as the East Indian Marine Society, has a fantastic collection of artifacts from those days. Famous Salem native **Nathaniel Hawthorne**—who added the "w" to his name to avoid being connected to his great-great-grandfather (a witch trial judge)—worked as a cargo surveyor for the customs authority and found inspiration for most of his works in his hometown.

HOUSE OF THE SEVEN GABLES

54 Turner St. Follow Derby St. 3 blocks past Central Wharf, then turn right on Hardy St. ***Contact:*** *☎978-744-0991; www.7gables.org.* ***Open:*** *daily July-Oct. 10am-7pm; Nov.-Dec. and Feb.-June 10am-5pm.* ***Admission:*** *$10, seniors $9, ages 5-12 $6.50, under 5 free. Combination ticket with "Salem 1630: Pioneer Village" $16, seniors $15, children $10.50. Admission by 30min. guided tour only.*

Surrounded by a colorful flower garden and endowed with magnificent views of Salem Harbor, the House of Seven Gables is one of the most beautiful (and most interesting) places to visit in Salem. Officially the Turner-Ingersoll Mansion—Capt. John Turner built it and the Ingersolls lived in it—this well-preserved pile of boards became famous after **Nathaniel Hawthorne** (whose cousin Susannah Ingersoll lived here) used it as the setting for his 1851 novel *The House of the Seven Gables*. The novel made Hawthorne famous, so when philanthropist Caroline Emmerton bought the house in 1908, she also bought the house where Hawthorne was born and moved it next door.

By a window in the dining room stands Susannah's grandfather's chair, which appears in both Hawthorne's short story "Tales from the Grandfather's Chair" and *The House of the Seven Gables*. During Emmerton's renovations, she discovered a hidden staircase and beneath it a slave's prayer book, which suggests that the Ingersolls may have helped slaves to escape via the Underground Railroad.

SALEM MARITIME NATIONAL HISTORIC SITE

193 Derby St., at Central Wharf. Walk 2 blocks downhill from Salem Common on Washington Sq. W., then turn left on Derby St. to reach the wharves. ***Contact:*** *☎978-740-1660; www.nps.gov/sama.* ***Open:*** *daily 9am-5pm.* ***Admission:*** *Free.* ***Tours:*** *$5, seniors and ages 6-15 $3, under 6 free. Tours run continuously in summer; off-season 2-3 per day.*

What little remains of Salem's once-bustling waterfront is on display within the Salem Maritime Park, including the 2000 ft. **Derby Wharf,** capped by a lighthouse. The shorter **Central Wharf** is where the *Friendship*, a reconstruction of a 3-masted Salem "East Indiaman" merchant ship, originally built in 1797, is moored. Tours of the *Friendship* include a visit to the **Customs House.** Rangers also lead tours of two other historic waterfront buildings—the **Derby House** and the **Narbonne House.** Other buildings, including the West India Goods Store, the 18th-century garden wharves, the Scale House, and the Rigging Shed are open to the public.

SALEM WITCH MUSEUM

19½ Washington Sq. N., opposite the Common off Hawthorne Blvd. ***Contact:*** *☎978-744-1692; www.salemwitchmuseum.com.* ***Open:*** *daily July-Aug. 10am-7pm; Sept.-June 10am-5pm.* ***Admission:*** *$6:50, seniors $6, ages 6-14 $4:50, under 6 free. Cash only.*

Billed as Salem's most touristed attraction, the Salem Witch Museum is housed in an imposing neo-Gothic church across from the Salem Common and beside the gloomy, windswept statue of Salem founder **Roger Conant.** A creepy audiovisual presentation (25min., every 30min.)—which uses grim, life-size wax figures and a god-like voice-over—graphically evokes the terror and hysteria of the dark days of 1692. Visitors are encouraged to explore the exhibit "Witches: Evolving Perceptions" on their own while they wait for the next show. Skeptical tourists may be interested to know that while the museum is undoubtedly profiting from Salem's reputation, the curators have clearly taken pains to present carefully planned, thoughtful exhibits that invite visitors to consider the larger role that scapegoating has played throughout American history.

PEABODY ESSEX MUSEUM

East India Sq., at the corner of Essex and New Liberty St., 1 block from the Visitors Center on the pedestrian walkway. ***Contact:*** *☎866-745-1876 or 978-745-9500; www.pem.org.* ***Open:*** *F-W 10am-5pm, Th 10am-9pm.* ***Admission:*** *$12, seniors $10, students $8, under 17 free. Admission includes house tours.*

Since Salem made its fortune from the sea, it is particularly appropriate that the best museum in town is dedicated to preserving the city's maritime history. The Peabody Essex Museum is the product of the 1992 merger of the **East Indian Marine Society,** founded in 1799, and the **Essex Historical Society,** established in 1821. The Essex half of the museum is retained in the Phillips Library, which houses more than 400,000 rare books, over 5200 ft. of manuscripts, and more than a million rare and vintage photographs, all of which document three centuries of New England life and culture.

The Peabody division concentrates on the artwork and cultural artifacts that the Marine Society collected from the four corners of the world, particularly from Asia. The permanent collection includes exhibits entitled "Maritime New England," "Port of Salem," and "East India Marine Hall." The museum also houses several galleries of Chinese and Japanese ceramics and decorative arts exported to European markets.

SALEM WAX MUSEUM OF WITCHES & SEAFARERS

288 Derby St. Walk 3 blocks downhill from Salem Common on Washington Sq. W. and turn right on Derby St.; the museum is on the 2nd block on the right. ***Contact:*** *☎800-298-2929; www.salemwaxmuseum.com.* ***Open:*** *daily Apr.-June and Sept. 10am-6pm; July-Aug. 10am-10pm; Oct. 10am-midnight; Nov.-Mar. 11am-4pm.* ***Admission:*** *$5.50, seniors $5, children $3. Combination "Hysteria" Pass for Wax Museum and Witch Village $10, seniors $9, students and children $5, under 5 free.*

The Wax Museum's dual focus on witches and seafarers gives it a broader perspective on Salem history than other witch-centric sites. The life-size wax representations of politicians, pirates, and scenes from the witch trials are displayed in a large, well-lit room. Alongside the villains are Roger Conant, Nathaniel Hawthorne, and America's first millionaire—a Salem merchant named Elias Hasket Derby.

PLYMOUTH

40 mi. (1hr.) southeast of Boston. ***By car:*** *Driving is preferable. Follow I-93S to Rte. 3, then take Exit 6A to Plymouth Center, via Rte. 44E (or Exit 4 to Plimoth Plantation).* ***By bus:*** *Plymouth & Brockton (☎508-746-0378; www.p-b.com) runs from T: South Station (Red) and Logan Airport, T: Airport (Blue), to the Exit 5 Info Ctr. ($9).* ***By public transportation:*** *The commuter rail runs from T: South Station (Red) to the Cordage Park Station (Plymouth/Kingston Line; 1hr., 3-4 per day, $5). From there, you can catch a local GATRA bus ($0.75, seniors and children $0.35, under 6 free) to Plymouth Center.* ***Visitors Center:*** *170 Water St.*

The story that the Pilgrims took their first steps in America on Plymouth Rock is mostly myth—but don't tell that to the droves of visitors and proprietors of cheesy "Olde Pilgrym" shops that populate this mecca of camera toters. An uninspiring chunk of the "famous" rock (a mere chip off the old block that was supposedly the first place they landed) is displayed under an elegant granite pavilion along the waterfront in Plymouth. However, the rock is little more than a place for people to toss their spare change: the Puritans were blown off course in their trip across the Atlantic, and actually first dropped anchor at Provincetown (p. 223), on Cape Cod, in mid-November. Since it was too late in the year to sail around the Cape, scouts chose Plymouth Harbor as the likeliest spot for them to survive the winter; no one bothered to "identify" their landing place until 1741. Nevertheless, Plymouth Rock was a symbol of liberty during the American Revolution, and eager tourists chipped most of it away before it was moved to its present location on Water St.

Though much of Plymouth proper is a tourist trap, the spirit and lifestyle of the original settlement is well preserved at **Plimoth Plantation,** a historical park that recreates the colony as it was in 1627. Visitors can also tour the reconstructed **Mayflower II,** which is docked off Water St., while the **Pilgrim Hall Museum** has some of the only remaining authentic artifacts from the Pilgrims on display. Cheap food and **free parking** abound along Water and North St.

Supplies

PLIMOTH PLANTATION

3 mi. south of town. ***Contact:*** *☎508-746-1622; www.plimoth.org.* ***By car:*** *Take Exit 4 off Rte. 3 and follow signs; from Cape Cod, take Exit 5 off Rte. 3N, then go under Rte. 3, get on Rte. 3S, and take Exit 4.* ***By public transportation:*** *Take the GATRA "Mayflower Link" bus from downtown Plymouth.* ***Open:*** *Apr.-Nov. daily 9am-5pm.* ***Admission:*** *$20, ages 6-12 $12. Combination discount ticket (valid for 2 consecutive days) for Plantation and* Mayflower II: *$22, students and seniors $20, ages 6-12 $14. $3 off combo pass/$2 off Plantation admission for AAA members.*

The Beautiful Atlantic

This painstakingly recreated (everything on the plantation is as authentic as possible) but painfully overpriced Pilgrim settlement has long been an annual pilgrimage for 4th graders across the Bay State. Given the price, the plantation is best suited to history buffs and families. Costumed interpreters play the parts of each of the settlement's actual inhabitants in 1627, the year when time—in the form of Gov. William Bradford's written record—stopped in "Plimoth." In winter, when the plantation is closed, the impostor Puritans must take special classes on Pilgrim lore and memorize every detail known about the individuals they represent, down to their regional English dialect and their views about religion and food. Nothing is labeled, and no tours are given, so come prepared to ask questions, but be aware that the "Pilgrims" you encounter here pretend not to know about anything that happened after 1627.

At the **Visitors Center,** a 15min. film introduces you to the world that you are about to enter. As you leave the theater, you'll pass the **Carriage House Crafts Center,** where artisans make reproductions of 17th-century goods. After exploring

Plimouth Plantation

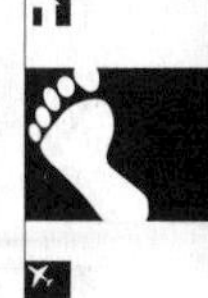

ON THE MENU

Cranberry Wine

Plymouth Colony Winery, *56 Pinewood Rd., 4 mi. west of Plymouth Center, off Rte. 44.* ***Contact:*** *☎508-747-3334; www.plymouthcolonywinery.com.* ***Open:*** *Apr.-Dec. Su noon-5pm, M-Sa 10am-5pm; Feb.-Mar. Sa 10am-4pm, Su noon-4pm.*

As the home of cranberry conglomerate Ocean Spray, the Plymouth region might as well be the unofficial cranberry capital of the world. Each year the tiny berry generates more than $200 million in revenue for Massachusetts farmers, making it the state's number one food crop. Visitors can witness the cranberry harvest season in full swing with a trip down Rte. 44 or Rte. 58. between mid-September and early November.

With that many cranberries, who needs grapes? If you miss the cranberry season, drown those sorrows with the one-of-a-kind cranberry wine. **Plymouth Colony Winery** offers free tastings at their nine acre cranberry winery. Tangy, crisp, refreshing—this may be the beginning of something big.

the village and meeting the locals, follow the **Eel River Nature Walk** down to the Wampanoag Indian campsite, known as **Hobbamock's Homesite.** Although most of the Native Americans kept their distance from the white strangers, Chief Hobbamock was enlisted to act as the liaison between the tribes and the newcomers. The small compound that he and his family built near the English encampment is faithfully reconstructed here, but the interpreters speak from a contemporary point of view about the experiences of their ancestors—a welcome break from the annoyance that hours of affected accents and feigned ignorance can imbue.

MAYFLOWER II

State Pier, off Water St., near Plymouth Rock. ***Open:*** *Apr.-Nov. daily 9am-5pm.* ***Admission:*** *$8, ages 6-12 $6.*

Three miles north of Plimoth Plantation sits a replica of the leaky vessel that brought the Pilgrims to Plymouth. In 1955, over 300 years after the original was scrapped, historians commissioned an English shipbuilder to rebuild the historic ship. In 1957, it made a 55-day voyage across the Atlantic and is now moored just a few feet from Plymouth Rock. By modern standards, the 106½ ft. ship seems far too small to have been the home of 102 Pilgrims, 25 crew members, various animals, and the supplies necessary to create a community from scratch. The boat tour proves an amusing and enlightening experience, enhanced by period actors borrowed from nearby Plimouth Plantation who sing songs and fix useless fishing nets.

PILGRIM HALL MUSEUM

75 Court St., on Rte. 3A. From the waterfront, walk north on Water St. and turn left on Chilton St. Free museum parking. ***Contact:*** *☎508-746-1620; www.pilgrimhall.org.* ***Open:*** *Feb.-Dec. daily 9:30am-4:30pm.* ***Admission:*** *$5, seniors $4.50, ages 5-17 $3; families $15.*

Founded in 1824 by the Pilgrim Society as a "monumental temple" to their ancestors, Pilgrim Hall claims to be the oldest continuously operating public museum in the country. That fact not withstanding, the museum proves to be remarkably dull. The architecture of the building, where Ralph Waldo Emerson once lectured, is the only real draw. Sure its stuffed to the gills with artifacts from Plymouth's (and America's) past, but they're all musty and relatively underwhelming—a chair here, a crib there. The main hall is dominated by what comes closest to a highlight, the wooden rib cage of the *Sparrow-Hawk*, a 17th-century transatlantic vessel that wrecked in 1626 and was preserved in Cape Cod sands for 250 years.

CAPE COD

It is wholly unknown to the fashionable world, and probably will never be agreeable to them.
—Henry David Thoreau, *Cape Cod*

Thoreau couldn't have been more wrong, and it is ironic that the book which held such a dire prediction would be the same book that would spark the stratospheric rise of the Cape's popularity. Originally named for its plentiful cod population, Cape Cod is now New England's premier vacation destination, drawing tourists in droves to its charming small towns and diverse, sun-drenched landscapes—everything from cranberry bogs and sandy beaches to salt marshes, hardwood forests, deep freshwater ponds, and even desert-like dunes.

Though parts of the Cape are known as the playground of the rich and famous—and the peninsula is in general geared toward bigger spenders—it can be an option for budget travelers, thanks to an emphasis on free activities (sunbathing, hiking, etc.) and a decent hostel and budget B&B system. The Cape also serves as the gateway to Martha's Vineyard (p. 228) and Nantucket (p. 236), two islands with unsurpassed natural beauty just off the southern coast.

ORIENTATION

Cape Cod resembles a bent arm, with Falmouth and Woods Hole (p. 213) at its armpit, transport hub Hyannis (p. 218) on its bicep, Chatham at the elbow, and queer mecca Provincetown (p. 223) at its clenched fist. Terminology for locations on the Cape can be confusing. **Upper Cape** refers to the more suburbanized and developed part of Cape Cod closer to the mainland. Proceeding eastward away from the mainland, you travel "down-Cape" to the **Middle Cape** and **Lower Cape,** finally reaching the **Outer Cape,** where remote towns like Eastham, Wellfleet, and Truro (home to the Cape's two HI-AYH hostels; see p. 224) reside, far enough out to have maintained the wind-blown charm of Thoreau's Cape Cod. The ocean beaches here, with sandy dunes and surfable waves, are the best on the peninsula. At the tip of the Cape lies picture-perfect **Provincetown** (p. 223), a former artists' colony that is now a large gay and lesbian community. For more information, visit the **Cape Cod Visitor's Information Center,** 3 Shoot Flying Hill Rd. in Hyannis. (☎508-362-3225. Open daily 8:30am-5pm.)

GETTING THERE

BY CAR

Driving is the best way to get to and around the Cape, as a car gives you much more flexibility than a bike or public transportation. Be sure to plan your driving schedule well: traffic from Boston to the Cape is heaviest on Friday afternoons, with traffic in the reverse direction heaviest on Sunday evenings. Gas is more expensive on the Cape, so fill up the tank before you get off the highway. For car rentals, see p. 282.

BY BUS

Buses to the Cape leave from Boston's South Station (T: South Station (Red); see p. 18). **Bonanza Bus** (☎888-751-8800; www.bonanzabus.com) runs express routes to most major towns (daily approx. every hr. 8am-10pm), while the **Plymouth & Brockton Street Railway** (schedules and fares ☎508-746-0378, office ☎508-746-4795; www.p-b.com) has more extensive bus service to most towns on Cape Cod. Schedules and prices change so frequently that it's best to call or check the website for the most up-to-date information. Note that buses from Boston to the Cape can run up to 30min. late because of traffic.

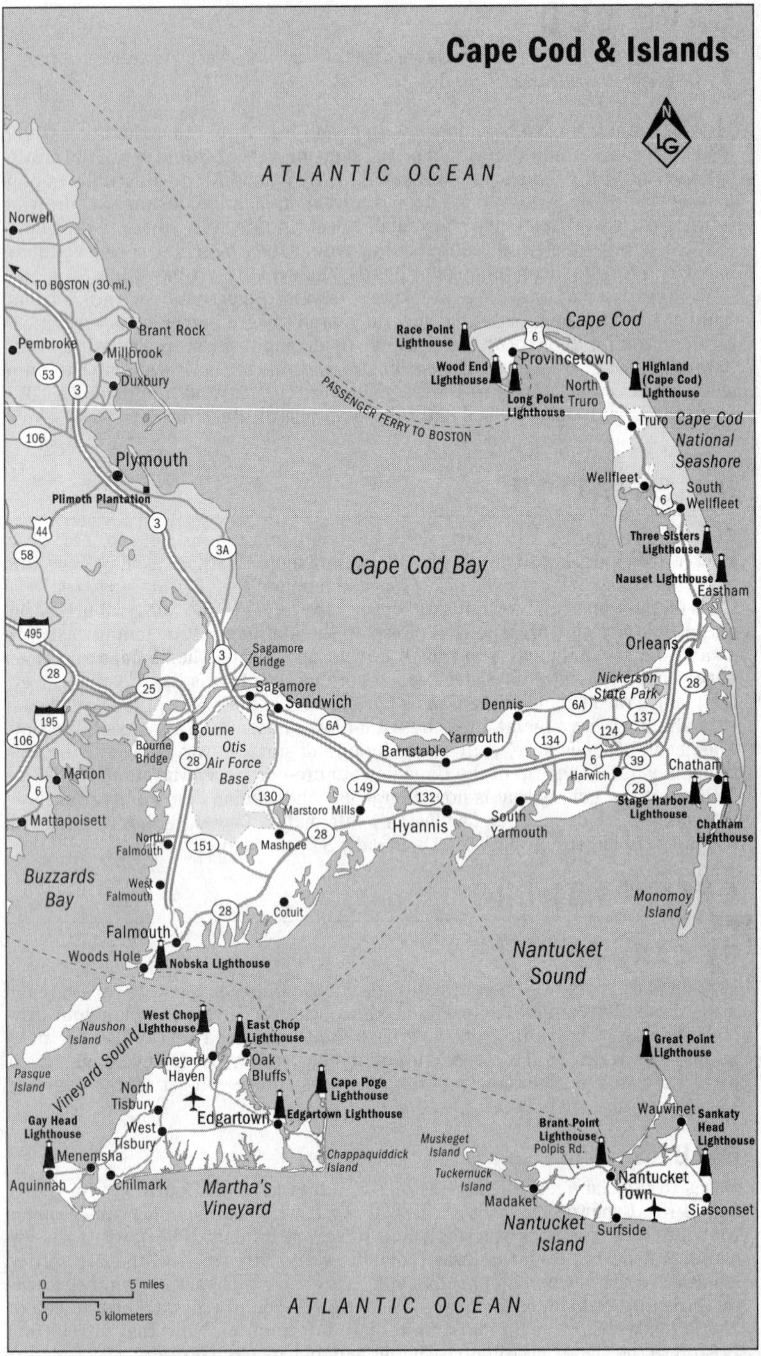

Cape Cod & Islands

ATLANTIC OCEAN

Norwell
TO BOSTON (30 mi.)
Brant Rock
Pembroke
Millbrook
Duxbury
Plymouth
Plimoth Plantation
Cape Cod
Race Point Lighthouse
Wood End Lighthouse
Provincetown
Long Point Lighthouse
Highland (Cape Cod) Lighthouse
North Truro
Truro
PASSENGER FERRY TO BOSTON
Cape Cod National Seashore
Wellfleet
South Wellfleet
Three Sisters Lighthouse
Nauset Lighthouse
Eastham
Cape Cod Bay
Orleans
Nickerson State Park
Sagamore Bridge
Sagamore
Sandwich
Dennis
Bourne
Bourne Bridge
Otis Air Force Base
Yarmouth
Barnstable
Harwich
Chatham
Marion
Mattapoisett
Marstons Mills
Hyannis
South Yarmouth
Stage Harbor Lighthouse
Chatham Lighthouse
North Falmouth
Mashpee
Buzzards Bay
West Falmouth
Cotuit
Monomoy Island
Falmouth
Woods Hole
Nobska Lighthouse
Nantucket Sound
Naushon Island
West Chop Lighthouse
East Chop Lighthouse
Vineyard Sound
Pasque Island
Vineyard Haven
Oak Bluffs
Great Point Lighthouse
North Tisbury
Cape Poge Lighthouse
Edgartown
Edgartown Lighthouse
Wauwinet
Gay Head Lighthouse
West Tisbury
Brant Point Lighthouse
Polpis Rd.
Sankaty Head Lighthouse
Muskeget Island
Menemsha
Chappaquiddick Island
Tuckernuck Island
Nantucket Town
Aquinnah
Chilmark
Martha's Vineyard
Madaket
Siasconset
Nantucket Island
Surfside
0 5 miles
0 5 kilometers

ATLANTIC OCEAN

BY FERRY

Ferries to the Cape run daily from Boston to Provincetown and are a fast, cheap way to reach the Outer Cape. **Boston Harbor Cruises** (☎617-227-4321 or 877-733-9425; www.bostonharborcruises.com) has high-speed catamarans that make the trip in only 90min. Ferries depart Boston from Long Wharf, near T: Aquarium (Blue). (May-Oct. daily 9am, returning 4pm; additional ferries at peak travel times—call or check the website for times. One-way $28, round-trip $49; students and seniors $21/$35.) *Let's Go* recommends BHC (all but officially known as the "Fairy Ferry") for their quick ride, well-appointed boats (including on-board bar), and proximity to the T.

Bay State Cruises (☎617-748-1428; www.baystatecruises.com) also runs regular and high-speed ferries from Boston's Commonwealth Pier, at the World Trade Center, on the Waterfront near T: South Station (Red), to MacMillian Wharf in P-town. There is a ticket and info desk at the Provincetown Chamber of Commerce. Regular ferries depart F-Su from Boston at 9:30am and leave from Provincetown at 3:30pm. (late June-Sept. F-Su. 3hr. One-way $18, round-trip $29; seniors $15/$23; children $14/$19. Bike $5 each way.) High-speed ferries depart Boston late May-Sept. daily at 8am, 1, and 5:30pm and return at 10am, 3, and 7:30pm. (1½hr. One-way $35, round-trip $55; seniors $30/$50; children $20/$45; bike $5 each way.)

BY BICYCLE

Once you're on the Cape, cycling is the most scenic way to travel the area's gentle slopes (as long as you're up for some exercise). Bus and ferry companies allow bikes to be taken on board for a $3-5 fee (Bonanza Bus requires bikes to be dismantled and stored in a bike box); there are also countless bike rental companies all over the Cape. The park service has a free map of trails, and the more detailed, very useful *Cape Cod Bike Book* ($3) is available at most Cape bookstores. The trails, which line either side of the Cape Cod Canal and the National Seashore, rank among the country's most picturesque, as does the 26 mi. **Cape Cod Rail Trail** (p. 222) from Dennis to Wellfleet. The 125 mi. **Boston-Cape Cod Bikeway** connects Boston to Provincetown; most cyclists do the trip in 1-2 days and then take the ferry back from Provincetown (p. 213).

FALMOUTH & WOODS HOLE

1½hr. from Boston. ***By car:*** *Take Rte. 3S to Rte. 6W to Rte. 28S.* ***By bus:*** *Bonanza Bus (☎888-751-8800; www.bonanzabus.com) leaves from Logan Airport and South Station in Boston and stops at Falmouth Bus Station, on Depot St. (1½hr.; one-way $22, round-trip $40.) The bus continues on to the ferry terminal in Woods Hole for the same price. Falmouth: Walk down Depot St., turn right onto N. Main St., then left onto Main St., and walk a couple of blocks to where most attractions are located. Woods Hole: Turn left out of the ferry terminal and walk up the road to Water St., turn right onto Water St.; most sights cluster there.*

Coming from Boston, Falmouth and Woods Hole are the first true Cape towns daytrippers encounter. Unlike other places on the Cape, these towns sustain a decent-sized year-round population and in summer tend to have less of a touristed feel, as most people bypass them to drive further up the Cape or catch the ferry to the Islands. However, Falmouth and Woods Hole have the same sun and sand as other towns, as well as some great local bars and restaurants, making it worthwhile to skip the long drive or ferry ride and park it here for a relaxing weekend.

PRACTICAL INFORMATION

Chamber of Commerce: 20 Academy Ln. (☎508-548-8500 or 800-526-8532; www.falmouth-capecod.com), off Main St. in Falmouth. Open M-Sa 9am-5pm.

Internet Access: Falmouth Public Library (☎508-457-2555), turn left of Main St. onto Library Ln. Free Internet access available to the public. Open M and Th 9:30am-5:30pm, Tu-W 9:30am-9pm, F-Sa 9:30am-5pm.

Post Office: 120 Main St. (☎508-548-3885). Open M-F 6am-6pm, Sa 6am-4:30pm.

Taxis: The only cab in town, **Falmouth All Village Taxi** (☎508-540-7200) goes from Falmouth center to Woods Hole for around $11.

Bike Rental: In summer traffic, the quickest way to get from Falmouth to Woods Hole and vice versa is often the bike path. To rent a bike, head to **Corner Cycle,** 115 Palmer Ave. (☎508-540-4195). Bikes $8 per hr.; $14 per day, return before close; overnight $18. Open M-F 10am-6pm, Sa-Su 9:30am-5:30pm.

ACCOMMODATIONS

Both Falmouth and Woods Hole are chock-full of quaint B&Bs, which serve as perfect respites for the traveler escaping the city. Peace doesn't come cheap though, as evidenced by the rates at most B&Bs. During the summer, reservations are needed far in advance. Below are the standouts, where the price of the stay is well worth it.

Village Green Inn, 40 Main St. (☎508-548-5621 or 800-237-1119; www.villagegreeninn.com). With so many accolades lining the walls, it almost seems as if this B&B couldn't possibly live up to the hype. However, they manage to exceed even the highest expectations. Excellent service and elegant, peaceful rooms, not to mention a full breakfast every morning at 8:30am, make this the best place to stay in Falmouth and Woods Hole. No children under 12. All rooms have phone, cable TV, private bath, and A/C; 2 rooms have working fireplaces. Check-in 3-6pm; check-out 11am. Doubles $90-175; 2-person suites $150-235; 3rd person additional $30. ❹

Inn at One Main, 1 Main St. (☎508-540-7469 or 888-281-6246; www.innatonemain.com). Though the rooms are a little on the cheesy side, with names like the Sunshine Room and the Blueberry Room, this friendly inn is reasonably priced and a great place to get some solid sleep or to relax on a porch. All rooms with private bath. Doubles $120-175. ❹

Ideal Spot Motel, 614 W. Falmouth Hwy. (☎508-548-2258 or 800-269-6910; www.idealspotmotel.com). North of Falmouth Center, this is the budget option for Falmouth. Unfortunately, the drop in price is reflected in the quality. Rooms lack the tasteful decor of more expensive B&Bs, but are still clean and functional. All rooms come with kitchenette, cable TV, and A/C. Doubles in summer $100-115; off-season $65-80; 3rd person additional $15. ❸

La Maison Cappellari at Mostly Hall, 27 Main St. (☎508-548-3786; www.mostlyhall.com). With a lovely porch overlooking a well-groomed lawn, a gazebo, and rooms decorated in both European and New England styles, La Maison is classy from floor to ceiling. But before you make reservations, remember that class comes with a price, and that price is usually rather high. No children under 16. TVs and phones in the common area. All rooms with private bath and A/C. Stays for 2 or more nights require 10% deposit. Check-in 3-7pm; check-out 11am. Reservations daily 10am-7pm. Doubles $165-225. ❺

FOOD

Though most meals in the area tend to be rather expensive, there are some innovative dinner menus and bargain lunch places that deserve a visit. Those looking for a midday snack, should stroll down Main St. to **Ben and Bill's Chocolate Emporium,** on Main St. at Walker St., for a sugary pick-me-up. Options include homemade fudge and tasty ice cream in creative flavors, including lobster. (☎508-548-7878. Two heaping scoops $4.25. Open June-Aug. Su 10am-11pm, M-Sa 9am-11pm; Sept.-May Su 10am-6pm, M-Sa 9am-6pm.)

Clam Shack, 227 Clinton Ave. (☎508-540-7758). Fresh, cheap seafood right on the waterfront. Need we say more? The Clam Shack may lack the prestigious facades of most Cape Cod eateries, but the food and prices are the best around. Seafood plates $10-13; seafood rolls $5-12. From the grill $2-6. Open June-Aug. daily 11:30am-8pm. ❷

Stir Crazy, 626 MacArthur Blvd (☎508-564-6464), in Pocasset, just north of Falmouth, in a strip mall (but don't let that deter you). If your appetite can't wait, stop in at Stir Crazy on your way from Boston to the Cape. In a region saturated with seafood places, Stir Crazy serves up unexpectedly innovative Cambodian and Vietnamese cuisine. Stir-fry $12-15. Open Tu-Th and Su 4-9pm, F 11am-2:30pm and 4-10pm, Sa 4-10pm. ❸

Betsy's Diner, 457 Main St. (☎508-540-0060). Their motto is "eat heavy," and their food makes that possible with generous portions at reasonable prices. Breakfast all day $5-7. Entrees $7-8. Open Su 6am-2pm, M-Sa 6am-8pm. ❶

Pie in the Sky, 10 Water St. (☎508-540-5475), by the ferry in Woods Hole. This veggie-friendly bakery puts together standard sandwiches with delightful twists. Sample "the Vermonter" (ham, green apples, cheddar, and dijon; $6). Sandwiches $4-6. Open daily 6am-9pm. ❶

Laureen's, 170 Main St. (☎508-540-9104), across from Town Hall. If you find yourself on Main St. around lunch time, stop in at Laureen's for gourmet sandwiches ($8-10). The sandwiches are a little pricey, but still one of the better options on Main St. Open in summer daily 8:30am-5pm; off-season M-Sa 8:30am-4pm. ❷

SIGHTS

The main attraction may be the area's beaches, but there are a few other sights to check out during a break from the sun, including the world-renowned WHOI.

WOODS HOLE OCEANOGRAPHIC INSTITUTE. WHOI (pronounced hoo-ey) is the nation's chief oceanographic institute. What exactly does an oceanographic institute do? Well, WHOI was responsible, among other things for discovering the sunken *Titanic*. Today, visitors can stop by the Information Center and find out more about their many undertakings. For more on educational and volunteer opportunities at WHOI, see **Alternatives to Tourism,** p. 276. *(Info Ctr.: 93 Water St. ☎508-289-2252. Open M-F 8am-5pm.)*

WOODS HOLE SCIENCE AQUARIUM. Though it has recently tightened security, the aquarium is still a fun and informative—not to mention air-conditioned—summer activity. It's especially popular with children, who enjoy watching the daily seal feedings. *(Follow Water St. past the ferry; the road will curve to the right and the aquarium will be on your left. ☎508-495-2001. Open Tu-Sa 11am-4pm. Seal feedings 11am and 4pm. Admission free; donations accepted.)*

NOBSKA LIGHTHOUSE. Between Buzzards Bay and Vineyard Sound in Woods Hole, the 42 ft. lighthouse is picture-perfect Cape Cod. The beaches around the lighthouse are private, but it is still a breathtaking scene to drive or bike past. *(Take Rte. 28 through Falmouth follow signs for Woods Hole, turn right onto Woods Hole Rd., then left onto Church St.)*

BEACHES

At times, the beach can become a bit of a social scene, making it difficult to find a patch of sand. The beaches may not be a secret, but don't let that stop you from basking in the healing powers of the Cape sun. For more information on the beaches or to purchase car passes, contact the **Surf Drive Beach Bathhouse** (☎508-548-8623; open mid-June to Aug. 9am-4pm) or **Falmouth Town Hall,** 59 Town Hall Sq. (☎508-548-7611), off Main St.

Chapoquoit, south of Old Silver, on the western shore of North Falmouth. "Chappy," as the beach is more affectionately called, is one of the more placid beaches and thus, more of a family scene.

Falmouth Heights, on the southern shore of Falmouth, along Grand Ave. The Heights, as the beach is more commonly known, more than any restaurant or bar, is the place to see and be seen. Expect a young and attractive crowd that is more into checking themselves out than anyone else. No parking without a sticker, though anyone can walk onto the beach.

Old Silver, on the western shore of North Falmouth, off Quaker Rd. A popular beach, expect hordes of beach-goers. Calmer water makes it less of a sporty beach and more of a tourist destination. Parking $15.

Stoney, in Woods Hole. Stoney is the only public beach in Woods Hole. Though it is quite tiny, the beach is not as well known as the Heights or Old Silver and provides a potential escape from the masses.

Surf Drive, west of Falmouth Heights Beach, along Surf Dr. What it lacks in shoreline, Surf Drive makes up in windsurfing (thus the name). Parking $10.

NIGHTLIFE

Far from Boston and its mock techno dance clubs, the nightlife options in Falmouth and Woods Hole are rather chill, ranging from local pubs to live music to bars for those waiting to catch the ferry to the Islands. So, pick a spot and ease that sunburn with a drink.

Captain Kidd's, 77 Water St. (☎508-548-8563), in Woods Hole. A local bar with no gimmicks, just strong drinks and a view of the harbor. The laid-back atmosphere is perfect for sitting around and enjoying the night. Off-season W open mic night. Beer $3-4; cocktails $4+. Open daily 11am-1am.

Liam Maguire's, 273 Main St. (☎508-548-0285), across from the library. Serving up standard American food (burgers $6-9) by day, Liam's becomes a packed live music venue by night, as namesake Liam plays to a devoted local crowd. Beer $3-4.50. Music nightly 9pm. Off-season W open mic night and Th R&B. Occasional cover. Open Su noon-1am, M-Sa 11:30am-1am.

Grumpy's Pub, 29 Locust St. (☎508-540-3930; www.grumpys.com), off Main St. Named for the owner's grandfather, Grumpy's is as local as you can get and probably as Irish. Generously poured drafts around $2.75. Live music (mostly blues) most F-Sa, sometimes Su. Th contraband—you'll have to go to figure out what it means—draws a younger crowd. Open daily 11am-1am.

Firefly, 271 Main St. (☎508-548-7953), next door to Liam Maguire's. Another bar on Main St., they have music on the weekends (F-Sa 10pm-1am) everything from bluegrass to rock 'n' roll. During the day they serve gourmet (read: over-priced) pizza ($12-17). W open mic night. Open daily 4:30pm-1am.

British Beer Co., 263 Grand Ave. (☎508-540-9600), right by the beach. Popular with the Heights Beach crowd who flood the pub in search of a drink after the sun has faded. Beer $2.75-3.50; 20oz. draft $4.50. Bar open Su noon-1am, M-Sa 11:30am-1am; food served Su-Th until 10pm, F-Sa 11pm.

Lee Side, 29 Railroad Ave. (☎508-548-9744), left on Luscombe Ave., off Water St. While you won't find any locals here, you will find lots of other Cape visitors cutting loose or biding their time until they can get on a ferry. Beer specials rotate, but they usually have a $2 pint and $7 pitcher. Sa nights in summer DJ. Open in summer Su noon-10pm, M-Sa 11:30am-10pm; off-season Su noon-10pm, M-Th and Sa 11:30am-9pm, F 11:30am-10pm.

SANDWICH

By car: *Take I-93S to Exit 7/Rte. 3S ("Braintree and Cape Cod"). Follow Rte. 3S 45 mi. until you come to a rotary. Cross the Sagamore Bridge and continue on Rte. 6. Take Exit 2, making a left at the end of the ramp onto Rte. 130N, which cuts through Sandwich center.*

Founded in 1627, Sandwich is the oldest town on the Cape and prides itself on being the most mature. Like an intellectual older sibling, Sandwich has spurned the miniature golf and go-karts that so fascinate some other Cape towns (cough, cough—Yarmouth; see p. 218), favoring instead antiques, art, and walks in the woods. Exuding a charm that can only be described as Old New England, Sandwich is the perfect place for a relaxing weekend in a cute B&B.

ORIENTATION

Bounded by Rte. 6 to the south and Rte. 6a to the north, most of quaint Sandwich can be found in and around the town's tiny center, at the intersection of **Main** and **Jarves** St. Main St. is littered with B&Bs, while Jarves houses the antique stores and galleries, all within walking distance. For food or outdoor adventure, a car is needed in order to go north to the beach or west to Hyannis.

ACCOMMODATIONS & CAMPING

Sandwich's main draw is its old-time feel. The best way to get the complete experience is to stay at one of the many cute family-run B&Bs that line the historic center.

INNS

The Belfry Inne, 6-8 Jarves St. (☎800-844-4542; www.belfryinn.com). Without a doubt, among the best B&Bs on the Cape, this former church has been converted into a luxurious inn with 6 comfortable, unique rooms. Maintaining a church-like decor, the rooms feature large stained glass windows, and headboards made from church pews. Do not fear, the rooms are beautiful, and the 2-person whirlpools help smooth away any of the awkwardness that may arise from sleeping on a pew. Rooms are also available in the 2 buildings flanking the church and are cheaper, though less interesting. Doubles $95-195. ❹

Captain Ezra Nye House, 152 Main St. (☎508-888-6142; www.captainezranyehouse). Cozy and quaint, the Captain Ezra Nye House has 4 large doubles and 2 suites. The rooms are comfortable, and the breakfast legendary. Doubles with bath May-Oct. $125-150; Nov.-Apr. $105-125. ❸

Isaiah Jones Homestead, 165 Main St. (☎508-888-9648; www.isaiahjones.com). Though there are 5 formally decorated rooms in the main house, the 2 sprawling doubles with whirlpool and fireplace in the adjacent carriage house are the choicest. May-Oct. $115-165; Nov.-Apr. $100-155. ❸

CAMPGROUNDS

Shawme-Crowell State Forest, Rte. 130 (☎508-888-0351; www.state.ma.us/dem/parks/shcr.htm), at Rte. 6. Provides 285 wooded campsites on 700 acres of parkland with restrooms, showers, campfires, and a swimming beach. $10-12 per site. Open year-round for camping. ❶

Scusset Beach, Scusset Beach Rd. (☎508-888-0859; www.state.ma.us/dem/parks/scus.htm), on the canal near the junction of Rte. 6 and Rte. 3. A coastal swimming locale outfitted with a fishing jetty and seaside campgrounds on Cape Cod Bay. Parking for beach-goers $7 per day. Tent sites $12-15. Open Apr.-Oct. ❶

Peters Pond Park Campground, 185 Cotuit Rd. (☎508-477-1775; www.peterspond.com), in south Sandwich. This family-oriented campground combines waterside sites with swimming, fishing, rowboat rentals ($15 per day), showers, and a grocery store. Sites $29-43. Teepees $250 per week. Open Apr.-Oct. ❶

FOOD & DRINK

Dunbar House & Tea Shop, 1 Water St. (☎508-833-2485; www.dunbarteashop.com). Built in an antique carriage house, the Tea Shop is the perfect atmosphere for feeling elite and English, ideal for a light lunch and a spot of tea. The food is usually "crusty bread and something," and the something may

inside
SECRETS TO...

Nantucket Baskets Made of Sandwich Glass

The **Pairpoint Glassworks** in Sandwich sells a small glass charm shaped like a **Nantucket Lighthouse Basket.** Combining two of Cape Cod's signature pieces into an odd hybrid, this charm is the perfect introduction to either medium.

Sandwich Glass, first produced by the Boston and Sandwich Glass Company in 1820, became hugely popular and at one point the factory of 500 craftsmen was turning out 100,000 pounds of glassware a week. Famous for its delicate carved glass, meticulously hand etched in a complicated flower and scroll pattern, "Sandwich Pattern Glass" would later be copied by other glassmakers across the USA.

The **Nantucket Basket** has more utilitarian roots. The strong wicker wood bottomed baskets were originally woven 150 years ago by sailors on lightships around Nantucket. The uniform size and shape of Nantucket Lightship Baskets was the result of the wooden molds, usually from the masts of old lightships, that the sailors used to aid their weaving. Like Sandwich Glass the unique pattern has since been copied and made into purses, jewelry, dog bowls, and of course, glass charms.

include cheeses, ham, or cod. The real draw is the decadent tea selection, and the snooty feeling you get sipping tea and eating "Shortbread Petticoats." Lunch $5-8. Crumpets $3.25. Open daily in summer and fall 8am-6pm; in winter and spring 11:30am-4pm. ❶

Marshland, 109 Rte. 6A (☎508-888-9824), near Tupper Rd. A diner-style delight and local favorite. The attached bakery composes indulgent fresh breakfasts, and the afternoon/evening menu has burgers ($5), fresh salads ($7), and rich entrees (from $9). Open Su 7am-1pm, M 6am-2pm, Tu-Sa 6am-9pm. Cash only. ❷

SIGHTS

Sandwich is most famous (among glassophiles and antiques collectors at least) for its colorful, expensive "Sandwich glass," which got rolling here in 1825 with the founding of the Boston & Sandwich Glass Co. Much of the town's history revolves around this industry.

HERITAGE PLANTATION OF SANDWICH. A completely unique parcel of land, Heritage Plantation can best be characterized as a sprawling estate sprinkled with eclectic activities and structures. The rolling grass and private groves are perfect for a day of picnicking. Heritage also boasts a working carousel, an epic auto museum (complete with Gary Cooper's Duesenberg), and the Cape Cod League Baseball Hall of Fame. Oh, and a windmill for good measure. *(67 Grove St. ☎508-888-3300. Open daily May-Oct. 9am-6pm; Nov.-Apr. 10am-1pm. $12, seniors $10, ages 6-18 $6. Wheelchair accessible.)*

PAIRPOINT CRYSTAL. Americas oldest operating glassworks, Pairpoint was founded as Mount Washington Glass Company in 1837 and later merged with Pairpoint Silver Company to become Pairpoint Crystal Company. The showroom is a small, expensive store that flanks the real draw, a fully functioning glass workshop. Windows in the shop allow patrons to view skilled artisans blowing and crafting intricate vases and carafes, all free of charge. *(851 Sandwich Rd., just off the Sagamore Bridge in Sagamore. ☎508-888-2344. Open Su 11am-6pm, M-F 9am-6pm, Sa 10am-6pm. Glass blowing M-F 9am-4pm, Sa 10am-2pm. Free.)*

SANDWICH GLASS MUSEUM. For those who love glass, and weren't all glassed out after seeing Pairpoint, this museum provides an engaging walk through the history of the art on Cape Cod. Various types and colors are explored, and occasional demonstrations are undertaken. Be forewarned, however, the museum is filled entirely with glass, and those who are clumsy or easily bored should probably stay away. *(129 Main St. ☎508-888-0251. Open Apr.-Dec. daily 9:30am-5pm; Feb.-Mar. W-Su 9:30am-4pm. $3.50, ages 6-16 $1.)*

HYANNIS & YARMOUTH

1½hr. from Boston. ***By car:*** *From Boston, take I-93S to Exit 7/Rte. 3S ("Braintree and Cape Cod"). Follow Rte. 3S 45 mi. until you come to the rotary. Cross the Sagamore Bridge and you are on Rte. 6E. Take Exit 7 and hang a left a the end of the ramp onto Willow St., which becomes Yarmouth Rd. Continue south to the intersection with Rte. 28. To reach Hyannis center cross over Rte. 28 and continue until it intersects Main St. To reach Yarmouth, take a left at Rte. 28 and continue for a few miles.* ***By bus:*** *Plymouth and Brockton Bus (☎508-746-0378, office ☎508-746-4795; www.p-b.com) runs from T: South Station (Red) to the brand new Hyannis Transportation Center, off Main St. (35 trips per day from 7am-midnight, $14.)*

Like a tattoo on the tricep of the cape, Hyannis and its neighbor Yarmouth are not exactly classy, yet remain strangely attractive and alluring. Hyannis' cute Main St. provides shopping and dining that is fun and friendly, while nearby Cape Cod Mall provides exactly the opposite. While the beaches just outside of town are natural and pristine, Rte. 28 in Yarmouth is a 5 mi. plastic paradise of miniature golf, batting cages, and deep fried food.

Though JFK spent his summers in nearby **Hyannisport** (which is still home to the Kennedy family's sprawling summer compound), Hyannis proper is now little more than a temporary destination for travelers en route to other cape locales. Buses to most other Cape towns leave from here, as do ferries to Martha's Vineyard (p. 228) and Nantucket (p. 236) islands.

ORIENTATION

Most of Hyannis can be found nuzzled snugly around **Main St.** and its sister streets **North St.** and **South St.** All are a short walk from the bus terminal or the ferry dock. To reach the beaches, expect a 1½ mi. walk. For the go, go, go-kart pace of Yarmouth, simply board the H20 Breeze, which departs from the Hyannis Transportation Center six times per day, and ride it along the mini-golf mecca that is Rte. 28. Parking along this epic road and in other parts of Hyannis and Yarmouth is plentiful, so those who possess cars should not feel shy about motoring.

ACCOMMODATIONS & CAMPING

Hyannis is full of cookie-cutter motels and inns with lots of amenities; most are downtown, with a few on the water in the southern part of town. Yarmouth can boast rows and rows of identical motor lodges, that while ugly and on a major thoroughfare, are also quite affordable.

Hyannis Inn Motel, 473 Main St. (☎508-775-0255; www.hyannisinn.com), near the ferries and bus station. The immense Hyannis Inn sports large, clean rooms with TVs and mini-fridges. Free parking, a great location, large pool and sauna, and on-site restaurant add to the appeal. Open mid-Mar. to mid-Oct. Doubles $62-126; deluxe suites $72-141; whirlpool rooms $97-165. ❷

FOOD & DRINK

Box Lunch, 357 Main St. (☎508-790-5855), in the heart of Hyannis center. Box lunch delivers what it promises—inexpensive delicious sandwiches perfect for a trip to the beach. Their specialty "Rollwiches" $4-6. Open Su 10am-5pm, M-F 9am-6pm, Sa 10am-10pm. ❶

Ocean Grill, 415 Main St. (☎508-778-7200) Right next to the Box Lunch is the best option for those looking to partake of the bounty of the sea. The Ocean Grill serves up typical American and seafood favorites in a 150-year-old sea captain's house, but ask for a seat on the airy patio if you can. Entrees (shrimp, scallops, fish, etc.; $12-22) are a bit pricey, but extremely fresh. ❹

SIGHTS

JFK MUSEUM. If the JFK museum in Dorchester is the permanent home of the memory of America's 35th president, then this is its summer cottage. Consisting mostly of old photographs, the museum presents the story of Kennedy's family life and offers unique insight into his ties to Cape Cod. Recommended primarily for those who are very interested in Kennedy, the museum tends to drag at times and is relatively small. *(397 Main St. ☎508-790-3077. Open in summer Su noon-5pm, M-Sa 9am-5pm; limited hours off-season. $5, ages 6-16 $2.50, under 6 free.)*

CAPE COD POTATO CHIP FACTORY. For the last 23 years the Cape Cod Potato Chip Co. has been churning out their signature homemade, kettle-cooked, salty snacks. Originally located in downtown Hyannis, the success of the company has pushed the potato barons to a larger more industrial location on the outskirts of town. Fortunately, you can still get an inside look at what makes these chips so addictive and tasty (so you'll at least know how they're made next time you finish a whole bag...alone). Tours include company history, views of the production process, and (there was much rejoicing) a free bag of chips. *(100 Breeds Hill Rd. ☎508-775-3358. Tours M-F 9am-5pm. Free.)*

PIRATE'S COVE. If miniature golf is what you crave, or even if it isn't, this ornate masterpiece of Astroturf and plaster is worth the trip. Pirate's Cove stands head and shoulders above all the other family amusement centers that lurk nearby, by doing it bigger and tackier than the rest. 36 holes dip around fake mountains, through pirate ships, and under waterfalls. *(728 Main St., on Rte. 28 in Yarmouth. ☎508-394-6200. Open May-Oct. daily 9am-11pm. Adults $7, children $6)*

BEACHES

All beaches in Hyannis are open 9am-9pm and charge $10 for parking during the summer and on weekends. Lifeguards are generally provided, but be aware that at times swimming is at your own risk.

Orrin Keyes Beach, at the end of Sea St. The best beach in Hyannis, Orrin Keyes is more secluded, and cuter than its western companions. Featuring a picnic area, bathhouse, snack-bar, and a mostly local crowd, Orrin Keyes is the place to relax, not necessarily to be seen.

Kalamus Park Beach, at the end of Ocean St. The exposed south face of Kalamus Park makes it *the* windsurfing spot in Hyannis. The sheltered cove side of the point makes it *the* pleasure beach in Hyannis. Something for everyone! Good thing Kalamus Park Beach has the most parking. Arrive early to secure a space, as the summer months get pretty cutthroat.

Veterans Park Beach, next to Kalamus Park Beach. Next to the somewhat uninspiring JFK memorial (looks a lot like a fountain in a mall atrium), whose parking lot abuts the 20 ft. wide beach, Veterans Park should be thought of more as a picnic spot and less as a relaxing outdoor opportunity. Picnic tables and hibachis are nestled in the shaded park across the asphalt and provide a wonderful place to eat your box lunch or grill up some burgers.

CAPE COD NATIONAL SEASHORE

2-3hr. from Boston. Rte. 6E follows the coast of the National Seashore passing through Eastham, Wellfleet, Truro, and Provincetown. ***By car:*** *Take Rte. 3 to Rte. 6E., cross the Sagamore Bridge, and follow signs for Eastham.* ***By bus:*** *Plymouth & Brockton Bus (schedules and fares ☎508-746-0378, office ☎508-746-4795; www.p-b.com) sends buses from T: South Station (Red) and Logan Airport to the Cape, with stops in Eastham (one-way $18-19, round-trip $35-37; children $9-9.50/$17.50-18.50), Wellfleet (one-way $20, round-trip $39; children $10/$19.50), and Truro (one-way $21-22, round-trip $41-43; children $10.50-11/$20.50-21.50).*

As early as 1825, the Cape had suffered so much manmade damage that the town of Truro required local residents to plant beach grass and keep their cows off the dunes. These conservation efforts culminated in 1961, when the National Park Service created the National Seashore, which includes much of the Lower and Outer Cape from Provincetown to Chatham. The heart of the seashore is their six beaches, which begin in **Eastham** (just above the elbow of the Cape), continue through **Wellfleet** and **Truro,** and run all the way to **Provincetown** (p. 223).

PRACTICAL INFORMATION

The best place to get information about the National Seashore are the various Chamber of Commerces and Visitors Centers.

Eastham Chamber of Commerce (☎508-240-7211; www.easthamchamber.com). For those wishing to stop in Eastham, the Chamber of Commerce has a helpful guide to the area; call or visit their website, and they'll send you a copy. The Chamber of Commerce also runs an **information booth** (☎508-255-3444), on Rte. 6 at Governor Prence Rd. Info booth open daily June and Sept. 10am-5pm; July-Aug. 9am-7pm.

Salt Pond Visitors Center (☎508-255-3421; www.nps.gov/caco), on Nauset Rd., in Eastham. Coming from Boston, turn right off Rte. 6 onto Nauset Rd. Run by the National Seashore, they have info on all 6 federal **beaches** (p. 222). Their main building is currently under construction, but normally it serves as a museum and theatre as well as an info center. Open daily 9am-5pm.

Truro Chamber of Commerce (☎508-487-1288), on Rte. 6A. Open July to mid-Sept. daily 10am-4pm; call for off-season hours.

Wellfleet Chamber of Commerce (☎508-349-2510; www.wellfleetchamber.com), on Rte. 6. The staff here knows absolutely everything about Wellfleet and will elaborate on their practical guide to the town. Open June-Sept. daily 9am-6pm; call ahead off-season.

ACCOMMODATIONS

Long the summertime getaway of New England's rich and famous, short-term accommodations don't come cheap on Cape Cod. Most visitors to the Cape rent bungalows for the entire summer, while those coming for only a few nights usually opt for pricey B&Bs. The following are the only three hostel-style (and priced) accommodations on the Cape, two of them HI-AYH accredited. (Martha's Vineyard (p. 228) and Nantucket (p. 236) also have HI-AYH hostels.) For more on Cape Cod hostels, look online at www.capecodhostels.org. Note that sleeping bags are not allowed in hostels by state law.

Race Point Light (☎508-487-9930), in **North Truro.** As atypical and remote a night's lodging as you're likely to find, Race Point is a lighthouse that has been converted into a B&B. There is no electricity, and after dark the entire house is lit by gas lanterns. What they lack in standard amenities, they make up for with the beach setting. Transportation to the location, which is 2½ mi. over sand dunes, is provided by the hosts. BYO linens, towels, food, and water. Doubles with shared bath $135-155; each additional person $25. ❹

Mid-Cape Hostel (HI-AYH), 75 Goody Hallet Dr. (☎508-255-2785, toll-free ☎888-901-2085), in **Eastham.** From Rte. 6, take the Rock Harbor exit at the Orleans Ctr. rotary, turn right onto Bridge Rd. (about a ½ mi.), then right again onto Goody Hallet Dr. (about ¼ mi.). If arriving by P&B bus, ask the driver to let you off at the Orleans Ctr. rotary or as close to the hostel as possible, and call the hostel for the "shortcut" directions along walking paths (following the driving directions above takes twice as long). It's a 15min. walk to the beach, but this hostel is close to the **Cape Cod Rail Trail** (p. 222). Communal bungalow living in a woodsy location complete the summer camp atmosphere. Shared bathrooms, kitchen, and BBQ facilities. Bike rental $5 per day. Check-in 4pm; check-out 11am. 21-day max. stay. Private cabins for 4-person families (2 adults, 2 children) members $88-96, nonmembers $91-99; dorms $22-24/$25-27. Rates lower off-season. Open mid-May to mid-Sept. 8-10am and 4-10pm. Reserve far in advance, especially for cabins. ❶

Truro Hostel (HI-AYH), 111 North Pamet Rd. (☎508-349-3889 or ☎888-901-2086), in **Truro.** From Rte. 6, take the Pamet Rd. exit, which becomes North Pamet Rd. Sitting on a bluff overlooking the ocean, this turn-of-the-century converted Coast Guard station offers a large kitchen, porch, and access to Ballston Beach. Close to such natural delights as bird sanctuaries, cranberry bogs, dunes, and marshes, the hostel is more for nature-lovers than those looking for a night out on the town. Men sleep downstairs; women sleep upstairs. Free linen. Check-in 4-9pm; check-out 7:30-10am. Curfew 10pm. Members $22, nonmembers $25. Open late June-early Sept. 8-10am and 4-10pm. ❶

FOOD & DRINK

Good places to eat are scarce in the towns of Eastham, Wellfleet, and Truro; Provincetown, to the north, has a broader variety and is worth the drive. However, for those stuck in one of these three towns after a day at the beach, there are options.

Beachcomber, 1120 Cahoon Hollow Rd. (☎508-349-6055; www.thebeachcomber.com), off Rte. 6. in **Wellfleet.** It's hard to determine whether the unbelievably fresh raw bar, nightly music (either a band or DJ), or the prime beach location is what gives the Beachcomber its popularity, but what is clear is its status as the best night spot in the National Seashore. Seafood plates $12-15. 21+ after 9pm. Cover for bands around $10. Open June-Aug. daily 11:30am-1am; closed Sa 8-9pm. ❸

Moby Dick's, Rte. 6 (☎508-349-9795; www.mobydicksrestaurant.com), across from Gull Pond Rd. in **Wellfleet.** Few restaurants are better than the books they're named after, but with fish fresher than Captain Ahab could have caught, Moby Dick's manages to surpass its namesake. Seafood $10-16; lobster $16+. Open daily in summer 11:30am-10pm; in spring and fall 11:30am-9pm. ❸

Bookstore, 50 Kendrick Ave. (☎508-349-3154; www.wellfleetoyster.com), in **Wellfleet.** From Rte. 6 (heading north), turn left onto Main St., left again onto Commercial St., and right onto Kendrick Ave. No trip to Wellfleet is complete without their famous oysters, and Bookstore is perhaps the best place to get them. Raw bar ½ dozen oysters $9. Entrees $13-17; lighter entrees $7-14. Seafood $15-21. Open daily in summer 8am-10pm; off-season 8am-9pm. ❹

The Village Café (☎508-487-5800), in **Truro.** For a quick but quality bite, stop in at the Village Café. Their wide selection of "Signature Sandwiches" ($5-12) include plenty of vegetarian options and have such area-appropriate names as "Route 6A" (roast beef, red onion, lettuce, tomato, and BBQ sauce). Open daily May-June and Sept.-late Oct. 7am-3pm; July-Aug. 7am-10pm. ❷

Box Lunch, 50 Briar Ln. (☎508-349-2178), in **Wellfleet.** The food and service are as simple and straight-forward as the name—order a sandwich and leave with a box lunch that is the perfect beach meal. Vegetarian menu available. Sandwiches $4.50-6. Open daily in summer 7am-7pm; off-season 7am-2:30pm. Another location on Rte. 6 in **Eastham** (☎508-255-0799). Open in summer daily 7am-8pm; off-season Su-W and F-Sa 9am-3pm. Cash only. For their **Hyannis** location, see p. 219. ❶

Lobster Shanty, 2905 Rte. 6 (☎508-255-9394), at Nauset Rd. **Eastham.** Shanty is the appropriate title for this restaurant, where the seafood is slightly sub-par by the Cape's standards, as well as a bit overpriced. If you're starving and in Eastham, this is your best bet. Appetizers $5-7. Seafood entrees $11-14. Burgers $6.50. Open mid-May to Oct. daily 10am-10pm; hours vary with business. Open mid-Apr. to mid-Nov. ❷

SIGHTS

LIGHTHOUSES. Cape Cod was one of the first stretches of land the Pilgrims saw on their voyage to America, and it remains a hub for ships today. Unlike the Pilgrims, today's seafarers get a little help from the Cape's lighthouses, which are some of the east coast's most scenic. Perhaps, the most famous of the Cape's lighthouses, **Nauset Light** can be found either in Eastham or at your local supermarket—on a bag of Cape Cod potato chips (for info on the Cape Cod Potato Chip Factory, see p. 219). **Race Point Light,** in North Truro, is now a B&B; see p. 221. Most lighthouses are open on erratic schedules, but they are always worth driving by. The third weekend in May marks **Maritime Week** when most major Cape lighthouses are open to the public. For more info, contact the Cape Cod Visitors Information Center (p. 211). **Highland Light** is the one light lighthouse open regularly to the public. *(Most lighthouses are just off Rte. 6. **Nauset Light:** turn right off Rte. 6 at the Salt Pond Visitors Center and then left on Ocean View Dr. ☎508-240-2612. **Highland Light:** in North Truro, turn onto Highland Rd. from Rte. 6 and then right onto Lighthouse Rd. ☎508-487-1121. Tours May-Oct. daily 10am-5:30pm.)*

CAPE COD RAIL TRAIL. If you're looking to see the Cape in something other than an automobile, this 26 mi. converted bike path that winds up the shore is the perfect alternative. Running from Dennis to Wellfleet, the trail is open to cyclists and runners and is clearly marked most of the way. Called the rail trail because it follows old railroad tracks, the trail passes by many area beaches. For more information, contact **Nickerson State Park.** *(State Park: on Rte. 6A in Brewster. Trail begins at Rte. 137 in Dennis and ends at LeCount Hollow Rd. in South Wellfleet. ☎508-896-3491.)*

WELLFLEET ART GALLERIES. Wellfleet would be just another quaint Cape town, if it weren't for its many art galleries, which make the town a conservative alternative to nearby Provincetown. In this town, with a population just over 3,000, there are at least 21 galleries. Though almost all are worth stopping by, the most renowned are: **Blue Heron Gallery,** specializing in contemporary art in a variety of forms; **Cove Gallery,** with a selection of international illustrators; **Kendall Art Gallery,** which houses paintings indoors and sculptures outdoors; and **Left-Bank Gallery,** with an astounding pottery selection in "The Potters Room." *(Most galleries located along Commercial St. **Blue Heron:** 20 Bank St. ☎508-349-6724. Open daily July-Oct. 10am-6pm; May-June 10am-6pm. **Cove:** on Commercial St. ☎508-349-2530. Open daily 10am-6pm. **Kendall:** 40 Main St. ☎508-349-2482. Open Su noon-4pm, M-Sa 10am-5:30pm. **Left-Bank:** 25 Commercial St. ☎508-349-9451. Open June-Oct. daily 10am-6pm.)*

BEACHES

The beaches run by the National Park Services require a parking pass (seasonal $30, daily $10). To purchase passes, stop in at the Salt Pond Visitors Center (p. 220). Beach camping is illegal. National Park beaches are listed in the order someone driving from Hyannis to Provincetown would encounter them. The six beaches run by the National Park are lifeguarded in the summer (July-Aug. 9am-5pm; Sept. to mid-Oct. Sa-Su 9am-5pm).

NATIONAL PARK BEACHES

Coast Guard, on Ocean View Dr. in **Eastham.** Limited parking; park in the lot by the Salt Pond Visitors Ctr. and shuttle to the beach. Coast Guard is a popular beach for surf and water sports because of its rough Atlantic waters. Showers and restrooms.

Nauset Light, on Ocean View Dr. in **Eastham.** Similar to Coast Guard, the main difference between the 2 beaches is Nauset's status as home to the Cape's most famous lighthouse (see p. 222). Showers and restrooms.

Marconi, off Rte. 6 in **Wellfleet.** Like the 2 Eastham beaches, Marconi draws large summer crowds to its picturesque sands and sizeable surf. Showers and restrooms.

Head of the Meadow, on Head of the Meadow Rd., off Rte. 6 in **Truro.** The least developed and crowded of the National Park beaches, this is the place to go to commune with nature, instead of throngs of beachgoers and their colorful umbrellas. No facilities.

Race Point, on Race Point Rd., off Rte. 6 in **Provincetown.** Unlike the more protected Herring Cove, Race Point is Provincetown's surf beach. Showers and restrooms.

Herring Cove, off either Rte. 6 or Rte. 6A in **Provincetown.** Herring Cove was for many years Provincetown's clothing-optional town beach. Things changed when the National Park Service took control. While you won't see as much skin, you will find calmer water than at most other National Seashore beaches. Showers and restrooms.

OTHER BEACHES

Great Island, on the peninsula in **Wellfleet,** accessible via the Chequesset Neck Rd.; it's then about a ¼ mi. jaunt to reach the beach. This is a terrific family beach. Well protected from the open water of the ocean, Great Island has really calm water and, during low-tide, excellent shell collecting. Free parking.

Mayo, along Chequesset Neck Rd. in **Wellfleet.** Another of the protected beaches in Wellfleet and near the captivating shops of the town center, Mayo is similar to a town beach, with a couple important exceptions–it is open to the public and has free parking.

PROVINCETOWN

3hr. from Boston. ***By car:*** *From Boston, take I-93S to Exit 7/Rte. 3S ("Braintree and Cape Cod"). Follow Rte. 3S 45 mi. until you come to the rotary. Cross the Sagamore Bridge and you are on route 6E, which ends in Provincetown.* ***By bus:*** *Plymouth & Brockton buses (schedules and fares ☎508-746-0378, office ☎508-746-4795; www.p-b.com) will take you all the way to Provincetown (3¼hr.; one-way $23, round-trip $45). Buses leave from T: South Station (Red) for Provincetown (M-F 6 per day 7am-5:40pm, Sa-Su 5 per day 7am-5:15pm) and return from MacMillian Wharf's Chamber of Commerce (5 per day 6:45am-5:45pm).* ***By ferry:*** *see p. 213.*

Provincetown—the clenched fist at the tip of the "arm" of Cape Cod—is anything but a typical Cape town; what sets Provincetown apart is its popularity as one of the premier gay and lesbian communities and vacation spots on the East Coast.

In the early 20th century, the town's popularity soared with artists, writers, and free thinkers. Norman Mailer, Tennessee Williams, and Edward Hopper are only a few of those who lived and worked in this artist enclave. In the 1960s and 70s, Provincetown's tradition of tolerance and open-mindedness began to attract a large gay community, who now fill the town to its rim in summer. Around the same time P-town became popular with queer folk, the government created the National Seashore (see p. 220), which protects two-thirds of P-town from development—making for fabulous stretches of pristine beaches just steps from the town's trendy restaurants, shops, galleries, and clubs.

ORIENTATION

Most people in P-town are very sure of their orientation, but maybe you need some help. **Commercial St.,** the town's main drag—home to countless art galleries, novelty shops, and trendy bars and eateries—runs along the harbor. **Brad-**

ford St., the other main street, runs parallel to Commercial St., one block inland. Standish St. divides P-town into the **East End** and **West End.** Across Rte. 6 from town, the **National Seashore** has beautiful beaches, forests, and sand dunes (for more info, see p. 220).

To get to the eastern edge of town, take the first left once you enter Provincetown onto Snail Rd. When you get to the water, turn right and then bear right onto Bradford St. **On-street parking** spots are hard-won in season, especially on cloudy days, when the Cape's frustrated sun-worshipers flock to Provincetown. You can try to find free public parking north of Bradford St. or at the east end of Commercial St., but it's probably better to pay to be closer to the center of things and park in the public lot on **MacMillian Wharf,** at the end of Standish St. off Commercial St., or in the private lot on the pier. Bradford St. also has parking lots.

PRACTICAL INFORMATION

Most of Provincetown is easily accessible on foot; for the outlying areas, the **Provincetown Shuttle** runs to Herring Cove Beach (p. 223) and North Truro. Tickets are available on the bus or at the Bay State Cruise desk in the Chamber of Commerce. Shuttles run late May to mid-Oct. All shuttles have bike racks and are fully wheelchair accessible. (☎800-352-7155; www.thebreeze.info. Late June-Aug. daily 7:30 and 8:30am and every 20min. 9am-12:30am; call or check online for non-peak season schedules. $1, seniors and ages 6-17 $0.50, under 6 free. One-day pass $3/$1.50.)

VISITOR INFORMATION

Provincetown Chamber of Commerce, 307 Commercial St. (☎508-487-3424; www.ptownchamber.com), on MacMillian Wharf., have info on everything and anything related to Provincetown. Open June-Sept. daily 9am-5pm; reduced off-season hours.

Province Lands Visitors Ctr. (☎508-487-1256), on Race Point Rd. off Rte. 6, has park info. Open May-Oct. daily 9am-5pm; call for off-season hours.

BIKES

Ptown Bikes, 42 Bradford St. (☎508-487-8735), rents mountain bikes, tandems, and beach cruisers. Rentals include free locks and maps. 2hr. minimum. Mountain bikes $3.50-4 per hr.; $10-17 per day. Cruisers $3/$10. Helmets also available for rental. Open mid-May to mid-Sept. daily 9am-7pm; call for off-season hours.

Gail Force Bikes, 144 Bradford St. (☎508-487-4849), at the corner of West Vine St., rents all bike styles and also provides free locks and helmets. 2hr. minimum, $3-4 per hr.; $14-17 per day. Open daily July-Aug. 8am-8pm; June and Sept. 9am-6pm; May and Oct. 9am-5pm.

ACCOMMODATIONS & CAMPING

Provincetown is teeming with expensive places to lay your head—guesthouses and B&Bs line Commercial St. and its side streets. There are a few moderately priced motels and the occasional less-expensive B&B, but unless you're staying at the hostel, be prepared to shell out at least $80 per night during the summer. Reservations are absolutely essential (especially on weekends and holidays), as accommodations fill up months in advance. If you have a car and can't find an affordable spot in Provincetown, consider the hostels (fairly) nearby in Truro and Eastham (see p. 220). Note that few of the accommodations in P-town offer free parking.

Dexter's Inn, 6 Conwell St. (☎508-487-1911 or 888-521-1999; www.ptowndextersinn.com), just off Bradford St. A few blocks from the town center, but well worth it. Dexter's offers hotel-quality rooms for quite reasonable prices, plus a lush garden, large sundeck, and free parking. Most of the 15 rooms have private bath, and the shared bath is immaculate. Doubles mid-June to mid-Sept. $75-125 (4-night min. stay); late May to Mid-June and mid-Sept. to early Oct. $70-90; mid-Oct. to late May $50-65. $25 each additional person. ❷

Sunset Inn, 142 Bradford St. (☎508-487-9810 or 800-965-1801; www.sunsetinnptown.com). When American artist and longtime P-town resident Edward Hopper wanted to paint a guesthouse, he used this inn for inspiration (it inspired his famous work *Rooms for Tourists*). Though the house has lost some of the romance and serenity of Hopper's painting, it still offers a comfortable night's sleep. Rooms are simple and well-kept (though nothing spectacular). Several sundecks (1 "clothing optional"). Free parking. mid-June to mid-Sept. with shared bath $79-89, with private bath and A/C $135-175; reduced rates ($49-109) in spring and fall. Open mid-Apr. to early Jan. ❸

Outermost Hostel, 28 Winslow St. (☎508-487-4378). The only budget accommodation in town, Outermost offers cheap beds only a short walk from the center of town—though it lacks in cleanliness and comfort what it offers in proximity and price. The 5 cottages are cramped and have less than pristine bathrooms (plus kitchen access and free parking), but just think of all that money you're saving to spend on P-town's more attractive offerings. Linen rental $3. Key deposit $10. Reception daily 8-9:30am and 5:30-10pm. Check-out 9:30am. Reservations recommended for weekends and July-Aug. Dorms $20. Open May to mid-Oct. ❶

CAMPGROUNDS

Dune's Edge Campground, 386 Rte. 6 (☎508-487-9815), on the right side at the East End, has 100 shady sites packed together in a pastoral setting. Office open daily July-Aug. 8am-10pm; May-June and Sept. 8am-8pm. Sites $30, with electricity $34. ❶

Coastal Acres Camping Court (☎508-487-1700), a 1 mi. walk from the center of town, go west on Bradford or Commercial St. and right on W. Vine, then follow W. Vine as it becomes Blueberry St. There are 120 crowded sites—try to snag one on the waterfront. Make reservations by mail; 3-night deposit required. Office with convenience store open daily 8am-9:30pm. Sites $24, with electricity $34; rates reduced in spring and fall by $1. Open Apr.-Nov. ❶

FOOD & DRINK

Sit-down meals in Provincetown tend to be expensive. A number of fast food joints line the Commercial St. extension (next to MacMillian Wharf) and the Aquarium Mall, farther west on Commercial St. For a gourmet picnic, head to the East End's **Angel Foods,** 467 Commercial St. (☎508-487-6666. Open in summer Su 8am-8pm, M-Sa 8am-9pm; reduced hours off-season.) Regular groceries are available at **Grand Union,** 28 Shankpainter Rd., in the West End. (☎508-487-4903. Open in summer Su 7am-10pm, M-Sa 7am-11pm; reduced hours off-season.)

Somerset House

378 Commercial St. ***Contact:*** *☎508-487-0383 or 800-575-1850; www.somersethouseinn.com.* ***Rates:*** *Doubles June-Aug. $110-245; Sept.-May $75-177. Nov.-Apr. 50% off 2nd day; 10% discount off 1st night if you mention* Let's Go. ❸

With a motto like "Get Serviced," the Somerset House is a wild ride from start to finish, from late nights in the jacuzzi to the latest gossip while taking in their bay view. The staff claims they'll do anything to keep the house packed and the party rocking. Fun and fabulous with a very social atmosphere, this 12-room "boutique-style" guesthouse caters to a mostly (95.8%) GLBT clientele (though they are extremely welcoming to all guests) and adds a touch of flair and sass to everything it does, making it more of a party than some of the clubs on Commercial St.

Funky modern decor with traditional touches gives the Somerset a decidedly young and edgy feel, while amenities—TV, fireplace, minifridge, DSL Internet, and A/C—ensure the highest level of comfort. However, not even the amenities can top the "proud to be out" staff, who embody the liberal carefree acceptance that is P-town's trademark.

Post Office Café, 303 Commercial St. (☎508-487-3892). Enjoy seafood, pasta, and sandwiches in this small, trendy eatery. Though the post office theme is somewhat inconsistently executed, the food is consistently good. Their clambake special (1¼lb. lobster and mussels), at market price, is the best deal is town. Entrees $7-20. Open daily 8am-midnight. ❸

Tofu A Go-Go, 338 Commercial St. (☎508-487-6237), upstairs. A casual restaurant with deliciously fresh vegetarian, vegan, and macrobiotic options. The tasty tofu tahini salad ($7.75), the hefty "Really Good Burrito" ($5.50), and all the daily specials are bargain eats. Lunch under $10; dinner under $13. Open Apr.-Oct.: in summer daily 11am-9pm; call for spring and fall hours. ❷

Chester Restaurant, 404 Commercial St. (☎508-487-8200; www.chesterrestaurant.com). Located in a gracious 19th-century Greek Revival house, Chester redefined fine dining in Provincetown when it opened a few years ago. Since then, it has been praised for its carefully prepared New American cuisine and flawless service. The warm yellow dining room is adorned with works by local artists–the perfect setting (as is the garden terrace) for the decadent cuisine and vast selection of wines. The menu changes frequently, but always includes a variety of seafood, chicken, and beef creations ($21-34). Don't miss the decadent homemade desserts (around $9). Reservations recommended, but walk-ins welcome. Dinner after 6pm. ❺

Karoo Kafe, 338 Commercial St. (☎508-487-6630). This self-described "fast-food safari" serves up South African and Mediterranean favorites, like falafel ($6.25) and tofu with *peri-peri* sauce (Swahili for "chili-chili;" $7). Get your meal to go or enjoy it on the small terrace. Open Mar.-Nov.: in summer daily 11am-9pm; spring and fall lunch hours only. ❶

Café Edwidge, 333 Commercial St. (☎508-487-20084020), offers an elegant yet casual dining experience. An airy candlelit dining room and small outdoor terrace offer respite from the masses on Commercial St. Though the dinner menu is loaded with delicious dishes ($8-22), it's Edwidge's breakfast that draws crowds ($6-10). The French toast with fresh fruit ($8) is the perfect morning-after treat–don't forget the mimosa. Open late June-Aug. 8am-1pm and 6-10pm; mid-May to late June and Sept. to mid-Oct. Sa-Su 8am-1pm and 6-10pm. ❸

Spiritus, 190 Commercial St. (☎508-487-2808), serves up spirit-lifting whole-wheat pizza. Sip coffee or enjoy some ice cream amid works by local artists, while scoping the crowds on Commercial St. from the front terrace. Slices $2-3. Open Apr.-Oct. daily noon-2am. ❶

Mayflower Family Dining, 300 Commercial St. (☎508-487-0121). Cheaper than it is good, Mayflower is worth seeking out in this haven of overpriced cuisine. Fish and chips $9.50, 1¼lb; lobster $14. Open Apr.-Nov. Su noon-10pm, M-Sa 11:30am-10pm. Cash only. ❸

SIGHTS

PILGRIM SIGHTS. Despite what they tell you at Plimoth Plantation (p. 209), the Puritan fugitives known as Pilgrims first arrived in America at Provincetown (before continuing on to Plymouth). The **Pilgrim Monument** (the tallest all-granite structure in the US at 253 ft.), and the **Provincetown Museum,** on High Pole Hill just north of the center of town, commemorate the Pilgrims' first landing. Hike up to the top of the tower for stunning views of the Cape and the Atlantic. As P-town idol Barbra Streisand will tell you, on a clear day, you can see to Boston. A large bas-relief **monument,** in the small park at Bradford and Ryder St. behind the town hall, depicts the signing of the Mayflower Compact on November 11, 1620 in Provincetown Harbor. This contract marked the beginning of Puritan rule. *(Pilgrim Monument & Provincetown Museum: ☎508-487-1310; www.pilgrim-monument.org. Open daily July-Aug. 9am-6:15pm; Apr.-June and Sept.-Nov. 9am-4:15pm. $7, ages 4-12 $3, under 4 free.)*

PROVINCETOWN ART ASSOCIATION & MUSEUM. Founded in 1914 during Provincetown's heyday as a seasonal artists' colony, the museum houses permanent and temporary exhibits and has an enchanting sculpture garden. In addition to the museum, Provincetown hosts over 20 **galleries**—most line Commercial St. near the museum. True to Provincetown's liberal past, most of the galleries are on the cutting-edge with some of the most contemporary and thought-provoking work in the Boston area. Throughout the peak tourist season, there are a slew of gallery openings and events. Pick up the *Provincetown Gallery Guide* from the Chamber of Commerce (p. 224) for a listing of events. *(**Museum:** 460 Commercial St., in the East End. ☎508-487-1750. Open June and Sept. Su-Th noon-5pm, F-Sa noon-5pm and 8-10pm; July-Aug. daily noon-5pm and 8-10pm; Oct.-May Sa-Su noon-5pm. Suggested donation $5, seniors and children free.)*

OUTDOORS

As part of the National Seashore, Provincetown's miles of shoreline provide spectacular scenery and more than enough space to catch some sun. From Race Point Rd., you can reach the **National Seashore** park (2 mi. from town) with its beaches, forest, and sand dunes. For more on the National Seashore, see p. 220. At **Race Point Beach** waves roll in from the Atlantic, while **Herring Cove Beach,** at the west end of town, offers calm, protected waters. For a complete list of National Seashore beaches, see p. 223. A number of walking and biking **trails** wind through the National Seashore. The **Province Lands Visitors Center** (p. 224) offers free daily guided tours and activities during the summer. Directly across from Snail Rd. on Rte. 6, an unlikely path leads to a world of rolling **sand dunes;** look for shacks where writers such as Tennessee Williams, Norman Mailer, and John Dos Passos spent their days. At the west end of Commercial St., the 1¼ mi. **Breakwater Jetty** takes you away from the crowds to a secluded peninsula, where there are two working lighthouses and the remains of a Civil War fort.

Today, Provincetown seafarers have traded harpoons for cameras, but they still enjoy whale-hunting—**whale-watching cruises** rank among P-town's most popular attractions. Most cruise companies guarantee whale sightings, with tickets averaging $22-25 for a 3hr. tour (a 3hr. tour); discount coupons are in most local publications and at the Chamber of Commerce. **Boston Harbor Cruises Whale Watch** (☎617-227-4321 or 877-733-9425; www.bostonharborcruises.com), **Dolphin Fleet** (☎508-349-1900 or 800-826-9300; www.whalewatch.com), and **Portuguese Princess** (☎508-487-2651 or 800-422-3188; www.princesswhalewatch.com) all leave from MacMillian Wharf. Morning, afternoon, and evening cruises are available.

NIGHTLIFE

Appropriately, the nightlife scene in P-town is almost totally gay- and lesbian-oriented. (Most places follow the "don't ask, don't tell" policy: you don't have to ask if a particular place is gay—more often than not, you can just tell.) Like in Boston, all bars and clubs close at the Puritanical hour of 1am; all are 21+.

A Provincetown tradition, the **Tea Dance** is a large, mostly male, beach dance party happening on weekends in July and August. To take part, head to the **Boatslip,** 161 Commercial St. (☎508-487-1669), between 4-7pm. If you miss the Tea Dance, don't fret—there's an **After Tea T-Dance,** at **The Pied,** 193A Commercial St. (☎508-487-1527), from 6-9:30pm, with an equally rowdy crowd.

Crown & Anchor, 247 Commercial St. (☎508-487-1430). A large complex with a restaurant, guesthouse, and 2 cabarets, alongside the **Wave** video bar and **Paramount** dance club. With several large video screens and a decidedly chill atmosphere, Wave is not exactly a raging scene, which makes it all the more striking in relation to **Paramount,** the closest P-town comes to a *real* club. An attractive (usually shirtless) male crowd heats up to house and techno inside and cools off on the harbor-front pool deck outside. All the pretty boys flock to Paramount on Sa for "Summer Camp." Beer $3-4; mixed drinks $4-8. Paramount cover usually $10, though varies with shows; no cover for Wave. Open in summer daily 11pm-1am; off-season Sa-Su 11pm-1am.

Atlantic House, 6 Masonic Place (☎508-487-3821), just off Commercial St. Founded in 1798 by gay whalers, the A-House continues to attract its fair share of seamen. Catering almost exclusively to men, this bar/club offers 3 different scenes—the "little bar" (low-key atmosphere, complete with a jukebox), the "macho bar" (catering to the Leather & Levis crowd), and the "big room" (full-on dance club). Patio deck open during the summer. Though not as modern or young as Paramount, the A-House still attracts a crowd every night. Beer $3; mixed drinks $4. Cover usually $10. Open daily 9pm-1am; "little bar" 11am-1am.

Vixen, 336 Commercial St. (☎508-487-6424). As the only major club in P-town catering to women, Vixen always draws a crowd. Nightly theme parties, like Th "Girls' Night Out" are very popular. W dance hits from the 70s and 80s get the weekend party started early. The front bar area is casual, with groups of women playing pool, while the dance floor in back gets hot and steamy as the night goes on. Beer $3; mixed drinks $5-7. Cover $5; more for live entertainment. Bar open daily noon-1am; club daily 10pm-1am; closed in winter.

Purgatory, 9-11 Carver St. (☎508-487-8442). Primarily a Leather & Levis spot, Purgatory is the place to be after a long day at church—thanks to "Bound Su," which attracts a more mainstream crowd (other days are quieter). This dark, subterranean venue has a small dance floor, a pool table, and lots of indiscriminate house music. Open daily until 1am.

Governor Bradford, 312 Commercial St. (☎508-487-2781). Boston's Axis Drag Night (p. 146) meets Long John Silver. Don't be fooled by the dark, traditional decor; the Governor has quite a wild side, hosting drag karaoke in summer nightly from 9:30pm (Sept.-Oct. karaoke F-Su only). Beer $3-4; mixed drinks $4-8. No cover. Open daily 11am-1am; food until 10pm.

MARTHA'S VINEYARD

When most people think of Martha's Vineyard, they think of swarms of the rich and famous who vacation on the island. However, the island hasn't always been so popular, and there is a lot more to be discovered on the Vineyard than the polo shirts who summer here. The Vineyard's population is, in fact, an interesting combination of Native American Wampanoags (who have long called the island home and reside mostly in the up-island town of Aquinnah), whalers and fishermen, and aging baby boomers (who seek to relive their liberal hippie days on the few remaining "clothing-optional" beaches). Since its tie-dyed heyday (also known as the 1960s), the Vineyard has seen an unbelievable boom in wealth and population. Each summer, the island population swells from 15,000 to over 105,000.

In peak season, beware of skyrocketing prices, as year-round Islanders work hard to make ends meet after the Vineyard's desolate winter. Savvy travelers might consider a weekend visit to the Vineyard in the spring or fall. As late as June and as early as September, the hordes of tourists thin out, while the beaches remain open and accommodations cut rates to nearly half-price.

GETTING THERE

The island is accessible by ferry or airplane only. Flights are very expensive (starting at $130 one-way), so the majority of visitors take ferries, which leave from various points on Cape Cod. The main ferry departs from Woods Hole (p. 213).

BY PLANE

Martha's Vineyard has only one airport, located in the middle of the island. **Cape Air** (☎800-352-0714, on the island ☎508-771-6944; www.flycapeair.com) flies year-round from Logan Airport (p. 17). Flights start at $130 one-way.

BY FERRY

FROM WOODS HOLE. The **Steamship Authority** (☎508-693-9130, on Martha's Vineyard ☎508-477-8600; www.islandferry.com) sends 12-17 boats per day from Woods Hole to either **Vineyard Haven** (45min.; May-Oct. 7am-10pm, Nov.-Apr. 7am-8:45pm; $5.50, ages 5-12 $2.75; cars May-Oct. $55, Nov.-Apr. $34; bikes $3) or **Oak Bluffs** (45min., mid-May to mid-Oct. 9:30am-5pm, $5.50, ages 5-12 $2.75; cars $55; bikes $3). Standby car travel is available late June to mid-Sept.; get in line early or risk waiting all day. For those looking to take a car on the ferry during peak season, reserve far in advance. Ferry information can vary; for exact schedules and fares, call or check the website.

To get to the Woods Hole ferry terminal **by car** (75 mi., 1½hr.), take I-93S to Rte. 3; just before the Sagamore Bridge, turn onto Rte. 6W and follow it to Buzzards Bay. Cross the Bourne Bridge and follow Rte. 28S to Woods Hole. In Woods Hole, follow signs for ferry parking (mid-May to mid-Oct. $10 per day; mid-Mar. to mid-May and mid-Oct. to Dec. $8; Jan. to mid-Mar. $6) at the Palmer Ave. lot (shuttle buses run continuously from here to the ferry); signs at the lot will direct you to other lots if it's full. If you're taking your car on the ferry, follow signs from Rte. 28S.

Bonanza Bus (☎888-751-8800; www.bonanzabus.com) runs from Boston's South Station (p. 18) and Logan Airport (p. 17) straight to the Woods Hole ferry terminal (1¾hr., 8-11 per day 8am-10pm, round-trip $40).

FROM ELSEWHERE ON CAPE COD. Ferries make the trip to the Vineyard from **Falmouth** on the Island Queen (☎508-548-4800; www.islandqueen.com), **Hyannis** on Hy-Line (☎800-492-8082 or 508-778-2600; www.hy-linecruises.com), and **New Bedford** on Schamonchi (☎508-997-1688; www.steamshipauthority.com). These companies do not allow vehicles on the ferry and run less frequently than Woods Hole's Steamship Authority, but are good options for those who don't want to park in the Steamship Authority lots. See directions for Falmouth (p. 213) and Hyannis (p. 218) earlier in this chapter.

PRACTICAL INFORMATION

Martha's Vineyard's 100 sq. mi. are made up of six communities. The relatively rural towns of **West Tisbury, Chilmark, Menemsha,** and **Aquinnah (Gay Head)** take up the southwestern side of the island, referred to as **up-island** because sailors have to tack up-wind to get to it. The three **down-island** towns—**Oak Bluffs, Edgartown,** and **Vineyard Haven**—are more developed and much busier. Oak Bluffs and Edgartown are the only "wet" (alcohol-selling) towns on the island. Vineyard Haven is the main ferry port, though ferries also dock in Oak Bluffs in summer.

In addition to the Chamber of Commerce, there are three **information booths**—at the ferry terminal in Vineyard Haven, at the foot of Circuit Ave. in Oak Bluffs, and on Church St. in Edgartown. For the latest news and events, pick up a copy of either the *Vineyard Gazette* (www.mvgazette.com; published in summer Tu and F) or *Vineyard Times* (www.mvtimes.com; published Th).

Chamber of Commerce (☎508-693-0085; www.mvy.com or www.marthasvineyardchamber.com), on Beach Rd. in **Vineyard Haven.** They provide innumerable handouts on everything from restaurants to seasonal events; their Visitor's Guide is particularly helpful. Open June-Oct. Su noon-4pm, M-F 9am-5pm, Sa 10am-4pm; Nov.-May M-F 9am-5pm, Sa 10am-2pm.

Leslie's Pharmacy, 65 Main St. (☎508-693-1010), in **Vineyard Haven.** Open Sept.-June Su 9am-3pm, M-Sa 8:30am-5:30pm; July-Aug. Su 9am-5pm, M-Sa 8am-6pm.

Post office, 1 Lagoon Pond Rd. (☎508-693-2818), opposite the Chamber of Commerce in **Vineyard Haven.** Window open M-F 8:30am-5pm, Sa 9:30am-1pm. Lobby open M-F 7am-5:50pm, Sa 7am-4pm.

LOCAL TRANSPORTATION

A car is the best way to get around the island, but fees for bringing vehicles on the ferry may make it prohibitively expensive. Bikes and/or public transportation are a cheaper option. In summer, most major places of interest are accessible by the buses run by the MVRTA (see below).

Public Transportation: Martha's Vineyard Regional Transit Authority (☎508-693-9440; www.vineyardtransit.com) runs summer shuttles between and within the 6 towns on the island. Pick up a free **schedule and map** of all 13 routes at the ferry terminal, Chamber of Commerce, or the info booths. Transportation between the 3 down-island towns is cheap, reliable, and convenient, but trips up-island often require shuttles that run more infrequently. Fare $1 per town, including town of origin. Unlimited travel passes 1-day $6, 3-day $11, 7-day $16.

Taxis: There are three major taxi companies on the island. **AdamCab** (☎508-693-3332 or 508-627-4462, toll-free ☎800-281-4462; www.adamcab.com). **Atlantic Cab** (☎508-693-7110 or 877-477-8294). **All Island** (☎508-693-2929 or 800-693-8294). Taxis are expensive and best shared with others. Vineyard Haven to Oak Bluffs $8-9; Vineyard Haven to Edgartown around $15 (prices for 1st 2 passengers; each additional passenger $2).

Bicycles: Bikes are the cheapest way to get around, though bike paths are not as comprehensive as the roads. Scenic **bike paths** run along the state beach and through the state forest between Edgartown and: Oak Bluffs (6 mi.), Vineyard Haven (8 mi.), South Beach (3¾ mi.), and West Tisbury (2 mi.). Traveling up-island means hills and narrow bike lanes; be careful when riding on the road shoulder. The Chamber of Commerce provides an excellent "Biking on Martha's Vineyard" map, complete with descriptions of the various roads.

Anderson's (☎508-693-9346), on Circuit Ave. Extension in **Oak Bluffs.** In a small shack right on the harbor, Anderson's is the best bet for a rental in Oak Bluffs. $15 per day. Open daily July-Aug. 8am-6pm; Apr.-June and Sept.-Oct. 9am-5pm.

Martha's Bike Rental (☎508-693-6593; www.marthasvineyardbikes.com), at Lagoon Pond Rd. and Beach Rd. in **Vineyard Haven.** $20 per day. Open daily Mar.-Nov. 8am-6pm; off-season by appointment.

Mopeds: Some car and bike rental agencies in Oak Bluffs rent mopeds, but *Let's Go* does not recommend driving them on Martha's Vineyard. The roads are not wide enough to handle moped traffic, and every year inexperienced moped riders are critically injured or killed.

Hitchhiking: *Let's Go* does not recommend hitchhiking, but it is a fairly common practice on the island. Hitchhikers report the most luck along State Rd. heading out of Vineyard Haven and in front of Alley's General Store in West Tisbury.

ACCOMMODATIONS & CAMPING

Budget accommodations are almost nonexistent in Martha's Vineyard. The Chamber of Commerce provides a list of inns and guest houses. Reserve far in advance.

Martha's Vineyard Hostel (HI-AYH), Edgartown-West Tisbury Rd. (☎508-693-2665 or ☎888-901-2087; www.capecodhostels.org), in **West Tisbury.** From Vineyard Haven, take MVRTA bus #3 to West Tisbury and then #6 to the hostel (call for biking or driving directions). Right next to a bike path, this environmentally-minded hostel has the 74 cheapest beds on the island. One of the cleanest and most comfortable hostels you're likely to encounter. The living quarters are tight but friendly. Free linen (bring your own towel). Lockers $0.75. Dorms and kitchen open in summer daily 7:30-10am and 4-10pm; off-season 7:30-10am and 5-10pm. Open mid-Apr. to mid-Nov. Dorms $18-24, nonmembers $21-27. Private room available for up to 4 people $65-95, depending on number of people and season. ❶

Nashua House, 30 Kennebec Ave. (☎508-693-0043 or 508-806-0290; www.nashuahouse.com), in **Oak Bluffs.** From the ferry terminal, walk straight along Lake Ave. and turn left onto Kennebec Ave. Though only 4 of the 15 rooms in this no-smoking old Victorian overlook the harbor, the staff is student-friendly, and the rooms are a stellar deal for those who want more privacy than a hostel can provide. Shared bath and daily maid service. Check-in 2pm; check-out 11am. Doubles in summer $99-129; 1 single available $79-109; each additional person $20. Rates lower off-season. Open year-round. ❸

Attleboro House, 42 Lake Ave. (☎508-693-4346), in **Oak Bluffs.** From the ferry terminal, walk 4 blocks straight down Lake Ave.; it's on your left, overlooking the harbor. Homey, no-frills atmosphere in one of Oak Bluffs' famous gingerbread houses, built in 1874. With balconies overlooking the water, the Attleboro house rents 11 tiny but cheerfully decorated rooms. No maid service; all rooms with shared bath. Check-in 1pm; check-out 11am. Doubles $75-115; suites $115-200; each additional person $15. Open June to mid-Sept. ❸

Martha's Vineyard Family Campground, 569 Edgartown-Vineyard Haven Rd. (☎508-693-3772; www.campmvfc.com), 1½ mi. from the ferry in **Vineyard Haven.** MVRTA bus #1 runs past the campground. The only campground on the island, their prices demonstrate their camping monopoly. It is mostly campers, though a few people do choose to rough it and stay in a tent. Check-in 2pm; check-out 11am. Reservations strongly recommended. Open mid-May to mid-Oct. 2-person site with water and electricity $40, with hook-up $44; each additional person up to 4 $10. Cabins: 1-room (max. 4 people) $100; 2-room (max. 6 people) $120. ❶

FOOD

For the most part, Vineyard food is mediocre and overpriced. Most upscale restaurants are popular for their scenic location, rather than their cuisine. The real deals on the island are the breakfast places and seafood shacks.

DOWN-ISLAND

Crowded with overpriced restaurants, there are plenty of places to watch dusk over the harbor, but all of them come with a hefty pricetag. Nevertheless, there are a few deals hidden among the tourist throngs.

Zapotec, 14 Kennebec Ave. (☎508-693-6800), in **Oak Bluffs.** From the ferry terminal, walk straight ahead on Lake Ave. and turn left at Kennebec Ave. Southwestern food in New England? Zapotec defies all expectations with delicious south-of-the-border dishes. Take advantage of the island location—fajitas with marinated swordfish ($17), lobster quesadillas ($13)—or stick to Tex-Mex favorites like burritos ($15-16). Open daily mid-June to Aug. noon-3pm and 5-10pm; May to mid-June and Sept.-Oct. noon-3pm. ❸

Murdicks Fudge, 21 N. Water St. (☎888-553-8343), in **Edgartown,** and 5 Circuit Ave. (☎508-693-2335), in **Oak Bluffs.** What's a trip to the Vineyard without fudge? Murdicks serves the best fudge you'll ever eat, from simple and sensuous chocolate to the more exotic Cape Cod Cranberry (around $6 per slice, $14 per 3 slices). Open daily July-Aug. 9am-11pm; Apr.-June and Sept.-Oct. 10am-5pm. Also in **Vineyard Haven,** 79 Main St. (☎508-693-7344). Open daily July-Aug. 10am-10pm; Apr.-June and Sept.-Oct. 10am-5pm.

Mad Martha's, 117 Circuit Ave. (☎508-693-9151), in **Oak Bluffs.** An island institution serving outstanding homemade ice cream and frozen yogurt (2 scoops $3.50). 2nd **Oak Bluffs** location on Lake Ave. Also in **Edgartown,** 7 N. Water St. (☎508-627-8761), and **Vineyard Haven,** 8 Union St. (☎508-693-5883). All branches open in summer daily 11am-11pm; Circuit Ave. location open July-Aug. 11am-midnight. Cash only.

Fresh Pasta Shoppe, 206 Upper Main St. (☎508-627-5582), in **Edgartown.** From the center of Edgartown, head towards Edgartown-Vineyard Haven Rd.; it's ½ mi. up on your left. Despite their name, the Fresh Pasta Shoppe is really known for serving the best pizza around. Pasta $3.50-7.50; large pizzas from $10, specialty pizzas like the Mexican or Bacon Double Cheeseburger around $16. Open May-Oct. Su 4-9pm, M-Sa 11am-9pm; stays open later if busy. ❶

Linda Jean's Restaurant, 34 Circuit Ave. (☎508-693-4093), in **Oak Bluffs.** Walk straight ahead from the ferry terminal and turn left onto Circuit Ave.; it's on the right. Popular with locals for their cheap breakfasts (under $7; served daily until 11:30am) and the friendliest service on the island. Sandwiches $3-7; light entrees around $10. Open daily 6am-8pm. ❶

Black Dog Bakery, Beach St. Extension (☎508-693-9223), in **Vineyard Haven.** Turn left out of the ferry terminal, then take your 1st left. Chances are you've seen their dog-emblazoned T-shirts and other paraphernalia everywhere, although wearing one here will guarantee that locals will look down at you as a tourist. Despite the tourist trap allure, the bakery still opens early in the morning to serve fresh baked goods ($0.40-3.25) to local fishermen. Open daily in summer 5:30am-8pm; off-season 5:30am-5pm. ❶

The Newes From America, 23 Kelley St. (☎508-627-4393), in **Edgartown.** From the Church St. bus stop, take a right onto Winter St., left onto N. Water St., and right onto Kelley St. Traditional pub fare served in an old-time Colonial tavern, replete with wooden cupboards and lanterns. Drink enough pints and they put your name on the wall of distinction. Grilled Salmon $10. Fish and chips $10.50. Beer $3.50-5; "rack of beers" (sample 5 of 13 drafts) $7.50. Open daily 11:30am-midnight; food served until 10:30pm. ❷

UP-ISLAND

Usually more subdued than the down-island towns, Gay Head and Menemsha Beach are choice spots to grab takeout from a seafood shack and have a romantic picnic.

Aquinnah Shop Restaurant, 27 Aquinnah Circle (☎508-645-3867), in **Aquinnah,** near the cliffs. Though they become ridiculously busy in peak season, if you go early or late enough in the season, it's possible to eat a picturesque meal outdoors overlooking the cliffs. The food is good, but the scenery is so breathtaking that it's hard to focus on your plate. Breakfast $4.50-7.50. Lunch sandwiches $5-8; seafood $12-15. Dinner $18-26. Open July-Aug. daily 8am-9pm; Apr.-June and Sept.-Oct. M-Th 8am-3pm, F-Su 8am to sunset. ❸

The Bite, Basin Rd. (☎508-645-9239), near the beach in **Menemsha.** Sporting a list of celebrity clientele that looks like the invite list to the Academy Awards, the Bite's phenomenal service in a low-key setting is topped only by their decadent fried seafood. Fish, clams, scallops, and shrimp for $8-16. Hearty chowder $2.50. Open in summer daily 11am-9pm; spring and fall M-F 11am-3pm, Sa-Su 11am-7pm. Cash only. ❷

Home Port, North Rd. (☎508-645-2679), by **Menemsha** Beach. Overlooking the Menemsha Harbor, this is *the* seafood restaurant on the island. They serve up a fresh and comprehensive *prix-fixe* menu (appetizer, beverage, salad, entree, and dessert). Always busy in the summer, the service is sometimes overworked and inattentive, but when the food arrives it's more than worth the wait. Dinner $35-42. Open mid-May to mid-Sept. daily 5-10pm. Reservations recommended. ❺

Larsen's, Basin Rd. (☎508-645-2680), on the dock of **Menemsha** Beach. This small seafood market/shop serves a few hot dishes and one of the best lobster rolls in town ("no filler, just lobster;" $8). Larsen's also sells delicious crabcakes ($2), oysters ($1), and steamers. Boiled lobsters near market price. Open May-Oct. daily 9am-7pm. One of the tastiest rivalries on the island, **Poole's Fish Market** (☎508-645-2282), next door, serves up equally fresh seafood. We'll leave the final verdict up to you. Open May-Oct. daily 10am-6pm. ❷

FARMS

A **farmers' market** takes over the Grange Hall Grounds on State Rd. in West Tisbury; take any MVRTA bus to West Tisbury or Alley's General Store. (Open June-Oct. Sa 9am-noon; late June-Aug. also W 2-5pm. Cash only.)

Morning Glory Farm (☎508-627-9003), on Edgartown-West Tisbury Rd. near Edgartown. Take MVRTA bus #6. They have the best farmstand on the island, selling hundreds of homemade baked goods ($1.50-4; pies $12). Open mid-June to Aug. Su 10am-5pm, M-Sa 9am-6pm; Sept.-late Nov. M-Sa 9am-6pm.

Thimble Farm (☎508-693-6396), from Vineyard Haven take a right on Head of the Pond Rd., off Edgartown-Vineyard Haven Rd. Visitors can pick their own seasonal fruit. In the early summer, it's raspberries and strawberries, but come fall, the farm preps for Halloween with pumpkins. Open late June-late Oct.; call for specific hours. Must be over 12 to pick raspberries.

SIGHTS

WEST TISBURY

West Tisbury is a hotbed of posh activity with the island's only vineyard and two leading art galleries. Despite the many galleries scattered along the main streets down-island, West Tisbury's Granary and Field are the two must-sees on Martha's Vineyard.

GRANARY GALLERY. Housed in a big red barn, the friendly staff loves to show visitors around the gallery's spectacular collection of sculpture and photography. On a grey day, the black-and-white photography provides better scenery than the beach.

(636 Old County Rd. Near Edgartown-West Tisbury Rd., on Old County Rd. ☎508-693-0455 or ☎800-472-6279; www.granarygallery.com. Open Su 11am-4pm, M-Sa 10am-5pm; shorter hours in winter, call ahead.)

FIELD GALLERY. Tom Maley's large, playful sculptures invite passersby to mimic his characters' vivid expressions. Maley began the gallery in 1972, and they have expanded beyond his sculptures, adding paintings and some photography to their collection. *(1050 State Rd. ☎508-693-5595; www.fieldgallery.com. Open July-Aug. daily 10am-7pm; May-June and Sept.-Dec. Su 11am-4pm, M-Sa 10am-5pm; Jan.-Apr. by appointment.)*

CHICAMA VINEYARDS. If you came to Martha's Vineyard looking for vineyards, here it is. Family-owned since 1971, this small vineyard is the oldest winery in Massachusetts. They offer free 25min. tours and wine tasting, and after the tour visitors can stop in at their small shop and purchase larger quantities of their home-grown wine. *(Driving or taking a taxi is the best option; otherwise take the MVRTA #3 bus and ask for Chicama Vineyards. Off State Rd., in West Tisbury, it's a 1 mi. walk up a dirt road. ☎508-693-0309; www.chicamavineyards.com. Open June-Oct. Su 1-5pm, M-Sa 11am-5pm; Nov.-May M-Sa 1-4pm. Tours June-Oct. Su 2 and 4pm; M-Sa noon, 2, 4pm.)*

OAK BLUFFS

Oak Bluffs, 3 mi. west of Vineyard Haven on Beach Rd., is the most youth-oriented of the Vineyard villages. For those with children, a trip to Oak Bluffs is a must, especially on a rainy day.

GINGERBREAD HOUSES. Playfully overlooking the harbor, the Gingerbread Houses are minutely detailed pastel Victorian cottages. Though the **Cottage Museum** offers a peek at the inside of a cottage, it is the facades that are most fascinating, and they can be seen just strolling around the town. *(Museum at 1 Trinity Park. Open mid-June to mid-Sept.)*

FLYING HORSES CAROUSEL. Built in 1876, the Flying Horses Carousel is the oldest continuously operating carousel in the country. For those still young at heart, the carousel provides 20 handcrafted horses for riders on the quest for the brass ring. Holsters, one on the outside and one on the inside, hold metal rings, among which are two lucky brass rings. Children gleefully shriek as they try to snatch the brass ring and win a free ride. *(At the end of Circuit Ave. ☎508-693-9481. Open daily late June-Aug. 10am-10pm; Sept.-late June 11am-4:30pm. Rides $1. 1 ride limit when busy.)*

OUTDOORS

Though Martha's Vineyard is best-known for its beaches, there is no shortage of alternative outdoor activities. From the thick inland greenery to the coasts and ponds, the island has an outdoor space for everyone.

TRAILS

Scattered throughout the island are trails that explore the lesser-appreciated beauty of the island's flora far from the overcrowded towns.

POLLY HILL ARBORETUM. At age 50, Polly started planting the exotic trees in her arboretum from seed. They've now grown into gigantic trees, flowers, and plants on 60 picturesque acres that are a must for anyone with a remote interest in botany. Visit during one of the Arboretum's special summer events and you might catch a glimpse of Polly, now age 96, as she rides around the property in her golf-cart. *(809 State Rd., in West Tisbury. ☎508-696-9538; www.pol-*

lyhillarboretum.org. Grounds open in summer Th-Tu 7am-7pm; off-season sunrise-sunset. Tours July-Sept. Th-Tu 10am and 2pm; June F-Su 10am and 2pm; early Oct. Th-Tu 2pm. Tours $5, under 12 free.)

MENEMSHA HILLS RESERVATION. The Menemsha Hills Reservation, off North Rd., has 4 mi. of trails that lead both to the rocky shores of the Vineyard Sound beach and the island's 2nd-highest point. Trails are perfect for joggers and walkers who want to take in the beauty of the island away from the crowds at the beach.

FELIX NECK WILDLIFE SANCTUARY. A birdwatcher's fantasy, Felix Neck provides five trails that meander through 350 acres, all leading to water. Though there's a gate, it is possible to walk onto the trails at anytime. *(On the Edgartown-Vineyard Haven Rd., 3 mi. outside Edgartown. ☎508-627-4850. Office open June-Sept. Su 12:30-4pm, M-F 8am-4pm, Sa 9am-4pm; Oct.-May Su 12:30-3pm, Tu-F 8am-4pm, Sa 9am-4pm. Gate opens with the office and closes around 7pm. $4, seniors and ages 3-12 $3.)*

OTHER TRAILS. Off Indian Hill Rd. on Menemsha's western shore, **Cedar Creek Tree Neck** harbors 250 acres of headland with trails throughout, while the **Long Point** park, in West Tisbury, preserves 633 acres and a shore on the Tisbury Great Pond.

ON THE WATERFRONT

With breathtaking cliff views, lighthouses, and every watersport yet invented, there's more to Martha's Vineyard waterfront than beaches. The quiet towns of Menemsha and Chilmark, a little northeast of Gay Head, share a scenic coastline and the best sunsets on the island. In addition to a public beach, Menemsha is home to a photogenic fishing village.

WATERSPORTS. Outside of Vineyard Haven, placid Lagoon Pond is a great spot for those new to the world of watersports. Both Edgartown Great Pond, off Herring Creek Rd., and Tisbury Great Pond, off Edgartown-West Tisbury Rd., are popular with kayakers. **Martha's Vineyard Kayak Co.,** at four island locations, rents single and double kayaks and leads expeditions to many of the island ponds. *(Call them to find the closest location. ☎508-693-0895. Kayak rental $30 per 3hr., $40 per ½ day, $50 per day. Free delivery. Open June-Sept. daily 8am-sunset.)*

Wind's Up is the spot for anyone looking to get out on the water in a boat. *(199 Beach Rd., near Lagoon Pond. ☎508-693-4252; www.windsupmv.com. Canoes $20 per hr. Windsurf boards $16 per hr., $50 per half-day. Sailboats $35-95. Kayaking, sailing, and windsurfing lessons available. Open daily late June to Sept. 9am-6pm; mid-May to late June and Oct. 10am-5:30pm.)*

GAY HEAD CLIFFS & LIGHTHOUSE. Aquinnah offers just about the best view of the sea in all of New England from the breathtaking **Gay Head Cliffs.** At sunset on weekends, be sure to visit the **Gay Head Lighthouse.** Originally built in 1799, a climb to the top of this still-operating lighthouse yields stunning views in all directions. *(**Cliffs:** 22 mi. southwest of Oak Bluffs, on State Rd. Parking $5 per hr., $15 max.; free if the attendant doesn't show up. **Lighthouse:** ☎508-645-2211. Open in summer F-Su 1½hr. before sunset to 30min. after sunset. $3, under 12 free.)*

BEACHES

Martha's Vineyard has some gorgeous beaches, especially in the up-island towns. Unfortunately, most of these are private or only open to residents of Martha's Vineyard. Here's a rundown of the best of the Vineyard's beaches that are open to the public. For a complete list of beaches, public and private, check out the Chamber of Commerce's Visitor's Guide.

DOWN-ISLAND

Katama Beach (South Beach), at the end of Katama Rd., a good 3 mi. south of **Edgartown.** Perhaps the most popular beach on the island, its sizeable surf attracts throngs of young people. Lifeguards on duty. Shuttle from Edgartown $2.

Lighthouse & Fuller St. Beach, in **Edgartown,** along North Water St. If you're looking for a younger crowd, Fuller is crawling with 20-somethings on summer days, while the Lighthouse is more subdued. The base of the Edgartown Lighthouse provides a scenic place to sit and gaze out over the harbor towards the mainland.

Oak Bluffs Town Beach & Joseph Sylvia State Beach, along Beach Rd. between Oak Bluffs ferry terminal and Edgartown. State Beach's warmer waters once set the stage for parts of *Jaws*. Ironically, the state beach (also called Bend-in-the-Road Beach) has safer waters (in terms of surf) than other down-island beaches, such as Katama.

UP-ISLAND

Aquinnah Beach, in **Aquinnah;** follow State Rd. all the way to the end of the island. Though many Aquinnah beaches are privately owned, this lovely public beach near the cliffs is one of the best and quietest public beaches on the island. The brilliant colors of the towering clay cliffs make this the Vineyard's best public beach, as well as New England's best clothing-optional stretch of sand. Surfers love Aquinnah for the rough waters that churn as the Atlantic meets the Sound, while kayakers and fishermen enjoy the calmer inland rivers and ponds. Parking $5 per hr., max. $15.

Menemsha Public Beach, in **Chilmark;** take State Rd. to North Rd. and follow signs to Menemsha. The calm waters of the Vineyard Sound are a safe swimming spot for children. Menemsha is the most popular spot on the island for watching the sunset, and rightfully so. Free parking and restrooms.

Long Point Beach, in **West Tisbury;** turn off 1 mi. beyond the airport on Edgartown-West Tisbury Rd., going away from Edgartown. This beach has great ocean waves and a fresh water pond. Parking $9.

Lobsterville Beach, in **Aquinnah,** along Lobsterville Rd., is a 2 mi. stretch of sand along the Vineyard Sound. There is nowhere close to the beach to park, so be prepared to walk.

NIGHTLIFE

All of the nightlife options are in the two alcohol-selling towns of **Edgartown** and **Oak Bluffs.** For those looking for a pint without the pre-

from the road

Bite it, Black Dog

For many people, Cape Cod and its islands—Martha's Vineyard and Nantucket—are synonymous with stuffy accents sporting Black Dog-emblazoned clothing and the clout of family names like Kennedy. Like most people, I went to Martha's Vineyard expecting to find an elite summer destination. Arriving early in the summer season, however, I was lucky enough to miss the tourist explosion that occurs in July and August. What I found instead was a misty June island that allowed for runs through shaded trails inland or along beaches and rocky shores on the coastline. This island, so often thought of as a summer destination of the rich and famous, is a place where people rarely know their addresses and the clerk at a grocery store is quick to spot you the difference when you come up short.

Though the tourist droves will invariably come with the heat of mid-summer, the charm of the island that isn't found blocks from the ferry has endured. Far from the Black Dog and its followers are the alluring shores and colored cliffs that many seem to have forgotten are the real reason to come.

—Megan Smith, 2003

tension of upscale and pricey bars, the island has some great pubs. For those itching to shake it to some live music, there are two decent clubs on the island. All bars shut down by 1am at the latest; last call usually 12:30am.

BARS & PUBS

Offshore Ale Co., 30 Kennebec Ave. (☎508-693-2626), in **Oak Bluffs.** From the ferry terminal, walk straight ahead and turn left onto Kennebec Ave. The staff couldn't be friendlier, and their 8 homemade beers (pints $4, pitchers $12) couldn't be smoother. The Amber Ale is by far the pub favorite, but it is impossible to make a bad choice. Gourmet American food $11-15. Local, regional, or even national music acts in summer 5 nights a week; off-season F-Sa. Usually no cover, big acts $10. Open daily May-Oct. noon-midnight; Nov.-Apr. 5pm-midnight; food until 10pm.

The Wharf, Lower Main St. (☎508-627-9966), in **Edgartown.** No gimmicks, this is simply the busiest bar in Edgartown. Packed with local fishermen by 7pm, the crowd becomes younger as the night wears on. Once the kitchen closes (10pm, on summer weekends 10:30pm) the bar spills over into the neighboring restaurant. Beer $3.50-4.50; mixed drinks $4.25-8.50. Open nightly until 1am.

The Lamppost, Circuit Ave. (☎508-696-9352), in **Oak Bluffs.** From the ferry terminal, walk straight ahead and turn left onto Circuit Ave. College kids pack this dim bar for events like "Best Male Body" and "Exotic Brazil Night." Upstairs is a dance club with live DJ Tu-W, while downstairs has pool tables, popcorn, and big-screen TVs. Adjacent **Rare Duck** caters to an older set with live rock nightly in summer. Beer $3.50-4.25; mixed drinks $5, each additional shot $1. 21+. No cover. Lamppost open Apr.-Oct. daily noon-12:30am; Rare Duck May-Sept. daily 8pm-12:30am.

CLUBS

The Hot Tin Roof, off Airport Rd. (☎508-693-1137). Take any MVRTA bus to the airport and ask to get off at the Roof turn-off. Back from a brief stint as a furniture shop, the Tin Roof is potentially empty and awkward or jammed with 600+ patrons. Carly Simon is a partial owner and may appear with celebrity friends. Live music, typically reggae, at least once a week, sometimes bringing in larger names like Ben Harper. Tickets available at stores throughout Martha's Vineyard. Drinks $4-6. Cover varies drastically depending on the act. Open late May-early Sept. shows usually Th-Sa, some mid-week; call ahead for schedule.

Atlantic Connection, 19 Circuit Ave. (☎508-693-7129), in **Oak Bluffs.** From the ferry terminal, walk straight ahead and turn left onto Circuit Ave. Strange things happen when you bring a big-city club scene to the small-town Vineyard; atmosphere varies drastically depending on the act–sometimes a local meat market, other times a quiet tourist hangout. Drinks $5-6. DJ spins most weekend nights. Mostly 21+, some exceptions–call ahead. Cover usually $5-10, more for larger acts. Open daily 9pm-12:30am.

NANTUCKET

Smaller, more expensive, more exclusive, and more beautiful than Martha's Vineyard, Nantucket has quickly become the premier Massachusetts island destination for the trendy, well-to-do city-dweller. Oozing both affluence and New England charm—complete with dune-covered beaches, beautiful wild flowers, cobblestone streets, and spectacular bike paths—Nantucket has grown from a tiny fishing and whaling village into a summer stomping ground for nearly 50,000 visitors. From those driving Land Rovers to those speeding by in Range Rovers, Nantucket vacationers tend to be a "diverse" group that may hail from as far as the Upper East Side or as nearby as Greenwich, Connecticut.

Over 36% of Nantucket is protected from development, and despite the incessant influx of obnoxiously wealthy summer tourists, the island often feels like a natural, peaceful paradise. The beaches, especially far from Nantucket Town, are breathtaking and often uncrowded. The best way to experience the real Nantucket, and to avoid those who may be prone to use the word "summer" as a verb, is a weekend visit in the spring or fall. As late as June and as early as September, the hordes of suits and trophy wives thin out, while the beaches remain open and accommodations cut rates to nearly half-price.

GETTING THERE

The island is accessible by ferry or airplane only. Flights are very expensive (starting at $220 round-trip), so the majority of visitors take ferries, which leave from various points on Cape Cod. The two major ferries depart from Hyannis (p. 218).

BY PLANE

As any fan of the now defunct TV show *Wings* (set in the airport at Nantucket's Tom Nevers Field) knows, Nantucket has only one airport, and it's filled with wacky characters and comical situations 365 days a year. **Cape Air** (☎800-352-0714; www.flycapeair.com) flies year-round from Logan Airport (p. 17). Flights start at $130 one-way. **Nantucket Airlines** (☎800-635-8787; www.nantucketairlines.com), owned by Cape Air, flies from Hyannis to the island for those who don't want to waste a whole hour taking the boat. (12min.; one-way $46).

BY FERRY

Hyannis is the cheapest most direct departure port for ferries to Nantucket. The town has two ferry companies, both near the bus station.

Hy-Line Cruises, Ocean St. Wharf (☎800-492-8082 or 508-778-2600; www.hylinecruises.com), runs to Nantucket's Straight Wharf on slow boats (2hr.; 3 per day 9am-6:10pm in summer, 1-3 per day other seasons; $13.50, ages 5-12 $6.75, bikes additional $5) and fast boats (1hr.; 6 per day 6:30am-8:45pm; $33, ages 5-12 $25, bikes additional $5).

The Steamship Authority, South St. Wharf (☎508-477-8600; www.islandferry.com), runs to Nantucket's Steamboat Wharf on slow boats (2hr.; May-Oct. 6 per day 7:15am-8:30pm, Oct.-Dec. 3 per day; $13, ages 5-12 $6.50, bikes additional $5) and fast boats (1hr.; 5 per day 6am-7:20pm; $26, ages 5-12 $19.50, bikes additional $5).

To get to the ferry terminals in Hyannis **by car** from Boston, follow directions to Hyannis on p. 218; parking ($10 per day) is available in lots. Taking a car on the ferry is not an affordable option (one-way $165), nor is it practical—you can get everywhere on tiny Nantucket by bike, and public transportation on the island is great. It's even easier and cheaper to take the **Plymouth & Brockton bus** (schedules and fares ☎508-746-0378, office ☎508-746-4795; www.p-b.com) from Boston's South Station to Hyannis, which lets you off a 5min. walk from the ferry terminal.

PRACTICAL INFORMATION

Nantucket is a tiny island floating in Nantucket Sound to the west of Martha's Vineyard. Just 18 mi. across and 3 mi. wide, Nantucket is made up of one town, also called Nantucket. The village area where the ferry docks is known to locals as Nantucket Town and is home to most attractions, restaurants, and accommodations. Steamship Authority ferries dock at **Steamboat Wharf,** which becomes **Broad St.** inland. To reach **Main St.,** walk straight up Broad St. and turn left on S. Water St. **Hy-Line** ferries dock at the base of Main St.

Nantucket Visitor Services, 25 Federal St. (☎508-228-0925; www.nantucket-ma.gov), left off Broad St. Provides maps and information on securing accommodations—though it's not a reservation service. Open in summer daily 9am-6pm; off-season M-Sa 9am-5:30pm.

Nantucket Chamber of Commerce, 48 Main St. (☎508-228-0925; www.nantucketchamber.org). They provide information on everything from restaurants to seasonal events; their Visitor's Guide is particularly helpful. Open M-F 9am-5pm,

Nantucket Pharmacy, 45 Main St. (☎508-228-0180), in town. Open daily 8am-10:30pm.

Post Office, 5 Federal St. (☎508-228-1067), next to the Nantucket Visitor Services. Window open M-F 8:30am-5pm, Sa 8:30am-12:30pm.

LOCAL TRANSPORTATION

On the island, SUVs are king. If you can't afford one, welcome to the club. Public transportation is abundant, and bikes are common, so getting around Nantucket is relatively simple.

Public Transportation: **Nantucket Regional Transit Authority** (☎508-228-7025; www.town.nantucket.ma.us) runs a variety of shuttle bus routes throughout the island. Buses to Siasconset and Surfside (where the hostel is) leave from Washington and Main St. (near the lamppost); buses to Miacomet leave from Washington and Salem St. (a block up from Straight Wharf); and buses to Madaket and Jetties Beach leave from Broad St. in front of the Peter Foulger Museum. (Buses depart every 30min. 7am-11:30pm; the Surfside bus runs every 40min. 10am-5:20pm. Fare is $0.50-2, seniors ½-price, under 6 free.) Each bus can accommodate 2 bikes; shuttles routinely stop along major bike paths. A bus map, schedules, and multi-day passes are available at the **Visitors Center.**

Bicycles: Bikes are the best way to get around Nantucket. There are relatively flat bike-trails everywhere, and signs give clear and useful directions. The island is so small that riding to and from the beach is a pleasant experience (and useful exercise on what is otherwise a lavish vacation).

Cook's Cycle, 6 S. Beach St. (☎508-228-0800), right off Broad St. One of the cheapest places to rent bicycles. Open Apr.-Nov. daily 9am-5pm. Bikes $20 per day, $50 per week.

Nantucket Bike Shop, Broad St. (☎508-228-1999). With 3 locations in Nantucket Town, it's by far the most convenient. Mountain bikes $25 per day or $90 per week.

Mopeds: Some car and bike rental agencies in Nantucket rent mopeds, and although they are speedy and really, really fun, *Let's Go* does not necessarily recommend driving them on Nantucket for 2 reasons. They are expensive and they are somewhat dangerous for beginners—though the roads are much more forgiving than those in Martha's Vineyard.

Hitchhiking: *Let's Go* does not recommend hitchhiking, but it is a fairly common practice on the island. Hitchhikers report the most luck along Broad St., heading out of Nantucket Town, and at any beach heading back.

ACCOMMODATIONS

There once was a hostel on Nantucket—and there still is. Unfortunately, most other accommodations on Nantucket are expensive. The best option in the super-busy summer is to contact one of the island's several reservation services, including the **Nantucket Accommodations Bureau** (☎508-228-9559) and **Nantucket & Martha's Vineyard Reservations** (☎800-649-5671). In summer, many places may have minimum-stay or advance payment policies. Most expensive guest houses are similar; be prepared to spend upwards of $200 per night during high season. Be forewarned, those looking to camp are out of luck, it is prohibited on the island due to environmental regulations. Those who sneak onto the beach after dark to sleep on the sly will find a $200 fine waiting when they wake up.

Nantucket Hostel (HI-AYH), 31 Western Ave. (☎508-228-0433 or 888-901-2084; www.hiayh.org). The hostel is best reached by bike; it's 3½ mi. from town, at the end of the unlit Surfside Bike Path. June-Sept. take the Surfside Shuttle to the beach, turn right, and walk down Western Ave. to the hostel; off-season take the Miacomet Loop Shuttle to Surfside Rd. and Fairground and walk 1 mi. south on Surfside before turning right on Western Ave. Taxis will also make the trek from town ($8). If you've come to Nantucket for the beach, Nantucket Hostel puts you closer than anywhere else—the beach is across the street. Housed in a gorgeous 128-year-old lifesaving station, the interior is less remarkable, with 3 large, clean, single-sex dorm rooms (49 beds). Full kitchen. Free linen. Check in 4-10pm. Lockout 10am-4pm. Curfew 10pm. Max. stay 7 days. Dorms $22, nonmembers $25. Open Apr.-Oct. ❶

Nesbitt Inn, 21 Broad St. (☎508-228-0156). This beautiful, centrally located Victorian (1 block from the wharf) is the oldest and one of the least expensive inns on Nantucket. Small rooms (with fan and sink) and shared baths explain the low price, but guests are kept comfortable with a fireplace, deck, common room with TV, and continental breakfast. Reception 7am-10pm. Check-in noon; check-out 11am. Singles $75; doubles $85, with king-sized bed $95; quads $125. Mar.-Apr. and Oct.-Dec. $20 less. Open Mar.-Dec. ❷

FOOD

Sit-down restaurants in Nantucket are pricey (entrees average $15-25), so the only cheap option is to join the crowds who flock to the takeout joints at the end of Steamboat Wharf (tacos, pizza, sandwiches, burgers, or ice-cream for under $5). For provisions, head to the **A&P Supermarket,** just off Straight Wharf. (☎508-228-9756. Open Su 7am-7pm, M-Sa 7am-10pm.)

Something Natural, 50 Cliff Rd. (☎508-228-0504), just outside town on Cliff Rd. A bakery at heart, this antique house turned sandwich shop makes the best sandwiches on the island. Each sandwich is served on delectable, freshly baked bread. Don't be fooled by the healthy name, the fare is far from vegetarian, masterfully incorporating lobster, ham, and bacon—though the avocado and chutney is also a favorite. A ½ sandwich makes for a filling lunch. Full sandwich $7-8; ½ sandwich $4-5. Open Su-Th 8am-6pm, F-Sa 8am-6:30pm. ❶

The Juice Bar, 12 Broad St. (☎508-228-5799), just up from Steamboat Wharf. Nantucket's answer to Mad Martha's serves up creamy, smooth ice cream. Nothing feels better than some ice cream after the beach, and this is the place to get it. Cone $3-4. Open summer 11am-11pm. ❶

The Atlantic Café, 15 S. Water St. (☎508-228-0570), left off Broad St. Nautical and nice, the food here is just standard American pub fare, but locals can't seem to get enough of this aquatic-themed restaurant/bar—friendly employees know the regulars by name. Sandwiches $8-15. Entrees $13-22. Open daily 11:30am-1am (closed M Nov.-Apr.); food until 11pm. ❸

Henry's, Steamboat Wharf (☎508-228-0123). The island's best, no nonsense sandwich shop, this less-than-inspirational spot is the first thing you'll see after getting off the ferry. No surprises here—just well-executed sandwiches ($4-5.25). Salads $5-7. Open May to mid-Oct. daily 8am-10pm. Cash only. ❶

SIGHTS

NANTUCKET WHALING MUSEUM. This one-of-a-kind museum explores the glories and hardships of the old whaling community through exhibits and talks on whales and whaling. The highlight is a 43 ft. skeleton of a finback whale that washed ashore in 1967. Next door, the **Peter Foulger Museum** has a rotating exhibit on Nantucket history. *(Whaling Museum ☎508-228-1736, Peter Foulger ☎508-228-1894; www.nha.org. Both open June-Sept. Su noon-5pm, M-Sa 10am-5pm; Oct.-May Sa-Su noon-4pm. Whaling museum only $10, ages 6-17 $6, under 6 free. Admission to Foulger Museum only available with a History Ticket ($15, ages 6-17 $8, under 7 free; family pass $35), which offers admission to both museums, 4 other historical sites, and a 90min. walking tour M-Sa 10:15am, 12:15, 2:15pm; June-Oct. also Su 2:15pm.)*

CONGREGATIONAL CHURCH TOWER. For a panorama of the island, climb the 92 stairs to the top of the bright white tower. On a clear day, you can see 14 mi. out to sea. About halfway up, you can take a rest at the small church museum. *(62 Centre St., the 3rd right off Broad St. ☎508-228-0950. Open mid-June-Oct. M-Sa 10am-4pm; Apr. to mid-June F-Sa 10am-2pm. $2.50, ages 5-12 $0.50.)*

the BIG $plurge

Bluefin

Nantucket: 15 South Beach St. ***Contact:*** *508-228-2033.* ***Open:*** *daily 5:30-9:30pm. Entrees $25-30; 2- to 8-pc. sushi $6-10.* ❺

On an island full of overpriced, over-hyped, overhyphenated cuisine, Bluefin, with its mix of pan-Asian and new American fare, is perhaps the only restaurant that delivers.

Housed in an ultra-modern minimalist-cool beachside shack, Bluefin boasts a lively bar, small dining area and even smaller sushi-bar. The waitstaff is as young and vibrant as the clientele, yet surprisingly experienced, knowledgeable, and friendly.

The food, however, is the real draw. The sumptuous sushi runs from traditional to bizarre, but the undisputed highlight is the inventive intersection of Japan (sushi) and New England (lobster) in the delicate Ninniku roll.

Also surprisingly worthy of note is the oft maligned, General Tso's chicken. Bluefin adds a flair seldom tasted in a takeout box, using ginger and peppers to create a lighter, fresher sauce.

After spending an arm and a leg on dinner, you might as well get dessert. All of the options are wonderful. The lemongrass crème brulée, however, is the best.

OUTDOORS

BEACHES

It's an island. It's surrounded by beaches, and they're some of the best in Massachusetts. Whether it's warm sand, big surf, or attractive, volleyball-playing beachgoers, the vast sands of Nantucket have something for everyone. The beaches below are all open to the public and offer free, if limited, parking.

Surfside, at the end of Surfside Rd. on the south shore of the island. Open to the vast North Atlantic, Surfside is famous for its large waves and cold water. The surf is heavy at times, but usually small enough to bodysurf comfortably. The beach is wide and perfect for sandcastles, kite flying, or volleyball. Full bathhouse amenities and a snack bar.

Cisco, at the end of Hummock Pond Rd. Cisco is a small beach devoted almost entirely to surfing. The waves are large for New England, if a bit messy. Nantucket Island Surf School (508-560-1020; www.surfack.com) is headquartered here and offers rentals ($40 per day, $25 per ½ day) and lessons ($65 for a 1hr. private lesson, $80 for a 2hr. group lesson).

Siasconset, on the eastern shore 6 mi. from town. Siasconset (pronounced 'sconset) is isolated and peaceful, with a lighter surf than Surfside. Never crowded, it is the perfect beach for relaxing or surfcasting. **Barry Thurston's,** 5 Salem St. (508-228-9595), in town at Candle St. (left off Straight Wharf), rents rods and reels and gives beginners enough advice to get started fishing. Open Apr.-Dec. Su 8am-5pm, M-F 8am-6pm. Equipment $20 per 24hr.

Madaket, 5 mi. west of town on Madaket Rd. Madaket is one of the only places on the eastern seaboard where you can see the sun set over the ocean, and thus, the perfect evening beach. Grab a sandwich from **Something Natural** (p. 239) on your way out here and enjoy a picnic. Surf is moderate, and the water is never crowded.

Dionis, on Eel Point Rd., 3 mi. out of town. Located on the calm, warm waters of Nantucket Sound, Dionis is a small hideaway ideal for families with small children. The water remains shallow for a good 40 ft. out.

Jetties, near town off Cliff Rd. Jetties is named for the large rock jetties that jut into the sound and create a harbor for ferries and sailboats to cavort in and out of. The beach itself is as crowded as Nantucket gets and offers numerous watersport options. Nantucket Community Sailing, (508-228-6600; www.nantucketcommunitysailing.org) rents kayaks ($15 per hr., $80 per day), windsurfers ($25 per hr., $80 per day), and small sailboats ($35 per hr., $85 per ½ day). Open late June-Aug. daily 9am-5pm.

TRAILS

SANFORD FARM HIKE. A single trail (round-trip 6 mi.) that can be made into a number of loops, this hike heads into the heart of the old Sanford Farm, which was bought and set aside as a nature preserve by the Nantucket Conservation Foundation. The entrance to the preserve lies on **Madaket Rd.** (follow directions for the Madaket bike path above). Once you are on Madaket Rd., stop at the second parking area on the left, which is marked as Sanford Farm. There are **maps** here that detail the three possible loops of the hike, which begins with a lowland loop through brush and meadow, heads uphill to a barn, then continues down through the meadows to the ocean.

TUPANCY LINKS. Originally a golf course (you can still see a putting green), the Links is now a walking trail with some of the best vistas overlooking Nantucket Sound. The short loop leads to 40 ft. cliffs that drop to inaccessible beaches. Look right to see Point Lighthouse 8 mi. away and also inaccessible (except by Jeep). The entrance to Tupancy is on **Cliff Rd.,** a short bike ride from town.

NIGHTLIFE

For a place popular with families, Nantucket has a fairly jumping nightlife, energized by the infusion of college kids who work on the island in the summer. Most of the bars are near the water between the 2 wharves.

The Chicken Box, 14 Daves St. (☎508-228-9717). From the bottom of Main St., walk away from the water and take a left onto Orange St. (15min.); Daves St. is on the right, 5 blocks after Orange St. becomes 2-way. The best and most popular nightlife spot on the island—just look around at the many cars sporting "BOX" bumper stickers. College students and 20-somethings flock here to dance to the surprisingly good live music, play pool ($1 per game), and mingle on the covered outdoor patio. Live music M-Tu and Th-Sa 9:45pm. Beer $3-4; mixed drinks $5-7. 21+. Cover $5-25. Open daily noon-1am. Cash only.

The Rose & Crown, 23 S. Water St. (☎508-228-2595; www.theroseandcrown.com). A left off Broad St. It's a standard pubby restaurant by day and a cheesy but popular nightspot by night. Frequented by islanders and tourists of all ages, the Rose and Crown is the closest Nantucket gets to a Top-40 dance club. Beer $3-4; mixed drinks $5-8. 21+ after 10pm. Cover $5. Open daily 11:30am-1am.

The Gazebo (☎508-228-1266), where Straight Wharf merges into Main St. (look for...the gazebo). Known around town as Nantucket's "meeting place," this fun-loving, drinks-only spot is the only bar that's as packed mid-afternoon as it is late at night. Casual but classy 20- and 30-somethings stop here for drinks and schmoozing before the nightly bar-hop. Beer $4-5; mixed drinks $4-6; frozen drinks (rumored to be the best on the island) $8. 21+ after 5pm. Open in summer daily 11:30am-12:30am.

PIONEER VALLEY (FIVE-COLLEGE AREA)

Aside from aggressive tourism, the best way to keep offbeat shops and eateries afloat is to pack a few square miles with college students. Centered on the Connecticut River, Pioneer Valley (also known as the "Five-College Area"), with nearly 30,000 college students, does just that. Preppy **Amherst,** free-wheeling **Hampshire,** sporty **Mt. Holyoke,** liberated **Smith,** and—the jewel of Massachusetts public education—the **University of Massachusetts at Amherst (UMass-Amherst)** make up the "Five College Consortium." True to form, the area has the best attributes of a college town: unique and cheap restaurants and cafés, impressive museums, and plenty of bike trails and parks to relieve the stress of a liberal arts education.

During the school year, the **University of Massachusetts Transit System** in conjunction with the **Pioneer Valley Transit Authority (PVTA)** runs free shuttles between all five campuses, the Holyoke mountain range, Sunderland, and South

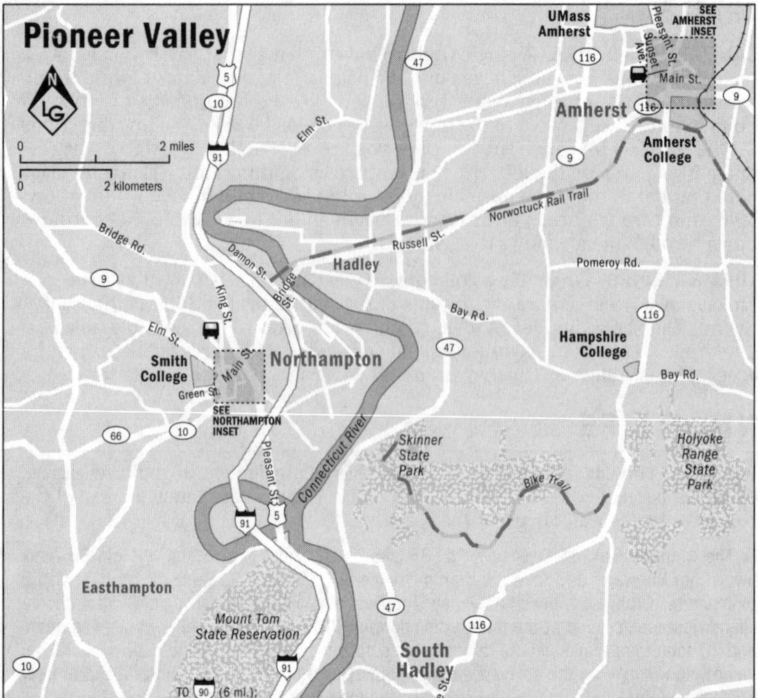

Pioneer Valley

UMass Amherst
SEE AMHERST INSET
Pleasant St.
Sunset Ave.
Main St.
Amherst
Amherst College
0 2 miles
0 2 kilometers
Elm St.
Norwottuck Rail Trail
Bridge Rd.
Damon St.
Russell St.
Hadley
Pomeroy Rd.
King St.
Bridge St.
Bay Rd.
Elm St.
Hampshire College
Smith College
Main St.
Northampton
Green St.
SEE NORTHAMPTON INSET
Bay Rd.
Pleasant St.
Connecticut River
Skinner State Park
Holyoke Range State Park
Bike Trail
Easthampton
Mount Tom State Reservation
South Hadley
TO 90 (6 mi.);
SPRINGFIELD (13 mi.)
Village Commons
College St.
Mt. Holyoke College

Northampton

TO 2
King St.
Bridge St.
Phillips Pl.
Center St.
Gothic St.
Gleason Plaza
Hawley St.
State St.
Masonic St.
Main St.
Smith College
Elm St.
JavaNet
Old South St.
Hampton Ave.
Green St.
New South St.
TO 14
Clark Ave.
Old South St.
Conz St.
Fruit St.
Smith St.
Pleasant St.
Wright Ave.
0 1000 feet
0 200 meters

Amherst

TO UMASS AMHERST
Fearing St.
E. Pleasant St.
Chestnut St.
High St.
Cottage St.
0 1000 feet
0 200 meters
McLellan St.
Pray St.
Triangle St.
Gray St.
Hallock St.
Lincoln Ave.
N Prospect St.
Taylor St.
Kellogg Ave.
JavaNet
Lessey St.
Main St.
TO 29
Sunset Ave.
Gaylord St.
Spring St.
Seelye St.
Railroad St.
Boltwood Ave.
College St.
N Pleasant St.
Dickinson St.
Amherst College
Northampton Rd.
Dana St.

ACCOMMODATIONS
Allen House Victorian Inn, **29**
Amherst Inn, **28**
Autumn Inn, **2**
Best Western, **16**
University Lodge, **17**

ENTERTAINMENT
Academy of Music, **10**
Calvin Theatre & Performing Arts Center, **3**
New Century Theatre, **14**

FOOD
Antonio's, **22**
Amanouz Café, **4**
Atlantis, **24**
Bart's Homemade, **9**
Black Sheep Deli, **26**
Fire & Water, **11**
Fresh Side, **25**
Henion Bakery, **19**
Ichiban, **13**
Northampton Brewery & Restaurant, **12**
Paul & Elizabeth's Natural Foods, **8**
Thai Corner, **23**

MUSUEMS
Emily Dickinson House, **27**
Historic Northampton Museum, **1**
Mead Art Museum, **30**
Pratt Museum of Natural History, **31**
Smith College Museum of Art, **5**

NIGHTLIFE
Amherst Brewing Co., **21**
Divas, **15**
The Monkey Bar, **20**
Pearl Street, **7**
The Pub, **18**

SHOPPING
The Mountain Goat, **6**

Deerfield (most routes run until 2:30am). There is reduced service during school breaks (in late Dec.-early Jan. and most of the summer). Schedules vary by bus route and are available online (www.umass.edu/campus_services/transit/) or at the Amherst Chamber of Commerce (☎413-586-5806).

NORTHAMPTON

Known for its independent film festivals, a liberal and gay-friendly populace, innumerable vegan restaurants and live music joints—as well as the incomparable Smith College—Northampton teaches the rest of the Valley how to really be a cool college town. The town is often referred to as "Lesbianville" by Valley students because it has the country's highest concentration of lesbians, with 20% of the female population identifying itself as queer. This scenic town is an ideal base camp to hike the surrounding Berkshires or a great place to just hang out and enjoy the ease of a welcoming and active community.

PRACTICAL INFORMATION

Driving by **car** from Boston (2hr.), take the Mass. Turnpike (I-90) to I-91N, get off at Exit 18, and follow Rte. 5 north into Northampton Ctr., which intersects with Main St., where most places of interest lie. Main St. curves to the right at the top of the hill, marking the beginning of the Smith College campus.

Buses: Peter Pan Bus Lines (☎800-343-9999; www.peterpanbus.com) runs service from Boston's South Station (p. 18) to Roundhouse Plaza (2¾hr., approx. every 90min. 10am-5pm, $25).

Bikes: Aside from the UMass/PVTA Shuttle (see above), bikes are the best way of getting out to see the valley, and rental shops abound. The best among them is **Valley Bicycle** in Hadley, 8 Railroad St. (☎413-584-4466), with another branch in Amherst.

Hiking: The Mountain Goat, 177 Main St. (☎413-586-0803), which stocks all sorts of athletic gear, footwear, and travel gear, is the perfect place to get outfitted if you feel like hiking instead of riding.

Tourist office: Get maps and info from the **Greater Northampton Chamber of Commerce,** 99 Pleasant St. (☎413-584-1900; www.gazettenet.com). Open Nov.-May M-F 9am-5pm; June-Oct. M-F 9am-5pm, Sa-Su 10am-2pm.

Internet Access: JavaNet, 241 Main St. (☎413-587-3401), in Northampton, with a second branch at 103 N. Pleasant St., in Amherst, provides Internet access ($2 per 20min.).

ACCOMMODATIONS

Chain motels are the cheapest bet in the Five-College Area. Accommodations can be hard to get during spring graduation time; reserve far in advance.

Best Western, 117 Conz St. (☎413-586-1500), Exit 18 off I-91, it is off Rte. 5. Free breakfast, cable TV, in-room fridges, jacuzzis, and an outdoor pool. Wheelchair accessible rooms available. Doubles in summer $89-139; in winter $69-99; under 15 free. ❷

Autumn Inn, 259 Elm St. (☎413-584-7660; www.autumninn.com), turn left off Main St. at Smith College. Forgo the region's many cookie-cutter motels in favor of the charming Autumn Inn, which provides guests with cable TV, an outdoor pool, and free parking. Singles $86; doubles $112; suites $150. ❸

FOOD

Restaurants of every variety line Main St., from expensive gourmet bistros to dirt-cheap vegan takeout counters. There is also a popular weekly **farmers' market** on Gothic St. (Sa 7am-12:30pm).

Northampton Brewery & Restaurant, 11 Brewster Ct. (☎413-584-9903). From Main St., turn onto Pleasant St., right onto Hampton Ave., then right again onto Brewster Ct. Billed as "The Valley's original brewpub," they have a standard array of pub grub favorites. Their quality lagers and ales are brewed on site. Burgers and sandwiches $6-7. Entrees $12-15. Open daily 11:30am-1am. ❸

Paul & Elizabeth's Natural Foods Restaurant, 150 Main St. (☎413-584-4832), in Thornes Market, serves delectable wheat rolls (reason enough to eat here) alongside fresh, veggie-friendly daily specials. If the grilled tofu kebabs ($11) sound too intimidating, plenty of seafood and pasta dishes await ($9-14). Beer and wine $4-5. Su-Th 11:30am-9pm, F-Sa 11:30am-10pm. ❸

Ichiban, 1 Roundhouse Plaza (☎413-585-1185), take a left down the hill at the Smith College campus; Ichiban is at the bottom, opposite the public parking lot. Tasty, affordable sushi (4-6pc. rolls $4) in a comfortable setting. Smith students rave about the dragon rolls ($8.50). Open M-Th, Su 11:30am-10pm; F-Sa 11:30am-2:30am. ❷

Fire & Water, 5 Old South St. (☎413-586-8336). Go up Main St. and take a left at the traffic light near the Smith College campus gate to get to this mellow and comfy café and performance space. A haven for vegans: everything on the menu is made with talent and care, but without a trace of animal products. Soups and sandwiches $5-8. Entrees $9-11. Earnest singer-songwriters—from local to national acts—perform nightly 7-8pm. No cover, but there are "mandatory donations." Open Su-Th 11am-midnight, F-Sa 11am-2am. ❷

Amanouz Café, 44 Main St. (☎413-585-9128). This tiny storefront serves up Moroccan and Mediterranean specialties and has a great selection of veggie-friendly delights ($8-12). The "Royal Feast" is a lot more hummus than you can eat for only $6, and the couscous entrees ($10-11) are fantastic. French night Th. Open Tu-Th, Su 8am-10pm; F-Sa 8am-11pm. ❷

Bart's Homemade, 235 Main St. (☎413-584-0721). A popular Ice cream shop/café/hangout with a global conscience (it's hard to find a restaurant in Northampton without a global conscience). Everything here is natural—the produce is locally grown, and the coffee is "Fair Trade." Their rich and creamy ice cream ($2-4) is always a crowd pleaser. Open M-Th 7:30am-11pm, F-Sa 7:30am-midnight, Su 8am-11pm. ❷

SIGHTS

Bikers, joggers, and in-line skaters should try the **Norwottuck Rail Trail,** a paved trail that begins on Damon Rd. in Northampton and runs 8½ mi. to Belchertown. The trail spans Northampton, Hadley, and Amherst, and follows the gentle curves and gradual hills of the old railroad beds that once existed here. For more rigorous cycling, visit www.ridenoho.com or call ☎888-817-6646.

SMITH COLLEGE. Built in the late 19th century, Smith College has become one of the largest and most prestigious women's colleges in the country. The campus is full of elegant wood and brick buildings attractively set on a hillside that overlooks downtown Northampton. The money to buy the land and construct the first buildings came from Sophia Smith and a fortune that she inherited at age 65. Smith sought to "furnish for [her] own sex means and facilities for education equal to those which are afforded now in our colleges to young men." One of the coolest facilities for that education is the **Lyman Plant House,** a beautiful botanical garden that makes a stop by the campus well worth your time. *(Opposite Helen Hills chapel. ☎413-585-2740. Open daily 8:30am-4pm. Free.)*

SMITH COLLEGE MUSEUM OF ART. Fresh from a $35 million face-lift, the popular museum reopened in 2003 with brand-new sky-lit galleries, additional studios and multimedia spaces, a new photography studio, and an expanded student art gallery. Strong in American art, the museum was the first to show painter Thomas Eakins, and still houses his masterpiece *Portrait of Edith Mahon*. A beautiful Cezanne and newly acquired Eastman Johnson are also not to be missed. *(Elm St. in the Brown Fine Arts Center. ☎413-585-2760; www.smith.edu/artmuseum. Open Su noon-5pm., Tu and Th-Sa 9am-5pm, W 9am-9pm.)*

HISTORIC NORTHAMPTON MUSEUM. This collection, housed in three restored homes from the 18th and 19th centuries, offers a local history of Northampton using over 10,000 photographs, manuscripts from the 17th to the 20th centuries, fine art, furniture, ceramics, glass, toys, textiles, and costumes. *(46 Bridge St. ☎413-584-6011; www.historic-northampton.org. Open Tu-F 10am-4pm, Sa-Su noon-4pm. Historic house tours Sa-Su noon-4pm.)*

ENTERTAINMENT

Academy of Music, 274 Main St. (☎413-584-8435), just down the hill from Smith College, is the place to stop for fine foreign and domestic film and stage entertainment. This attractive building features great performances on and off the screen.

Calvin Theatre & Performing Arts Center, 19 King St. (☎413-586-0851), books big-name performers, which have recently included Lou Reed, BB King, Tracy Chapman, and Bill Cosby. Tickets $28-45.

New Century Theatre (NCT) (☎413-585-3220; www.smith.edu/theatre/nct), on Green St., hosts professional summer theatre. June-Aug. NCT presents 4 productions in the Hallie Flanagan Studio Theatre on the Smith Campus. Shows $20, seniors $18.

NIGHTLIFE

Divas, 492 Pleasant St., (☎413-586-8161; www.divasofnoho.com). The queer hot-spot of the moment, Divas boasts an outdoor patio, two full bars, and a large dance floor with a young, hip, gay and lesbian crowd flashing as much flesh as attitude. Tu Goth night. Su-W 18+, Th-Sa 21+. Cover varies, but is never over $7. Open Su-W 8pm-1am, Th-Sa 8pm-2am.

Pearl Street, 10 Pearl St. (☎413-584-7771; www.ihcg.com/pearl_street_main.asp), right off Main St. This popular nightclub features DJs and dancing, as well as the best live music in town. Rotating schedules showcase a diverse fare, from local hippie jam bands to national hip-hop acts. Shows $8-20. Open daily 7pm-1am.

AMHERST

If you want to see how 25,000 college kids can take over a small Western Massachusetts town, Amherst is your place. The presence of Amherst College and the University of Massachusetts ensures that what would have otherwise been a two-lane country town has been transformed into a a vibrant and active college scene. Cradled in the Berkshires, the town somehow manages to remain quaint and old-fashioned, while packing countless diversions into its small downtown. From a rowdy pub crawl, countless independent bookstores, and fabulously diverse restaurants to stoic art museums and colonial churches, Northampton is a charming contrast of a progressive present and a Puritan past.

PRACTICAL INFORMATION

By car (2hr.), take the Mass. Pike (I-90) west to Exit 4 (W. Springfield), then I-91N to Exit 19, and then the Rte. 9/Amherst exit east. Continue east on Rte. 9 about 9 mi. to the intersection of Rte. 9 and Rte. 116. From here, take a left to reach UMass or continue straight towards Amherst College. Once you reach South Pleasant St., Amherst College is on the right and the town center is on the left. Most of the main shops and restaurants lie along Main St., which runs parallel to Rte. 9. The town center and common lie at the intersection of Main and Pleasant St., directly north of Amherst College.

Trains: Amtrak runs trains once a day from South Station (p. 18) to Amherst via Springfield (6hr., daily 9:50am, $40), while the **Valley Transporter** (Amherst ☎413-253-1350, Springfield ☎413-733-9700) runs shuttles from Springfield to Amherst ($30). The **Amtrak station,** 13 Railroad St., comes up on your right as you go down Rte. 9 just past Amherst College.

Buses: There is no direct bus service to Amherst.

Amherst Area Chamber of Commerce, 409 Main St. (☎413-253-0700; www.amherstcommon.com), by the Amtrak station. Open M-F 9am-3:30pm.

Internet Access: JavaNet, 103 N. Pleasant St. $2 per 20min.

ACCOMMODATIONS

As in Boston and Cambridge, it's impossible to get housing in May, when all the colleges in the area hold their graduation ceremonies. If you wish to visit at that time, be sure to plan months in advance.

Allen House Victorian Inn, 599 Main St. (☎413-253-5000; www.allenhouse.com). Voted the Valley's best B&B, the Allen House offers rooms with A/C, telephones with modems, goose-down comforters, complimentary full breakfast and proximity to Amherst's many galleries, museums, and shops. Rooms in summer Su-Th $100-125; F-Sa $135-170; off-season as low as $75. Owned and operated by the same proprietors, **The Amherst Inn,** 251 Main St., opposite the Emily Dickinson homestead (p. 247) is a similarly old-fashioned experience. ❸

University Lodge, 345 N. Pleasant St. (☎413-256-8111), is only a block from downtown and features 20 large rooms with double beds. Rooms $69-139, depending on time of year and day of week. ❷

Country Belle Motel, 329 Russell St. (☎413-586-0715; www.countrybellemotel.com), between Northampton and Amherst on Rte. 9, in Hadley. A convenient and economical alternative, this homey motel has an outdoor pool, free continental breakfast, easy access to the Norwottuck Bike Trail (p. 244), cable TV, and A/C. May-Dec. $60-80; Nov.-Apr. $50. ❶

FOOD

Food in Amherst is diverse, cheap, and plentiful. Restaurants cluster around the intersection of Main and Pleasant St. A **farmers' market** is held in the Spring St. lot on the Amherst Common every Saturday (7:30am-1:30pm). For a guide to all the area's restaurants, try www.amherstcommon.com or http://amherst.dailyjolt.com/food.

Antonio's, 31 N. Pleasant St. (☎413-253-0808), serving what is no doubt the best pizza in Western Massachusetts and arguably the best in the Northeast, Antonio's is always crowded. Try the Spicy Chicken and Blue Cheese pizza. Slices $1.50-3; whole pizzas from $9. Open daily 10am-1am. Cash only. ❶

Thai Corner, 31 Boltwood Walk (☎413-253-1639). Fiery Thai curries and noodle dishes (all $5-8) meet quick service to make this ordinary looking restaurant a great dinner spot. Open M-Th 11:30am-9pm, F-Sa 11:30am-10pm, Su 5-9pm. ❷

Fresh Side, 61 Main St., (☎413-256-0296), offers a cozy and tasteful atmosphere in which to enjoy a host of other Asian-influenced noodle and rice dishes (most under $7). Also a tea café, Fresh Side serves numerous teas with their signature flower petals. Delicious chicken satay tea rolls $4.25. Open daily 10am-10pm. Cash only. ❷

Black Sheep Deli, 79 Main St. (☎413-253-1706, www.blacksheepdeli.com). Don't let the needlessly complicated ordering system and claustrophobic deli counter discourage you, the Black Sheep fixes up a wide variety of great sandwiches at cheap prices ($4-6). Fresh European-style breads, cakes, tarts, and pastries—with vegan options—baked every morning ($2-4). Open mic poetry F-Sa 7pm. Open Su 8am-9pm, M-Sa 7am-11pm. $5 min. for credit cards. ❶

Atlantis, 41 Boltwood Walk (☎413-253-0025). Begun as a UMass student's senior thesis, Atlantis was voted the Valley's best new restaurant in 2001. Concocting plenty of inventive American options, vegans can dig into the dairy-free mushroom and spinach lasagna ($11). Su Jazz Brunch 11:30am-3pm. DJ spins nightly. Entrees $13-18. Open Tu-Su 11:30am-10pm. ❹

The Henion Bakery, 174 N. Pleasant St. (☎413-253-4909), is simple and decadently delicious. A host of fresh-baked delights are packed into this small bakery. Open M-F 7am-5:30pm, Sa 8am-4pm. ❶

SIGHTS

Founded by Noah Webster in 1821, **Amherst College**, near the intersection of Rte. 9 and 116, was originally intended to be a ministry for young men with great intelligence and few funds. It is now a top coeducational liberal arts institution ornamented with beautiful classical architecture, including an eye-catching Greek Revival chapel. Below are the area's most impressive sights.

To learn more about the campus and the college's history, take a **campus tour,** offered four times per day departing the Admissions Office (☎413-542-2529), at the southern corner of the campus.

AMHERST COLLEGE WILDLIFE SANCTUARY. Amherst College's charms extend beyond the architecture of its buildings and the elegance of its landscaping to the **Wildlife Sanctuary,** located to the east of the tennis courts on campus. With the Norwottuck Rail Trail running through the sanctuary, there are plenty of hiking and jogging opportunities.

MEAD ART MUSEUM. The museum has an impressive 12,000-piece permanent collection strong in early American and European Renaissance art. Though many of the specific portraits prove forgettable, there are memorable highlights, including an eerie Monet and the bawdy *Salome* by Robert Henri. *(Next to Stearns Steeple on the east side of the main quadrangle. ☎413-542-2335. Open Sept.-May Tu-Su 10am-4:30pm; June-Aug. Tu-Su 1-4pm. Free.)*

PRATT MUSEUM OF NATURAL HISTORY. An appealing, albeit rather archaic museum, they have displays of fossilized vertebrates and invertebrates as well as a large collection of minerals, meteorites, and anthropological materials. *(Southeast corner of the quad. ☎413-542-2165. Open Sept.-May Su noon-5pm, M-F 9am-3:30pm, Sa 10am-4pm; June-Aug. Sa 10am-4pm, Su noon-5pm. Free.)*

EMILY DICKINSON HOUSE. A visit to Amherst would hardly be complete without paying tribute to Emily Dickinson at her family's homestead at 280 Main St. Born here on December 10, 1830, Dickinson lived here nearly all her life and composed almost 1800 poems. Wandering around the grounds should be enough for all but the most diehard fans. *(☎413-542-8161. Grounds open in summer W-Sa 10am-5pm; off-season W-Sa 1-5pm. Homestead open only for guided tours. Tours $5, students and seniors $4, ages 6-18 $3, under 6 free.)*

ENTERTAINMENT

Much of the area's active cultural life is within the two colleges. Each hosts weekly concerts, theater and dance shows, performances, and lectures, all by nationally renowned artists and scholars. Call the Amherst Box Office (☎413-542-2277) for detailed schedules or check http://amherst.dailyjolt.com. For an updated events calender for the University (UMass-Amherst), check www.umass.edu/umhome/arts/index.html.

Hampshire Shakespeare hosts an annual festival of "Shakespeare Under the Stars," performed between late June and early August. The performance venue is at the Hartsbrook School, on Bay Rd., next to Atkins Farm. From Rte. 9E, turn south on Rte. 47, then turn left onto Bay Rd.; the school is on the right. (☎413-548-8118. Tickets $15, students and seniors $10, children $6.)

NIGHTLIFE

Though small in size, Amherst has a hefty selection of bars and pubs catering to the student population. Many nights are 18+ and all the venues tend to be laid-back and filled with a cheery student crowd. Most of the bars/pubs are right next to each other along Rte. 116 between Amherst College and the University of Massachusetts.

The Monkey Bar, 63 N. Pleasant St. (☎413-259-1600; www.mymonkeybar.com), is the swanky, new place in town. A ritzy restaurant serving swordfish and crab by day (entrees $11-15), the Monkey pulses at night with hot DJs (W-Sa; 21+). Open daily 11:30am-1am.

Amherst Brewing Company, 24-36 N. Pleasant St., (☎413-253-4400), has 2 fl. of drinks, good food, and (of course) W night karaoke. Upstairs is exclusively 21+ with a full bar, pool tables, ping-pong, and a lounge area. Downstairs has a full restaurant, bar, and outside patio and is open to everyone. Students swear by the Honey Pilsner ($4). Local bands and live music F-Sa. Mixed drinks $5-6. Open daily 11:30am-1am.

The Pub, 15 East Pleasant St., (☎413-549-1200), popular for its Long Island Iced Teas in pint glasses ($5.50), is your standard college bar. A young, chill crowd plays pool, while watching *Law & Order* reruns on multiple TV screens. 21+ after 10pm. Open Su-W 11:30am-9:30pm, Th-Sa 11:30am-1am.

THE BERKSHIRES

Comprising the western third of Massachusetts, the Berkshires mountain region is bordered to the north by Rte. 2 (Mohawk Trail) and Vermont and to the south by the Mass. Pike and Connecticut. ***Contact: Berkshire Visitors Bureau,*** *3 Hoosac St. (☎413-743-4500 or 800-237-5747; www.berkshires.org), in Adams. Open M-F 8:30am-5pm. For hiking and outdoor information, try* ***Region 5 Headquarters,*** *740 South St. (☎413-442-8928), in Pittsfield. Open M-F 8am-5pm.*

Major cultural institutions and gorgeous fall foliage make the Berkshires an attractive destination for a weekend getaway—the area's distance from Boston makes it impractical as a mere daytrip. Sprinkled with classic small towns, the Berkshires offer typical New England fare—fudge shops, country stores, scenic drives, and pristine liberal arts colleges—in a gorgeous mountain setting. The Berkshires are best known as the site of **Tanglewood,** the Boston Symphony Orchestra's summer home, and for **MASS. MoCA,** the country's largest contemporary art museum.

NORTH ADAMS

130 mi. (2½hr.) west of Boston. ***By car:*** *North Adams is only accessible by car. Take Rte. 2 (Mohawk Trail) westward through Greenfield; it passes through N. Adams. Alternatively, take I-90 west past Springfield, then take Exit 2 (for Lee/Pittsfield) to Rte. 7.* ***Contact: Visitors Center*** *(☎617-663-9204), on Union St. (Rte. 2/Rte. 8), on the east side of town, easily accessible by following Rte. 2 east from Mass MoCA. Open daily 10am-4pm.*

Once a large industrial center, North Adams went into decline after its factories fell into disuse. The city is now on the upswing again thanks to the opening of the phenomenal Massachusetts Museum of Contemporary Art (better known as MASS. MoCA), a giant contemporary art complex.

SIGHTS

MASS. MOCA. Housed in 27 former factory buildings, sprawling MASS. MoCA is the largest center for contemporary visual and performing arts in the country. Thanks to its overwhelming gallery space (MASS. MoCA makes even Boston's MFA (p. 86) feel like a weekend cottage), the museum is capable of exhibiting art that—because of its size and complexity—can't be shown anywhere else in the country. The museum is most popular in the fall, when the tourists come west to watch the leaves change. *(1040 Mass MoCA Way. ☎413-662-2111; www.massmoca.org. Open June-Oct. daily 10am-6pm; Nov.-May Su-W 11am-5pm. June-Oct. $9, ages 6-16 $3; Nov.-May $7, students and seniors $5, ages 6-16 $2.)*

The **Contemporary Artists Center** also displays stunning modern art. *(189 Beaver St. (Rte. 8N). ☎413-663-9555. Open Su noon-5pm, W-Sa 11am-5pm. Free.)*

WESTERN GATEWAY. The Western Gateway is a small complex comprised of a Visitors Center, railroad museum, a gallery, and one of Massachusetts's five Heritage State Parks. *(On the Furnace St. bypass off Rte. 8. ☎413-663-6312. Open daily 10am-5pm. Live music in summer Th 7pm. Free; donations accepted.)*

NATURAL BRIDGE STATE PARK. Natural Bridge State Park is home to a white marble bridge over a 60 ft. deep chasm that formed during the last Ice Age. The 30 ft. wide bridge is not the only attraction in the park; glacial potholes and waterfalls flowing through the chasm are also among the area's natural wonders. *(On Rte. 8, ½ mi. north of downtown. May-Oct. ☎413-663-6392; Nov.-Apr. ☎413-663-8469. Open late May to mid-Oct. daily 9am-5pm. Parking $2.)*

CAMPING

Clarksburg State Park, 1199 Middle Rd. (☎413-664-8345), a few mi. north of town on Rte. 8, has 44 wooded campsites and over 346 acres of woods and water. The park, also open for day use, is an ideal place to cool off on a hot summer day by taking a dip in the water at the small sand beach. Camping $12, state residents $10. Day use $5. ❶

WILLIAMSTOWN

135 mi. (2½hr.) from Boston. ***Contact:*** *Chamber of Commerce (☎413-485-9077; www.williamstownchamber.com). Open July-Aug. daily 10am-6pm; Sept. F-Su 10am-6pm.* ***By car:*** *Follow Rte. 2 (Mohawk Trail) westward through Greenfield; it passes through Williamstown. Alternatively, take I-90 west past Springfield, then take Exit 2 (for Lee/Pittsfield) to Rte. 7.* ***By bus: Peter Pan Bus Lines*** *(☎800-343-9999) runs from South Station to Springfield, where there is a* ***Bonanza*** *connection to Williamstown, via a transfer in Pittsfield. (4hr., daily 10am, $33 total).*

Williams College injects youth and preppiness into what would otherwise be a quaint little town surrounded by beautiful hills. In summer, this sleepy hamlet is host to the Tony award-winning **Williamstown Theater Festival,** which produces plays and musicals on its three stages, one of which is free. (☎413-597-3400, info line 413-597-3399; www.WTFestival.org. Box office open June-Aug. Su 11am-4pm, Tu-Sa 11am-after curtain. Performances Tu-Su. Main Stage $20-48; Nikos Stage $21-23, F afternoons $3.)

ACCOMMODATIONS

Williamstown has many affordable motels east of town on Rte. 2, making it the best non-camping option in the Berkshires.

Maple Terrace Motel, 555 Main St./Rte. 2 (☎413-458-9677), has bright, welcoming rooms with cable TV and VCR, a heated outdoor pool, and continental breakfast. Reception daily 8am-10:30pm. Check-in 1pm; check-out 11am. Rooms in summer $79-108; off-season $53-63. Reservations strongly recommended. ❷

Chimney Mirror Motel, 295 Main St. (☎413-458-5202), is a cheaper but less lavish choice, with A/C and breakfast. Rooms in summer Su-Th $68-78, F-Sa $89-99; off-season $52-65. ❷

FOOD

For affordable meals in Williamstown, stroll down Spring St., where the cheap eats cluster.

Pappa Charlie's, 28 Spring St. (☎413-458-5969). The sandwiches ($5) bear the names of celebrities, like the "Gwyneth Paltrow" (an eggplant parmigiana with a side salad) and the "Mary Tyler Moore"—a gimmick perfected by Cambridge's Bartley's Burger Cottage (p. 112). Open Su-Th 8am-8pm, F-Sa 8am-9pm. Cash only. ❶

Lickety Split, 69 Spring St. (☎413-458-1818), serves up Herrell's ice cream ($1.75-2.50; see p. 113 for more on Herrell's), incredibly thick milkshakes ($3.25), and delightful lunchtime specials. Sandwiches $5. Quiche $3.50. Open Feb.-Nov. Su noon-10pm, M-Sa 11:30am-10pm; Dec.-Jan. M-Sa 11:30am-4pm; lunch until 3pm. Cash only. ❶

Tanglewood

297 West St., in Lenox MA. Tanglewood is really only accessible ***by car.*** *Take Mass. Pike (I-90) west to Exit 2, drive through the town of Lee (4 mi.), and finally turn left onto Rte. 183S, (which merges with Rte. 7A-N before emerging again). The main entrance is a few miles up on the left.* ***Contact:*** *box office ☎617-637-5165; www.bso.org.* ***Concerts:*** *late June-late Aug. F 8:30pm with 6pm prelude, Sa 8:30pm, Su 2:30pm; open rehearsals Sa 10:30am.* ***Tickets:*** *Auditorium or "Music Shed" $17-90; lawn seats $15-18, under 12 free. Students with valid ID ½-price F lawn tickets.*

Tanglewood is the summer residence of the **Boston Symphony Orchestra** (p. 156), who perform at various venues tucked away among the rolling hills and pristine meadows of the Berkshires. One of the best-regarded and most beloved music festivals in the world, Tanglewood attracts more than 300,000 visitors each summer, not to mention a celestial array of classical music celebrities, including Yo-Yo Ma and Itzhak Perlman.

Concerts include a variety of musical genres (folkie James Taylor's annual concert here is very popular) and take place at several locations around the Tanglewood estate. However, the focus of most performances is the BSO's tried-and-true classical repertoire. For an unforgettable summer concert, purchase the eminently affordable lawn tickets ($15-18) online, arrive early (with lawn chairs and a picnic), and wait for the music to begin.

SIGHTS

WILLIAMS COLLEGE. Nicknamed "Ephs", after college founder Ephraim Williams, Williams students rally behind their unlikely mascot, the purple cow, when competing with rival Amherst College (see p. 245). Maps of the campus are available from the admissions office. While on campus, pay a visit to the **Williams College Museum of Art,** which houses artwork that spans the medieval and contemporary eras, but focuses mostly on American and modern works. *(**Admissions:** 33 Stetson Court, in Bascom House. ☎413-597-2211; www.williams.edu. Open M-F 8:30am-4:30pm. Tours daily; contact the office for a schedule, as times change frequently. **Art Museum:** 15 Lawrence Hall Dr. ☎413-597-2429; www.williams.edu/WCMA. Open Su 1-5pm, Tu-Sa 10am-5pm. Free.)*

CLARK ART INSTITUTE. This formidable collection is made up of 19th-century French paintings as well as a variety of 14th- to 19th-century American and European art. With over 140 acres of grounds, the institute also encourages patrons to enjoy a picnic in the gardens or to explore the many trails. *(225 South St., ½ mi. down South St. from the rotary. ☎413-458-2303; www.clarkart.edu. Open July-Aug. daily 10am-5pm; Sept.-June Tu-Su 10am-5pm. June-Oct. $10, students and under 19 free; Nov.-May free.)*

OUTDOORS

Williamstown's surrounding wooded hills beckon from the moment visitors arrive. The **Hopkins Memorial Forest** (☎413-597-2346) offers 2425 acres and 15 mi. of free hiking and cross-country skiing trails. To reach Hopkins: take Rte. 7N (North St.), turn left on Bulkley St., follow Bulkley to the end, and turn right onto Northwest Hill Rd. For bike, snowshoe, or cross-country ski rentals, check out **The Mountain Goat,** 130 Water St. (☎413-458-8445. Open Su, 11am-5pm. M-W and F-Sa 10am-6pm, Th 10am-7pm. Bike and ski rentals $25 per day, $35 for 2 days.)

LENOX

Lenox lends the Berkshires a touch of sophistication and class, a la Tanglewood, the summer home of the Boston Symphony Orchestra. There really isn't any other reason to come all the way to Lenox, but if you do come for a concert, the area is home to a few other sights that are of interest. Beyond the musical arts, Lenox has a place of prominence in the theatrical arts. Every summer at the Founders Theater, the **Shakespeare & Company,** 70 Kemble St. (Rte. 7A), performs enchanting productions of Shakespeare's plays as well as other plays written by Berkshires authors like Edith Wharton and Henry James. (☎413-637-3353. Box office open late May-late Oct. daily 10am-2pm or until performance. $10-100.)

SIGHTS

THE MOUNT. Though best known for her literary works of fiction, such as "Ethan Frome" and *The House of Mirth*, Edith Wharton also dabbled in architecture, designing and building her own home in 1902. Newly restored and containing three acres of formal gardens and a stable, the Mount offers tours, special events, and lecture series. *(2 Plunkett St., at the southern junction of Rte. 7 and 7A. ☎413-637-1899; www.edithwharton.org. Open late May-Nov. daily 9am-5pm. Tours M-F every hr., Sa-Su every ½hr. from 9:30am-3:30pm. $16, students $8, under 12 free. Special events $16 if reserved in advance, $18 at the door.)*

PLEASANT VALLEY WILDLIFE SANCTUARY. Amble through the 1500 acres and 7 mi. of trails in this Massachusetts Audubon Society Sanctuary, and you'll experience the natural beauty that the hardwood forests, meadows, wetlands, and the slopes of Lenox Mountain have to offer. *(From Pittsfield, take Rte. 20S. to W. Dugway Rd. Follow W. Dugway 1½ mi. to the Nature Center. ☎413-637-0320. Open July-Sept. daily dawn-dusk. Nature Center open late Oct.-late June Su, 10am-4pm, M 9am-4pm, Tu-Sa 9am-5pm; July-late Oct. Su-M 10am-4pm, Tu-Sa 9am-5pm. $4, ages 3-12 $3.)*

STOCKBRIDGE

Like many other small towns in the Berkshires, Stockbridge is rich in culture natural beauty, and history. For those looking to sample the elegant country feel of the Berkshires, Stockbridge is home to a remarkable museum and a staggering mansion.

SIGHTS

NORMAN ROCKWELL MUSEUM. Bring back memories of days gone by at this highly focused museum, where it's all Norman, all the time. Visit the artist's studio and see the largest single collection of his original works, including many Saturday Evening Post covers. *(☎ 9 Glendale Rd. (Rte. 183.) ☎ 413-298-4100; www.nrm.org. Open May-Oct. daily 10am-5pm; Nov.-Apr. M-F 10am-4pm, Sa-Su 10am-5pm. $12, students $7, under 18 free.)*

BERKSHIRE BOTANICAL GARDENS. If you like plants then you'll love spending a pleasant afternoon at the 15 acre Berkshire Botanical Gardens, enjoying soothing aromas and stunning flower arrangements. *(At the intersection of Rte. 2 and Rte. 183. ☎ 413-298-3926; www.berkshirebotanical.org. Open daily May-Oct. 10am-5pm. $7, students and seniors $5, under 12 free.)*

NAUMKEAG. From Newport to West Egg, the Gilded Age produced luxurious mansions all along the east coast, even in quaint, New-Englandy, Stockbridge. Naumkeag is the 44-room shrine to decadence built by the rich, influential, Choate family in 1885. Especially lavish and noteworthy are the mansion's gardens, which were designed and built by noted landscape architect Fletcher Steele over a 30 year period. *(5 Prospect Hill Rd. ☎ 413-298-3239; www.thetrustees.org. Open daily 10am-5pm; last tour 4pm. Admission and tour $10, ages 3-12 $3. Admission to the garden only, no tour $8/$3.)*

MISSION HOUSE. Home to John Sergeant, the first missionary to the Stockbridge Mohican tribe, the Mission House offers a tour detailing the history of the area as well as facts about the home, built in 1739. *(19 Main St. ☎ 413-298-3239; www.thetrustees.org. $5, ages 6-12 $3. Open June-late Oct. daily 10am-5pm; last tour 4pm.)*

SKIING NEW ENGLAND

Folks say that if you can handle the narrow, icy steeps of New England skiing, you can ski anywhere. In general, expect the unexpected—ice, slush, rocks, bumps—on trails with natural snow. The inconsistent weather conditions have led most mountains to rely heavily on man-made snow, which is granular and less interesting than natural snow, but necessary for providing base coverage that will last through the season. In northern New England, the season usually starts in mid-November and lasts until late March. Check individual mountain websites for updated conditions.

The listings below, in order of proximity to Boston, provide information about each mountain and pick out the defining characteristics of each. Every mountain has a ski school and equipment rental in the base lodge (and frequently on the highways leading up to the mountain), and most have ski-and-stay packages that include accommodations and lift tickets (see individual websites for details and reservations). In terms of staying on a budget, the best advice is to bring your own food. Ski lodge food is mediocre and overpriced—you'll be glad you brought your own sandwiches when you see your neighbor glumly picking at his soggy $5 fries.

A note on passes: while **multi-day passes** may offer a small price break, stay away from half-day passes (they're never more than a few dollars off a day pass). If you'll be taking frequent daytrips, you might consider the **Threedom Pass,** which allows unlimited skiing at Waterville Valley, Loon, and nearby Cranmore (http://exchange.waterville.com). Lift ticket prices increase (often drastically) for the holiday skiing season (Dec. 25-Jan. 1, Jan. 19-21, and Feb. 16-24).

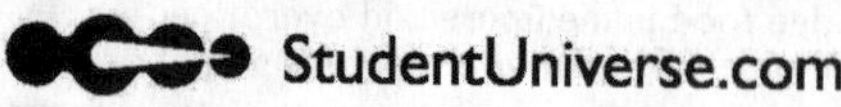
StudentUniverse.com

DAYTRIPS FROM BOSTON

WATERVILLE VALLEY

Ski Area Rd., Waterville Valley, NH (130 mi., 2hr). ***Contact:*** *☎800-468-2553; www.waterville.com/winter.* ***By car:*** *Take I-93N to Exit 28, then 11 mi. via Rte. 49 to the resort village.* ***Trails:*** *52 trails; 20% beginner, 60% intermediate, 20% expert.* ***Snowboarding:*** *Exhibition Park with new Superpipe, the Boneyard and Little Slammer kids' park.* ***Lift tickets:*** *Adult $39, students $29, ages 6-12 and 66+ $19.*

The ability to dodge rich suburban kids in North Face Jackets who think they can ski is a must for someone looking to ski or ride Waterville. While *True Grit* and a few other trails provide excitement and solitude for more advanced skiers, Waterville is a solidly intermediate mountain. Its well-groomed trails and varied terrain seem promising on paper, but windy conditions and long lift lines are not uncommon and can often spoil the fun. Its proximity to Boston makes it suitable for daytrips, but for longer stays, advanced skiers may find more amusement farther north. The Exhibition Park and new Superpipe, as well as the Little Slammers kids' park, make Waterville a good option for snowboarders.

LOON MOUNTAIN

Kancamagus Hwy, Lincoln, NH (130 mi., 2hr.). ***By car:*** *Take I-93N to Exit 32, on the western end of the Kancamagus Hwy. (Rte. 112).* ***Contact:*** *☎603-745-8111; www.loonmtn.com/winter.* ***Trails:*** *44 trails and 5 tree-skiing areas; 15% beginner, 65% intermediate, 20% expert.* ***Snowboarding:*** *Loon Mountain Park.* ***Lift tickets:*** *M-F adult $43, ages 13-17 $36, ages 6-12 $29, 70+ $10; Sa-Su $51/$45/$33.*

Populated by the same suburban set as Waterville, Loon manages to provide a more enjoyable skiing experience with the same tools. Faster lifts and an all-advanced peak mean less waiting in line for the experts. About the same distance from Boston as Waterville Valley, Loon makes a great daytrip for beginners and intermediate skiers as well. Five tree-skiing zones offer variety for more advanced skiers. Long lift lines for the gondola can be tiresome, but on cold days the enclosed space offers welcome relief.

MOUNT SNOW

Rte. 100, West Dover, VT (130 mi., 2½hr.). ***Contact:*** *☎800-245-7669; www.mountsnow.com.* ***By car:*** *Take Rte. 2W to I-91. Follow I-91N to Exit 2 in Vermont. Take Rte. 9W 20 mi. to Wilmington, VT. Turn right at the stoplight onto Rte. 100N. Continue for 9mi. to Mount Snow/Haystack.* ***Trails:*** *145 trails; 22% beginner, 49% intermediate, 29% expert.* ***Snowboarding:*** *4 parks and 2 superpipes.* ***Lift tickets:*** *M-F adult $52, ages 13-18 $47, senior and under 13 $36; Sa-Su $61/$54/$41.*

Mount Snow offers vast, wide-open skiing on a good range of terrain, including 130 acres of tree-skiing. Proximity to Boston makes the mountain a popular weekend getaway, but there are ample opportunities to elude the crowds. Snowboarders love the wide trails, not to mention the 4 terrain parks and 2 half-pipes.

CANNON

Franconia Notch State Park. ***Contact:*** *☎603-823-8800; www.cannonmt.com/winter.htm.* ***Trails:*** *55 trails; 17% beginner, 48% intermediate, 35% expert.* ***Snowboarding:*** *No special facilities, although snowboarding is allowed on all trails.* ***Lift tickets:*** *M-F adult $34, ages 6-17, students and seniors $23; Sa-Su $45, ages 13-17 and students $37, ages 6-12 and 66+ $29. Tu and Th 2 adults for $40. Prices increase for holiday season.*

The best mountain in New Hampshire. Owned and operated as a New Hampshire State Park rather than a glitzy ski resort, Cannon offers real rugged New England skiing with no lift lines and no suburban posers. Though Cannon doesn't spend as much on snowmaking as other mountains, the low-key, authentic feel and uncrowded slopes more than make up for sometimes inconsistent snow conditions. Adventurous skiers with well-sharpened edges love the challenge of Cannon's steeps and the ability to ski for about half the price of most other resorts.

FOR A WEEKEND OR LONGER

KILLINGTON

4763 Killington Rd., Killington, VT (160 mi, 3hr.). ***Contact:*** *800-621-6867; www.killington.com.* ***By car:*** *Take I-93 to just south of Concord, NH. Exit onto I-89N and follow to Rte. 4 Rutland, Exit 1 in Vermont. Follow Rte. 4W to Killington.* ***Trails:*** *200 trails; 30% beginner, 39% intermediate, 31% expert.* ***Snowboarding:*** *3 alpine parks, 1 half-pipe, 1 superpipe, and 1 Palmer-Rider Cross course.* ***Lift tickets:*** *M-F adult $59, ages 13-18 $54, ages 6-12 and 66+ $36; Sa-Su $62/$57/$39. Prices increase for holidays. Discount multiple-day pass.*

Killington is—in a word—huge. Its spacious slopes give Killington more of an "out west" quality. The terrain is pretty evenly divided among beginner, intermediate, and expert trails, which makes it popular for families looking for a mix of everything. Snowboarders will find bliss in the three terrain parks and well-groomed slopes. After the sun goes down, those looking for *après* ski can choose from over 100 nearby bars and restaurants.

SUNDAY RIVER

Sunday River Rd., Bethel, ME (180 mi., 3hr.). ***Contact:*** *800-543-2754; www.sundayriver.com.* ***By car:*** *Take Rte. 1N to I-95N; I-95N to the Maine Turnpike; Maine Turnpike North to Exit 11 (Gray); Rte. 26N to Bethel. Follow Rte. 2E for 2½ mi. Take a left onto Sunday River Rd., marked by the large Sunday River Brewery (big building with red roof).* ***Trails:*** *128 trails; 25% beginner, 35% intermediate, 40% expert.* ***Snowboarding:*** *3 parks plus a kids' park, a superpipe, and a mini-pipe.* ***Lift tickets:*** *M-F adult $49, ages 13-18 $44, ages 6-12 and 66+ $32; Sa-Su $52/$47/$34. Prices increase $2 for holiday season and decrease for spring skiing; check website for daily updates.*

Sunday River prides itself on snowmaking, which provides good coverage on trails late into the season. The consistent conditions draw a surprising number of crowds, considering its distance from Boston. The variety of trails provides something for everyone: expert skiers are dared to try the infamous *White Heat* (although some experienced skiers say don't believe the hype). Snowboarding is also taken seriously here: the **Rocking Chair** park under the main lift gives daredevils a chance to show off on the jumps and rails; **American Express** is a medium-sized park with medium-sized jumps; and **Starlight** is a long park with ever-changing features.

SUGARBUSH

Rte. 100, Warren, VT (190 mi., 3½hr.). ***Contact:*** *800-537-8427; www.sugarbush.com.* ***By car:*** *Take I-89N to Exit 9 Middlesex, then to Rte. 100S (Warren, VT).* ***By train:*** *Trains stop in Waterbury, VT (Waterbury-Stowe station), but the route from Boston is not direct and may take all day.* ***Trails:*** *115 trails; 22% beginner, 46% intermediate, 32% expert.* ***Snowboarding:*** *2 terrain parks, a learning park, and a regulation half-pipe.* ***Lift tickets:*** *Adult $55, ages 13-18 $53, ages 6-12 and 66+ $35. Prices increase $2 on holidays. Discounted multiple-day pass.*

With six mountain peaks and more than 50 mi. of bumps, steeps, and cruisers, Sugarbush offers plenty of great skiing for a weekend or longer. Sugarbush is certainly one of the ritzier resorts, but that doesn't keep the locals and long-time regulars from enjoying the slopes. The drive through the Mad River Valley to the town of Warren is so picture-perfect Vermont you'll be drooling maple syrup.

STOWE

5781 Mountain Rd., Stowe, VT (205 mi., 3½hr.). ***Contact:*** *802-253-3500; www.stowe.com/winter.* ***By car:*** *Take I-93N to I-89N (Lebanon/White River Junction, VT). Take I-89 to Exit 10 and take Rte. 100N into Stowe Village (about 15min.). Turn left onto Rte. 108, Mountain Rd. Stowe*

Mountain Resort is 6 mi. up on the left. ***By train:*** *Trains stop in Waterbury, VT (Waterbury-Stowe station), but the route from Boston is not direct and may take all day.* ***Trails:*** *47 trails; 16% beginner, 59% intermediate, 25% expert.* ***Snowboarding:*** *2 parks and a superpipe.* ***Lift tickets:*** *Adult $60, ages 6-12 and seniors $40; holidays $62/$42.*

Stowe is a smaller, more European-style ski resort in a storybook Vermont town. Although the terrain is weighted toward intermediate blues, advanced skiers will love the challenge of the classic tree-lined New England runs, narrow and winding, with plenty of steeps and bumps. Rarely crowded, you'll be able to enjoy Stowe's remote beauty. Night skiing is offered until 9pm, weather permitting.

SUGARLOAF/USA

Rte. 27 and Sugarloaf Access Rd., Carrabassett Valley, ME (230 mi., 4-4½hr.). ***Contact:*** *☎800-843-5623; www.sugarloaf.com.* ***By car:*** *Take I-95N to Augusta Exit 31B. Follow Rte. 27N through Farmington and Kingfield, straight to Sugarloaf.* ***Trails:*** *129 trails plus 14 tree-skiing glades; 27% beginner, 30% intermediate, 43% expert.* ***Snowboarding:*** *Terrain park and superpipe.* ***Lift tickets:*** *Adult $56, ages 13-18 $51, ages 6-12 and 66+ $38. Prices increase $1 for holiday season (Dec. 25-Jan. 1 and Feb. 16-22 only).*

Sugarloaf is definitely off the beaten path (when you get off the highway after two hours you're only halfway there), but when you get there you'll understand why the devoted few wouldn't think of going anywhere else. The snow is sublime, and there is certainly enough variety to keep skiers and riders of all levels in a state of bliss. Those nostalgic for the snow bowls out west will feel right at home when they discover the expert-only King Pine Bowl. Expecting that most people come for a week or at least a long weekend, the mountain has plenty of ski-and-stay packages, including "ski-in, ski-out" condos right on the lift lines.

INSIDE

Planning Your Trip

WHEN TO GO

Boston is like a chameleon, changing colors and appearance drastically with each of the seasons. **Fall** (Sept.-early Nov.) is the best time to visit Boston: the weather is temperate, the foliage is beautiful, prices are lower, and the summer tourist hordes have largely dissipated. Late **spring** (Apr.-early June) is also enjoyable, as there is plenty of sunshine and many exciting festivals and other events; unfortunately, finding a place to stay in Boston this time of year is next to impossible thanks to the area's many college graduations. **Summer** (late June-Aug.) is at times unbearably hot and humid, but it remains the peak tourist season in Boston, nearby Cape Cod, and the islands of Martha's Vineyard and Nantucket. Nightlife is much more sedate during these months, as most college students clear out by late May. Though snowfall is lighter than it is further inland, **winter** (late Nov.-Mar.) in Boston is dark, cold, cruel, and wet. On the positive side, winter means accommodations are cheap. For more information on seasonal highlights (holidays, festivals, etc.), see p. 11 in Discover Boston.

Unpredictable, moody weather changes—snowfall in late April or morning beach weather giving way to evening hailstorms—tend to be the rule rather than the exception. In order to be prepared for anything always pack rain gear and keep a sweater handy.

Below is a range of average temperatures for Boston (in °C and °F), by month:

	JANUARY	APRIL	JULY	OCTOBER
Celsius (°C)	-5 - 2°C	4 - 13°C	18 - 27°C	8 - 17°C
Farenheit (°F)	22 - 36°F	40 - 56°F	65 - 82°F	47 - 63°F

EMBASSIES & CONSULATES

Embassies and consulates are the places to contact for information regarding visas and permits to the United States. Offices are only open limited hours, so call before you visit. The US State Department provides contact information for US diplomatic missions on the Internet at http://foia.state.gov/keyofficers.asp. If you're not sure whether to call the embassy or consulate, contact the embassy, as they can direct you to the appropriate consular services. The addresses below are locations only; most embassies and consulates have separate mailing addresses that can be obtained by calling the numbers below or checking the websites. For information on foreign consulates in Boston, see p. 25 in "Once In Boston."

US CONSULATES ABROAD

Australia: Embassy & Consulate: Moonah Pl., **Yarralumla** (Canberra), ACT 2600 (☎02 6214 5600; http://usembassy-australia.state.gov). **Other Consulates:** MLC Centre, Level 59, 19-29 Martin Pl., **Sydney,** NSW 2000 (☎02 9373 9200); 553 St. Kilda Rd., P.O. Box 6722, **Melbourne,** VIC 3004 (☎03 9526 5900); 16 St. George's Terr., 13th fl., **Perth,** WA 6000 (☎08 9202 1224).

Canada: Embassy & Consulate: 490 Sussex Dr., **Ottawa,** ON K1N 1G8 (☎613 238 5335; www.usembassycanada.gov). **Other Consulates:** 615 Macleod Trail SE, Room 1000, **Calgary,** AB T2G 4T8 (☎403 266 8962); 1969 Upper Water St., Purdy's Wharf Tower II #904, **Halifax,** NS B3J 3R7 (☎902 429 2480); 1155 St. Alexandre St., **Montréal,** QC H2Z 1Z2 (☎514 398 9695); 2 Place Terr. Dufferin, C.P. 939, **Québec City,** QC G1R 4T9 (☎418 692 2095); 360 University Ave., **Toronto,** ON M5G 1S4 (☎416 595 1700); 1095 West Pender St., 21st fl., **Vancouver,** BC V6E 2M6 (☎604 685 4311, ext. 257).

Ireland: Embassy & Consulate: 42 Elgin Rd., Dublin 4 (☎353 668 8777 or 353 668 7122; www.usembassy.ie).

New Zealand: Embassy & Consulate: 29 Fitzherbert Terr., **Thorndon,** Wellington (☎04 462 6000; http://usembassy.org.nz). **Consulate:** 23 Customs St., Citibank Building, 3rd fl., **Auckland** (☎64 9336 0870).

South Africa: Embassy & Consulate: 877 Pretorius St., Pretoria 0001 (☎27 12 342 1048; http://usembassy.state.gov/pretoria). **Other Consulates:** Broadway Industries Center, Heerengracht, Foreshore, **Cape Town** (☎27 21 421 4280); 303 West St., Old Mutual Bldg., 31st fl., **Durban** (☎27 31 305 7600); 1 River St., Killarney, **Johannesburg** (☎011 644 8000).

UK: Embassy and Consulate: 24 Grosvenor Sq., **London** W1A 1AE (☎0207 499 9000; www.usembassy.org.uk). **Other Consulates:** Queen's House, 14 Queen St., **Belfast,** N. Ireland BT1 6EQ (☎0289 032 8239); 3 Regent Terr., **Edinburgh,** Scotland EH7 5BW (☎0131 556 8315).

DOCUMENTS & FORMALITIES

PASSPORTS

All foreign visitors to the United States (except Canadians) need valid passports to enter the US and to re-enter their home countries. The US does not allow entrance if the holder's passport expires in under six months; returning home with an expired passport is often illegal and could result in a fine. **Canadians** need only demonstrate proof of Canadian citizenship (such as a citizenship card) to enter the US.

If your passport is lost or stolen, immediately notify the police (☎911) and the nearest consulate of your home government (for a list, see p. 258). Any visas stamped in your old passport will be irretrievably lost. If you can't wait for your replacement passport request to be processed, you can ask for immediate temporary traveling papers, which allow you to re-enter your home country. Before you leave home for Boston, photocopy your passport including visas and any other important travel documents. Carry one set of copies with you apart from the originals, and leave another set at home.

VISAS

A visa is a stamp, sticker, or insert in your passport that specifies the purpose of your travel and the duration of your stay.

VISA WAIVERS. As of August 2003, citizens of **South Africa** need a non-immigrant visa ($100) to enter the United States for pleasure travel. To obtain a visa, contact the US embassy or consulate nearest you: there are US diplomatic missions in Johannesburg, Cape Town, and Durban. You can also call the visa helpline (☎083 900 0800) from anywhere in the country. Through the US's Visa Waiver Program, citizens of the **European Union** and most other Western European countries, **Australia,** and **New Zealand** do not need a visa to enter the US if they are traveling to the US only for business or pleasure (*not* for work or study) and are staying in the US for 90 days or fewer. They must show proof of a pre-purchased return ticket and submit a visa waiver (I-94W) form, issued upon arrival at the airport. **Canadians** need only show proof of citizenship to enter or exit the US.

WORK/STUDY VISAS. If you plan to stay in the US for more than 90 days (180 days for Canadians), or if you're coming to the US to work or study, you'll need to apply at a US consulate for a **B-1 visa.** All documents required for applying for a visa are available online at the **US State Department's Visa Services** webpage (http://travel.state.gov/visa_services.html). If you know ahead of time that you'll be staying in the US longer than 90 days, you should visit the closest US consulate in your home country (see p. 258 for a listing of these) for the proper documents and processing.

TOURIST VISAS. If you want to extend your stay in Boston longer than 90 days (180 days for Canadians), but are not planning on working or traveling during that time, you must obtain a 6-month, non-immigrant **B-2 visa** ("pleasure tourist" visa). B-2 applicants must prove they do not intend to immigrate by demonstrating the following: that the purpose of their trip is for business, pleasure, or medical treatment; that they plan to remain in the US for a limited period of time; and that they have a residence outside the US. National law dictates that travelers known to be HIV-positive cannot obtain visas. Holders of B-2 visas or those who entered the US visa-free under the Visa Waiver Program (see p. 259) cannot enter into full-time study or paid employment without a student visa or a work permit (see p. 273).

If you need to apply for a visa once you're in Boston, contact the Bureau of Citizenship and Immigration Services:

Bureau of Citizenship and Immigration Services (BCIS), JFK Federal Bldg., Government Ctr. (toll-free ☎800-375-5283; www.bcis.gov). T: Government Ctr. (Blue/Green). Formerly known as the Immigration and Naturalization Services (INS), the BCIS is now the division of the US government that processes all documents for immigrants and long-term visitors in cooperation with the Department of Homeland Security (DHS). Check their website to keep abreast of any developments or changes in visa requirements and procedures that have occurred with the shift in government departments. Open M-F 7am-noon.

IDENTIFICATION

Always carry one photo ID with you while traveling. Never carry all your forms of ID together, in case of theft or loss; split them up and leave some behind in the safe at your place of accommodation.

The **International Student Identity Card (ISIC)** is the most widely accepted form of student ID in the world. Although a valid student ID issued by your school will get you the student discounts offered at nearly all of the attractions in Boston, an ISIC also comes with insurance benefits (see **Travel Insurance,** p. 262), access to a 24hr. emergency helpline (☎877-370-ISIC in the US), and discounts on sights, accommodations, food, and transport. To qualify for an ISIC, you must be a degree-seeking student of a secondary or post-secondary school and at least 12 years old.

The **International Teacher Identity Card (ITIC)** offers teachers the same insurance coverage as the ISIC and similar cards, but more limited discounts. The **International Youth Travel Card (IYTC)**—for travelers under the age of 26 who are not students—offers almost all of the same benefits as the ISIC. The **International Student Exchange ID Card (ISE)** provides discounts, medical benefits, and the ability to purchase student airfares.

Though cost differs from one issuer to another, each of these identity cards costs approximately $22. ISIC and ITIC cards are valid for about 1½ academic years; IYTC cards are valid for one year from the date of issue. Most youth-oriented travel agencies (including those listed in the **Service Directory** on p. 285 or in this chapter on p. 263) issue cards. For the location of the issuer nearest you, check www.istc.org or contact the **International Student Travel Confederation (ISTC)** Herengracht 479, 1017 BS Amsterdam, The Netherlands (☎+31 20 421 28 00; fax 421 28 10; istcinfo@istc.org).

PACKING

Pack lightly: put out only what you absolutely need, then take half the clothes and twice the money. As you pack, here are some important things to keep in mind.

CONVERTERS & ADAPTERS

In the US and Canada, electricity is **110V,** and 220V electrical appliances don't like 110V current. Visit a hardware store for an adapter (which changes the shape of the plug) and a converter (which changes the voltage). Don't make the mistake of using only an adapter unless appliance instructions explicitly state otherwise. See http://kropla.com/electric.htm for more info.

FILM & CAMERAS

Less serious photographers may want to bring a **disposable camera** or two rather than an expensive permanent one. Always pack film in your carry-on luggage, since higher-intensity X-rays are used on checked luggage; these can, despite disclaimers, fog film. All types of film for all types of cameras are available in Boston, but 35mm is the most common.

IMPORTANT DOCUMENTS

Don't forget your passport, traveler's checks, ATM and/or credit cards, and adequate ID (see p. 259). Also check that you have any of the following that might apply: an ISIC card, driver's license, and travel insurance forms.

MONEY

The unit of currency in the US is the **dollar ($),** which is divided into 100 **cents (¢).** Many first-time visitors to the US who are used to their home country's easily distinguishable, multicolored currency are tripped up by US currency: the various denominations of US bills ($1, $5, $10, $20, and $50 are the most common) seem identical except for the amount written in the 4 corners of the bill's face. Check bills carefully before handing them over to cashiers.

Most establishments in Boston accept payment via **credit card** or **ATM card,** although some places have $10-15 minimums for credit card purchases. If an establishment is listed as **cash only** in this guide, the establishment only accepts payment in bills and coins.

Traveler's checks are accepted at some establishments (credit cards and ATM cards are more widely accepted). Before you leave for Boston, you'll need to arrange for your bank or a private agency (American Express, Visa, and Travelex/Thomas Cook are the most common) to issue you a set. Traveler's "checks" are actually issued like cash in set denominations (typically $20) and meant to be used like cash or turned in for cash at banks. The benefit of traveler's checks is that, unlike cash, if they're stolen or lost, they can be replaced.

CURRENCY EXCHANGE

As noted above, the best rates for converting money are found at **ATMs** (automatic teller machines), which are everywhere in Boston including the airport. ATMs allow you to either access money in your national or international bank account or get cash advances for a rather high fee using a credit card. Contact your credit card company about advances before attempting it, as there are various restrictions. **Banks** offer less favorable rates and post these rates in their windows; they are also the only place to cash traveler's checks. Avoid at all costs the exorbitant exchange rates offered at the **currency exchange booths** at Logan Airport and elsewhere in the city. The chart below lists August 2003 exchange rates between the US dollar and various non-US currencies. The most up-to-date rates are posted online, in bank windows and in newspapers.

US DOLLAR ($)	
AUS$1 = US$0.64	US$1 = AUS$1.55
CDN$1 = US$0.71	US$1 = CDN$1.40
NZ$1 = US$0.58	US$1 = NZ$1.72
ZAR1 = US$0.13	US$1 = ZAR7.43
UK£1 = US$1.60	US$1 = UK£0.62
€1 = US$0.88	US$1 = €1.13

BUDGETING

The cost of living in (and visiting) Boston is the highest in the US after New York City and San Francisco. An average, modest budget for Boston (sticking to free and cheap sights, hosteling or sharing a cheap room, eating at restaurants once a day, and occasionally going out at night) falls somewhere around $60-70 per day. Here's a breakdown of what costs to expect and tips on keeping those costs down:

Accommodations: If you have a friend or acquaintance in Boston, stay with them, as accommodations will be your biggest expense. The city's six hostel-style accommodations cost $25-35 per person per night, while a double room in a budget hotel or guest house starts at $80 per night (plus a 12.75% tax). For long-term accommodations, see p. 191.

Sights & Museums: Thankfully, most sights worth seeing in Boston are free or inexpensive. Museums have discounted admission and/or offer days and times when admission is free. If you're planning a museum binge, you should consider buying a CityPass (p. 87), which offers 50% off museum admission fees.

Food: Restaurant meals average $5 for breakfast, $10 for lunch entrees, and $12-15+ for dinner entrees. Eating frugally, you could get away with spending $15 per day on food. If you want to make your own meals, see the list of grocers and supermarkets on p. 129.

Nightlife: Nightlife gets pricey thanks to the $10-15 "cover" charge (entrance fee) levied by every dance club in town. Many bars also charge a smaller $3-8 cover on weekends, but remember that Boston's many college students and young people are as ready to party on (cover-free) weeknights as they are on weekends. Liquor is also expensive: beers average $4 and cocktails $5-6, but prices drop at the city's oft-neglected Happy Hours (usually 4-6pm on weekdays at bars downtown and near college campuses).

Public Transportation (MBTA; p. 20): Boston's far-reaching public transportation system (the "T") will get you anywhere you need to go for just $1 per ride. The catch is that the T shuts down by 1am (F-Sa 2:30am), meaning you'll need to pay for an expensive taxi if you plan to stay out late and live far from nightlife. For info on unlimited-travel T passes, see p. 21.

PRICES

Within each neighborhood, *Let's Go Boston* ranks all establishments by value; the best places get a thumbs-up (☒). At the end of each food and accommodation listing in this guide, you'll find a marker indicating a price range, as follows:

	①	②	③	④	⑤
ACCOMMODATIONS based on average rate per person, per night, double occupancy	**under $35**	**$35-50**	**$50-70**	**$70-90**	**$90+**
FOOD based on average price for an entree (main dish) at dinner	**under $7**	**$7-11**	**$11-16**	**$16-22**	**$22+**

HEALTH CARE

PRESCRIPTIONS & SUPPLIES

There is no need to bring extra health supplies (tampons, contact lens solution, etc.) to Boston, as there is no shortage of drugstores and pharmacies in Boston. Even convenience stores sell non-prescription drugs (for a listing of 24hr. pharmacies, see p. 283). For any health aid requiring a **prescription**—contact lenses, medication, birth control, etc.—bring an extra copy of that prescription with you on your trip. While traveling, always keep prescription medication in your carry-on luggage. In your passport, write the names of people that should be contacted in a medical emergency, and list allergies or medical conditions a doctor should be aware of.

TRAVEL INSURANCE

Travel insurance generally covers four basic areas: medical/health problems, property loss, trip cancellation/interruption, and emergency evacuation. Your regular medical insurance policy may well extend to travel-related accidents (this is true of most nationally subsidized policies and university policies, but not true of US Medicare). However, you might consider purchasing extra travel insurance if the cost of potential trip cancellation or emergency evacuation is greater than you can afford.

Buying travel insurance independently (apart from a larger insurance package) generally costs about $50 per week for full coverage, while trip cancellation/interruption may be purchased separately at a rate of about $5.50 per $100 of coverage. The international student and youth ID cards **ISIC, IYTC,** and **ITIC** (see p. 259) provide basic insurance benefits, including $100 per day of in-hospital sickness for up to 60 days, $3000 of accident-related medical reimbursement, and $25,000 for emergency medical transport. Cardholders also have access to a useful toll-free 24hr. helpline (in the US and Canada ☎877-370-4742, elsewhere ☎715-345-0505) for medical, legal, and financial emergencies.

GETTING TO BOSTON

BY PLANE

You should have no problem finding flights to and from Boston: although Boston's Logan Airport (airport code BOS) is not a major hub for any specific airline, almost every major national and international airline carrier serves Logan (see p. 17 for more info on Logan.)

Discounts and price wars are so common in the airline industry that students, seniors, and those under 26 should never pay full price for an airline ticket. In the US, flights can often be found at prices near those of ground transportation. A **standby** ticket—which isn't confirmed but dependent on there being an open seat on the plane—can also be a good deal, but **last-minute specials** (mostly available over the Internet) often beat these fares. Your best bets for finding a cheap fare are the budget travel agencies (listed below) and your own sleuthing on the Internet.

Logan is only 5 mi. from downtown Boston, so there's no need to plan ahead for your transportation from the airport to wherever you're going in Boston. There are plenty of private and public transportation options to and from the airport, but travelers whose flights arrive after the subway (T) closes at 1am (F-Sa 2:30am) will find themselves shelling out a pretty penny ($20-30) for a taxi to the city proper.

TRAVEL AGENCIES ABROAD

Below is a list of the most common budget travel-oriented travel agencies throughout the English-speaking world. Most are based primarily in one country but have branches throughout the world. In addition to selling international ID cards, all the following book airline tickets at their branch offices and through the phone numbers listed (STA Travel also books online); some also book arranged tours and sell travel-related gear (rucksacks, phone cards, etc.). Travelers holding **ISIC** or **IYTC** (see p. 259) qualify for major discounts.

STA Travel (www.sta-travel.com). The largest worldwide youth travel agency, with countless offices worldwide. Also books tickets online at www.sta-travel.com.

usit world (www.usitworld.com). A collection of youth travel agencies that faced bankruptcy a few years ago but is still up and running. usit Campus offices in the UK are all out of business. Remaining branches include: nearly 20 **usit NOW** offices in the Republic of Ireland (☎01 602 1600; www.usitnow.ie) and N. Ireland (☎028 9032 7111; www.usitnow.com); usit World-run offices throughout Europe (check www.usitworld.com); and 10 **usit Adventures** in South Africa (☎086 000 0111; www.usitadventures.co.za).

CTS Travel (anywhere in Europe ☎020 7290 0621; www.ctstravel.co.uk). A London-based budget travel agency with branches all over Europe and a US office at 350 Fifth Ave. #7813, New York City, NY (toll-free US ☎877-287-6665; www.ctstravelusa.com).

Travel CUTS (www.travelcuts.com). **Canada's** own budget and student travel agency with roughly 60 agencies near college campuses throughout Canada. Also has several branches in **London** (☎020 7255 2082; www.travelcuts.co.uk).

Council Travel (☎800-329-9537; www.counciltravel.com). A **US-only** youth travel agency that went bankrupt in 2002, but was bought out by STA Travel and is now back up and running. Their hundreds of US offices (there are several in every state) are still in existence and transacting business through STA.

Student UNI Travel (www.sut.com.au). **Australia-** and **New Zealand-**based budget travel agency. The branch at 92 Pitt St., Level 8, Sydney (☎02 9232 8444) is the main office for the 6 Australian offices, while the branch at 5-7 Victoria St. E., Auckland (☎09 379 4224) heads the New Zealand offices.

TRAVEL AGENCIES IN BOSTON

Carlson Wagonlit, Cambridge. 30 JFK St. (☎617-868-1818). T: Harvard (Red). Open M-F 10am-6pm, Sa 11am-3pm.

STA Travel: Back Bay, 297 Newbury St. (☎617-266-6014; www.sta-travel.com). T: Hynes/ICA (Green-B,C,D). **Cambridge,** 65 Mt. Auburn St. (☎617-576-4623). T: Harvard (Red). Both open M-F 9am-7pm, Sa 10am-6pm, Su 10am-5pm. **Cambridge,** 714 Mass. Ave. (☎617-497-1497). T: Central (Red). Open M-Sa 10am-6pm. Kenmore Sq., 738 Commonwealth Ave. (☎617-264-2030). T: BU Central (Green-B). Open M-Sa 10am-6pm.

BY BUS

The bus is the best budget travel option if you're visiting Boston from elsewhere in New England or from New York City or Washington, D.C. It's cheaper and faster than a train and just as safe and clean. All national bus lines arrive and depart from South Station, south of Downtown Boston (for more info, see p. 19); some also stop at North Station and Logan Airport (see p. 17).

Concord Trailways (☎800-639-3317; www.concordtrailways.com) runs to Boston from northern New England, while **Bonanza Bus** (☎888-751-8800; www.bonanza-bus.com) runs from southern New England with frequent trips to and from New York City (5hr., round-trip $64). **Greyhound** (☎800-231-2222; www.greyhound.com) has routes across America, including a frequent express service between Boston and New York City that can be as expensive as a train ticket depending on what time you travel (4-5hr.; round-trip can cost as much as $80, but don't pay more than $40).

Several accredited transport services run coaches and 15-passenger vans between the Chinatowns of Boston and New York City (4hr., 10-18 per day, round-trip $20). The companies are small but much faster and about as safe as national carriers like Greyhound. The most well known of these carriers is **Fung Wah Transport Vans,** 139 Canal St., New York (☎212-925-8889 or 718-438-3300; www.fungwahbus.com), which runs between its Canal St. ticket office and Boston's Crown Royal Bakery, 68 Beach St. (☎617-338-0007) T: Chinatown (Orange). Roundtrip tickets can be bought at either destination; and the bus runs roughly hourly, on the hour, until 10 pm.

BY TRAIN

If you are visiting Boston from elsewhere in the US or Canada and considering traveling by train, you may want to reconsider. Visitors used to the efficient, swift train service of Europe will be sorely disappointed by the near-monopoly of the US rail system held by slow-moving **Amtrak** (☎800-872-7245; www.amtrak.com). Trains are safe and fairly clean, but fall short of European standards. A bus trip may be bumpier than a train trip, but it will be cheaper and shorter in duration and just as safe. The one exception to this rule is Amtrak's new **Acela Express,** which offers high speed travel between Boston and New York (3¾hr., one-way $99).

Trains arrive at and depart from Boston's South Station (see p. 19); some also stop at Back Bay Station.

BY CAR

If you're visiting Boston from elsewhere in North America, it may be cheaper to drive to the city than to take buses or trains, depending on where you're coming from. Driving is definitely cheaper than air travel, and America's autoerotic love of cars means the US highway system is well maintained and easy to navigate. However, the tangled mess of the highway system around Boston—not to mention the interminable construction project known as the Big Dig (see p. 99)—is not for the faint of heart. Once you get to Boston, arrange to park your car in an airport garage (there's little free on-street parking for non-residents in Boston) or return it to the rental agency, as only a fool would try to get around Boston in an automobile.

If you don't have a US or Canadian driver's license, you'll need an **International Driving Permit (IDP),** which must be issued in your home country before you depart. As long as you have a current local license, the IDP is easily obtainable from your country's automobile association (fees vary) and is valid for one year.

Most credit cards cover standard **car insurance.** If you rent, lease, or borrow a car, you will need an **International Insurance Certificate**—a.k.a. a "green card" (not to be confused with immigration green cards)—to certify that you have liability insurance and that it applies abroad. Green cards do not need to be obtained abroad; they are issued by rental agencies, car dealers (for leasers), and some travel agents.

SPECIFIC CONCERNS

WOMEN TRAVELERS

Boston is as safe for women as any other large urban area in the United States. There is no sure-fire set of precautions that will protect you when you travel. However, you should feel safe visiting Boston as long as you exercise common sense: stick to busy, well-lit areas; avoid suspicious characters; don't walk alone anywhere at night; and always let someone at home know your itinerary. In the case of verbal harassment, the best answer is usually no answer at all. Always carry extra cash for a phone call or a taxi home at night—and remember that public transportation in Boston shuts down at 1am (F-Sa 2:30am), before most nightlife establishments close. Accommodations throughout the city are secure and safe for solo women. The T (subway system) may not be sparkling clean, but it is relatively safe. A self-defense course—although not necessary for a visit to Boston—will give you more options for dealing with the unexpected. Contact your local hospital, police, or community center for info on such courses in your area.

GAY & LESBIAN TRAVELERS

Boston is nowhere near San Francisco or Amsterdam as far as acceptance of gays and lesbians goes, but it is a queer-friendly city with a decent-sized, though rather dispersed, gay and lesbian population. Like most of the communities in Boston, the gay and lesbian community is very insular, although it is in no way unwelcoming to strangers. Except for in the South End and parts of Cambridge and Somerville, same-sex displays of affection are uncommon in Boston, but typically won't draw too much unwarranted attention.

It is more common to see gays and lesbians out and about across the river in Cambridge and Somerville than it is in Boston proper, but most establishments in Boston proper are welcoming of same-sex couples. The heart of the gay male community in Boston is the **South End** (p. 4), home to most of the city's exclusively gay bars, countless out and proud gay couples, and an endless array of gay-friendly and gay-owned shops, restaurants, and cafes. Any accommodations in the neighborhood are also likely to be gay-friendly (including the gay-owned Chandler Inn; see p. 189). There is a healthy lesbian presence across the river—in Inman Sq. (p. 7) and Davis Sq. (p. 8)—and a growing community in **Jamaica Plain** (p. 6), which is also home to the feminist rag *Sojourner.* Queer folk are much rarer in the city's outer southern neighborhoods—such as South Boston, Roxbury, and Dorchester—so gays and lesbians may feel less welcome there.

The gay community tends to gather less in specific areas and more often at their favorite gay-friendly haunts—mostly coffeeshops, bars, and dance clubs (which are some of the city's best); check the boxes **Girls' Night Out** (p. 144) and **Boys' Night Out** (p. 138) for info on these places. Flyers in the South End advertise gay and lesbian community events and activities. Most of the free publications available in street-side boxes—especially the *Boston Phoenix* (www.bostonphoenix.com), *Stuff@Night*, and the *Improper Bostonian*—also have special sections with listings of gay and lesbian events. The exclusively gay and totally free publications **Bay Windows** (www.baywindows.com, based in Boston) and **In News Weekly** (www.innewsweekly.com) have comprehensive coverage of gay nightlife and news in Boston and throughout New England; they can be found in street-side boxes and in many shops and restaurants.

For a list of queer resources in Boston, see **Gay & Lesbian Resources,** p. 283.

TRAVELERS WITH DISABILITIES

Most establishments and nearly every sight of interest in Boston is wheelchair accessible, but the city's tangle of narrow, cobblestoned sidewalks makes getting from place to place rather difficult. Thankfully, the T (subway and bus system) gets you anywhere you want to go for just $1 per ride; most T stations and subway cars and certain designated T buses are accessible to travelers with disabilities. For more info, these are two useful online resources:

Disability Resource Ctr. (www.dac.neu.edu/drc/bostonrc.htm) is an extensive online directory, run by Boston's Northeastern University, of Boston-area advocacy, counseling and accessible transportation resources.

MossRehab Resource Net (www.mossresourcenet.org/travel.htm) is packed with hard information on accessibility service providers and general advice on travel-related concerns for those with disabilities.

MATURE TRAVELERS

Senior citizens are eligible for a wide range of discounts on transportation, museums, movies, theaters, concerts, restaurants, and accommodations; this guide lists entrance discounts for mature travelers heading to various sights all over the city. If you don't see a senior citizen price listed, ask, and you may be delightfully surprised. The books *No Problem! Worldwise Tips for Mature Adventurers*, by Janice Kenyon (Orca Book Publishers; $16) and *Unbelievably Good Deals and Great Adventures That You Absolutely Can't Get Unless You're Over 50*, by Joan Rattner Heilman (NTC/Contemporary Publishing; $13) are both excellent resources. For more information on senior citizen deals, contact one of the following organizations:

Elderhostel, 11 Ave. de Lafayette, Boston, MA 02111 (☎877-426-8056; www.elderhostel.org). Organizes 1- to 4-week "educational adventures" on varied subjects in its home city and other locales all over the globe for those 55+.

The Mature Traveler, P.O. Box 15791, Sacramento, CA 95852 (☎800-460-6676; www.thematuretraveler.com). Deals, discounts, and travel packages for the 50+ traveler. Subscription $30.

TRAVELERS WITH CHILDREN

Boston is an excellent city for families: it's safe and small with countless kid-friendly, hands-on museums and activities, lots of living history, plenty of outdoor play space, and discounted kids' prices on everything. However, Boston isn't called "America's Walking City" for nothing: take it slow and make sure you and your children are ready to do a good bit of walking. Cheaper accommodations don't usually see young children, but most hotels are happy to make young travelers feel at home.

TRAVELERS WITH DIETARY RESTRICTIONS

VEGETARIANS & VEGANS

Boston's founding fathers may have eaten mostly meat and potatoes, but the city now has countless veggie-friendly spots. *Let's Go* lists three major veggie-only spots (see p. 103). The large number of Indian and cheap pan-Asian restaurants are safe bets if you're looking for vegetarian options, and vegans will find hearty animal product-free cuisine at Middle Eastern restaurants (p. 103). Most restaurants have non-meat options, especially establishments in Cambridge, Somerville, and Jamaica Plain. The **Boston Vegetarian Society** (www.bostonveg.org) lists eateries and info on holiday events, outdoor activities, vegan cooking classes, and the annual autumn **Boston Vegetarian Food Festival.**

KEEPING KOSHER

Travelers who keep kosher should have no problem in Boston—or rather, in **Brookline** (accessible by T from downtown; see p. 6), a largely Jewish city nearby that offers everything from kosher Chinese food, groceries, and pizza to orthodox synagogues and Judaica shops. You can find a comprehaensive list of local resources at www.kashrut.com/travel/Boston and www.shalomboston.com.

HALAL & *ZABIBAH*

There is a string of halal butchers downstairs at the weekend Haymarket (T: Haymarket (Green/Orange); see p. 81); most stay open throughout the week. There is a strong Middle Eastern (mostly Levantine) community in **Watertown** (just west of Cambridge), home to halal eateries and info about Muslim community events. Buses #502 from T: Copley (Green), #57 from T: Kenmore (Green-B,C,D), and #71 from T: Harvard (Red) will get you to Watertown in 30min. (for more on buses, see p. 20). The directory at www.zabibah.com/ma.shtml offers an admittedly incomplete list of establishments throughout the state that offer halal and *zabibah* meat.

ONLINE RESOURCES

Boston.com (www.boston.com). Mostly local and national news, including the online version of the *Boston Globe,* one of the city's 2 major newspapers.

Boston Online (www.boston-online.com). Countless insider travel tips on Boston and quirky facts about the city. Excellent links and photos, a healthy hatred of snooty Cantabrigians, and the "wicked good" guide to understanding Bostonian dialect.

Boston Phoenix (www.bostonphoenix.com). The online version of indisputably the best resource for living cheaply and happily in Boston. For more info, see p. 28.

Cambridge Smart Yellow Pages (http://cambridge.zami.com). An exhaustive listing of nearly every establishment in Cambridge, from bike shops to bagel shops. Restaurant listings come complete with online menus.

City of Boston (www.cityofboston.gov). The city's official website.

Citysearch Boston (www.boston.citysearch.com). A list-loving, easily searchable directory that reviews pretty much everything there is in Boston, from restaurants and shops to sights and nature trails. Reader-submitted reviews range from the drunken bar write-up to the insightful fashionista manifesto.

Greater Boston Convention & Visitors Bureau (www.bostonusa.com). Basic tourist information, including online hotel and dining reservations.

Let's Go (www.letsgo.com). Our website now includes introductory chapters from all our guides and a wealth of information on a monthly featured destination. As always, our website also has info about our books, a travel forum buzzing with stories and tips, and additional links that will help you make the most of a trip to Boston. In addition, all nine Let's Go City Guides are available for download on Palm OS PDAs.

INSIDE

Alternatives to Tourism

Despite a population just over 500,000, Boston draws over 12 million visitors a year, and of those over 1 million come from outside the US. With a diverse mix of domestic and foreign travelers as well as city-dwellers, tiny Boston has turned to sustainable travel in the form of **community-based tourism.** Like most American cities, Boston feels the effects of having a large population in a small space—though many people have prospered from the city's many economic opportunities, others are left wanting. Those looking to **volunteer** in the efforts to resolve these issues have many options, from serving food in a soup kitchen to explaining Boston's historical sites to other travelers.

There are other ways to integrate yourself into the Boston community. As America's largest college town, Boston has more students per square mile than any other US city. For those who want a real native Bostonian experience, **studying** at one of the city's many colleges is an option worth considering. For those coming to Boston for a summer, most universities offer summer programs (p. 274). If you prefer income to books, consider **working** while you travel. Boston doesn't have the political internships of Washington, D.C. or the financial internships of New York City, but with a little online perseverance, there is work to be found.

For those who seek more active involvement, Earthwatch International, Operation Crossroads Africa, and Habitat for Humanity offer fulfilling volunteer opportunities all over the world. For more on volunteering, studying, and working in Boston and beyond, consult Let's Go's alternatives to tourism web site, **www.beyondtourism.com.**

A NEW PHILOSOPHY OF TRAVEL

We at *Let's Go* have watched the growth of the 'ignorant tourist' stereotype with dismay, knowing that the majority of travelers care passionately about the state of the communities and environments they explore—but also knowing that even conscientious tourists can inadvertently damage natural wonders, rich cultures, and impoverished communities. We believe the philosophy of **sustainable travel** is among the most important travel tips we could impart to our readers, to help guide fellow backpackers and on-the-road philanthropists. By staying aware of the needs and troubles of local communities, today's travelers can be a powerful force in preserving and restoring this fragile world.

Working against the negative consequences of irresponsible tourism is much simpler than it might seem; it is often self-awareness, rather than self-sacrifice, that makes the biggest difference. Simply by trying to spend responsibly and conserve local resources, all travelers can positively impact the places they visit. Let's Go has partnered with **BEST** (**Business Enterprises for Sustainable Travel,** an affiliate of the Conference Board; see www.sustainabletravel.org), which recognizes businesses that operate based on the principles of sustainable travel. Below, they provide advice on how ordinary visitors can practice this philosophy in their daily travels, no matter where they are.

TIPS FOR CIVIC TRAVEL: HOW TO MAKE A DIFFERENCE

Travel by train when feasible. Rail travel requires only half the energy per passenger mile that planes do. On average, each of the 40,000 daily domestic air flights releases more than 1700 pounds of greenhouse gas emissions.

Use public mass transportation whenever possible; outside of cities, take advantage of group taxis or vans. Bicycles are an attractive way of seeing a community first-hand. And enjoy walking–purchase good maps of your destination and ask about on-foot touring opportunities.

When renting a car, ask whether fuel-efficient vehicles are available. Honda and Toyota produce cars that use hybrid engines powered by electricity and gasoline, thus reducing emissions of carbon dioxide. Ford Motor Company plans to introduce a hybrid fuel model by the end of 2004.

Reduce, reuse, recycle–use electronic tickets, recycle papers and bottles wherever possible, and avoid using containers made of styrofoam. Refillable water bottles and rechargable batteries both efficiently conserve expendable resources.

Be thoughtful in your purchases. Take care not to buy souvenir objects made from trees in old-growth or endangered forests, such as teak, or items made from endangered species, like ivory or tortoise jewelry. Ask whether products are made from renewable resources.

Buy from local enterprises, such as casual street vendors. In developing countries and low-income neighborhoods, many people depend on the "informal economy" to make a living.

Be on-the-road-philanthropists. If you are inspired by the natural environment of a destination or enriched by its culture, join in preserving their integrity by making a charitable contribution to a local organization.

Spread the word. Upon your return home, tell friends and colleagues about places to visit that will benefit greatly from their tourist dollars, and reward sustainable enterprises by recommending their services. Travelers can not only introduce friends to particular vendors but also to local causes and charities that they might choose to support when they travel.

VOLUNTEERING

Though Boston is considered wealthy in worldwide terms, the city still faces the problems of homelessness and hunger. The important work done by those fighting the city's problems, preserving history, and generally making life easier for Bostonians is incalculable. Volunteering can be one of life's most fulfilling experiences, especially if you combine it with the thrill of traveling in a new place.

Most people who volunteer in Boston do so on a short-term basis at organizations that make use of drop-in or once-a-week volunteers. The best way to find opportunities that match up with your interests and schedule is to call one of the organizations listed below. Most organizations welcome help, be it for a couple hours or full-time.

More intensive volunteer services may charge you a fee to participate. These costs can be surprisingly hefty (although they frequently cover airfare and most, if not all, living expenses). Most people choose to go through a parent organization that takes care of logistical details and frequently provides a group environment and support system. There are two main types of organizations—religious and non-sectarian—although there are rarely restrictions on participation in either.

The following list identifies the three largest issues facing Boston in the 21st century. Below each issue are contacts and organizations that welcome volunteers.

FIND THE PATH. To read more on specific organizations that are working to better their communities, look for our **Giving Back** features throughout the book. We recommend: the interview with Kaitlyn Greenidge of the National Park Service, p. 64, and a personal narrative about one volunteer's experience in a soup kitchen, p. 129.

HOMELESSNESS

On any given day, there are approximately 6,210 homeless people living in Boston. Needless to say, homelessness is one of the leading problems in the city. As the city's cost of living rises, more and more individuals and families are being forced from their homes by high rents. Over 50% of those who are homeless in Boston today have full-time jobs and still can not afford a place to live. The organizations below exist to combat this problem through education, job placement, lobbying, construction, and—most importantly—providing shelter to those who need it. Volunteers drive these organizations.

Rosie's Place, 889 Harrison Ave. (☎617-442-9322; www.rosies.org). **South End.** Founded in 1974, Rosie's place was the first homeless shelter in America dedicated to women's concerns and open to women only. Rosie's provides shelter, meals, groceries, and counseling to hundreds of women each year at their headquarters in the South End. Run by a permanent staff and over 800 volunteers, opportunities to help exist year-round and range from cooking to folding clothes to tutoring.

Habitat Boston, 273 Summer St., 3rd fl. (☎617-423-2223; www.habitatboston.org). Habitat Boston is a faith-based organization affiliated with Habitat For Humanity International and dedicated to alleviating the housing shortage in Boston. Their activities include the construction and renovation of houses and apartments in the Boston area in order to create affordable housing for those in need. Opportunities to volunteer are available year-round and usually consist of construction, landscaping, and painting. Non-manual labor opportunities are also available.

Horizons Initiative, 90 Cushing Ave. (☎617-287-1900; www.horizonsinitiative.org). **Dorchester.** Horizons Initiative has provided homeless children in Boston with early education and recreation programs for the last 15 years. Volunteers work mostly in the Playspace program, a network of playrooms in homeless shelters. They also sponsor programs to help support homeless parents.

Pine Street Inn, 444 Harrison Ave. (☎617-482-4944; www.pinestreetinn.com). **South End.** The Pine Street Inn is a network of almost 20 different shelters scattered across the Boston area. The inn's mission is to provide food, shelter, and moral support to homeless people living in Boston. Volunteers are always welcome and are needed to serve meals, make sandwiches, teach interesting skills, and even play music.

Father Bill's Place, 38 Broad St. (☎617-770-3314; www.fatherbillsplace.org). **Quincy.** Father Bill's Place is dedicated to serving the homeless community that lives outside the city limits. Easily accessible via the Red Line of the T, Father Bill's focuses on helping those who need assistance in the city of Quincy and the surrounding suburban area known as the "South Shore." Volunteers are needed to help with all aspects of the shelter from meal preparation to direct work with guests.

HUNGER

Like any major metropolitan area, the city of Boston is faced each year with hundreds of thousands of individuals that do not have the food they need. In recent years the problem has gotten worse, with a full six percent of the population of Eastern Massachusetts seeking help in the last five years. Organizations like those below have attempted to provide food and help those in need, but the state only provides so much funding. Volunteers are the lifeblood of these organizations.

Project Bread, 160 North Washington St. (☎617-723-5000; www.projectbread.org). **North End.** Project Bread is most famous in Boston for its annual "Walk for Hunger," a 20 mi. walk in May that attracts 42,000 people and raises over $3 million. The money they raise is used to fund emergency food pantries and soup kitchens across Massachusetts, where they provide 31 million emergency meals annually. Though volunteers are welcome year-round, in April and May, they are needed to compose the bulk of the logistical support for the annual walk.

The Food Project, 555 Dudley St. (☎781-259-8621; www.thefoodproject.org). **Dorchester.** The Food Project is a unique organization that uses sustainable agriculture to combat the hunger problem in Boston. With farms downtown and in the surrounding suburbs, volunteers and members of the community work together to grow produce which is donated to soup kitchens or sold at market to benefit local community initiatives. Volunteers are needed year-round in the offices and in the summer and fall to plant and harvest.

Community Servings, 125 Magazine St. (☎617-445-7777; www.servings.org). **Roxbury.** Community Servings is a program established to provide hot meals to individuals living with AIDS in the Boston area. Of those served, 95% live at or below the poverty line and would otherwise have little access to the food required to meet their complex dietary needs. Volunteers are needed to help cook and deliver meals year-round.

Greater Boston Food Bank, 99 Atkinson St. (☎617-427-5200; www.gbfb.org). The largest food bank in Eastern Massachusetts, it provides a staggering 15 million meals a year to over 283,000 people. This enormous feat is accomplished only through the 38,000 hours donated by over 10,000 volunteers each year. Help is vital to stocking and supplying food to hungry individuals and families.

HISTORICAL PRESERVATION

Boston is a unique city because of its place in American history. The historical sights found across Boston are a testament to the living history of both the city of Boston and the United States, but their preservation is a continuous struggle. Without a highly dedicated group of individuals donating their time, many of these landmarks would not exist today. If you feel that you might be one of those individuals, numerous opportunities exist to interact with and help preserve Boston's history.

Boston by Foot, 77 North Washington St. (☎617-367-2345; www.bostonbyfoot.com). Boston by Foot is a non-profit, educational corporation established to promote awareness of Boston landmarks and architecture. Volunteer guides give daily tours during the summer months. For a fee anyone can take a course to become a tour guide; courses consist of lectures by prominent Bostonians, mock tours, and a written exam.

Boston Historical Society and Museum, 206 Washington St. (☎617-720-1713; www.bostonhistory.org). The Boston Historical Society is responsible for the maintenance and upkeep of the Old State House museum and library. Volunteers are needed to staff the museum shop, act as gallery guides, and conduct educational programs for school children.

Boston National Historical Park, Charlestown Navy Yard (☎617-242-5601; www.nps.gov/bost/volunteer_opps.htm). The Boston National Historical Park is a collection of Boston sites run by the National Park Service. Sites include the Freedom Trail, the USS *Constitution*, and Dorchester Heights. Volunteer opportunities are available year-round.

GENERAL SOCIAL ISSUES

Some organizations dedicate themselves to the general health and well-being of the city and its people. From establishing after-school programs to funding other charitable endeavours, the following organizations and resources offer a variety of ways to serve the city of Boston.

Boston Online: Non-Profit Groups (www.boston-online.com/Volunteer). A lengthy list of area organizations that need volunteers—everything from AIDS outreach groups and literacy advocates to volunteer-run movie theaters and homeless shelters.

United Way of Massachusetts Bay, 245 Summer St. #1401 (☎617-624-8000; www.uwmb.org). The United Way is a major volunteer organization in the US. They match non-profit groups with interested volunteers. **Volunteer Solutions** (www.volunteersolutions.org/boston) is their affiliate website, with a comprehensive listing of individual volunteer job openings in the Greater Boston area.

City Year, 285 Columbus Ave. (☎617-927-2500; www.cityyear.org/sites/boston). Opened in Boston in 1988, this civic-minded group now has red-coated corps all over the country. In addition to the annual City Year Serve-A-Thon—a city-wide, community-oriented day of public service—City Year has a "youth service corps" of several hundred 17-24 year-olds who spend a year living together in a city and engaging in rigorous community service and community-building activities. Contact them if you are interested in joining a City Year corps or working in their corporate offices.

Oxfam America, Inc., 26 West St. (☎617-482-1211; www.oxfamamerica.org). Headquartered in Boston, Oxfam America is the American arm of Oxfam International, an organization dedicated to educating people about world hunger and poverty and encouraging them to get involved in issues of international development.

American Red Cross of Massachusetts Bay, 285 Columbus Ave. (☎617-375-0700; www.bostonredcross.org/volunteer/volunteer.cfm). The Red Cross is an international organization dedicated to issues of health and disaster relief. The Massachusetts Bay Chapter serves 78 communities and is New England's leading volunteer organization. Volunteers are always needed to help with blood drives, disaster relief, and office work.

STUDYING

Boston has the highest concentration of colleges and universities in the world: college students make up a quarter of the population of the city, and there are 28 accredited bastions of higher education within the city limits alone. Many of these universities have international exchange student programs, which allow thousands of international students to come to Boston every year to spend a semester or full year living the life of an American college student. Most every college or university in the city has an international student office that will be your best resource before and during your time in America; contact schools for details.

As far as **duration,** a year-long or summer program is ideal. If you have to pick a single semester, though, spring is far better. Boston's weather is actually tolerable then, and it leaves open the option of sticking around the city through the summer. As far as **accommodations,** most students elect to live in a dormitory with their fellow students. In the US, a homestay with a family is only com-

STUDENT VISA INFORMATION To secure a student visa, you must already be accepted into a full course of study at an educational institution approved by the Immigration and Naturalization Services (INS; see p. 259). Once you are accepted to a school, they should help in arranging your visas and other formalities. Two types of student visas are available: the **F-1,** for academic studies (this includes language schools), and the **M-1,** for non-academic and vocational studies. All F-1 applicants must also prove they have enough readily available funds to meet all expenses for the first year of study; M-1 applicants must have evidence that sufficient funds are immediately available to pay all tuition and living costs for the entire period of intended stay. Applications should be processed by the American embassy or consulate in your country of residence (see p. 258 for a list of these).

mon in high school/secondary school exchanges, and may isolate you too much from the communal college experience. If you'll be looking for housing on your own, see **Long-Term Accommodations,** p. 191.

The best way to study in Boston is to contact colleges and universities in your home country to see what kind of exchanges they have with schools in Boston. With any major university, chances are good that there will be some sort of exchange program. Research is best done through your own school's study abroad or international office, which can also help you to arrange your visas, transportation, and the like.

Below are the main schools in the Boston area and a listing of the summer and exchange programs they offer.

SUMMER PROGRAMS

Boston College Summer Session, 140 Commonwealth Ave. (switchboard ☎617-552-8000; www.bc.edu/schools/summer). **Newton.** Co-ed Jesuit 4-year college. Offers two 6-week summer sessions; the first running from early May to mid-June, and the second mid-June to July. Enrollment is open to anyone with a high school degree or equivalent. Starting in mid-June on-campus housing is available for $75-100 per week. A special program is available for high school students who have completed the 11th grade (or equivalent), and is called **the Boston College Experience.** Boston College has exchange partnerships with universities around the world.

Boston University Summer Term, Commonwealth Ave. (☎617-353-2300; www.bu.edu/summer). **Fenway.** A private university with 15 schools and colleges. Summer programs are available to high school and college students in two 6-week sessions, though some courses may run through both sessions. International exchange programs also available.

Harvard Summer School, 51 Brattle St. (☎617-495-4024; www.summer.harvard.edu). **Cambridge.** America's oldest private institution, they have a list of summer courses available on a per credit rate to college students; an application is required to enter the program. A Secondary School Program invites high school junior and seniors to take college-level courses.

Massachusetts College of Art, 621 Huntington Ave. (☎617-879-7200; www.massart.edu). **The Fenway.** The nation's only state-sponsored art school, they have summer-school courses in everything from fashion design to ceramics to film.

Summer at Simmons (visiting undergraduates ☎617-521-2500, graduates ☎617-521-2910; www.simmons.edu/summer). **The Fenway.** Summer courses are offered at a reduced tuition rate in two sessions. The first session runs mid-May to late June; the second session from late June to early Aug.

Tufts Summer, 108 Packard Ave. (☎617-627-3454; www.ase.tufts.edu/summer). **Medford,** near Davis Sq. Private 4-year university. Over 250 course offerings in two summer sessions. The first session runs late May to late June, the second, July to early Aug.

BEFORE YOU GO Before handing your money over to any volunteer or study program, make sure you know exactly what you're getting into. It's a good idea to get the name of **previous participants** and ask them about their experience, as some programs sound much better on paper than in reality. The **questions** below are a good place to start:

-Will you be the only person in the program? If not, what are the other participants like? How old are they? How much will you be expected to interact with them?

-Is room and board included? If so, what is the arrangement? Will you be expected to share a room? A bathroom? What are the meals like? Do they fit any dietary restrictions?

-Is transportation included? Are there any additional expenses?

-How much free time will you have? Will you be able to travel?

-What kind of safety network is set up? Will you still be covered by your home insurance? Does the program have an emergency plan?

Summer Learning UMass Boston, 100 Morrissey Blvd. (☎617-287-7900; www.ccde.umb.edu). **Dorchester.** Public University. Within their more than 500 summer course listings are the exciting "field study programs," like *Nantucket Light: Oil Painting*. Two summer sessions.

CONTINUING EDUCATION

For those coming to the city in the fall, winter, or spring, there are other study opportunities available through continuing education programs at the various universities. Most of these departments allow for open enrollment in courses, while also providing more serious degree programs.

Emerson College Division of Continuing Education, 100 Beacon St. (☎617-824-8500; www.emerson.edu/ce). **Downtown.** Private 4-year college of communication and performing arts. The college provides a variety of programs from 1-day seminar workshops to open-enrollment courses to graduate programs.

Harvard Extension School, 51 Brattle St. (617-495-4024; www.extension.harvard.edu). **Cambridge.** Offers both open enrollment courses and degree programs in a variety of subjects.

Lesley University, 29 Everett St. (☎617-868-9600 or 800-999-1959; www.lesley.edu). **Cambridge.** Degree programs available in education, human services, management, and the arts. Open enrollment courses are offered in similar areas of study.

Simmons College Continuing Education (☎617-521-2051; www.simmons.edu/ce). **Fenway.** Private 4-year women's college. Degree programs and short-term courses available.

Suffolk University (☎617-573-8000; www.suffolk.edu). **Beacon Hill.** Offers mostly certificate learning programs in computer science, education and human services, accounting, art and design, and management.

OTHER PROGRAMS & COLLEGES

Some universities in the area lack organized departments or summer programs, but still provide opportunities for travelers. Most universities have seminars or lectures that are open to the community, and some even allow people to audit classes by sitting in on lectures without receiving credit.

Massachusetts Institute of Technology (MIT), 77 Massachusetts Ave. (☎617-253-1000; www.mit.edu). **Cambridge.** Premiere institution of science and technology. Though they recently dissolved their formal continuing education department, they still have many summer research and course options.

Northeastern University, 360 Huntington Ave. (617-373-2200; www.northeastern.edu). **Kenmore Sq.** Private 4-year college with programs combining classwork and internships. No formal summer school or continuing education programs, but they still offer community learning opportunities in the form of seminars and research year-round.

ProArts Consortium, 1140 Boylston St. (☎617-236-8617; www.proarts.org). **Fenway.** For those interested in the dramatic or performing arts, this consortium allows for cross-registration between Emerson College, the Boston Conservatory, the School of the Museum of Fine Arts, Berklee College of Music, the Boston Architectural Center, and the Massachusetts College of Art.

Tufts Institute for Learning in Retirement (TILR), 95 Talbot Ave. (☎617-627-3532; www.tufts.edu/alumni). **Medford,** near Davis Sq. Run through the alumni office, TILR has on-campus study groups that are open to members of the community. An application to become a member of the organization is required. The classes, though supported by Tufts University, are volunteer-driven.

Woods Hole Oceanographic Institute (WHOI), 360 Woods Hole Rd. (☎508-289-2219; www.whoi.edu), in Woods Hole. Visit their website to survey the many summer or year-round volunteer opportunities available for students with an interest in marine biology.

WORKING

Many young people just out of university choose to move to Boston to look for work, as the area's 200,000+ college students ensure a lively, young, casual social scene, making the transition into the cruel real world a little easier. Although Boston is not the American headquarters for any major industries like New York City (publishing, finance, etc.) or Los Angeles (film), most national and international companies have branches in the city or in the area.

WORKING VISA INFORMATION If you are not a US citizen, you need a work permit or "green card" to work in the US. Your employer must obtain this document. Work visas cannot be obtained unless you have first acquired some form of employment in the United States. Friends in Boston can sometimes help expedite work permits or arrange work-for-accommodations exchanges. There are three general categories of work visas: employment-based visas, issued to skilled or highly educated workers who already have job offers in the US; temporary worker visas, which have fixed time limits and specific classifications (for instance, "artists or entertainers who perform under a program that is culturally unique" or "persons who have practical training in the education of handicapped children"); and cultural exchange visas, which allow participation in either fellowships or reciprocal work programs with the aim of promoting cultural and historical exchange. For young adults in the English-speaking world, the simplest way to get legal permission to work abroad is through the **Council Exchanges** (www.councilexchanges.org) and their Work Abroad Programs. For a hefty but worthwhile fee (typically $300-425), Council Exchanges will obtain a 3- to 6-month work visa for you and assist you in finding permanent jobs and housing.

The following sections explain both the complicated process of securing a long-term job with a firm in Boston, as well as options for quick and easy short-term work for those looking to make a little extra money. For reliable information about the job search in America (everything from resume tips to interview strategies), check the **Riley Guide** (www.rileyguide.com).

LONG-TERM WORK

LOGISTICS

As noted above, Boston is not the headquarters for any American industry, but as a major American city, it has plenty of job opportunities. The **minimum wage** in Boston is $6.75 per hr. (the 2nd highest minimum wage in the nation), but you should look for a job that pays at least $10-11 per hr. if you expect to support yourself. When you are hired for a full-time job, you will have to fill out W-2 and I-9 tax forms, which authorize the government to take state and national taxes out of your paycheck. The combined state and federal income taxes in Massachusetts usually amount to about 25% of your income annually.

Those used to the less strict working requirements of European firms—casual hours, long lunch breaks, frequent holidays, etc.—will be surprised by the typical American company. Holidays are infrequent, and the work week is set firmly at 40hr., typically M-F 9am-5pm, with a 30-60min. lunch break. If you work more than this, you are usually entitled to **overtime pay,** typically 1½ times your hourly wage.

LOOKING FOR WORK

The easiest way to look for jobs is through the Internet: start by checking the job sites listed below. If you're in Boston, the classified ads of the *Boston Globe* ($0.50, daily) and the *Boston Herald* ($0.50, daily) are valuable resources—both are available at newsstands and streetside boxes.

If you're looking for a job in Boston from somewhere outside the US, international placement agencies are usually the best place to start. **Internships** are unpaid or poorly paid experiences working for a company in various capacities, from menial to meaningful, and are a good way to segue into working abroad. Be wary of advertisements or companies that claim they can get you a job abroad for a fee—often the same listings are available online or in papers, and some firms even provide out-of-date information.

If you are interested in **teaching,** the only real option is to teach at a **private school,** a co-ed or single-sex school not funded by the government. All Massachusetts public schools (similar to British state schools, free and subsidized) hire only state-certified teachers, and obtaining certification is an arduous process. Fortunately for armchair teachers, the Boston area is chock full of private schools. Most are in nearby towns and not in Boston proper, though they're often accessible by public transportation. Teachers' salaries at private schools are generally lower than those at public schools. Moreover, at a private school, you will most likely be required to lead extracurricular activities, such as coaching a school sport or advising a publication or group, for no extra compensation.

GENERAL JOB SEARCH RESOURCES

Most of the following general Internet resources are free, though registration is usually required before you can post a resume.

About.com (jobsearch.about.com). Links to hundreds of job-searching resources, from sample cover letters to actual job databases.

Careerbuilder.com (www.careerbuilder.com). Over 400,000 jobs in database.

Craigslist (http://boston.craigslist.org). An invaluable resource. Post your resume, search available jobs and apartment listings, and learn about community resources.

Employment Guide (www.employmentguide.com). Instead of posting your resume, you answer a series of questions that form an interview in the industry of your choice. You can build a resume at the completion of your interview. Also has extensive job database.

Foreignborn.com (www.foreignborn.com/career_ctr.htm). Foreignborn.com's career center lets you submit your resume for viewing by US-based companies looking specifically for foreign-born employees. Also has visa information.

HotJobs (www.hotjobs.com). Resume posting and a huge job database.

Monster.com (www.monster.com). Search the database and post your resume on this highly acclaimed site known for its catchy Super Bowl commercials.

Recruiters Online Network (www.recruitersonline.com). Find thousands of current, open job listings. Post your resume; locate recruiters and headhunters in your industry and location.

BOSTON-SPECIFIC RESOURCES

Typing "Boston" and "jobs" into a search engine yields thousands of results. Aside from the list of sites under **General Job Search Resources,** here are the best places on the Internet to search for a job in Boston:

www.theatlantic.com/about/bosintern lists publishing internships available in the Boston area.

www.bostonworks.com Online classifed ads for *The Boston Globe.*

www.bostonsearch.com lists thousands of jobs with fast-growing Boston-area companies.

www.bostonjobs.com lets you search their job listings and post a resume at no charge.

www.bostonhire.com is similar to a recruitment firm—they try to match the best applicants with the most appropriate employer. You can also post a resume, search listings, and read company profiles on their site.

boston.preferredjobs.com has the usual resume postings and job listings, as well as interview tips and listings of internships and job fairs.

INTERNSHIPS

Boston Globe, 135 Morrissey Blvd. (☎617-929-3120). **Dorchester.** For over 40 years, the Globe has been hiring summer interns who are interested in learning more about the newspaper industry. Must be an undergraduate to be eligible; some experience preferable. Paid a weekly wage.

Health Career Connections (☎714-808-1677). Partnered with many renowned medical facilities in Boston, it places undergraduate students who have an interest in healthcare in internships at various facilities, including Massachusetts General Hospital and the Boston Medical Center.

SHORT-TERM WORK

TEMP AGENCIES

A popular option for those just starting out is a temporary employment agency, known as a temp agency. Companies approach these agencies (who have databases of potential temporary workers) to fill short-term openings in their staff, such as those created when employees go on maternal or sick leave. These jobs are typically secretarial and often menial (answering phones, typing, stapling, filing, etc.), but they do pay well ($8-14 per hr.) and have been known to lead to more lucrative permanent positions.

To register with an agency and add your name to their temp worker database, first call to set up an appointment. In general it is a good idea to treat this appointment as you would a job interview—that is, come to the appointment dressed professionally, with resume and information on personal and professional references in hand. After you take several simple tests (typing tests, questionnaires on your interests and skills, etc.), they'll put you in their database and contact you if and when a job that matches your interests comes along. There is no fee for registering, so it's best to register with several agencies and increase your chances. Popular Boston-area temp agencies include the following; for a full list, check the yellow pages of the phone book under "employment agencies."

OfficeTeam, 101 Arch St. (☎800-804-8367 or 617-951-0036). **Downtown.** T: Downtown Crossing (Orange/Red). Another location in **Cambridge (Harvard Sq.),** 14 Story St. (☎617-876-9000). Both locations open M-F 8am-6pm.

PSG/Professional Staffing Group, 89 Devonshire St. (☎617-250-1000; www.psgboston.com), at Water St. **Downtown.** T: State (Blue/Orange). They take walk-ins, but strongly recommend that you make an appointment. Open M-F 7am-7pm, Su 9am-4pm.

Spherion Personnel, 75 Federal St., #200 (☎617-482-5996), at Franklin St. **Downtown.** T: State (Blue/Orange). Open M-F 8am-5pm.

FOOD SERVICE & BARTENDING

A popular option for finding short-term work is in food service, as either a waiter/waitress or bartender. Check for "help wanted" signs in windows of bars and restaurants, as food service vacancies are hardly ever posted in newspapers or with employment agencies. Those who **wait tables** usually make less than minimum wage because their salary is supplemented by tips (gratuity). In the US, tips are typically 15-20% of the food bill, so the more expensive the restaurant, the more money the waitstaff makes in tips (nicer restaurants usually hire people with previous food service experience). Hit the streets around the nicer parts of town—Beacon Hill (p. 3), the Back Bay on and around Newbury St. (p. 58) or the establishments lining Boston Common (p. 44)—if you're looking to work for high-end establishments.

Those working behind a counter or as a **greeter/host** don't make much in tips, so their salary is usually in excess of minimum wage. Most **bartenders** make big money in tips, and some manage to earn up to $20 per hr. Some establishments require their bartenders to have national TIP or TAM certification, which certifies the holder as a responsible alcohol server; these certificates are available only through accredited bartending schools.

FOR FURTHER READING ON ALTERNATIVES TO TOURISM

Alternatives to the Peace Corps: A directory of third world and U.S. Volunteer Opportunities, by Joan Powell. Food First Books, 2000 ($10).

International Directory of Voluntary Work, by Whetter and Pybus. Peterson's Guides and Vacation Work, 2000 ($16).

International Jobs, by Kocher and Segal. Perseus Books, 1999 ($18).

Work Your Way Around the World, by Susan Griffith. Worldview Publishing Services, 2001 ($18).

Invest Yourself: The Catalogue of Volunteer Opportunities, published by the Commission on Voluntary Service and Action (☎718-638-8487).

R-24
YELLOW
YELLOW
TAXI

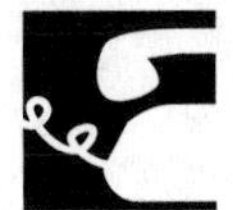

Service Directory

ACCOMMODATION AGENCIES

Boston Reservations: ☎617-332-4199.

Central Reservation Service: ☎800-332-3026 or 617-569-3800; www.bostonhotels.net.

Citywide Reservation Services: ☎617-267-7424 or 800-468-3593; www.cityres.com.

Hotel Distribution Network: ☎866-563-8913; www.hdn.com.

Hotel Reservations Network: ☎800-715-7666, Europe toll-free ☎00800 1066 1066; www.hoteldiscount.com.

AMERICAN EXPRESS

Back Bay: 432 Stuart St. (☎617-236-1331), at Trinity Pl. T: Copley (Green B,C,D,E). Open M-F 8:30am-5:30pm, Sa 9am-3pm.

Cambridge: 39 JFK St. (☎617-868-2600). T: Harvard (Red). Open M-Sa 9am-5:30pm.

Downtown: 1 State St. (☎617-723-8400). T: State (Blue/Orange). Open M-F 8:30am-5:30pm.

Financial District: 170 Federal St. (☎617-439-4400), at High St. T: South Station (Red). Open M-F 8:30am-6pm.

BICYCLE RENTAL

Back Bay Bikes, 336 Newbury St. (☎617-247-2336; www.backbaybicycle.com). **Back Bay.** T: Hynes/ICA (Green-B,C,D). $20 per day. Open in summer Su noon-5pm, M-F 10am-7pm, Sa 10am-6pm; off-season Su noon-5pm, M-Sa 10am-6pm.

Bicycle Exchange, 2067 Massachusetts Ave. (☎617-864-1300). **Cambridge.** T: Porter (Red). $20 per day. Open Su noon-5pm, M-W and F-Sa 9am-6pm, Th 9am-9pm.

Cambridge Bicycle, 259 Massachusetts Ave. (☎617-876-6555). **Cambridge.** T: Central (Red). $25 per 24hr. Open Su noon-6pm, M-Sa 10am-7pm.

Community Bicycle, 496 Tremont St. (☎617-542-8623). **South End.** T: N.E. Medical Center (Orange) or T: E. Berkeley St. (Silver). $20 per 24hr. Open Su noon-5pm, M-F 10am-7pm, Sa 10am-6pm.

BUSES

Bonanza Bus: ☎888-751-8800.

Concord Trailways: ☎800-639-3317.

Greyhound: ☎800-231-2222.

Peter Pan: ☎800-343-9999.

Plymouth & Brockton: ☎508-746-0378.

CABS

*See **Taxis***

CAR RENTAL AGENCIES

Prices and availability vary from day to day and agency to agency; check www.rentalcar-guide.com/boston.htm to compare prices across companies. All rental companies below are at Logan Airport (see p. 17), unless otherwise specified.

Adventure Rent-a-Car, 139 Brighton Ave. (☎617-783-3825). **Allston.** T: Harvard Ave. (Green-B). From $34 per day (100 mi. included). Insurance $13. Must be 21+; $5 per day surcharge for under 25. Open M-Sa 8am-5:30pm.

Alamo (☎800-462-5266, in Boston ☎617-561-4100; www.alamo.com). Must be 21+; $25 per day surcharge for under 25. Open 24hr.

Avis (☎800-331-1212, in Boston ☎617-561-3500; www.avis.com). Locations throughout the city, including a 24hr. site at the airport. 25+ only.

Budget (☎800-527-0700; www.budget.com). Locations throughout the city. Must be 21+; $30 per day surcharge for under 25.

Dollar (☎800-800-3665, in Boston ☎617-634-0006; www.dollar.com). Locations throughout the city, including a 24hr. site at the airport. Must be 21+; $30 per day surcharge for under 25.

Enterprise (☎800-736-8222, in Boston ☎617-561-4488; www.enterprise.com). Locations throughout the city, including the airport (M-F 7am-10pm, Sa-Su 9am-10pm). Must be 21+; $25 per day surcharge for under 25.

Hertz (☎800-654-3131; www.hertz.com). Locations throughout the city. 25+ only.

National (☎800-227-7368; www.nationalcar.com). 2 locations in the Boston area, 1 in Cambridge and another at the airport. Must be 21+; $30 per day surcharge for under 25.

Thrifty (☎800-847-4389, in Boston ☎877-283-0898; www.thrifty.com). Airport location. Must be 21+; $30 per day surcharge for under 25.

CONSULATES & EMBASSIES

All embassies to the US are in Washington, D.C.; the following consulates have offices in Boston:

Canada: 3 Copley Pl., #400 (☎617-262-3760). T: Copley (Green).

Ireland: 535 Boylston St., 3rd fl. (☎617-267-9330), at Clarendon St. T: Copley (Green).

United Kingdom: 1 Memorial Dr. (☎617-245-4500). T: Kendall (Red).

CRISIS LINES

*See **Emergency***

CURRENCY EXCHANGE

*Also see **American Express***

The best exchange rates are at 24hr. streetside ATMs. Avoid the high rates at the airport and train station exchange booths.

DRY CLEANING

Back Bay: 316 Newbury St. (☎617-266-5607). Open Su 10am-5pm, M-Sa 7am-7pm.

Brookline: 281 Harvard St. (☎617-739-5440). Open Su 10am-5pm, M-Sa 7am-7:30pm.

EMBASSIES

*See **Consulates***

EMERGENCY

*Also see **Hospitals** and **Pharmacies***

AIDS Action Hotline: ☎800-235-2331.

Fire, Police, Ambulance: ☎911.

MBTA Police: ☎617-222-1000.

Rape Crisis Ctr.: ☎617-492-7273.

GAY & LESBIAN RESOURCES

BAGLY (Boston Alliance of Gay and Lesbian Youth): ☎617-227-4313.

Bisexual Resource Ctr., Living Ctr., 29 Stanhope St. (☎617-424-9595).

Boston GLASS Community Ctr., 93 Massachusetts Ave. (☎617-266-3349).

Fenway Community Health Ctr., 7 Haviland St. (☎617-267-0900).

Gay, Lesbian, Bisexual, & Transgendered Help Line: ☎617-267-9001. Open M-F 6-11pm, Sa-Su 5-10pm.

Greater Boston PFLAG (Parents, Families, and Friends of Lesbians and Gays): ☎866-427-3524.

HELP LINES

*See **Emergency***

HOSPITALS

*Also see **Emergency** and **Pharmacies***

Beth Israel-Deaconess Medical Ctr., 330 Brookline Ave. (☎617-667-7000). **Fenway.**

Boston Medical Ctr., 1 Boston Medical Ctr. Pl. (☎617-638-8000). **South End.**

Brigham & Women's Hospital, 75 Francis St. (☎617-732-5500). **Fenway.**

Children's Hospital, 300 Longwood Ave. (☎617-355-6000). **Fenway.**

Faulkner Hospital, 1153 Centre St. (☎617-983-7000). **Jamaica Plain.**

Mass. Eye & Ear Infirmary, 243 Charles St. (☎617-523-7900). **Beacon Hill.**

Mass. General Hospital (MGH), 55 Fruit St. (☎617-726-2000). **Beacon Hill.**

Tufts-New England Medical Ctr., 800 Washington St. (☎617-636-5000). **Downtown.**

INTERNET ACCESS

Adrenaline Zone, 40 Brattle St. (☎617-876-1314). **Cambridge.** Exit T: Harvard (Red) onto Brattle St. and follow it as it veers right; the Zone is downstairs from the Algiers coffeehouse. $5 per hr. Open Su-Th 11am-11pm, F-Sa 11am-midnight.

Boston Public Library, Copley Sq., 700 Boylston St. (☎617-536-5400; www.bpl.org). **Back Bay.** T: Copley (Green). Enter via Dartmouth St. 7 terminals of free 15min. Internet access. See p. 61.

Brookline Public Library, 31 Pleasant St. (☎617-730-2380). T: Washington Sq. (Green-D). 30 min., by appointment. Open M and W 10am-6pm, Tu and Th 10am-9pm, F-Sa 9:30am-5pm.

Cambridge Public Library, 449 Broadway (☎617-349-4040; www.ci.cambridge.ma.us/~CPL). T: Harvard (Red). Walk against traffic up Mass. Ave., turn left onto Quincy St., then right onto Broadway. Free Internet access with sign-up for free library card. 1 first-come, first-served terminal with 15min. access; reserve terminals with 1hr. Internet access by calling ☎617-349-4425. Open M-F 9am-9pm, Sa 9am-5pm; Sept.-May also Su 1-5pm.

Somerville Public Library (West Branch), 40 College Ave. (☎617-623-5000). T: Davis (Red). 7 terminals free 30min. Internet access (limit 1hr. per day). Open M and Th 10am-9pm, Tu 10am-6pm, F 2-6pm.

LIBRARIES

*See **Internet Access***

MAIL

*See **Post Offices***

PASSPORTS

*See p. 258. For passports, renewals, and visas needed in 15+ days, see **Post Offices.***

US Passport Agency, Thomas O'Neill Federal Building, 10 Causeway St., #247 (☎617-878-0900). T: North Station (Green). New US passports, US passport renewals, and visas for non-US countries issued to those who need such documents in under 14 days and have proof of travel. Those traveling in 14+ days must apply at a US post office (see **Post Offices** below). Passports $80 (under 16 $70), renewals $55, plus $35 fee to expedite. Bring proof of citizenship (old passport or birth certificate) and 2 2"-by-2" passport photos. Office open M-F 9am-4pm.

PHARMACIES

*Also see **Hospitals***

Drugstores and pharmacies are everywhere in Boston; CVS and Walgreens are the most common. The 2 **24hr.** pharmacies are:

CVS, 35 White St. (☎617-876-5519). **Cambridge.** T: Porter (Red). Pharmacy and drugstore.

CVS, 155 Charles St. (☎617-227-0437 or 617-523-1028). **Beacon Hill.** T: Charles/MGH (Red). Only drugstore 24hr.; pharmacy open daily until 9pm.

POST OFFICES

US Postal Service (☎800-275-8777; www.usps.gov). Most branches open M-F 7:30am-5:30pm, Sa 8am-noon.

Downtown: Main Office, 25 Dorchester Ave. (☎617-654-5302). Behind T: South Station (Red). **Open 24hr.**

Airport: T: Airport (Blue). **Open 24hr.**

Back Bay: 390 Stuart St. (☎617-236-7800). T: Copley (Green). Also in the Prudential Ctr. (☎617-267-4164). T: Prudential (Green-E).

Beacon Hill: 24 Beacon St. (☎617-575-8700). T: Park St. (Green). Also at 136 Charles St. (☎617-723-7434). T: Charles/MGH (Red).

Cambridge: Central Sq., 770 Massachusetts Ave. (☎617-876-0550). T: Central (Red). **Harvard Sq.,** 125 Mt. Auburn St. (☎617-876-3883). T: Harvard (Red).

Kenmore Sq.: 11 Deerfield St. (☎617-437-1113). T: Kenmore (Green-B,C,D).

North End: 217 Hanover St. (☎617-723-6397). T: Haymarket (Green/Orange).

South End: 59 W. Dedham St. (☎617-266-0989). T: Back Bay (Orange) or T: Union Park St. (Silver).

REGISTRY OF MOTOR VEHICLES

Most forms can be filled out online at www.state.ma.us/rmv.

Boston: 630 Washington St. **Chinatown.** T: Chinatown (Orange). Open M-W and F 8:30am-5pm, Th 8:30am-7pm.

Cambridge: CambridgeSide Galleria Mall (p. 179), 100 CambridgeSide Pl. T: Lechmere (Green). Open M-F 10am-7pm.

TAXIS

Boston Cab: ☎617-536-5010.

Checker Taxi: ☎617-495-8294.

Taxi complaints: ☎617-343-4475.

Town Taxi: ☎617-536-5000.

TICKETS

*Also see **Entertainment,** p. 155*

Bostix (☎617-723-5181). ½-price day-of-show theater tickets sold 11am. **Faneuil Hall:** T: Government Center (Blue/Green). Open Su 11am-4pm, Tu-Sa 10am-6pm. **Copley Sq.:** T: Copley Sq. (Green), at Boylston and Dartmouth St. Open Su 11am-4pm, M-Sa 10am-6pm.

Fleet Center Box Office (☎617-624-1750). Tickets for Celtics (basketball) and Bruins (hockey) games. Also available from Ticketmaster (see below).

Hub Tickets, 240 Tremont St. (☎617-426-8340). **Theatre District.** T: Boylston (Green). Theater and sports tickets. Open M-F 9am-5pm, Sa 10am-noon.

NEXT Ticketing (☎617-423-6398, operator ☎617-423-6000; www.nextticketing.com).

Red Sox Ticket Office, 4 Yawkey Way (☎617-482-4769; www.redsox.com). **Fenway.** From T: Kenmore (Green-B,C,D), walk down Brookline Ave. (with the Hotel Buckminster on your right) and turn left onto Yawkey Way.

Ticket City, 128 Harvard Ave. (☎617-787-2370; www.tixboston.com). **Allston.** T: Harvard Ave. (Green-B). Music and sports. Open Su noon-5pm, M-F 10:30am-7pm, Sa 10:30am-6pm.

Ticketmaster (☎617-931-2000; www.ticketmaster.com). Tickets for the Celtics, Bruins, and Patriots, as well as for most musical events.

TOURIST OFFICES

Cambridge Office For Tourism runs a Visitor Information Booth (☎617-441-2884; www.cambridge-usa.org) outside T: Harvard (Red). Open Su 1-5pm, M-F 9am-5pm, Sa 10am-3pm.

Greater Boston Convention & Visitors Bureau, 2 Copley Pl., #105 (☎617-536-4100; www.bostonusa.com). **Back Bay.** T: Copley (Green). Open M-F 8:30am-5pm. Runs 2 info booths, 1 on Boston Common (p. 44), just outside T: Park St. (Green/Red), and the other in the Prudential Center, T: Prudential (Green).

National Historic Park Visitor Ctr., 15 State St. (☎617-242-5642 or 617-242-5601; www.nps.gov/bost). **Downtown.** T: State (Blue/Orange). Freedom Trail info and tours. Open daily 9am-5pm.

TOURS

See p. 97 for prices, hours, and complete tour descriptions

Big Dig (☎617-951-6400; www.big-dig.com).

Black Heritage Trail (☎617-742-5415). See p. 66.

Boston By Foot (☎617-367-2345, recorded tour info ☎617-367-3766; www.bostonbyfoot.com).

Boston Duck Tours (☎617-723-3825; www.bostonducktours.com).

Boston Harbor Cruises, 1 Long Wharf (☎617-227-4321; www.bostonharborcruises.com).

Freedom Trail. (☎617-242-5642; www.thefreedomtrail.org). See p. 43.

Literary Trail (☎617-350-0358; www.lit-trail.org).

MYTOWN: Multicultural Youth Tours of What's Now (☎617-536-8696; www.mytowninc.com).

North End Market Tours (☎617-523-6032; www.cucinare.com).

Old Town Trolley Tours (☎617-269-7010; www.historictours.com/boston).

TRANSPORTATION

Also see ***Taxis, RMV,*** *and* ***Buses.***

Airport: Logan International (☎800-235-6426). T: Airport (Blue).

Buses: *See* ***Buses.***

MBTA: ☎617-222-3200.

Trains: Amtrak (☎800-872-7245). T: South Station (Red).

TRAVEL AGENCIES

Carlson Wagonlit, 30 JFK St. (☎617-868-1818). **Cambridge.** T: Harvard (Red). Open M-F 10am-6pm, Sa 11am-3pm.

STA Travel: Back Bay, 297 Newbury St. (☎617-266-6014; www.sta-travel.com). T: Hynes/ICA (Green-B,C,D). **Cambridge,** 65 Mt. Auburn St. (☎617-576-4623). T: Harvard (Red). Both open Su 10am-5pm, M-F 9am-7pm, Sa 10am-6pm. **Cambridge,** 714 Mass. Ave. (☎617-497-1497). T: Central (Red). Open M-Sa 10am-6pm. **Kenmore Sq.,** 738 Commonwealth Ave. (☎617-264-2030). T: BU Central (Green-B). Open M-Sa 10am-6pm.

Index

A

B

C

D

E

F

I

J

K

N

P

T

U

W

Z

Map Appendix

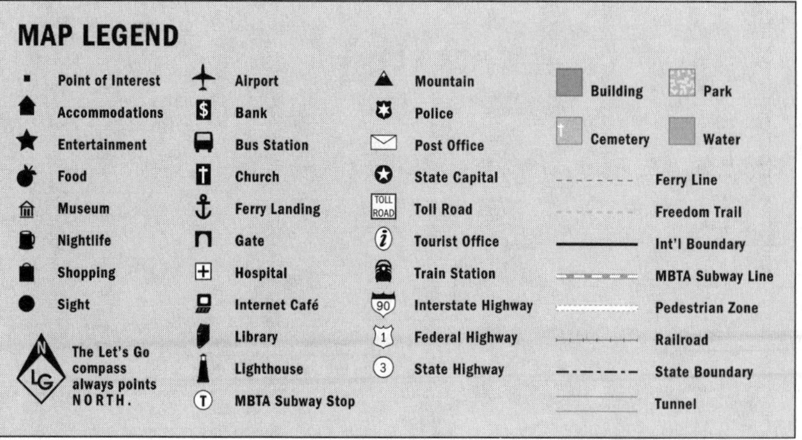

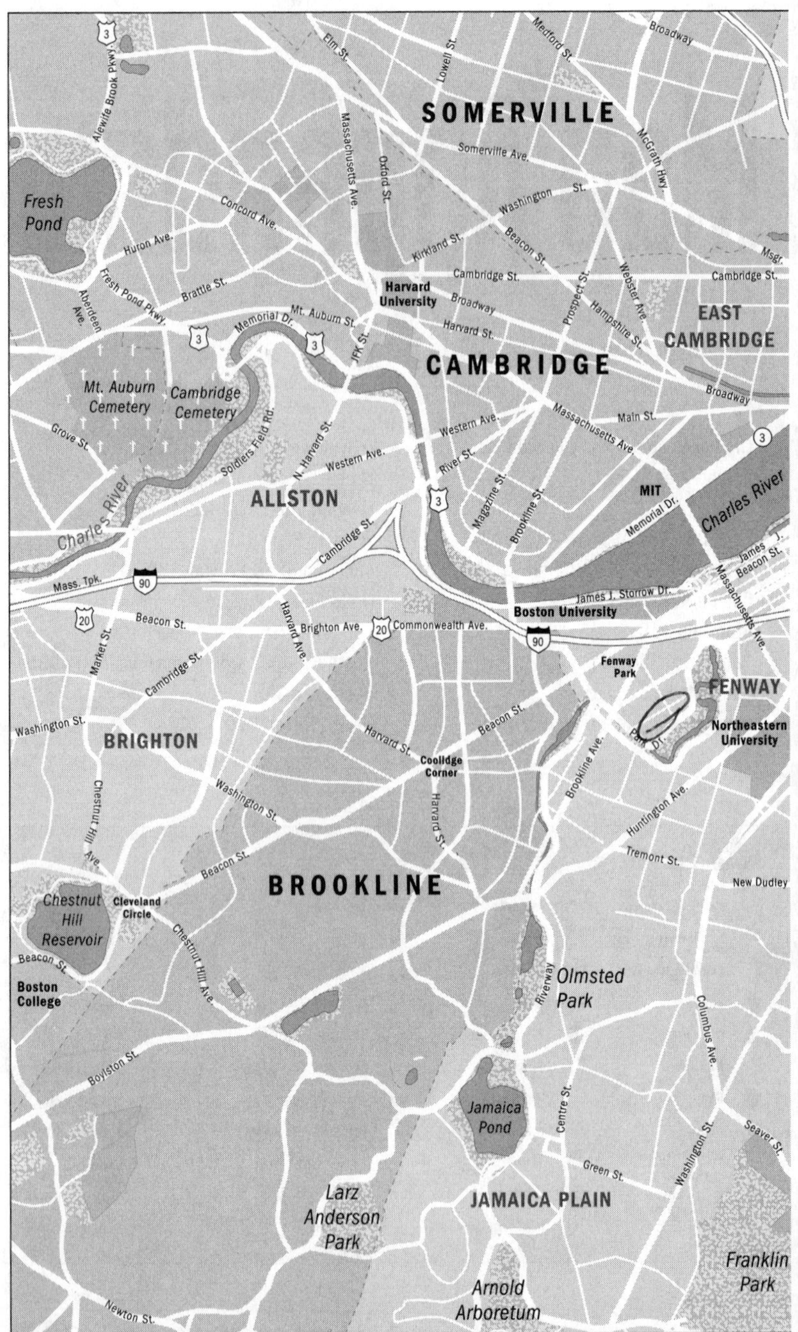
SOMERVILLE
CAMBRIDGE
EAST CAMBRIDGE
ALLSTON
BRIGHTON
BROOKLINE
JAMAICA PLAIN
FENWAY
Harvard University
MIT
Boston University
Northeastern University
Boston College
Fenway Park
Coolidge Corner
Cleveland Circle
Fresh Pond
Mt. Auburn Cemetery
Cambridge Cemetery
Charles River
Chestnut Hill Reservoir
Olmsted Park
Jamaica Pond
Larz Anderson Park
Arnold Arboretum
Franklin Park
Medford St.
Broadway
Elm St.
Lowell St.
Alewife Brook Pkwy.
Massachusetts Ave.
Oxford St.
Somerville Ave.
McGrath Hwy.
Washington St.
Concord Ave.
Kirkland St.
Beacon St.
Huron Ave.
Cambridge St.
Prospect St.
Webster Ave.
Msgr.
Fresh Pond Pkwy.
Brattle St.
Aberdeen Ave.
Memorial Dr.
Mt. Auburn St.
Harvard St.
Hampshire St.
JFK St.
Grove St.
Soldiers Field Rd.
N. Harvard St.
Western Ave.
River St.
Main St.
Magazine St.
Brookline St.
Mass. Tpk.
James J. Storrow Dr.
Beacon St.
Market St.
Harvard Ave.
Brighton Ave.
Commonwealth Ave.
Washington St.
Chestnut Hill Ave.
Park Dr.
Brookline Ave.
Huntington Ave.
Tremont St.
New Dudley
Harvard St.
Riverway
Columbus Ave.
Boylston St.
Centre St.
Green St.
Washington St.
Seaver St.
Newton St.
James J.
3
20
90

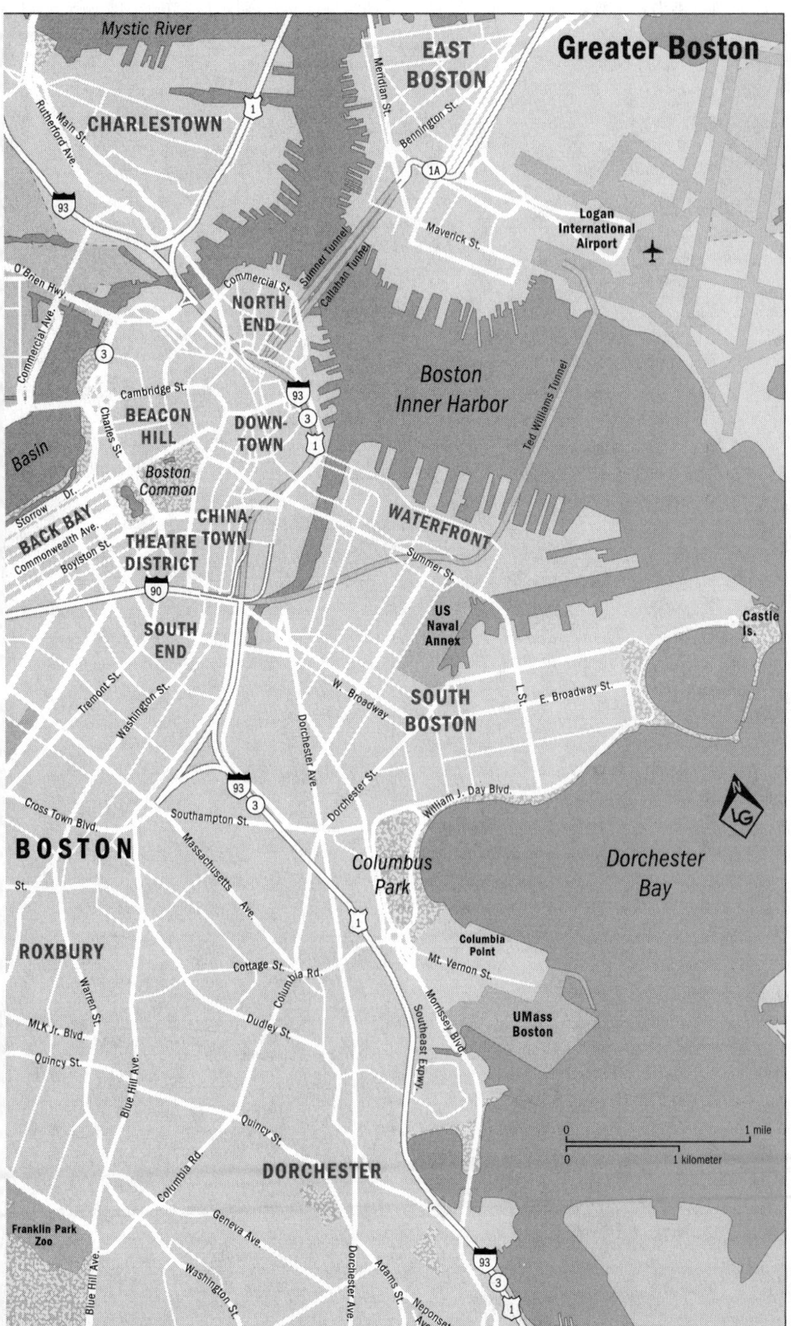
Greater Boston
Mystic River
CHARLESTOWN
EAST BOSTON
Meridian St.
Bennington St.
Main St.
Rutherford Ave.
Logan International Airport
Maverick St.
Sumner Tunnel
Callahan Tunnel
Commercial St.
O'Brien Hwy.
Commercial Ave.
NORTH END
Boston Inner Harbor
Ted Williams Tunnel
Cambridge St.
BEACON HILL
DOWN-TOWN
Charles St.
Basin
Boston Common
Storrow Dr.
BACK BAY
Commonwealth Ave.
Boylston St.
THEATRE DISTRICT
CHINA-TOWN
WATERFRONT
Summer St.
US Naval Annex
Castle Is.
SOUTH END
Tremont St.
Washington St.
W. Broadway
SOUTH BOSTON
L St.
E. Broadway St.
Dorchester Ave.
Dorchester St.
William J. Day Blvd.
Cross Town Blvd.
Southampton St.
BOSTON
Massachusetts Ave.
Columbus Park
Dorchester Bay
ROXBURY
Columbia Point
Mt. Vernon St.
Cottage St.
Columbia Rd.
Warren St.
Morrissey Blvd.
Southeast Expwy.
UMass Boston
MLK Jr. Blvd.
Dudley St.
Quincy St.
Blue Hill Ave.
0
1 mile
1 kilometer
DORCHESTER
Franklin Park Zoo
Geneva Ave.
Washington St.
Adams St.
Neponset Ave.

CAMBRIDGE
Massachusetts Institute of Technology
MIT Museum
Charles River
BACK BAY
FENWAY
Back Bay Fens
SOUTH END
Northeastern University
Museum of Fine Arts
Fenway Park
Hynes Convention Center
Prudential Tower
Boston Public Library
Trinity Church
John Hancock Tower
Christian Science Plaza
Symphony Hall
Hatch Shell
Briggs Field
Ahearn Field
TECHNOLOGY SQ.
KENDALL SQ.
KENMORE SQ.
COPLEY SQ.
KENDALL/MIT
KENMORE
HYNES/ICA
COPLEY
BACK BAY
PRUDENTIAL
SYMPHONY
MASSACHUSETTS AVE.
NORTHEASTERN
MUSEUM
NEWTON ST.
Longfellow Br.
Harvard Br.
Memorial Dr.
James J. Storrow Memorial Drive
Massachusetts Ave.
Commonwealth Ave.
Boylston St.
Newbury St.
Beacon St.
Marlborough St.
Back St.
Huntington Ave.
Columbus Ave.
Main St.
Broadway
0 400 yards
0 400 meters

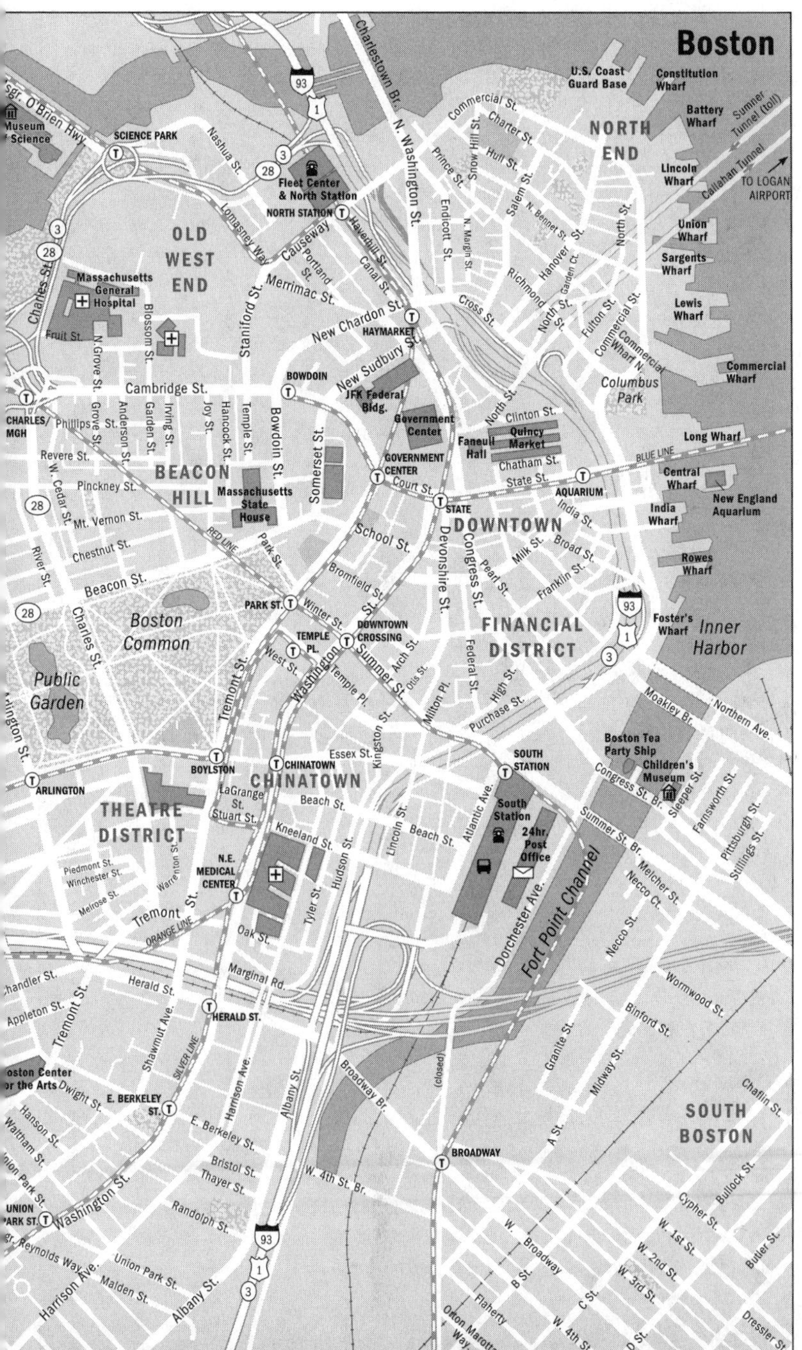
Boston
U.S. Coast Guard Base
Constitution Wharf
Battery Wharf
Sumner Tunnel (toll)
Callahan Tunnel
TO LOGAN AIRPORT
NORTH END
Lincoln Wharf
Union Wharf
Sargents Wharf
Lewis Wharf
Commercial Wharf
Columbus Park
Long Wharf
BLUE LINE
Central Wharf
New England Aquarium
India Wharf
Rowes Wharf
Foster's Wharf
Inner Harbor
Charlestown Br.
N. Washington St.
Commercial St.
Charter St.
Snow Hill St.
Hull St.
Prince St.
Salem St.
N. Bennet St.
Endicott St.
N. Margin St.
Hanover St.
North St.
Richmond St.
North Garden Ct.
Fulton St.
Commercial Wharf N.
Cross St.
Museum of Science
SCIENCE PARK
Nashua St.
Fleet Center & North Station
NORTH STATION
Lomasney Way
Causeway St.
Haverhill St.
Portland St.
Canal St.
Merrimac St.
OLD WEST END
Massachusetts General Hospital
Charles St.
Fruit St.
N. Grove St.
Blossom St.
Staniford St.
New Chardon St.
HAYMARKET
New Sudbury St.
BOWDOIN
JFK Federal Bldg.
Government Center
Faneuil Hall
Quincy Market
Clinton St.
Chatham St.
State St.
AQUARIUM
Cambridge St.
CHARLES/MGH
Phillips St.
Grove St.
Anderson St.
Garden St.
Irving St.
Joy St.
Hancock St.
Temple St.
Bowdoin St.
Somerset St.
GOVERNMENT CENTER
Court St.
STATE
Revere St.
W. Cedar St.
Pinckney St.
BEACON HILL
Massachusetts State House
Mt. Vernon St.
Chestnut St.
River St.
RED LINE
Park St.
School St.
Devonshire St.
Congress St.
DOWNTOWN
India St.
Broad St.
Milk St.
Pearl St.
Franklin St.
Beacon St.
Bromfield St.
PARK ST.
Winter St.
Boston Common
DOWNTOWN CROSSING
TEMPLE PL.
West St.
Washington St.
Temple Pl.
Summer St.
Arch St.
Otis St.
FINANCIAL DISTRICT
Federal St.
High St.
Purchase St.
Public Garden
Arlington St.
Tremont St.
Kingston St.
Milton Pl.
Moakley Br.
Northern Ave.
Boston Tea Party Ship
Children's Museum
Congress St. Br.
Sleeper St.
Farnsworth St.
Essex St.
BOYLSTON
CHINATOWN
SOUTH STATION
ARLINGTON
THEATRE DISTRICT
LaGrange St.
Stuart St.
Beach St.
Kneeland St.
Lincoln St.
Atlantic Ave.
South Station
24hr. Post Office
Summer St. Br.
Pittsburgh St.
Stillings St.
Melcher St.
Necco Ct.
Warrenton St.
Piedmont St.
Winchester St.
N.E. MEDICAL CENTER
Melrose St.
Hudson St.
Tyler St.
Dorchester Ave.
Fort Point Channel
Necco St.
ORANGE LINE
Oak St.
Marginal Rd.
Chandler St.
Herald St.
HERALD ST.
Appleton St.
Shawmut Ave.
SILVER LINE
Wormwood St.
Binford St.
Granite St.
Midway St.
Boston Center for the Arts
Dwight St.
E. BERKELEY ST.
Harrison Ave.
Albany St.
Broadway Br.
(closed)
E. Berkeley St.
Hanson St.
Waltham St.
Union Park St.
Bristol St.
Thayer St.
W. 4th St. Br.
BROADWAY
A St.
SOUTH BOSTON
Chaflin St.
Bullock St.
UNION PARK ST.
Randolph St.
Cypher St.
W. 1st St.
W. 2nd St.
W. 3rd St.
Butler St.
W. Broadway
B St.
C St.
Reynolds Way
Union Park St.
Malden St.
Flaherty Way
Orton Marotta Way
W. 4th St.
D St.
Dresser St.

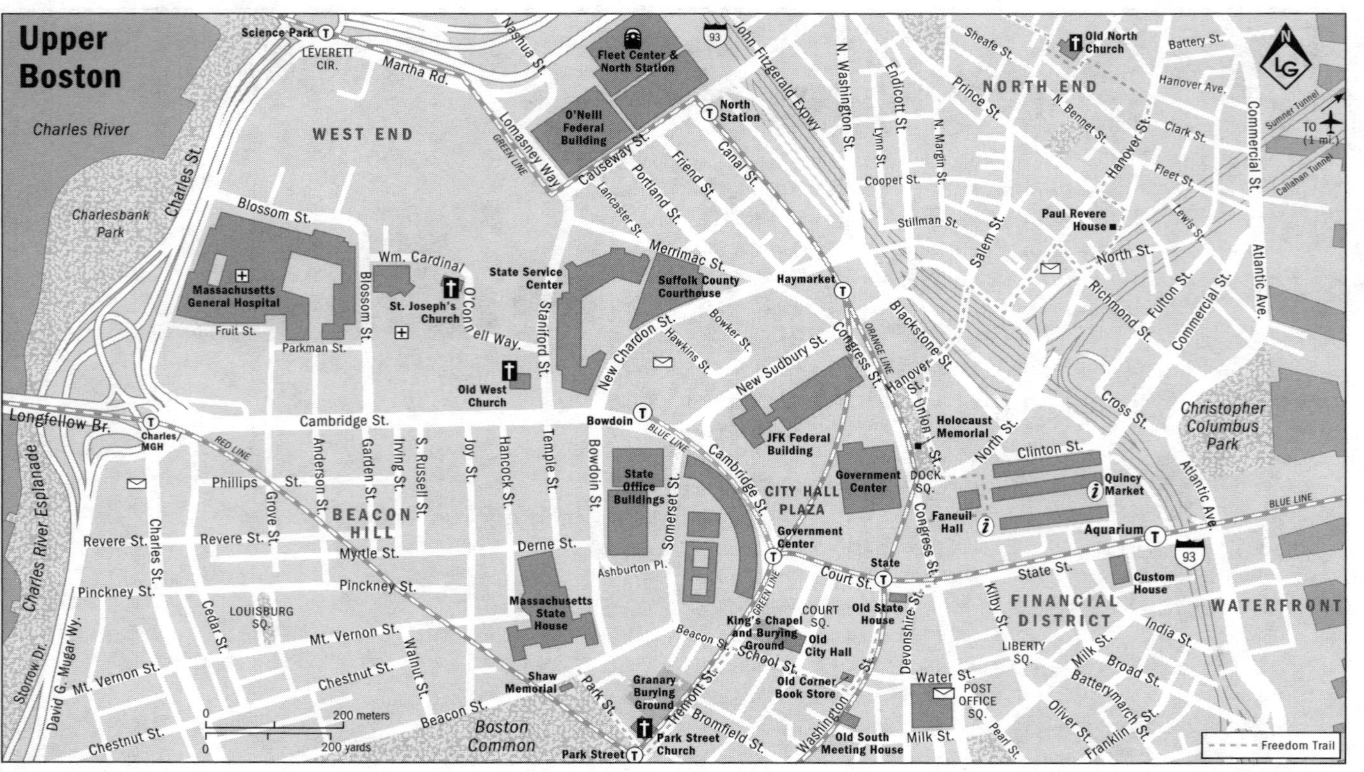
Upper Boston
Charles River
Charlesbank Park
Charles River Esplanade
Storrow Dr.
David G. Mugar Wy.
Longfellow Br.
Charles/MGH
RED LINE
Charles St.
Science Park
LEVERETT CIR.
Martha Rd.
Nashua St.
Lomasney Way
GREEN LINE
Fleet Center & North Station
O'Neill Federal Building
Causeway St.
North Station
93
John Fitzgerald Expwy
Canal St.
Friend St.
Portland St.
Lancaster St.
Merrimac St.
Haymarket
N. Washington St.
Lynn St.
Endicott St.
Cooper St.
N. Margin St.
Stillman St.
Salem St.
Prince St.
Sheafe St.
NORTH END
N. Bennet St.
Old North Church
Hanover St.
Paul Revere House
North St.
Battery St.
Hanover Ave.
Clark St.
Fleet St.
Lewis St.
Commercial St.
Atlantic Ave.
Fulton St.
Richmond St.
Cross St.
Christopher Columbus Park
Sumner Tunnel
Callahan Tunnel
TO (1 mi.)
BLUE LINE
WATERFRONT
Aquarium
Custom House
Quincy Market
Clinton St.
Faneuil Hall
Holocaust Memorial
Union St.
DOCK SQ.
Blackstone St.
Hanover St.
ORANGE LINE
Congress St.
New Sudbury St.
JFK Federal Building
Government Center
CITY HALL PLAZA
Cambridge St.
State
Court St.
Old State House
Devonshire St.
State St.
Kilby St.
FINANCIAL DISTRICT
LIBERTY SQ.
India St.
Milk St.
Broad St.
Batterymarch St.
Oliver St.
Franklin St.
Pearl St.
POST OFFICE SQ.
Water St.
Milk St.
Old South Meeting House
Washington St.
COURT SQ.
Old City Hall
Old Corner Book Store
King's Chapel and Burying Ground
School St.
Bromfield St.
Tremont St.
Beacon St.
Park Street Church
Park Street
Granary Burying Ground
Park St.
Somerset St.
Ashburton Pl.
State Office Buildings
Bowdoin
Bowdoin St.
New Chardon St.
Hawkins St.
Bowker St.
Suffolk County Courthouse
State Service Center
Staniford St.
Temple St.
Derne St.
Massachusetts State House
Shaw Memorial
Boston Common
Hancock St.
Joy St.
Old West Church
O'Connell Way
St. Joseph's Church
Wm. Cardinal
S. Russell St.
Irving St.
Myrtle St.
BEACON HILL
Pinckney St.
Walnut St.
Mt. Vernon St.
Chestnut St.
Garden St.
Blossom St.
WEST END
Parkman St.
Massachusetts General Hospital
Fruit St.
Anderson St.
Grove St.
Phillips St.
Revere St.
LOUISBURG SQ.
Cedar St.
Freedom Trail
0
200 meters
0
200 yards

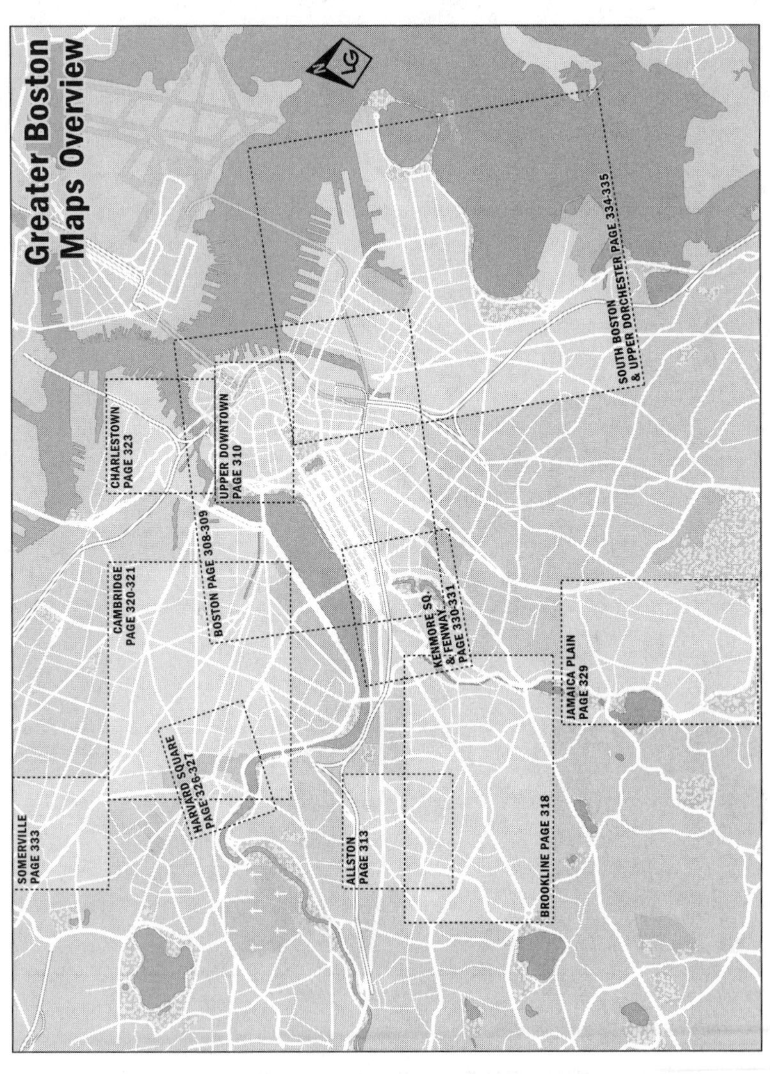
Greater Boston
Maps Overview
CHARLESTOWN
PAGE 323
UPPER DOWNTOWN
PAGE 310
SOUTH BOSTON
& UPPER DORCHESTER PAGE 334-335
CAMBRIDGE
PAGE 320-321
BOSTON PAGE 308-309
KENMORE SQ.
& FENWAY
PAGE 330-331
JAMAICA PLAIN
PAGE 329
SOMERVILLE
PAGE 333
HARVARD SQUARE
PAGE 326-327
ALLSTON
PAGE 313
BROOKLINE PAGE 318

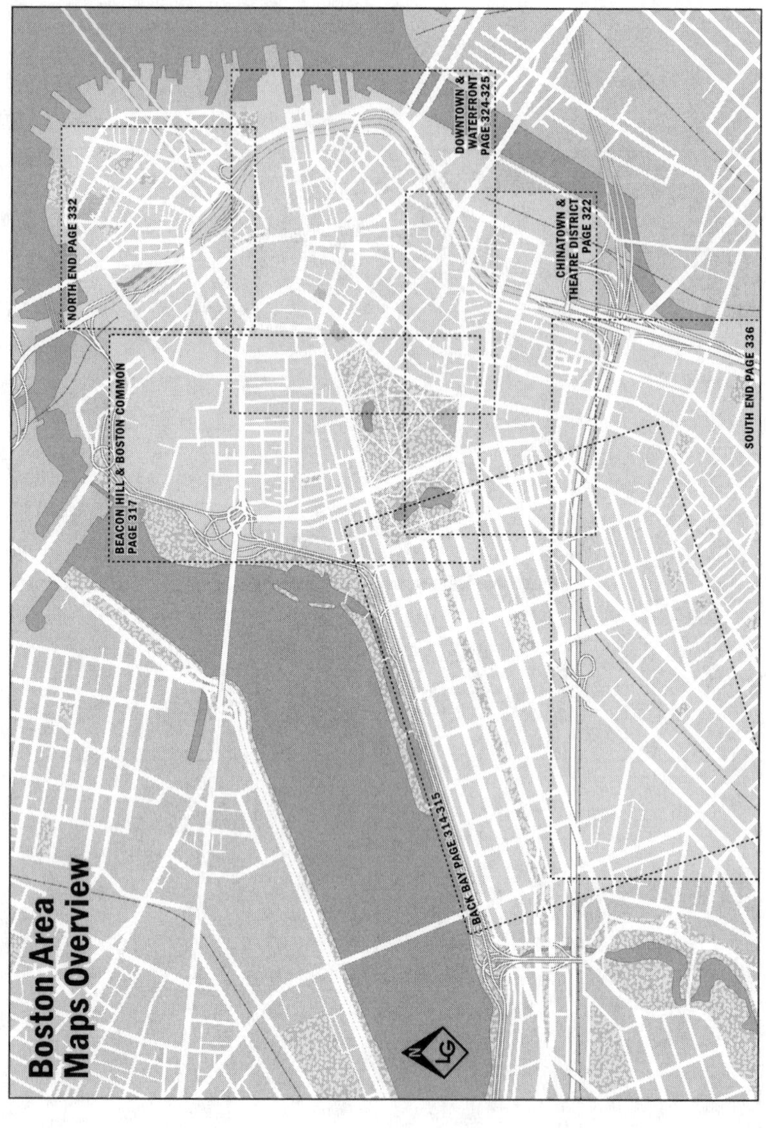
Boston Area
Maps Overview
NORTH END PAGE 332
DOWNTOWN & WATERFRONT PAGE 324-325
CHINATOWN & THEATRE DISTRICT PAGE 322
BEACON HILL & BOSTON COMMON PAGE 317
SOUTH END PAGE 336
BACK BAY PAGE 314-315

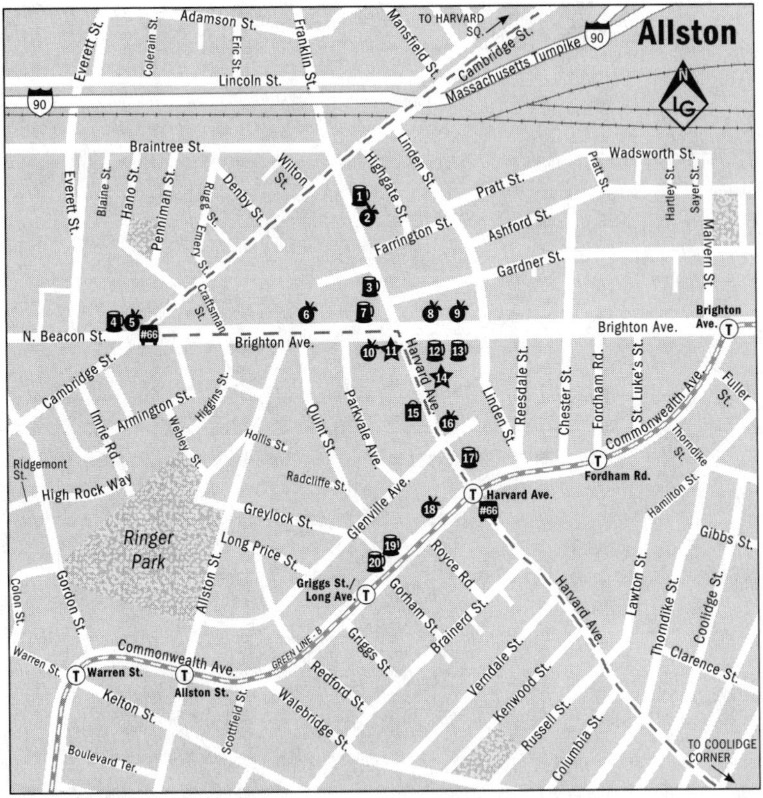

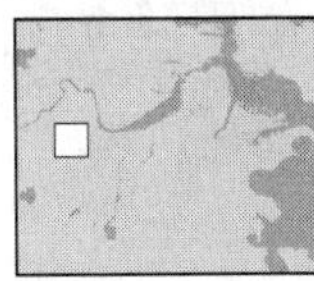

Allston

★ ENTERTAINMENT
Harper's Ferry, **11**
Mr. Music/Ticket City, **14**

FOOD
Bagel Rising, **18**
Café Belo, **6**
Camino Real, **2**
Grasshopper, **5**
Grecian Yearning Restaurant, **16**
Pho Pasteur, **8**
Rangoli, **9**
V. Majestic, **10**

NIGHTLIFE
The Avenue Bar & Grill, **19**
Common Ground Bar & Grill, **3**
The Kells, **7**
The Kinvara, **1**
Model Café, **4**
Our House, **20**
Sunset Grill & Tap, **12**
White Horse Tavern, **13**
Wonder Bar, **17**

SHOPPING
Flyrabbit, **15**

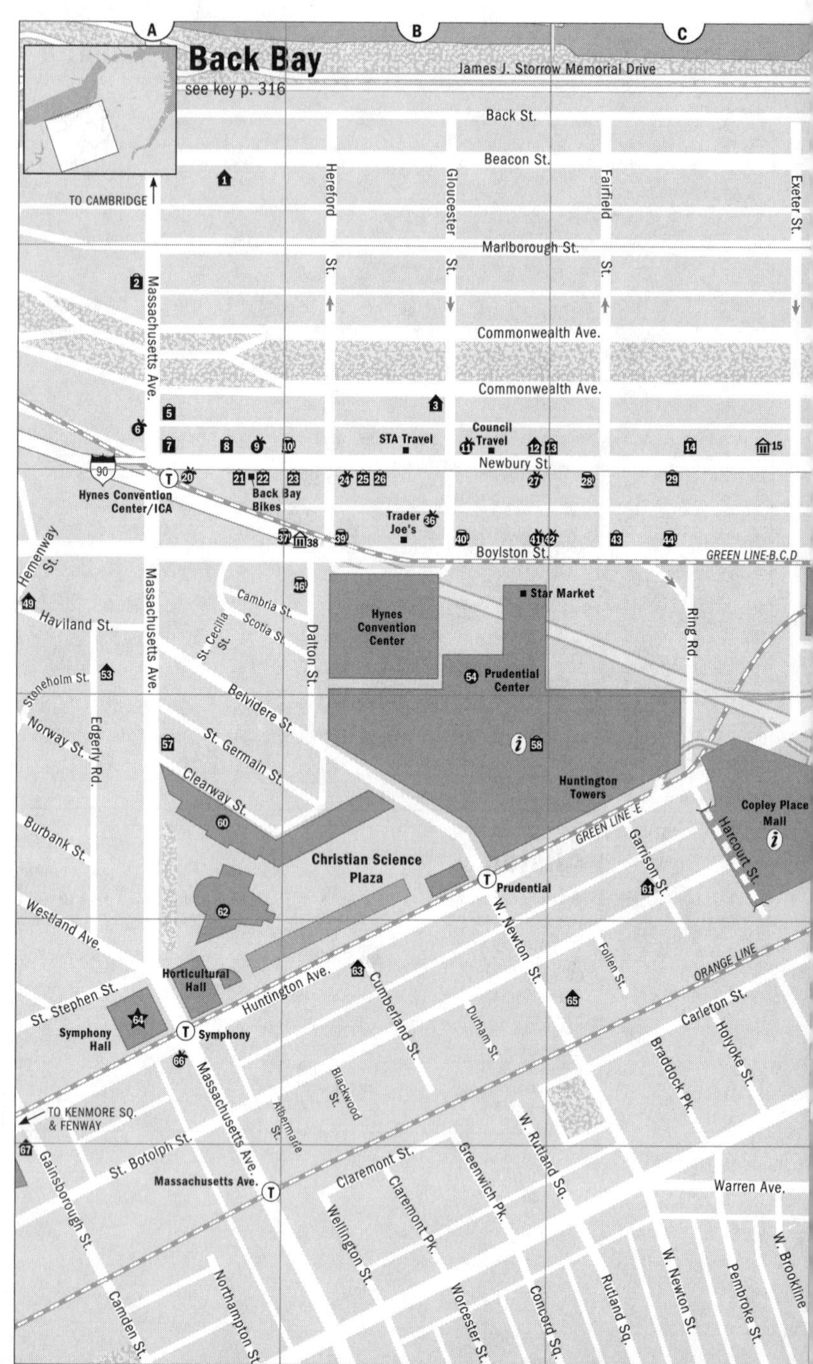
Back Bay
see key p. 316
A
B
C
James J. Storrow Memorial Drive
Back St.
Beacon St.
Hereford St.
Gloucester St.
Fairfield St.
Exeter St.
TO CAMBRIDGE
Marlborough St.
Massachusetts Ave.
Commonwealth Ave.
Commonwealth Ave.
STA Travel
Council Travel
Newbury St.
90
Hynes Convention Center/ICA
Back Bay Bikes
Trader Joe's
Boylston St.
GREEN LINE-B,C,D
Hemenway St.
Haviland St.
Cambria St.
Scotia St.
St. Cecilia St.
Dalton St.
Hynes Convention Center
Star Market
Prudential Center
Ring Rd.
Stoneholm St.
Belvidere St.
Norway St.
Edgerly Rd.
St. Germain St.
Clearway St.
Huntington Towers
Copley Place Mall
Burbank St.
GREEN LINE-E
Garrison St.
Harcourt St.
Christian Science Plaza
Prudential
Westland Ave.
W. Newton St.
Follen St.
ORANGE LINE
Horticultural Hall
Huntington Ave.
Cumberland St.
St. Stephen St.
Symphony Hall
Symphony
Durham St.
Carleton St.
Holyoke St.
Braddock Pk.
Blackwood St.
TO KENMORE SQ. & FENWAY
Albermarle St.
W. Rutland Sq.
St. Botolph St.
Claremont St.
Greenwich Pk.
Massachusetts Ave.
Claremont Pk.
Warren Ave.
Gainsborough St.
Wellington St.
W. Brookline
W. Newton St.
Pembroke St.
Northampton St.
Camden St.
Worcester St.
Concord Sq.
Rutland Sq.

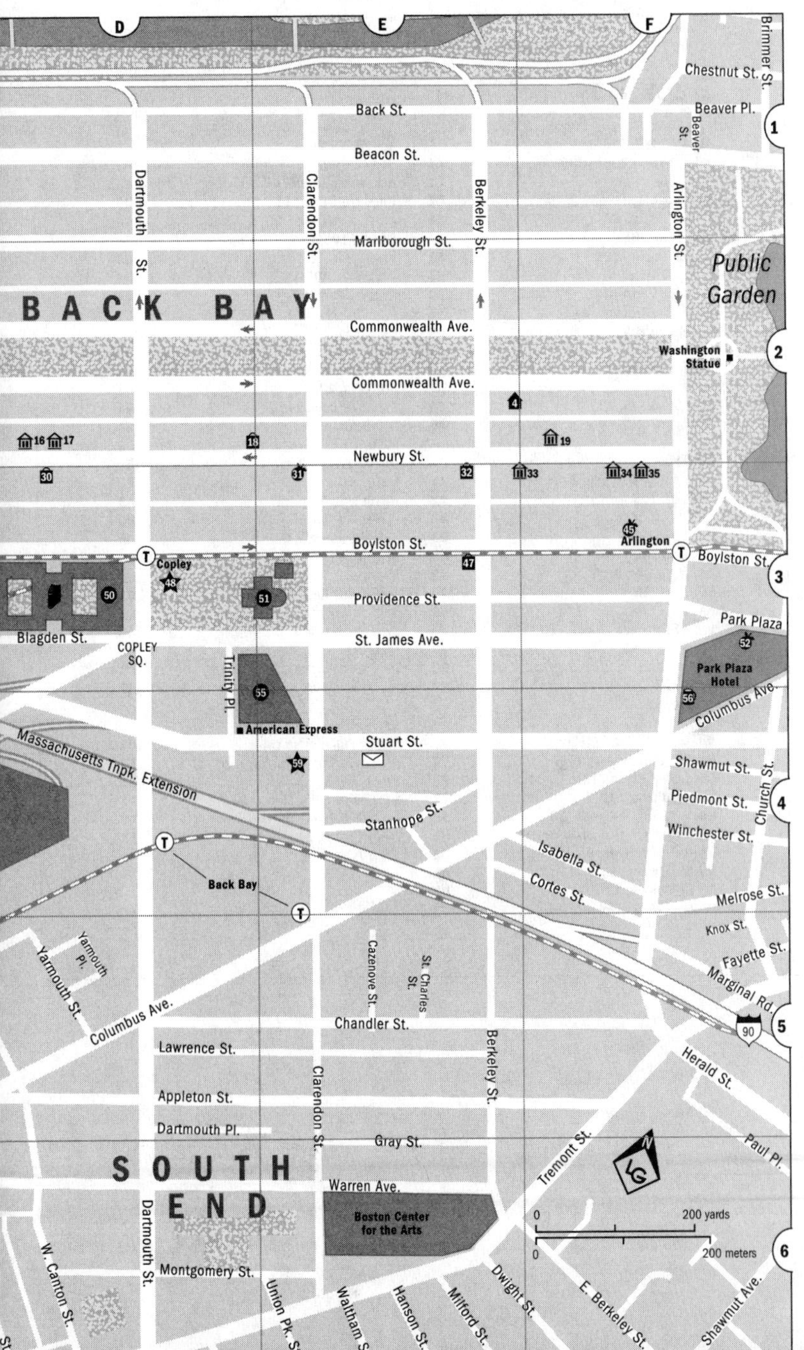

D
E
F
1
2
3
4
5
6
Brimmer St.
Chestnut St.
Beaver Pl.
Beaver St.
Back St.
Beacon St.
Marlborough St.
Commonwealth Ave.
Commonwealth Ave.
Newbury St.
Boylston St.
Providence St.
St. James Ave.
Stuart St.
Dartmouth St.
Clarendon St.
Berkeley St.
Arlington St.
Public Garden
Washington Statue
BACK BAY
Arlington
Boylston St.
Copley
Blagden St.
COPLEY SQ.
Trinity Pl.
American Express
Park Plaza
Park Plaza Hotel
Columbus Ave.
Massachusetts Tnpk. Extension
Shawmut St.
Piedmont St.
Winchester St.
Church St.
Stanhope St.
Isabella St.
Cortes St.
Melrose St.
Knox St.
Fayette St.
Marginal Rd.
Back Bay
Yarmouth Pl.
Yarmouth St.
Cazenove St.
St. Charles St.
Columbus Ave.
Chandler St.
Lawrence St.
Appleton St.
Dartmouth Pl.
Gray St.
Herald St.
Paul Pl.
Tremont St.
SOUTH END
Warren Ave.
Boston Center for the Arts
Montgomery St.
W. Canton St.
Union Pk. St.
Waltham St.
Hanson St.
Milford St.
Dwight St.
E. Berkeley St.
Shawmut Ave.
0 200 yards
0 200 meters
90

Back Bay

see map p. 314-315

ACCOMMODATIONS

463 Beacon St. Guest House, **1**	**A1**
The College Club, **4**	**E2**
Commonwealth Court Guest House, **3**	**B2**
Copley House, **65**	**C5**
Copley Inn, **61**	**C4**
HI-Boston (HI-AYH), **49**	**A3**
MidTown Hotel, **63**	**B5**
Newbury Guest House, **12**	**B2**
Oasis Guest House, **53**	**A3**
YMCA of Greater Boston, **67**	**A6**

ENTERTAINMENT

Bostix, **48**	**D3**
Lyric Stage Co., **59**	**E4**
Symphony Hall, **64**	**A5**

FOOD

Betty's Wok & Noodle Diner, **66**	**A5**
Bodhi Café, **9**	**A2**
Cafe Jaffa, **36**	**B3**
Chilli Duck, **41**	**B3**
Gyuhama, **42**	**C3**
Island Hopper, **6**	**A2**
J.P. Licks, **20**	**A3**
Kashmir, **11**	**B2**
Legal Sea Foods (Park Plaza), **52**	**F3**
Parish Café, **45**	**F3**
Steve's Greek Cuisine, **24**	**B3**
Tapéo, **27**	**B3**
Tealuxe, **31**	**E3**

MUSEUMS & GALLERIES

Barbara Krakow Gallery, **35**	**F3**
Chappell & Alpha Galleries, **34**	**F3**
Galerie d'Orsay, **19**	**F2**
Howard Yezerski Gallery, **34**	**F3**
Institute of Contemporary Art, **38**	**B3**
International Poster Gallery, **15**	**C2**
Nielsen Gallery, **16**	**D2**
Pucker Gallery, **17**	**D2**
Robert Klein & Pepper Galleries, **33**	**F3**

NIGHTLIFE

Barcode, **37**	**A3**
Bukowski's Tavern, **46**	**B3**
The Cactus Club, **39**	**B3**
Daisy Buchanan's, **28**	**C3**
Sonsie, **10**	**B2**
Vox Populi, **44**	**C3**
Whiskey's, **40**	**B3**
Whiskey Park, **56**	**F4**

SHOPPING

Anthropologie, **43**	**C3**
Ave. Victor Hugo Books, **8**	**A2**
CD Spins, **23**	**B3**
Dorothy's Boutique, **57**	**A4**
FAO Schwartz, **47**	**E3**
fresh, **18**	**D2**
Louis Boston, **32**	**E3**
Matsu, **13**	**C2**
Newbury Comics, **22**	**A3**
Planet Aid, **25**	**B3**
Satellite Records, **2**	**A2**
Second Time Around, **30**	**D3**
Shops at Prudential Center, **58**	**B4**
Smash City Records, **26**	**B3**
Spenser's Mystery Book Shop, **14**	**C2**
Sweet 'n' Nasty, **5**	**A2**
Teuscher Chocolatier, **29**	**C2**
Trident Booksellers, **21**	**A3**
Urban Outfitters, **7**	**A2**

SIGHTS

Boston Public Library, **50**	**D3**
First Church of Christ, Scientist, **62**	**A4**
Hancock Tower, **55**	**E3**
Mary Baker Eddy Library, **60**	**A4**
Prudential Center Tower & Skywalk, **54**	**B3**
Trinity Church, **51**	**E3**

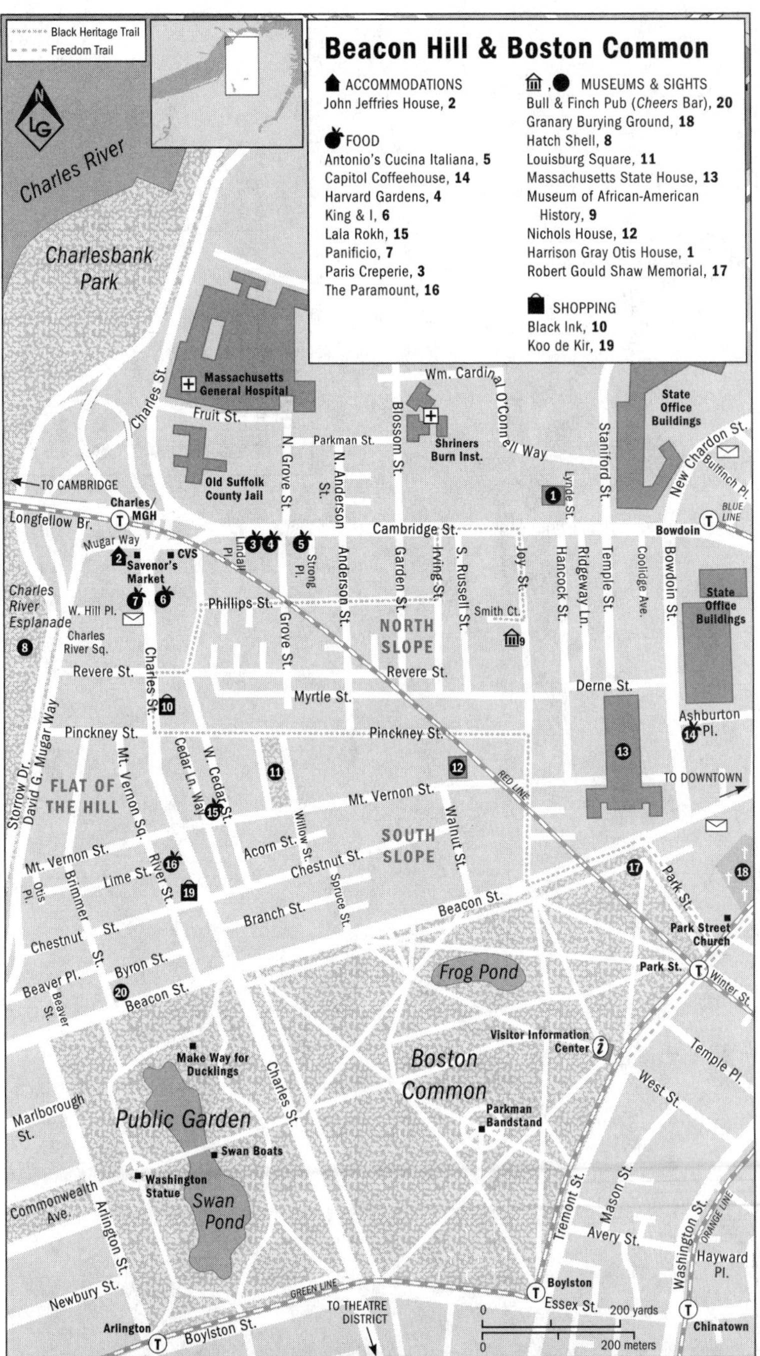

Beacon Hill & Boston Common
Black Heritage Trail
Freedom Trail
ACCOMMODATIONS
John Jeffries House, 2
FOOD
Antonio's Cucina Italiana, 5
Capitol Coffeehouse, 14
Harvard Gardens, 4
King & I, 6
Lala Rokh, 15
Panificio, 7
Paris Creperie, 3
The Paramount, 16
MUSEUMS & SIGHTS
Bull & Finch Pub (Cheers Bar), 20
Granary Burying Ground, 18
Hatch Shell, 8
Louisburg Square, 11
Massachusetts State House, 13
Museum of African-American History, 9
Nichols House, 12
Harrison Gray Otis House, 1
Robert Gould Shaw Memorial, 17
SHOPPING
Black Ink, 10
Koo de Kir, 19
Charles River
Charlesbank Park
Massachusetts General Hospital
Old Suffolk County Jail
Shriners Burn Inst.
State Office Buildings
TO CAMBRIDGE
Charles/MGH
Longfellow Br.
Bowdoin
BLUE LINE
Savenor's Market
CVS
Charles River Esplanade
Charles River Sq.
NORTH SLOPE
SOUTH SLOPE
FLAT OF THE HILL
TO DOWNTOWN
RED LINE
Park Street Church
Park St.
Frog Pond
Visitor Information Center
Boston Common
Parkman Bandstand
Make Way for Ducklings
Public Garden
Swan Boats
Washington Statue
Swan Pond
Boylston
Arlington
GREEN LINE
TO THEATRE DISTRICT
ORANGE LINE
Chinatown
Hayward Pl.
200 yards
200 meters

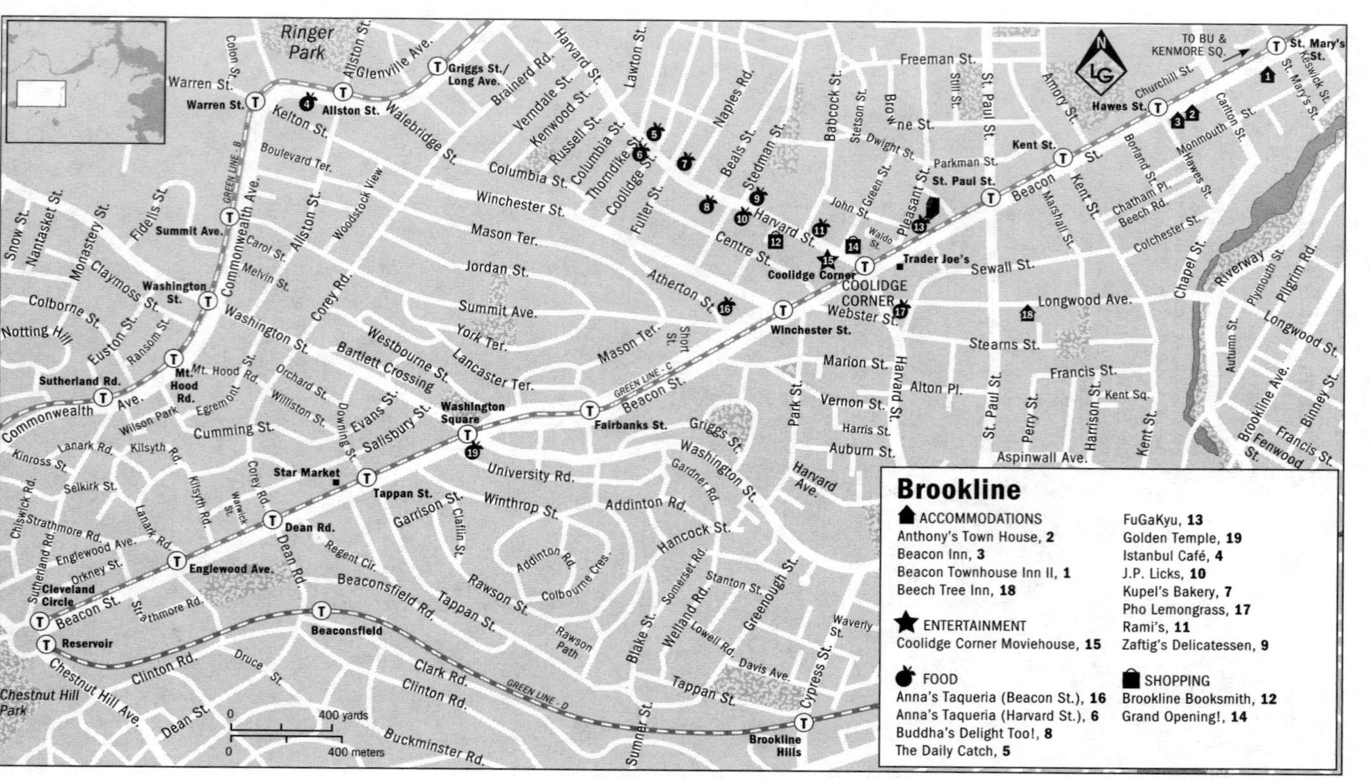
Brookline
ACCOMMODATIONS
Anthony's Town House, 2
Beacon Inn, 3
Beacon Townhouse Inn II, 1
Beech Tree Inn, 18
ENTERTAINMENT
Coolidge Corner Moviehouse, 15
FOOD
Anna's Taqueria (Beacon St.), 16
Anna's Taqueria (Harvard St.), 6
Buddha's Delight Too!, 8
The Daily Catch, 5
FuGaKyu, 13
Golden Temple, 19
Istanbul Café, 4
J.P. Licks, 10
Kupel's Bakery, 7
Pho Lemongrass, 17
Rami's, 11
Zaftig's Delicatessen, 9
SHOPPING
Brookline Booksmith, 12
Grand Opening!, 14
TO BU & KENMORE SQ.
COOLIDGE CORNER
Ringer Park
Trader Joe's
Star Market
St. Mary's St.
Hawes St.
Kent St.
St. Paul St.
Coolidge Corner
Winchester St.
Fairbanks St.
Washington Square
Tappan St.
Dean Rd.
Englewood Ave.
Cleveland Circle
Reservoir
Beaconsfield
Brookline Hills
Griggs St./ Long Ave.
Allston St.
Warren St.
Summit Ave.
Washington St.
Mt. Hood Rd.
Sutherland Rd.
GREEN LINE - B
GREEN LINE - C
GREEN LINE - D
400 yards
400 meters

Cambridge see map p. 320-321

ACCOMMODATIONS

Harding House, **22**	**D4**
Mary Prentiss Inn, **1**	**A1**

ENTERTAINMENT

Kendall Café, **19**	**F4**
Kendall Sq. Cinema, **18**	**F4**
Lizard's Lounge, **3**	**A2**
The Middle East, **45**	**E6**
T.T. the Bear's Place, **47**	**E6**
Western Front, **49**	**C6**

FOOD

1369 Coffee House (Central Sq.), **30**	**D5**
1369 Coffee House (Inman Sq.), **7**	**E3**
Asmara Ethiopian, **31**	**D5**
Atasca (Broadway), **21**	**E4**
Atasca (Hampshire), **23**	**F4**
The Blue Room, **20**	**F4**
Christina's Homemade Ice Cream, **10**	**E3**
CityGirl Caffè, **15**	**E3**
Dalí, **4**	**C2**
East Coast Grill & Raw Bar, **9**	**E3**
Emma's Pizza, **24**	**F5**
Helmand Restaurant, **11**	
India Castle, **28**	**C5**
Korea Garden, **39**	**E5**
Legal Seafood, **27**	
Moody's Falafal Palace, **37**	**D5**
Oleana, **16**	**E4**
Picante, **32**	**D5**
Punjabi Dhaba, **6**	**D3**
Rangzen, **42**	**E6**
Rosie's Bakery, **5**	**D3**
S&S Deli, **13**	**E3**
Toscanini's, **46**	**E6**

NIGHTLIFE

B-Side Lounge, **17**	**F4**
Cambridge Common, **3**	**A2**
The Cantab Lounge, **34**	**D5**
The Cellar, **25**	**C5**
The Enormous Room, **38**	**E5**
The Good Life, **35**	**D5**
Green St. Grill, **41**	**D6**
The Field, **33**	**D5**
ManRay, **48**	**E6**
Miracle of Science, **50**	**E6**
Paradise, **51**	**F6**
The People's Republik, **29**	**D5**
The Phoenix Landing, **44**	**E6**
Ryles, **14**	**E3**
Temple Bar, **2**	**A1**

SHOPPING

Buckaroo's Mercantile, **8**	**E3**
CambridgeSide Galleria, **12**	
Cheapo Records, **36**	**D5**
The Garment District, **26**	**F5**
Hubba Hubba, **43**	**E6**
Skippy White's, **40**	**E5**

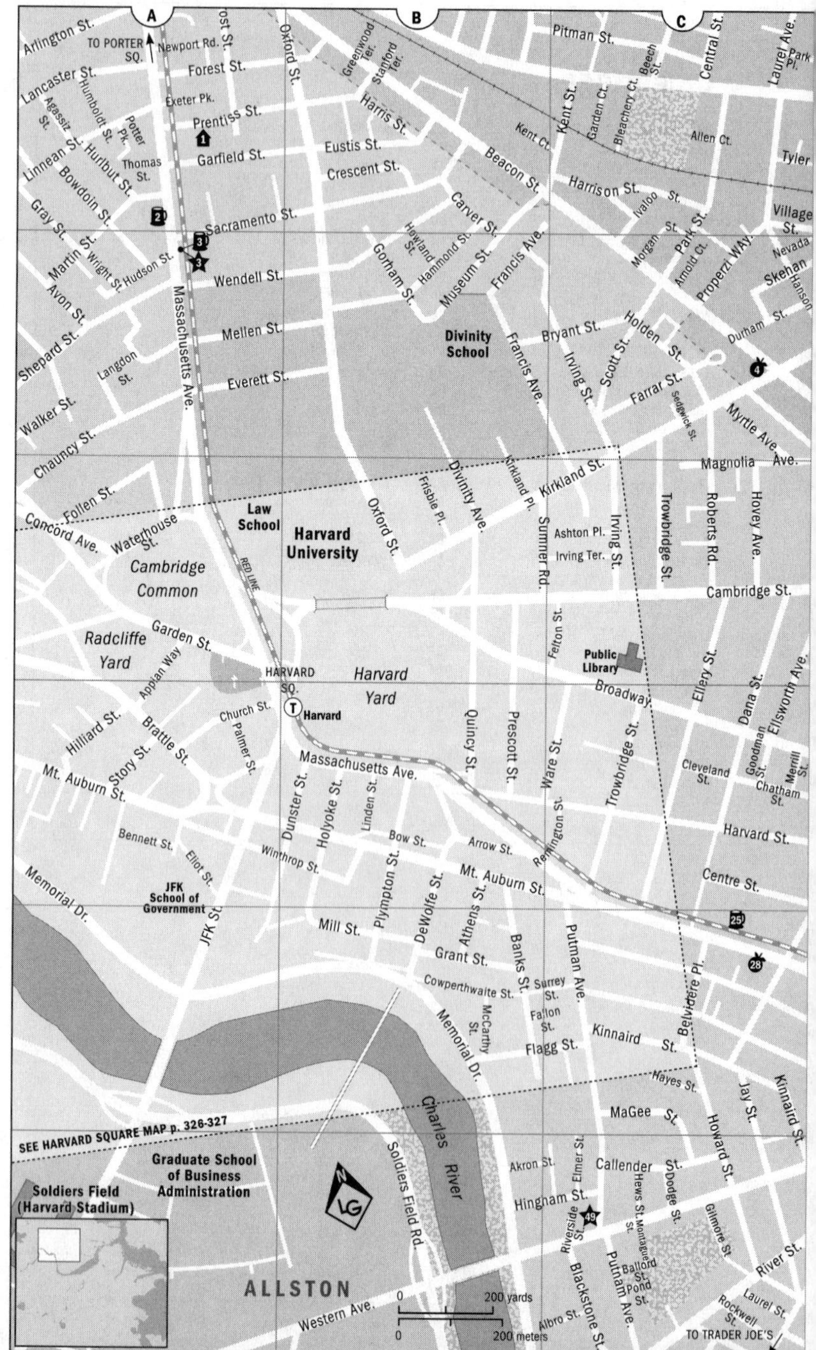

A
B
C
TO PORTER SQ.
Harvard University
Law School
Divinity School
Cambridge Common
Radcliffe Yard
Harvard Yard
HARVARD SQ.
Harvard
RED LINE
Public Library
JFK School of Government
Graduate School of Business Administration
Soldiers Field (Harvard Stadium)
ALLSTON
Charles River
SEE HARVARD SQUARE MAP p. 326-327
TO TRADER JOE'S
0 200 yards
0 200 meters
Massachusetts Ave.
Oxford St.
Kirkland St.
Cambridge St.
Broadway
Mt. Auburn St.
Memorial Dr.
Brattle St.
Garden St.
Concord Ave.
JFK St.
Western Ave.
Soldiers Field Rd.
Putnam Ave.
Howard St.
River St.

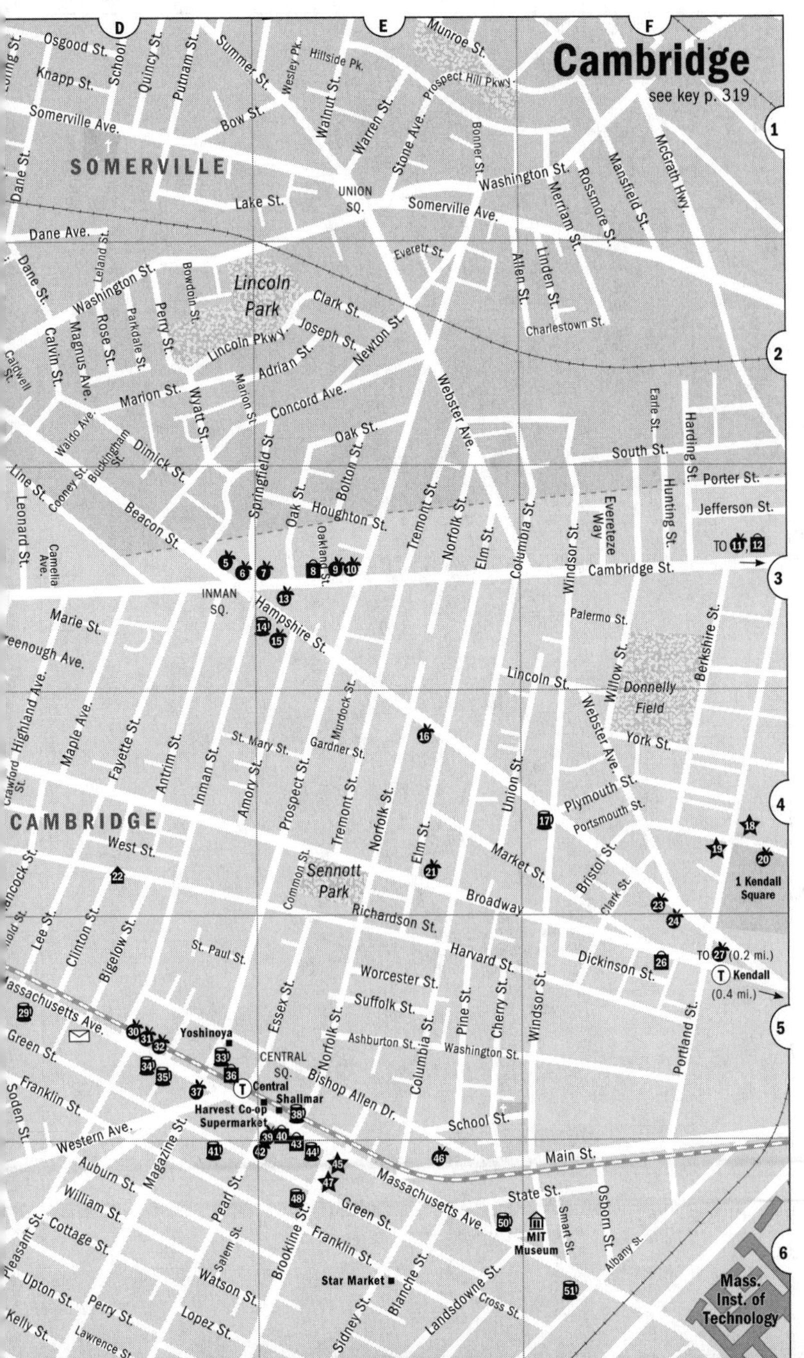
Cambridge
see key p. 319
SOMERVILLE
CAMBRIDGE
UNION SQ.
INMAN SQ.
CENTRAL SQ.
Lincoln Park
Sennott Park
Donnelly Field
1 Kendall Square
TO 27 (0.2 mi.)
Kendall (0.4 mi.)
Yoshinoya
Central
Shalimar
Harvest Co-op Supermarket
Star Market
MIT Museum
Mass. Inst. of Technology
Massachusetts Ave.
Cambridge St.
Hampshire St.
Broadway
Main St.
Somerville Ave.
Washington St.
Beacon St.
Webster Ave.
Prospect St.
Windsor St.
Columbia St.

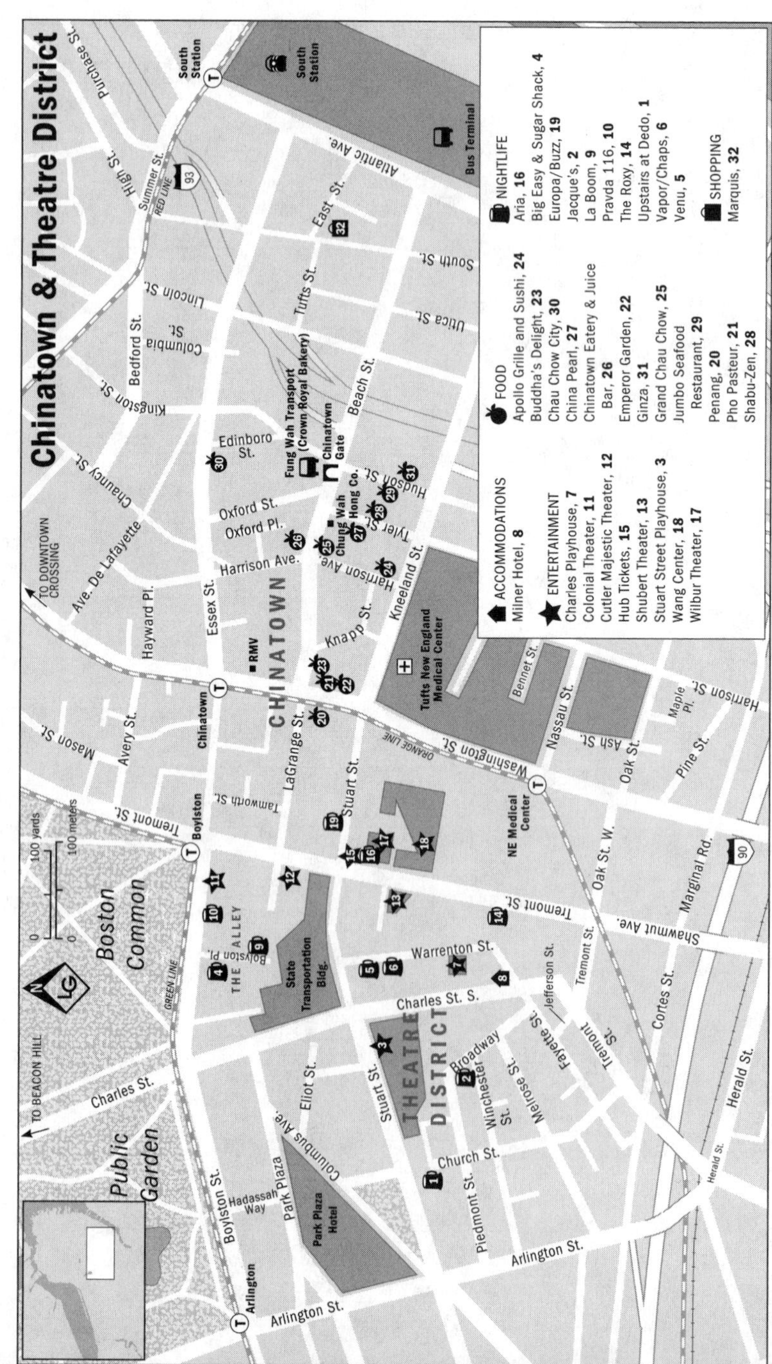

Chinatown & Theatre District
ACCOMMODATIONS
Milner Hotel, 8
ENTERTAINMENT
Charles Playhouse, 7
Colonial Theater, 11
Cutler Majestic Theater, 12
Hub Tickets, 15
Shubert Theater, 13
Stuart Street Playhouse, 3
Wang Center, 18
Wilbur Theater, 17
FOOD
Apollo Grille and Sushi, 24
Buddha's Delight, 23
Chau Chow City, 30
China Pearl, 27
Chinatown Eatery & Juice Bar, 26
Emperor Garden, 22
Ginza, 31
Grand Chau Chow, 25
Jumbo Seafood Restaurant, 29
Penang, 20
Pho Pasteur, 21
Shabu-Zen, 28
NIGHTLIFE
Aria, 16
Big Easy & Sugar Shack, 4
Europa/Buzz, 19
Jacque's, 2
La Boom, 9
Pravda 116, 10
The Roxy, 14
Upstairs at Dedo, 1
Vapor/Chaps, 6
Venu, 5
SHOPPING
Marquis, 32
South Station
Bus Terminal
Purchase St.
High St.
Summer St.
RED LINE
93
Atlantic Ave.
East St.
South St.
Utica St.
Lincoln St.
Columbia St.
Bedford St.
Kingston St.
Tufts St.
Beach St.
Fung Wah Transport (Crown Royal Bakery)
Chinatown Gate
Edinboro St.
Chauncy St.
Oxford St.
Oxford Pl.
Hudson St.
Tyler St.
Chung Wah Hong Co.
Harrison Ave.
Kneeland St.
TO DOWNTOWN CROSSING
Ave. De Lafayette
Hayward Pl.
Essex St.
CHINATOWN
RMV
Knapp St.
Tufts New England Medical Center
Bennet St.
Nassau St.
Harrison St.
Maple Pl.
Ash St.
Oak St.
Pine St.
Chinatown
Mason St.
Avery St.
LaGrange St.
ORANGE LINE
Washington St.
Tamworth St.
Stuart St.
NE Medical Center
Oak St. W.
Marginal Rd.
90
Tremont St.
Boylston
0 100 yards
0 100 meters
Boston Common
THE ALLEY
Boylston Pl.
State Transportation Bldg.
Warrenton St.
Shawmut Ave.
Jefferson St.
Tremont St.
Cortes St.
GREEN LINE
Charles St. S.
THEATRE DISTRICT
Broadway
Fayette St.
Melrose St.
Winchester St.
Herald St.
TO BEACON HILL
Charles St.
Eliot St.
Columbus Ave.
Church St.
Public Garden
Park Plaza
Hadassah Way
Boylston St.
Park Plaza Hotel
Piedmont St.
Arlington St.
Arlington

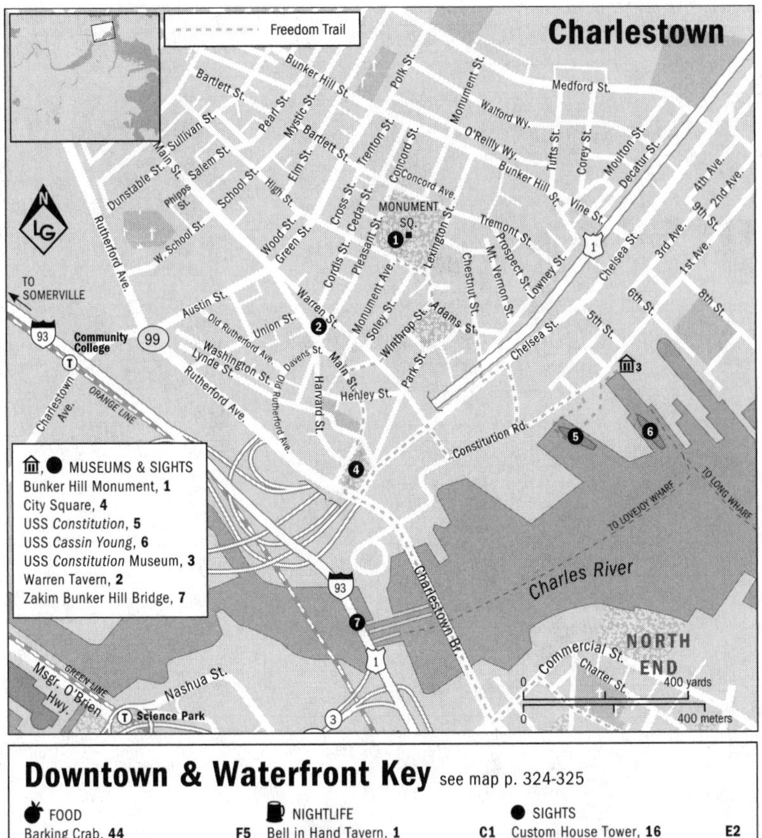

Downtown & Waterfront Key see map p. 324-325

FOOD

- Barking Crab, **44** — **F5**
- Ben's Café, **21** — **B3**
- Country Life Vegetarian, **29** — **E3**
- Durgin Park, **7** — **D1**
- Jimbo's Fish Shanty, **45**
- Legal Sea Foods, **14** — **E2**
- Milk St. Café, **37** — **D4**
- No Name, **47**
- Radius, **43** — **C5**
- South Street Diner, **49**
- Sultan's Kitchen, **24** — **E3**
- Ye Olde Union Oyster House, **3** — **C1**

ENTERTAINMENT

- BosTix, **11** — **D2**

MUSEUMS

- Boston Tea Party Ship, **48** — **E6**
- Children's Museum, **52**
- Immigration Museum, **30** — **C3**

NIGHTLIFE

- Bell in Hand Tavern, **1** — **C1**
- Black Rhino, **18** — **D2**
- The Black Rose, **13** — **E2**
- Emily's/SW1, **36** — **A4**
- Felt, **41** — **A5**
- The Good Life, **42** — **B5**
- Green Dragon Tavern, **2** — **C1**
- The Littlest Bar, **26** — **B3**
- Mantra/OmBar, **39** — **A4**
- Purple Shamrock, **6** — **C1**
- The Rack, **5** — **D1**

SHOPPING

- Brattle Book Shop, **40** — **A5**
- CD Spins, **35** — **A4**
- DSW, **33** — **B4**
- Filene's Basement, **38** — **B4**
- H&M, **31** — **B3**
- Hip Zepi USA, **34** — **B4**
- Marquis, **50**
- Newbury Comics, **12** — **C2**

SIGHTS

- Custom House Tower, **16** — **E2**
- Faneuil Hall, **10** — **C2**
- Government Center, **9** — **C1**
- Granary Burying Ground, **25** — **B3**
- Harpoon Brewery, **46**
- Holocaust Memorial, **4** — **C1**
- Hood's Milk Bottle, **51**
- King's Chapel & Burying Ground, **19** — **B3**
- New England Aquarium, **15** — **F2**
- Old City Hall, **20** — **B3**
- Old Corner Bookstore, **23** — **C3**
- Old South Meeting House, **28** — **C3**
- Old State House, **17** — **C2**
- Omni Parker House, **22** — **B3**
- Park at Post Office Sq., **32** — **D4**
- Park St. Church, **27** — **A3**
- Quincy Market, **8** — **D1**

Freedom Trail

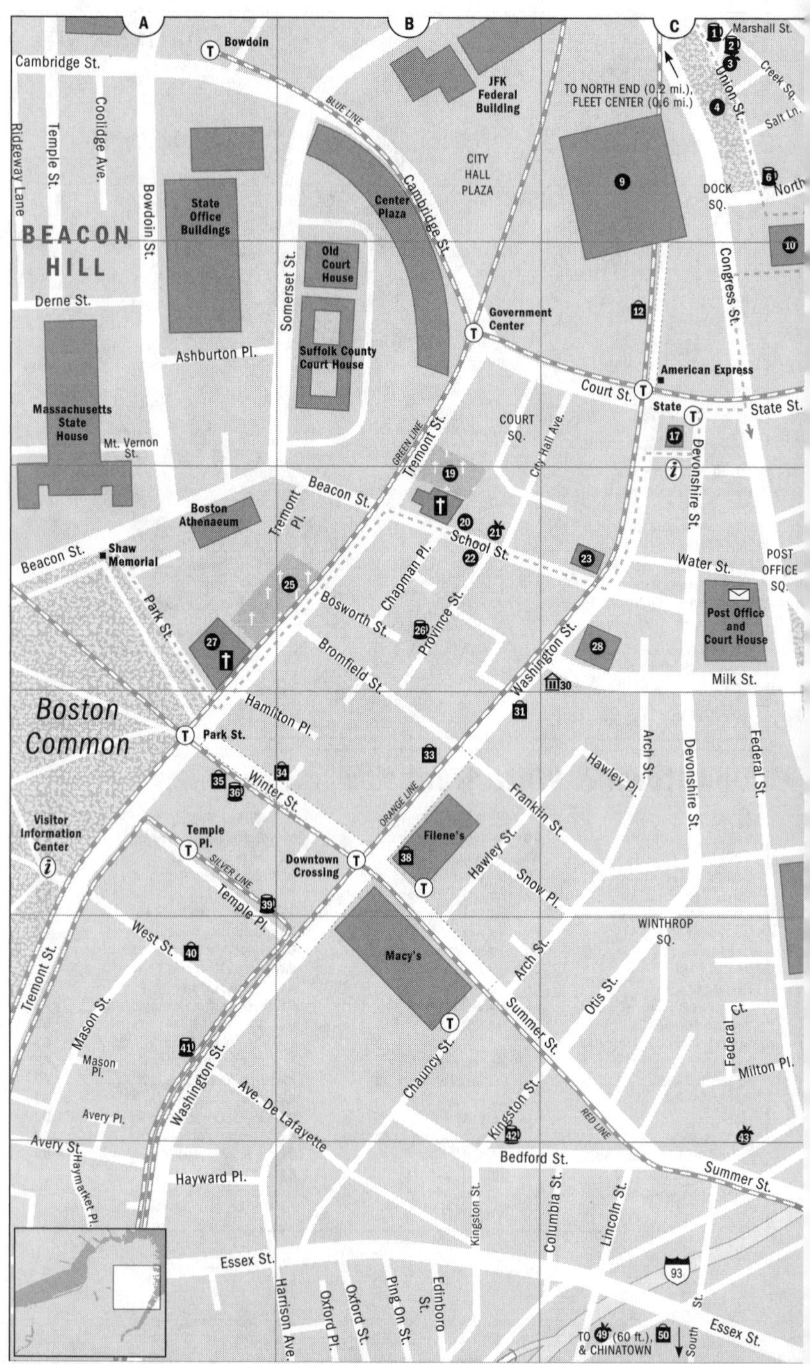

A
B
C
Bowdoin
Cambridge St.
Coolidge Ave.
Temple St.
Ridgeway Lane
Bowdoin St.
BEACON HILL
Derne St.
State Office Buildings
Ashburton Pl.
Massachusetts State House
Mt. Vernon St.
BLUE LINE
Cambridge St.
Center Plaza
Old Court House
Somerset St.
Suffolk County Court House
JFK Federal Building
CITY HALL PLAZA
TO NORTH END (0.2 mi.), FLEET CENTER (0.6 mi.)
Marshall St.
Creek Sq.
Union St.
Salt Ln.
DOCK SQ.
North
Congress St.
Government Center
American Express
Court St.
State
State St.
COURT SQ.
City Hall Ave.
GREEN LINE
Tremont St.
Beacon St.
Tremont Pl.
Boston Athenaeum
Beacon St.
Shaw Memorial
Park St.
School St.
Chapman Pl.
Province St.
Bosworth St.
Bromfield St.
Washington St.
Water St.
Devonshire St.
POST OFFICE SQ.
Post Office and Court House
Milk St.
Boston Common
Park St.
Hamilton Pl.
Winter St.
Visitor Information Center
Temple Pl.
SILVER LINE
Temple Pl.
Downtown Crossing
ORANGE LINE
Filene's
Franklin St.
Hawley Pl.
Arch St.
Devonshire St.
Federal St.
Hawley St.
Snow Pl.
WINTHROP SQ.
West St.
Macy's
Arch St.
Tremont St.
Mason St.
Mason Pl.
Washington St.
Summer St.
Otis St.
Federal Ct.
Milton Pl.
Chauncy St.
Avery Pl.
Ave. De Lafayette
Kingston St.
RED LINE
Avery St.
Haymarket Pl.
Hayward Pl.
Bedford St.
Summer St.
Kingston St.
Columbia St.
Lincoln St.
Essex St.
93
Harrison Ave.
Oxford Pl.
Oxford St.
Ping On St.
Edinboro St.
Essex St.
South St.
TO 49 (60 ft.), 50 & CHINATOWN

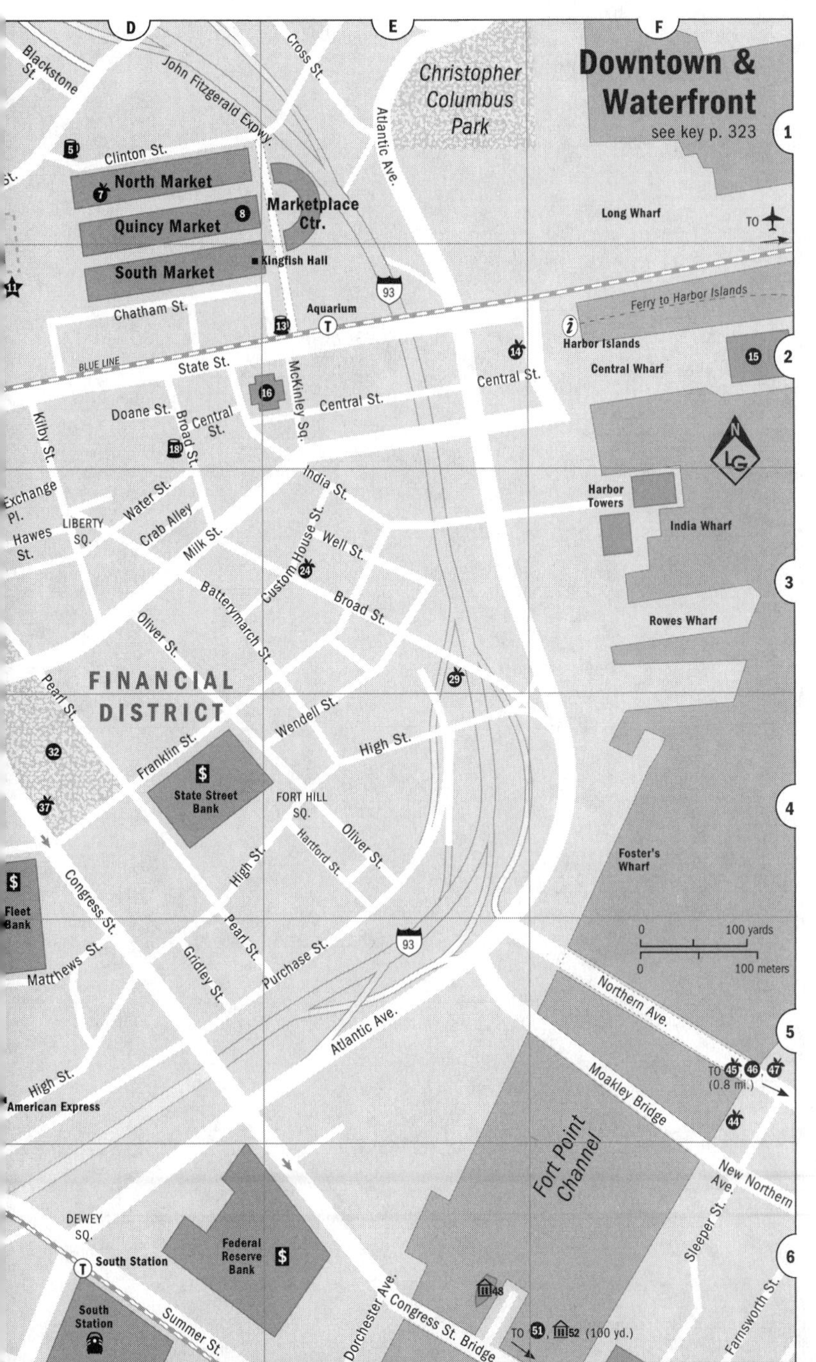
Downtown & Waterfront
see key p. 323
D
E
F
1
2
3
4
5
6
Blackstone St.
John Fitzgerald Expwy.
Cross St.
Christopher Columbus Park
Atlantic Ave.
Clinton St.
North Market
Quincy Market
South Market
Marketplace Ctr.
Kingfish Hall
Long Wharf
TO
Chatham St.
Aquarium
Ferry to Harbor Islands
Harbor Islands
Central Wharf
BLUE LINE
State St.
McKinley Sq.
Central St.
Doane St.
Broad St.
Kilby St.
India St.
Harbor Towers
India Wharf
Exchange Pl.
Water St.
Hawes St.
LIBERTY SQ.
Crab Alley
Milk St.
Custom House St.
Well St.
Batterymarch St.
Broad St.
Rowes Wharf
Oliver St.
Pearl St.
FINANCIAL DISTRICT
Wendell St.
High St.
Franklin St.
State Street Bank
FORT HILL SQ.
Hartford St.
Oliver St.
Foster's Wharf
Fleet Bank
Congress St.
High St.
Pearl St.
Purchase St.
Gridley St.
Matthews St.
0
100 yards
100 meters
Northern Ave.
Atlantic Ave.
Moakley Bridge
TO 45, 46, 47 (0.8 mi.)
High St.
American Express
Fort Point Channel
New Northern Ave.
Sleeper St.
DEWEY SQ.
South Station
Federal Reserve Bank
South Station
Summer St.
Dorchester Ave.
Congress St. Bridge
TO 51, 52 (100 yd.)
Farnsworth St.

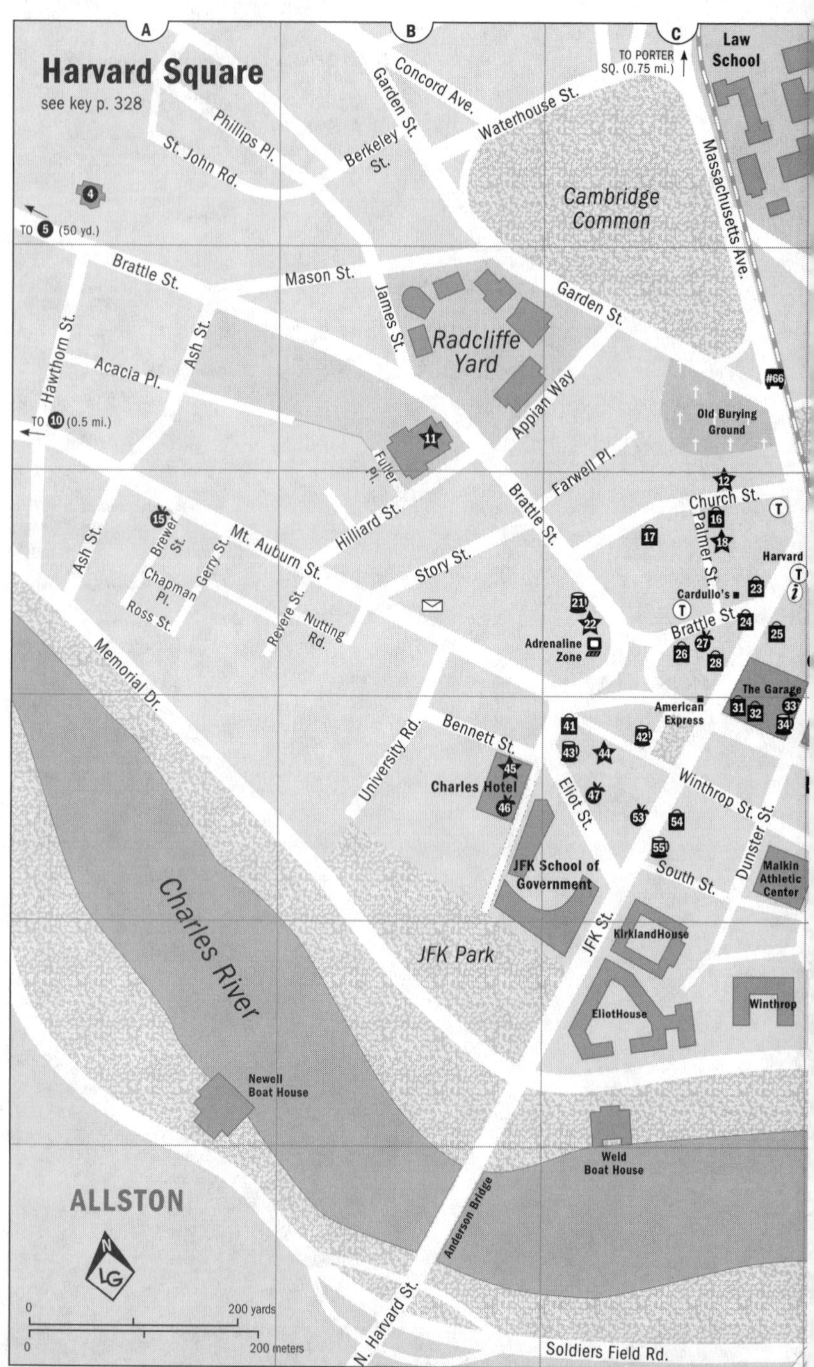
Harvard Square
see key p. 328
A
B
C
TO PORTER SQ. (0.75 mi.)
Law School
Concord Ave.
Garden St.
Phillips Pl.
St. John Rd.
Berkeley St.
Waterhouse St.
Cambridge Common
Massachusetts Ave.
TO 5 (50 yd.)
Brattle St.
Mason St.
James St.
Garden St.
Radcliffe Yard
Hawthorn St.
Ash St.
Acacia Pl.
Appian Way
#66
Old Burying Ground
TO 10 (0.5 mi.)
Fuller Pl.
Farwell Pl.
Brattle St.
Church St.
Ash St.
Brewer St.
Gerry St.
Mt. Auburn St.
Hilliard St.
Palmer St.
Harvard
Chapman Pl.
Ross St.
Story St.
Cardullo's
Revere St.
Nutting Rd.
Brattle St.
Adrenaline Zone
Memorial Dr.
The Garage
American Express
University Rd.
Bennett St.
Charles Hotel
Eliot St.
Winthrop St.
Dunster St.
JFK School of Government
South St.
Malkin Athletic Center
Charles River
JFK St.
KirklandHouse
JFK Park
EliotHouse
Winthrop
Newell Boat House
Weld Boat House
Anderson Bridge
ALLSTON
N
LG
0
200 yards
0
200 meters
N. Harvard St.
Soldiers Field Rd.

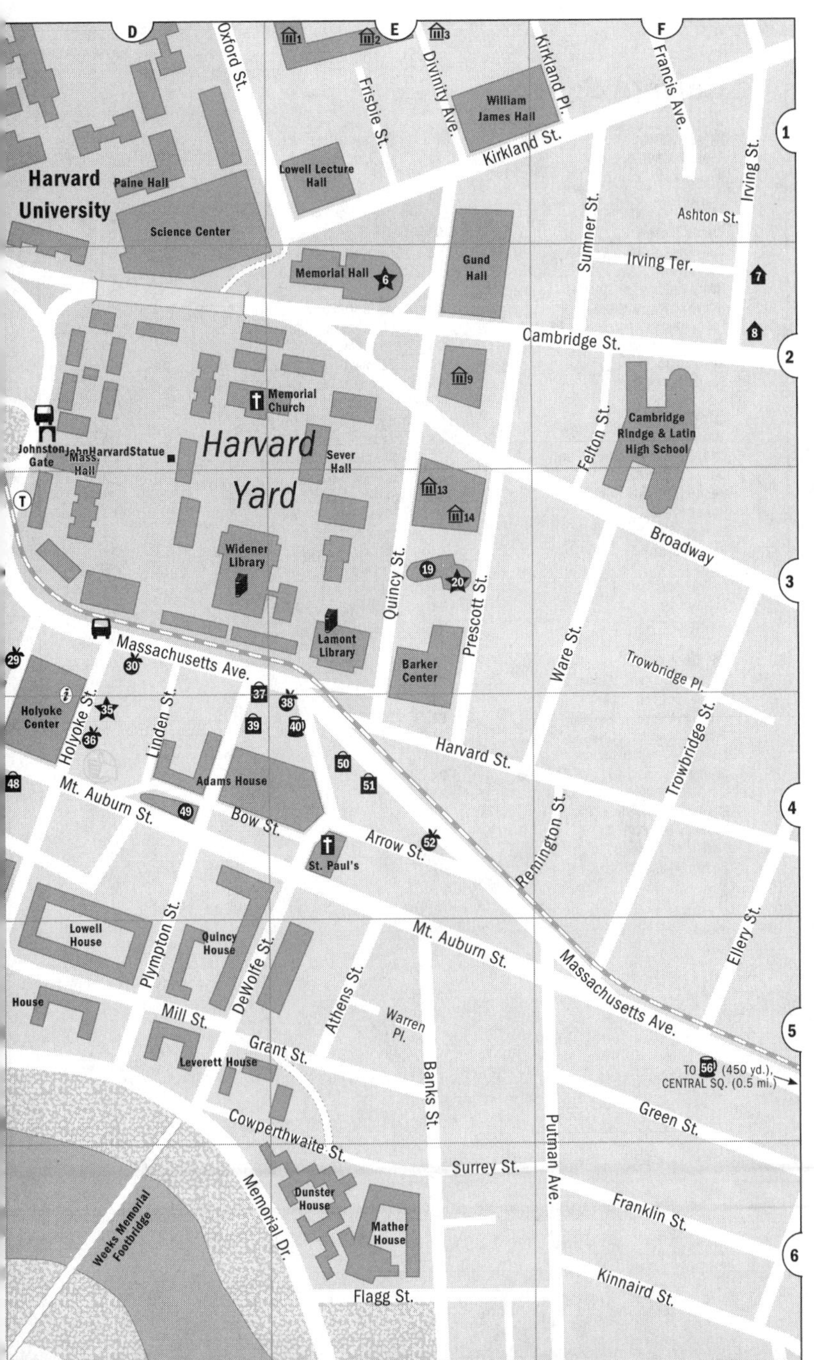
Harvard University
Paine Hall
Science Center
Lowell Lecture Hall
William James Hall
Memorial Hall
Gund Hall
Memorial Church
Harvard Yard
Johnston Gate
John Harvard Statue
Mass. Hall
Sever Hall
Widener Library
Lamont Library
Barker Center
Cambridge Rindge & Latin High School
Holyoke Center
Adams House
St. Paul's
Lowell House
Quincy House
House
Leverett House
Dunster House
Mather House
Weeks Memorial Footbridge
Oxford St.
Divinity Ave.
Frisbie St.
Kirkland Pl.
Francis Ave.
Kirkland St.
Irving St.
Ashton St.
Sumner St.
Irving Ter.
Cambridge St.
Felton St.
Broadway
Quincy St.
Prescott St.
Ware St.
Trowbridge Pl.
Trowbridge St.
Massachusetts Ave.
Holyoke St.
Linden St.
Harvard St.
Mt. Auburn St.
Bow St.
Arrow St.
Remington St.
Plympton St.
DeWolfe St.
Athens St.
Ellery St.
Warren Pl.
Mill St.
Grant St.
Banks St.
Cowperthwaite St.
Surrey St.
Putman Ave.
Green St.
Franklin St.
Memorial Dr.
Kinnaird St.
Flagg St.
TO 56 (450 yd.), CENTRAL SQ. (0.5 mi.)
D
E
F
1
2
3
4
5
6

Harvard Square see map p. 326-327

ACCOMMODATIONS

A Friendly Inn, **8**	**F2**
Irving House, **7**	**F2**

ENTERTAINMENT

Brattle Theatre, **22**	**C3**
Club Passim, **18**	**C3**
Harvard Film Archive, **20**	**E3**
Hasty Pudding Theatricals, **35**	**D4**
House of Blues, **44**	**C4**
Loeb Drama Center (ART), **11**	**B2**
Nameless Coffehouse, **12**	**C3**
Regattabar, **45**	**B4**
Sanders Theatre, **6**	**E2**

FOOD

1 Arrow St. Crêpes, **55**	**E4**
Bartley's Burger Cottage, **38**	**E4**
Darwin's Ltd., **15**	**A3**
Henrietta's Table, **46**	**B4**
Herrell's, **29**	**D3**
Penang, **53**	**C4**
Pho Pasteur, **33**	**C4**
Spice, **36**	**D4**
Tanjore, **47**	**C4**
Tealuxe, **27**	**C3**
Toscanini's, **30**	**D3**

MUSEUMS & SIGHTS

Busch-Reisinger Museum, **14**	**E3**
Carpenter Center, **19**	**E3**
Fogg Art Museum, **13**	**E3**
Harvard Museum of Natural History, **1**	**E1**
Hooper-Lee-Nichols House, **5**	
Lampoon Castle, **49**	**D4**
Longfellow House, **5**	**A1**
Mt. Auburn Cemetery, **10**	
Peabody Museum, **2**	**E1**
Sackler Museum, **9**	**E2**
Semitic Museum, **3**	**E1**

NIGHTLIFE

Casablanca, **21**	**C3**
Charlie's Kitchen, **43**	**C4**
The Cellar, **56**	
Grafton St., **40**	**E4**
Grendel's Den, **42**	**C4**
John Harvard's Brew House, **34**	**C4**
Shay's, **55**	**C4**

SHOPPING

Black Ink, **23**	**C3**
CD Spins, **17**	**C3**
Curious George Goes To WordsWorth, **24**	**C3**
Globe Corner Bookstore, **16**	**C3**
Grolier Poetry Bookshop, **39**	**D4**
Harvard Book Store, **37**	**D3**
Hootenanny, **31**	**C4**
Newbury Comics, **32**	**C4**
Oona's, **51**	**E4**
Planet Aid, **25**	**C3**
Planet Records, **54**	**C4**
Revolution Books, **50**	**E4**
Schoenhof's Foreign Books, **48**	**D4**
Second Time Around, **41**	**C4**
Urban Outfitters, **28**	**C3**
WordsWorth Books, **26**	**C3**

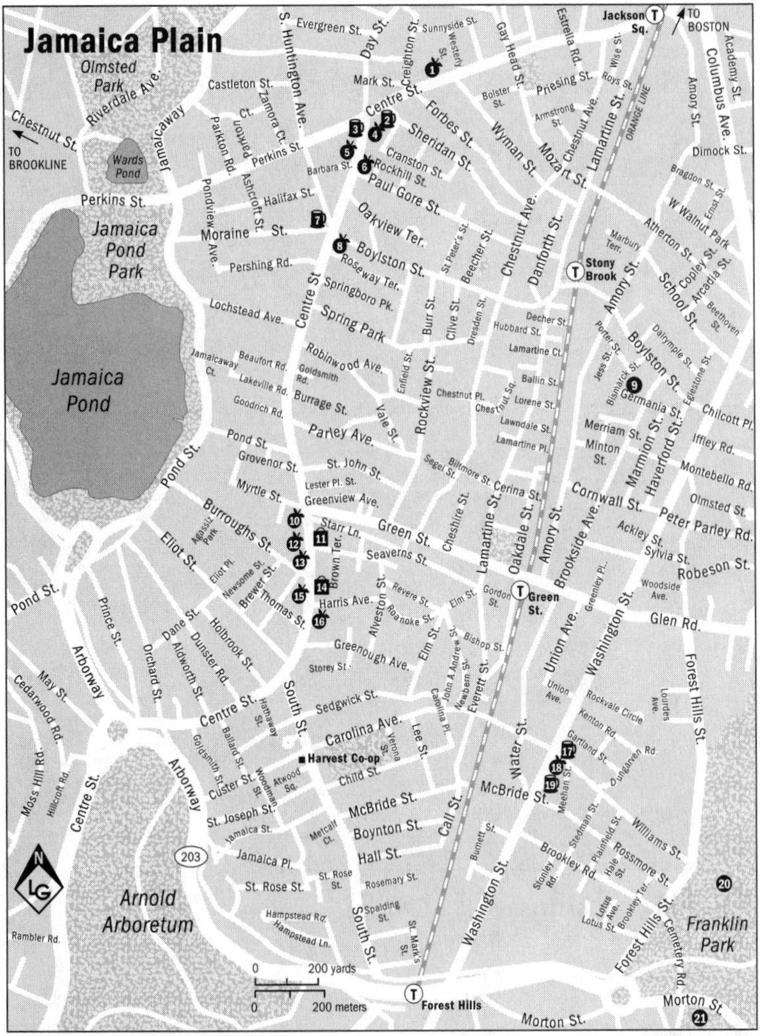

Jamaica Plain

Jamaica Plain

FOOD
- Acapulco Mexican, **8**
- Bella Luna, **5**
- Bukhara, **15**
- Centre St. Café, **12**
- El Oriental de Cuba, **6**
- Jake's Boss BBQ, **18**
- J.P. Licks, **10**
- JP Seafood Café, **16**
- Sorella's, **4**
- Tacos el Charro, **1**
- Wonder Spice Café, **13**

NIGHTLIFE
- Brendan Behan Pub, **2**
- F. J. Doyle & Co., **17**
- Midway Café, **19**
- Milky Way Lounge & Lanes, **3**
- Triple D's Fine Food & Drink, **7**

SHOPPING
- Boomerangs, **14**
- CD Spins, **11**

SIGHTS
- Forest Hills Cemetery, **21**
- Franklin Park Zoo, **20**
- Sam Adams Brewery, **9**

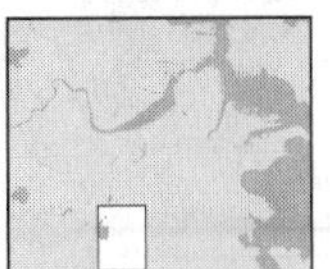

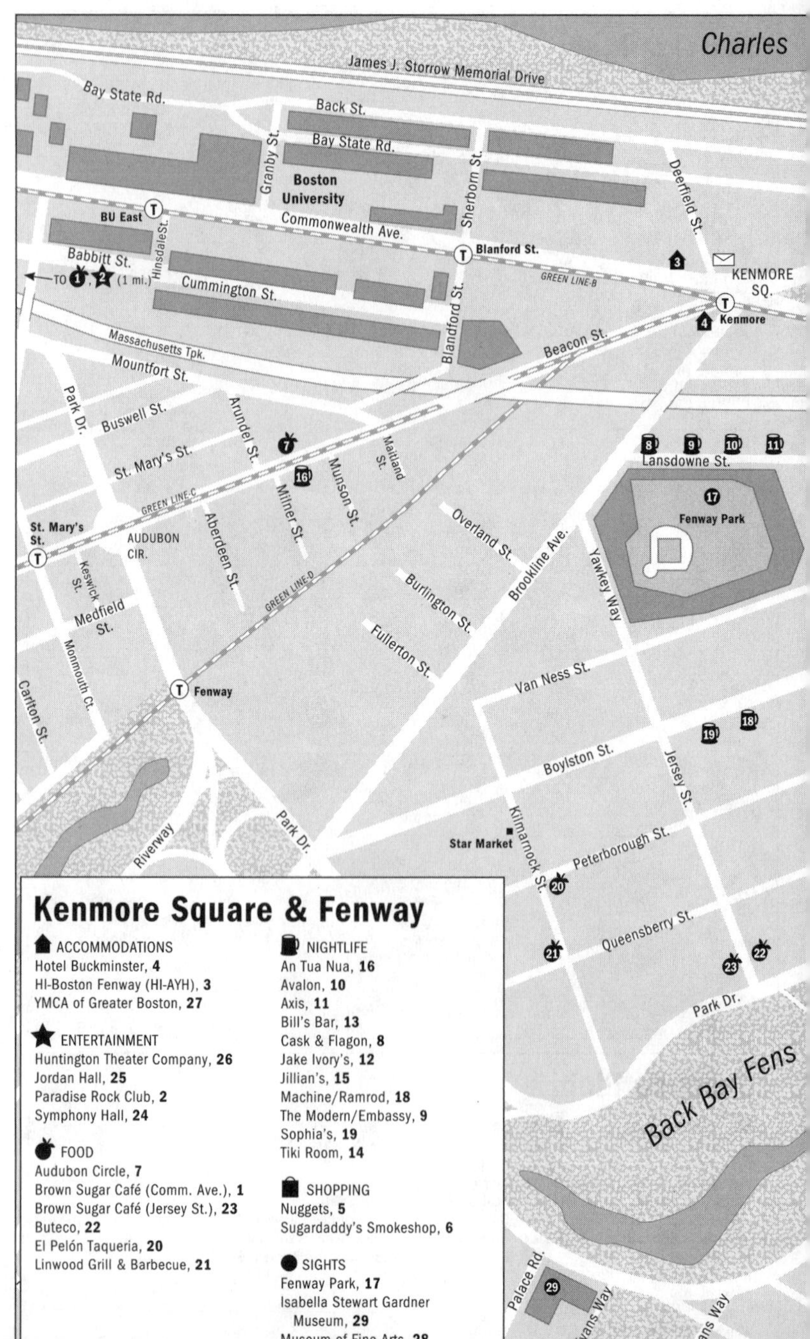
Charles
James J. Storrow Memorial Drive
Bay State Rd.
Back St.
Granby St.
Boston University
Sherborn St.
Deerfield St.
BU East
Commonwealth Ave.
Blanford St.
GREEN LINE-B
KENMORE SQ.
Kenmore
Babbitt St.
Hinsdale St.
TO 1, 2 (1 mi.)
Cummington St.
Blandford St.
Massachusetts Tpk.
Mountfort St.
Beacon St.
Park Dr.
Buswell St.
Arundel St.
Maitland St.
St. Mary's St.
Munson St.
Lansdowne St.
Fenway Park
GREEN LINE-C
Milner St.
St. Mary's St.
AUDUBON CIR.
Aberdeen St.
Overland St.
Brookline Ave.
Yawkey Way
Keswick St.
Medfield St.
GREEN LINE-D
Burlington St.
Fullerton St.
Monmouth Ct.
Carlton St.
Fenway
Van Ness St.
Boylston St.
Jersey St.
Riverway
Park Dr.
Star Market
Kilmarnock St.
Peterborough St.
Queensberry St.
Park Dr.
Back Bay Fens
Palace Rd.
Evans Way
Evans Way

Kenmore Square & Fenway

ACCOMMODATIONS
Hotel Buckminster, 4
HI-Boston Fenway (HI-AYH), 3
YMCA of Greater Boston, 27

ENTERTAINMENT
Huntington Theater Company, 26
Jordan Hall, 25
Paradise Rock Club, 2
Symphony Hall, 24

FOOD
Audubon Circle, 7
Brown Sugar Café (Comm. Ave.), 1
Brown Sugar Café (Jersey St.), 23
Buteco, 22
El Pelón Taqueria, 20
Linwood Grill & Barbecue, 21

NIGHTLIFE
An Tua Nua, 16
Avalon, 10
Axis, 11
Bill's Bar, 13
Cask & Flagon, 8
Jake Ivory's, 12
Jillian's, 15
Machine/Ramrod, 18
The Modern/Embassy, 9
Sophia's, 19
Tiki Room, 14

SHOPPING
Nuggets, 5
Sugardaddy's Smokeshop, 6

SIGHTS
Fenway Park, 17
Isabella Stewart Gardner Museum, 29
Museum of Fine Arts, 28

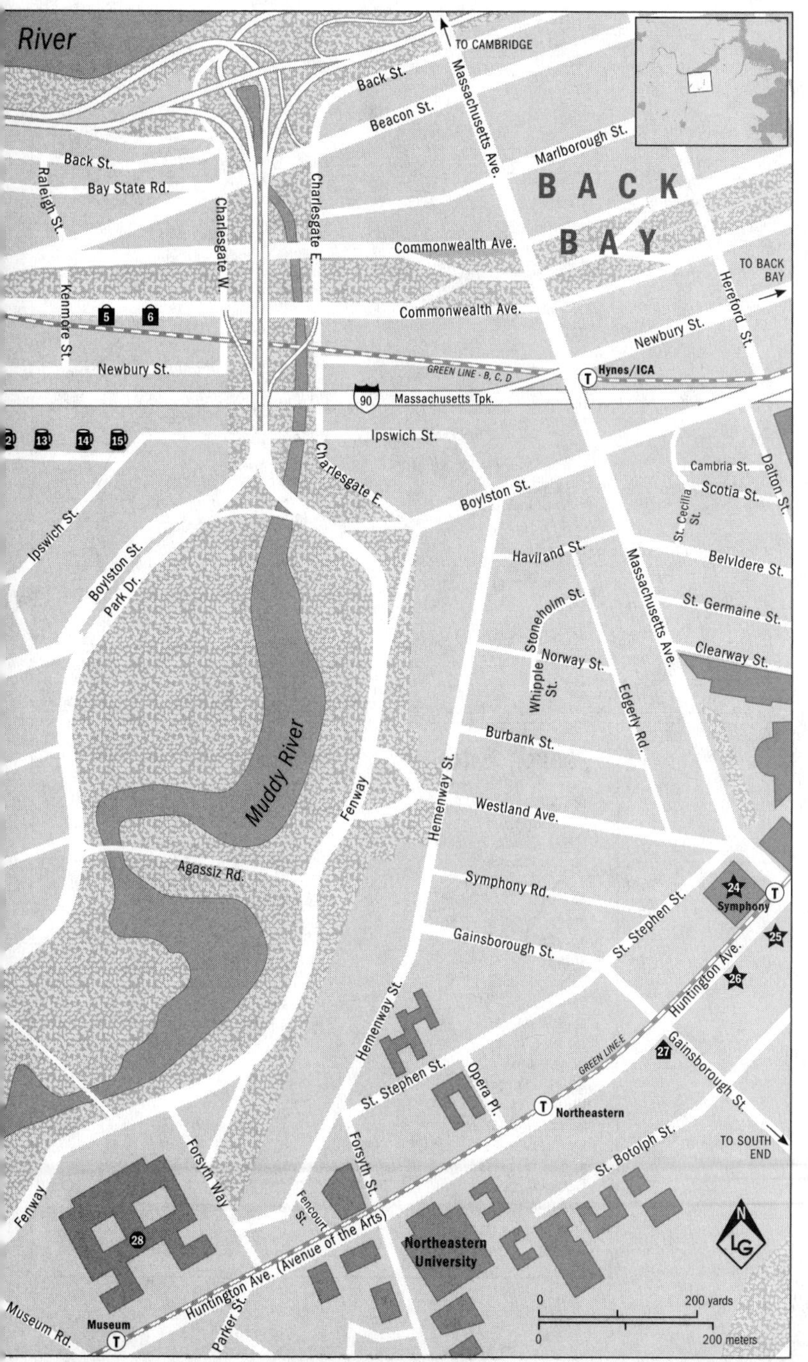
River
TO CAMBRIDGE
Back St.
Beacon St.
Massachusetts Ave.
Marlborough St.
BACK BAY
Back St.
Raleigh St.
Bay State Rd.
Charlesgate W.
Charlesgate E.
Commonwealth Ave.
Commonwealth Ave.
TO BACK BAY
Hereford St.
Kenmore St.
Newbury St.
Newbury St.
GREEN LINE - B, C, D
Hynes/ICA
Massachusetts Tpk.
90
Ipswich St.
Charlesgate E.
Boylston St.
Cambria St.
Scotia St.
Dalton St.
St. Cecilia St.
Ipswich St.
Boylston St.
Park Dr.
Haviland St.
Belvidere St.
Stoneholm St.
Massachusetts Ave.
St. Germaine St.
Clearway St.
Norway St.
Whipple St.
Edgerly Rd.
Burbank St.
Muddy River
Fenway
Hemenway St.
Westland Ave.
Agassiz Rd.
Symphony Rd.
St. Stephen St.
Symphony
Gainsborough St.
Huntington Ave.
Hemenway St.
GREEN LINE-E
Gainsborough St.
St. Stephen St.
Opera Pl.
Northeastern
TO SOUTH END
Forsyth Way
Forsyth St.
St. Botolph St.
Fenway
Fencourt St.
Huntington Ave. (Avenue of the Arts)
Northeastern University
Parker St.
Museum
Museum Rd.
0
200 yards
0
200 meters
N
LG

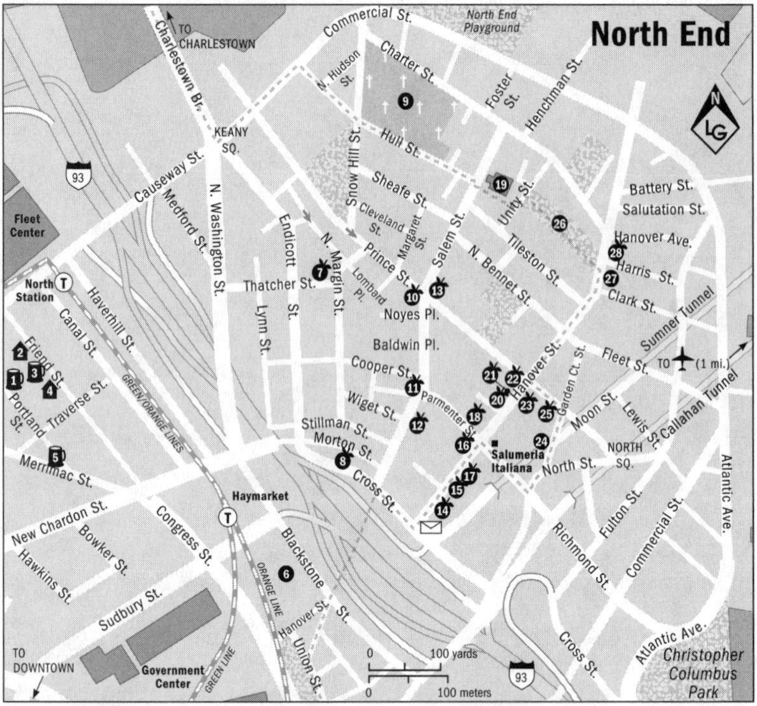

North End

TO CHARLESTOWN
Charlestown Br.
Commercial St.
North End Playground
Charter St.
N. Hudson St.
Foster St.
Henchman St.
Hull St.
KEANY SQ.
Snow Hill St.
Sheafe St.
Unity St.
Battery St.
Salutation St.
Hanover Ave.
Harris St.
Clark St.
Causeway St.
Medford St.
N. Washington St.
Endicott St.
N. Margin St.
Cleveland St.
Margaret St.
Salem St.
N. Bennet St.
Tileston St.
Prince St.
Lombard Pl.
Thatcher St.
Noyes Pl.
Baldwin Pl.
Lynn St.
Cooper St.
Hanover St.
Garden Ct. St.
Fleet St.
Sumner Tunnel
TO (1 mi.)
Fleet Center
North Station
Haverhill St.
Canal St.
Friend St.
Portland St.
Traverse St.
GREEN/ORANGE LINES
Wiget St.
Parmenter St.
Stillman St.
Morton St.
Moon St.
Lewis St.
Callahan Tunnel
Salumeria Italiana
North St.
NORTH SQ.
Merrimac St.
Cross St.
Haymarket
New Chardon St.
Congress St.
Bowker St.
Hawkins St.
Blackstone St.
ORANGE LINE
Sudbury St.
Hanover St.
Union St.
Richmond St.
Fulton St.
Commercial St.
Atlantic Ave.
TO DOWNTOWN
Government Center
GREEN LINE
0 100 yards
0 100 meters
93
Cross St.
Atlantic Ave.
Christopher Columbus Park

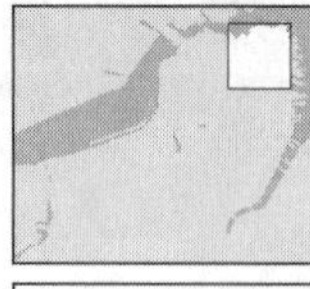

Freedom Trail

North End

ACCOMMODATIONS
Beantown Hostel / Irish Embassy Hostel, **4**
The Shawmut Inn, **2**

FOOD
Antico Forno, **12**
Artú, **25**
Bova's Bakery, **10**
Caffé dello Sport, **22**
Caffé Paradiso, **15**
Caffé Vittoria, **20**
The Daily Catch, **23**
Dolce Vita, **14**
Il Panino Express, **16**
L'Osteria, **11**
Maria's Pastry Shop, **8**
Mike's Pastry, **21**
Modern Pastry, **17**
Pizzeria Regina, **7**
Ristorante Lucia, **28**
Sage, **13**
Trattoria Il Panino, **18**

NIGHTLIFE
Irish EmbassyPub, **3**
McGann's, **1**
Paddy Burke's, **5**

SIGHTS
Copp's Hill Burying Ground, **9**
Haymarket, **6**
Old North Church, **19**
Paul Revere House, **24**
Paul Revere Mall, **26**
St. Stephen's Church, **27**

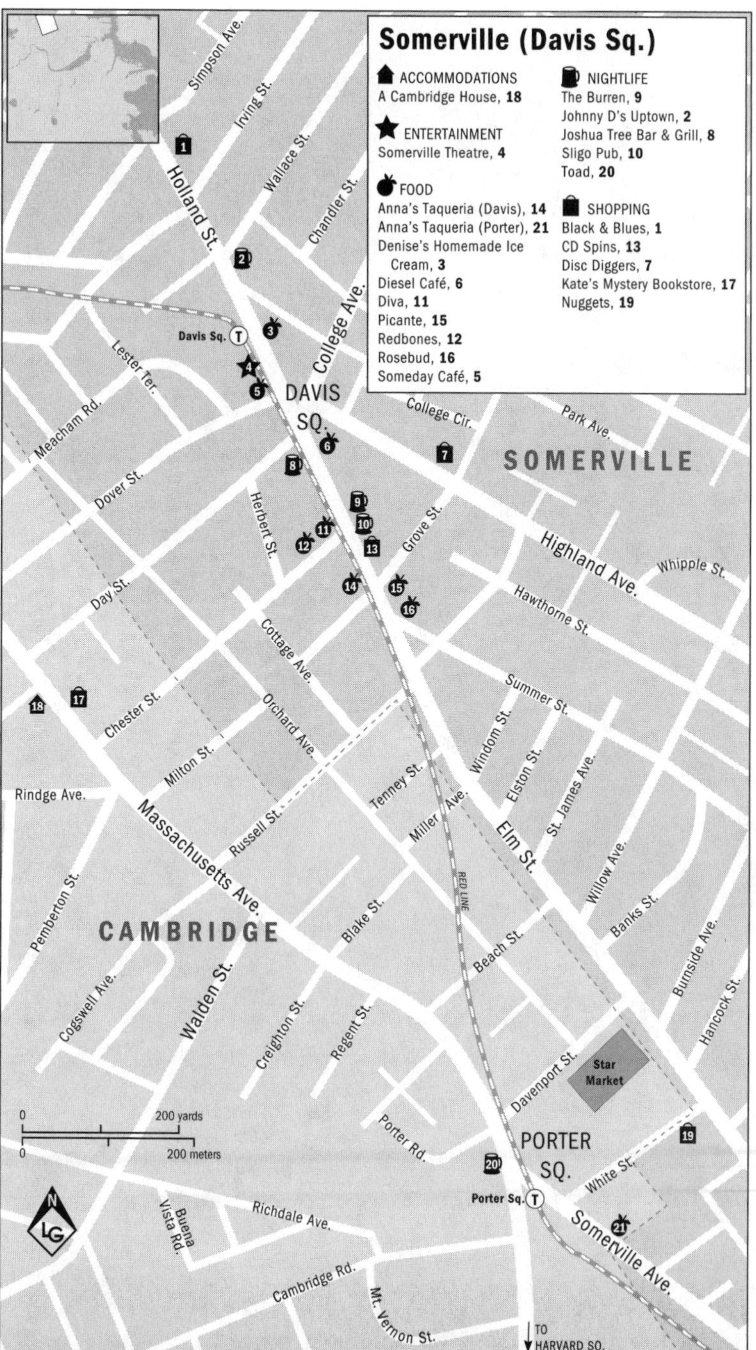

Somerville (Davis Sq.)
ACCOMMODATIONS
A Cambridge House, 18
ENTERTAINMENT
Somerville Theatre, 4
FOOD
Anna's Taqueria (Davis), 14
Anna's Taqueria (Porter), 21
Denise's Homemade Ice Cream, 3
Diesel Café, 6
Diva, 11
Picante, 15
Redbones, 12
Rosebud, 16
Someday Café, 5
NIGHTLIFE
The Burren, 9
Johnny D's Uptown, 2
Joshua Tree Bar & Grill, 8
Sligo Pub, 10
Toad, 20
SHOPPING
Black & Blues, 1
CD Spins, 13
Disc Diggers, 7
Kate's Mystery Bookstore, 17
Nuggets, 19
DAVIS SQ.
Davis Sq.
SOMERVILLE
CAMBRIDGE
PORTER SQ.
Porter Sq.
Star Market
RED LINE
TO HARVARD SQ.
0 200 yards
0 200 meters
Simpson Ave.
Irving St.
Wallace St.
Chandler St.
Holland St.
College Ave.
Lester Ter.
Meacham Rd.
Dover St.
College Cir.
Park Ave.
Herbert St.
Grove St.
Highland Ave.
Whipple St.
Hawthorne St.
Day St.
Cottage Ave.
Summer St.
Chester St.
Orchard Ave.
Windom St.
Elston St.
St. James Ave.
Milton St.
Tenney St.
Miller Ave.
Rindge Ave.
Russell St.
Elm St.
Willow Ave.
Massachusetts Ave.
Banks St.
Pemberton St.
Blake St.
Burnside Ave.
Beach St.
Hancock St.
Cogswell Ave.
Walden St.
Creighton St.
Regent St.
Davenport St.
Porter Rd.
White St.
Somerville Ave.
Richdale Ave.
Buena Vista Rd.
Cambridge Rd.
Mt. Vernon St.

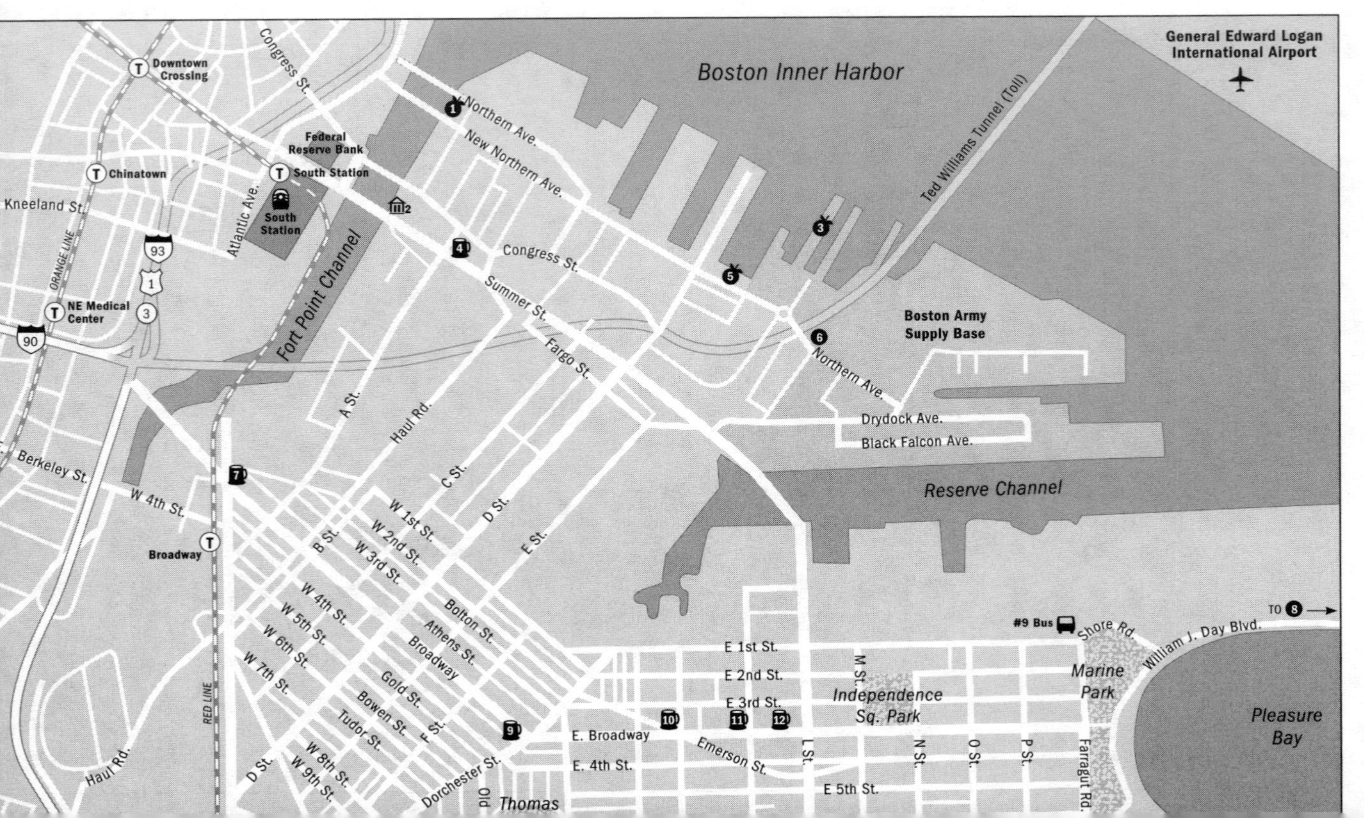
General Edward Logan International Airport
Boston Inner Harbor
Ted Williams Tunnel (Toll)
Downtown Crossing
Congress St.
Northern Ave.
New Northern Ave.
Federal Reserve Bank
South Station
Chinatown
Kneeland St.
Atlantic Ave.
South Station
Congress St.
Summer St.
Fargo St.
Fort Point Channel
ORANGE LINE
NE Medical Center
Boston Army Supply Base
Northern Ave.
Drydock Ave.
Black Falcon Ave.
Reserve Channel
A St.
Haul Rd.
C St.
D St.
E St.
E. Berkeley St.
W 4th St.
Broadway
W 1st St.
W 2nd St.
W 3rd St.
B St.
W 4th St.
W 5th St.
W 6th St.
W 7th St.
Bolton St.
Athens St.
Broadway
Gold St.
Bowen St.
Tudor St.
F St.
W 8th St.
W 9th St.
D St.
Dorchester St.
Old
Thomas
Haul Rd.
RED LINE
TO 8
#9 Bus
Shore Rd.
William J. Day Blvd.
Marine Park
Pleasure Bay
E 1st St.
E 2nd St.
E 3rd St.
M St.
Independence Sq. Park
E. Broadway
E. 4th St.
Emerson St.
L St.
E 5th St.
N St.
O St.
P St.
Farragut Rd.

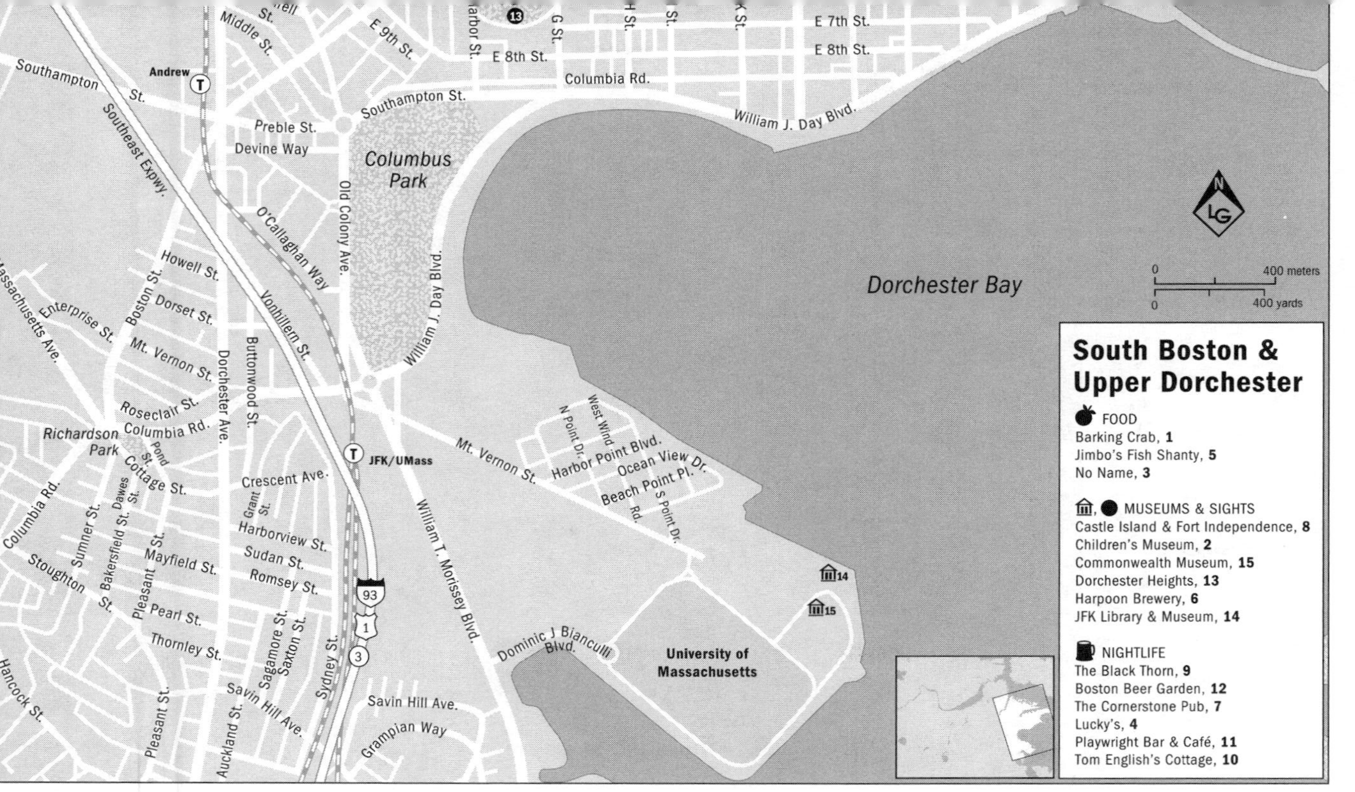
South Boston & Upper Dorchester
FOOD
Barking Crab, 1
Jimbo's Fish Shanty, 5
No Name, 3
MUSEUMS & SIGHTS
Castle Island & Fort Independence, 8
Children's Museum, 2
Commonwealth Museum, 15
Dorchester Heights, 13
Harpoon Brewery, 6
JFK Library & Museum, 14
NIGHTLIFE
The Black Thorn, 9
Boston Beer Garden, 12
The Cornerstone Pub, 7
Lucky's, 4
Playwright Bar & Café, 11
Tom English's Cottage, 10
0
400 meters
0
400 yards
N
LG
Dorchester Bay
University of Massachusetts
Columbus Park
William J. Day Blvd.
William T. Morissey Blvd.
Mt. Vernon St.
Dominic J Bianculli Blvd.
West Wind
N Point Dr.
Harbor Point Blvd.
Ocean View Dr.
Beach Point Pl.
S Point Dr.
Rd.
JFK/UMass
Andrew
Old Colony Ave.
O'Callaghan Way
Vonhillern St.
Buttonwood St.
Dorchester Ave.
Southeast Expwy.
Southampton St.
Massachusetts Ave.
Boston St.
Columbia Rd.
Richardson Park
Pond St.
E 7th St.
E 8th St.
E 9th St.
G St.
Middle St.
Preble St.
Devine Way
Howell St.
Dorset St.
Mt. Vernon St.
Roseclair St.
Enterprise St.
Cottage St.
Dawes St.
Bakersfield St.
Sumner St.
Stoughton St.
Crescent Ave.
Grant St.
Harborview St.
Sudan St.
Romsey St.
Mayfield St.
Pleasant St.
Pearl St.
Thornley St.
Sydney St.
Saxton St.
Sagamore St.
Savin Hill Ave.
Auckland St.
Hancock St.
Grampian Way
93
1
3
13
14
15

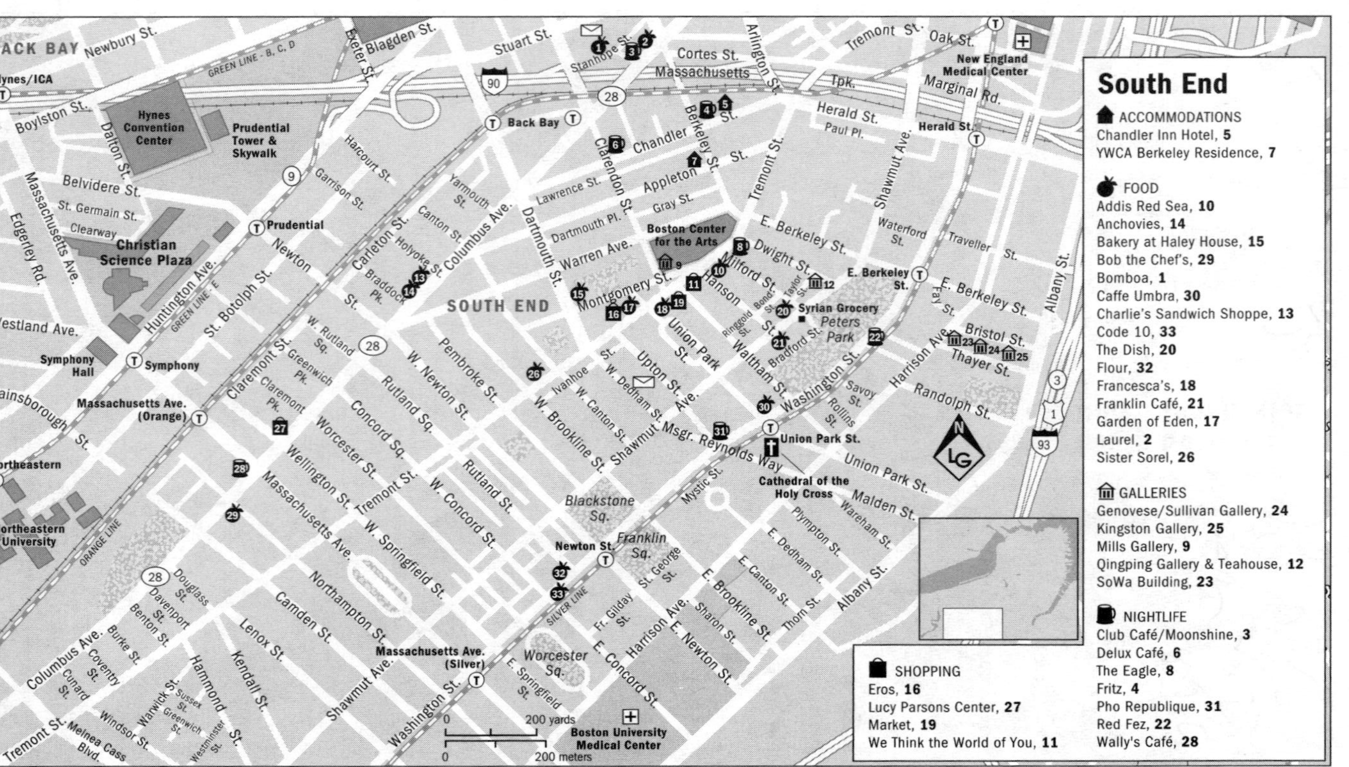
South End
ACCOMMODATIONS
Chandler Inn Hotel, 5
YWCA Berkeley Residence, 7
FOOD
Addis Red Sea, 10
Anchovies, 14
Bakery at Haley House, 15
Bob the Chef's, 29
Bomboa, 1
Caffe Umbra, 30
Charlie's Sandwich Shoppe, 13
Code 10, 33
The Dish, 20
Flour, 32
Francesca's, 18
Franklin Café, 21
Garden of Eden, 17
Laurel, 2
Sister Sorel, 26
GALLERIES
Genovese/Sullivan Gallery, 24
Kingston Gallery, 25
Mills Gallery, 9
Qingping Gallery & Teahouse, 12
SoWa Building, 23
NIGHTLIFE
Club Café/Moonshine, 3
Delux Café, 6
The Eagle, 8
Fritz, 4
Pho Republique, 31
Red Fez, 22
Wally's Café, 28
SHOPPING
Eros, 16
Lucy Parsons Center, 27
Market, 19
We Think the World of You, 11
BACK BAY
SOUTH END
Hynes Convention Center
Prudential Tower & Skywalk
Christian Science Plaza
Symphony Hall
Boston Center for the Arts
Syrian Grocery
Cathedral of the Holy Cross
New England Medical Center
Boston University Medical Center
Northeastern University
200 yards
200 meters

pictures - reports - friends - discounts
GLOBOsapiens.net
travel community